Handbook of
ECONOMIC FIELD EXPERIMENTS

Handbook of Field Experiments

VOLUME 1

Handbook of
ECONOMIC FIELD EXPERIMENTS

Handbook of Field Experiments

VOLUME 1

Edited by

ABHIJIT VINAYAK BANERJEE
Massachusetts Institute of Technology
Cambridge, MA, United States

ESTHER DUFLO
Massachusetts Institute of Technology
Cambridge, MA, United States

ELSEVIER

N·H North-Holland
An imprint of Elsevier

North-Holland is an imprint of Elsevier
Radarweg 29, PO Box 211, 1000 AE Amsterdam, Netherlands
The Boulevard, Langford Lane, Kidlington, Oxford OX5 1GB, United Kingdom

Notices

Knowledge and best practice in this field are constantly changing. As new research and experience broaden our understanding, changes in research methods, professional practices, or medical treatment may become necessary.

Practitioners and researchers must always rely on their own experience and knowledge in evaluating and using any information, methods, compounds, or experiments described herein. In using such information or methods they should be mindful of their own safety and the safety of others, including parties for whom they have a professional responsibility.

To the fullest extent of the law, neither the Publisher nor the authors, contributors, or editors, assume any liability for any injury and/or damage to persons or property as a matter of products liability, negligence or otherwise, or from any use or operation of any methods, products, instructions, or ideas contained in the material herein.

ISBN: 978-0-444-63324-8
ISSN: 2214-658X

For information on all Elsevier publications visit our website at https://www.elsevier.com/books-and-journals

Publisher: Zoe Kruze
Acquisition Editor: Kirsten Shankland
Editorial Project Manager: Edward Payne
Production Project Manager: Stalin Viswanathan
Designer: Mark Rogers

Typeset by TNQ Books and Journals
Transferred to Digital Printing in 2017

INTRODUCTION TO THE SERIES

The aim of the *Handbooks in Economics* series is to produce Handbooks for various branches of economics, each of which is a definitive source, reference, and teaching supplement for use by professional researchers and advanced graduate students. Each Handbook provides self-contained surveys of the current state of a branch of economics in the form of chapters prepared by leading specialists on various aspects of this branch of economics. These surveys summarize not only received results but also newer developments, from recent journal articles and discussion papers. Some original material is also included, but the main goal is to provide comprehensive and accessible surveys. The Handbooks are intended to provide not only useful reference volumes for professional collections but also possible supplementary readings for advanced courses for graduate students in economics.

Founding Editors
Kenneth J. Arrow and Michael D. Intriligator

CONTENTS

Volume 1

Section II. Methodology and Practice of RCTs

Section III. Understanding Preferences and Preference Change

VOLUME 2

Section I. The Challenge of Improving Human Capital

CONTRIBUTORS

Volume 1

O. Al-Ubaydli
Bahrain Center for Strategic, International and Energy Studies, Manama, Bahrain; George Mason University, Fairfax, VA, United States; Mercatus Center, Arlington, VA, United States

S. Athey
Stanford University, Stanford, CA, United States; NBER (National Bureau of Economic Research), Cambridge, MA, United States

A.V. Banerjee
Massachusetts Institute of Technology, Cambridge, MA, United States; NBER (National Bureau of Economic Research), Cambridge, MA, United States

M. Bertrand
University of Chicago Booth School of Business, Chicago, IL, United States

S. Chassang
New York University, New York, NY, United States

E. Duflo
Massachusetts Institute of Technology, Cambridge, MA, United States

A.S. Gerber
Yale University, New Haven, CT, United States

R. Glennerster
Massachusetts Institute of Technology, J-PAL, Cambridge, MA, United States

U. Gneezy
University of California, San Diego, La Jolla, CA, United States; University of Amsterdam, Amsterdam, Netherlands

D.P. Green
Columbia University, New York, NY, United States

J.M. Gueron
President Emerita, MDRC, New York, NY, United States

A. Imas
Carnegie Mellon University, Pittsburgh, PA, United States

G.W. Imbens
Stanford University, Stanford, CA, United States; NBER (National Bureau of Economic Research), Cambridge, MA, United States

J.A. List
University of Chicago, Chicago, IL, United States; NBER (National Bureau of Economic Research), Cambridge, MA, United States

E.L. Paluck
Princeton University, Princeton, NJ, United States

D. Simester
MIT Sloan School of Management, Cambridge, MA, United States

E. Shafir
Princeton University, Princeton, NJ, United States

E. Snowberg
California Institute of Technology, Pasadena, CA, United States; NBER (National Bureau of Economic Research), Cambridge, MA, United States

Volume 2

W.J. Congdon
ideas42, New York, NY, United States

A. de Janvry
University of California, Berkeley, Berkeley, CA, United States

P. Dupas
Stanford University, Stanford, CA, United States; NBER (National Bureau of Economic Research), Cambridge, MA, United States; Center for Education Policy Research, Cambridge, MA, United States

F. Finan
University of California, Berkeley, Berkeley, CA, United States

R.G. Fryer, Jr.
Harvard University, Cambridge, MA, United States; NBER (National Bureau of Economic Research), Cambridge, MA, United States

R. Hanna
Harvard University, Cambridge, MA, United States

D. Karlan
Yale University, New Haven, CT, United States

J.R. Kling
Congressional Budget Office, Washington, DC, United States; NBER (National Bureau of Economic Research), Cambridge, MA, United States

J. Ludwig
NBER (National Bureau of Economic Research), Cambridge, MA, United States; University of Chicago, Chicago, IL, United States

E. Miguel
University of California, Berkeley, Berkeley, CA, United States; NBER (National Bureau of Economic Research), Cambridge, MA, United States

S. Mullainathan
NBER (National Bureau of Economic Research), Cambridge, MA, United States; Harvard University, Cambridge, MA, United States

K. Muralidharan
University of California, San Diego, La Jolla, CA, United States; NBER (National Bureau of Economic Research), Cambridge, MA, United States; Jameel Poverty Action Lab, Cambridge, MA, United States

B.A. Olken
Massachusetts Institute of Technology, Cambridge, MA, United States

R. Pande
Harvard University, Cambridge, MA, United States

J. Rothstein
University of California, Berkeley, Berkeley, CA, United States; NBER (National Bureau of Economic Research), Cambridge, MA, United States

E. Sadoulet
University of California, Berkeley, Berkeley, CA, United States

T. Suri
MIT Sloan School of Management, Cambridge, MA, United States

T. von Wachter
NBER (National Bureau of Economic Research), Cambridge, MA, United States; University of California, Los Angeles, Los Angeles, CA, United States

CHAPTER 1

An Introduction to the "Handbook of Field Experiments"

A.V. Banerjee[1], E. Duflo[1]

Massachusetts Institute of Technology, Cambridge, MA, United States
[1]Corresponding authors: E-mail: eduflo@mit.edu; banerjee@mit.edu

Contents

Many (though by no means all) of the questions that economists and policymakers ask themselves are causal in nature: What would be the impact of adding computers in classrooms? What is the price elasticity of demand for preventive health products? Would increasing interest rates lead to an increase in default rates? Decades ago, the statistician Fisher (1925) proposed a method to answer such causal questions: Randomized Controlled Trials (RCTs). In an RCT, the assignment of different units to different

Handbook of Economic Field Experiments, Volume 1
ISSN 2214-658X, http://dx.doi.org/10.1016/bs.hefe.2016.09.005

treatment groups is chosen randomly. This ensures that no unobservable characteristics of the units are reflected in the assignment, and hence that any difference between treatment and control units reflects the impact of the treatment. While the idea is simple, the implementation in the field can be more involved, and it took some time before randomization was considered to be a practical tool for answering questions in economics.

By many accounts, the first large-scale social experiment was the New Jersey Income Maintenance Experiment, which was initiated in 1968 and tested the impact of income transfers and tax rates on labor supply. The next few decades, as Chapter 2 in Volume 1 (Gueron, 2017) and Chapter 8 in Volume 2 (von Wachter and Rothstein, 2017) remind us, were a sometime tortuous journey eventually leading to a more widespread acceptance of RCTs, both by policymakers and by academic researchers. While this acceptance first took hold in the US, starting in the mid-1990s it extended to developing countries, where the RCT revolution took the field by storm.

At this point, the method has gained widespread acceptance (though there continue to be vocal critics and active debates, many of which this Handbook covers), and there is now a large body of research on field experiments, both in developed and developing countries. We feel that we have collectively learnt an enormous amount from this literature, both in terms of not only how to conduct and analyze experiments, but also about the methodological contributions experiments have made to economics and about the world. For this volume, we asked some of the foremost experts in the field to distill these learnings, as well as discuss the most important challenges, and open questions for future work. In this short introduction, we provide what is our (admittedly personal, subjective, and somewhat biased towards our own field, development economics) assessment of the impacts that the past 20 years of field experiment research have had, both on how we do research and how we understand the world.

1. THE IMPACT ON THE WAY WE DO RESEARCH[1]

The remarkable growth in the number of RCTs is, in itself, a dramatic change in some fields. The type of development research that is carried out today is significantly different from research conducted even 15 years ago. A reflection of this fact is that many researchers who were openly skeptical of RCTs, or simply belonged to an entirely different tradition within development economics, are now involved in one or more RCTs (e.g., Daron Acemoglu, Derek Neal, Martin Ravallion, Mark Rosenzweig).

Early discussions of the merits (or lack thereof) of randomization put significant emphasis on its role in the reliable identification of internally valid causal effects and the external validity of such estimates. We and others have already had these discussions

[1] This section draws on Banerjee et al. (2016a).

in various forums (Heckman, 1992; Banerjee et al., 2007; Duflo et al., 2007; Banerjee and Duflo, 2009; Deaton, 2010), and we will not reproduce them here. As we had also begun to argue in Banerjee and Duflo (2009), we actually think that these discussions somewhat miss the point about why RCTs are really valuable, and why they have become so popular with researchers.

1.1 A greater focus on identification across the board

Starting with Neyman (1923) (who used it as a theoretical device) and Fisher (1925) (who was the first to propose physically randomizing units), the original motivation of randomized experiments was a focus on the credible identification of causal effects. As Imbens and Athey (2017) write in Chapter 3 of Volume 1:

> There is a long tradition viewing randomized experiments as the most credible of designs to obtain causal inferences. Freedman (2006) writes succinctly that experiments offer more reliable evidence on causation than observational studies. On the other hand, some researchers continue to be skeptical about the relative merits of randomized experiments. For example, Deaton (2010) argues that evidence from randomized experiments has no special priority. …Randomized experiments cannot automatically trump other evidence, they do not occupy any special place in some hierarchy of evidence. Our view aligns with that of Freedman and others who view randomized experiments as playing a special role in causal inference. Whenever possible, a randomized experiment is unique in the control that the researcher has over the assignment mechanism, and by virtue of this control, selection bias in comparisons between treated and control units can be eliminated. That does not mean that randomized experiments can answer all causal questions. There are a number of reasons why randomized experiments may not be suitable to answer particular questions.

For a long time, observational studies and randomized studies progressed largely on parallel paths: In agricultural science, and then biomedical studies, randomized experiments were quickly accepted, and a vocabulary and statistical apparatus to think about them were developed. Despite the adoption of randomized studies in other fields, most researchers in the social sciences continued to reason exclusively in terms of observational data. The main approach was to estimate associations, and then to try to assess the extent to which these associations reflect causality (or to explicitly give up on causality). Starting with Rubin's (1974) fundamental contribution, researchers started to use the experimental analog to reason about observational data, and this set the stage for thinking about how to analyze observational data through the lens of the ideal experiment.

Through the 1980s and 1990s, motivated by this clear thinking about causal effects, labor economics and public finance were transformed by the introduction of new empirical methods for estimating causal effects, namely: matching, instrumental variables, difference-in-differences, and regression discontinuity designs. Development economics also embraced these methods starting in the 1990s, but some researchers further decided that it may be possible to go straight to the ideal experiments (RCTs), and therefore researchers began to go back and forth between experimental and non-experimental studies. This means that the experimental and non-experimental literature developed in close relationship, constantly cross-fertilizing each other.

In development economics, the non-experimental literature was completely transformed by the existence of this large RCT movement. When the gold standard is not just a twinkle in someone's eyes, but the clear alternative to a particular empirical strategy or at least well-defined benchmark for it, researchers feel compelled to think harder about identification strategies, and to be more inventive and rigorous about them. As a result, researchers have become increasingly more clever at identifying and using natural experiments, and at the same time, much more cautious in interpreting the results from them. Not surprisingly, the standards of the nonexperimental literature have therefore improved tremendously over the last few decades, without necessarily sacrificing its ability to ask broad and important questions. To highlight some examples, Alesina et al. (2013) use suitability to the plow to study the long-run determinants of the social attitudes towards the role of women; Padró i Miquel et al. (2012) use a difference-in-differences strategy to study village democracy; and Banerjee and Iyer (2005) and Dell (2010) each use a spatial discontinuity to look at the long-run impact of extractive institutions. In each of these cases, the questions are approached with the same eye for careful identification as other more standard program evaluation questions.

Meanwhile, the RCT literature was also influenced by work done in the non-experimental literature. The understanding of the power (and limits) of instrumental variables allowed researchers to move away from the basic experimental paradigm of the completely randomized experiment with a perfect follow-up and use more complicated strategies, such as encouragement designs. Techniques developed in the non-experimental literature offered ways to handle situations in the field that are removed from the ideal setting of experiments (imperfect randomization, clustering, non-compliance, attrition, spillovers, and contamination, etc.). These methods are very clearly exposed in Chapter 3 of Volume 1 (Imbens and Athey, 2017) on the econometrics of experiments, and most chapters provide examples of their uses.

Structural methods are also increasingly combined with experiments to estimate counterfactual policies [see Chapter 8 of Volume 2 (von Wachter and Rothstein, 2017) for a number of examples from the developed world, as well as Todd and Wolpin (2006) and Attanasio et al. (2012) for developing country examples].

More recently, machine learning techniques have also been combined with experiments to model treatment effect heterogeneity [see Chapter 3 of Volume 1 (Imbens and Athey, 2017)].

Of course, the broadening offered by these new techniques comes with the cost of making additional assumptions on top of the original experimental assignment, and those assumptions may or may not be valid. This means that the difference in the quality of identification between a very well-identified, non-experimental study and a randomized evaluation that ends up facing lots of constraints in the field or tries to estimate parameters that are not pure treatment effects is a matter of degree. In this sense, there has been a convergence across the empirical spectrum in terms of the quality of identification, though mostly because experiments have pulled the remaining study designs up with them.

Interestingly, somewhat counter to this tendency to blur the boundaries between experiments and non-experiments, in Chapter 3 of Volume 1, Imbens and Athey (2017) provide a coherent framework for designing and analyzing experiments that puts randomization at the center:

> *A major theme of the chapter is that we recommend using statistical methods that are directly justified by randomization, in contrast to the more traditional sampling-based approach that is commonly used in econometrics. In essence, the sampling-based approach considers the treatment assignments to be fixed, while the outcomes are random. Inference is based on the idea that the subjects are a random sample from a much larger population. In contrast, the randomization-based approach takes the subject's potential outcomes (that is, the outcomes they would have had in each possible treatment regime) as fixed, and considers the assignment of subjects to treatments as random.*

Thus, the methods they propose to analyze experiments sometimes differ from traditional econometrics: For example, instead of controlling for covariates (what researchers routinely do), which can easily lead to bias in finite samples, they suggest placing the data into strata, analyzing the within group experiments, and averaging the results. This is directly justified by the randomization of the treatment and does not require any additional assumptions. They also suggest doing as much as possible ex-ante through the design of the experiment to avoid any ex-post adjustment.

1.2 Assessing external validity

In the words of Imbens and Athey (2017) (Chapter 3 in Volume 1): "external validity is concerned with generalizing causal inferences, drawn for a particular population and setting, to others, where these alternative settings could involve different populations, different outcomes, or different contexts." The question of the external validity of RCTs is even more hotly debated than that of their internal validity. This is perhaps because, unlike internal validity, there is no clear endpoint to the debate. Other individuals could always be different and react differently to the treatment, and any future treatment could be ever so slightly different from what has been tested. As Banerjee et al. (2017) (Chapter 4 in Volume 1) acknowledge: "External policy advice is unavoidably subjective. This does not mean that it needs to be uninformed by experimental evidence, rather, judgment will unavoidably color it."

It is worth noting that there is very little here that is specific about RCTs (Banerjee and Duflo, 2009). The same problem afflicts all empirical analysis with the one exception of what Heckman (1992) calls the randomization bias. Randomization bias refers to the fact that experiments require the consent of both the subjects and the organization that is carrying out the program, and these people may be special, and non-representative of the future population that could be treated. Chapter 5 in Volume 1 (Glennerster, 2017) provides a list of the characteristics of an ideal partner: They must have sufficient scale, be flexible, and technically competent in the area of the program; have expertise and reputation; have low staff turnover; and possess a desire to know the truth. In other words, they are clearly not representative of the typical NGO or government, and this has clear implications on what can be generalized from those studies.

On the other hand, it is worth pointing out that any naturally occurring policy that gets evaluated (i.e., not an RCT) is also selected: The evaluation requires that the policy did take place, and that was presumably because someone thought it was a good idea to try it out. In general, any study takes place in a particular time and place, and that might affect results. This does not imply that subjective recommendations by experts, based both on their priors and the results of their experiments, should not be of some use for policymakers. Most policymakers are not stupid, and they do know how to combine data that are presented to them with their own prior knowledge of their settings. From our experience, when presented with evidence from a program of interest, the immediate reaction of a policymaker is typically to ask whether an RCT could be done in their own context.

There is one clear advantage that RCTs do offer for external validity, although it is not often discussed and has not been systematically exploited as yet. To assess any external validity issues, it is helpful to have well-identified causal studies in multiple settings. These settings should vary in terms of the distribution of characteristics of the units, and possibly in terms of the specific nature of the treatments or the treatment rate, to assess the credibility of generalizing to other settings. With RCTs, because we can, in principle, control where and over what sample experiments take place (and not just how to allocate the treatment within a sample), we can, also in principle, get a handle on how treatment effects might vary by context. Of course, if we allow the world to vary in infinite ways, this is not sufficient to say anything much on its own. But there are several ways to make progress.

1.2.1 Combine existing evaluations and conduct meta-analyses

A first approach is to combine existing evaluations, and make assumptions about the possible distribution of treatment effects. There are a variety of ways of doing so, ranging from the explicitly parametric—Rubin (1981) proposes modeling treatment effect heterogeneity as stemming from a normal distribution: In each site, the causal effect of the treatment is a site-specific effect drawn from a normal distribution—to more non-parametric procedures, such as those based on revealed preference. Chapter 8 in Volume 2 (von Wachter and Rothstein, 2017) contains an extensive discussion of the trade-offs between the various approaches in the context of the evaluation of social programs in developed countries. Chapter 2 in Volume 2 (Fryer, 2017) provides a systematic meta-analysis of 196 RCTs in education in the US in three domains.

One issue that arises with trying to do any kind of meta-analysis is the access to an un-selected sample of results from an unselected sample of studies. Since there is publication bias in economics, the worry is that the sample of published studies may not be representative of all the studies that exist; furthermore, since researchers have some flexibility in the analyses to run, the available results may themselves be selected. This is where another advantage of RCTs kicks in: Since they have a defined beginning and end, they can in principle be registered. To this end, Chapter 5 in Volume 1 (Glennerster, 2017) discusses how the American Economic Association recently created a registry of randomized trials (www.socialscienceregistry.org), which listed over 800 entries as of August 10, 2017. The hope is that all projects are registered, preferably before they are launched, and that results are clearly linked to their respective study, so that in the future meta-analysts can work from the full universe of studies. Chapter 5 (Glennerster, 2017) and Chapter 4 (Banerjee et al., 2017) in Volume 1 also have a useful exchange on the value to go further than registration and pre-analysis plan, where researchers lay out in advance the hypotheses to be tested and the regressions to be run.[2] Overall, both chapters not only point out the value in tying the hands of a partner, who may be too eager to show success, but also emphasize that this comes with the cost of losing the flexibility to explore the data. In Chapter 4 of Volume 1, Banerjee et al. (2017) point out that, if the data are available to others, there is in principle no reason to pre-specify a specific analysis, since anyone can decide what to run. This ties in to another issue that is discussed in Chapter 5 of Volume 1 (Glennerster, 2017): The need for open access of complete and usable data, both for reproducing existing analyses and for running others. This is an area where a lot of progress has been made, and hopefully more will be made in years to come.

1.2.2 Use other experiments to understand mechanisms
A second approach is to use the results from other experiments to test specific channels, and support the conclusions from the policy experiment. One way to do is to draw parallels between those results and results from laboratory experiments conducted in comparable settings [see Chapter 10 in Volume 1 (Gneezy and Imas, 2017)]. Another option involves carrying out additional field experiments that provide support for the causal channels that underlie the policy claim [see Chapter 4 in Volume 2 (Kling et al., 2017)].

1.2.3 Multi-site projects
A third approach is to conceive projects as multi-site projects from the start. One recent example of such an enterprise is the Graduation approach—an integrated, multi-faceted program with livelihood promotion at its core that aims to graduate individuals out of

---

[2] Paluck and Shafir (2017) also discuss the merit of pre-registration and pre-analysis plan for an experimenter who has some construal of what the results should be.

extreme poverty and onto a long-term, sustainable higher consumption path, which is discussed in Chapter 7 of Volume 2 (Hanna and Karlan, 2017). BRAC, perhaps the world's largest nongovernmental organization, has scaled-up this program in Bangladesh (Bandiera et al., 2013), while NGOs around the world have engaged in similar livelihood-based efforts. Six randomized trials were undertaken over the same time period across the world (Ethiopia, Ghana, Honduras, India, Pakistan, and Peru). The teams regularly communicated with each other and with BRAC to ensure that their local adaptations remained true to the original program. The results suggest that the integrated multi-faceted program was sufficient to increase long-term income, where long-term is defined as 3 years after the productive asset transfer (Banerjee et al., 2015a,b). Using an index approach to account for multiple hypotheses testing, positive impacts were found for consumption, income and revenue, asset wealth, food security, financial inclusion, physical health, mental health, labor supply, political involvement, and women's decision-making after 2 years. After a third year, the results remained the same in 8 out of 10 outcome categories. There is country-by-country variation (e.g., the program was ineffective in Honduras), and the team is currently working on a meta-analysis to quantify the level of heterogeneity.

1.2.4 Structured speculation

One issue is that there is little the researcher can do ex-post to causally identify the source of differences in findings across countries. An option for multi-site projects would be to take guidance from the first few sites to make a prediction on what the next sites would find. To discipline this process, researchers would be encouraged to use the results from existing trials to make some explicit predictions about what they expect to observe in other samples (or with slightly different treatments). These can serve as a guide for subsequent trials. This idea is discussed in Chapter 4 of Volume 1 (Banerjee et al., 2017), where it is called structured speculation. They propose the following broad guidelines for structured speculation:

1. Experimenters should systematically speculate about the external validity of their findings.
2. Such speculation should be clearly and cleanly separated from the rest of the paper, maybe in a section called speculation.
3. Speculation should be precise and falsifiable.

According to Banerjee et al. (2017), structured speculation has three advantages: First, it ensures that the researcher's specific knowledge is captured. Second, it creates a clear sense of where else experiments should be run. Third, it creates incentives to design research that has greater external validity. They write the following:

> To address scalability, experimenters may structure local pilot studies for easy comparison with their main experiments. To identify the right sub-populations for generalizing to other environments, experimenters can identify ahead of time the characteristics of groups that can be generalized, and stratify on those. To extend the results to populations with a different distribution of unobserved

characteristics, experimenters may elicit the former using the selective trial techniques discussed in Chassang et al. (2012), and run the experiments separately for each of the groups so identified.

As this idea of structured speculation is just being proposed, there are few examples as yet. A notable example is Dupas (2014), who studies the effect of short-term subsidies on long-run adoption of new health products and reports that short-term subsidies had a significant impact on the adoption of a more effective and comfortable class of bed nets. The paper then provides a clear discussion of external validity. It first spells out a simple and transparent argument relating the effectiveness of short-run subsidies to (1) the speed at which various forms of uncertainty are resolved; (2) the timing of a user's costs and benefits. If the uncertainty over benefits is resolved quickly, short-run subsidies can have a long-term effect. If uncertainty over benefits is resolved slowly, and adoption costs are incurred early on, short-run subsidies are unlikely to have a long-term effect.

Dupas (2014) then answers the question "For what types of health products and contexts would we expect the same results to obtain?" It does so by classifying potential technologies into three categories based on how short-run (or one-time) subsidies would change adoption patterns. Clearly, there could be such discussions at the end of all papers, not just ones featuring RCTs. But because RCTs can be purposefully designed and placed, there is a higher chance of follow-up in this case.

1.3 Testing theories

This discussion makes clear that the talking about external validity only makes sense once we understand the lesson that we want to generalize. Reflecting on the problem of partner selection that we mentioned earlier, in Chapter 5 of Volume 1, Glennerster (2017) writes the following:

> *Whether we want to prioritize having a representative partner or a highly committed partner depends on the objective of the research. If we are testing an underlying human behavior—such as a willingness to pay now for benefits in the future—the representativeness of the partner may be less relevant. If we want to know whether a type of program, as it is usually implemented, works, we will want to prioritize working with a representative partner. Note that does this type of program work is not necessarily a more policy-relevant question than a more general question about human behavior. By their nature, more general questions generalize better and can be applied to a wider range of policy questions.*

A big contribution of field experiments has been the ability to test theory. In Chapter 3 of Volume 1, Imbens and Athey (2017) argue a randomized experiment is unique in the control that the researcher has over the assignment mechanism. We would take the argument one step further: Randomization is also unique in the control that the researcher (often) has on the treatment itself. In observational studies, however beautifully designed, the researcher is limited to evaluating what has been implemented in the world. In a randomized experiment, she can manipulate the treatment in ways that we do not observe in reality. This has a number of advantages. First, she can innovate, i.e., design new policies or interventions that she thinks will be effective based on prior knowledge or theory, and test them even if no policymaker is thinking of putting them in practice yet. Development economists have many ideas, often inspired by what they have read or researched, and many of the randomized experiment projects come out of those: They test in the field an intervention that simply did not exist before (a kilogram of lentil for parents who vaccinate their kids; stickers to encourage riders to speak up against a bad driver; free chlorine dispensers, etc.).

Second, she can introduce variations that will help her test implications of existing theories or establish facts that could not otherwise be established. The well-known Negative Income Tax (NIT) experiment was designed with precisely that idea in mind: In general, when wages are raised, this creates both income and substitution effects, which cannot easily be separated (Heckman, 1992). But randomized manipulation of the slope and the intercept of a wage schedule make it possible to estimate both together. Interestingly, after the initial NIT and the Rand Health Insurance Experiment, the tradition of social experiments in the US has mainly been to obtain causal effect of social policies that were often fairly comprehensive packages (Gueron, 2017), though according to Chapter 4 of Volume 2 (Kling et al., 2017) there has been a recent revival of what they call mechanism experiments which they define to be the following:

> ...an experiment that tests a mechanism—that is, it tests not the effects of variation in policy parameters themselves, directly, but the effects of variation in an intermediate link in the causal chain that connects (or is hypothesized to connect) a policy to an outcome. That is, where there is a specified policy that has candidate mechanisms that affect an outcome of policy concern, the mechanism experiment tests one or more of those mechanisms. There can be one or more mechanisms that link the policy to the outcome, which could operate in parallel (for example when there are multiple potential mediating channels through which a policy could change outcomes) or sequentially (if for example some mechanisms affect take-up or implementation fidelity). The central idea is that the mechanism experiment is intended to be informative about some policy but does not involve a test of that policy directly.

In other words, mechanism experiments are a specific version of experiments that test theories, which distinctively have a relatively direct implication for the design of some policy.

Experiments that test theories, including mechanism experiments, have always had an important place in development economics and are now also used in developed countries. Banerjee and Duflo (2009) discuss some early examples of mechanism experiments including the justly influential papers on observing unobservables by Karlan and Zinman (2009). A number of these are discussed in Chapter 8 of Volume 1 (Bertrand and Duflo, 2017), Chapter 1 of Volume 2 (Dupas and Miguel, 2017), and Chapter 7 of Volume 2 (Hanna and Karlan, 2017).

Another area where it is now standard to use field experiments to test theories is in the growing literature on replicating tests of theories that were previously conducted in the laboratory in more realistic settings. Chapter 7 (Al-Ubaydli and List, 2017) and Chapter 10 (Gneezy and Imas, 2017) in Volume 1 are both excellent introduction to this literature, with the first focusing on theoretical predictions about market outcomes while the second is more about understanding preferences. By moving from the lab to the field, the studies that are reviewed in these two chapters aim to select a more relevant population, and to place them in situations that are not artificial, to test these theories in the contexts that are relevant in practice. The idea is that, in the lab, people do not behave as they would in reality. Chapter 6 in Volume 1 (Paluck and Shafir, 2017) goes one step further in helping us think about how an experimenter must design an experiment to successfully test a theory. They place the notion of construal at the center of their approach. They write: "Construal is defined as the individual's subjective interpretation of a stimulus, whether the stimulus is a choice set, a situation, another person group of people, or an experimental intervention." To successfully test a theory, the experiment must be designed such that the participants understand the world (and the different treatments) in the way the experimenter intended, and therefore their action and behavior in the different conditions can be interpreted. Of course, construal is relevant for other research as well (it affects how people will respond to a survey). But it is particularly important in an experimental set up, when a researcher is thinking about relevant manipulation. There is no magic recipe to do this, but Paluck and Shafir emphasize and encourage us to use this lens to think about basic experimental practice: Piloting, as well as open-ended and open-minded observations, in the early phase of an experiment to ensure that the participants' construal is the same as the researchers; a manipulation check to make sure that participants understood that they were being treated; and decisions on whether to be present or not during an experiment.

1.4 Data collection

Data collection is at the core of experimental work, since administrative data are not always available or sufficient to obtain information on the relevant outcome. Considerable progress has been made on this front. Chapter 5 in Volume 1 (Glennerster, 2017) gives specific and useful guidance on how researchers can insure the validity of the data that they have collected, summarizing best practices on monitoring, back checking, and effective use of information technology. Experiments have also spurred creativity in measurement, and Glennerster's chapter, as well as almost all the other chapters, covers these innovations. We elaborate a bit more on these issues here.

In principle, there is no automatic link between careful and innovative collection of microeconomic data and the experimental method. However, one specific feature of experiments that serves to encourage the development of new measurement methods is high take-up rates and a specific measurement problem. In many experimental studies, a large fraction of those who are intended to be affected by the program are actually affected. This means that the number of units on which data need to be collected to assess the impact of the program does not have to be very large and that data are typically collected especially for the purpose of the experiment. Elaborate and expensive measurement of outcomes is then easier to afford than in the context of a large multipurpose household or firm survey. By contrast, observational studies must often rely on identification on variation (policy changes, market-induced variation, natural variation, supply shocks, etc.) that cover large populations, requiring the use of a large dataset often not collected for a specific purpose. This makes it more difficult to fine-tune the measurement to the specific question at hand. Moreover, even if it is possible ex post to do a sophisticated data collection exercise specifically targeted to the question, it is generally impossible to do it for the preprogram situation. This precludes the use of a difference-in-differences strategy for these types of outcomes, which again limits the incentives to collect them ex-post.

Some of the most exciting recent developments related to field experiments have to do with measurement. Researchers have turned to other sub-fields of economics as well as different fields altogether to borrow tools for measuring outcomes. Examples include soil testing for quality and remote sensing for real time data in agriculture [see Chapter 5 in Volume 2 (de Janvry et al., 2017) for a review on agriculture]; techniques developed by social psychologists for difficult to measure outcomes such as discrimination and prejudice—audit and correspondence studies, implicit association tests, Goldberg experiments, and List experiments [see Chapter 8 in Volume 1 (Bertrand and Duflo, 2017) for a review on discrimination]; tools developed by cognitive psychologists for child development (Attanasio et al., 2014); tools inspired by economic theory, such as Becker—DeGroot—Marshak games to infer willingness to pay [see a discussion in Chapter 1 in Volume 2 (Dupas and Miguel, 2017)]; biomarkers in health, beyond the traditional height, weight, and hemoglobin (cortisol to measure stress for example); wearable devices to measure mobility or effort (Rao et al.,2016; Kreindler, 2016).

Specific methods and devices that exactly suit the purpose at hand have also been developed for experiments. Olken (2007) is one example of the kind of data that can be collected in an experimental setting. The objective was to determine whether audits or community monitoring was an effective way to curb corruption in decentralized construction projects. Getting a reliable measure of actual levels of corruption was thus necessary. Olken focused on roads and had engineers dig holes in the road to measure the material used. He then compared that with the level of material reported to be used. The difference is a measure of how much of the material was stolen, or never purchased but invoiced, and thus an objective measure of corruption. Olken then demonstrated that this measure of missing inputs is affected by the threat of audits, but not, except under one specific condition, by encouraging greater participation in community meetings. Rigol et al. (2016) provide another example of innovative data collection practices. For their experiment, to accurately measure if and when people wash their hands, they designed soap dispensers that could track when the pump was being pushed and hired a Chinese company to manufacture them. Similar audit methodologies are used to measure the impact of interventions in health, such as patients posing with specific diseases to measure the impact of training (Banerjee et al., 2016b,c,d) or ineligible people attempting to obtain free bed nets (Dupas et al., 2016). Even a partial list of such examples would be very long.

In parallel, greater use is being made of administrative data, which are often combined with large-scale experiments. Administrative data are often at the core of the analysis of experiments in the US [see Chapter 2 in Volume 1 (Gueron, 2017) and Chapter 8 in Volume 2 (von Wachter and Rothstein, 2017)], and the more recent availability of tax data has allowed to examine long-term impacts of interventions (Chetty et al., 2011, 2016). Recently, the practice has also spread to developing countries. For example, Banerjee et al. (2016b,c,d) make use of both publicly available administrative data on a workfare program in India and restricted expenditure data made available to them as part of the experiment; Olken et al. (2016) use administrative tax data from Pakistan; and Attanasio et al. (2016) use unemployment insurance data to measure the long-term effect of job training in Colombia.

Another increasingly important source of data comes from the use of lab-in-the-field experiments either as predictors of the treatment effect (e.g., commitment devices should help those who have self-control problems more than others) or as an outcome (e.g., cooperation in a public goods game as a measure of success in creating social capital). Chapter 10 in Volume 1 (Gneezy and Imas, 2017) not only provides a number of examples, but also warns against blindly trusting lab-in-the-field experiments to unearth deep preferences—for example, behavior in a dictator game may not necessarily predict pro-social behaviors in real-life contexts.

The bottom line is that there has been great progress in our understanding of how to creatively and accurately collect or use existing data that goes beyond the traditional surveys, and these insights have led both to better projects and to innovations in data collection that have been adopted in non-randomized work as well.

1.5 Iterate and build on previous research in the same settings

Another methodological advantage of RCTs also relates to the control that researchers have over the assignment and, often enough, over the treatments themselves. Well-identified policy evaluations often raise more questions than they can actually answer. In particular, we are often left wondering why things turned out the way they did and how to change the intervention to make things (even) better.

This is where the ability to keep trying different interventions can be enormously valuable. Chapter 2 in Volume 2 (Fryer, 2017) on education in the developed world is in part a history of such a quest. Fryer details the process of trying to figure out what actually works in closing the black—white achievement gap, describing the long line of experiments that failed to deliver or deliver enough, and the slow accretion of learnings from successes and failures. Through this process, the main directions eventually became clear and he is able to conclude the following:

> *These facts provide reason for optimism. Through the systematic implementation of randomized field experiments designed to increase human capital of school-aged children, we have substantially increased our knowledge of how to produce human capital and have assembled a canon of best practices.*

We see a very similar process of dynamic discovery in Chapter 9 of Volume 1 (Gerber and Green, 2017) on the question of how to influence voter turnout. Marketing experiments also feature dynamically evolving treatments [see Chapter 11 in Volume 1 (Simester, 2017)], as do some agricultural experiments [see Chapter 5 in Volume 2 (de Janvry et al., 2017)].

1.6 Unpacking the interventions

Finally, RCTs allow the possibility to unpack a program to its constituent elements. Here again the work may be iterative. For example, all the initial evaluations of the BRAC ultra poor program were done using their full package, as were a large number of evaluations of the Mexican conditional cash transfer (CCT) program (PROGRESA). But both for research and for policy, once we know that the full program works, there is a clear interest in knowing what are the elements that are key to its success. In recent years, a number of papers have looked inside CCTs, relaxing the conditionality and altering it in other ways which are discussed in Chapter 7 of Volume 2 (Hanna and Karlan, 2017). Hanna and Karlan also highlight the challenge of fully unpacking a program in the context of their discussion of the graduation program, mentioned above, which provides beneficiaries with the gift of an asset, as well as access to a savings opportunity, health services and information, life coaching, and a small stipend. They write the following:

> *The ideal method, if unconstrained by budget and organizational constraints, is a complex experimental design that randomizes all permutations of each component. The productive asset transfer, if the only issue were a credit market failure, may have been sufficient to generate these results, and if no other component enabled an individual to accumulate sufficient capital to acquire the asset, the transfer alone may have been a necessary component. The savings component on the other hand may have been a substitute for the productive asset transfer, by lowering transaction costs to save and serving as a behavioral intervention which facilitated staying on task to accumulate savings. Clearly it is not realistic in one setting to test the necessity or sufficiency of each component, and interaction across components: Even if treated simplistically with each component either present or not, this would imply $2 \times 2 \times 2 \times 2 = 16$ experimental groups.*

As this paragraph implies, the way forward is clearly going to be the development of a mosaic, rather than any one definitive study that both tests each component and also includes sufficient contextual and market variations so that it can help set the policy for a myriad of countries and populations. More work is needed to tease apart the different components: asset transfer (addresses capital market failures), savings account (lowers savings transaction fee), information (addresses information failures), life-coaching (addresses behavioral constraints, and perhaps changes expectations and beliefs about possible return on investment), health services and information (addresses health market failures), consumption support (addresses nutrition-based poverty traps), etc. Furthermore, for several of these questions, there are key open issues for how to address them; for example, life-coaching can take on an infinite number of manifestations. Some organizations conduct life-coaching through religion, others through interactive problem-solving, and others through psychotherapy approaches (Bolton et al., 2003, 2007; Patel et al., 2010) Much remains to be learned not only just in regard to the promise of such life-coaching components, but also how to make them work (if they work at all).

In some settings, particularly when working on a large scale with a government, it is actually possible to experiment from the beginning with various versions of a program. This serves two purposes: It gives us a handle on the theory behind the program and it has operational value for the government, who can pick the most cost-effective combination. The evaluation of potential reforms of Indonesia's Raskin program by Banerjee et al. (2016b,c,d), discussed in Chapter 7 of Volume 2 (Hanna and Karlan, 2017), is an example.

2. THE IMPACT ON THE WAY WE THINK ABOUT THE WORLD

Whether or not the main point of a particular RCT was to test a theory, its results end up altering our theories about the world. While this is true of all credible empirical work, it is especially true of RCT results. This is because one advantage of RCTs and RCT-like natural experiments is that they do not rely on any theory for identification and therefore open the door to questioning even the most basic assumptions of the field. In this section, we list some of the areas where there are robust insights derived from the RCT literature, mostly building upon the material discussed in various chapters throughout this volume.

2.1 On the value of better human capital

The literature from health RCTs in developing countries [summarized in Chapter 1 of Volume 2 (Dupas and Miguel, 2017)] confirms what one would suspect that serious ailments such as HIV and malaria have large income/productivity consequences (this is based on the random assignment of scarce treatments). Dupas and Miguel also report on some RCTs that look at longer-term outcomes for children, who received health interventions in childhood. In some instances, such as deworming, there are striking long-term effects on, for example, earnings as an adult. The long-term follow-up of the Moving to Opportunity experiment in the United States, described in some detail in Chapter 8 of Volume 2 (von Wachter and Rothstein, 2017), has similarly large earnings positive consequences for those who benefitted from the move to a less poor neighborhood at young ages. Both chapters suggest that the magnitude of the long-term effects has not been explained fully, given the relatively small short-term effects.

Unfortunately, there seems to be very little else in the RCT literature on either health or education, either in the developed or the developing world, that can help us understand the channels through which interventions at relatively young ages can have persistent and large effects. This remains an important area for future work.

2.2 On reforming education

The one very clear message from the RCT literature on education summarized in Chapter 2 (Fryer, 2017) (for the developed world) and in Chapter 3 (Muralidharan, 2017) of Volume 2 (for the developing world) is that Teaching at the Right Level (TaRL) is perhaps the central ingredient of programs that succeed in helping the average school-age student perform substantially better. The idea behind the intervention is very simple: The student's specific deficiencies need to be identified and addressed, even if they do not align with what he or she is expected to know at his or her age or grade. This might seem obvious, but both chapters make the point that it is often precluded by the compulsions of school systems—in particular the need to keep up with the curriculum.

The right way to implement TaRL, however, differs across the two contexts. Fryer makes the case for expensive high-intensity tutoring while Muralidharan describes the success of a number of low-cost interventions, where a limited amount of focused teaching by minimally trained volunteers seems to have had large positive effects. This difference could reflect, among other things, differences in the starting point (the kids in the developing world are so much further behind that it is easy to move them) or the fact that the right kind of low-intensity tutoring has not yet been arrived at in the developed countries.

It is also striking how many well-regarded interventions either do not work at all or give relatively weak positive results. These include various aspects of school infrastructure, student incentives, increasing the teacher–student ratio, standard teacher training/professional development, altering the teacher selection process, and perhaps most strikingly, school vouchers. Other interventions, like computer-assisted learning, seem to deliver mostly zero or negative results, but there are also a few large, significantly positive results, all from the developing world. The difference may come from the opportunity cost of the time—perhaps the alternatives to learning from the computer are worse in developing countries, where teachers are often completely disengaged and frequently missing. Another mixed bag is teacher incentives, where both Fryer and Muralidharan report a few very large positive effects and many small or zero effects. The reason for the variation may lie in the details of how the incentives were implemented, or in the internal culture or management of the school.

2.3 On the design of redistributive programs

Income and incentive (substitution) effects on labor supply are at the heart of the design of redistributive and social insurance programs. If these effects are strong and negative, the extent of possible income transfer may be severely limited and the constrained optimal insurance will tend to be very partial. Reassuringly, from the point of view of the efficiency of redistributive policies, the evidence from the developed world summarized in Chapter 8 of Volume 2 (von Wachter and Rothstein, 2017) suggests that both elasticities are negative, but tend to be small (around 0.1). The evidence from the developing world, summarized in Chapter 7 of Volume 2 (Hanna and Karlan, 2017), finds in fact no clear evidence of negative income effects on labor supply. Interestingly, the unconditional income transfers seem to have no effect on labor supply, while the transfer of assets, such as in the so-called graduation programs, seems to encourage people to work harder, if anything.[3] It should be recognized, however, that these are impure income effects, since the assets potentially increased the marginal product of labor, though that still supports the case for redistribution. In addition, two recent review articles of the evidence from developing countries suggest that the additional income is often used to boost nutrition (Banerjee, 2016) and does not increase the consumption of temptation goods (Evans and Popova, 2014), which further reinforces the case for redistribution.

Given this, it is not surprising that the beneficiaries of a variety of asset transfer programs have been found to be durably better off as much as 5 years after they ceased to have any contact with the program itself. It remains to be seen whether this is the effect of the asset transfer per se or the whole package, which nudges beneficiaries to use their assets for long-run economic betterment.

On the flip side, the absence of strong incentive effects means that it is costly to use financial incentives to change behavior. Chapter 8 in Volume 2 (von Wachter and Rothstein, 2017) summarizes the evidence on a range of social programs in developed countries, which try to use incentives to alter the job search and job retention behavior of those at the margins of the labor market and find limited effects at best. The experience from CCTs in the less-developed world [as discussed in Chapter 7 of Volume 2 (Hanna and Karlan, 2017)] is a bit more varied; most of the programs do alter behavior but, with some exceptions, the cost of doing so tends to be substantial.

2.4 On the design of incentives for public officials

A somewhat related literature that is mainly focused on developing countries [though there are echoes in Chapter 2 (Fryer, 2017) and Chapter 8 (von Wachter and Rothstein, 2017) of Volume 2] emphasizes the difficulty of using incentives to get better performance from public officials. This is the subject of a small but growing literature that is reviewed in Chapter 6 of Volume 2 (Olken et al., 2017). The chapter starts by demonstrating that government employees are paid a premium in developing countries, which is not true in the developed world. Efficiency wage theory would suggest that this would

---

[3] Banerjee et al. (2016b,c,d) provide a summary of the evidence on income effects on labor supply.

make it easier to give incentives to government employees, but that does not seem to be the case. Incentives based on job termination are very rarely used and there is lots of prima facie evidence of delinquency by these well-paid officials, which has inspired a body of recent RCTs focused on trying to improve government performance by providing better incentives and other means. One main take-away from this literature is that it is difficult to design proper incentives for these officials (because of the risk of perverse responses) and perhaps even more difficult to make sure that these incentives are actually implemented.

2.5 On access to financial products

Given the success of asset transfer programs in raising earnings, the natural presumption is that improved access to reasonably priced credit would have similar effects. Yet, as Chapter 7 in Volume 2 (Hanna and Karlan, 2017) makes clear [see also Chapter 5 in Volume 2 (de Janvry et al., 2017)], there is essentially no support from RCTs for this view (this particular literature is almost exclusively focused on the developing world). Improving access to micro-credit, to take the obvious example, seems to have some effects on direction of consumer spending but no effects on earnings or even business earnings. This might be because the microcredit product is poorly designed, or because credit discourages risk-taking, or because the loan amounts are too small to permit the borrowers to invest in projects that earn high returns (or for a variety of other reasons), but the fact itself is striking.

On the other hand, in the case of agriculture, there is a clear RCT evidence of positive impacts on earnings from access to subsidized crop insurance [see Chapter 5 in Volume 2 (de Janvry et al., 2017)]. The study by Karlan et al. (2014) on agriculture in Ghana (discussed in Chapter 5 of Volume 2) is especially striking in this context because it finds large investment and productivity effects from access to subsidized insurance, but no investment or productivity effects from a cash transfer. The authors interpret this as saying that these farmers are not credit constrained, however it is then not clear as to why these farmers do not invest and self-insure by borrowing and lending. It is true that self-insurance is not as good as getting insurance from the market, but the welfare loss seems small relative to the productivity gains. We believe that there exist important modeling issues here that have yet to be resolved.

2.6 On the demand for insurance and other prophylactic products

While insurance seems to be very useful to low income beneficiaries—who are happy to purchase insurance when it is highly subsidized, and change their behavior to take advantage of it—there is very little demand for it at the market price or anywhere close to it. This is true of both crop insurance [see Chapter 5 in Volume 2 (de Janvry et al., 2017)] and health insurance [see Chapter 1 in Volume 2 (Dupas and Miguel, 2017)]. de Janvry, Sadoulet, and Suri suggest that this is in part because of a trust deficit between the insurer and the insured, who think that the insurer would refuse to pay ex post. However, Dupas and Miguel make the point that the same lack of demand is also seen in the case of most health protection goods—such as deworming pills, insecticide-treated bed nets, and vaccination—suggesting that the problem may be more general.

One possibility is that there is not enough information about the efficacy of these products. While there is prima facie evidence of an information deficit, Chapter 1 in Volume 2 (Dupas and Miguel, 2017) finds the impact of providing information on the demand for healthcare to be quite mixed. The alternative is that the lack of demand is related to the widely documented phenomenon of present bias: Essentially the problem is that prophylactic products require the buyer to pay now and for uncertain future benefits. However, we are clearly some distance from a full resolution of the problem of demand and further research is clearly necessary.

2.7 On preferences and preference change

Deviations like these from the standard model of rational behavior in economic models are the inspiration for the three chapters: Chapter 7 (Al-Ubaydli and List, 2017), Chapter 10 (Gneezy and Imas, 2017), and Chapter 11 (Simester, 2017) of Volume 1, though from somewhat different angles. Al-Ubaydli and List explicitly take on the question of robustness of these deviations. In particular, they focus on whether or not these deviations survive strong incentives and long practice, both of which are characteristics of long-term market participants (of course this is not the only population of interest—mothers, for example, only need to vaccinate their children a few times in their lives). They conclude that while some of these deviations go away with practice or when properly incentivized, many of them are indeed quite robust—e.g., professionals are not necessarily less likely to deviate than students—and point out that despite this, many individual markets still deliver outcomes that are quite close to what the conventional equilibrium would predict.

Gneezy and Imas (Chapter 10 in Volume 1) have a somewhat different concern: Do we actually pick up the deep preference parameter we are looking for when we use the outcomes from lab-in-the-field experiments? For example, they conclude that:

The results suggest that incentivized lottery experiments typically used to elicit risk attitudes lack predictive power over the unincentivized general survey questions in predicting relevant real-world behavior such as investment choices.

On the other hand, they find that the gender difference in competitiveness as measured by performance in games does correlate strikingly with how patriarchal the society is.

Chapter 11 in Volume 1 (Simester, 2017) describes field experiments in marketing. The marketing field takes as given that consumers have biases and use simple heuristics to make decisions. A significant part of marketing effort goes into exploiting those to push the product. Moreover, there is advertising, which is in part directed towards altering preferences.

The experimental evidence described in Chapter 11 of Volume 1 (Simester, 2017) is in part about understanding the nature of people's heuristics and biases, how marketers respond to these heuristics and biases, and what kinds of advertising are most effective in changing preferences. There seems to be no general lesson other than the fact that many contextual factors seem to matter and therefore experimentation is quite valuable. As a result, there are now dynamic models of targeted marketing where the specific intervention varies based on the past experience with that particular client or group of clients, and these models are tested using experimental methods. This is a very different approach from most of the field experiment literature, where the interventions to be tested are chosen based on priori thinking rather than experimentation. This is in part possible because in this age of high internet penetration and big data, marketing instruments (prices, offers, advertising, etc.) can be varied at a high frequency and the reaction to the changes can be tracked and processed immediately. This is obviously not always the case in other areas of economics, but it is worth thinking about how to design more experiments which follow the marketing model.

Finally, Chapter 8 in Volume 1 (Bertrand and Duflo, 2017) focuses on one specific kind of preferences: those that lead to prejudice and discrimination. The chapter starts by showing that there is robust experimental evidence of prejudice and discrimination, including self-discrimination based on audit studies, willingness to pay studies, and various psychological tools such as IATs and Goldberg Paradox experiments. On the more difficult question of whether these are based on innate preferences rather than statistical discrimination, they find less clear-cut experimental evidence. However, the balance of the evidence taken together suggests that preferences do play an important role. The second part of the chapter describes the experimental evidence showing that these identity-based preferences (whether innate or induced) have significant negative consequences both for those who are viewed negatively as a result and for productivity in general. The final section then goes into the question of whether these preferences can be altered by an appropriate choice of interventions. This is perhaps where the experimental evidence is the most valuable and the scarcest. Laboratory work suggests that preference change is indeed possible, but too few convincing field studies have been conducted.

2.8 On the role of the community

Discrimination is of course one important reason why the structure of communities can have significant negative effects. However, there is now a large experimental literature that looks for positive effects. Chapter 5 in Volume 2 (de Janvry et al., 2017) reports on the literature on learning from friends and neighbors in agriculture. Chapter 7 in Volume 2 (Hanna and Karlan, 2017) discusses the possibility of using the community's knowledge about its members to identify the poor. Chapter 1 (Dupas and Miguel, 2017), Chapter 3

(Muralidharan, 2017), and Chapter 6 (Olken et al., 2017) in Volume 2 all discuss the possibility of a specific type of collective action: using the community to monitor and incentivize local government officials. Our overall assessment of this evidence is that it is disappointing. There are few very successful examples, but in most cases there is surprisingly little transmission/use of collective knowledge or collective action. There are of course plausible explanations—many of which are mentioned in the chapters—but understanding why the community does not make use of the information and access it clearly remains an important agenda item for the future.

2.9 On getting people to vote

One form of collective action that many people do engage in is voting. In fact, so-called rational models of voting find it very difficult to explain why quite so many people vote. Given that, theory is unlikely to be a very good guide to the question of how to enfranchise even more people, especially from socially excluded groups. Starting from this observation, political scientists Alan Gerber and Don Green decided to take a radically empiricist approach to understanding how to influence turnout: They essentially organized a long series of RCTs where they tried out all the standard approaches and combinations thereof. This effort inspired a large and growing literature in political science which is detailed in Chapter 9 in Volume 1 (Gerber and Green, 2017). They summarize the main learnings from it in the following succinct paragraph:

> One is that encouragements to vote tend to be more effective when delivered in person than via direct mail or email. Another is that advocacy messages that give voters reasons to support or oppose a given candidate or cause tend not to increase turnout. Yet another is that messages that forcefully assert the social norm of civic participation are often highly effective at stimulating turnout, especially in low salience elections.

3. CONCLUSION

Overall, these chapters provide an incredibly rich overview of the remarkable progress that has occurred over the last 20 years in regard to field experimentation, reflecting both on advances and the issues that remain, as well as providing useful research tips and insights into what the next steps should be. We hope that this Handbook provides guidance, identifies knowledge gaps, spurs further creativity, and leads to research that continues to challenge our assumptions and helps us understand the world better.

REFERENCES

Al-Ubaydli, O., List, J., 2017. Field experiments in markets. In: Banerjee, A.V., Duflo, E. (Eds.), Handbook of Field Experiments, vol. 1, pp. 271–307.

Alesina, A., Giuliano, P., Nunn, N., 2013. On the origins of gender roles: women and the plough. Q. J. Econ. 128 (2), 469–530.

Attanasio, O.P., Meghir, C., Santiago, A., 2012. Education choices in Mexico: using a structural model and a randomized experiment to evaluate progresa. Rev. Econ. Stud. 79 (1), 37–66.

Attanasio, O.P., Fernández, C., Fitzsimons, E.O., Grantham-McGregor, S.M., Meghir, C., Rubio-Codina, M., 2014. Using the infrastructure of a conditional cash transfer program to deliver a scalable integrated early child development program in Colombia: cluster randomized controlled trial. BMJ 349, g5785.

Attanasio, O.P., Medina, A., Meghir, C., 2016. Long term impact of vouchers for vocational training: experimental evidence for Colombia. Am. Econ. J. (forthcoming).

Bandiera, O., Burgess, R., Das, N., Gulesci, S., Rasul, I., Sulaiman, M., 2013. Can basic entrepreneurship transform the economic lives of the poor? IZA Discuss. Pap. 7386.

Banerjee, A.V., Duflo, E., 2009. The experimental approach to development economics. Annu. Rev. Econ. 1, 151–178.

Banerjee, A.V., Iyer, L., 2005. History, institutions, and economic performance: the legacy of colonial land tenure systems in India. Am. Econ. Rev. 95 (4), 1190–1213.

Banerjee, A.V., Amsden, A.H., Bates, R.H., Bhagwati, J.N., Deaton, A., Stern, N., 2007. Making Aid Work. MIT Press.

Banerjee, A.V., Duflo, E., Goldberg, N., Karlan, D., Osei, R., Parienté, W., Shapiro, J., Thuysbaert, B., Udry, C., 2015a. A multifaceted program causes lasting progress for the very poor: evidence from six countries. Science 348 (6236), 1260799.

Banerjee, A.V., Hanna, R., Kyle, J.C., Olken, B.A., Sumarto, S., 2015b. The power of transparency: information, identification cards and food subsidy programs in Indonesia. Natl. Bureau Econ. Res. (No. w20923).

Banerjee, A.V., Duflo, E., Kremer, M., 2016a. The influence of randomized controlled trials on development economics research and on development policy. Mimeo MIT.

Banerjee, A.V., Duflo, E., Imbert, C., Mathew, S., Pande, R., 2016b. Can e-governance reduce capture of public programs? Experimental evidence from India's employment guarantee. Mimeo.

Banerjee, A.V., Das, J., Hussam, R., 2016c. Improving the Quality of Private Sector Health Care in West Bengal (forthcoming in Science).

Banerjee, A.V., Hanna, R., Olken, B.A., Kreindler, G., 2016d. Debunking the stereotype of the lazy welfare recipient: evidence from cash transfer programs worldwide. Mimeo.

Banerjee, A.V., Chassang, S., Snowberg, E., 2017. Decision theoretic approaches to experiment design and external validity. In: Banerjee, A.V., Duflo, E. (Eds.), Handbook of Field Experiments, vol. 1, pp. 141–174.

Banerjee, A.V., 2016. Policies for a better-fed world. Rev. World Econ. 152 (1), 3–17.

Bertrand, M., Duflo, E., 2017. Field experiments on discrimination. In: Banerjee, A.V., Duflo, E. (Eds.), Handbook of Field Experiments, vol. 1, pp. 309–393.

Bolton, P., Bass, J., Neugebauer, R., Verdeli, H., Clougherty, K.F., Wickramaratne, P., Speelman, L., Ndogoni, L., Weissman, M., 2003. Group interpersonal psychotherapy for depression in rural Uganda: a randomized controlled trial. JAMA 289 (23), 3117–3124.

Bolton, P., Bass, J., Betancourt, T., Speelman, L., Onyango, G., Clougherty, K.F., Neugebauer, R., Murray, L., Verdeli, H., 2007. Interventions for depression symptoms among adolescent survivors of war and displacement in northern Uganda: a randomized controlled trial. JAMA 298 (5), 519–527.

Chassang, S., Padró i Miquel, G., Snowberg, E., 2012. Selective trials: a principal-agent approach to randomized controlled experiments. Am. Econ. Rev. 102 (4), 1279–1309.

Chetty, R., Friedman, J.N., Hilger, N., Saez, E., Schanzenbach, D.W., Yagan, D., 2011. How does your kindergarten classroom affect your earnings? Evidence from project STAR. Q. J. Econ. 126 (4), 1593–1660.

Chetty, R., Hendren, N., Katz, L.F., 2016. The effects of exposure to better neighborhoods on children: new evidence from the moving to opportunity experiment. Am. Econ. Rev. 106 (4), 855–902.

de Janvry, A., Sadoulet, E., Suri, T., 2017. Field experiments in developing country agriculture. In: Banerjee, A.V., Duflo, E. (Eds.), Handbook of Field Experiments, vol. 2, pp. 175–243.

Deaton, A., 2010. Instruments, randomization, and learning about development. J. Econ. Literature 48 (2), 424–455.

Dell, M., 2010. The persistent effects of Peru's mining mita. Econometrica 78 (6), 1863–1903.

Duflo, E., Glennerster, R., Kremer, M., 2007. Using randomization in development economics research: a toolkit. Handb. Dev. Econ. 4, 3895–3962.

Dupas, P., Miguel, T., 2017. Impacts and determinants of health levels in low-income countries. In: Banerjee, A.V., Duflo, E. (Eds.), Handbook of Field Experiments, vol. 2, pp. 3–94.

Dupas, P., Robinson, J., Dizon-Ross, R., 2016. Governance and the Effectiveness of Public Health Subsidies (forthcoming). http://web.stanford.edu/~pdupas/Governance&Effectiveness_PublicHealthSubsidies.pdf.

Dupas, P., 2014. Short-run subsidies and long-run adoption of new health products: evidence from a field experiment. Econometrica 82 (1), 197–228.

Evans, D.K., Popova, A., 2014. Cash transfers and temptation goods: a review of global evidence. In: World Bank Policy Research Working Paper (6886).

Fisher, R.A., 1925. Statistical Methods for Research Workers. Genesis Publishing Pvt Ltd.

Freedman, D.A., 2006. Statistical models for causation what inferential leverage do they provide? Eval. Rev. 30 (6), 691–713.

Fryer, R., 2017. The production of human capital in developed countries: evidence from 196 randomized field experiments. In: Banerjee, A.V., Duflo, E. (Eds.), Handbook of Field Experiments, vol. 2, pp. 95–322.

Gerber, A., Green, D., 2017. Field experiments on voter mobilization: an overview of a burgeoning literature. In: Banerjee, A.V., Duflo, E. (Eds.), Handbook of Field Experiments, vol. 1, pp. 395–438.

Glennerster, R., 2017. The practicalities of running randomized evaluations: partnerships, measurement, ethics, and transparency. In: Banerjee, A.V., Duflo, E. (Eds.), Handbook of Field Experiments, vol. 1, pp. 175–244.

Gneezy, U., Imas, A., 2017. Lab in the field: measuring preferences in the wild. In: Banerjee, A.V., Duflo, E. (Eds.), Handbook of Field Experiments, vol. 1, pp. 439–464.

Gueron, J., 2017. The politics and practice of social experiments: seeds of a revolution. In: Banerjee, A.V., Duflo, E. (Eds.), Handbook of Field Experiments, vol. 1, pp. 27–70.

Hanna, R., Karlan, D., 2017. Designing social protection programs: using theory and experimentation to understand how to help combat poverty. In: Banerjee, A.V., Duflo, E. (Eds.), Handbook of Field Experiments, vol. 2, pp. 515–554.

Heckman, J., 1992. Randomization and social policy evaluation. In: Manski, C., Garfinkel, I. (Eds.), Evaluating Welfare and Training Programs. Harvard University Press, Cambridge.

Imbens, G., Athey, S., 2017. The econometrics of randomized experiments. In: Banerjee, A.V., Duflo, E. (Eds.), Handbook of Field Experiments, vol. 1, pp. 73–140.

Karlan, D., Zinman, J., 2009. Observing unobservables: identifying information asymmetries with a consumer credit field experiment. Econometrica 77 (6), 1993–2008.

Karlan, D., Osei, R., Osei-Akoto, I., Udry, C., 2014. Agricultural decisions after relaxing credit and risk constraints. Q. J. Econ. 129 (2).

Kling, J., Ludwig, J., Congdon, B., Mullainathan, S., 2017. Social policy: mechanism experiments and policy evaluations. In: Banerjee, A.V., Duflo, E. (Eds.), Handbook of Field Experiments, vol. 2, pp. 389–426.

Kreindler, G., 2016. Driving Delhi? The impact of driving restrictions on driver behavior. Working Paper. (in progress).

Muralidharan, K., 2017. Field experiments in education in the developing countries. In: Banerjee, A.V., Duflo, E. (Eds.), Handbook of Field Experiments, vol. 2, pp. 323–388.

Neyman, J., 1923 [1990]. On the application of probability theory to agricultural experiments. Essay on principles. Section 9. Stat. Sci. 5 (4), 465–472. http://people.hss.caltech.edu/~jiji/Causation-Explanation/Rubin.pdf.

Olken, B.A., Khan, A.Q., Khwaja, A., 2016. Tax farming redux: experimental evidence on performance pay for tax collectors. Q. J. Econ. 131 (1), 219–271.

Olken, B.A., Pande, R., Finan, F., 2017. The personnel economics of the developing state. In: Banerjee, A.V., Duflo, E. (Eds.), Handbook of Field Experiments, vol. 2, pp. 467–514.

Olken, B.A., 2007. Monitoring corruption: evidence from a field experiment in Indonesia. J. Political Econ. 115 (2).

Padró i Miquel, G., Qian, N., Yao, Y., 2012. Social Fragmentation, Public Goods and Elections: Evidence from China. NBER Working Paper No. 18633.

Paluck, E.L., Shafir, E., 2017. The psychology of construal in the design of field experiments. In: Banerjee, A.V., Duflo, E. (Eds.), Handbook of Field Experiments, vol. 1, pp. 245–268.

Patel, V., Weiss, H.A., Chowdhary, N., Naik, S., Pednekar, S., Chatterjee, S., De Silva, M.J., Bhat, B., Araya, R., King, M., et al., 2010. Effectiveness of an intervention led by lay health counsellors for depressive and anxiety disorders in primary care in Goa, India (MANAS): a cluster randomised controlled trial. Lancet 376 (9758).

Rao, G., Schilbach, F., Schofield, H., 2016. Sleepless in Chennai: the economic effect of sleep deprivation among the poor. Working Paper. (in progress).

Rigol, N., Hussam, R., Regianni, G., 2016. Slipped my mind: Handwashing and habit formation. Working Paper. (in progress).

Rubin, D.B., 1974. Estimating causal effects of treatments in randomized and nonrandomized studies. J. Educ. Psychol. 66 (5), 688.

Rubin, D.B., 1981. Estimation in parallel randomized experiments. J. Educ. Behav. Statistics 6 (4), 377–401.

Simester, D., 2017. Field experiments in marketing. In: Banerjee, A.V., Duflo, E. (Eds.), Handbook of Field Experiments, vol. 1, pp. 465–497.

Todd, P.E., Wolpin, K.I., 2006. Assessing the impact of a school subsidy program in Mexico: using a social experiment to validate a dynamic behavioral model of child schooling and fertility. Am. Econ. Rev. 96 (5), 1384–1417.

von Wachter, T., Rothstein, J., 2017. Social experiments in the labor market. In: Banerjee, A.V., Duflo, E. (Eds.), Handbook of Field Experiments, vol. 2, pp. 555–630.

SECTION I

Some Historical Background

CHAPTER 2

The Politics and Practice of Social Experiments: Seeds of a Revolution

J.M. Gueron[a]

President Emerita, MDRC, New York, NY, United States
E-mail: judy.gueron@gueron.org

Contents

[a] The views expressed herein are the author's and do not necessarily reflect those of MDRC.

Handbook of Economic Field Experiments, Volume 1
ISSN 2214-658X, http://dx.doi.org/10.1016/bs.hefe.2016.11.001

Abstract

Between 1970 and the early 2000s, there was a revolution in support for the use of field experiments to evaluate social programs. Focusing on the welfare reform studies that helped to speed that transformation in the United States, this chapter describes the major challenges to implementing randomized controlled trials (RCTs) in real world conditions, how they emerged and were overcome, and how initial conclusions about conditions necessary to success—strong financial incentives, tight operational control, and small scale—proved to be wrong. Drawing on specific evaluations that were turning points in this 40-year story, the chapter highlights how these studies demonstrated the feasibility of using high-quality RCTs to address important problems, produced results that many considered unusually persuasive, and contributed to the conclusion that alternatives were less credible. It also examines how experimental methods evolved (for example, in the reliance on administrative records and multiarm designs) to meet political, financial, and research needs. The final section discusses lessons from this experience for other fields.

Keywords

Evaluation; Field experiments; Randomized controlled trials; Social experiments; Social policy—United States; Welfare policy; Welfare reform—United States

JEL Codes

C93; I32; I38; J20

Between 1970 and the early 2000s, there was a revolution in support for the use of randomized experiments to evaluate social programs. Focusing on the welfare reform studies that helped to speed that transformation in the United States, this chapter describes the major challenges to randomized controlled trials (RCTs), how they emerged and were overcome, and how initial conclusions about conditions necessary to success—strong financial incentives, tight operational control, and small scale—proved to be wrong. The final section discusses lessons from this experience for other fields.

1. WHY FOCUS ON WELFARE?

Substantive and personal reasons explain my focus on welfare. It is the field of social policy research that pioneered large-scale RCTs and in which they have had the longest uninterrupted run (almost 50 years). Many view these evaluations as having had an unusual impact on legislation, practice, research methods, and the current enthusiasm for evidence-based policy (Angrist and Pischke, 2010, p. 5; Baron, 2013, p. 2; DeParle, 2004, p. 111; Greenberg et al., 2003, p. 238; Haskins, 2006, p. 11; Manzi, 2012, p. 181). The second reason is more parochial: I know this history firsthand and can provide an insider's perspective on why and how the art that sustained RCTs developed.

Although numerous books and articles present findings from or describe how to design experiments,[1] my task is different: to lay out what it took to move them from the laboratory into the real world of social programs. In doing so, I draw, often directly, from *Fighting for Reliable Evidence* (Gueron and Rolston, 2013), which centers on MDRC (formerly, the Manpower Demonstration Research Corporation) and the United States Department of Health and Human Services (HHS), the two organizations that played outsized roles in shaping this story.[2] The focus on HHS (a direct or indirect funder of most of these studies) is obvious; that on a private, nonprofit company makes sense because over a critical 20 years that organization conducted many of the major evaluations and, with HHS, shaped the research agenda. Although in what follows I have sought to be objective and draw on a vast archive of contemporaneous documents and subsequent interviews and publications, I am not an impartial observer. I was an actor in these events, first as MDRC's Research Director (1974–85) and then as its President (1986–2004).

This chapter does not cover the scores of relevant studies but highlights the turning points in a tale in which successive experiments built on the lessons and success of prior ones. Gueron and Rolston (2013) provide the details behind the headlines, including the crucial role played by particular entrepreneurs and supporters and the limited importance in the most influential evaluations of the federal policy of requiring random assignment as a condition for granting states flexibility to reform welfare.[3]

2. WHY EXPERIMENT?

To varying degrees, the proponents of welfare experiments at MDRC and HHS shared three mutually reinforcing goals. The first was to obtain reliable and—given the long and heated controversy about welfare reform—defensible evidence of what worked and, just as importantly, what did not. Over a pivotal 10 years from 1975 to 1985, these individuals became convinced that high-quality RCTs were uniquely able to produce such evidence and that there was simply no adequate alternative. Thus, their first challenge was to demonstrate *feasibility*: that it was ethical, legal, and possible to implement this untried— and at first blush to some people immoral—approach in diverse conditions. The other two goals sprang from their reasons for seeking rigorous evidence. They were not

---

[1] For example, see Bloom (2005), Bloom (2008), Gerber and Green (2012), Glennerster and Takavarasha (2013), Greenberg and Shroder (2004), Grogger and Karoly (2005), Gueron and Pauly (1991), Gueron and Rolston (2013), and Orr (1999).

[2] This chapter uses "HHS" as shorthand for shifting subdivisions within the agency, including the Office of Family Assistance in the Social Security Administration, variously titled offices in the Family Support Administration and the Administration for Children and Families, and the Office of the Assistant Secretary for Planning and Evaluation.

[3] The view that clout from the federal waiver authority (what came to be called the welfare waiver quid pro quo) explains the flourishing of RCTs is a mistaken one. (For a more detailed discussion, see footnote 18.)

motivated by an abstract interest in methodology or theory; they wanted to inform policy and make government more effective and efficient. As a result, they sought to make the body of studies *useful*, by assuring that it addressed the most significant questions about policy and practice, and to structure the research and communicate the findings in ways that would increase the potential that they might actually be *used*.

These three goals took shape over time, in part opportunistically and in part strategically, as the conditions that had nurtured the earliest experiments disappeared. The result was an agenda of increasingly audacious RCTs—a ratcheting up in scale (from pilots for several hundred people to evaluations of full-scale, statewide reforms involving tens of thousands), in complexity (from tests of stand-alone programs to tests of multidimensional system wide reforms using multiarm experimental designs), and in the hostility of the context (from testing funded and voluntary services offered by special programs to mandatory obligations in mainstream public agencies). Each of these steps, in turn, raised new controversies and objections and reduced centralized control. This agenda, and a resistance to conducting one-off studies or to evaluating interesting but not central issues, helped demonstrate the feasibility of RCTs under increasingly demanding conditions.

This chapter recounts how the challenges, practices, and lessons evolved in response to the shifting political, funding, and programmatic context, the knowledge gains and goals, the acquired experience, the evidence of feasibility, and the reactions to the findings. It also shows how the three goals became mutually reinforcing: the more the findings proved useful and used, the greater the likelihood that the relevant actors would agree to the demands of quality.

3. THE STORY

In the 1970s, knowledge about efforts to move people from welfare to work could be accurately described as in the dark ages, with no answers to the most basic questions about whether reforms had any effect, for whom, and at what cost. The prevailing mood was skepticism. The problem was not a lack of evaluations, but that studies of effectiveness all too often ended with experts gathered around a table debating methodology, an outcome that not only was the kiss of death for having an impact on policymakers but also fed the conviction that this research was just another form of advocacy and not "scientific."

The main obstacle to obtaining persuasive evidence of effectiveness comes from the reality that people on welfare do not stand still waiting for some program to give them a helping hand. Many factors influence behavior. When a woman gets a job, for example, how can one tell if it is because of the help she received or because the economy improved, she got her children into day care, she simply hated the stigma and hassle of public assistance, or some combination of these or other reasons? Is it possible for an evaluation to answer this question convincingly? Can it sort out the effect of one intervention from the web of other factors? Because of this reality, the "outcomes" for people enrolled in an activity (for example, the number of individuals who get a job, earn a diploma, or leave welfare) may accurately tell you their status but will not tell you the change in status that the program caused, what researchers call its value added or "impact." The logic is clear: if some people move from welfare to work on their own, outcomes will overstate impacts. But, by how much?

To answer that question, one needs a "counterfactual," a reliable measure of what the same people would have done without the intervention. During the 1970s, researchers tried various strategies to mimic this "what if" behavior. They compared the conduct of participants with their own actions before they enrolled, or with that of people who resembled them on measured characteristics but did not volunteer, were not selected or served, or lived in a different but similar community. The main weakness of such designs was "selection bias," the risk that people in the comparison group would differ in some systematic but unmeasured and influential way from people in the experimental treatment. If selection bias occurred, the context, motivation of people in the two groups, or both would not be the same, and a comparison of their subsequent outcomes would produce a biased estimate of the program's impact.

The unique strength of random assignment is that it both solves the problem of selection bias and is transparent. Since eligible people are assigned by chance to the treatment or control group, there is no systematic difference in the groups or in the conditions they face initially or over time. If the numbers are large enough and the study is done well (two big "ifs"), the result is the right answer. On transparency, RCTs allow researchers to estimate impacts using arithmetic. Basically, all one has to do is calculate the average behavior of people in the two groups after random assignment and subtract. There may be some straightforward adjustments (which rarely affect the basic findings), but no fancy statistics, no mumbo jumbo of arcane expertise, and scant potential for researcher bias. Everyone could—and did—understand this simple process.

But the question of whether or not it was feasible remained. In the 1960s and 1970s, researchers knew about random assignment, but most saw it as a laboratory tool that was not a realistic means to address important problems in everyday conditions. By the early 2000s, it had become clear that it was both feasible and uniquely credible. It was also increasingly clear that alternatives would not reliably produce the right answer or make evident when they did and did not. How this change happened was not the result of some decades-long master plan but of the iterative actions of entrepreneurs inside and outside of government.

The chapter tells the story of these individuals' push to determine causality. It does not focus on a simultaneous and coordinated effort that was of equal importance: the attempt to find out how and why programs succeeded or failed. This effort included documenting the extent to which the test treatments were implemented (their operational achievements) and determining (using varied methods) why they did or did not achieve their goals and what changes would make them more effective (Gueron and Rolston, 2013, pp. 58–59, 291, 426).

4. MAJOR CHALLENGES

Implementing a high-quality RCT means overcoming numerous obstacles[4]:

1. gaining the initial and ongoing cooperation of the relevant administrators and organizations (including their frontline staff) with conducting intake via a lottery, defining and sustaining a distinct treatment, enforcing the research groups (which usually means not helping the control group members) initially and over time, enrolling an appropriate and adequate sample, and cooperating with various research protocols;
2. securing funds for the research and, sometimes, the test program, especially if it is a special demonstration;
3. obtaining the cooperation of the research subjects;
4. acquiring reliable and comparable data for people in the program and control groups in order to track outcomes for a long enough time to detect key effects;
5. meeting high ethical and legal standards;
6. assuring that the operating program has a fair test, in particular, that it has moved beyond the start-up phase; and
7. getting all the details right and keeping the endeavor on track for the years necessary to determine potential effects.

The first challenge is the most fundamental. The researcher needs the cooperation of people in the agencies involved. But what is in it for them? Success hinges on an ability to assure them that this approach—which for some evokes horrific images of "experimenting" with human beings—is ethical, legal, and actually necessary (that is, that a less intrusive and possibly less expensive design would not do just as well). In the 1970s and 1980s, this was a tough sell. There was limited academic support and plenty of vocal naysayers, including high-powered econometricians (who claimed that they could solve selection bias via statistical modeling or alternative designs) and researchers from diverse disciplines who argued that experiments addressed limited or secondary questions (Gueron and Rolston, 2013, pp. 270–272, 455–468). This skepticism was before newspapers routinely reported on how randomized clinical trials in medicine overturned long-standing practices based on observational studies and before it had become almost trite to say that correlation did not imply causation.

As a result, the risk-to-reward calculation was stacked against experiments. Why would any politician or administrator chance adverse publicity, a potential lawsuit,

---

[4] During the years discussed in this chapter, almost all of the studies involved the random assignment of individuals, not intact groups or clusters.

bureaucratic backlash, or even staff revolt? The trick was to somehow persuade people that the benefit from being involved in the RCT exceeded these obvious dangers and that, as a result, they wanted you as much as you wanted them. To gain this cooperation, managers of randomized experiments needed to create a win—win situation. As shown in the rest of this chapter, they employed diverse tools that drew on operational, research, and political skills and savvy—a combination that I have elsewhere called an art (Gueron, 2002, p. 32). By these means, MDRC and others were able to reverse incredulity and get many to agree to join and, in some cases in later years, even seek out participation in such studies.

5. DEMONSTRATING FEASIBILITY: THE NATIONAL SUPPORTED WORK DEMONSTRATION

Starting in 1975, the first large random assignment study of a multisite employment program, the National Supported Work Demonstration, offered a year of carefully structured, paid work to hard-to-employ people—former prisoners, former addicts, young school dropouts, and single mothers who were long-term recipients of welfare [at the time called Aid to Families with Dependent Children (AFDC) and now Temporary Assistance for Needy Families (TANF)].[5] The hope was that participants would develop some combination of habits, attitudes, self-worth, skills, and credentials that would produce a long-term increase in employment and reduction in criminal activities, drug abuse, or welfare receipt.

Even though the country had already successfully launched several path-breaking social experiments—the negative income tax (NIT), health insurance, and housing allowance demand experiments in the 1960s and 1970s—those experiments tested variations in economic incentives: treatments that could be defined by a small number of parameters (guarantee levels, tax rates, coinsurance requirements, and so on) and that were tightly controlled and administered by the researchers. The Supported Work challenge promised to be harder, with much less researcher control, and included convincing 10 mission-driven, community-based nonprofit organizations to operate a complex program and use an intake lottery. With a 45-year track record of success, it is easy to get blasé, but at the time random assignment in such a context was unheard of. The message was clear: it simply cannot be done. Program operators would implacably oppose turning people away based on some random process. The approach would be viewed as cold hearted, immoral, and akin to asking a doctor to deny a patient a known cure.

---

[5] AFDC, the federal—state cash welfare program created by Franklin D. Roosevelt's New Deal, was replaced by TANF in 1996. Although the Supported Work demonstration included welfare recipients, it was viewed as a highly targeted employment program, not as a pretest for welfare reform (Gueron and Rolston, 2013, p. 29).

Given the uncertain outcome, why did this project even attempt random assignment? As envisioned by its original proponent, Mitchell (Mike) Sviridoff at the Ford Foundation, the Supported Work demonstration would assess whether a promising one-site program could be replicated in other locations and for different populations. Sviridoff envisioned a "respectable research component" and saw it as part of a try-small-before-you-spend-big vision of policymaking. But Sviridoff, who always thought big, had assembled a consortium of six federal funding partners and created an illustrious advisory committee, of which two members (Robert Solow and Robert Lampman) backed up by staff at HHS took the project in an unanticipated direction by insisting that "testing" meant using random assignment. When asked about it 35 years later, Solow attributed his determination to his training, saying "My first job was as a professor of statistics! I favored it because I wanted to have a defensible response." He and Lampman also shared the conviction that the research design had to be strong enough to detect what they anticipated would be, at best, small and complex effects (Gueron and Rolston, 2013, pp. 32, p. 483, note 13).

The result was a hybrid: Supported Work was both a demonstration and an experiment. As a demonstration, the project sought to provide sites with enough flexibility to create a realistic test of the administrative and other obstacles to replicating the multifaceted program. As a social experiment, it needed sufficient standardization to define a "model" (the treatment), allow pooling data from multiple programs, and reduce the risk of evaluating a poorly implemented start-up period.

Why did 10 sites ultimately accept random assignment? As expected, initial opposition was strong. To do their jobs well, local staff had to believe they were helping people. Any intake procedure involves some form of rationing—first come first served, enrolling the more motivated first, allowing for caseworker discretion, or limiting recruitment so that no one is actually rejected. Staff overwhelmingly preferred those approaches to a random process in which they personally had to confront and turn away people they viewed as eligible and deserving. Yet for a social experiment to succeed, these staff had to be converted. They had to buy into the process or at least agree to cooperate fully with it. Otherwise, the study would be doomed, which is what many feared would happen to Supported Work. But the project did not fail. Relatively quickly, the process became familiar, complaints diminished, and random assignment was accepted. A high-quality RCT was implemented, and the findings were not subject to the familiar methodological debate.

At the time, I and others attributed the ability to induce and discipline compliance to four conditions. The first and most important was money. Community organizations received millions of dollars to run a new and distinctive program conditional upon them playing by the rules, the most important of which was random assignment. There was also generous funding for research and data collection, including for in-person interviews to track 6500 people for up to 3 years.

The second was strong nonfinancial incentives. The local Supported Work operators, referral agencies, and interest groups all viewed the program positively: it was voluntary; it offered paid jobs to underserved and hard-to-employ people at a time when others were advocating mandatory, unpaid work-for-your-benefits (workfare) programs; and there was an explicit commitment to high ethical and legal standards. Thus, the pitch used to recruit sites and train frontline staff stressed the rationale for and morality of random assignment. It was a specially funded demonstration that would provide enriched services that would not otherwise exist. It would not reduce service levels or deny people access to benefits to which they were entitled. It had the resources to enroll only a small number of those interested. It would increase services for one group without reducing them for another. Finally, though the program sounded like an idea that could not fail, there was as yet no evidence that it would actually help people. In these conditions, the demonstration's managers argued (1) a lottery was actually fairer than other ways to allocate scarce opportunities and (2) getting a reliable answer on effectiveness (and thus abiding by the study rules, including not helping controls) was consistent with the program operators' mission. Supported Work reaffirmed this message in its procedures, as it was the first social experiment to be covered by new federal regulations on the protection of human subjects. (At intake, through a process of informed consent, applicants were told about the lottery and the possible risks and advised of both the kind of data that would be collected in surveys—in some cases on illegal activities—and the strict procedures that would be put in place to protect confidentiality and limit data access.)

A third factor was the management structure and people involved. Given Supported Work's complexity, a new organization, MDRC, was created to impose tight central control on the project and balance operational and research priorities. MDRC, in turn, selected a team, which included people at Mathematica Policy Research and the University of Wisconsin's Institute for Research on Poverty who had played lead roles in the NIT experiments, to conduct the impact and benefit–cost analyses. This staffing decision was an early example of the continuity that persisted over the years, with later studies drawing, often directly, on the wisdom gained in earlier ones. Another force for continuity lay in MDRC's Board of Directors, of which one leading member, Robert Solow, served for a remarkable 40-plus years. Throughout his tenure, Solow was a consistent advocate for rigor and for the organization's pioneering use of random assignment in the evaluation of an expanding range of social and educational programs.

The fourth factor was the intentionally low profile. The location of random assignment in relatively small (several hundred volunteers per site) pilot programs run by community agencies gave the project a stealth quality that helped it fly below the potentially ruinous political and press radar.

In retrospect, Supported Work was an auspicious debut for using large-scale RCTs to evaluate operating programs. The incentives, commitment to ethical practices, and over-subscribed program won allies and gave MDRC clout to call the shots. The generous

Table 1 Percentage working 2 years after random assignment: supported work evaluation

Hard-to-employ group	Treatment group	Control group	Difference (impact)
Long-term Aid to Families with Dependent Children recipients	49.1	40.6	8.5[a]
Ex-addicts	56.5	53.0	3.5
Ex-offenders	56.5	53.3	3.2
Young high school dropouts	62.6	62.6	0.0

[a]Statistically significant at the 5% level.
Author's compilation based on MDRC Board of Directors, 1980. Summary and Findings of the National Supported Work Demonstration. Ballinger, Cambridge, MA, Tables 9-1 to 9-4.

funding assured local interest and a large treatment-control treatment difference. The behind-the-scenes nature of the project averted controversy. Compared with what was to follow, it was a step out of the laboratory but not a movement into the real world of mainstream public agencies. From this experience, I and others concluded that the conditions that favored success were not just helpful but necessary for RCTs. Although it is probably true that, at the time, MDRC would not have succeeded without them (particularly the generous operating funds), subsequent events proved that these conditions were not indispensable.

In addition to demonstrating feasibility, the Supported Work findings (released in 1980) showed the value of using a control group to reach conclusions on effectiveness. Table 1 (which gives the percent of people in the treatment and control groups who were employed for some time between the nineteenth and twenty-seventh months after random assignment, as well as the difference or impact) points to three telling insights.[6]

First, social programs can work, but not all prima facie good ideas do. Supported Work significantly increased the postprogram employment of single mothers on AFDC and (not shown in Table 1) reduced their receipt of cash welfare. Given the prevailing skepticism, this success was heralded. But, the program did not have impacts on the three other groups.

Second, even for the AFDC group, impacts were modest. Although Supported Work boosted employment, the employment rate of the control group revealed that the big gain over the 2 years came from the economy and the myriad other factors that led people (almost all of whom were unemployed at the start of the study) to take a job.

Third, high outcomes may not reflect high impacts. The demonstration's planners had expected that Supported Work would be least effective for AFDC women, since they had a harder time finding work, had competing child care responsibilities, and faced lower work incentives (they not only got jobs with lower wages but received

---

[6] For more detail on the program and the findings, see Hollister et al. (1984) and MDRC Board of Directors (1980).

welfare as an alternative source of income and their benefits would be cut if they worked). The data in column one appear to support this hunch: AFDC recipients were the least likely of the four groups to be working after participating in the program. However, evidence from the control groups disproves this expectation: the mostly male former addicts, offenders, and young school dropouts were also more likely to get jobs on their own, with the program making no significant difference. Thus, Supported Work succeeded with AFDC women not because the participants did so well (as measured by their outcomes) but because the corresponding control group members (without program aid) did so poorly. One implication was clear: traditional outcome-based performance measures (for example, how many enrollees were placed in jobs or left welfare) would have sent a false signal and led to wasted funds and less effective programs.

The magnitude, unpredictability, and complexity of the findings brought themes into focus that sharpened with time: (1) impacts, if they occur, are likely to be modest; (2) pay attention to the service differential, that is, do not focus only on the treatment group and the quality of the test program, but keep your eye on the control group (both their outcomes and the alternative services they and treatment group members receive); (3) beware of overreliance on outcome-based performance standards; and (4) look at impacts for key subgroups.

Supported Work also offered good news to people searching for ways to bring rigorous evidence to policy debates often dominated by claims made on a hunch or discredited on an anecdote. Once it became clear that the study had been meticulously implemented, there was widespread acceptance of the findings. The transparency of the method and the simplicity with which the results could be explained made random assignment a powerful communications tool. People differed on the implications for policy and questioned whether the impacts could be replicated on a larger scale, but there was not the familiar back and forth among experts that followed studies using more complex, and ultimately less interpretable, methods.

Nonetheless, even though Supported Work was a beautiful study that pioneered many methods used in subsequent RCTs, there was little pick up on the encouraging impacts for welfare mothers. We at MDRC attributed that to several factors: the project's origin (designed by elites with little state ownership), the nature of the program and findings (an expensive and complex model that produced gains similar to those later found for lower-cost approaches), and the 1980 election that ended federal interest. Although we had always known that positive results would not automatically lead to expansion and were chary about becoming advocates of the program rather than of the research, we went away thinking we had failed to build a constituency in the existing systems that would be waiting for the results and primed to act on them. Determined not to repeat that mistake, MDRC took a more inclusive and grassroots approach in subsequent experiments.

6. SOCIAL EXPERIMENTS REINCARNATED AS A PARTNERSHIP: TESTING FEASIBILITY ANEW BY EVALUATING STATE INITIATIVES

What happened next was driven by long-term trends, the 1980 election, and institutional priorities. From the 1970s through the 1990s, welfare reform was a bitterly contentious political wedge issue stoked by increasing anger at a system that many felt encouraged dependency, undermined family structure, and unfairly supported people who could work but did not while others struggled in low-wage jobs. During these years, politicians ran for president or the state house on their record and claims as welfare reformers.

Several factors had spurred the erosion of support for AFDC as an open-ended entitlement. One was the dramatic growth in the rolls and costs. Created in 1935 as a program intended to support a small number of poor widows and wives of disabled workers (people not expected to work), it had swelled from 270,000 families in 1945 to 1,000,000 in 1965; 3,400,000 in 1975; 3,700,000 in 1985; and 4,900,000 in 1995 (Gueron and Rolston, 2013, p. 481, note 3). A second was the change in who received welfare. The vast majority were not widows but divorced, separated, or never married women, reflecting what was widely perceived as an alarming dissolution of the family.[7] A third was that women across the country (including single parents with young children) were flooding into the labor force, often not by choice.

Together, these changes raised questions about the equity of long-term support for one group of single mothers and whether the very design of the program was having a range of unintended side effects. These effects potentially included encouraging family breakup and teen pregnancy, discouraging women from earning a living, and making it easier for fathers to leave their families and avoid supporting their children. The result was that, over time, public debate shifted from whether mothers on welfare should work to who should work and how to make that happen, from voluntary programs such as Supported Work to mandates and obligations that would require people to work or participate in diverse work-directed activities, and later (in the 1990s) to whether there should be a limit on how long people could remain on the rolls.

Ronald Reagan's election in 1980—following a campaign that capitalized on this hot-button issue—produced a dramatic change in welfare policy, the role of the states, and the nature and origin of research funds. The new administration saw workfare (work-for-your-benefits) as the solution and, convinced of its benefits, was not interested in any rigorous evaluation. In Congress, however, there was no consensus on how to structure such a program or what different approaches might cost or yield. Consequently, rather than impose a nationwide vision, federal legislation in 1981 gave the states

---

[7] The proportion of children under 18 living with an unmarried mother had increased from 5% of white children (25% of black children) in 1965 to 15% of white children (50% of black children) by the early 1980s (McLanahan and Jencks, 2015, p. 16).

increased flexibility to undertake their own initiatives. At the same time, the administration, which viewed social science researchers with suspicion and as advocates for the liberal policies they typically assessed, ended most funding for demonstrations and evaluations.

As a result, prospects for experiments looked bleak. The conditions that had nurtured Supported Work—generous funding, centralized clout, and an oversubscribed voluntary program—disappeared, in some cases permanently. More parochially, stunned by the cancelation of multiple studies (for an example, see Elmore, 1985, p. 330) and having let go 45% of its staff, MDRC debated the chances and choices for survival. With a determination to maintain its focus on rigorous studies of programs for low-income people, MDRC dreamed up a partnership vision that proved to be the major turning point in the design of welfare experiments and within a decade both produced results of greater relevance and policy impact than the NIT or Supported Work experiments and became the model that flourished for the next 20 years.

With the specter of controversial state welfare reforms and no planned federal evaluation, MDRC sought Ford Foundation funding for an objective, outside assessment. The concept was to make a reality of Supreme Court Justice Brandeis's famous statement that the states were laboratories for experiments by taking the word "experiment" literally; that is, MDRC would convert into actual RCTs the initiatives that emerged as governors across the country responded enthusiastically to the opportunity to put their stamp on welfare.[8] Instead of one experiment that would test a centrally defined model in multiple sites (as in Supported Work), MDRC's resulting Work/Welfare Demonstration used RCTs to assess programs that reflected each state's particular values, resources, goals, and capabilities—but primarily required people to search for a job or work for their benefits—with random assignment integrated into the helter-skelter of normal agency operations (Gueron and Rolston, 2013, pp. 97–117).[9]

MDRC identified three key research questions to address in parallel studies in each state: Would the state run a mandatory program (and what would high participation

---

[8] To appreciate why governors played such a prominent role in welfare reform, it is important to understand how AFDC differed from some other programs. For example, in contrast to Social Security, which is fully funded by the federal government and operates under standard, nationwide rules, AFDC was designed as a federal–state partnership. On the one hand, the program was a federal entitlement, meaning that no person who satisfied the eligibility criteria and program rules could be denied benefits. On the other hand, it was a state program, insofar as the states retained substantial discretion over those rules and shared the cost with the federal government. Consequently, both states and the federal government had a strong financial incentive to reduce the rolls and, potentially, an appetite for reliable evidence on cost-effectiveness. Simultaneously, the unpopularity of the program created a political incentive for governors to compete for leadership as reformers.

[9] MDRC sought to place random assignment as early as feasible in the intake process (preferably at welfare application) because the reforms were expected to change the behavior not only of people who actually participated in the required activities but also of those who did not but were subject to the monitoring, the messaging, and the threat or reality of financial sanctions.

and workfare look like in practice)? Would the reform reduce welfare or increase work and, if so, for whom? Would the reform cost more or save money? The nature of the programs and the absence of the key enablers of the Supported Work study drove a radically different vision for the evaluation. Because the new mandates were intensely controversial, MDRC staff knew they would need the most rigorous evidence to defend any findings and thus chose random assignment. Because they anticipated at most modest impacts and had to assess each state initiative as a separate experiment, they knew they would need large samples, which ultimately involved 28,500 people. Because of the relatively limited research budget (the Ford Foundation's $3.6 million grant, which MDRC hoped to double, ultimately lasted more than 5 years), staff knew they could not track this vast sample using surveys but, for the first time in a large-scale RCT, would have to estimate impacts solely from existing administrative records.[10] This decision meant seeking reliable answers to the first order questions covered by these records and leaving the rest to future studies.

A social experiment had never before been attempted at this scale, in mainstream offices run by large bureaucracies, in mandatory programs, with no direct federal funds or role, with no special operating funds, and with no researcher leverage.[11] Further, MDRC would be testing relatively high-profile political initiatives that—although still viewed as demonstrations implemented in one or a few locations in a state—were hyped in gubernatorial and even presidential campaigns (one program was Governor Bill Clinton's initiative in Arkansas).

At a time when they were under pressure to launch new programs, why did some welfare commissioners accept the added work and potentially explosive risk of inserting a lottery into the stressful welfare intake process and participating in a demanding and independent study that could as easily show failure as success? Not surprisingly, their initial reaction was disbelief. You want us to do what? Is this ethical? Will it impede operations? Will it explode?

In a courtship that extended over 30 states and lasted 2 years, MDRC gradually overcame these concerns, in eight states that met its requirements, by making specific design

---

[10] Albeit a decision of necessity, it had the advantage of limiting sample attrition and recall problems over the eventual 5 years of follow-up, although it raised some coverage issues, for example, by not tracking people after they left a state.

[11] It is useful to distinguish two aspects of social experiments that could be more or less subject to centralized control: the treatment being tested and the design and implementation of the research. On the former, the NITs were at one end of the continuum (total researcher control of the treatment), Supported Work a few steps along the continuum (a centrally defined model, with some room for local variation), and the Work/Welfare Demonstration at the other extreme (treatments defined by the states, with no researcher role). Along the research design control continuum, there was less variation. Researchers had full control of the design, random assignment process, data collection, analysis, and reporting in the NITs and Supported Work. In the Work/Welfare Demonstration, MDRC used the Ford Foundation funding to insist on a consistent research agenda and control of random assignment and data requirements, but also sought, in the partnership mode, to answer questions that were of interest to particular states.

decisions, building relationships that nurtured trust, and marshalling five arguments to sell the project as a win—win opportunity.[12] As a group, these eight states were representative of both nationwide responses to the 1981 law and the variety of local conditions (Gueron and Rolston, 2013, pp. 118—131).

The first selling point was the promise of a new style: a partnership that would answer *their* questions about *their* reforms, combined with a pitch on why getting answers required estimating impacts. The 1981 law's flexibility had put welfare commissioners on the spot. The system was unpopular and they were under pressure to get tough, but they understood the difficulty of implementing change and the diversity of people on the rolls. Although they had almost no reliable data on the likely cost and results of specific policies, at least some of them suspected that the job entry or case closure measures they typically touted would overstate success. The commissioners could grasp how the evidence from control groups in prior RCTs confirmed their doubts. But the challenge remained to explain why one needed an experiment, rather than some less intrusive design, to determine success, especially given the limited academic support and often outright opposition.[13] MDRC's response was fourfold: pretend there was a consensus and assume that welfare administrators would not follow or understand the econometric debate; educate them on the outcome—impact distinction and why outcomes would not answer their questions; expose the weaknesses of alternative designs; and offer a study that would accurately measure the real accomplishments of their programs, address other questions they cared about (for example, the impact on state budgets and insights on what may explain success or failure), and produce results that would be simple, credible, and defensible.

The second selling point was that random assignment was not some wacko scheme dreamed up by ivory-tower purists. It had been done before; it had not disrupted operations; and it had not blown up in the courts or in the press. The Supported Work experience got MDRC part way, but more powerful evidence for welfare administrators came from a small project, called the Work Incentive (WIN) Laboratories, that MDRC had managed in the late 1970s and that had lodged random assignment in a few local welfare-to-work program offices and thus involved civil servants facing normal

---

[12] MDRC sought states that planned initiatives of sufficient scale to generate the needed samples, agreed to cooperate with research demands (not only random assignment but also monitoring and restricting services for a large share of the caseload), maintained and would share administrative records of sufficient quality, and could somehow provide 50% of the funds for the evaluation. This last condition proved by far the toughest, and most of the state contribution came from other sources. For a description of the programs and findings, see the individual state reports published by MDRC, Friedlander and Burtless 1995, Gueron and Pauly 1991, and Gueron and Rolston 2013.

[13] The opposition came from both qualitative and institutional researchers who said we were addressing narrow and relatively unimportant questions and economists who argued that statistical modeling could produce equally reliable answers at lower cost and that experimental results were likely to be biased (because random assignment altered the programs being analyzed) or of dubious scientific value (because they yielded no basic or cumulative knowledge). See Gueron and Rolston 2013, pp. 270—272, 455—457.

pressures and performance requirements (Gueron and Rolston, 2013, pp. 66—87). However, the proposed state studies upped the ante: larger and much more political initiatives and the integration of random assignment into the high stakes welfare eligibility review process. To overcome these obstacles, MDRC promised to work with state staff and local community advocates to develop procedures that would be fair, ethical, and not overly burdensome; to provide extensive training so that frontline staff would understand the rationale for random assignment; and to produce results that would address pragmatic concerns.

The final three selling points were the offering of a subsidized study that met the then vague but useful federal requirement for an independent assessment of the waivers to welfare rules, which most states needed to implement their initiatives[14]; modest assistance on program design; and prestige from selection for a high-profile Ford Foundation initiative (although at the time no one remotely anticipated the visibility that would come to participating states).

Nonetheless, enlisting states was a tough sell. There was always pressure to use weaker, less intrusive research designs. That the pitch ultimately worked is why I have called the welfare commissioners the heroes of the survival and reincarnation of welfare experiments. Their unflinching support once they had signed on was the major reason why random assignment was the dog that did not bark and why no state dropped out of or sought to undermine the studies, despite the relentless beating some of them took from having their programs assessed using the new and tough metric (impacts) and at a time when governors in other states trumpeted their success and built their reputations based on misleading but numerically vastly higher outcomes (Gueron and Rolston, 2013, pp. 128—31, 256). In an effort to assist participating states and debunk these claims, MDRC repeatedly sought to educate the press, advocacy groups, congressional staff, and senior state and federal policymakers about the erroneous use of outcome data, the unrealistic expectations generated by hyping those data, and the truth of the more modest results from the RCTs.

Collaboration and partnership are often empty slogans masking business as usual. However, in 1982 it was clear that MDRC's powerlessness vis-à-vis the states required a genuinely new style, in which leverage was based not on holding the purse strings, and as a result calling the shots, but on the quality of working relationships, the usefulness of the findings, and the creation of a strong mutual interest in and commitment to obtaining credible answers. The outcome was positive: by trading control and uniformity of the operating programs for relevance and ownership, the states had a greater commitment to

---

[14] The subsidy came mostly from the Ford Foundation and, indirectly, federal special demonstration and matching funds. For a discussion on the critical role of the 50% uncapped federal match for state evaluations under AFDC, see Gueron and Rolston 2013, pp. 134, 258—259, 386.

the treatments and ultimately the RCTs, which in turn provided a built-in constituency for the results (Gueron and Rolston, 2013, p. 105; Blum and Blank, 1990).

The partnership model also had the unanticipated benefit of treatment replication. Six of the initial states (plus a second RCT in San Diego that HHS initiated and MDRC conducted) sought to implement variations on the theme of work requirements, with job search as the first and major activity followed (for some) by unpaid work experience. But in the context of welfare experiments, replication did not mean reproducing an identical, centrally specified model. Just as welfare benefit levels differed greatly across the country, so did the reforms' specific design, targeting, goals, cost, and implementation (the messaging, participation rates, and intensity and nature of services). (For example, the nature of job search varied from individual job searches, in which people were expected, on their own, to follow up, and report back on job leads, to job clubs, in which program staff might provide instruction on resume preparation and interviewing, a phone room for contacting prospective employers, and job leads.) They also differed in context: urban or rural, labor market conditions, and the extent of alternative services available to people in the treatment and control groups. Since each state program was a separate RCT, this created a form of replication that, as discussed below, greatly increased the influence of the findings, as it became clear that most of the reforms had impacts in the desired direction.

However, the shift in authority (the studies were conducted under state contracts), combined with the mandatory nature of the initiatives and the commitment to providing useful findings, prompted a controversial departure from past RCTs. Because states insisted on learning the effect of their reforms on the full range of people required to participate (not just those who might volunteer to be in the study or the program, if given a choice), eligible people could not opt out of the program, or of random assignment, or of any follow-up that relied on the states' own administrative records. This stipulation assured generalizability of the results to the universe of people subject to the new requirements and made the studies more akin to natural field experiments.[15]

The strategy of state-based experiments was a success. Random assignment worked, as did the reliance on administrative records (Gueron and Rolston, 2013, pp. 185–90). More importantly for the participating states, the findings were judged encouraging.

---

[15] At each site, random assignment was used to create a treatment group that was subject to the new program and its requirements and a control group that was excused from both the newly required services and the threatened financial penalties for noncooperation. People in both groups would be told they were in the study and subject to a lottery, informed of the grievance procedures, and given a choice about responding to any special surveys. Most welfare advocates did not object to the elimination of a general informed consent because at the time they viewed the new mandates as punitive and were glad that the control group was excused from potential sanctions (Gueron and Rolston, 2013, pp. 186–188). For a discussion of the level of control in laboratory experiments (where people are aware of their participation and give informed consent) versus natural field experiments (where people are assigned covertly, without their consent), see Al-Ubaydli and List (2014).

States had sought, to varying degrees, to make progress on four goals: increase employment, reduce dependence on public assistance, save money, and make families better off. Although not articulated as such, they likely also shared a fifth goal, cost-effectiveness, defined as the impact per dollar spent or the "bang for the buck." (This last goal is particularly relevant to welfare reform initiatives, since they are, by intent, mass interventions that seek both to change individual behavior and to reduce the welfare rolls.)[16]

The findings, released between 1984 and 1988, showed progress on most fronts. The programs generally increased average employment rates and earnings and, somewhat less consistently, reduced welfare receipt. Surprisingly, most of them also saved money, generating cumulative reductions in AFDC payments and other transfers that within a few years exceeded the programs' net costs. The combination of modest impacts on behavior and low costs also made most of them highly cost-effective. There were, however, minimal or no impacts on family income or poverty (Friedlander and Burtless, 1995, pp. 32, 87—101; Gueron, 1990; Gueron and Pauly, 1991, pp. 142—154; Gueron and Rolston, 2013, pp. 182—185).

An in-depth analysis of the four programs that had 5 years of follow-up showed that average impacts (ranging from 3 to 7 percentage point increases in quarterly employment rates and 0 to 8 percentage point reductions in the monthly rate of AFDC receipt) remained strong for 3—4 years, after which the controls began to catch up with the treatment group.[17] The study concluded that the programs encouraged more people to start working and to leave welfare sooner than they would have without the reforms, but generally did not help them get higher-paying or more stable jobs (leaving many with little income and back on the rolls) and did little to reduce welfare for more disadvantaged, potential long-term recipients (Friedlander and Burtless, 1995, pp. 2—3, 16, 88—101).

[16] The cost-effectiveness of social programs always matters, but it is made particularly salient by a fundamental difference between the 1980s welfare reforms and programs such as Supported Work. Most of the state initiatives were viewed as a dry run in a few locations of potential statewide (or even nationwide) reforms. The evaluations were designed explicitly to assess the impact of changing the service delivery system—including mandatory administrative practices, case management, and multiple components—for all eligible people in the demonstration areas. In contrast, the Supported Work evaluation assessed a single activity intended to reach a fixed number of volunteers. The more cost-effective a state's initiative, the greater is its ability to reach a larger share of the caseload within a given budget and hence to produce a bigger aggregate or total impact. This consideration (which highlights the importance of cumulative welfare savings) is fundamental when comparing results for higher- and lower-cost approaches (Gueron and Rolston, 2013, pp. 103, 207—208, 425; Gueron and Pauly, 1991, pp. 70—78; Friedlander and Burtless, 1995, p. 71; and Friedlander and Gueron, 1992).

[17] Friedlander and Burtless (1995, pp. 8—9, 58—60) caution readers to view this "catch-up" as a lower-bound estimate of the long-term effects of permanent programs. Because the original evaluation plans had envisioned a relatively short follow-up, the embargo on enrolling controls in the test programs lasted for only 2 years following random assignment, although the programs generally continued after that time. As a result, the 5-year follow-up included years during which some people in the control group might have been subject to the mandates and services, possibly reducing the late-year estimates and making impacts appear less long lasting.

7. USING RANDOMIZED CONTROLLED TRIALS TO TEST FULL-SCALE PROGRAMS: THE FIGHT GOT TOUGHER

By 1986, the terrain for welfare experiments had changed. MDRC had shown that RCTs testing state initiatives were feasible. A number of senior people in the Reagan administration had become strong supporters. Some governors and commissioners had seen firsthand that such studies not only were not toxic but also could contribute to their claim for leadership as welfare reformers and produce valuable lessons that brought them unanticipated renown.

What followed over the next 15 years made the welfare saga exceptional: a flowering of RCTs that has been called the "golden age of social welfare experimentation" (Manzi, 2012, p. 184). Separately and in interaction, MDRC, other research firms, HHS, and state administrators built a coherent body of evidence about the effectiveness of the major policy alternatives. After identifying what it considered the key policy options, MDRC sought to assemble clusters of places planning or willing to try out those approaches, aiming to repeat its early 1980s strategy of turning the dynamic state reform context into an opportunity to learn (at times, by again leveraging Ford Foundation grants). Staff at HHS led by Howard Rolston in what was then the Family Support Administration and Michael Fishman and others in the Office of the Assistant Secretary for Planning and Evaluation launched increasingly ambitious experiments, culminating in the largest and most complex welfare RCT, and embarked on a 5-year journey with the US Office of Management and Budget (OMB) to require states that sought waivers to modify standard policy to assess their initiatives using a control group created through random assignment. In 1992, after ups and downs, an RCT became the required yardstick by which to measure the fiscal neutrality of the explosion of waivers that states requested in a push for more—and more ambitious—reforms.[18]

The result was an accretive agenda that looked carefully orchestrated but in reality emerged from a feedback loop, in which experiments generated findings and raised substantive and methodological questions and hypotheses that prompted successive tests. (See Table 2 for examples.)

The initial effect of this expanding agenda was that a tough fight got tougher. The strongest opposition arose after senior officials in California and Florida, in late 1985 and 1989, invited MDRC to conduct random assignment evaluations of their respective

---

[18] Since 1962, HHS had had the authority to grant states waivers of AFDC program requirements in order to try out innovations. But only after 1992, and thus after the most influential of the welfare experiments, was a quid pro quo firmly implemented, in which states could not get waivers without conducting an RCT. The logic was straightforward: HHS and OMB had learned that RCTs were feasible and much more reliable than alternative research designs. As a result, and in order to assure that waivers did not become an intended or unintended drain on federal budgets, they insisted that they be used to measure fiscal impact and to allocate costs between federal and state budgets (Gueron and Rolston, 2013, pp. 156–159, 217–261).

Table 2 Evolution of welfare research agenda

Findings from prior studies	Prompted new questions and tests
The early 1980s low-cost mandatory job search/workfare programs produced small-to-modest increases in employment and (less consistently) reductions in welfare for single mothers with school-aged children	Would remediation of basic education deficits increase success, particularly for more disadvantaged recipients?
	Would similar approaches succeed with mothers of younger children or with teen parents?
	Would work-related mandates help or hurt young children in welfare families?
	Would impacts increase if ongoing participation was required as long as people remained on welfare?
Single- or multicounty demonstrations and pilot programs produced encouraging results	Could success be replicated or improved upon in full-scale, statewide programs?
Programs requiring some combination of job search, workfare, and basic education increased work but did little to reduce poverty	Would programs that supplemented earnings increase work, reduce poverty, and benefit children?
	Would extending services or mandates to the noncustodial fathers of children on welfare increase child support payments or improve outcomes for children?
Comparisons of impacts across sites suggested certain approaches were more effective than others	Could this be confirmed in multiarm randomized controlled trials testing varied approaches in the same sites?

Author's compilation.

statewide programs: Greater Avenues for Independence (GAIN) and Project Independence (PI). The officials' reasons differed, but neither state was driven by the need for waivers. In California, some people in the legislature and state agencies had seen firsthand the problem-free implementation of MDRC's earlier RCTs in San Diego and the usefulness and influence of the findings. As a result, once they agreed that GAIN had to be rigorously evaluated, they quickly concurred across party lines that rigor meant random assignment.

In Florida, after the agency charged by the legislature to determine effectiveness had been attacked for producing conflicting findings from successive studies using nonexperimental methods, Don Winstead, the key state official, sought guidance from Robinson Hollister, the chair of a recent National Academy of Sciences panel, who advised him to do it the right way and use random assignment. In contrast to the situation in California, Winstead had no familiarity with RCTs but, after reading reports from earlier experiments and Senator Daniel Patrick Moynihan's statements about the role of such research in the 1988 federal legislation, was persuaded that "the only way to get out of the pickle of these dueling unprovable things…and salvage the credibility of the program…was to get an evaluation of unquestioned quality and go forward" (Gueron and Rolston, 2013, p. 301).[19]

Yet, despite strong support at the top and for the first time having random assignment written into legislation in California and Florida, what followed were legal and ethical objections that went way beyond those raised in the first generation of state studies. In Florida, a firestorm of opposition flared up that almost led the legislature to ban control groups and in the process would have both jeopardized a major federal research project and potentially poisoned the well for future studies (Gueron and Rolston, 2013, pp. 281−287, 298−309).

What explains the fierce reaction? The California GAIN and Florida PI programs were not just more of the same. They were more ambitious in scale, permanence, and prominence, and they also shifted the balance between opportunity and obligation. Earlier experiments had assessed reforms designed by researchers or funders (such as Supported Work and the NITs) or state-run initiatives that though large compared with prior evaluations were implemented on a trial basis in a few locations. Now, for the first time, random assignment was proposed to evaluate two programs that were intended to be universal (covering all who met the mandatory criteria), full scale, ongoing, and statewide. Further, the numbers were huge: GAIN was the largest and most ambitious welfare-to-work program in the nation, with a projected budget of over $300 million a year and targeting 200,000 people, 35,000 of whom were ultimately subject to random assignment (Gueron and Rolston, 2013, pp. 276−278).

As a result, both evaluations raised an ethical red flag: Would the creation of a control group reduce the number of people served? Would it in effect deny people access to a quasi or real entitlement? The specific activities added another element. In earlier RCTs of mandatory programs, most welfare advocates had not objected to excluding controls from the services and penalties, in part because the programs were viewed primarily as imposing burdens not offering opportunities. Now, when the required activities included remedial education, denial of service became more controversial.

In combination, these differences meant that, far from being stealth evaluations, they appeared immediately and vividly on the political and press radars. In California, MDRC staff were called Nazis and a senior legislator who believed deeply in the value of education threatened to close down the study. In Florida, a lethal combination of gubernatorial

---

[19] Critically important, Winstead had strong support from the Secretary of Florida's Department of Health and Rehabilitative Services, Gregory Coler, who, notwithstanding negative findings from MDRC's earlier random assignment evaluation of the program he had run in Illinois, sought out such a study when he took over in Florida, having seen firsthand the credibility that Congressional staff and the press accorded to findings from experiments.

politics, a concerned legislator, and ill will between the advocacy community and the welfare agency fed an explosion of inflammatory press. Headlines accused the state and MDRC of treating welfare recipients like guinea pigs and implementing practices that were shameful, inhuman, and akin to those used in the infamous Tuskegee syphilis study. Even in this pre-Internet era, the flare-up ricocheted to newspapers across the country, threatening other HHS experiments.

Proponents in the two states, MDRC, and HHS ultimately prevailed (showing the fallacy of claims that random assignment can be used only to assess small-scale operations) by both drawing on know-how gained in the earlier state studies and leveraging new forces. The first, and most important, was the unflinching stand taken by California and Florida officials who did not walk away when attacked, despite withering criticism. No researcher or research firm could have overcome this level of opposition alone. The determination of state officials to get an independent and credible evaluation—one that would address their questions but that they were well aware could expose their failure—was inspiring. Thus, when threatened with lawsuits, Carl Williams, California's GAIN administrator, said he was simply unwilling to supervise a program of that size and complexity unless it had a really sound evaluation, declaring, "We were going to get random assignment one way or another." When asked why he fought for the study, Winstead replied, "It sounds sort of naïve, but I became convinced that it was the right thing to do…If we're going to put thousands of people through something, we ought to be willing to find out whether or not it works" (Gueron and Rolston, 2013, pp. 281, 285, 307).

The second new factor was the slow shift in academic backing for random assignment, reflected in and prodded by two events. The first, in 1985, was the release of authoritative reports from the National Academy of Sciences and the Department of Labor, publications that MDRC cited over and over again to encourage allies and convert opponents (Betsey, Hollister, and Papageorgiou and Job Training Longitudinal Survey Research Advisory Panel). Both expert panels concluded that they did not believe the results of most comparison group studies—including the Department of Labor's $50 million or so outlay on conflicting econometric evaluations of the nation's major job-training program—and saw no alternative to random assignment given existing statistical techniques if one wanted to produce credible data on effectiveness. The second event was an unexpected legacy from Supported Work. Not only did the demonstration show that it was feasible to use a field experiment to evaluate a large-scale employment program, but it also provided a public use file that, for the first time, offered an intriguing way to find out if alternatives could have done as well. Robert LaLonde's groundbreaking study, published in the *American Economic Review* in 1986, did just that by testing whether econometric estimates—using eight carefully constructed comparison groups drawn from the Current Population Survey and the

Panel Study of Income Dynamics—could reliably reproduce the experimental findings. His negative conclusion had a profound influence.[20]

The third factor was the successful effort to build and then mobilize a community of converts and fans (including advocates, public officials, funders, academics, practitioners, and state and federal legislative, congressional, and agency staff) who recognized and valued the distinctive quality of the evidence from RCTs and became allies in defending the studies and their results. This factor became particularly important when MDRC and state staff in Florida, fearful that a successful lawsuit or ban on control group research in the state risked widespread contagion, used endorsements from these sources and one-on-one meetings with dozens of legislators to sell the merits and ethics of RCTs.

The final and most decisive factor in both states was a budget shortfall. Despite the rhetoric of universal mandates, the reality was that there were not enough funds to reach everyone. Once it became clear that services would have to be rationed and some eligible people denied access (but not as a result of the study), a lottery struck the objecting legislators as a fair way to give everyone an equal chance. (The California and Florida experience also led HHS to prohibit using RCTs to test entitlements.)

The findings from the GAIN evaluation addressed a number of the issues raised by the early 1980s state studies (see Table 2). The GAIN approach reflected the hope that emphasizing basic education for those with limited academic skills and helping the rest get a job quickly would produce better results (particularly for long-term welfare recipients) than would the shorter-term, primarily job search programs, and that the higher cost would be worth it. The effects for the six study counties combined were mixed. GAIN outperformed the earlier programs on some measures, generating larger, longer-lasting impacts (still robust 5 years later) and having greater success with more disadvantaged recipients. Nonetheless, the big picture remained in the range of modest but positive: in the average 3 months during the 5 years of follow-up, 28% of single mothers assigned to the program worked, compared with 24% of control group members; by the last 3 months, 39% received some AFDC benefits compared with 42% of control group members. Further, in contrast to most of the earlier state studies, GAIN did not pay for itself, returning $0.76 in budget savings for every public dollar spent to run it (with net costs calculated as the difference in the average cost of all services received by program and control group members). On the other hand, GAIN did better in raising participants' income, leading to a 3 percentage point reduction in the share of families in poverty (Gueron and Rolston, 2013, pp. 287—289; Freedman et al., 1996).

---

[20] LaLonde (1986, p. 604) states: "This comparison shows that many of the econometric procedures do not replicate the experimentally determined results, and it suggests that researchers should be aware of the potential for specification errors in other nonexperimental evaluations." Subsequently, Fraker and Maynard (1987) also used the Supported Work data and reached similar conclusions. Bloom et al. (2005b) describe the numerous studies that followed, drawing on data from other experiments.

The findings for one county, Riverside, however, were strikingly more positive, with better results overall and among low-skilled recipients, lower costs, and a highly cost-effective program that returned to taxpayers almost three dollars for every dollar invested. For the first time, a welfare-to-work program produced effects that broke out of the modest range. These findings raised an obvious question: What explained Riverside's success?

GAIN had given counties substantial discretion in how they implemented the program. Although Riverside provided a mix of activities (and had other special features), it emphasized getting a job quickly and, for those deemed to need basic education, offered work-focused short-term education or training. In the early years of the study, welfare directors in counties that had made a greater investment in education argued that it would pay off in the long term, particularly for people without skills or a high school degree. But the 2-, 3-, and 5-year results confirmed a different story: though impacts in the other counties grew over time, Riverside stayed in the lead on most measures and, crucially, proved to be the most successful with more disadvantaged recipients (Riccio et al., 1994; Freedman et al., 1996; Gueron and Rolston, 2013, pp. 289—290; Gueron, 1996; Gueron and Hamilton, 2002).

8. WHAT WORKS BEST? A MULTIARM TEST OF LABOR FORCE ATTACHMENT VERSUS HUMAN CAPITAL DEVELOPMENT

This counterintuitive finding along a major liberal-conservative fault line—work first versus education first—attracted attention in Washington and across the country (DeParle, 2004, p. 111). However, since it came from comparing RCT results across California counties that differed not only in their program designs but also in labor market conditions, alternative services, and welfare populations—a nonexperimental comparison—it cried out for more rigorous confirmation. Hotz et al. (2006) sought to do this in a study that extended the GAIN follow-up to 9 years and controlled statistically for county differences in pre- and postprogram background and local conditions. They concluded that the other counties eventually caught up with and then surpassed Riverside's employment and earnings impacts and called for a reconsideration of the value of "training components that stress the development of work-related skills."[21]

Although an important extension to the GAIN evaluation, the Hotz, Imbens, and Klerman conclusion was still based on a nonexperimental analysis in six counties in one state. It raised a challenge: Was it possible to get a more definitive, experimental

---

[21] Hotz, Imbens, and Klerman did not address the relative success of the counties in meeting GAIN's other goals, including reducing cumulative welfare outlays and increasing cost-effectiveness. (See footnote 16.)

answer to this key policy question? Fortunately, a response was already in the works. In mid-1989, HHS had launched and MDRC was selected to conduct the most ambitious of the welfare experiments: randomly assigning 57,000 individuals to 11 programs at seven sites to evaluate the Job Opportunities and Basic Skills Training (JOBS) program, the major component of the 1988 federal welfare legislation. JOBS extended the requirement for participation in work-directed activities to mothers with younger children and emphasized serving people at risk of long-term dependency (Hamilton et al., 2001; Gueron and Rolston, 2013, pp. 311−352). The major hypothesis underlying JOBS (as with GAIN) was that providing remedial education to people with low basic skills was the strategy of choice for helping them to get better and more stable jobs, increase their family's income, and reduce the likelihood of their returning to the rolls. It was expected that programs emphasizing education and training would be longer and more costly. The central questions, as in GAIN, included whether they would produce greater or longer-lasting impacts and be cost-effective in budgetary or other terms.

The centerpiece of the JOBS evaluation was an innovative and daring head-to-head test at three sites in which welfare recipients were randomly assigned either to a no-JOBS control group or to one of two different approaches: mandatory job-search-first programs, called labor force attachment (LFA) programs, that encouraged people to find employment quickly, or mandatory education-or-training-first programs, called human capital development (HCD) programs, that emphasized longer-term skill-building activities, primarily basic or remedial education, GED preparation, and, to a lesser extent, vocational training (but not college).[22] In contrast to the GAIN evaluation, this three-group design could produce *experimental* estimates of not only the impacts of each of the strategies (LFA versus a control group and HCD versus a control group) but also their differential effectiveness (LFA versus HCD). Overcoming MDRC's and HHS's initial concerns about feasibility, the two treatments and the multiarm research design were successfully implemented at three very different sites: Grand Rapids, Michigan; Riverside, California; and Atlanta, Georgia (Hamilton et al., 1997).[23]

[22] The LFA strategy reflected the view that the best way to build work habits and skills was by working, even at low wages; the HCD strategy was based on the belief that education and training should come first so that people could gain the skills required for them to get better jobs. Although both approaches included elements of the other (for example, people in the LFA programs who did not find work through job clubs could be assigned to short-term education or training or to unpaid work and people in the HCD stream could later be assigned to job clubs), they conveyed different messages and emphasized different activities (Hamilton et al., 1997).

[23] Although MDRC had employed multiarm designs in three welfare RCTs during the early 1980s, these RCTs had tested whether adding workfare after job search increased effectiveness. The JOBS evaluation was much more ambitious. It required welfare agencies to operate two distinct comprehensive programs simultaneously. In addition, the JOBS evaluation used multiarm designs to assess alternative case management strategies and to determine the separate effect of the program's services and its participation mandate (Gueron and Pauly, 1991, p. 164, note 37; Gueron and Rolston, 2013, pp. 322−338).

Fig. 1 shows the impacts (the difference between averages for the treatment and control groups) on single mothers' earnings and welfare receipt of the LFA and HCD programs at the three sites combined for each of the 5 years following random assignment. Both approaches increased earnings and reduced welfare, but the time trends differed. The LFA programs moved people into jobs and off welfare more quickly and thus had larger short-term impacts (that is, the LFA and HCD impacts differed significantly from each other in the first year or two, depending on the outcome measure). However, by the third year, the HCD programs had caught up: The gap between the two lines narrowed and was no longer statistically significant (Hamilton, 2002, p. 32). But Hotz, Imbens, and Klerman had suggested that 5 years would not do justice to the HCD strategy. MDRC's final report on the JOBS evaluation concluded that the 5-year trends made it unlikely that the story would change, if longer follow-up were available. This conclusion was confirmed when Freedman and Smith (2008a,b) tracked impacts up to 15 years after random assignment.

Since the HCD programs did not surpass the LFA programs in the out years, the earnings gains and welfare savings over the entire 5-year period (for both the three sites combined and in each site) were either the same for the two approaches or larger for the

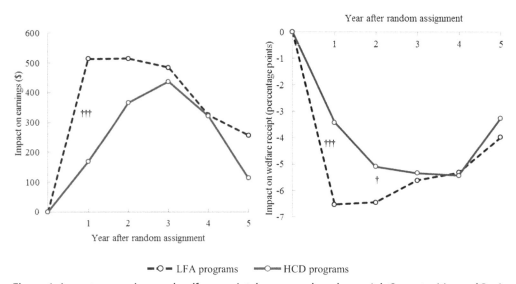

Figure 1 *Impact on earnings and welfare receipt, by approach and year: Job Opportunities and Basic Skills Training evaluation.* The impacts shown are averages for sample members in the three LFA and HCD programs. *Daggers* (†) denote statistical significance levels for LFA–HCD differences: †, 10%; ††, 5%; †††, 1%. (Hamilton, G., 2002. Moving People from Welfare to Work: Lessons from the National Evaluation of Welfare-to-Work Strategies. U.S. Department of Health and Human Services and U.S. Department of Education, Washington, DC, Figs. 8 and 9.)

LFA programs. Furthermore, because the HCD programs were from one-third more expensive to nearly twice as expensive as the LFA programs that operated in the same site, the LFA programs proved to be much more cost-effective. As a result, for the same cost, the programs could reach more people and have larger aggregate impacts.[24] Particularly disappointing for advocates of the HCD approach, these findings held true both for program enrollees who lacked a high school diploma or a General Educational Development (GED) certificate—the subgroup of welfare recipients who were expected to derive the greatest benefit from the initial investment in basic education—as well as for those who already possessed one of those credentials (Hamilton, 2002; Hamilton et al., 2001; Gueron and Rolston, 2013).

The JOBS evaluation demonstrated the value of the multiarm, multisite designs by providing convincing evidence that, in mandatory programs for welfare mothers, the rigid job-search-first approach was more successful than the rigid education-or-training-first approach. However, this finding did not mean that there should be no role for education or training in welfare-to-work programs. [A cross-site comparison of results from 20 welfare RCTs suggests that the most successful ones used a mixed strategy, in which some people were urged to get a job quickly and others required to enroll in work-focused, short-term education or training (Gueron and Hamilton, 2002).] It also did not imply that other types of training or postsecondary education or programs targeting different populations or volunteers would not be more effective. (for example, see Card et al., 2015; Hamilton, 2012.)

9. THE MOMENTUM SHIFTS

By the early 1990s, four changes had shifted the momentum further in favor of random assignment: the evidence of the feasibility and payoff from the more ambitious and sophisticated tests, the visibility of the completed experiments and participating states, the final success of the HHS/OMB effort to make random assignment the quid pro quo for waivers, and the slowly gathering support among academics.

The result was that, instead of researchers or funders having to sell RCTs to states that accepted them reluctantly as the new price for HHS waivers, the reverse sometimes occurred. This outcome was most notable when the Canadian government, the New Hope program in Milwaukee, and the state of Minnesota proposed reforms to make

---

[24] Advocates of the LFA and HCD strategies had anticipated that administrators might face a tradeoff in advancing different goals, with LFA more successful in saving money and HCD more successful in reducing poverty. However, the HCD programs did not have larger impacts on either outcome. This reflects the finding that, contrary to their goal, the HCD programs did not produce more earnings growth or increase the likelihood of sample members' getting more stable or higher-paying jobs. They also did not differentially affect the well-being of sample members' children.

work pay more than welfare by supplementing people's earnings if (in most cases) they worked full time. All three sought random assignment evaluations as the way to convince a wider audience of the value of their approaches. For them, despite the challenges (particularly in implementing multiarm designs to determine which aspects of complex programs drove any impacts), experiments had been transformed from high-risk endeavors to pathways to recognition.

Because MDRC used consistent measures and research designs in these and many of its earlier state studies, it was relatively easy to contrast the success of different strategies in advancing reformers' diverse goals. Such comparisons of two approaches—mandatory welfare-to-work programs and earnings supplements—revealed that the former did better in reducing welfare dependency and government spending, the latter did better in reducing poverty and benefiting young children, and no single policy maximized all goals (Gueron and Rolston, 2013, p. 385).[25]

Starting in 1996, when AFDC was replaced by a block grant to states, the incentive structure for RCTs shifted again. States could now redesign welfare on their own (no federal waivers needed) but could not tap federal matching funds for evaluation.[26] Fortunately, HHS's commitment to RCTs did not change. After a few years, during which it focused on sustaining the most valuable waiver experiments, HHS shifted gears and took the lead in launching multisite experiments that addressed questions of interest to states in the new TANF environment. By the early 2000s—signaled in part by the creation of the Institute of Education Sciences in the US Department of Education in 2002—the explosion of interest in experiments was in full swing (Gueron and Rolston, 2013, pp. 388—422, 455—471).

10. USEFUL AND USED

As stated above, the architects of the welfare experiments sought not only to obtain reliable evidence of effectiveness but to make the studies useful and to increase the potential that they would be used. A number of people close to the transformation of the U.S. welfare system—both the radical 1996 law that ended the AFDC entitlement and imposed tough work requirements and the 1988 bill that required participation in activities designed to enhance employability—have suggested that the experiments were unusually influential in shaping attitudes, legislation, and practice. For example,

---

[25] For more information about the treatments, findings, and tradeoffs, see Bloom and Michalopoulos (2001), Gueron and Rolston (2013), Berlin (2000), Greenberg et al. (2010), Morris et al. (2001), and Morris et al. (2005).

[26] Thus, the block grant structure increased states' financial incentive to reduce the rolls, since they would reap all of the savings if people left welfare and bear all the costs for any expansion, but reduced the incentive for evaluation.

Ron Haskins, head of the Republican staff on the welfare subcommittee of House Ways and Means during these years, stated:

> *Work really is the central issue of welfare reform, and the idea of work took on even more significance as an important, achievable goal because of the experiments. They took that potentially contentious issue off the table by showing that states could actually do things to get more people to work and save money. As a result of the experiments, by something like osmosis everybody in Congress came to understand this, it became the new conventional wisdom, and this had a dramatic effect on the welfare debate…It is the best story I know of how research influenced policy (Gueron and Rolston, 2013, pp. 296–297).*[27]

None of these people claimed that the legislation tracked the experiments (central parts of both bills reflected hunches that went way beyond the findings) or that politics, philosophy, and values were not much more important, but they did offer four reasons why this group of studies had an outsized effect (Gueron and Rolston, 2013, pp. 190–216, 436–443).

10.1 The credibility of random assignment, replication, and relevance

A major rationale for RCTs was the belief that policymakers could distinguish—and might privilege—the uncommon quality of the evidence. For a number of reasons, it seems that this hypothesis was often the case: the simplicity and transparency of the method; the growing consensus in the research community that alternative designs would fall short; the indication that performance measures such as job placements overstated success; and the replication of results in diverse conditions and in small-, medium-, and full-scale programs.[28] All of these contributed to a bipartisan agreement that the RCTs offered an unusually reliable and objective yardstick.

The reaction to the studies suggested that policymakers valued external validity, though not in any formal statistical sense. The strategy described earlier—judgmentally selecting states which were representative along the dimensions that politically savvy folks viewed as likely to affect success (for example, strong and weak labor markets and administrative capacity), conducting experiments in ordinary offices, and having samples that were unscreened and large enough to produce valid estimates for each location—provided convincing face validity that the findings could be generalized beyond the study sites. As an example, Erica Baum (recruited by Senator Moynihan to draft the Senate's version of the 1988 legislation) points to the importance of finding positive results across nearly all the states studied, despite the variation in design, conditions, cost, population,

---

[27] For different views on how and why these studies did or did not influence policy and practice, see Gueron and Rolston (2013), pp. 190–215, 292–298; Baron (2013); Baum (1991); Greenberg et al. (2003); Haskins (1991); Rogers-Dillon (2004), p. 46; Szanton (1991); Weaver (2000).

[28] This high rate of replication contrasts with low rates in other fields (Manzi, 2012) and what Begley and Ioannidis (2015) call the "reproducibility crisis" in biomedical research.

attitudes, and administrative capacity. She particularly highlighted that regular staff in regular offices delivered the programs:

> *This is no minor matter. In the past, elaborate programs pilot-tested by sophisticated social scientists or a small number of program experts produced worthwhile findings. But when the programs were transplanted to real-world social agencies…the positive results disappeared. Since MDRC found that diverse state and local administrators could succeed on their own…we could be relatively confident that…other cities, counties, and states could do likewise (Gueron and Rolston, 2013, p. 195).*

10.2 The findings from comprehensive studies

The experiments had been structured strategically to test the major reform options and address the key concerns of liberals and conservatives. Although the effectiveness findings were the centerpiece (and the focus of this chapter), they were by no means the only evidence that the designers had thought would be important. Random assignment was always viewed as the skeleton on which to build studies using multiple techniques to answer a range of questions about program implementation and the factors that made programs more or less effective. The reaction showed that varied parts of the research did indeed matter to different audiences.

The fact that the impacts from mandatory welfare-to-work programs were relatively consistent and in the desired direction (increased work and reduced welfare) was critical. However, their absolute magnitude also mattered and played out differently in 1988 and 1996. In the early period, the modest gains prompted expanded funding for work programs; 10 years later, limited success in the face of an increase in the rolls and the more stridently partisan context convinced some policymakers that a kind of shock therapy was called for.[29]

The findings on participation rates, suggesting that states could be trusted to impose serious obligations, contributed to the push for block grants. The finding that, under certain conditions, welfare recipients considered workfare fair changed the views of some originally hostile to requiring unpaid work. The counterintuitive evidence that programs emphasizing rapid employment had larger impacts than those requiring basic education contributed to a transformation of state programs. And the benefit-cost lesson—that up-front outlays were sometimes more than offset by rapid savings from reduced transfer payments and increased taxes as people went to work—provided unanticipated confirmation that social programs could be worthwhile investments and affected the all-important Congressional Budget Office estimates of the cost of legislative proposals (Gueron and Rolston, 2013, p. 173).

---

[29] Many factors explain this shift, but personalities and the change in who controlled Congress likely played a role. During the late 1980s when Senator Moynihan, a welfare expert and exceptionally nuanced research consumer, chaired the relevant subcommittee, he consistently sought the latest findings and argued that, given the complexity of the problem, incremental improvements were to be expected (Gueron and Rolston, 2013, pp. 199–200). Because of his approach, I took as a compliment his obviously two-sided description of me as "Our Lady of Modest but Positive Results" (*New York Times*, March 9, 1993).

10.3 The timeliness of results

The timing of results also mattered. Two preconditions of research having an impact on policy are relevance and timeliness. On the former, although there was an element of luck, two design choices drove success. One was the explicit effort to anticipate issues and launch studies of enduring policy options. A second was that most of the RCTs did not assess reforms dreamed up by policy wonks. The partnership vision meant that the initiatives tested had bubbled up from governors, their staffs, and community activists—people with finely calibrated judgment on political timing.

On the latter, there is an inherent tension between getting the story out soon and getting it right. Under the state contracts, there was always pressure to produce results quickly, but we were determined not to repeat the negative income tax experiments' experience, where people struggled with limited success to retract findings that had been released prematurely (Coyle and Wildavsky, 1986, p. 179). Yet MDRC faced the reality that it takes time before an adequate number of people are enrolled in a program and can be followed for long enough to judge impacts; it also takes time to obtain, analyze, and accurately report on the data. We sought to address the impatience by dividing up the research: identifying some meaty issues (participation rates, the nature of workfare, implementation challenges) that could be addressed quickly and delaying findings on impacts and cost-effectiveness.

10.4 Forceful, nontechnical, and even-handed communication

Finally, people point to the influence of several aspects of MDRC's communication strategy. One was aggressive marketing and outreach to people across the political spectrum. Although this started with lengthy technical reports, it evolved to include pamphlets, press releases, summaries, and more than 100 presentations—briefings, lectures, and frequent testimony—during 1 year alone. There was also an explicit drive to keep results simple by using easy-to-understand outcome measures and rudimentary and uniform charts and tables that drew, as much as possible, on the transparency of random assignment.

In addition, there was the conscious choice not to take sides and to share positive and negative results.[30] As with many social policy issues, the various factions in the welfare debate differed in their diagnosis of the problem and thus the priority they placed on achieving different goals (for example, reducing dependency or poverty). As a result, good news for some could be judged neutral or bad news by others. MDRC's strategy

---

[30] Although many studies produced positive findings, some were clearly negative. State officials, program administrators, and funders did not welcome reports that progress depended on discarding approaches (particularly their favorite approaches) because they were found not to work. However, though state officials at first may not have grasped that a failed program was not a failed study, we found they did learn and move on from disappointing findings, even to the point of volunteering for subsequent experiments. (See footnote 19.)

was not to push people to agree on a goal, but to agree on the facts. Thus, we sought to get reliable estimates of what approaches produced what results and to flag trade-offs but not to promote or advocate for one policy over another (Gueron and Rolston, 2013, pp. 208–211, 443). This style encouraged people with divergent views to see the researchers as neutral parties with no ax to grind.

During the 1980s, the most difficult communication challenge was explaining why, in the face of a competing narrative from prominent governors, high outcomes did not automatically mean success. Staff in states with RCTs begged for cover, as they heard from their own governors who—on reading news articles about how other states got tens of thousands of people off of welfare and into jobs—demanded comparably big numbers. How could an RCT suggesting impacts of 5–10 percentage points compete? We and the state staff knew from the control groups that most of the people counted in the other states' statistics would have gotten off of welfare anyway, but could they sell that politically? The war of claims played out in the press, but by the late 1980s, after MDRC's relentless outreach effort, key reporters and staff in Congress and Congressional agencies came to recognize that the big numbers could as easily reflect a strong economy as the particulars of welfare reform. However, this argument was not one that was permanently won, and governors continued to duel using competing measures to claim success (Gueron and Rolston, 2013, pp. 128–131, 195; Gueron, 2005).

This type of active, ongoing communication—to state and federal officials, public interest groups, practitioners, policy analysts, academics, and the press—takes time and money. Throughout these years, MDRC was fortunate to obtain foundation funding to support staff (including communications professionals) in this role. This effort was not viewed as a sideshow, but integral to the organization's two-part mission: to learn what works to improve the well-being of low-income people and to communicate what was learned in ways that would enhance the effectiveness of social policies and programs.

The effect of these four factors was that, despite the highly politicized debate, random assignment was generally accepted as unbiased, impartial, and scientific, rather than as another form of pressure group noise. Further, the findings were not seriously contested and became almost common knowledge. Finally, this result led some people to conclude that the widespread press coverage had an effect on Congress and in states and that the studies contributed to the consensus that made reform possible. As an example, Jo Anne Barnhart, Associate Commissioner/Assistant Secretary of HHS during the Reagan and first Bush administrations, stated:

> The debate over how to reform welfare could aptly be described as contentious, emotional, and partisan. When President Reagan brought his ideas about Community Work Experience (work-fare) to Washington, a stark line was drawn in the sand…Without the incremental insights provided by the random assignment experiments, it is difficult to imagine the two conflicting sides coming together…[F]act-based information gleaned from the research provided a "neutral"

common language for the divided political rhetoric. Thus, although [the 1996 bill] did not exactly mirror the research findings, it would never have been possible without them...The shift in thinking with respect to welfare reform was the reward [for] the research effort (Gueron and Rolston, 2013, p. 298).[31]

11. LESSONS AND CHALLENGES

In the field of welfare policy, a long fight showed that random assignment could be used to assess major policy options and that the distinctive quality of the evidence was recognized and valued. This experience provides lessons for others seeking similar rigor.

11.1 A confluence of supportive factors

In the critical years before 1996, six factors sustained welfare experiments: (1) public hostility to AFDC combined with state/federal cost-sharing to create strong political and financial incentives for governors to innovate and achieve success; (2) the discovery that RCTs were not overly burdensome and could be used to determine the effectiveness of state reforms, plus a growing consensus that alternative methods would fall short; (3) momentum from sufficiently positive findings (success fed success); (4) the active dissemination of results; (5) sustained research funding from Congress, the AFDC formula, and the Ford Foundation; and (6) zealots in the federal government and research firms who stayed involved for decades, consciously built a constituency for experiments, and used the waiver approval process to encourage and ultimately require random assignment.

Researchers in other fields will neither have the same advantages nor have to fight the same battles. The transformation in academic support for experiments is unlikely to be fully reversed and, in combination with the track record of successful RCTs, has contributed to a remarkable federal commitment to scientific, evidence-based policy as a route to more effective government (Gueron and Rolston, 2013, pp. 461–68; Haskins and Baron, 2011; Haskins and Margolis, 2015). Moreover, as reflected in this volume, hundreds of social experiments are now underway worldwide. The challenge remains to preserve this momentum against future objections and budget cuts and in fields that may be less susceptible to testing.

11.2 The payoff to building an agenda

The power of the welfare experiments flowed from their logic, relevance, and consistency of findings. In part, this resulted from the independent determination of a small number of people at HHS and MDRC to ensure that successive experiments be accretive

---

[31] Reflecting on the 1988 debate, Henry Aaron (1990, p. 278) offers a contrary view: "The lesson of this experience seems to be that social science can facilitate policy when it finds that measures congenial to the values of elected officials are at least modestly beneficial."

rather than a collection of scatter-shot tests (Gueron and Rolston, 2013, pp. 431–433). The experiments also responded to the reality of devolution, in which neither the federal government nor any outside actor could impose what would be tested. Welfare reform was too political; the options too controversial. The paradigm of partnership with states, forged out of necessity and that reflected this devolution, had the important benefit of producing results relevant to the diverse and dynamic policy context of state-based welfare programs. Rather than seeking to identify a single, most effective model that no state might have been willing or able to subsequently fund and implement, policy-makers pursued evaluations of similar (but not identical) reforms in multiple states as well as a strategically structured agenda that by the end allowed them to see the trade-offs among the major options.

The influence of the experiments also came from the breadth of the research. These experiments were not bare-bones RCTs that spoke only to whether reforms did or did not work. The state and foundation partners would never have gotten involved or stayed the course just for that. They would have found the results insufficiently useful. Although the how and why questions were not answered with the rigor of the yes or no ones (and by how much and for whom), a little insight went a long way toward sustaining momentum and commitment.

Developing this agenda took time. In 1974, it would have been inconceivable to implement RCTs of the scale or complexity of what was done 10 or 15 years later. Researchers did not have the skill or the nerve, nor had they identified the relevant questions. Another reason it took time was that the array of models tested reflected both findings from prior RCTs and the values and beliefs that hardened into policy options after years of debate within states. As a result, constructing the agenda (which eventually encompassed most of the reform proposals advanced during these years) depended on the actual evolution of policy, politics, and evidence.

Over time, there was also a ratcheting up in methodological demands, in terms of the questions asked and the conditions faced. Designs tended to become more ambitious, researchers sometimes had less money and control, and the results became more visible. At each stage, researchers drew lessons on the tools (the art, craft, and risk-taking) they judged key to overcoming the challenges—lessons that were often later revised or reversed.

Implementing this agenda also took long-term funding. High-quality, longitudinal studies (experimental or not) cost money, and the continuity and breadth of the welfare RCTs benefited from there being multiple funders. Most notable, at times when federal enthusiasm waned, support from the Ford Foundation financed the survival of RCTs, the testing of approaches that were of little initial interest to the federal government, and the innovation of the partnership paradigm. Fortunately for those advocating evidence-based policy, there are encouraging signs that public agencies and diverse foundations continue to recognize the vital role they can play in informing policy through supporting rigorous evaluations in the United States and abroad. It remains to be seen whether this role will be sustained and what people and organizations will step up to assure that, as in welfare, the individual studies feed a larger learning agenda.

11.3 The need for realistic expectations

The welfare experiments tell a surprisingly upbeat story. A range of reforms produced relatively consistent effects: employment rates went up, welfare rolls went down, and there was almost no collateral harm.[32] Some strategies also benefited young children and even substantially reduced poverty. Given the skepticism about social programs prevalent in the 1970s—reflected in researchers' fear that the studies would yield null findings (Gueron and Rolston, 2013, pp. 45, 205)—and the failure to replicate success in RCTs in other fields, the ability repeatedly to beat the status quo is encouraging.

However, the results also send another message. Average success was generally modest (for example, employment gains of 5 percentage points). Many members of the control groups eventually got jobs or left welfare, either on their own or with the assistance of (or incentives provided by) existing programs and systems. This normal behavior—the counterfactual—set a steep hurdle that reformers had to clear to have an impact.

Over the years, defenders of experimental results faced the repeated challenge of setting realistic expectations, especially when politically powerful reformers claimed greater success based on outcomes.[33] But there was one way in which welfare researchers had it easy compared with colleagues in other fields. Reforms that caused people to leave welfare sooner produced real budget savings. Even if controls subsequently caught up, this fading out of impacts did not wipe out past savings. This savings in part explains why almost all states implemented what came to be called "work first" programs.

If RCTs show modest impacts in other fields, will they be viewed as useful building blocks (as is the case for welfare-to-work programs or in medicine) or discarded as signs of failure? Fortunately, the increasing sophistication of public funders (led in the United States by the Office of Management and Budget's push for high-quality evidence of effectiveness) offers reason for optimism (see Haskins and Margolis, 2015).

---

[32] A few studies, however, showed small (sometimes temporary) negative effects on the school performance of adolescents from their mothers' participation in welfare-to-work programs (Gennetian et al., 2002).

[33] Robert Solow (1980, p. 16) expressed well the frustration of defending reliably measured impacts against hyped outcomes in his discussion of the Supported Work results: "No one who cares seriously about the employment of disadvantaged groups will sneer at those results. They are not at all trivial…Somehow we have to learn to make a convincing case for policy initiatives based on reasonable estimates of the probability of success and the quantitative meaning of success. If the professional policy community allows itself to promise more than it can deliver, it will end up not delivering what it promises, and eventually the promises will be disbelieved and there will be no delivery at all."

11.4 Maintaining a culture of quality

The welfare experiments were unusual in the extent to which their findings were accepted as objective truth. There were many reasons for this wide acceptance, but two flowed from the shared culture of the relatively small number of people conducting the studies in the early decades. The first was their almost religious devotion to high standards for the myriad aspects that make a quality RCT. The second was their shared vision that the purpose of such studies was to learn *whether* a test treatment worked, not to *prove* that it worked. This eschewing of advocacy research included a commitment to sharing both good and bad news and a view that failure was not learning that a promising program did not work, but of not bothering to learn whether it worked (Gueron, 2008). It is this culture—combined with randomness—that contributed to the view of experiments as the gold standard.

With social experiments now a growth industry, there is a risk that researchers claim the RCT brand, but do not enforce the multitude of hidden actions vital to the distinctive value of such studies. Just as all that glitters is not gold, the magic does not come from flipping a properly balanced coin. The angel is in the details, and it takes experience to discover and master the details. As policing of RCTs falls to the familiar terrain of peer review, what protects against a debasing of the metal?[34]

11.5 The advantage of transparent measures and relatively short treatments

People evaluating welfare reforms had several advantages compared with those in some other fields. First, the outcomes that most policymakers cared about—the percent of people working, on welfare, or in poverty and the average dollar earnings or benefits—could be measured in easily understood units (no proxies for what really mattered years later and no hard-to-interpret "effect size") that in most cases could be directly incorporated in a benefit–cost calculation. Second, the treatments were often comparatively simple and short—or usually front-loaded when long or open-ended—so that useful results could be produced with a few years (and sometimes less) of follow-up data. Third, although control group members could and did access competing (and sometimes similar) services provided by other agencies in the community, they were not systematically enrolled in an alternative treatment.

The first advantage had a major impact on communications. At the state level, the studies would likely have had less impact if, at the end, welfare commissioners—who

---

[34] As a warning of the potential seriousness of this risk, Begley and Ioannidis (2015) discuss how the failure to apply well-established guidelines for experimental research may have contributed to the inability to replicate 75–90% of the preclinical biomedical research published in high-profile journals. In an effort to address this danger, the Institute of Education Sciences created the What Works Clearinghouse to serve as the "central and trusted source of scientific evidence on what works in education" (Gueron and Rolston, 2013, p. 463).

are political appointees—had been told that their programs had an effect size of 0.15 on a measure that was not their ultimate goal (for example, on getting a training credential) and then, in response to the resulting blank stare, been told that this effect was small. My guess is that they would not have acted on the results or volunteered (as some did) to be in another random assignment study. Instead, welfare researchers could make statements such as "Your program increased earnings by 25% and reduced the welfare rolls by 4 percentage points. This cost $800 per person. Over 5 years, you saved $1.50 for every $1 invested." Since most states wanted to restructure welfare to increase work and save money, this approach was a clear winner. It did not matter that the impacts were called modest or small, the results pointed to a better way to run the system and the response was often direct.

It may be hard to replicate these advantages in other fields, such as education, where the treatments are both more complex and may last many years, the ultimate outcomes are further in the future, the control group members are systematically receiving services, and the goals are more diverse and not convertible to dollar measures. In such cases, studies often rely on intermediate or proximate measures that are an uncertain stand-in for the ultimate goals and are usually calibrated in measures that are not as readily interpretable.

11.6 The payoff to multiple studies and synthesis

Experience has shown that no single experiment is definitive. Uncertainty shrinks with replication in different contexts and times. The real payoff comes when there are enough high-quality studies to allow for different types of syntheses to identify the trade-offs and refine the evidence on what works best for whom under what conditions.

The welfare area was unusual in the extent and nature of experiments and the use of consistent measures. The resulting volume of work and richness of data affected the need and potential for high-level syntheses. The result was various kinds of literature reviews, secondary analysis of pooled data, and metaanalyses, including a ground-breaking study by Bloom et al. (2003, 2005a) that applied a multilevel model to pooled data from 69,000 people at 59 offices for which there were identical measures of individual characteristics, management practices, services, economic conditions, and outcomes (examples of syntheses include Greenberg and Cebulla, 2005; Grogger and Karoly, 2005; Gueron and Pauly, 1991; Michalopoulos and Schwartz, 2001; Morris et al., 2001). Among the lessons from this work were that almost all subgroups saw increased earnings from the various welfare reform initiatives, earnings impacts were smaller in places with higher unemployment, and program effectiveness was positively associated with the extent to which staff emphasized rapid job entry and negatively correlated with the extent of participation in basic education (Gueron and Rolston, 2013, pp. 348−352).

It will be important to encourage a similar replication of high-quality experiments and uniform data in other fields (see, for example, Banerjee et al., 2015a; Banerjee et al., 2015b).

11.7 Major challenges remain

The beginning of this chapter posed the fundamental evaluation question: Is it possible to isolate the effect of a social program from the many other factors that influence human behavior? For welfare policy, the answer is clearly yes. Across the country, from small- to full-scale reforms, and under varied conditions, experiments provided convincing answers to the basic question of whether an intervention changed behavior. Moreover, the body of experiments also addressed another question: Is context so important that results cannot be replicated? The answer appears to be no. For reasons that are unclear and in contrast to other areas (Manzi, 2012), when the welfare RCTs were repeated (using related, not identical models) in different circumstances, the average results were relatively consistent, providing confidence in the reliability of the findings.

Although the welfare experiments moved the field out of the dark ages of the 1970s, the lack of headway in two key areas suggests some humility. First, despite repeated efforts, the body of work does not adequately explain why programs succeed or fail and thus how to make them more effective. Lurking behind the modest average and broadly consistent impacts is substantial variation. It remains unclear how much of this variation is due to features of people, programs, context, or control services. The uncertainty is not for lack of trying. All the major RCTs used multiple techniques to address this question. Over time, techniques have evolved, including innovative multiarm tests and the Bloom, Hill, and Riccio study cited above. On-going work promises to move the field further (for example, see Weiss et al., 2014; Bloom and Weiland, 2015).

The second challenge concerns how to make random assignment a more useful management tool. Systematic and repeated RCTs of the type discussed in this chapter offer one approach to improving program effectiveness. Ideally, one would use such evaluations to identify successful approaches, replicate those that worked and reject those that did not, modify and retest programs, and employ this trial-and-error culling as a means of continuous improvement. Although a dramatic advance, critics object that this approach is too costly, slow, and static to serve as a realistic tool to foster innovation. There is another approach to using evidence to strengthen social programs—the performance management movement—that seems to overcome these drawbacks. It relies on the real-time tracking of outcome metrics (such as job placements or welfare case closures) as a way to achieve multiple goals, including holding managers accountable and inspiring and rewarding progress. Performance management is a bottoms-up approach that sets expectations and leaves managers and staff free to figure out how to use their time and resources to meet or exceed the standards.

As I stated elsewhere (Gueron and Rolston, 2013, p. 445):

Ideally, since they share a common goal of promoting effectiveness by creating a positive feedback loop, these two movements would reinforce each other, with performance metrics serving as a short- or intermediate-term way to inspire higher outcomes that would, in turn, result in higher impacts and cost effectiveness (to be periodically confirmed by experiments). But for this to be true, outcome standards must be a good proxy for impacts. If they are, they will send signals that are likely to make programs more effective; if not, they will increase the risk of unintended, negative effects. Unfortunately, the welfare experiments show that outcomes are not good predictors of impacts. As a result—by making apparent winners out of actual losers—outcomes can potentially send false signals about whom to serve, what managers or practices are most effective, or whether programs are improving over time.

This poses a serious dilemma. It cannot mean that outcomes are unimportant, since by definition higher outcomes, if nothing else changes, translate directly into higher impacts. It also cannot mean that workers and managers should not try out and track the results of new ideas unless they are verified by an experiment, since this would deny the obvious value of hands-on experience, high expectations, and incentives. It also cannot mean that setting stretch goals and encouraging people on the ground to figure out ways to achieve them is useless, since that is the way most successful businesses foster innovation and high performance. But it raises a bright red flag that emphasizing outcomes can prompt people to game the system in a multitude of counterproductive ways. (The press is filled with examples of this response to high-stakes testing in education.)

At present, these two strategies do not connect. The strengths of one are the flaws of the other. Experiments produce convincing evidence about effectiveness but have not been useful as a management tool. Performance standards provide timely lower-cost data and tap into the "you-get-what-you-measure" mantra, but since by definition they measure the wrong thing (outcomes not impacts), any resulting innovations may be implemented in pursuit of a mistaken target.

During the 40 years described in this chapter, scholars have accumulated evidence of this problem but have made only limited progress toward a solution.[35] Although periodic, comprehensive RCTs represent enormous progress, the challenge remains to more successfully put the tool of social experimentation at the service of managers. One way to accomplish this would be to convince managers to integrate random assignment into their routine testing of small and modest changes in administrative procedures or services, in the process producing treatment and control groups that they or others could follow using existing and low-cost administrative records. This approach resembles the private sector model of rapid and repeated testing, involving hundreds or thousands of

---

[35] Demonstrating the problem, Heckman et al. (2011, pp. 273–74) conclude, using data from the large-scale RCT testing the nation's job-training system, that "the short-run labor market outcomes commonly used as performance measures do not predict long-run impacts. Indeed, in some cases we find a perverse relationship, indicating that the performance measures actually provide an incentive for program staff to move away from, rather than toward, economic efficiency."

RCTs, that Manzi (2012) describes and advocates be applied in the public sector. There is recent interest in this approach, including the creation in 2014 of the first-ever Social and Behavioral Sciences Team in the White House.[36] The concept seems simple, but the tough job remains to convince managers to adopt a culture of evidence-driven innovation and to accept that lotteries are easy to conduct, ethical, and a particularly reliable technique to build that evidence. If managers buy into this approach, then rapid-cycle RCTs, with short-term follow-up, could serve as a powerful tool to improve and refine programs, which could then be tested more definitively through comprehensive and longer-term evaluations.

These two challenges are not unique to welfare, pointing to a demanding agenda for future researchers.

ACKNOWLEDGMENTS

The author thanks Lawrence Katz, Esther Duflo, Howard Rolston, and John Hutchins for helpful comments on an earlier draft of this chapter.

REFERENCES

Aaron, H.J., 1990. Social science research and policy: review essay. J. Hum. Resour. 25 (2), 276—280.

Al-Ubaydli, O., List, J.A., 2014. Do Natural Field Experiments Afford Researchers More or Less Control than Laboratory Experiments? A Simple Model. NBER Working Paper No. 20877. National Bureau of Economic Research, Cambridge, MA.

Angrist, J.D., Pischke, J.-S., 2010. The credibility revolution in empirical economics: how better research design is taking the con out of econometrics. J. Econ. Perspect. 24 (2), 3—30.

Banerjee, A., et al., 2015a. A multi-faceted program causes lasting progress for the very poor: evidence from six countries. Science 348 (6236), 772.

Banerjee, A., Karlan, D., Zinman, J., 2015b. Six randomized evaluations of microcredit: introduction and further steps. Am. Econ. J. Appl. Econ. 7 (1), 1—21.

Baron, J., 2013. Statement: House Committee on Ways and Means, Subcommittee on Human Resources Hearing on What Works/Evaluation, July 17, 2013. Coalition for Evidence-Based Policy, Washington, DC. http://waysandmeans.house.gov/UploadedFiles/Jon_Baron_Testimony_071713.pdf.

Baum, E.B., 1991. When the witch doctors agree: the Family Support Act and social science research. J. Policy Anal. Manag. 10 (4), 603—615.

Begley, C.G., Ioannidis, J.P.A., 2015. Reproducibility in science: improving the standard for basic and preclinical research. Circ Res. 116 (1), 116—126.

Berlin, G.L., 2000. Encouraging Work and Reducing Poverty: The Impact of Work Incentive Programs. MDRC, New York.

Betsey, C.L., Hollister Jr., R.G., Papageorgiou, M.R., 1985. Youth Employment and Training Programs: The YEDPA Years. National Academy Press, Washington, DC.

Bloom, D., Michalopoulos, C., 2001. How Welfare and Work Policies Affect Employment and Income: A Synthesis of Research. MDRC, New York.

---

[36] See "A Better Government, One Tweak at a Time," *The New York Times*, September 25, 2015; Social and Behavioral Sciences Team. 2015.

Bloom, H.S. (Ed.), 2005. Learning More from Social Experiments: Evolving Analytic Approaches. Russell Sage Foundation, New York.

Bloom, H.S., 2008. The core analytics of randomized experiments for social research. In: Alasuutari, P., Bickman, L., Brannen, J. (Eds.), The SAGE Handbook of Social Research Methods. SAGE Publications, Thousand Oaks, CA.

Bloom, H.S., Hill, C.J., Riccio, J.A., 2003. Linking program implementation and effectiveness: lessons from a pooled sample of welfare-to-work experiments. J. Policy Anal. Manag. 22 (4), 551–575.

Bloom, H.S., Hill, C.J., Riccio, J.A., 2005a. Modeling cross-site experimental differences to find out why program effectiveness varies. In: Bloom, H.S. (Ed.), Learning More from Social Experiments: Evolving Analytic Approaches. Russell Sage Foundation, New York.

Bloom, H.S., Michalopoulos, C., Hill, C.J., 2005b. Using experiments to assess nonexperimental comparison-group methods for measuring program effects. In: Bloom, H.S. (Ed.), Learning More from Social Experiments: Evolving Analytic Approaches. Russell Sage Foundation, New York.

Bloom, H.S., Weiland, C., 2015. Quantifying Variation in Head Start Effects on Young Children's Cognitive and Socio-emotional Skills Using Data from the National Head Start Impact Study. MDRC, New York.

Blum, B.B., Blank, S., 1990. Bringing administrators into the process. Public Welf. 48 (4), 4–12.

Card, D., Kluve, J., Weber, A., 2015. What Works? A Meta Analysis of Recent Active Labor Market Program Evaluations. Working Paper 21431. National Bureau of Economic Research, Cambridge, MA.

Coyle, D.J., Wildavsky, A., 1986. Social experimentation in the face of formidable fables. In: Munnell, A. (Ed.), Lessons from the Income Maintenance Experiments: Proceedings of a Conference. Federal Reserve Bank of Boston, Boston, MA. Conference Series 30.

DeParle, J., 2004. American Dream: Three Women, Ten Kids, and a Nation's Drive to End Welfare. Viking Press, New York.

Elmore, R.F., 1985. Knowledge development under the Youth Employment and Demonstration Projects Act, 1977–81. In: Betsey, C.L., Hollister Jr., R.G., Papageorgiou, M.R. (Eds.), Youth Employment and Training Programs: The YEDPA Years. National Academy Press, Washington, DC.

Fraker, T.M., Maynard, R.A., 1987. The adequacy of comparison group designs for evaluations of employment-related programs. J. Hum. Resour. 22 (2), 194–227.

Freedman, S., Smith, J., 2008a. Examining the Effectiveness of Different Welfare-to-Work Approaches: Extended Follow-up of TANF and Employment Outcomes for the National Evaluation of Welfare-to-Work Strategies (NEWWS) Project. Memo 1 — Long-term Impacts on Employment and Earnings for the Full Sample and Key Subgroups. Internal Working Paper. MDRC, New York.

Freedman, S., Smith, J., 2008b. Examining the Effectiveness of Different Welfare-to-Work Approaches: Extended Follow-up of TANF and Employment Outcomes for the National Evaluation of Welfare-to-Work Strategies (NEWWS) Project. Memo 2 — Long-term Impacts on TANF and UI Benefits Receipt for the Full Sample and Key Subgroups. Internal Working Paper. MDRC, New York.

Freedman, S., et al., 1996. The GAIN Evaluation: Five-year Impacts on Employment, Earnings, and AFDC Receipt. Working Paper 96.1. MDRC, New York.

Friedlander, D., Gueron, J.M., 1992. Are high-cost services more effective than low-cost services. In: Manski, C.E., Garfinkel, I. (Eds.), Evaluating Welfare and Training Programs. Harvard University Press, Cambridge, MA.

Friedlander, D., Burtless, G., 1995. Five Years After: The Long-term Effects of Welfare-to-Work Programs. Russell Sage Foundation, New York.

Gennetian, L.A., et al., 2002. How Welfare and Work Policies for Parents Affect Adolescents: A Synthesis of Research. MDRC, New York.

Gerber, A.S., Green, D.P., 2012. Field Experiments. W.W. Norton and Company, New York.

Glennerster, R., Takavarasha, K., 2013. Running Randomized Evaluations: A Practical Guide. Princeton University Press, Princeton, NJ.

Greenberg, D.H., Linksz, D., Mandell, M., 2003. Social Experimentation and Public Policymaking. Urban Institute Press, Washington, DC.

Greenberg, D.H., Shroder, M., 2004. The Digest of Social Experiments, third ed. Urban Institute Press, Washington, DC.

Greenberg, D.H., Cebulla, A., 2005. Report on a Meta-analysis of Welfare-to-Work Programs. U.S. Department of Health and Human Services, Washington, DC.

Greenberg, D.H., Deitch, V., Hamilton, G., 2010. A synthesis of random assignment benefit-cost studies of welfare-to-work programs. J. Benefit-Cost Anal. 1 (1). Article 3.

Grogger, J., Karoly, L.A., 2005. Welfare Reform: Effects of a Decade of Change. Harvard University Press, Cambridge, MA.

Gueron, J.M., 1990. Work and welfare: lessons on employment programs. J. Econ. Perspect. 4 (1), 79—98.

Gueron, J.M., 1996. A research context for welfare reform. J. Policy Anal. Manag. 15 (4), 547—561.

Gueron, J.M., 2002. The politics of random assignment: implementing studies and affecting policy. In: Mosteller, F., Boruch, R. (Eds.), Evidence Matters: Randomized Trials in Education Research. Brookings Institution Press, Washington, DC.

Gueron, J.M., Fall 2005. Throwing good money after bad: a common error misleads foundations and policymakers. Stanf. Soc. Innov. Rev. 69—71.

Gueron, J.M., Winter 2008. Failing well: foundations need to make more of the right kind of mistakes. Stanf. Soc. Innov. Rev. 25.

Gueron, J.M., Pauly, E., 1991. From Welfare to Work. Russell Sage Foundation, New York.

Gueron, J.M., Hamilton, G., 2002. The role of education and training in welfare reform. In: Welfare Reform and Beyond. The Brookings Institution, Washington, DC.

Gueron, J.M., Rolston, H., 2013. Fight for Reliable Evidence. Russell Sage Foundation, New York.

Hamilton, G., 2002. Moving People from Welfare to Work: Lessons from the National Evaluation of Welfare-to-Work Strategies. U.S. Department of Health and Human Services and U.S. Department of Education, Washington, DC.

Hamilton, G., 2012. Improving Employment and Earnings for TANF Recipients. Urban Institute, Washington, DC.

Hamilton, G., et al., 1997. Evaluating Two Welfare-to-Work Program Approaches: Two-year Findings on the Labor Force Attachment and Human Capital Development Programs in Three Sites. U.S. Department of Health and Human Services, Washington, DC.

Hamilton, G., et al., 2001. How Effective Are Different Welfare-to-Work Approaches? Five-year Adult and Child Impacts for Eleven Programs. U.S. Department of Health and Human Services and U.S. Department of Education, Washington, DC.

Haskins, R., 1991. Congress writes a law: research and welfare reform. J. Policy Anal. Manag. 10 (4), 616—632.

Haskins, R., 2006. Work over Welfare: The Inside Story of the 1996 Welfare Reform Law. Brookings Institution Press, Washington, DC.

Haskins, R., Baron, J., 2011. Building the Connection between Policy and Evidence: The Obama Evidence-based Initiatives. Paper Commissioned by the UK National Endowment for Science, Technology, and the Arts. September. Available at: http://coalition4evidence.org/wordpress/wp-content/uploads/Haskins-Baron-paper-on-fed-evid-based-initiatives-2011.pdf.

Haskins, R., Margolis, G., 2015. Show Me the Evidence: Obama's Fight for Rigor and Results in Social Policy. Brookings Institution Press, Washington, DC.

Heckman, J.J., Heinrich, C.J., Smith, J., 2011. Do short-run performance measures predict long-run impacts? In: Heckman, et al. (Eds.), The Performance of Performance Standards. W.E. Upjohn Institute for Employment Research, Kalamazoo, MI.

Hollister, R.G., Kemper, P., Maynard, R.A. (Eds.), 1984. The National Supported Work Demonstration. University of Wisconsin Press, Madison, WI.

Hotz, V.J., Imbens, G.W., Klerman, J.A., 2006. Evaluating the differential effects of alternative welfare-to-work training components: a reanalysis of the California GAIN program. J. Labor Econ. 24 (3), 521—566.

Job Training Longitudinal Survey Research Advisory Panel, 1985. Recommendations: Report Prepared for the Office of Strategic Planning and Policy Development, Employment and Training Administration. U.S. Department of Labor, Washington, DC.

LaLonde, R., 1986. Evaluating the econometric evaluations of training programs with experimental data. Am. Econ. Rev. 76 (4), 604—620.

Manzi, J., 2012. Uncontrolled: The Surprising Payoff of Trial-and-Error for Business, Politics, and Society. Basic Books, New York.

McLanahan, S., Jencks, C., 2015. Was Moynihan right? What happens to children of unmarried mothers. Educ. Next 15 (2), 14–20.

MDRC Board of Directors, 1980. Summary and Findings of the National Supported Work Demonstration. Ballinger, Cambridge, MA.

Michalopoulos, C., Schwartz, C., 2001. What Works Best for Whom? Impacts of 20 Welfare-to-Work Programs by Subgroup. U.S. Department of Health and Human Services and the U.S. Department of Education, Washington.

Morris, P.A., et al., 2001. How Welfare and Work Policies Affect Children: A Synthesis of Research. MDRC, New York.

Morris, P.A., Gennetian, L.A., Duncan, G.J., 2005. Effects of welfare and employment policies on young children: new findings on policy experiments conducted in the early 1990s. Soc. Policy Rep. 19 (11), 3–18.

Orr, L.L., 1999. Social Experiments: Evaluating Public Programs with Experimental Methods. Sage Publications, Thousand Oaks, CA.

Riccio, J., Friedlander, D., Freedman, S., 1994. GAIN: Benefits, Costs, and Three-year Impacts of a Welfare-to-Work Program. MDRC, New York.

Rogers-Dillon, R.H., 2004. The Welfare Experiments: Politics and Policy Evaluation. Stanford University Press, Stanford, CA.

Social and Behavioral Sciences Team, 2015. Annual Report. Executive Office of the President, National Science and Technology Council, Washington.

Solow, R.M., 1980. The Story of a Social Experiment and Some Reflections. Thirteenth Geary Lecture. Economic and Social Research Institute, Dublin, Ireland.

Szanton, P.L., 1991. The remarkable 'Quango': knowledge, politics, and welfare reform. J. Policy Anal. Manag. 10 (4), 590–602.

Weaver, R.K., 2000. Ending Welfare as We Know it. Brookings Institution Press, Washington, DC.

Weiss, M.J., Bloom, H.S., Brock, T., 2014. A conceptual framework for studying the sources of variation. J. Policy Anal. Manag. 33 (3), 778–808.

Methodology and Practice of RCTs

CHAPTER 3

The Econometrics of Randomized Experiments[a]

S. Athey[*,§,1], G.W. Imbens[*,§,1]
*Stanford University, Stanford, CA, United States
§NBER (National Bureau of Economic Research), Cambridge, MA, United States
[1]Corresponding authors: E-mail: athey@stanford.edu; imbens@stanford.edu

Contents

[a]   We are grateful for comments by Esther Duflo.

Handbook of Economic Field Experiments, Volume 1
ISSN 2214-658X, http://dx.doi.org/10.1016/bs.hefe.2016.10.003

Abstract

In this chapter, we present econometric and statistical methods for analyzing randomized experiments. For basic experiments, we stress randomization-based inference as opposed to sampling-based inference. In randomization-based inference, uncertainty in estimates arises naturally from the random assignment of the treatments, rather than from hypothesized sampling from a large population. We show how this perspective relates to regression analyses for randomized experiments. We discuss the analyses of stratified, paired, and clustered randomized experiments, and we stress the general efficiency gains from stratification. We also discuss complications in randomized experiments such as noncompliance. In the presence of noncompliance, we contrast intention-to-treat analyses with instrumental variables analyses allowing for general treatment effect heterogeneity. We consider, in detail, estimation and inference for heterogenous treatment effects in settings with (possibly many) covariates. These methods allow researchers to explore heterogeneity by identifying subpopulations with different treatment effects while maintaining the ability to construct valid confidence intervals. We also discuss optimal assignment to treatment based on covariates in such settings. Finally, we discuss estimation and inference in experiments in settings with interactions between units, both in general network settings and in settings where the population is partitioned into groups with all interactions contained within these groups.

Keywords

Causality; Potential outcomes; Random assignment; Randomized experiments; Regression analyses

JEL Codes
C01; C13; C18; C21; C52; C54

1. INTRODUCTION

Randomized experiments have a long tradition in agricultural and biomedical settings. In economics, they have a much shorter history. Although there have been notable experiments over the years, such as the RAND health care experiment (Manning et al., 1987; see the general discussion in Rothstein and von Wachter, 2016), the *negative income tax* experiments (e.g., Robins, 1985), as well as randomized experiments in laboratory settings (Kagel et al., 1995), it is only recently that there has been a large number of randomized field experiments in economics, and development economics in particular. See Duflo et al. (2006) for a survey. As digitization lowers the cost of conducting experiments, we may expect that their use may increase further in the near future. In this chapter, we discuss some of the statistical methods that are important for the analysis and design of randomized experiments.

Although randomized experiments avoid many of the challenges of observational studies for causal inference, there remain a number of statistical issues to address in the design and analysis of experiments. Even in the simplest case with observably homogenous, independent subjects, where the experiment is evaluated by comparing sample means for the treatment and control group, there are questions of how to conduct inference about the treatment effect. When there are observable differences in characteristics among units, questions arise about how best to design the experiment and how to account for imbalances in characteristics between the treatment and control groups in analysis. In addition, it may be desirable to understand how the results of an experiment would generalize to different settings. One approach to this is to estimate heterogeneity in treatment effects; another is to reweigh units according to a target distribution of characteristics. Finally, statistical issues arise when units are not independent, as when they are connected in a network. In this chapter, we discuss a variety of methods for addressing these and other issues.

A major theme of the chapter is that we recommend using statistical methods that are directly justified by randomization, in contrast to the more traditional sampling-based approach that is commonly used in econometrics. In essence, the sampling-based approach considers the treatment assignments to be fixed, while the outcomes are random. Inference is based on the idea that the subjects are a random sample from a much larger population. In contrast, the randomization-based approach takes the subject's potential outcomes (that is, the outcomes they would have had in each possible treatment regime) as fixed, and considers the assignment of subjects to treatments as random. Our focus on randomization follows the spirit of Freedman (2006, p. 691), who wrote: "Experiments should be analyzed as experiments, not as observational studies. A simple comparison of rates might be just the right tool, with little value added by 'sophisticated' models." Young (2016) has recently applied randomization-based methods in development economics.

As an example of how the randomization-based approach matters in practice, we show that methods that might seem natural to economists in the conventional sampling paradigm (such as controlling for observable heterogeneity using a regression model) require additional assumptions in order to be justified. Using the randomization-based approach suggests alternative methods, such as placing the data into strata according to covariates, analyzing the within-group experiments, and averaging the results. This is directly justified by randomization of the treatment assignment, and does not require any additional assumptions.

Our overall goal in this chapter is to collect in one place some of the most important statistical methods for analyzing and designing randomized experiments. We will start by discussing some general aspects of randomized experiments, and why they are widely viewed as providing the most credible evidence on causal effects. We will then present a brief introduction to causal inference based on the potential outcome perspective. Next we discuss the analysis of the most basic of randomized experiments, what we call completely randomized experiments where, out of a population of size N, a set of N_t units are selected randomly to receive one treatment and the remaining $N_c = N - N_t$ are assigned to the control group. We discuss estimation of, and inference for, average as well as quantile treatment effects. Throughout, we stress randomization-based rather than model-based inference as the basis of understanding inference in randomized experiments. We discuss how randomization-based methods relate to more commonly used regression analyses, and why we think the emphasis on randomization-based inference is important. We then discuss the design of experiments, first considering power analyses and then turning to the benefits and costs of stratification and pairwise randomization, as well as the complications from rerandomization. We recommend using experimental design rather than analysis to adjust for covariates' differences in experiments. Specifically, we recommend researchers to stratify the population into small strata and then randomize within the strata and adjust the standard errors to capture the gains from the stratification. We argue that this approach is preferred to model-based analyses applied after the randomization to adjust for differences in covariates. However, there are limits on how small the strata should be: we do not recommend to go as far as pairing the units, because it complicates the analysis due to the fact that variances cannot be estimated within pairs, whereas they can within strata with at least two treated and two control units. We also discuss in detail methods for estimating heterogenous treatment effects. We focus on methods that allow the researcher to identify subpopulations with different average treatment effects, as well as methods for estimating conditional average treatment effects. In both cases, these methods allow the researcher to construct valid confidence intervals.

This chapter draws from a variety of literature, including the statistical literature on the analysis and design of experiments, e.g., Wu and Hamada (2009), Cox and Reid

(2000), Altman (1991), Cook and DeMets (2008), Kempthorne (1952, 1955), Cochran and Cox (1957), Davies (1954), and Hinkelmann and Kempthorne (2005, 2008). We also draw on the literature on causal inference, both in experimental and observational settings, Rosenbaum (1995, 2002, 2009), Rubin (2006), Cox (1992), Morgan and Winship (2007), Morton and Williams (2010), Lee (2005), and Imbens and Rubin (2015). In the economics literature, we build on recent guides to practice in randomized experiments in development economics, e.g., Duflo et al. (2006), Glennerster (2016), and Glennerster and Takavarasha (2013) as well as the general empirical microliterature (Angrist and Pischke, 2009).

There have been a variety of excellent surveys of methodology for experiments in recent years. Compared to Duflo et al. (2006), Glennerster and Takavarasha (2013), Bertrand and Duflo 2016, Banerjee and Duflo 2009, and Glennerster (2016), this chapter focuses more on formal statistical methods and less on issues of implementation in the field. Compared to the statistics literature, we restrict our discussion largely to the case with a single binary treatment. We also pay more attention to the complications arising from noncompliance, clustered randomization, and the presence of interactions and spillovers. Relative to the general causal literature, e.g., Rosenbaum (1995, 2009) and Imbens and Rubin (2015), we do not discuss observational studies with unconfoundedness or selection-on-observables in depth, and focus more on complications in experimental settings.

This chapter is organized as follows. In Section 2 we discuss some general issues related to randomized experiments, followed by a discussion of causality and the potential outcome framework or Rubin Causal Model in Section 3. In Section 4 we discuss the analysis of the simplest form of randomized experiments, completely randomized experiments using randomization inference. In Section 5 we extend the randomization analyses to regression estimators for completely randomized experiments. Next, in Section 6 we discuss more complicated designs, stratified and paired experiments that have superior power properties compared to completely randomized experiments. In Section 7 we discuss the power implications of stratification and pairing. In Section 8 we discuss the complications arising from cluster-level randomization. We discuss how the use of clustering required the researcher to make choices regarding the estimands. We also focus on the choice concerning the unit of analysis, clusters or lower-level units. We recommend in general to focus on cluster-level analyses as the primary analyses. Section 9 contains a discussion of noncompliance to treatment assignment and its relation to instrumental variables methods. In Section 10 we present some recent results for analyzing heterogeneity in treatment effects. Finally, in Section 11 we discuss violations of the no-interaction assumption, allowing outcomes for one unit to be affected by treatment assignments for other units. These interactions can take many forms, some through clusters, and some through general networks. We show that it is possible to calculate exact p-values for tests of null hypotheses of no interactions while allowing for direct effects of the treatments. Section 12 concludes.

2. RANDOMIZED EXPERIMENTS AND VALIDITY

In this section we discuss some general issues related to the interpretation of analyses of randomized experiments and their validity. Following Cochran (1972), we define randomized experiments as settings where the assignment mechanism does not depend on characteristics of the units, either observed or unobserved, and the researcher has control over the assignments. In contrast, in observational studies (Rosenbaum, 1995; Imbens and Rubin, 2015), the researcher does not have control over the assignment mechanism, and the assignment mechanism may depend on observed and or unobserved characteristics of the units in the study. In this section we discuss four specific issues. First, we elaborate on the distinction between randomized experiments and observational studies. Second, we discuss internal validity, and third, external validity. Finally, we discuss the issues related to finite population versus infinite superpopulation inference.

2.1 Randomized experiments versus observational studies

There is a long tradition in viewing randomized experiments as the most credible of designs to obtain causal inferences. Freedman (2006) writes succinctly "Experiments offer more reliable evidence on causation than observational studies." On the other hand, some researchers continue to be skeptical about the relative merits of randomized experiments. For example, Deaton (2010, p. 426) argues, that "I argue that evidence from randomized experiments has no special priority. ... Randomized experiments cannot automatically trump other evidence, they do not occupy any special place in some hierarchy of evidence." Our view aligns with that of Freedman and others who view randomized experiments as playing a special role in causal inference. A randomized experiment is unique in the control the researcher has over the assignment mechanism, and by virtue of that control, selection bias in comparisons between treated and control units can be eliminated. That does not mean that randomized experiments can answer all causal questions. There are a number of reasons why randomized experiments may not be suitable to answer particular questions.

First, consider a case where we are interested in the causal effect of a particular intervention on a single unit: what would the outcome have been for a particular firm in the absence of a merger compared to the outcome given the merger. In that case, and similarly for many questions in macroeconomics, no randomized experiment will provide us with the answer to the causal question. Once the interest is in an intervention that can be applied repeatedly, however, it may be possible to conduct experiments, or find data from quasi-experiments, even in macroeconomics. Angrist and Kuersteiner (2011), building on work by Romer and Romer (2004), use the potential outcome framework to discuss causal analyses in a macroeconomic time series context. Second, it may not be ethical to conduct an experiment. In educational settings, it is often impossible to withhold particular educational services to individuals in order to evaluate their benefits. In such cases, one may need to do observational studies of some kind, possibly randomizing inducements to participate in the programs.

2.2 Internal validity

In a classic text, Shadish et al. (2002) discuss various aspects of the validity of studies of causal effects. Here we focus on two of the most important ones, internal validity and external validity. Shadish et al. (2002) define a study to have internal validity if the observed covariance between a treatment and an outcome reflects "a causal relationship … in which the variables were manipulated," (p. 53). Internal validity refers to the ability of a study to estimate causal effects within the study population. Shadish et al. (2002) then continue to observe that "the (internal validity) problem is easily solved in experiments because they force the manipulation of A to come before the measurement of B." Essentially they argue that well-executed randomized experiments by definition have internal validity, and that the problem of internal validity is one that plagues only observational studies or compromised random experiments. This is not necessarily true in experimental settings where interference between units is a concern.

2.3 External validity

The second aspect of validity that Shadish et al. (2002) consider is that of external validity. They write that "external validity concerns inferences about the extent to which a causal relationship holds over variation in persons, settings, treatments, and outcomes." (p. 83). Thus, external validity is concerned with generalizing causal inferences, drawn for a particular population and setting, to others, where these alternative settings could involve different populations, different outcomes, or different contexts.

Shadish, Cook, and Campbell argue for the primacy of internal validity, and claim that without internal validity, causal studies have little value. This echos Neyman's comment that without actual randomization a study would have little value, as well as Fisher's observation that randomization was what he called "the reasoned basis" for inference. It stands in sharp contrast with a few researchers who have recently claimed that there is no particular priority for internal validity over external validity (e.g., Manski, 2013).

The first important point is that external validity cannot be guaranteed, neither in randomized experiments, nor in observational studies. Formally, one major reason for that in experiments involving human subjects is that one typically needs informed consent: individuals typically need to agree to participate in the experiment. There is nothing that will guarantee that subjects who agree to do so will be similar to those that do not do so, and thus there is nothing that can guarantee that inferences for populations that give informed consent will generalize to populations that do not. See also the discussion in Glennerster (2016). This argument has been used to question the value of randomized experiments. However, as Deaton (2010, p. 449) notes, the same concern holds for nonexperimental studies: "RCTs, like nonexperimental results, cannot automatically be extrapolated outside the context in which they were obtained." There is nothing in nonexperimental methods that makes them superior to randomized experiments with the same population and sample size in this regard.

Fundamentally, most concerns with external validity are related to treatment effect heterogeneity. Suppose one carries out a randomized experiment in setting A, where the setting may be defined in terms of geographic location, or time, or subpopulation. What value have inferences about the causal effect in this location regarding the causal effect in a second location, say setting B? Units in the two settings may differ in observed or unobserved characteristics, or treatments may differ in some aspect. To assess these issues, it is helpful to have causal studies, preferably randomized experiments, in multiple settings. These settings should vary in terms of the distribution of characteristics of the units, and possibly in terms of the specific nature of the treatments or the treatment rate, in order to assess the credibility of generalizing to other settings. An interesting case study is the effect of microfinance programs. Meager (2015) analyzes data from seven randomized experiments, including six published in a special issue of the American Economic Journal (Applied) in 2015, and finds remarkable consistency across these studies.

Another approach is to specifically account for differences in the distributions of characteristics across settings. Hotz et al. (2005) and Imbens (2010) set up a theoretical framework where the differences in treatment effects between locations arise from differences in the distributions of characteristics of the units in the locations. Adjusting for these differences in unit-level characteristics (by reweighting the units) enables the researcher to compare the treatment effects in different locations. Allcott (2015) assess the ability of similar unconfoundedness/selection-on-observable conditions to eliminate differences in treatment effects between 111 energy conservation programs. Recently developed methods for assessing the treatment effect heterogeneity with respect to observables, reviewed below in Section 10, can in principle be used to flexibly estimate and conduct inference about treatment effects conditional on observables.

Finally, Bareinboim et al. (2013) develop graphical methods to deal with external validity issues.

2.4 Finite population versus random sample from superpopulation

It is common in empirical analyses to view the sample analyzed as a sample drawn randomly from a large, essentially infinite superpopulation. Uncertainty is viewed as arising from this sampling, with knowledge of the full population leading to full knowledge of the estimands. In some cases, however, this is an awkward perspective. In some of these cases the researcher observes all units in the entire population, and sampling uncertainty is absent. In other cases, it is not clear what population the sample can be viewed as being drawn from.

A key insight is that viewing the statistical problem as one of causal inference allows one to interpret the uncertainty as meaningful without any sampling uncertainty. Instead the uncertainty is viewed as arising from the unobserved (missing) potential outcomes: we view some units in the population exposed to one level of the treatment, but do not observe what would have happened to those units had they been exposed to another treatment level, leaving some of the components of the estimands unobserved. Abadie (2014) discuss these issues in detail.

In part of the discussion in this chapter, therefore, we view the sample at hand as the full population of interest, following the approaches taken by Fisher (1925, 1935), Neyman et al. (1935), and subsequently by Rubin (1974, 1978, 2007). The estimands are defined in terms of this finite population. However, these estimands depend on all the potential outcomes, some observed and others not observed, and as a result we cannot infer the exact values of the estimands even if all units in the population are observed. Consider an experiment with 10 individuals, five randomly selected to receive a new treatment, and the remaining five assigned to the control group. Even if this group of 10 individuals is the entire population of interest, observing realized outcomes for these 10 individuals will not allow us to derive the estimand, say the difference in the average outcome if all individuals were treated and the average outcome if all 10 individual were to receive the control treatment, without uncertainty. The uncertainty is coming from the fact that for each individual we can only see one of the two relevant outcomes. In many cases the variances associated with estimators based on random assignment of the treatment will be similar to those calculated conventionally based on sampling uncertainty. In other cases the conventional sampling-based standard errors will be unnecessarily conservative. When covariates are close to uncorrelated with the treatment assignment (as in a randomized experiment), the differences are likely to be modest. See Abadie et al. (2014) for details.

3. THE POTENTIAL OUTCOME/RUBIN CAUSAL MODEL FRAMEWORK FOR CAUSAL INFERENCE

The perspective on causality we take in this chapter is associated with the potential outcome framework (for a textbook discussion see Imbens and Rubin, 2015). This approach goes back to Fisher (1925) and Neyman (1923). The work by Rubin (1974, 1975, 1978) led Holland (1986) to label it the Rubin Causal Model (RCM).

3.1 Potential outcomes

This RCM or potential outcome setup has three key features. The first is that it associates causal effects with potential outcomes. For example, in a setting with a single unit (say an individual), and a single binary treatment, say taking a drug or not, we associate two potential outcomes with this individual, one given the drug and one without the drug. The causal effect is the comparison between these two potential outcomes. The problem, and in fact what Holland (1986) in a widely quoted phrase called the "fundamental problem of causal inference" (Holland, 1986, p. 947), is that we can observe at most one of these potential outcomes, the one corresponding to the treatment received. In order for these potential outcomes to be well defined, we need to be able to think of a manipulation that would have made it possible to observe the potential outcome that corresponds to the treatment that was not received, which led Rubin to claim "no causation without manipulation" (Rubin, 1975, p. 238). Because for any single unit we can observe at most one of the potential outcomes, we need to observe outcomes for multiple units. This is the second feature of the potential outcomes framework, the necessity of the presence of multiple units. By itself the presence of multiple units does not solve the problem because with multiple units the number of distinct treatments increases: with N units and two treatment levels for each unit there are 2^N different values for the full vector of treatments, with any comparison between two of them a valid causal effect. However, in many cases, we are willing to make assumptions that interactions between units is limited so that we can draw causal inferences from comparisons between units. An extreme version of this is the assumption that the treatment for one unit does not affect outcomes for any other unit, so that there is no interference whatsoever. The third key feature of the RCM is the central role of the assignment mechanism. Why did a unit receive the treatment it did receive? Here randomized experiments occupy a special place in the spectrum of causal studies: in a randomized experiment the assignment mechanism is a known function of observed characteristics of the units in the study. The alternatives, where parts of the assignment mechanism are unknown, and may possibly depend on unobserved characteristics (including the potential outcomes) of the units, are referred to as observational studies (Cochran, 1972).

There are alternative approaches to causality. Most notably there has been much work recently on causal graphs, summarized in the book by Pearl (2000, 2009). In this approach, causal links are represented by arrows and conditional independencies are captured by the absence of arrows. These methods have been found useful in studies of identification questions as well as for using data to discover causal relationships among different variables. However, the claims in this literature (e.g., Pearl, 2000, 2009) that the concept of a causal effect does not require the ability to at least conceptually manipulate treatments remains controversial.

Let us now add some specifics to this discussion. Suppose we start with a single unit, say "I". Suppose we have a binary treatment, denoted by $W \in \{0,1\}$ for this unit, which may correspond to taking a drug or not. The two potential outcomes are $Y(0)$, the outcome for me if I do not take the drug, and $Y(1)$, the outcome if I do take the drug. The causal effect is a comparison of the two potential outcomes, say the difference, $Y(1) - Y(0)$, or the ratio, $Y(1)/Y(0)$. Once we assign the treatment, one of the potential outcomes will be realized and possibly observed:

$$Y^{\text{obs}} = Y(W) = \begin{cases} Y(0) & \text{if } W = 0, \\ Y(1) & \text{if } W = 1 \end{cases}$$

We can only observe one of the potential outcomes, so drawing credible and precise inferences about the causal effect, say the difference $Y(1) - Y(0)$, is impossible without additional assumptions or information. Now let us generalize to the setting with N units, indexed by $i = 1,\ldots,N$. Each of the units can be exposed to the two treatments, no drug or drug, with W_i denoting the treatment received for unit i. Let $\mathbf{W}$ be the N-vector of assignments with typical element W_i. The problem is that in principle the potential outcomes can depend on the treatments for all units, so that for each unit we have 2^N different potential outcomes $Y_i(\mathbf{W})$. In many cases it is reasonable to assume that the potential outcomes for unit i depend solely on the treatment received by unit i. This is an important restriction on the potential outcomes, and one that is unrealistic in many settings, with a classic example being that of vaccinations for infectious diseases. For example, exposing some students to educational interventions may affect outcomes for their class mates, or training some unemployed individuals may affect the labor market prospects for other individuals in the labor market. We will discuss the complications arising from interactions in Section 11. Note that the interactions can be a nuisance for estimating the effects of interest, but they can also be the main focus.

If we are willing to make the no-interference assumption, or *sutva* (stable unit treatment value assumption, Rubin, 1978), we can index the potential outcomes by the own treatment only, and write without ambiguity $Y_i(w)$, for $w = 0,1$. For each of the N units the realized outcome is now $Y_i^{\mathrm{obs}} = Y_i(W_i)$. Now with some units exposed to the active treatment and some exposed to the control treatment, there is some hope for drawing causal inferences. In order to do so, we need to make assumptions about the assignment mechanism. To be formal, let $\mathbb{Y}$ be the range of values for the potential outcomes, and let $\mathbb{X}$ be the range of values for the covariates or pretreatment variables. In general, we write this as a function

$$p : \{0, 1\}^N \times \mathbb{Y}^{2N} \times \mathbb{X}^N \mapsto [0, 1],$$

so that $p(\mathbf{W}|\mathbf{Y}(0), \mathbf{Y}(1), \mathbf{X})$ is the probability of the assignment vector $\mathbf{W}$, as a function of all the potential outcomes and covariates.

We limit the general class of assignment mechanism we consider. The most important limitation is that for randomized experiments we disallow dependence on the potential outcomes, and we assume that the functional form of the assignment mechanism is known. Analyzing observational studies where the assignment mechanism depends in potentially complicated ways on the potential outcomes is often a challenging task, typically relying on controversial assumptions.

3.2 A classification of assignment mechanisms

Let us consider four assignment mechanisms that we will discuss in subsequent sections in this chapter.

3.2.1 Completely randomized experiments

In completely randomized experiment, a fixed number of units, say N_t, is drawn at random from the population of N units to receive the active treatment, with the remaining $N_c = N - N_t$ assigned to the control group. It satisfies

$$p(\mathbf{W}|\mathbf{Y}(0), \mathbf{Y}(1), \mathbf{X}) = \binom{N}{N_t}^{-1} \quad \text{for all } \mathbf{W} \text{ such that } \sum_{i=1}^{N} W_i = N_t.$$

3.2.2 Stratified randomized experiments

The next two experimental designs, stratification and pairing, are intended to improve the efficiency of the design by disallowing assignments that are likely to be uninformative about the treatment effects of interest. In a stratified randomized experiment, we first partition the population on the basis of covariate values into G strata. Formally, if the covariate space is $\mathbb{X}$, we partition $\mathbb{X}$ into $\mathbb{X}_1, \ldots, \mathbb{X}_G$, so that $\cup_g \mathbb{X}_g = \mathbb{X}$, and $\mathbb{X}_j \cap \mathbb{X}_{g'} = \varnothing$ if $g \neq g'$. Let G_{ig} be an indicator for unit i belonging to stratum g, so that $G_{ig} = 1_{X_i \in \mathbb{X}_g}$. Let N_g be the number of units in stratum g. Then we fix the number of treated units in each stratum as $N_{t,g}$, so that the total number of treated units is $N_t = \sum_{g=1}^{G} N_{t,g}$. The assignment probability is then

$$p(\mathbf{W}|\mathbf{Y}(0), \mathbf{Y}(1), \mathbf{X}) = \prod_{g=1}^{G} \binom{N_j}{N_{t,g}}^{-1}, \text{ for all } \mathbf{W} \text{ such that } \forall g \sum_{i=1}^{N} G_{ig} \cdot W_i = N_{t,g}.$$

This design rules out some assignments that are allowed in a completely randomized design, with the hope that the assignment vectors that are disallowed are relatively uninformative compared to assignment vectors that are allowed, for example where all men are in the treatment group and all women in the control group.

3.2.3 Paired randomized experiments

In a paired randomized experiment, we pair units together and randomize within the pairs. We can think of this as an extreme case of stratification where each stratum contains exactly one treated unit and exactly one control unit. In that case, there are $G = N/2$ strata, and $N_g = 2$ and $N_{t,g} = 1$ for all g. Then

$$p(\mathbf{W}|\mathbf{Y}(0), \mathbf{Y}(1), \mathbf{X}) = \left(\frac{1}{2}\right)^{N/2} \text{ for all } \mathbf{W} \text{ such that } \forall g, \sum_{i=1}^{N} G_{ig} \cdot W_i = 1.$$

3.2.4 Clustered randomized experiments

The last design we discuss is not intended to be more informative than a completely randomized experiment with the same sample size. Rather it is a design that attempts to avoid complications with local interactions at the unit level, as well as disallow assignments that are may be relatively expensive in terms of data collection, and thus indirectly may attempt to increase the sample size to improve precision. In a clustered randomized experiment, as in a stratified randomized experiments, we start with a partitioning of the covariate space. Now, however, instead of assigning treatments randomly to units within a cluster (the same as the stratum in the stratified randomized experiment), treatments are assigned randomly to entire clusters, with all units within a cluster receiving the same level of the treatment.

This design may be motivated by concerns that there are interactions between units. For example, for educational programs, it may be that exposing some children in a classroom to an intervention has spillover effects on children in the same classroom who were not exposed to the intervention. For that reason, it may make sense to expose all children in a classroom or school to the same treatment. Alternatively, it may be expensive to randomize at the individual level compared to randomizing at the classroom or geographic unit level.

Again, let G_{ig} denote the indicator for unit i belonging to cluster g, with G the total number of clusters. Although we may vary the probability of a cluster being assigned to the treatment group, here we focus on the simplest case where G_t out of the G clusters are selected randomly to be assigned to the treatment group. Thus, at the cluster level, we have a completely randomized experiment. Let $\overline{W}_g = \sum_{i:G_{ig}=1} W_i/N_g$ be the average value of W_i for units in cluster g, so that the clustering implies that $\overline{W}_g \in \{0, 1\}$. More generally, one may vary the probability of being assigned to the treatment by cluster, without requiring that all units in the same cluster having the same treatment, although we do not consider that case here. Then

$$p(\mathbf{W}|\mathbf{Y}(0), \mathbf{Y}(1), \mathbf{X}) = \binom{G}{G_t}^{-1},$$

for all $\mathbf{W}$ such that if $G_{ig} = G_{i'g} = 1$, then $W_i = W_{i'}$, and $\sum_{g=1}^{G} \overline{W}_g = G_t$.

4. THE ANALYSIS OF COMPLETELY RANDOMIZED EXPERIMENTS

In this section, we discuss the analysis of the simplest form of randomized experiments, completely randomized experiments. In this setting, we have a sample of N units, N_t of whom are selected at random to receive the active treatment, and the remaining $N_c = N - N_t$ of whom receive the control treatment. We consider four sets of analyses. First, we study the calculation of exact p-values for sharp hypotheses, based on the work by Fisher (1925, 1935). Second, we consider estimation of and inference for average treatment effects, following the original work by Neyman (1928, 1990) and Neyman et al. (1935). Third, we study the relation between the Neyman approach and linear regression, showing how randomization justifies conventional regression analyses. Fourth, we look at quantile treatment effects. Central to our discussion is the view of the potential outcomes as fixed, leading to a focus on inference based on the randomization distribution, keeping fixed the total number of units assigned to treatment and control. We will sometimes view the sample as identical to the population of interest, and sometimes as a random sample from an infinitely sized population of interest. Although randomization inference is still relatively uncommon in economics, we view it as strongly preferable for data from randomized experiments. The properties of the methods follow directly from the design, without reliance on auxiliary modeling assumptions that are typically more difficult to assess.

Initially, we focus on the case without pretreatment variables. In Section 4.4, we allow for the presence of covariates but maintain the focus on global targets such as the average effect of the treatment. In Section 10, we explore the benefits of observing covariates that are not affected by the treatment, also known as pretreatment variables. We will illustrate some of the discussions with analyses of an experimental evaluation of a labor market program, first analyzed by Lalonde (1986). The data set contains information on 445 individuals, 185 in the treatment group, and 260 in the control group. The outcome is post-training earnings, and pretreatment variables include lagged earnings and individual characteristics.

4.1 Exact *p*-values for sharp null hypotheses

The first analysis is based on Fisher's (1925, 1935) work on exact *p*-values for sharp null hypotheses. See, for recent discussions, Rosenbaum (1995), Gail et al. (1988), Imbens and Rubin (2015), and in economics Young (2016). Fisher was interested in testing sharp null hypotheses, that is, null hypotheses under which we can infer all the missing potential outcomes from the observed ones. The leading null hypothesis in this class is the null hypothesis that the treatment has no effect whatsoever, as

$$H_0 : Y_i(0) = Y_i(1) \quad \forall\ i = 1, ..., N. \tag{1}$$

The implicit alternative hypothesis is that there is at least one unit i such that $Y_i(0) \neq Y_i(1)$. Other sharp null hypothesis corresponds to known constant treatment effects, but in many cases these are less interesting and natural. However, in some cases, one can use the exact *p*-values in settings without sharp null hypotheses by redefining the experiment, as shown by Athey et al. (2015) in the context of network experiments (see Section 11.3 for further discussion).

Given the sharp null hypothesis, we can infer all the missing potential outcomes. As a result we can infer, for any statistic that is a function of $\mathbf{Y}^{obs}$, $\mathbf{W}$, and $\mathbf{X}$, the exact distribution of that statistic under the null hypothesis. So, suppose we choose as our statistic the difference in means by treatment status, as

$$T^{ave}\left(\mathbf{W}, \mathbf{Y}^{obs}, \mathbf{X}\right) = \overline{Y}^{obs}_t - \overline{Y}^{obs}_c = \frac{1}{N_t} \sum_{i:W_i=1} Y^{obs}_i - \frac{1}{N_c} \sum_{i:W_i=0} Y^{obs}_i. \tag{2}$$

We can calculate the probability, over the randomization distribution, of the statistic taking on a value as large, in absolute value, as the actual value given the actual treatment assigned. This calculation gives us the p-value for this particular null hypothesis:

$$p = \text{pr}\left(\left|T^{\text{ave}}\left(\mathbf{W}, \mathbf{Y}^{\text{obs}}, \mathbf{X}\right)\right| \geq \left|T^{\text{ave}}\left(\mathbf{W}^{\text{obs}}, \mathbf{Y}^{\text{obs}}, \mathbf{X}\right)\right|\right). \tag{3}$$

Let us illustrate this using data from National Supported Work program, previously analyzed by Lalonde (1986), Dehejia and Wahba (1999) and many others. The simple difference in average posttreatment earnings between treated and control is 1.79 (in thousands of dollars). To calculate the p-value associated with this difference of 1.79, we reassign the treatment, keeping the number of treated and control units fixed at 185 and 240, respectively. Given the reassigned treatment, we calculate what the value of the statistic would have been. Although the observed outcomes do not change for any unit under the null hypothesis, the value of the statistic changes because who is in the treatment group and who is in the control group changes. Repeating this many times, we calculate the fraction of reassignment vectors that leads to a statistic that is at least as large as 1.79 in absolute value. The p-value associated with this statistic is 0.0044, suggesting we should clearly reject the null hypothesis that the program had no effect on earnings whatsoever.

The main choice to be made in this procedure is the choice of statistic. A natural statistic is the one we choose in the illustration, the difference in means by treatment status. Another attractive choice is the difference in means of the ranks by treatment status. Here the outcomes are first converted to ranks, normalized to have zero mean as

$$R_i = R\left(i; Y_1^{\text{obs}}, \ldots, Y_N^{\text{obs}}\right) = \sum_{j=1}^{N} 1_{Y_j^{\text{obs}} < Y_i^{\text{obs}}} + \frac{1}{2}\left(1 + \sum_{j=1}^{N} 1_{Y_j^{\text{obs}} = Y_i^{\text{obs}}}\right) - \frac{N+1}{2}.$$

The term in the middle deals with the presence of ties in the data. For the Lalonde data, this statistic leads to a p-value of 0.01. In this application the robustness to outliers does not actually buy very much, and the presence of many zeros has a bigger impact on the difference between the mean and rank statistics.

This transformation improves the power of the tests in settings with outliers and thick-tailed distributions. It is less arbitrary than, for example, simply transforming the outcome by taking logarithms, especially in settings where such transformations are not feasible, for example, in settings with thick-tailed distribution and a mass point at zero. There are some settings where the transformation to ranks does not work well. An example would be a case with a large proportion of zeros, and a very thick-tailed distribution for the outcomes for units with nonzero outcomes.

In some cases the researcher has multiple outcomes. One can calculate exact p-values for each of the outcomes, but obviously the probability that at least one of the p-values is less than 0.05 even if the treatment has no effect on any of the outcomes is generally larger than 0.05. There are two modifications one can implement to address this. The simplest is to modify the test statistic to take account of all the outcomes. For example, one could use an F-statistic, that is, a quadratic form in the difference in average outcomes by treatment status, with the inverse of the covariance matrix in the middle. For that statistic, one can calculate the exact p-value under the null hypothesis that there is no effect of the treatment whatsoever using the Fisher randomization distribution. See for example Young (2016). Alternatively one can use adjustments to the p-values to take account of the multiple testing. Traditionally such adjustments are based on Bonferroni bounds. However, there are tighter bounds available, although they tend to be more conservative than the exact Fisher p-values. See Romano et al. (2010) for a review of this literature.

Rosenbaum (1995) discusses estimators for treatment effects based on rank statistics, as opposed to simply doing tests, following Hodges and Lehmann (1970) and Doksum (1974). Specifically, he looks for values for the common treatment effect that set the rank correlation between the residuals and the treatment equal to zero, leading to confidence intervals based on inverting test statistics.

4.2 Randomization inference for average treatment effects

In this section, we continue the analysis of completely randomized experiments, taking as fixed the potential outcomes in the population. Here, we follow the line of research that originates in the work by Neyman (1923, 1990) and Neyman et al. (1935). Neyman was interested in estimating the average effect of the treatment for the sample at hand as

$$\tau = \frac{1}{N}\sum_{i=1}^{N}(Y_i(1) - Y_i(0)) = \overline{Y}(1) - \overline{Y}(0). \tag{4}$$

In addition, Neyman was interested in constructing confidence intervals for such average effects. Initially, we focus purely on the finite sample, with no assumptions on any sampling that may have led to the particular sample at hand.

As an estimator, Neyman proposed the difference in average outcomes by treatment status as

$$\widehat{\tau} = \overline{Y}_{\mathrm{t}}^{\mathrm{obs}} - \overline{Y}_{\mathrm{c}}^{\mathrm{obs}}, \quad \text{where } \overline{Y}_{\mathrm{t}}^{\mathrm{obs}} = \frac{1}{N_{\mathrm{t}}}\sum_{i:W_i=1}Y_i^{\mathrm{obs}}, \text{ and } \overline{Y}_{\mathrm{c}}^{\mathrm{obs}} = \frac{1}{N_{\mathrm{c}}}\sum_{i:W_i=0}Y_i^{\mathrm{obs}}. \tag{5}$$

Defining

$$D_i = W_i - \frac{N_{\mathrm{t}}}{N} = \begin{cases} \dfrac{N_{\mathrm{c}}}{N} & \text{if } W_i = 1 \\[2mm] -\dfrac{N_{\mathrm{t}}}{N} & \text{if } W_i = 0, \end{cases}$$

so that $\mathbb{E}[D_i] = 0$, we can write this estimator as

$$\widehat{\tau} = \tau + \frac{1}{N} \sum_{i=1}^{N} D_i \cdot \left(\frac{N}{N_t} \cdot Y_i(1) + \frac{N}{N_c} \cdot Y_i(0) \right). \tag{6}$$

Because all potential outcomes are fixed, the only stochastic components are the D_i, and with $\mathbb{E}[D_i] = 0$, the second term has expectation zero, which immediately implies that this estimator is unbiased for the average treatment effect, τ. A more tedious calculation (e.g., Imbens and Rubin, 2015), shows that the sampling variance of $\widehat{\tau}$, over the randomization distribution, is

$$\mathbb{V}(\widehat{\tau}) = \frac{S_c^2}{N_c} + \frac{S_t^2}{N_t} - \frac{S_{tc}^2}{N}, \tag{7}$$

where S_c^2 and S_t^2 are the variances of $Y_i(0)$ and $Y_i(1)$ in the sample, defined as

$$S_c^2 = \frac{1}{N-1} \sum_{i=1}^{N} (Y_i(0) - \overline{Y}(0))^2, \quad \text{and} \quad S_t^2 = \frac{1}{N-1} \sum_{i=1}^{N} (Y_i(1) - \overline{Y}(1))^2,$$

and S_{tc}^2 is the sample variance of the unit-level treatment effects, defined as

$$S_{tc}^2 = \frac{1}{N-1} \sum_{i=1}^{N} (Y_i(1) - Y_i(0) - (\overline{Y}(1) - \overline{Y}(0)))^2.$$

We can estimate the first two terms as

$$s_c^2 = \frac{1}{N_c - 1} \sum_{i:W_i=0} \left(Y_i(0) - \overline{Y}_c^{obs} \right)^2 = \frac{1}{N_c - 1} \sum_{i:W_i=0} \left(Y_i^{obs} - \overline{Y}_c^{obs} \right)^2,$$

and

$$s_t^2 = \frac{1}{N_t - 1} \sum_{i:W_i=1} \left(Y_i(1) - \overline{Y}_t^{obs} \right)^2 = \frac{1}{N_t - 1} \sum_{i:W_i=1} \left(Y_i^{obs} - \overline{Y}_t^{obs} \right)^2.$$

These estimators are unbiased for the corresponding terms in the variance of $\widehat{\tau}$. The third term, S_{tc}^2 [the population variance of the unit-level treatment effects $Y_i(1) - Y_i(0)$] is generally impossible to estimate consistently because we never observe both $Y_i(1)$ and $Y_i(0)$ for the same unit. We therefore have no direct observations on the variation in the treatment effects across the population and cannot directly estimate S_{tc}^2.

In practice, researchers therefore use the estimator for $\mathbb{V}(\widehat{\tau})$ based on estimating the first two terms by s_c^2 and s_t^2, and ignoring the third term as

$$\widehat{\mathbb{V}}_{neyman} = \frac{s_c^2}{N_c} + \frac{s_t^2}{N_t}. \tag{8}$$

This leads in general to an upwardly biased estimator for $\mathbb{V}(\hat{\tau})$, and thus to conservative confidence intervals. There are two important cases where the bias vanishes. First, if the treatment effect is constant, the third term is zero, and so ignoring it is immaterial. Second, if we view the sample at hand as a random sample from an infinite population, then $\mathbb{V}(\hat{\tau})$ is unbiased for the variance of $\hat{\tau}$ viewed as an estimator of the population average treatment effect $\mathbb{E}[Y_i(1) - Y_i(0)]$, rather than as an estimator of the sample average treatment effect $\sum_{i=1}^{N}(Y_i(1) - Y_i(0))/N$ (See Imbens and Rubin, 2015).

To construct confidence intervals, we do need to make large sample approximations. One way to do this is to assume that the sample can be viewed as a random sample from a large population and use a standard central limit theorem for independent and identically distributed random variables. An alternative is to make assumptions on the properties of the sequence of $[Y_i(0), Y_i(1)]$ so that one can use a Lindenberg-type central limit theorem for independent, but not identically distributed, random variables for the second term in Eq. (6). The main condition is that the sequence of averages of the squares of $Y_i(0) + Y_i(1)$ does not diverge. The large sample approximations do play a very different role though than in standard discussions with random sampling. Most importantly, the estimand is defined in terms of the finite sample, not in terms of the infinite superpopulation.

For the Lalonde data, the estimate and Neyman standard error, which are up to a degrees-of-freedom adjustment equal to the White robust standard errors (White, 1980; Eicker, 1967; Huber, 1967; Eckles et al., 2014), are

$$\hat{\tau} = 1.794 \ (\widehat{\text{se}} \ 0.671).$$

The p-value based on the normal approximation to the distribution of the t-statistic is 0.0076, compared to an exact p-value of 0.0044 based on the Fisher approach.

4.3 Quantile treatment effects

Much of the theoretical as well as the empirical literature on treatment effects has focused on average causal effects. An exception is Firpo (2007). However, there are other causal effects that might be of interest. Of particular interest are quantile treatment effects. These can be used as a systematic way to uncover treatment effects that may be concentrated in tails of the distribution of outcomes, or to estimate more robustly constant treatment effects in settings with thick-tailed distributions. For this case, there are no finite sample results in the spirit of Neyman's results for the average treatment effect, so we focus on the case where the sample can be viewed as a random sample from an infinite population.

In general, let $q_Y(s)$ denote the s-th quantile of the distribution of the random variable Y. Formally,

$$q_Y(s) = \inf_y 1_{F_Y(y) \geq s}.$$

Now define the s-th quantile treatment effect as the difference in quantiles between the $Y_i(1)$ and $Y_i(0)$ distributions:

$$\tau_s = q_{Y(1)}(s) - q_{Y(0)}(s). \tag{9}$$

Such quantile treatment effects have been studied in Doksum (1974) and Lehman (1974), and more recently in Abadie et al. (2002), Chernozhukov and Hansen (2005), Firpo (2007), and Bitler et al. (2002).

Note that τ_s is a difference in quantiles, and in general, it is different from the quantile of the differences, that is, the corresponding quantile of the unit-level treatment effects, $q_{Y(1)-Y(0)}(s)$. Specifically, although the mean of the difference of $Y_i(0)$ and $Y_i(0)$ is equal to the difference in the means of $Y_i(1)$ and $Y_i(0)$, in general, the median of the difference $Y_i(1)-Y_i(0)$ is not equal to the difference in the medians of $Y_i(1)$ and $Y_i(0)$. There are three important issues concerning the quantile of the treatment effects in relation to the differences in quantiles. First, the two estimands, $q_{Y(1)}(s)-q_{Y(0)}(s)$ and $q_{Y(1)-Y(0)}(s)$, are equal if there is perfect rank correlation between the two potential outcomes. In that case,

$$Y_i(1) = F_{Y(1)}^{-1}\left(F_{Y(0)}(Y_i(0))\right).$$

A special case of this is that where the treatment effect is additive and constant. This assumption is implausible in many settings. However, in general, it has no testable implications.

The second, related, issue is that in general the quantile of the unit-level treatment effects, $q_{Y(1)-Y(0)}(s)$, is not identified. Even with large-scale experiments, we can only infer the two marginal distributions of $Y_i(0)$ and $Y_i(1)$. Nothing about the joint distribution that cannot be expressed in terms of these two marginal distributions can be inferred from the data.

A third issue is the question which of the two quantile treatment effects, the difference in quantiles, $q_{Y(1)}(s)-q_{Y(0)}(s)$, or the quantile of the difference, $q_{Y(1)-Y(0)}(s)$, is the more interesting object for policymakers. To discuss that question, it is useful to think about the possible decisions faced by a policy maker. If a policy maker is committed to making one of the two treatments universal and is deciding between exposing all units to the control treatment or to the active treatment, the answer should depend only on the two marginal distributions, and not on aspects of the joint distribution that cannot be expressed in terms of the two marginal distributions. This suggests that the difference in quantiles may be a more natural object to consider, although there are some cases, such as legal settings, where unit-level treatment effects are of primary interest.

For these reasons, we focus on the difference in quantiles, τ_s. Inspecting this estimand for different values of s may reveal that a particular treatment affects the lower or upper tail more than the center of the distribution. In addition, in cases where the average effects of the treatment may be imprecisely estimated because of thick-tailed distributions, quantile treatment-effect estimates may be very informative.

Here, we estimate quantile effects for the Lalonde data for the quantiles 0.10, 0.25, 0.50, and 0.75. For each quantile, we estimate the average effect and calculate standard errors using the bootstrap. We also use the difference in quantiles as a statistic in an exact p-value calculation (Table 1).

The results for the exact tests are quite different from those based on estimating the effects and calculating standard errors. The reason is that the quantile estimates are far from normally distributed. Mainly because of the 30% zeros in the outcome distribution, the distribution of the difference in the lower quantiles has a substantial point mass at zero. Because of the substantial proportion of individuals with zero earnings, the bootstrap standard error for the 0.10 quantile is essentially zero.

4.4 Covariates in completely randomized experiments

In this section, we discuss some additional analyses that a researcher may wish to carry out if covariates are recorded for each unit. Later, we discuss regression methods, but here we discuss some general principles. We focus here on the case where the randomization took place without taking into account the covariates. In fact, as we discuss in Section 3.2.2, if one has covariates observed prior to the randomization, one should modify the design of the experiment and carry out a stratified randomized experiment rather than as a completely randomized experiment. If one has a well-conducted randomized experiment where the randomization did not take into account the covariates, one does not need regressors in order to estimate average treatment effects. The simple difference in means by treatment status, $\widehat{\tau} = \overline{Y}_t^{obs} - \overline{Y}_c^{obs}$, is unbiased for the average effect. So, the question is what the role is of covariates. There are two principal roles.

First, incorporating covariates may make analyses more informative. For example, one can construct test statistics in the Fisher exact p-value approach that may have more power than statistics that do not depend on the covariates. Similarly, by estimating average treatment effects within subpopulations, and then averaging up the estimates appropriately, the results will be more precise if the covariates are sufficiently strongly

Table 1 Estimates of quantile treatment effects for Lalonde data

Quantile	est	Bootstrap s.e.	Exact p-value
0.10	0.00	(0.00)	1.000
0.25	0.49	(0.35)	0.003
0.50	1.04	(0.90)	0.189
0.75	2.34	(0.91)	0.029
0.90	2.78	(1.97)	0.071

correlated with the potential outcomes. There is potentially a small-sample cost to ex-post adjustment. For example, if the covariates are independent of the potential outcomes, this ex-post adjustment will lower precision slightly. In practice, the gains in precision tend to be modest.

Second, if the randomization was compromised, adjusting for covariate differences may remove biases. Even if the original randomization was done appropriately, this may be relevant if there are missing data and the analysis uses only complete cases where there is no guarantee of ex-ante comparability between treated and control units.

To illustrate this, let us consider the Lalonde data, and focus on the indicator that the lagged earnings are positive as a covariate. The overall estimate of the average treatment effect is

$$\widehat{\tau} = 1.79 \quad (\widehat{\mathrm{se}} = 0.67).$$

For the individuals with positive prior earnings the effect is

$$\widehat{\tau}_p = 1.69 \quad (\widehat{\mathrm{se}}_p = 1.31).$$

For the individuals with zero prior earnings the effect is

$$\widehat{\tau}_z = 1.71 \quad (\widehat{\mathrm{se}}_z = 0.74).$$

Combining the two estimates leads to

$$\widehat{\tau} = \widehat{p} \cdot \widehat{\tau}_p + (1 - \widehat{p}) \cdot \widehat{\tau}_z = 1.70 \quad (\widehat{\mathrm{se}} = 0.66),$$

with a standard error that is barely smaller than that without adjusting for positive prior earnings, 0.67.

The two arguments regarding the role of covariates in the analysis of randomized experiments also raise the question whether there is any reason to compare the covariate distributions by treatment status as part of the analysis. There are a couple of reasons why such a comparison may be useful. If there is some distance between the agencies carrying out the original randomization and the researcher analyzing the data, it may be useful as a check on the validity of the randomization to assess whether there are any differences in covariates. Second, even as the randomization was carried out appropriately, it may be informative to see whether any of the key covariates were by chance relatively imbalanced between treatment and control groups, so that prior to seeing the outcome data an analysis can be designed that addresses these presumably modest imbalances. Third, if there is reason to believe that the sample to be analyzed is not identical to the population that was randomized, possibly because of attrition, or item nonresponse with incomplete observations dropped from the analysis, it is useful to assess how big the imbalances are that resulted from the sample selection. Table 2 presents the differences in covariates for the experimental Lalonde data.

Table 2 Covariates in Lalonde data

Covariate	Average		Difference	s.e.	Exact *p*-value
	Treated	Controls			
African–American	0.84	0.83	0.02	(0.04)	0.700
Hispanic	0.06	0.11	−0.05	(0.03)	0.089
Age	25.8	25.0	0.8	(0.7)	0.268
Education	10.3	10.1	0.3	(0.2)	0.139
Married	0.19	0.15	0.045	(0.04)	0.368
No-degree	0.71	0.84	−0.13	(0.04)	0.002
Earnings 1974	2.10	2.11	−0.01	(0.50)	0.983
Unemployed 1974	0.71	0.75	−0.04	(0.04)	0.329
Earnings 1974	1.53	1.27	0.27	(0.31)	0.387
Unemployed 1975	0.60	0.69	−0.09	(0.05)	0.069

We see that despite the randomization, there is substantial evidence that the proportion of individuals with a degree in the treatment group is lower than in the control group. This conclusion survives adjusting for the multiplicity of testing.

5. RANDOMIZATION INFERENCE AND REGRESSION ESTIMATORS

In this section, we discuss regression and more generally modeling approaches to estimation and inference in the context of completely randomized experiments. Although these methods remain the most popular way of analyzing data from randomized experiments, we suggest caution in using them. Some of these comments echo the concerns raised by others. For example, in the abstract of Freedman (2008), he writes "Regression adjustments are often made to experimental data. Since randomization does not justify the models, almost anything can happen" (Freedman, 2008; abstract) and similar comments are made by Deaton (2010), Young (2016), and Imbens and Rubin (2015). Regression methods were not originally developed for analyzing data from randomized experiments, and the attempts to fit the appropriate analyses into the regression framework requires some subtleties. In particular, there is a disconnection between the way the conventional assumptions in regression analyses are formulated and the implications of randomization. As a result, it is easy for the researcher using regression methods to go beyond analyses that are justified by randomization, and end up with analyses that rely on a difficult-to-assess mix of randomization assumptions, modeling assumptions, and large sample approximations. This is particularly true once one uses nonlinear methods. See for additional discussions Lesaffre and Senn (2003), Samii and Aronow (2012), Rosenbaum (2002), Lin (2013), Schochet (2010), Bloniarz et al. (2015), Young (2016), Wager et al. (2016), and Senn (1994).

Ultimately, we recommend that researchers wishing to use regression or other model-based methods, rather than the randomization-based methods we prefer, do so with care. For example, using only indicator variables based on partitioning the covariate space, rather than using multivalued variables as covariates in the regression function preserves many of the finite sample properties that simple comparisons of means have, and leads to regression estimates with clear interpretations. In addition, in many cases the potential gains from regression adjustment can also be captured by careful ex-ante design, that is, through stratified randomized experiments to be discussed in the next section, without the potential costs associated with ex-post regression adjustment.

5.1 Regression estimators for average treatment effects

In ordinary least squares, one regresses the observed outcome Y_i^{obs} on the indicator for the treatment, W_i, and a constant:

$$Y_i^{\text{obs}} = \alpha + \tau \cdot W_i + \varepsilon_i, \tag{10}$$

where ε_i is an unobserved error term. The least squares estimator for τ is based on minimizing the sum of squared residuals over α and τ,

$$(\widehat{\tau}_{\text{ols}}, \widehat{\alpha}_{\text{ols}}) = \arg\min_{\tau, \alpha} \sum_{i=1}^{N} \left(Y_i^{\text{obs}} - \alpha - \tau \cdot W_i \right)^2,$$

with solution

$$\widehat{\tau}_{\text{ols}} = \frac{\sum_{i=1}^{N} (W_i - \overline{W}) \cdot \left(Y_i^{\text{obs}} - \overline{Y}^{\text{obs}} \right)}{\sum_{i=1}^{N} (W_i - \overline{W})^2} = \overline{Y}_{\text{t}}^{\text{obs}} - \overline{Y}_{\text{c}}^{\text{obs}}, \quad \text{and}$$

$$\widehat{\alpha}_{\text{ols}} = \overline{Y}^{\text{obs}} - \widehat{\tau}_{\text{ols}} \cdot \overline{W}.$$

The least squares estimate of τ is identical to the simple difference in means, so by the Neyman results discussed in Section 4.2, the least squares estimator is unbiased for the average causal effect. However, the assumptions that are typically used to justify linear regression are substantially different from the randomization that justifies Neyman's analysis. In addition, the unbiasedness claim in the Neyman analysis is conceptually different from the one in conventional regression analysis: in the first case the repeated sampling paradigm keeps the potential outcomes fixed and varies the assignments, whereas in the latter the realized outcomes and assignments are fixed but different units with different residuals, but the same treatment status, are sampled. The assumptions typically used in regression analyses are that, in the infinite population the sample was drawn from, the error terms ε_i are independent of, or at least uncorrelated with, the treatment indicator W_i. This assumption is difficult to evaluate, as the interpretation of these residuals is rarely made explicit beyond a vague notion of capturing unobserved factors affecting the outcomes of interest. Textbooks therefore often stress that regression estimates measure only association between the two variables, and that causal interpretations are not in general warranted.

It is instructive to see the formal implications of the randomization for the properties of the least squares estimator, and to see how the randomization relates to the standard versions of the regression assumptions. To build this connection between the two repeated sampling paradigms, it is very convenient to view the sample at hand as a random sample from an infinite population. This allows us to think of all the variables as random variables, with moments defined as population averages and with a distribution induced by random sampling from this infinite population. Define

$$\tau = \mathbb{E}[Y_i(1) - Y_i(0)], \quad \text{and} \quad \alpha = \mathbb{E}[Y_i(0)].$$

Then define the residual as

$$\begin{aligned}
\varepsilon_i &= Y_i(0) - \alpha + W_i \cdot \{Y_i(1) - Y_i(0) - \tau\} \\
&= (1 - W_i) \cdot \{Y_i(0) - \mathbb{E}[Y_i(0)]\} + W_i \cdot \{Y_i(1) - \mathbb{E}[Y_i(1)]\}.
\end{aligned}$$

This implies we can write the regression as in Eq. (10). Now the error term has a clear meaning as the difference between potential outcomes and their population expectation, rather than as the difference between the realized outcome and its conditional expectation given the treatment. Moreover, the independence of W_i and $[Y_i(0), Y_i(1)]$, directly implied by the randomization, now has implications for the properties of the error term. Specifically, the randomization implies that the average residuals for treated and control units are zero:

$$\mathbb{E}[\varepsilon_i | W_i = 0] = 0, \quad \text{and} \ \mathbb{E}[\varepsilon_i | W_i = 1] = 0.$$

Note that random assignment of the treatment does *not* imply that the error term is independent of W_i. In fact, in general, there will be heteroskedasticity, and we need to use the Eicker-Huber-White robust standard errors to get valid confidence intervals.

It may appear that this is largely semantics, and that using regression methods here makes no difference in practice. This is certainly true for estimation in this simple case without covariates, but not necessarily for inference. The conventional least squares approach suggests using the robust (Eicker-Huber-White) standard errors. Because the general robust variance estimator has no natural degrees-of-freedom adjustment, these standard robust variance estimators differ slightly from the Neyman unbiased variance estimator $\widehat{\mathbb{V}}_{\text{neyman}}$:

$$\widehat{\mathbb{V}}_{\text{robust}} = \frac{s_c^2}{N_c} \cdot \frac{N_c - 1}{N_c} + \frac{s_t^2}{N_t} \cdot \frac{N_t - 1}{N_t}. \tag{11}$$

The Eicker-Huber-White variance estimator is not unbiased, and in settings where one of the treatment arms is rare, the difference may matter. For the Duflo-Hanna-Ryan data on the effect of teacher presence on educational achievement (Duflo et al., 2012), this leads to

$$\widehat{Y}_i^{\text{obs}} = \underset{(0.0256)}{0.5805} + \underset{(0.0308)}{0.2154} \times W_i,$$
$$[0.0311]$$

with the Eicker-Huber-White standard errors in parentheses and the Neyman standard error in brackets. Because both subsample sizes are large enough ($N_c = 54$ and $N_t = 53$), there is essentially no difference in the standard errors. However, if we modify the sample so that there are $N_c = 54$ control units but only $N_t = 4$ treated units, the standard errors are quite different, 0.1215 for the Eicker-Huber-White standard errors, and 0.1400 for the Neyman standard errors.

Although there are refinements of the general Eicker-Huber-White variance estimator, there are none that are unbiased in general. The difference with the Neyman variance estimator relies on the fact that the only regressor in the Neyman variance estimator is a binary indicator. Moreover, the Neyman variance estimator, fitting into the classic Behrens-Fisher problem, suggests using a t-distribution rather than a normal distribution with the degrees of freedom dependent on the size of the two treatment groups. See Imbens and Kolesár (2016) and Young (2016) for recent discussions with illustrations how the distribution of the covariates matters for the standard errors.

5.2 Regression estimators with additional covariates

Now let us turn to the case with additional covariates beyond the treatment indicator W_i, with these additional covariates denoted by X_i. These additional covariates are not affected by the treatment by definition, that is, they are pretreatment variables. Moreover, we assume here that these covariates did not affect the assignment, which we continue to assume is completely random. It is the presence of these covariates that often motivates using regression methods rather than simple differences by treatment status. There are generally three motivations for including these covariates into the analysis. First, they may improve the precision of the estimates. Second, they allow for estimation of average effects for subpopulations and in general for assessments of heterogeneity in treatment effects. Third, they may serve to remove biases in simple comparisons of means if the randomization was not adequate. These are somewhat distinct, although related, goals, however, and regression methods are not necessarily the optimal choice for any of them. In general, again, we wish to caution against the routine way in which regression methods are often applied here.

There are two ways covariates are typically incorporated into the estimation strategy. First, they can be included additively through the regression model

$$Y_i^{\text{obs}} = \alpha + \tau \cdot W_i + \beta' \dot{X}_i + \varepsilon_i. \tag{12}$$

Here $\dot{X}_i = X_i - \overline{X}$ is the covariate measured in deviations from its mean. Using deviations from means does not affect the point estimates of τ or β, only that of the intercept α, but this transformation of the covariates is convenient once we allow for interactions. Estimating this regression function for the Duflo-Hanna-Ryan data changes the point estimate of the average effect to 0.1921 and leaves the standard error unchanged at 0.0298. The R-squared in the original regression was 0.3362, and the two additional covariates increase this to 0.3596, which is not enough to make a difference in the standard error.

Second, we can allow for a model with a full set of interactions:

$$Y_i^{\text{obs}} = \alpha + \tau \cdot W_i + \beta' \dot{X}_i + \gamma' \dot{X}_i \cdot W_i + \varepsilon_i. \tag{13}$$

In general the least squares estimates based on these regression functions are not unbiased for the average treatment effects over the randomization distribution given the finite population. There is one exception. If the covariates are all indicators and they partition the population, and we estimate the model with a full set of interactions, Eq. (13), then the least squares estimate of τ is unbiased for the average treatment effect. To see this, consider the simplest case with a single binary covariate. In that case, we can think of average treatment effects τ_x for each value of x. We can also think of $\hat{\tau}_x$ estimated separately on the corresponding part of the subpopulation. If $\overline{X}$ is the average value of X_i in the sample, then

$$\hat{\tau} = \hat{\tau}_1 \cdot \overline{X} + \hat{\tau}_0 \cdot (1 - \overline{X}), \quad \text{and} \quad \hat{\gamma} = \hat{\tau}_1 - \hat{\tau}_0.$$

Below in Section 10.3.1, we discuss machine-learning methods for partitioning the covariate space according to treatment effect heterogeneity; if we construct indicators for the element of the partition derived according to an "honest causal tree" (Athey and Imbens, 2016) and incorporate them into Eq. (13), then the resulting average treatment effect (estimated on what Athey and Imbens (2016) refer to as the estimation sample) is unbiased over the randomization distribution. This result extends conceptually to the case where all regressors are indicators. In that case, all least squares estimates are weighted averages of the within-cell estimated average effects.

If we are willing to make large sample approximations, we can also say something about the case with multivalued covariates. In that case, $\hat{\tau}$ is (asymptotically) unbiased for the average treatment effect. Moreover, and this goes back to the first motivation for including covariates, the asymptotic variance for $\hat{\tau}$ is less than that of the simple difference estimator by a factor equal to $1 - R^2$ from including the covariates relative to not including the covariates. It is important that these two results do not rely on the regression model being true in the sense that the conditional expectation of Y_i^{obs} is actually linear in the covariates and the treatment indicator in the population. Because of the randomization, there is zero correlation in the population between W_i and the covariates X_i, which is sufficient for the lack of bias from including or excluding the covariates. However, the large sample approximation needs to be taken seriously here. If in fact the covariates have very skewed distributions, the finite sample bias in the linear regression estimates may be substantial, as

Freedman (2008) points out. At the same time, the gain in precision is often modest as the covariates often only have limited explanatory power.

The presence of nonzero values for γ imply treatment effect heterogeneity. However, the interpretation of the γ depends on the actual functional form of the conditional expectations. Only if the covariates partition the population do, these γ have a clear interpretation as differences in average treatment effects. For that reason, it may be easier to convert the covariates into indicator variables. It is unlikely that the goodness of fit of the regression model is much affected by such transformations, and both the interpretation and the finite sample unbiasedness would be improved by following that approach.

For the Duflo et al. (2012) data,

$$\widehat{Y}_i^{\text{obs}} = \underset{(0.02)}{0.59} + \underset{(0.03)}{0.192} \times W_i + \underset{(0.002)}{0.001} \times X_{1i} - \underset{(0.01)}{0.004} \times X_{2i} - \underset{(0.003)}{0.006} \times X_{1i} \times W_i + \underset{(0.01)}{0.017} \times X_{2i} \times W_i$$

The inclusion of the two covariates with the full set of interactions does not affect the point estimate of the average treatment effect, nor its standard error.

Alternatively, if we run the regression with an indicator for $X_{1i} > 37$ (teacher score greater than the median), we get

$$\widehat{Y}_i^{\text{obs}} = \underset{(0.02)}{0.60} + \underset{(0.03)}{0.188} \times W_i + \underset{(0.05)}{0.10} \times 1_{\{X_{1i}>37\}} - \underset{(0.06)}{0.06} \times 1_{\{X_{1i}>37\}} \times W_i$$

Now the coefficient on the interaction is directly interpretable as an estimate of the difference in the average effect for teachers with a score higher than 37 versus teachers with a score less than or equal to 37. Ultimately, there is very little gain in precision in the estimator for the average treatment effect. If one wants to interpret the estimates of the coefficients on the interactions in addition to the main effect, one should take into account the multiplicity of comparisons and adjust the p-values accordingly. See, for example, Benjamini and Hochberg (1995).

6. THE ANALYSIS OF STRATIFIED AND PAIRED RANDOMIZED EXPERIMENTS

In this section, we discuss the analyses for two generalizations of completely randomized experiments. First, consider stratified randomized experiments. In that case the covariate space is partitioned into a finite set. Within each of these subsets, a completely randomized experiment is carried out. In the extreme case where the partition is such that within each subset, there are exactly two units, and the designs correspond to randomly assigning exactly one of these two units to the treatment and the other to the control group we have a paired randomized experiment. Such experiments are more powerful than completely randomized experiments. Both these designs can be thought of as attempting to capture the gains from adjusting from observable differences between units by design, rather than by model-based analysis as in the previous section. As such, they capture the gains from ex-post regression adjustment without the potential costs of linear regression, and therefore stratification is generally to be preferred over regression adjustment. In the current section, we discuss the analyses of such experiments, and in Section 7.2 the design aspects.

6.1 Stratified randomized experiments: analysis

In a stratified randomized experiment the covariate space is partitioned into a finite set of subsets. Within each of these subsets a completely randomized experiment is carried out, after which the results are combined. If we analyze the experiment using Neyman's repeated sampling approach the analysis of stratified randomized experiments is straight-forward. Suppose there are G strata within which we carry out a completely randomized experiment, possibly with varying treatment probabilities. Let τ_g be the average causal effect of the treatment for all units within stratum g. Within this stratum, we can estimate the average effect as the difference in average outcomes for treated and control units:

$$\widehat{\tau}_g = \overline{Y}_{t,g}^{obs} - \overline{Y}_{c,g}^{obs},$$

and we can estimate the within-stratum variance, using the Neyman results, as

$$\widehat{\mathbb{V}}\left(\widehat{\tau}_g\right) = \frac{s_{t,g}^2}{N_{t,g}} + \frac{s_{c,j}^2}{N_{c,g}},$$

where the j-subscript indexes the stratum. We can then estimate the overall average effect of the treatment by simply averaging the within-stratum estimates weighted by the stratum share N_g/N as

$$\widehat{\tau} = \sum_{g=1}^{G} \widehat{\tau}_g \cdot \frac{N_g}{N}, \quad \text{with estimated variance} \quad \widehat{\mathbb{V}}_{strat}(\widehat{\tau}) = \sum_{g=1}^{G} \widehat{\mathbb{V}}\left(\widehat{\tau}_g\right) \cdot \left(\frac{N_g}{N}\right)^2.$$

There is a special case that is of particular interest. Suppose the proportion of treated units is the same in all strata. In that case the estimator for the average treatment effect is equal to the difference in means by treatment status,

$$\widehat{\tau} = \sum_{g=1}^{G} \widehat{\tau}_g \cdot \frac{N_g}{N} = \overline{Y}_t^{obs} - \overline{Y}_c^{obs},$$

which is the estimator we used for the completely randomized experiment. In general, however, the variance based on the completely randomized experiment setup,

$$\widehat{\mathbb{V}}_{neyman} = \frac{s_t^2}{N_t} + \frac{s_c^2}{N_c},$$

will be conservative compared to the variance that takes into account the stratification, $\widehat{\mathbb{V}}_{strat}(\widehat{\tau})$: the latter takes into account the precision gain from stratification.

6.2 Paired randomized experiments: analysis

Now let us consider a paired randomized experiment. Starting with N units in our sample, $N/2$ pairs are constructed based on covariate values so that within the pairs the units are more similar in terms of covariate values. Then, within each pair a single unit is chosen at random to receive the active treatment and the other unit is assigned to the control group. The average treatment effect within the pair is estimated as the difference in outcome for the treated unit and the control unit as

$$\widehat{\tau}_g = \sum_{i:G_{ig}=1,W_i=1} Y_i^{\text{obs}} - \sum_{i:G_{ig}=1,W_i=0} Y_i^{\text{obs}}.$$

The overall average effect is estimated as the average over the within-pair estimates as

$$\widehat{\tau} = \frac{1}{N/2} \sum_{g=1}^{N/2} \widehat{\tau}_g = \overline{Y}_{\text{t}}^{\text{obs}} - \overline{Y}_{\text{c}}^{\text{obs}}.$$

So far, this is similar to the analysis of a general stratified experiment, and conceptually the two designs are closely related.

The complications arise when estimating the variance of this estimator, as an estimator of the average effect over the strata, $\tau = \sum_{g=1}^{N/2} \tau_g \cdot 2/N$. In the stratified randomized experiment case, we estimated the variance in two steps, first estimating the within-stratum variance for stratum g as

$$\widehat{\mathbb{V}}\left(\widehat{\tau}_g\right) = \frac{s_{\text{t},g}^2}{N_{\text{t},g}} + \frac{s_{\text{c},g}^2}{N_{\text{c},g}},$$

followed by averaging this over the strata. However, this variance estimator requires at least two treated and at least two control units in each stratum, and thus is not feasible in the paired randomized experiment case with only one treated and one control unit in each stratum or pair.

Instead, typically the following variance estimator is used:

$$\widehat{\mathbb{V}}\left(\widehat{\tau}\right) = \frac{1}{N/2 \cdot (N/2 - 1)} \sum_{g=1}^{N/2} \left(\widehat{\tau}_g - \widehat{\tau}\right)^2, \tag{14}$$

the variance of the $\widehat{\tau}_g$ over the pairs. This variance estimator is conservative if viewed as an estimator of $\tau = \sum_{g=1}^{N/2} \tau_g \cdot 2/N$. However, suppose we view the pairs as being randomly drawn from a large superpopulation, with population average treatment effect equal to $\tau^* = \mathbb{E}[\tau_g]$. Then the variance of $\widehat{\tau}$, viewed as an estimator of τ^*, can be estimated using $\widehat{\mathbb{V}}\left(\widehat{\tau}\right)$.

Because in this case the proportion of treated units is the same in each pair, namely 1/2, we can also use the variance based on analyzing this as a completely randomized experiment, leading to

$$\widehat{\mathbb{V}}_{\text{neyman}} = \frac{s_t^2}{N_t} + \frac{s_c^2}{N_c}. \tag{15}$$

In general, this will be conservative, and more so than necessary.

Let us illustrate this with data from the Children's Television Workshop experiment. See Imbens and Rubin (2015) for details. There are eight pairs of classrooms in this experiment, with one classroom in each pair shown the Electric Company, a children's television program. The outcome is a posttest score, leading to

$$\widehat{\tau} = 13.4, \quad \left(\widehat{\text{se}}_{\text{pair}} = 4.6\right),$$

where the standard error is calculated as in Eq. (14), taking into account the paired design. The variance estimate based on the interpretation as a completely randomized experiment as in Eq. (15), rather than a paired experiment, is $\widehat{\text{se}}_{\text{neyman}} = 7.8$, almost twice the size. There is a substantial gain from doing the paired randomized experiment in this case.

7. THE DESIGN OF RANDOMIZED EXPERIMENTS AND THE BENEFITS OF STRATIFICATION

In this section, we discuss some issues related to the design of randomized experiments. First, we discuss the basic power calculations for completely randomized experiments. Second, we discuss the benefits of stratification, and its limit, pairwise randomization, in terms of the expected precision of the resulting experiments. Finally, we discuss issues related to rerandomization if one feels the randomization did not produce the desired balance in covariates between treatment and control groups. Ultimately, our recommendation is that one should always stratify as much as possible, up to the point that each stratum contains at least two treated and two control units. Although there are in principle some benefits in terms of expected precision to using paired designs rather than stratified designs with two treated and two control units, these tend to be small and because there are some real costs in terms of analyses we recommend the stratified rather than paired designs. If the stratification is done appropriately, there should be no need for rerandomization.

7.1 Power calculations

In this section, we look at some simple power calculations for randomized experiments. These are intended to be carried out prior to any experiment, in order to assess whether the proposed experiment has a reasonable chance of finding results of the size that one might reasonably expect. These analyses depend on a number of inputs, and can focus on various outputs. Here we largely focus on the formulation where the output is the minimum sample size required to find treatment effects of a prespecified size with a pre-specified probability. Alternatively, one can also focus on the treatment size one would be likely to find given a particular sample size. For details on these and similar calculations a standard reference is Cohen (1988). See also Murphy et al. (2014).

Let us consider a simple case where for a sample of size N, we would observe values for an outcome for the N units, $Y_1^{\text{obs}}, \ldots, Y_N^{\text{obs}}$, and a treatment indicator $W_1, \ldots, W_N$. We are interested in testing the hypothesis that the average treatment effect is zero as

$$H_0 : \mathbb{E}[Y_i(1) - Y_i(0)] = 0,$$

against the alternative that the average treatment effect differs from zero as

$$H_a : E[Y_i(1) - Y_i(0)] \neq 0.$$

We restrict the size of the test, the probability of rejecting the null hypothesis when it is in fact true, to be less than or equal to α. Often, following Fisher (1925), we choose $\alpha = 0.05$ as the statistical significance level. In addition, we want the power of the test, the probability of rejecting the null when it is in fact false, to be at least equal to β, in the case where the true average treatment effect is $\tau = \mathbb{E}[Y_i(1) - Y_i(0)]$ for some prespecified value of τ. Let $\gamma = \sum_i W_i/N$ be the proportion of treated units.

For simplicity, we assume that the conditional outcome variance in each treatment arm is the same, $\sigma^2 = \mathbb{V}(Y_i(0)) = \mathbb{V}(Y_i(1))$. We look for the minimum sample size $N = N_c + N_t$, as a function of α, β, τ, σ^2, and γ.

To test the null hypothesis of no average treatment effect, we look at the T-statistic as

$$T = \frac{\overline{Y}_t^{\text{obs}} - \overline{Y}_c^{\text{obs}}}{\sqrt{S_Y^2/N_t + S_Y^2/N_c}} \approx \frac{\overline{Y}_t^{\text{obs}} - \overline{Y}_c^{\text{obs}}}{\sqrt{\sigma^2/N_t + \sigma^2/N_c}}.$$

We reject the null hypothesis of no difference if the absolute value of this t-statistic, $|T|$, exceeds $\Phi^{-1}(1 - \alpha/2)$. Thus, if $\alpha = 0.05$, the threshold would be $\Phi^{-1}(1 - \alpha/2) = 1.96$. We want the rejection probability to be at least β, given that the alternative hypothesis is true with the treatment effect equal to τ. In general, the difference in means minus the true treatment effect τ, scaled by the standard error of that difference, has approximately a standard normal distribution as

$$\frac{\overline{Y}_t^{\text{obs}} - \overline{Y}_c^{\text{obs}} - \tau}{\sqrt{\sigma^2/N_t + \sigma^2/N_c}} \approx \mathcal{N}(0, 1).$$

This implies that the t-statistic has an approximately normal distribution as

$$T \approx \mathcal{N}\left(\frac{\tau}{\sqrt{\sigma^2/N_t + \sigma^2/N_c}}, 1\right).$$

Now, a simple calculation implies that the null hypothesis will be rejected with probability as

$$\mathrm{pr}\left(|T| > \Phi^{-1}(1 - \alpha/2)\right) \approx \Phi\left(-\Phi^{-1}(1 - \alpha/2) + \frac{\tau}{\sqrt{\sigma^2/N_{\mathrm{t}} + \sigma^2/N_{\mathrm{c}}}}\right)$$

$$+\Phi\left(-\Phi^{-1}(1 - \alpha/2) - \frac{\tau}{\sqrt{\sigma^2/N_{\mathrm{t}} + \sigma^2/N_{\mathrm{c}}}}\right).$$

The second term is small, so we ignore it. Thus we want the probability of the first term to be equal to β, which requires

$$\beta = \Phi\left(-\Phi^{-1}(1 - \alpha/2) + \frac{\tau}{\sqrt{\sigma^2/N_{\mathrm{t}} + \sigma^2/N_{\mathrm{c}}}}\right),$$

leading to

$$\Phi^{-1}(\beta) = -\Phi^{-1}(1 - \alpha/2) + \frac{\tau\sqrt{N}\sqrt{(\gamma(1 - \gamma))}}{\sigma}.$$

This leads to a required sample size as

$$N = \frac{\left(\Phi^{-1}(\beta) + \Phi^{-1}(1 - \alpha/2)\right)^2}{(\tau^2/\sigma^2) \cdot \gamma \cdot (1 - \gamma)}. \tag{16}$$

For example, let us consider a setting close to the Lalonde data. The standard deviation of the outcome is approximately 6, although that may have been difficult to assess before the experiment. Suppose we choose $\gamma = 0.5$ (equal sample sizes for treated and controls, which is optimal in the case with homoskedasticity, and typically close to optimal in other cases), $\alpha = 0.05$ (test at 0.05 level). Suppose also that we are looking to be able to find an effect of 1 (1000 dollars), which is a substantial amount given the average preprogram earnings of these individuals, and that we choose $\beta = 0.8$ (power of 0.8). Then

$$N = \frac{\left(\Phi^{-1}(\beta) + \Phi^{-1}(1 - \alpha/2)\right)^2}{(\tau^2/\sigma_Y^2) \cdot \gamma \cdot (1 - \gamma)} = \frac{\left(\Phi^{-1}(0.8) + \Phi^{-1}(0.975)\right)^2}{0.167^2 \cdot 0.5^2} = 1{,}126,$$

so that the minimum sample size is 1,126, with 563 treated and 563 controls. If the effect we wish to have power of 0.8 for is 2, then the required sample size would be substantially smaller, namely 282, split equally between 141 treated and 141 controls.

7.2 Stratified randomized experiments: benefits

In this section, we discuss the benefits of stratification in randomized experiments. Mostly this discussion is based on the special case where the ratio of the number of treated units to the total number of units is the same in each stratum. In this case the intended benefit of the stratification is to achieve balance in the covariates underlying the stratification. Suppose there are only two strata, containing, respectively, women and men. If the total sample size is 100, with 50 women and 50 men, and there are 60 individuals to be assigned to the treatment group and 40 to the control group, stratification would ensure that in the treatment group there are 30 women and 30 men, and the 20 of each sex in the control group. This would avoid a situation where, by chance, there were 25 women and 35 men in the treatment group, and 25 women and 15 men in the control group. If the outcomes were substantially correlated with the sex of the individual, such a random imbalance in the sex ratio in the two treatment groups would reduce the precision from the experiment. Note that without stratification, the experiment would still be valid, and, for example, still lead to exact p-values. Stratifying does not remove any bias, it simply leads more precise inferences than complete randomization.

Although it is well known that stratification on covariates is beneficial if based on covariates that are strongly correlated with the outcomes, there appears to be confusion in the literature concerning the benefits of stratification in small samples if this correlation is weak. Bruhn and McKenzie (2009) document this in a survey of researchers in development economics, but the confusion is also apparent in the statistics literature. For example, Snedecor and Cochran (1967,1989, p. 101) write:

> If the criterion has no correlation with the response variable, a small loss in accuracy results from the pairing due to the adjustment for degrees of freedom. A substantial loss may even occur if the criterion is badly chosen so that member of a pair are negatively correlated.

Box et al. (2005, p. 93) also suggest that there is a tradeoff in terms of accuracy or variance in the decision to stratify, writing:

> Thus you would gain from the paired design only if the reduction in variance from pairing outweighed the effect of the decrease in the number of degrees of freedom of the t distribution.

This is somewhat counterintuitive: if one stratifies on a covariate that is independent of all other variables, then stratification is obviously equivalent to complete randomization. In the current section, we argue that this intuition is correct and that in fact there is no tradeoff. We present formal results that show that in terms of expected-squared error, stratification (with the same treatment probabilities in each stratum) cannot be worse than complete randomization, even in small samples, and even with little, or even no, correlation between covariates and outcomes. Ex ante, committing to stratification can only improve precision, not lower it. There are two important qualifications to this result. First, ex post, given the joint distribution of the covariates in the sample, a particular stratification may be inferior to complete randomization. Second, the result requires that the sample can be viewed as a (stratified) random sample from an infinitely large population, with the expectation in the expected-squared-error taken over this population. This requirement guarantees that outcomes within strata cannot be negatively correlated.

The lack of any finite sample cost to (ex-ante) stratification in terms of expected-squared-error contrasts with the potential cost of ex-post stratification, or regression adjustment. Ex-post adjustment for covariates through regression may increase the finite sample variance, and in fact it will strictly increase the variance for any sample size, if the covariates have no predictive power at all.

However, there is a cost to stratifying on a variable that has no association with the potential outcomes. Although there is no cost to stratification in terms of the variance, there is a cost in terms of estimation of the variance. Because there are unbiased estimators for the variance, it follows that if the variance given stratification is less than or equal to the variance without stratification, it must be that the expectation of the estimated variance given stratification is less than or equal to the expectation of the estimated variance without stratification. However, the estimator for the variance given stratification typically has itself a larger variance, related to the degrees of freedom adjustment. In our view, this should not be interpreted, however, as an argument against stratification. One can always use the variance that ignores the stratification: this is conservative if the stratification did in fact reduce the variance. See Lynn and McCulloch (1992) for a similar argument in the context of paired randomized experiments.

We state the formal argument for a simplified case where we have a single binary covariate, $X_i \in \{f,m\}$ (females and males). We start with a large (infinitely large) superpopulation that expectations and variances refer to. We will draw a sample of size N from this population and then assign treatments to each unit. For simplicity, we assume that $N/4$ is an integer. Each unit is characterized by a triple $[Y_i(0), Y_i(1), X_i]$, where X_i is a binary indicator. In the superpopulation X_i has a binomial distribution with support $\{f, m\}$ (females and males) with $\mathrm{pr}(X_i = f) = 1/2$. Let $\mu_{ft} = \mathbb{E}[Y_i(1)|X_i = f]$, $\mu_{fc} = \mathbb{E}[Y_i(0)|X_i = f]$, $\mu_{mt} = \mathbb{E}[Y_i(1)|X_i = m]$, and $\mu_{mc} = \mathbb{E}[Y_i(0)|X_i = m]$, and similarly for the variances.

We consider the following sampling scheme. We randomly sample $N/2$ units from each of the two strata. Given a sample of $X_1,\ldots,X_N$ we consider two randomization schemes. In the first, we randomly select $N/2$ units out of the sample of N units to be assigned to the treatment group. We refer to this as the completely randomized assignment, $\mathbb{C}$. Second, we consider the following stratified randomization scheme, denoted by $\mathbb{S}$. For the stratified design randomly select $N/4$ from each stratum to be assigned to the treatment, and assign the remainder to the control group. In both cases, we estimate the average treatment effect as

$$\hat{\tau} = \overline{Y}_t^{\mathrm{obs}} - \overline{Y}_c^{\mathrm{obs}}.$$

We consider the properties of this estimator over repeated randomizations, and repeated random samples from the population. It follows trivially that under both designs, the estimator is unbiased for the population average treatment effect under the randomization distribution. The differences in performance between the estimators and the designs are solely the result of differences in the variances. The exact variance for a completely randomized experiment can be written as

$$\mathbb{V}_{\mathbb{C}} = \frac{1}{4 \cdot N} \cdot \left(\left(\mu_{fc} - \mu_{mc} \right)^2 + \left(\mu_{ft} - \mu_{mt} \right)^2 \right) + \frac{1}{N} \cdot \left(\sigma_{ft}^2 + \sigma_{fc}^2 \right)$$
$$+ \frac{1}{N} \cdot \left(\sigma_{mt}^2 + \sigma_{mc}^2 \right).$$

The variance for the corresponding stratified randomized experiment is

$$\mathbb{V}_{\mathbb{S}} = \frac{1}{N} \cdot \left(\sigma_{ft}^2 + \sigma_{fc}^2 \right) + \frac{1}{N} \cdot \left(\sigma_{mt}^2 + \sigma_{mc}^2 \right).$$

Thus, the difference in the two variances is

$$\mathbb{V}_{\mathbb{C}} - \mathbb{V}_{\mathbb{S}} = \frac{1}{4 \cdot N} \cdot \left(\left(\mu_{fc} - \mu_{mc} \right)^2 + \left(\mu_{ft} - \mu_{mt} \right)^2 \right) \geq 0.$$

Therefore, stratification leads to variances that cannot be higher than those under a completely randomized experiment. There can only be equality if neither of the potential outcomes is correlated with the covariate, and $\mu_{fc} = \mu_{mc}$ and $\mu_{ft} = \mu_{mt}$. This is the main argument for our recommendation that one should always stratify.

The inability to rank the conditional variance is useful in understanding the Snedecor and Cochran's quote in the introduction. If the strata are defined in terms of a continuous covariate than in a particular sample, it is possible that stratification leads to larger variances conditional on the covariate values (and in the special case of paired experiments, to negative correlations within pairs). That is not possible on average, that is, over repeated samples randomly drawn from large strata, rather than conditional on the covariate values in a single sample. As mentioned before, the large strata qualification here is important: if the strata we draw from are small, say litters of puppies, it may well be that the within-stratum correlation is negative, but that is not possible if all the strata are large: in that case the correlation has to be nonnegative.

Now let us consider two estimators for the variance. First define, for $w = $ c, t, and $x = $ f, m,

$$s_{xw}^2 = \frac{1}{N_{xw} - 1} \sum_{i: W_i = 1_{\{w=t\}}, X_i = x} \left(Y_i^{obs} - \overline{Y}_{xw}^{obs} \right)^2 \text{ and}$$
$$s_w^2 = \frac{1}{N_w - 1} \sum_{i: W_i = 1_{\{w=t\}}} \left(Y_i^{obs} - \overline{Y}_w^{obs} \right)^2.$$

The natural estimator for the variance under the completely randomized experiment is

$$\widehat{\mathbb{V}}_{\mathbb{C}} = \frac{s_c^2}{N_c} + \frac{s_t^2}{N_t}, \quad \text{with } \mathbb{E}\big[\widehat{\mathbb{V}}_{\mathbb{C}}\big] = \mathbb{V}_{\mathbb{C}}.$$

For a stratified randomized experiment the natural variance estimator, taking into account the stratification, is

$$\widehat{\mathbb{V}}_{\mathbb{S}} = \frac{N_f}{N_f + N_m} \cdot \left(\frac{s_{fc}^2}{N_{fc}} + \frac{s_{ft}^2}{N_{ft}} \right) + \frac{N_m}{N_f + N_m} \cdot \left(\frac{s_{mc}^2}{N_{mc}} + \frac{s_{mt}^2}{N_{mt}} \right) \text{ with } \mathbb{E}\big[\widehat{\mathbb{V}}_{\mathbb{S}}\big] = \mathbb{V}_{\mathbb{S}}.$$

Hence, $\mathbb{E}[\widehat{\mathbb{V}}_{\mathbb{S}}] \leq \mathbb{E}[\widehat{\mathbb{V}}_{\mathbb{C}}]$. Nevertheless, in a particular sample, with values $(\mathbf{Y}, \mathbf{W}, \mathbf{X})$, it may well be the case that the realized value of the completely randomized variance estimator $\widehat{\mathbb{V}}_{\mathbb{C}}(\mathbf{Y}, \mathbf{W}, \mathbf{X})$ is less than that of the stratified variance $\widehat{\mathbb{V}}_{\mathbb{S}}(\mathbf{Y}, \mathbf{W}, \mathbf{X})$. To be more specific, consider the case where the stratification is not related to the potential outcomes at all. In that case the two variances are identical in expectation, $\mathbb{E}[\widehat{\mathbb{V}}_{\mathbb{S}}] \geq \mathbb{E}[\widehat{\mathbb{V}}_{\mathbb{C}}]$, but the variance of $\widehat{\mathbb{V}}_{\mathbb{S}}$ is larger than the variance of $\widehat{\mathbb{V}}_{\mathbb{C}}$, $\mathbb{V}(\widehat{\mathbb{V}}_{\mathbb{S}}) > \mathbb{V}(\widehat{\mathbb{V}}_{\mathbb{C}})$. As a result the power of a t-test based on $\widehat{\mathbb{V}}_{\mathbb{S}}$ will be slightly lower than the power of a t-test based on $\widehat{\mathbb{V}}_{\mathbb{C}}$. Nevertheless, in practice, we recommend to always stratify whenever possible.

7.3 Rerandomization

Suppose one is conducting a randomized experiment. For the study population the researcher has collected some background characteristics and has decided to assign the units to the treatment or control group completely at random. Although this would in general not be optimal, it may be that the researcher decided it was not worth the effort investigating a better design, and just went ahead with the complete randomization. Now, however, suppose that after the random assignment has been decided, but prior to the actual implementation of the assignment, the researcher compares average pre-treatment values by treatment status. In expectation, these should be identical for all covariates, but obviously in reality these will differ somewhat. Now suppose that one of the most important covariates does actually show a substantial difference between the assigned treatment and control group. It need not be, although it may be statistically significant at conventional levels even if the randomization was done properly, simply because there is a substantial number of covariates, or simply by chance. What should one do in that case? More specifically, should one go back to the drawing board and rerandomize the treatment assignment so that the important covariate is better balanced? This question of rerandomization has received some attention in the empirical development literature. One paper that raised the question forcefully in this literature is

Bruhn and McKenzie (2009). Theoretical papers discussing some of the formal aspects are Morgan and Rubin (2012) and Banerjee et al. (2016).

Here, we offer some comments. First of all, implicitly many designs for randomized experiments can be thought of as based on rerandomization. Consider the case where the population of $N = 100$ individuals consists of 50 women and 50 men. Suppose we do a completely randomized experiment, with 60 individuals to be assigned to the treatment group and the remaining 40 assigned to the control group. Now suppose we reject and rerandomize any randomization vector that does not correspond to 30 men and 30 women being assigned to the treatment group. Then, in an indirect manner, we end up with a stratified randomized experiment that we know how to analyze, and that in general offers better sampling properties in terms of variance. The point is that in this case the rerandomization does not create any complications, although the appropriate analysis given the rerandomization is different from the one based on ignoring the rerandomization. Specifically, p-values need to be adjusted for the rerandomization, although ignoring the adjustment simply leads to conservative p-values. Both statements hold more generally.

In order for the subsequent analysis to be able to take account of the rerandomization, however, the details of the rerandomization need to be spelled out. This is most easily seen if we consider a Fisher exact p-value analysis. In order to calculate the exact p-value, we need to know the exact distribution of the assignment vector. In the case of possible rerandomization, we would therefore need to know exactly which assignment vectors would be subject to rerandomization, and which would be viewed as acceptable. The actual criterion may be complicated, and involve calculation of t-statistics for differences in average covariates between treatment groups, but it needs to be completely spelled out in order for the exact p-value calculation to be feasible. Doing this is ultimately equivalent to designing an experiment that guarantees more balance, and it would most likely take a form close to that of a stratified randomized experiment. We recommend simply taking care in the original design so that assignments that correspond to unacceptable balance are ruled out from the outset, rather than ruled out ex post, which complicates inference.

8. THE ANALYSIS OF CLUSTERED RANDOMIZED EXPERIMENTS

In this section, we discuss clustered randomized experiments. Instead of assigning treatments at the unit level, in this setting the population is first partitioned into a number of clusters. Then all units in a cluster are then assigned to the same treatment level. Clusters may take the form of schools, where within a school district a number of schools are randomly assigned to an educational intervention rather than individual students, or villages, or states, or other geographical entities. For general discussions, see Donner (1987), Gail et al. (1996), and Murray (2012).

Given a fixed sample size, this design is in general not as efficient as a completely randomized design or a stratified randomized design. The motivation for such clustered designs is different. One motivation is that in some cases there may be interference between units at the unit level. If there is no interference between units in different clusters, then the cluster-level randomization may allow for simple, no-interference type analyses, whereas a unit-level analysis would require accounting for the within-cluster interactions. A second motivation is that in many cases it is easier to sample units at the cluster level. For the same cost, or level of effort, it may be therefore be possible to collect data on a larger number of units.

In practice, there are quite different settings where clustered randomization may take place. In some cases the number of units per cluster is similar, for example in educational settings where the clusters are classrooms. In other settings where clusters are geographical units, e.g., states, or towns, there may be a substantive amount of variation in cluster size. Although theoretically this does not make much of a difference, in practice it can affect what effective strategies are available for dealing with the clustering. In the first case, our main recommendation is to include analyses that are based on the cluster as the unit of analysis. Although more sophisticated analyses may be more informative than simple analyses using the clusters as units, it is rare that these differences in precision are substantial, and a cluster-based analysis has the virtue of great transparency. Analyzing the data at the unit level has the benefit that one can directly take into account unit-level characteristics. In practice, however, including unit-level characteristics generally improves precision by a relatively modest amount compared to including cluster-averages as covariates in a cluster-level analysis, so our recommendation is to focus primarily on cluster-level analyses. For the second case where there is substantial variation in cluster sizes, a key component of our recommended strategy is to focus on analyses with cluster averages as the target in addition to analysis with unit averages that may be the main target of interest. The former may be much easier to estimate in settings with a substantial amount of heterogeneity in cluster sizes.

8.1 The choice of estimand in clustered randomized experiments

As before, let G be the number of clusters, and let $G_{ig} \in \{0, 1\}$, $i = 1, \ldots, N$, $g = 1, \ldots, G$ denote the binary indicator that unit i belongs to cluster g. $N_g = \sum_{i=1}^{N} G_{ig}$ is the number of units in cluster g, so that N_g/N is the share of cluster g in the sample. W_i continues to denote the treatment assignment for unit i, but now $\overline{W}_g$ denotes the average value of the treatment assignment for all units in cluster g, so that by the definition of clustered randomized assignment, $\overline{W}_g \in \{0, 1\}$. Let G_t be the number of treated clusters, and $G_c = G - G_t$ the number of control clusters.

The first issue in clustered randomized experiments is that there may be different estimands to consider. One natural estimand is the overall population average treatment effect,

$$\tau^{\text{pop}} = \frac{1}{N} \sum_{i=1}^{N} (Y_i(1) - Y_i(0)),$$

where we average over all units in the population. A second estimand is the unweighted average of the within–cluster average effects as

$$\tau^{\mathbb{C}} = \frac{1}{G} \sum_{g=1}^{G} \tau_g, \quad \text{where} \ \ \tau_g = \frac{1}{N_g} \sum_{i:G_{ig}=1} (Y_i(1) - Y_i(0)).$$

We can think of $\tau^{\mathbb{C}}$ as a weighted average of the unit-level treatment effects, with the weight for units in cluster g proportional to the inverse of the cluster sample size, $1/N_g$. Similarly, the population average treatment effect can be thought of as a weighted average of the cluster-level average treatment effects with weights proportional to the cluster sample size N_g.

There are two issues regarding the choice of estimand. One is which of the estimands is of most substantive interest. In many cases, this will be the un-weighted, population average treatment effect τ^{pop}. A second issue is the ease and informativeness of any analysis. Because the randomization is at the cluster level, simply aggregating unit-level outcomes to cluster-level averages simplifies the analysis substantially: all the methods developed for completely randomized experiments apply directly to a cluster-level analysis for clustered randomized experiments. In addition, inferences for $\tau^{\mathbb{C}}$ are often much more precise than inferences for τ^{pop} in cases where there are a few large clusters and many small clusters. Consider an extreme case where there is one extremely large cluster that in terms of size is larger than the other clusters combined. Inference for τ^{pop} in that case is difficult because all the units in this mega cluster will always be in the same treatment group. Inference for $\tau^{\mathbb{C}}$, on the other hand, may well be precise. Moreover, if the substantive question is one of testing for the presence of any treatment effect, answering this question by focusing on a statistic that averages over clusters without weighting is just as valid as comparing weighted averages over clusters.

In practice a researcher may therefore want to report analyses for τ^{pop} in combination with analyses for $\tau^{\mathbb{C}}$. In cases where τ^{pop} is the estimand that is of most substantive interest, the more precise inferences for $\tau^{\mathbb{C}}$ may complement the noisy analyses for the substantively more interesting τ^{pop}.

8.2 Point estimation in clustered randomized experiments

Now let us consider the analysis of cluster randomized experiments. We focus on the case where unit-level outcomes and possibly covariates are available. The first choice facing the researcher concerns the choice of the unit of analysis. One can analyze the data at the unit level or at the cluster level. We first do the latter, and then return to the former.

If we are interested in the average effect $\tau^{\mathbb{C}}$, we can directly use the methods for completely randomized experiments discussed in Section 4. Let $\overline{Y}_g^{\mathrm{obs}}$ be the average of the observed outcomes in cluster g. We can simply average the averages for the treated and control clusters as

$$\widehat{\tau}^{\mathbb{C}} = \frac{1}{G_{\mathrm{t}}} \sum_{g:\overline{W}_g=1} \overline{Y}_g^{\mathrm{obs}} - \frac{1}{G_{\mathrm{c}}} \sum_{g:\overline{W}_g=0} \overline{Y}_g^{\mathrm{obs}}.$$

The variance of this estimator can be estimated as

$$\widehat{\mathbb{V}}\left(\widehat{\tau}^{\mathbb{C}}\right) = \frac{s_{\mathbb{C},\mathrm{c}}^2}{G_{\mathrm{c}}} + \frac{s_{\mathbb{C},\mathrm{t}}^2}{G_{\mathrm{t}}},$$

where the variance for the averages of

$$s_{\mathbb{C},\mathrm{c}}^2 = \frac{1}{G_{\mathrm{c}} - 1} \sum_{g:\overline{W}_g=0} \left(\overline{Y}_g^{\mathrm{obs}} - \frac{1}{G_{\mathrm{t}}} \sum_{g':\overline{W}_{g'}=1} \overline{Y}_{g'}^{\mathrm{obs}} \right)^2,$$

and similarly for $s_{\mathbb{C},\mathrm{c}}^2$. We can also get the same estimates using regression methods for the regression function as

$$\overline{Y}_g^{\mathrm{obs}} = \alpha + \tau^{\mathbb{C}} \cdot \overline{W}_g + \eta_g. \tag{17}$$

We can generalize the specification of this regression function to include cluster-level covariates, including cluster characteristics or averages of unit-level characteristics.

Using a unit-level analysis obtaining an estimate for $\tau^{\mathbb{C}}$ is more complicated. Consider the regression

$$Y_i^{\mathrm{obs}} = \alpha + \tau \cdot W_i + \varepsilon_i. \tag{18}$$

We can estimate this regression function using weighted least squares with the weight for unit i, belonging to cluster $g(i)$, equal to $1/N_{g(i)}$ as in the Cox (1956) analysis of weighted randomized experiments. This weighted least squares estimator is identical to $\widehat{\tau}^{\mathbb{C}}$.

Now consider the case where we are interested in τ^{pop}. In that case, we can estimate the regression function in Eq. (18) without any weights. Alternatively, we can get the same numerical answer by estimating the regression (Eq. 17) at the cluster level with weights proportional to the cluster sample sizes N_g. To get the variance for the estimator for the population average treatment effect, we can use the unit-level regression, but we need to take into account the clustering. We can do so using the robust clustering standard errors proposed by Liang and Zeger (1986). Let $\widehat{\alpha}$ and $\widehat{\tau}$ be the least squares estimators for α and τ based on Eq. (18), and let $\widehat{\varepsilon}_i = Y_i^{\mathrm{obs}} - \widehat{\alpha} - \widehat{\tau} \cdot W_i$ be the residual. Then the covariance matrix for $(\widehat{\alpha}, \widehat{\tau})$ can be estimated as

$$\left(\sum_{i=1}^{N} \begin{pmatrix} 1 & W_i \\ W_i & W_i^2 \end{pmatrix} \right)^{-1} \left(\sum_{g=1}^{G} \sum_{i:C_{ig}=1} \begin{pmatrix} \widehat{\varepsilon}_i \\ W_i \cdot \widehat{\varepsilon}_i \end{pmatrix} \right.$$

$$\left. \times \sum_{i:C_{ig}=1} \begin{pmatrix} \widehat{\varepsilon}_i \\ W_i \cdot \widehat{\varepsilon}_i \end{pmatrix}' \right) \left(\sum_{i=1}^{N} \begin{pmatrix} 1 & W_i \\ W_i & W_i^2 \end{pmatrix} \right)^{-1}.$$

The key difference with the Eicker-Huber-White robust standard errors is that before taking the outer product of the product of the residuals and the covariates they are summed up within clusters. This cluster-robust variance estimator is implemented in many regression software packages, sometimes with *ad-hoc* degrees of freedom adjustments.

If we compare unit-level and cluster-level analyses in the form described so far, our preference is for cluster-level analysis, as it is more transparent and more directly linked to the randomization framework. However, unit-level analysis allows the analyst to impose additional modeling assumptions; for example, a unit-level regression can incorporate covariates and impose additional assumptions, such as restricting the effect of covariates to be common across clusters. If justified, imposing such restrictions can increase efficiency. One could accomplish the same goal by first doing a unit-level regression and constructing residuals for each unit, and then performing cluster-level analysis on the residuals, but at that point the inference would become more complex and depart from the pure randomization-based analysis, reducing the benefits of a cluster-based approach.

8.3 Clustered sampling and completely randomized experiments

A second issue related to clustering is that the original sample may have been obtained through clustered sampling. This issue is discussed in more detail in Abadie et al. (2016). Suppose we have a large population. The population is divided into G clusters, as in the previous discussion. Instead of a random sample from this population, we first sample a number of clusters from the population of clusters. Within each of the sampled clusters, we sample a fixed fraction of the units within that cluster. Given our sample, we conduct a completely randomized experiment, without regard to the cluster these units belong to.

There is a subtle issue involved in defining what the estimand is. The first alternative is to focus on the sample average treatment effect, that is, the average difference for the two potential outcomes over all the units in the sample. A second alternative is to analyze the population average treatment effect for all the units in the population, including those in nonsampled clusters. For both alternatives, the simple difference in average outcomes by treatment status is unbiased for the estimand.

Abadie et al. (2016) show that we are interested in the sample average treatment effect, we can ignore the clustering and use the conventional Neyman variance estimator discussed in Section 4. In contrast, if we are interested in the population average treatment effect, we need to take into account the implications of the clustering sampling design. We can adjust the standard errors for the clustered sampling by using the Liang and Zeger (1986) clustered standard errors.

9. NONCOMPLIANCE IN RANDOMIZED EXPERIMENTS

Even if a randomized experiment is well designed, there may be complications in the implementation. One of the most common of these complications is noncompliance. Some units assigned to the treatment group may end up not taking the treatment, and some units assigned to the treatment group may manage to acquire the active treatment. If there are only violations of the treatment assignment of the first type, we refer to it as one-sided noncompliance. This may arise when individuals assigned to the control groups can be effectively be embargoed from the active treatment. If some units assigned to the control group do manage to receive the active treatment, we have two-sided noncompliance.

The concern is that noncompliance is not random or accidental, but the result of systematic differences in behavior or characteristics between units. Units that are assigned to the treatment but that choose not receive it may do so because they are different from the units assigned to the treatment that do receive it. These differences may be associated with the outcomes of interest, thereby invalidating simple comparisons of outcomes by treatment received. In other words, the randomization that validates comparisons by treatment status does not validate comparisons by posttreatment variables such as the treatment received. These issues come up both in randomized experiments as well as in observational studies. The general term for these complications in the econometric literature is endogeneity of the receipt of treatment. Random assignment ensures that the assignment to treatment is exogenous, but it does not bear on the exogeneity of the receipt of treatment if the receipt of treatment is different from the assignment to treatment.

In this chapter, we discuss three distinct approaches to dealing with noncompliance, all of which are valid under fairly weak assumptions. First, one can ignore the actual receipt of the treatment and focus on the causal effects of assignment to the treatment, in an intention-to-treat analysis. Second, we can use instrumental variables methods to estimate the local average treatment effect, the causal effect of the receipt of treatment for the subpopulation of compliers. Third, we can use a partial identification or bounds analysis to obtain the range of values for the average causal effect of the receipt of treatment for the full population. Another approach, not further discussed here, is the randomization-based approach to instrumental variables developed in Imbens and Rosenbaum (2005). There are also two types of analyses that require much stronger assumptions in order to be valid. The first of these is an as-treated analysis, where units are compared by the treatment received; this relies on an unconfoundedness or selection-on-observables assumption. A second type of analysis is a per protocol analysis, where units are dropped who do not receive the treatment they were assigned to.

We need some additional notation in this section. Let $Z_i \in \{0,1\}$ denote the randomly assigned treatment. We generalize the notation for the treatment received, to reflect its status as an (intermediate) outcome. Let $W_i(z) \in \{0,1\}$ denote the potential treatment outcome given assignment z, with $W_i^{obs} = W_i(Z_i)$ the realized value for the treatment received. For the outcome of primary interest, there are different setups possible. One approach, e.g., Angrist et al. (1996), is to let $Y_i(z, w)$ denote the potential outcome corresponding to assignment z and treatment received w. Alternatively, we could index the potential outcomes solely by the assignment, with $\tilde{Y}_i(z)$ denoting the outcome corresponding to the treatment assigned to unit i. The two notations are closely related, with $\tilde{Y}_i(z) = Y_i(z, W_i(z))$. Here we mainly use the first setup. The realized outcome is $Y_i^{obs} = Y_i(Z_i, W_i(Z_i)) = \tilde{Y}_i(Z_i)$. To simplify notation, we index sample sizes, averages, and variances by 0,1 when they are indexed by values of the assignment Z_i, and by c, t when they are indexed by values of the treatment received W_i. For example, $\overline{Y}_{0,t}^{obs}$ is the average of the observed outcome for units assigned to the control group ($Z_i = 0$) but who received the active treatment ($W_i^{obs} = 1$).

9.1 Intention-to-treat analyses

In an intention-to-treat analysis, the receipt of treatment is ignored, and outcomes are compared by the assignment to treatment (Imbens and Rubin, 2015; Fisher et al., 1990). The intention-to-treat effect is the average effect of the assignment to treatment. In terms of the notation introduced above, the estimand is

$$\tau^{itt} = \frac{1}{N} \sum_{i=1}^{N} (Y_i(1, W_i(1)) - Y_i(0, W_i(0))).$$

We can estimate this using the difference in averages of realized outcomes by treatment assignment as

$$\hat{\tau}^{itt} = \overline{Y}_1^{obs} - \overline{Y}_0^{obs}, \quad \text{where } \overline{Y}_z^{obs} = \frac{1}{N_z} \sum_{i:Z_i=z} Y_i^{obs} \text{ for } z = 0, 1.$$

To construct valid confidence intervals for τ^{itt}, we can use the standard methods discussed in Section 4.2. The exact variance for $\hat{\tau}^{itt}$ is

$$\mathbb{V}\left(\hat{\tau}^{itt}\right) = \frac{S_0^2}{N_0} + \frac{S_1^2}{N_1} - \frac{S_{01}^2}{N},$$

where S_0^2 and S_1^2 are the variances of $Y_i[0, W_i(0)]$ and $Y_i[1, W_i(1)]$ in the sample, defined as

$$S_0^2 = \frac{1}{N-1} \sum_{i=1}^{N} \left(Y_i(0, W_i(0)) - \overline{Y}(0)\right)^2, \text{ and}$$

$$S_1^2 = \frac{1}{N-1} \sum_{i=1}^{N} \left(Y_i(1, W_i(1)) - \overline{Y}(1)\right)^2,$$

and S_{01}^2 is the sample variance of the unit-level treatment effects, defined as:

$$S_{01}^2 = \frac{1}{N-1} \sum_{i=1}^{N} \left(Y_i(1, W_i(1)) - Y_i(0, W_i(0)) - (\overline{Y}(1) - \overline{Y}(0))\right)^2.$$

We can estimate the first two terms as

$$s_0^2 = \frac{1}{N_0 - 1} \sum_{i:Z_i=0} \left(Y_i^{obs} - \overline{Y}_0^{obs}\right)^2,$$

and

$$s_1^2 = \frac{1}{N_1 - 1} \sum_{i:Z_i=1} \left(Y_i^{obs} - \overline{Y}_1\right)^2.$$

As discussed in Section 4.2, the third term, S_{01}^2 is generally impossible to estimate consistently because we never observe both $Y_i[1, W_i(1)]$ and $Y_i[0, W_i(0)]$ for the same unit. In practice, we therefore use the estimator for $\mathbb{V}(\hat{\tau}^{itt})$ based on estimating the first two terms by s_0^2 and s_1^2, and ignoring the third term as

$$\widehat{\mathbb{V}}\left(\hat{\tau}^{itt}\right) = \frac{s_0^2}{N_0} + \frac{s_1^2}{N_1}.$$

This leads to valid confidence intervals in large samples, justified by the randomization and *sutva* without additional assumptions.

The main drawback associated with the intention-to-treat approach is that the corresponding estimand is typically not the object of primary interest. The researcher may be interested in settings where the assignment mechanism may be different, and the incentives for individuals to take the treatment might change. For example, in medical drug trials the compliance rate is often very different from what would happen if a drug is released to the general population. In the trial phase individuals, knowing that the efficacy of the drug has not been established may be more likely to stop adhering to the protocol. As a result the intention-to-treat effect would not provide much guidance to the effects in the new setting. In other words, intention-to-treat effects may have poor external validity. The presumption is that causal effects of the receipt of treatment are more generalizable to other settings, though of course there is no formal result that proves that this is so.

9.2 Local average treatment effects

An alternative approach that deals directly with the noncompliance is to use instrumental variables methods and related methods based on principal stratification (Frangakis and Rubin, 2002; Barnard et al., 1998). Bloom (1984), Zelen (1979, 1990), Baker (2000), Baker and Lindeman (1994), and Cuzick et al. (1997) contain early and independent discussions of the instrumental variables approach, some in the special case of one-sided noncompliance, and Imbens and Angrist (1994) and Angrist et al. (1996) develop the general setup in the potential outcomes framework. See also Imbens and Rubin (2015) and Lui (2011) for textbook discussions and Baker et al. (2016) for a biostatistical perspective. The first step is to consider the possible patterns of compliance behavior. Let $C_i \in \{c, d, a, n\}$ denote the compliance behavior, where

$$
C_i = \begin{cases}
c & \text{if } W_i(0) = 0, W_i(1) = 1, \\
d & \text{if } W_i(0) = 1, W_i(1) = 0, \\
a & \text{if } W_i(0) = 1, W_i(1) = 1, \\
n & \text{if } W_i(0) = 0, W_i(1) = 0,
\end{cases}
$$

where c stands for complier, d for defier, n for never-taker, and a for always-taker. These labels are just definitional, not requiring any assumptions.

Now we consider two key assumptions. The first is monotonicity (Imbens and Angrist, 1994), or no-defiance, which requires

$$
W_i(1) \geq W_i(0).
$$

This rules out the presence of defiers, units that always (that is, whether assigned to control or treatment) do the opposite of their assignment. In the setting we consider in this chapter, where the instrument is the random assignment to treatment, this appears a very plausible assumption: assigning someone to the active treatment increases the incentive to take the active treatment, and it would appear unusual for there to be many units who would respond to this increase in incentives by declining to take the treatment where they would otherwise have done so. In other settings, monotonicity may be a more controversial assumption. For example, in studies in criminal justice, researchers have used random assignment of cases to judges to identify the causal effect of prison terms on recidivism (reference). In that case, even if one judge is more strict than another in the sense that the first judge has a higher rate of sentencing individuals to prison terms, it is not necessarily the case that any individual who would be sentenced to time in prison by the on-average more lenient judge would also be sentenced to prison by the stricter judge.

The second key assumption is generally referred to as the exclusion restriction. It requires that there is no direct effect of the assignment on the outcome without passing through the receipt of treatment. Formally, using the form used in Angrist et al. (1996),

$$Y_i(z, w) = Y_i(z', w), \quad \text{for all } z, z', w.$$

The key components on the assumption is that for never-takers,

$$Y_i(0,0) = Y_i(1,0), \quad \text{and for always} - \text{takers } Y_i(0,1) = Y_i(1,1).$$

For compliers and defiers, the assumption is essentially about the interpretation of the causal effect of the assignment to treatment to the causal effect of the receipt of treatment. The exclusion restriction is a strong one, and its plausibility needs to be argued on a case-by-case basis. It is not justified by, and in fact not related to, the random assignment. Given the exclusion restriction, we can drop the dependence of the potential outcomes on z, and simply write $Y_i(w)$, for $w = 0, 1$.

Given the monotonicity assumption and the exclusion restriction, we can identify the average causal effect of the receipt of treatment on the outcome, what is known as the local average treatment effect (Imbens and Angrist, 1994) as

$$\tau^{\text{late}} = \mathbb{E}[Y_i(1) - Y_i(0)|C_i = c] = \frac{\mathbb{E}[Y_i^{\text{obs}}|Z_i = 1] - \mathbb{E}[Y_i^{\text{obs}}|Z_i = 0]}{\mathbb{E}[W_i^{\text{obs}}|Z_i = 1] - \mathbb{E}[W_i^{\text{obs}}|Z_i = 0]}.$$

Given the setting, it is clear that we cannot identify the average effect for always-takers or never-takers without additional assumptions: we do not observe outcomes for always-takers without the receipt of treatment, and we do not observe outcomes for never-takers given the receipt of treatment. As a result, we need assumptions to extrapolate the treatment effects for compliers to other compliance groups in order to identify the overall average treatment effect.

9.3 Generalizing the local average treatment effect

One major concern with the local average treatment effect is that it reflects only on a subpopulation, the compliers. In many cases the researcher may be more interested in the overall average effect of the treatment. Here, we discuss some supplementary analyses that can be done to assess the generalizability of the local average treatment effect. This section builds on the discussions in Angrist (2004), Hirano et al. (2000), Imbens and Rubin (1997a,b), and Bertanha and Imbens (2014). The Bertanha and Imbens (2014) discussion is primarily in the context of fuzzy regression discontinuity designs, but their results apply directly to other instrumental variables settings.

We use the same setup as in the previous section, but explicitly allow for the presence of exogenous covariates X_i. Instead of using instrumental variables methods to estimate the local average treatment effect, an alternative approach is to adjust for differences in the covariate to estimate the average effect of the treatment, assuming unconfoundedness as

$$W_i \perp (Y_i(0), Y_i(1))|X_i.$$

If this assumption is valid, we can estimate the average effect of the treatment, as well as average effects for any subpopulation using an as-treated analysis. One natural analysis is to compare the local average treatment effect to the covariate-adjusted difference by treatment status. A formal comparison of the two estimates, in a linear model setting, would be a Hausman test (Hausman, 1983). In the absence of covariates the Hausman test would be testing the equality as

$$\frac{\pi_a}{\pi_a + \pi_c \cdot p_z} \cdot \Big(\mathbb{E}[Y_i(1)|G_i = a] - \mathbb{E}[Y_i(1)|G_i = c] \Big)$$

$$= \frac{\pi_n}{\pi_n + \pi_c \cdot (1 - p_z)} \cdot \Big(\mathbb{E}[Y_i(0)|G_i = n] - \mathbb{E}[Y_i(0)|G_i = c] \Big),$$

where π_a, π_c, and π_n are the population shares of always-takers, compliers, and never-takers, respectively. This equality is difficult to interpret. A particular weighted average of the difference between the expected outcomes given treatment for always-takers and compliers is equal to a weighted average of the difference between the expected outcomes without treatment for compliers and never-takers.

Compared to the Hausman test, a more natural and interpretable approach is to test the equality of the unweighted differences, between always-takers and treated compliers and never-takers and not-treated compliers as

$$\mathbb{E}[Y_i(1)|G_i = a] - \mathbb{E}[Y_i(1)|G_i = c] = \mathbb{E}[Y_i(0)|G_i = n] - \mathbb{E}[Y_i(0)|G_i = c],$$

as suggested in Angrist (2004).

Bertanha and Imbens suggest testing the pair of equalities, rather than just the difference, as

$$\mathbb{E}[Y_i(1)|G_i = a] - \mathbb{E}[Y_i(1)|G_i = c] = 0, \quad \text{and}$$
$$\mathbb{E}[Y_i(0)|G_i = n] - \mathbb{E}[Y_i(0)|G_i = c] = 0.$$

If this pair of equalities hold, possibly after adjusting for differences in the covariates, it means that always-takers are comparable to compliers given the treatment, and never-takers are comparable to compliers without the treatment. That would suggest that always-takers without the treatment might also be comparable to compliers without the treatment, and that never-takers with the treatment might be comparable to compliers with the treatment, although neither claim can be tested. If those equalities were to hold, however, then the average effect for compliers, adjusted for covariates, can be generalized to the entire population.

9.4 Bounds

To get estimates of, or do inference for, the average causal effect of the receipt of treatment in settings with noncompliance an alternative to making additional assumptions is to focus on getting ranges of values for the estimand that are consistent with the data in a bound or partial identification approach in a line of research associated with Manski (1990, 1996, 2003a,b, 2013).

The simplest approach without any additional assumptions recognizes that because of the noncompliance the receipt of treatment is no longer exogenous. We can therefore analyze this as an observational study without any assumptions on the assignment process. Consider the average difference in potential outcomes if all units are assigned to the treatment versus no one is assigned to the treatment as

$$\tau = \frac{1}{N} \sum_{i=1}^{N} (Y_i(1) - Y_i(0)) = \overline{Y}(1) - \overline{Y}(0).$$

To estimate this object, it is useful to look at both terms separately. The first term is

$$\overline{Y}(1) = \frac{N_t}{N} \cdot \overline{Y}_{t}^{obs} + \frac{N_c}{N} \cdot \frac{1}{N} \sum_{i:W_i=0} Y_i(1).$$

The last term is what is causing the problems. The data are not directly informative about this term. Let us look at the special case where the outcome is binary. In that case

$$\overline{Y}(1) \in \left[\frac{N_t}{N} \cdot \overline{Y}_{t}^{obs}, \frac{N_t}{N} \cdot \overline{Y}_{t}^{obs} + \frac{N_c}{N} \right].$$

We can do the same thing for the second term in the estimand, leading to

$$\tau \in \left[\frac{N_t}{N} \cdot \overline{Y}_{t}^{obs} - \frac{N_c}{N} \cdot \overline{Y}_{c}^{obs} - \frac{N_t}{N}, \frac{N_t}{N} \cdot \overline{Y}_{t}^{obs} + \frac{N_c}{N} - \frac{N_c}{N} \cdot \overline{Y}_{c}^{obs} \right].$$

This is not a very informative range. By construction, it always includes zero, so we can never be sure that the treatment has any effect on the outcome of interest.

Next, let us consider how the bounds change when we add information in the form of additional assumptions maintaining the binary outcome assumption. Under the full set of instrumental variables assumptions, that is, the monotonicity assumption and the exclusion restriction, we can tighten the bounds substantially. To derive the bounds, and at the same time develop intuition for their value, it is useful to think of the average treatment effect as the sum of the averages over the three compliance groups, compliers, never-takers and always-takers, with shares equal to π_c, π_n, and π_a, respectively. Under monotonicity and the exclusion restriction, the average effect for compliers is identified. For always-takers, we can identify $\mathbb{E}[Y_i(1)|C_i = a]$, but the data are uninformative about $\mathbb{E}[Y_i(0)|C_i = a]$, so that the average effect for always-takers is bounded by

$$\tau_a \in \left[\mathbb{E}[Y_i^{\text{obs}}|Z_i = 0, W_i = 1] - 1, \mathbb{E}[Y_i^{\text{obs}}|Z_i = 0, W_i = 1]\right].$$

Similarly,

$$\tau_n \in \left[-\mathbb{E}[Y_i^{\text{obs}}|Z_i = 1, W_i = 0], 1 - \mathbb{E}[Y_i^{\text{obs}}|Z_i = 1, W_i = 0]\right].$$

Combining these leads to

$$\tau \in \left[\pi_a \cdot \left(\mathbb{E}[Y_i^{\text{obs}}|Z_i = 0, W_i = 1] - 1\right) - \pi_n \cdot \mathbb{E}[Y_i^{\text{obs}}|Z_i = 1, W_i = 0]\right.$$
$$+ \left(\mathbb{E}[Y_i^{\text{obs}}|Z_i = 1] - \mathbb{E}[Y_i^{\text{obs}}|Z_i = 1]\right),$$
$$\pi_a \cdot \mathbb{E}[Y_i^{\text{obs}}|Z_i = 0, W_i = 1] + \pi_n \cdot \left(1 - \mathbb{E}[Y_i^{\text{obs}}|Z_i = 1, W_i = 0]\right)$$
$$\left. + \left(\mathbb{E}[Y_i^{\text{obs}}|Z_i = 1] - \mathbb{E}[Y_i^{\text{obs}}|Z_i = 1]\right)\right].$$

Under these assumptions, these bounds are sharp (Balke and Pearl, 1997).

9.5 As-treated and per protocol analyses

There are two older methods that have sometimes been used to analyze experiments with noncompliance that rely on strong assumptions, as-treated and per-protocol analyses. See, for example, McNamee (2009) and Imbens and Rubin (2015). In an *as-treated* analysis, units are compared by the treatment received, rather than the treatment assigned, essentially invoking an unconfoundedness assumption. Because it was the assignment that was randomized, rather than the receipt of treatment, this is not justified by the randomization. It is useful to consider in a setting where the instrumental variables assumptions, that is, the monotonicity assumption and the exclusion restriction, hold, and assess what the as-treated analysis leads to.

The estimand in an as-treated analysis is

$$\tau^{\text{at}} = \mathbb{E}[Y_i^{\text{obs}}|W_i = 1] - \mathbb{E}[Y_i^{\text{obs}}|W_i = 0].$$

If the monotonicity assumption holds, the first term is an average of outcomes given treatment for always-takers and compliers. If the fraction of units with $Z_i = 1$ is equal to p_Z, then we can write the first term as

$$\mathbb{E}[Y_i^{\text{obs}}|W_i = 1] = \frac{\pi_a}{\pi_a + \pi_c \cdot p_Z} \cdot \mathbb{E}[Y_i(1)|C_i = a]$$
$$+ \frac{\pi_c \cdot p_Z}{\pi_a + \pi_c \cdot p_Z} \cdot \mathbb{E}[Y_i(1)|C_i = c].$$

Similarly,

$$\mathbb{E}\left[Y_i^{\mathrm{obs}}|W_i = 0\right] = \frac{\pi_{\mathrm{n}}}{\pi_{\mathrm{n}} + \pi_{\mathrm{c}} \cdot (1 - P_Z)} \cdot \mathbb{E}[Y_i(0)|C_i = \mathrm{n}]$$
$$+ \frac{\pi_{\mathrm{c}} \cdot (1 - p_Z)}{\pi_{\mathrm{n}} + \pi_{\mathrm{c}} \cdot (1 - P_Z)} \cdot \mathbb{E}[Y_i(0)|C_i = \mathrm{c}].$$

The difference is then

$$\mathbb{E}\left[Y_i^{\mathrm{obs}}|W_i = 1\right] - \mathbb{E}\left[Y_i^{\mathrm{obs}}|W_i = 0\right]$$
$$= \mathbb{E}[Y_i(1) - Y_i(0)|C_i = \mathrm{c}]$$
$$+ \frac{\pi_{\mathrm{a}}}{\pi_{\mathrm{a}} + \pi_{\mathrm{c}} \cdot P_Z} \cdot (\mathbb{E}[Y_i(1)|G_i = \mathrm{a}] - \mathbb{E}[Y_i(1)|C_i = \mathrm{c}])$$
$$- \frac{\pi_{\mathrm{n}}}{\pi_{\mathrm{n}} + \pi_{\mathrm{c}} \cdot (1 - P_Z)} \cdot (\mathbb{E}[Y_i(0)|G_i = \mathrm{n}] - \mathbb{E}[Y_i(0)|C_i = \mathrm{c}]).$$

These last two terms in expression are compared to zero in a Hausman test for the exogeneity of the treatment. The form is in general difficult to interpret.

The second is a per protocol analysis, where units who do not comply with their assigned treatment are simply dropped from the analysis. Again it is instructive to see what this method is estimating under the monotonicity assumption and the exclusion restriction. In general,

$$\tau^{\mathrm{pp}} = \mathbb{E}\left[Y_i^{\mathrm{obs}}|W_i = 1, Z_i = 1\right] - \mathbb{E}\left[Y_i^{\mathrm{obs}}|W_i = 0, Z_i = 0\right].$$

Similar calculations as for the as-treated analysis show that given the monotoniticy and the exclusion restriction, this is equal to

$$\tau^{\mathrm{pp}} = \mathbb{E}[Y_i(1) - Y_i(0)|C_i = \mathrm{c}] + \frac{\pi_{\mathrm{a}}}{\pi_{\mathrm{a}} + \pi_{\mathrm{c}}} \cdot (\mathbb{E}[Y_i(1)|G_i = \mathrm{a}] - \mathbb{E}[Y_i(1)|C_i = \mathrm{c}])$$
$$- \frac{\pi_{\mathrm{n}}}{\pi_{\mathrm{n}} + \pi_{\mathrm{c}}} \cdot (\mathbb{E}[Y_i(0)|G_i = \mathrm{n}] - \mathbb{E}[Y_i(0)|C_i = \mathrm{c}]).$$

This expression is again difficult to interpret in general, and the analysis is not recommended.

10. HETEROGENOUS TREATMENT EFFECTS AND PRETREATMENT VARIABLES

Most of the literature has focused on estimating average treatment effects for the entire sample or population. However, in many cases, researchers are also interested in the presence or absence of heterogeneity in treatment effects. There are different ways to study such heterogeneity. Here, we discuss some approaches. Note that this is different from the way covariates or pretreatment variables were used in Section 4.4, where the focus remained on the overall average treatment effect and the presence of pretreatment variables served solely to improve precision of the estimators. In observational studies, covariates also serve to make the identifying assumptions more credible.

As discussed at the outset of this chapter, a key concern with randomized experiments is external validity. If we apply the treatment in a different setting, will the effect be the same? Although there are many factors that vary across settings, one common way that settings differ is that the populations of individual units may be different. If these differences can be captured with observable pretreatment variables, then it is in principle possible to address this element of external validity as in Hotz et al. (2005). In particular, if we obtain an estimate of the treatment effect for each potential value of the covariate vector x, then we can estimate average treatment effects in any population be accounting for the differences in distributions. That is, given an estimate for $\tau(x) = \mathbb{E}[Y_i(1) - Y_i(0)|X_i = x]$, it is straightforward to estimate $\mathbb{E}[\tau(X_i)]$ if the distribution of X_i is known.

10.1 Randomized experiments with pretreatment variables

Traditionally, researchers specified particular subpopulations based on substantive interest, and estimated average treatment effects for those subpopulations, as well as tested equality of treatment effects across these subpopulations. For example, one may be interested separately in the effect of an educational program on girls versus boys. In such cases the analyses are straightforward. One can simply analyze the data separately by subpopulation using the methods developed in Section 6.1. In these cases there is often some concern that the subpopulations were selected ex post, so that p-values are no longer valid because of multiple testing concerns. For example, suppose one has a randomized experiment, with a 100 independent binary pretreatment variables that are in fact unrelated to the treatments or the outcomes. One would expect that for five of them the t-statistic for testing the null hypothesis that the average treatment effect was different by the value of that covariate was larger than two in absolute value, even though none of the covariates are related to the treatment effect. Preanalysis plans (Casey et al., 2012; Olken, 2015) are one approach to alleviate such concerns; another is to correct for multiple testing (List et al., 2016). Below, we describe some recently developed alternatives that work not only when the number of covariates is small, but also when the number is large relative to the sample size or the true underlying model of treatment effect heterogeneity may be quite complex.

10.2 Testing for treatment effect heterogeneity

A second approach is to simply test for the presence of heterogeneity in the average treatment effect as a function of the covariates, $\tau(x) = \mathbb{E}[Y_i(1) - Y_i(0)|X_i = x]$.

One type of test considers whether there is any evidence for observable heterogeneity. Crump et al. (2008) develop nonparametric tests for the null hypothesis as

$$H_0 : \tau(x) = \tau, \quad \text{for all } x \in \mathbb{X},$$

against the alternative

$$H_0 : \tau(x) \neq \tau(x'), \quad \text{for some } x, x' \in \mathbb{X}.$$

The setup of Crump et al. uses a sequence of parametric approximations to the conditional expectation

$$\mathbb{E}\left[Y_i^{\text{obs}} | W_i = w, X_i = x\right] = \beta_0' h(x) \cdot (1 - w) + \beta_1' h(x) \cdot w,$$

for vector-valued functions $h(x)$ and then tests the null hypothesis the equality $\beta_1 = \beta_0$. By increasing the dimension of $h(x)$, with a suitable basis of functions, one can nonparametrically test the null hypothesis that the average treatment effect $\tau(x)$ is a constant as a function of the covariates under the assumption of unconfoundedness, which is implied by randomized assignment.

A researcher might also like to understand which, if any, covariates are associated with treatment effect. A natural approach would be to evaluate heterogeneity with respect to each covariate, one by one. For example, each covariate could be transformed into a binary indicator for whether the value of the covariate is above or below the median, and then the researcher could test the hypothesis that the treatment effect is higher when the covariate is high than when it is low. Conducting a large number of hypothesis tests raises issues of multiple testing, and confidence intervals should be corrected to account for this. However, standard approaches (e.g., the Bonferroni correction) assume that each test is independent, and thus may be overly conservative in an environment where many covariates are correlated with one another (which will imply that the test statistics are also correlated with one another). List et al. (2016) propose a computationally feasible approach to the multiple testing problem in this context. The approach uses bootstrapping, and it accounts for correlation among test statistics. One challenge with this approach is that the researcher must prespecify the set of hypothesis tests to conduct; thus, it is hard to explore all possible interactions among covariates and all possible ways to discretize them. In the next section, we consider methods that explore more complex forms of heterogeneity.

10.3 Estimating the treatment effect heterogeneity

There are several possible approaches for exploring the treatment effect heterogeneity. The first is to specify a parametric model of treatment effect heterogeneity (as in Eq. 13) and report the estimates. For example, one simple approach would be to specify a regression of the outcome on an indicator for treatment status as well as interactions of the indicator with the treatment indicator. With a small number of covariates relative to the sample size, all linear interactions with the treatment indicator could be considered, partially alleviating concerns about multiple testing. Below, we discuss generalizations of this idea to regularized regression (e.g., LASSO) where a systematic method is used to select covariates.

A second approach is to construct a fully nonparametric estimator for $\tau(x)$. We will develop this approach further below; with sufficiently large datasets and a relatively small number of covariates, this approach can be effective, and recent work-building on techniques from machine learning (Wager and Athey, 2015) has lead to improvements in how many covariates can be handled without sacrificing the coverage of confidence intervals. For the case where there may be many covariates relative to the sample size, a third approach proposed by Athey and Imbens (2016) uses the data to select a set of subgroups (a "partition" of the covariate space) such that treatment effect heterogeneity across subgroups is maximized in a particular sense.

Whether a fully nonparametric approach or an approach based on subgroups is preferred may be partially determined by the constraints of the data; valid confidence intervals may not be available (at least with existing methods) with too many covariates relative to sample size. But even if both methods are potentially feasible, it may be desirable to learn about subgroups rather than a fully nonparametric estimate of $\tau(x)$ if the results of the experiment will be used in a context where people with limited processing capability/memory will make decisions based on the experiment. For example, doctors might use a simple flowchart to determine which patients should be prescribed a drug. Results about subgroups may also be more easily interpretable by researchers.

Relative to testing all covariates one by one, an approach that selects a single partition of the covariate space will not, in general, discover all heterogeneity that exists, since the algorithm will focus on the covariates with the biggest impact to the exclusion of others. In addition, in the process of constructing a partition, once we have divided the data into two groups according to the value of one covariate, further divisions will be considered on subsamples of the data, reducing the power available to test heterogeneity in additional covariates. Thus, constructing a single partition does not answer the question of which covariates are associated with heterogeneity; rather, it identifies a particular way to divide the data into meaningful groups. If a researcher wanted to explore all covariates, while maintaining a data-driven approach to how to discretize them, an approach would be to construct distinct partitions that restrict attention to one covariate at the time. For interactions, one could consider small subsets of covariates. If the results of such an exercise were reported in terms of which covariates are associated with significant heterogeneity, multiple testing corrections would be warranted. The approach of List et al. (2016) works for an arbitrary set of null hypotheses, so the researcher could generate a long list of hypotheses using the causal tree approach restricted to different subsets of covariates, and then test them with a correction for multiple testing. Since in datasets with many covariates, there are often many ways to describe what are essentially the same subgroups, we expect a lot of correlation in test statistics, reducing the magnitude of the correction for multiple hypothesis testing.

We begin by describing the third approach, where we construct a partition of the covariate space, and then return to the second and first approaches.

10.3.1 Data-driven subgroup analysis: recursive partitioning for treatment effects

Athey and Imbens (2016) develop a method for exploring heterogeneity in treatment effects without having to prespecify the form of the heterogeneity, and without having to worry about multiple testing. Their approach builds on "regression tree" or "recursive partitioning" methods, where the sample is partitioned in a number of subgroups, defined by the region of the covariate space each unit belongs to. The data are used to determine which partition produces subgroups that differ the most in terms of treatment effects. The method avoids introducing biases in the estimated average treatment effects and allows for valid confidence intervals using "sample splitting," or "honest" estimation. The idea of sample splitting to control significance levels goes back a long way in statistics; see, e.g., Cox (1975), or for a more recent discussion, see Fithian et al. (2015). In a sample splitting approach, in a first step, one sample is used to select the partition, while in a second step, an independent sample is used to estimate treatment effects and construct confidence intervals for each subgroup (separately) given the partition from the first step. The output of the method is a set of subgroups, selected to optimize for treatment effect heterogeneity (to minimize expected mean-squared error of treatment effects), together with treatment effect estimates and standard errors for each subgroup.

Let us illustrate some of the issues in a simple case to develop more intuition. Suppose we consider only a single split of the covariate space in a setting with a substantial number of covariates. We specify a criterion that determines whether one split (that is, a combination of a choice of the covariate and a threshold) is better than another. We return to the choice of criterion below. Given a criterion, we select the covariate and threshold that maximize the criterion. If we estimate the average treatment effect on the two subsamples using the same sample, the fact that this particular split led to a high value of the criterion would often imply that the average treatment effect estimate is biased. Athey and Imbens (2016) therefore suggest, in what they call an honest approach, to estimate the treatment effects on a separate sample. The implication is that the treatment effect estimates are unbiased on the two subsamples, and the corresponding confidence intervals are valid, even in settings with a large number of pretreatment variables or covariates.

A key issue is the choice of criterion. In principle, one would like to split in order to obtain more precise estimates of the average treatment effects. A complicating factor is that the standard criterion for splitting optimized for prediction rely on observing the outcome whose expectation one wants to estimate. That is not the case here because the unit-level treatment effect is not observed. There have been various suggestions in the literature to deal with this. One simple solution is to transform the outcome from Y_i^{obs} to

$$Y_i^* = Y_i^{obs} \cdot \frac{W_i - p}{p \cdot (1 - p)}.$$

This transformed outcome has the property that $\mathbb{E}[Y_i^* | X_i = x] = \tau(x) = \mathbb{E}[Y_i(1) - Y_i(0) | X_i = x]$ so that standard methods for recursive partitioning based on prediction apply (see Weisburg and Pontes, 2015; Athey and Imbens, 2016). Su et al. (2009) suggest using test statistics for the null hypothesis that the average treatment effect in the two subsamples is equal to zero. Zeileis et al. (2008) suggest using model fit, where the model corresponds to a linear regression model in the partitions with an intercept and a binary treatment indicator. Athey and Imbens (2016) show that neither of the two criteria is optimal, and derive a new criterion that focuses directly on the expected squared error of the treatment effect estimator, and which turns out to depend both on the t-statistic and on the fit measures. The criterion is further modified to anticipate honest estimation, that is, to anticipate that the treatment effects will be reestimated on an independent sample after the subgroups are selected. This modification ends up penalizing the expected variance of subgroup estimates; for example, if subgroups are too small, the variance of treatment effect estimates will be large. It also rewards splits for covariates that explain outcomes but not treatment effect heterogeneity, to the extent that controlling for such covariates enables a lower-variance estimate of the treatment effect.

Other related approaches include Wager and Walther (2015), who discuss corrections to confidence intervals (widening the confidence intervals by a factor) as an alternative to sample splitting; however, since confidence intervals need to be inflated fairly substantially, it is not clear whether there is a wide range of conditions where it improves on sample splitting. Relative to the approach of List et al. (2016) discussed above, the methods in this section focus on deriving a single partition, rather than considering heterogeneity one covariate at the time with prespecified discretizations of the covariates; the approaches in this section will have the advantage of exploring interaction effects and using the data to determine a meaningful partition in terms of mean-squared error of treatment effects.

10.3.2 Nonparametric estimation of treatment effect heterogeneity
There are (at least) four possible goals for using nonparametric estimation to estimate heterogeneous treatment effects. The first is descriptive: the researcher can gain insight about what types of units have the highest and lowest treatment effects, as well as visualize comparative statics results, all without imposing a prior restrictions. The second, discussed earlier, is that the researcher wishes to estimate the impact of applying the treatment in a

setting with a different distribution of units. A third is that the researcher wishes to derive a personalized policy recommendation. A fourth is that the researcher wishes to test hypotheses and construct confidence intervals. If confidence intervals are desired, the set of potential methods is quite small. For optimal policy evaluation, a Bayesian framework may have some advantages, since it is natural to incorporate the uncertainty and risk involved in alternative policy assignments. For description or estimation where confidence intervals are not important, there are a wide variety of approaches.

Classical nonparametric approaches to treatment effect heterogeneity would include K-nearest neighbor matching and kernel estimation (Härdle, 2002). In the case of K-nearest neighbor matching, for any x, we can construct an estimate of the treatment effect at that x by averaging the outcomes of the K-nearest neighbors that were treated, and subtracting the average outcomes of the K-nearest neighbors that were control observations. Kernel estimation does something similar, but uses a smooth weighting function rather than uniformly reweighting nearby neighbors and giving 0 weight to neighbors that are farther away. In both cases, distance is measured using Euclidean distance for the covariate vector. These methods can work well and provide satisfactory coverage of confidence intervals with one or two covariates, but performance deteriorates quickly after that. The output of the nonparametric estimator is a treatment effect for an arbitrary x. The estimates generally must be further summarized or visualized since the model produces a distinct prediction for each x.

A key problem with kernels and nearest neighbor matching is that all covariates are treated symmetrically; if one unit is close to another in 20 dimensions, the units are probably not particularly similar in any given dimension. We would ideally like to prioritize dimensions that are most important for heterogeneous treatment effects, as is done in many machine learning methods, including the highly successful random forest algorithm. Unfortunately, many popular machine learning methods that use the data to select covariates may be bias-dominated asymptotically (including the standard random forest). Recently, Wager and Athey (2015) propose a modified version of the random forest algorithm that produces treatment effect estimates that can be shown to be asymptotically normal and centered on the true value of the treatment effect, and they propose a consistent estimator for the asymptotic variance. The method averages over many "trees" of the form developed in Athey and Imbens (2016); the trees differ from one another because different subsamples are used for each tree, and in addition, there is some randomization in the choice of which covariates to split on. Each tree is "honest," in that, one subsample is used to determine a partition and an independent subsample is used to estimate treatment effects within the leaves. Unlike the case of a single tree, no data are "wasted" because each observation is used to determine the partition in some trees and used to estimate treatment effects in other trees, and subsampling is already an inherent part of the method. The method can be understood as a generalization of kernels and nearest neighbor-matching methods, in that the estimated treatment effect at x is the difference between a weighted average of nearby treated units and nearby control units; but the choice of what dimensions are important for measuring distance is determined by the data. In simulations, this method can obtain nominal coverage with more covariates than K-nearest neighbor matching or kernel methods, while simultaneously producing much more accurate estimates of treatment effects. However, this method also eventually becomes bias-dominated when the number of covariates grows. It is much more robust to irrelevant covariates than kernels or nearest neighbor matching.

Another approach to the problem is to divide the training data by treatment status, and apply supervised learning methods to each group separately. For example, Foster et al. (2011) use random forests to estimate the effect of covariates on outcomes in treated and control groups. They then take the difference in predictions as data and project treatment effects onto units' attributes using regression or classification trees. The approach of Wager and Athey (2015) can potentially gain efficiency by directly estimating heterogeneity in causal effects, and further the off-the-shelf random forest estimator does not have established statistical properties (so confidence intervals are not available).

Taking the Bayesian perspective, Green and Kern (2012) and Hill (2011) have proposed the use of forest-based algorithms for estimating heterogeneous treatment effects. These papers use the Bayesian additive regression tree method of Chipman et al. (2010), and report posterior credible intervals obtained by Markov chain Monte Carlo (MCMC) sampling based on a convenience prior. Although Bayesian regression trees are often successful in practice, there are currently no results guaranteeing posterior concentration around the true conditional mean function, or convergence of the MCMC sampler in polynomial time. In a related paper, Taddy et al. (2015) use Bayesian nonparametric methods with Dirichlet priors to flexibly estimate the data-generating process, and then project the estimates of heterogeneous treatment effects down onto the feature space using regularization methods or regression trees to get low-dimensional summaries of the heterogeneity; but again, asymptotic properties are unknown.

10.3.3 Treatment effect heterogeneity using regularized regression

Imai and Ratkovic (2013), Signovitch (2007), Tian et al. (2014), and Weisburg and Pontes (2015) develop lasso-like methods for causal inference and treatment effect heterogeneity in a setting where there are potentially a large number of covariates, so that regularization methods are used to discover which covariates are important. When the treatment effect interactions of interest have low dimension (that is, a small number of covariates have important interactions with the treatment), valid confidence intervals can be derived (without using sample splitting as described above); see, e.g., Chernozhukov et al. (2015) and references therein. These methods require that the true underlying model is (at least approximately) "sparse": the number of observations must be large relative to the number of covariates (and their interactions) that have an important effect on the outcome and on treatment effect heterogeneity. Some of the methods (e.g., Tian et al., 2014) propose modeling heterogeneity in the treatment and control groups separately, and then taking the difference; this can be inefficient if the covariates that affect the level of outcomes are distinct from those that affect treatment effect heterogeneity. An alternative approach is to incorporate interactions of the treatment with covariates as covariates, and then allow LASSO to select which covariates are important. Interaction terms can be prioritized over terms that do not include treatment effect interactions through weighting.

10.3.4 Comparison of methods

Although the LASSO-based methods require more a-priori restrictions on sparsity than the random forest methods, both types of methods will lose nominal coverage rates if the models become too complex. The LASSO methods have some advantages with datasets where there are linear or polynomial relationships between covariates and outcomes; random forest methods do not parsimoniously estimate linear relationships and use them for extrapolation, but are more localized. The random forest methods are well designed to capture complex, multidimensional interactions among covariates, or highly nonlinear interactions. LASSO has the advantage that the final output is a regression, which may be more familiar to researchers in some disciplines; however, it is important to remember that the conditions the justify the standard errors are much more stringent when the model selection was carried out on the same data that are used for estimation. If valid confidence intervals are the first priority in an environment where the model is not known to be sparse and there are many covariates, the recursive partitioning approach provides confidence intervals that do not deteriorate (at all) as the number of covariates grow. What suffers, instead, is the mean-squared error of the predictions of treatment effects.

Another point of comparison between the regression-based methods and tree-based methods (including random forests) relates to our earlier discussions of randomization-based inference versus sampling-based inference. Tree-based methods construct estimates by dividing the sample into subgroups and calculating sample averages within the groups; thus, the estimates and associated inference can be justified by random assignment of the treatment. In contrast, regression-based approaches require additional assumptions.

10.3.5 Relationship to optimal policy estimation

The problem of estimating heterogeneous treatment effects is closely related to the problem of estimating, as a function of the covariates, what the optimal policy is. Heuristically, with a binary treatment, we would want to assign an individual with covariates x to a treatment if $\tau(x) > 0$. However, the optimal policy literature addresses additional issues that might arise when there are multiple potential treatments, as well as when the loss function may be nonlinear (so that there is, for example, a mean-variance tradeoff between different policies). More broadly, the criterion used in estimation may be modified to account for the goal of policy estimation; when regularization approaches are used to penalize model complexity, the methods may deprioritize discovering heterogeneity that is not relevant for selecting an optimal policy. For example, if a treatment clearly dominates another for some parts of the covariate space, understanding heterogeneity in the magnitude of the treatment's advantage may not be important in those regions.

Much of the policy estimation literature takes a Bayesian perspective; this allows the researcher to evaluate welfare and to incorporate risk aversion in the loss function in an environment where there is uncertainty about the effects of the policy.

In the machine learning literature, Beygelzimer and Langford (2009) and Dudik et al. (2011) discuss procedures for transforming outcomes that enable off-the-shelf loss minimization methods to be used for optimal treatment policy estimation. In the econometrics literature, Graham et al. (2014), Dehejia (2005), Hirano and Porter (2009), Manski (2003a,b), and Bhattacharya and Dupas (2012) estimate parametric or semiparametric models for optimal policies, relying on regularization for covariate selection in the case of Bhattacharya and Dupas (2012). See also Banerjee et al. (2016).

11. EXPERIMENTS IN SETTINGS WITH INTERACTIONS

In this section, we discuss the analysis of randomized experiments in settings with interference between units. Such interference may take different forms. There may be spillovers from the treatment assigned to one unit to other units. A classic example of that is that of agricultural experiments where fertilizer applied to one plot of land may leach over to other plots and thus affect outcomes in plots assigned to different treatments. It may also take the form of active and deliberate interactions between individuals, for example in educational settings, where exposing one student to a new program may well affect the outcomes for students the first student is friends with.

There are many different versions of these problems, and many different estimands. An important theoretical paper in an observational setting is Manski (1993) who introduced terminology to distinguish among contextual effects, exogenous effects, and endogenous effects. Contextual effects arise when individuals are exposed to similar environmental stimula as their peers. Exogenous effects refer to effects from fixed characteristics of an individual's peers. Endogenous effects in Manski's terminology refer to direct causal effects of the behavior of the peers of an individual.

The interactions may be a nuisance that affects the ability to do inference, with the interest in the overall average effect, or the interactions may be of primary interest to the researcher. This is an active area of research, with many different approaches, where it not clear what will ultimately be the most useful results for empirical work. In fact, some of the most interesting work has been empirical.

11.1 Empirical work on interactions

Here, we discuss some of the questions raised in empirical work on interactions. These provide some of the background for the discussions of the theoretical work by suggesting particular questions and settings where these questions are of interest. There are a number of different settings. In some cases the peer group composition is randomized, and in other cases treatments are randomized. An example of the first case is Sacerdote (2001) where individual students are randomly assigned to dorm rooms and thus matched to a roommate. An example of the second is Duflo and Saez (2003) where individuals in possibly endogenously formed groups are randomly assigned to treatments, with the treatments clustered at the group level.

Miguel and Kremer (2004) were interested in the effects of deworming programs on children's educational outcomes. There are obviously direct effects of deworming on the outcomes for individuals who are exposed to these programs, but just as in the case of infectious diseases in general, there may be externalities for individuals not exposed to the program if individuals they interact with are exposed. Miguel and Kremer find evidence of substantial externalities.

Crepon et al. (2013) were interested in the effects of labor market-training programs. They were concerned about interactions between individuals through the labor market. Part of the effect of providing training to an unemployed individual may be that this individual becomes more attractive to an employer relative to an untrained individual. If, however, the total number of vacancies is not affected by the presence of more trained individuals, the overall effect may be zero even if the trained individuals are more likely to be employed than the individuals in the control group. Crépon et al. studied this by randomizing individuals to training programs in a number of labor markets. They varied the marginal rate at which the individuals were assigned to the training program between the labor markets. They then compared the difference in average outcomes by treatment status within the labor markets, across the different labor markets. In the absence of interactions, here in the form of equilibrium effects, the average treatment effects should not vary by the marginal treatment rate. Evidence that the average treatment effects were higher when the marginal treatment rate was lower suggests that part of the treatment effect was based on redistributing jobs from control individuals to trained individuals.

Sacerdote (2001) studies the effect of roommates on an individual's behavior in college. He exploits the random assignment of incoming students to dorm rooms at Dartmouth (after taking account of some characteristics such as smoking behavior). The treatment can be thought of here as having a roommate of a particular type, such as a roommate with a relatively high or low level of high school achievement. If roommates are randomly assigned, then finding that individuals with high achieving roommates have outcomes that are systematically different from those of individuals with low achieving roommates is evidence of causal interactions between the roommates.

Carrell et al. (2013) analyze data from the US Air Force Academy. They control the assignment of incoming students to squadrons to manipulate the distribution of characteristics of fellow squadron students that an incoming student is faced with. They find that the outcomes for students vary systematically with this distribution of fellow student characteristics, which is evidence of causal effects of interactions.

11.2 The analysis of randomized experiments with interactions in subpopulations

One important special case of interference assumes the population can be partitioned into groups or clusters, with the interactions limited to units within the same cluster. This is a case studied by, among others, Manski (2013), Hudgens and Halloran (2008), and Liu and Hudgens (2013). Ugander et al. (2013) discuss graph cutting methods in general network settings to generate partitions of the basic network where such an assumption holds, at least approximately. Hudgens and Halloran define in this setting direct, indirect, total, and overall causal effects, and consider a two-stage randomized design where in the first stage clusters are selected randomly and in the second stage units within the clusters are randomly assigned. The direct causal effect for a particular unit corresponds to the difference between potential outcomes where only the treatment effect for that unit is changed, and all other treatments are kept fixed. Indirect effects correspond to causal effects of changes in the assignments for other units in the same group, keeping fixed the own assignment. The total effect combines the direct and indirect effects. Finally, the overall effect in the Hudgens and Halloran framework is the average effect for a cluster or group, compared to the baseline where the entire group receives the control treatment.

Hudgens and Halloran also stress the widely used assumption that for unit i it matters only what fraction of the other units in their group are treated, not the identity of the treated units. Without such an assumption the proliferation of indirect treatment effects makes it difficult to obtain unbiased estimators for any of them. This assumption is often made, sometimes implicitly, in empirical work in this area.

They consider designs where the marginal rate of treatment varies across groups. In the first stage of the assignment the groups are randomly assigned to different treatment rates, followed by a stage in which the units are randomly assigned to the treatment.

11.3 The analysis of randomized experiments with interactions in networks

Here, we look at a general network setting where the population of units is not necessarily partitioned into mutually exclusive groups. With N individuals in the population of interest, we have a network characterized by an $N \times N$ adjacency matrix G, with $G_{ij} \in \{0, 1\}$ a binary indicator for the event that units i and j are connected. The matrix

G is symmetric with all diagonal elements equal to zero. The question here is what we can learn about presence of interaction effects by conducting a randomized experiment on this single network, with a binary treatment. Unlike the Manski (1993) and Hudgens and Halloran (2008) setting, we have only a single network, but the network is richer in the sense that it need not be the case that friends of friends are also friends themselves. The types of questions Athey et al. (2015) are interested in are, for example, whether there is evidence that changing the treatment for friends affects an individual's outcome, or whether manipulating treatments for friends of an individual's friends changes their outcome. They do so by focusing on exact tests to avoid the reliance on large sample approximations, which can be difficult to derive in settings with a single network. (There is not even a clear answer to the question of what it means for a network to grow in size; specifying this would require the researcher to specify what it means for the network to grow, in terms of new links for new units.)

Let us focus in this discussion on the two main hypotheses Athey et al. (2015) consider. First, the null hypothesis of no interactions whatsoever, that is the null hypothesis that changing the treatment status for friends does not change an individual's outcome, also considered in Aronow (2012), and second, the null hypothesis that the treatment of a friend of a friend does not have a causal effect on an individual's outcome. Like Liu and Hudgens (2013) and Athey et al. (2015), they consider randomization inference.

We focus on the setting where in the population treatments are completely randomly assigned. The network itself is analyzed as given. Initially let us focus on the null hypothesis of no interactions whatsoever. Athey et al. (2015) introduce the notion of an artificial experiment. The idea is to select a number of units from the original population, whom they call the focal units. Given these focal units, they define a test statistic in terms of the outcomes for these focal units, say the correlation between outcomes and the fraction of treated friends. They look at the distribution of this statistic, induced by randomizing the treatments only for the nonfocal or auxiliary units. Under the null hypothesis of no treatment effects whatsoever, changing the treatment status for auxiliary units would not change the value of the outcomes for the focal units.

For the second null hypothesis, that friends of friends have no effect, they again consider a subset of the units to be focal. A second subset of units are termed "buffer" units: these are the friends of the focal unit. If we allow that friends can have an impact on focal units, then their treatments cannot be randomized in the artificial experiment designed to test the impact of friends of friends. The complement of focal and buffer units, termed the auxiliary units, are the units whose treatments are randomized in the artificial experiment. The randomization distribution over the treatment assignments of auxiliary units induces a distribution on the test statistic, and this approach thus enables the researcher to test the hypothesis that friends of friends have no effect, without placing any restrictions on direct effects or the effect of friends.

Athey et al. (2015) also consider richer hypotheses, such as hypotheses about what types of link definitions correspond to meaningful peer effects; they propose a test of the hypothesis that a sparser definition of the network is sufficient to capture relationships for which treating a friend influences a unit.

Aronow and Samii (2013) study estimation in this general network setting. They assume that there is a structure on the treatment effects so that only a limited number of unit-level treatment assignments have a nonzero causal effect on the outcome for unit i. The group structure that Hudgens and Halloran (2008) use is a special case where it is only the treatments for units in the same group as unit i can have nonzero effects on the outcome for unit i.

12. CONCLUSION

In this chapter, we discuss statistical methods for analyzing data from randomized experiments. We focus primarily on randomization-based, rather than model-based methods, starting with classic methods developed by Fisher and Neyman, up to recent work on noncompliance, clustering and methods for identifying treatment effect heterogeneity, as well as experiments in settings with interference.

REFERENCES

Abadie, A., Angrist, J., Imbens, G., 2002. Instrumental variables estimates of the effect of subsidized training on the quantiles of trainee earnings. Econometrica 70 (1), 91−117.

Abadie, A., Athey, S., Imbens, G., Wooldridge, J., 2014. Finite Population Causal Standard Errors. NBER working paper 20325.

Abadie, A., Athey, S., Imbens, G., Wooldridge, J., 2016. Clustering as a Design Problem. Unpublished working paper.

Allcott, H., 2015. Site selection bias in program evaluation. Q. J. Econ. 1117−1165.

Altman, D., 1991. Practical Statistics for Medical Research. Chapman and Hall/CRC.

Angrist, J., 2004. Treatment effect heterogeneity in theory and practice. Econ. J. 114 (494), C52−C83.

Angrist, J., Kuersteiner, G., 2011. Causal effects of monetary shocks: semiparametric conditional independence tests with a multinomial propensity score. Rev. Econ. Stat. 93 (3), 725−747.

Angrist, J., Pischke, S., 2009. Mostly Harmless Econometrics. Princeton University Press, Princeton, NJ.

Angrist, J., Imbens, G., Rubin, D., 1996. Identification of causal effects using instrumental variables. J. Am. Stat. Assoc. 91, 444−472.

Aronow, P., 2012. A general method for detecting interference between units in randomized experiments. Sociol. Methods Res. 41 (1), 3−16.

Aronow, P., Samii, C., 2013. Estimating Average Causal Effects under Interference between Units. arXiv: 1305.6156(v1).

Athey, S., Eckles, D., Imbens, G., 2015. Exact P-values for Network Interference. NBER working paper 21313.

Athey, S., Imbens, G., 2016. Recursive partitioning for heterogeneous causal effects. arXiv:1504.01132 Proc. Nat. Acad. Sci. U.S.A. (Forthcoming).

Baker, S., 2000. Analyzing a randomized cancer prevention trial with a missing binary outcome, an auxiliary variable, and all-or-none compliance. J. Am. Stat. Assoc. 95 (449), 43−50.

Baker, S.G., Kramer, B.S., Lindeman, K.S., 2016. Latent class instrumental variables: a clinical and biostatistical perspective. Stat. Med. 35 (1), 147−160.

Baker, S.G., Lindeman, K.S., 1994. The paired availability design: a proposal for evaluating epidural analgesia during labor. Stat. Med. 13, 2269–2278.

Balke, A., Pearl, J., 1997. Bounds on treatment effects from studies with imperfect compliance. J. Am. Stat. Assoc. 92 (439), 1171–1176.

Banerjee, A., Chassang, S., Snowberg, E., 2016. Decision theoretic approaches to experimental design and external validity. In: Banerjee, Duflo (Eds.), Handbook of Development Economics. Elsevier, North Holland.

Banerjee, A., Duflo, E., 2009. The experimental approach to development economics. Annu. Rev. Econ. 1, 151–178.

Bareinboim, E., Lee, S., Honavar, V., Pearl, J., 2013. Causal transportability from multiple environments with limited experiments. Adv. Neural Inf. Process. Syst. 26 (NIPS Proceedings), 136–144.

Barnard, J., Du, J., Hill, J., Rubin, D., 1998. A broader template for analyzing broken randomized experiments. Sociol. Methods Res. 27, 285–317.

Benjamini, Y., Hochberg, Y., 1995. Controlling the false discovery rate: a practical and powerful approach to multiple testing. J. R. Stat. Soc. Series B (Methodological), 289–300.

Bertanha, M., Imbens, G., 2014. External Validity in Fuzzy Regression Discontinuity Designs. NBER working paper 20773.

Bertrand, M., Duflo, E., 2016. Field Experiments on Discrimination. NBER working paper 22014.

Beygelzimer, A., Langford, J., 2009. The Offset Tree for Learning with Partial Labels. http://arxiv.org/pdf/0812.4044v2.pdf.

Bhattacharya, D., Dupas, P., 2012. Inferring welfare maximizing treatment assignment under budget constraints. J. Econ. 167 (1), 168–196.

Bitler, M., Gelbach, J., Hoynes, H., 2002. What mean impacts miss: distributional effects of welfare reform experiments. Am. Econ. Rev. 96 (4), 988–1012.

Bloniarz, A., Liu, H., Zhang, C.H., Sekhon, J.S., Yu, B., 2015. Lasso adjustments of treatment effect estimates in randomized experiments. arXiv preprint arXiv:1507.03652.

Bloom, H., 1984. Accounting for no-shows in experimental evaluation designs. Eval. Rev. 8, 225–246.

Box, G., Hunter, S., Hunter, W., 2005. Statistics for Experimenters: Design, Innovation and Discovery. Wiley, New Jersey (Chapter 4 and 9).

Bruhn, M., McKenzie, D., 2009. In pursuit of balance: randomization in practice in development field experiments. Am. Econ. J. Appl. Econ. 1 (4), 200–232.

Carrell, S., Sacerdote, B., West, J., 2013. From natural variation to optimal policy? The importance of endogenous peer group formation. Econometrica 81 (3), 855–882.

Casey, K., Glennerster, R., Miguel, E., 2012. Reshaping institutions: evidence on aid impacts using a pre-analysis plan. Q. J. Econ. 1755–1812.

Chernozhukov, V., Hansen, C., 2005. An IV model of quantile treatment effects. Econometrica 73 (1), 245–261.

Chernozhukov, V., Hansen, C., Spindler, M., 2015. Post-selection and post-regularization inference in linear models with many controls and instruments. Am. Econ. Rev. 105 (5), 486–490.

Chipman, H., George, E., McCulloch, R., 2010. BART: Bayesian additive regression trees. Ann. Appl. Stat. 4 (1), 266–298.

Cochran, W., 1972. Observational studies. In: Bancroft, T.A. (Ed.), Statistical Papers in Honor of George W. Snedecor. Iowa State University Press, pp. 77–90. Reprinted in *Observational Studies*, 2015.

Cochran, W., Cox, G., 1957. Experimental Design, Wiley Classics Library.

Cohen, J., 1988. Statistical Power for the Behavioral Sciences, second ed.

Cook, T., DeMets, D., 2008. Introduction to Statistical Methods for Clinical Trials. Chapman and Hall/CRC.

Cox, D., 1956. A note on weighted randomization. Ann. Math. Stat. 27 (4), 1144–1151.

Cox, D., 1975. A note on data-splitting for the evaluation of significance levels. Biometrika 62 (2), 441–444.

Cox, D., 1992. Causality: some statistical aspects. J. R. Stat. Soc. Ser. A 155, 291–301.

Cox, D., Reid, N., 2000. The Theory of the Design of Experiments. Chapman and Hall/CRC, Boca Raton, Florida.

Crepon, B., Duflo, E., Gurgand, M., Rathelot, R., Zamora, P., April 24, 2013. Do labor market policies have displacement effects? Evidence from a clustered randomized experiment. Q. J. Econ. 128 (2), 531–580.

Crump, R., Hotz, V.J., Imbens, G., Mitnik, O., 2008. Nonparametric tests for treatment effect heterogeneity. Rev. Econ. Stat. 90 (3), 389–405.

Cuzick, J., Edwards, R., Segnan, N., 1997. Adjusting for non-compliance and contamination in randomized clinical trials. Stat. Med. 16, 1017–1039.

Davies, O., 1954. The Design and Analysis of Industrial Experiments. Oliver and Boyd, Edinburgh.

Deaton, A., 2010. Instruments, randomization, and learning about development. J. Econ. Lit. 424–455.

Dehejia, R., 2005. Program evaluation as a decision problem. J. Econ. 125 (1), 141–173.

Dehejia, R., Wahba, S., 1999. Causal effects in nonexperimental studies: reevaluating the evaluation of training programs. J. Am. Stat. Assoc. 94, 1053–1062 (Chapters 8,11,16 and 17).

Donner, A., 1987. Statistical methodology for paired cluster designs. Am. J. Epidemiol. 126 (5), 972–979.

Doksum, K., 1974. Empirical probability plots and statistical inference for nonlinear models in the two-sample case. Ann. Stat. 2, 267–277.

Dudik, M., Langford, J., Li, L., 2011. Doubly robust policy evaluation and learning. In: Proceedings of the 28th International Conference on Machine Learning (ICML-11).

Duflo, E., Glennerster, R., Kremer, M., 2006. Using randomization in development economics research: a toolkit. In: Handbook of Development Economics. Elsevier.

Duflo, E., Hanna, R., Ryan, S., 2012. Incentives work: getting teachers to come to school. Am. Econ. Rev. 102 (4), 1241–1278.

Duflo, E., Saez, E., 2003. The role of information and social interactions in retirement decisions: evidence from a randomized experiment. Q. J. Econ. 815–842.

Eckles, D., Karrer, B., Ugander, J., 2014. Design and Analysis of Experiments in Networks: Reducing Bias from Interference (Unpublished working paper).

Eicker, F., 1967. Limit theorems for regression with unequal and dependent errors. In: Proceedings of the Fifth Berkeley Symposium on Mathematical Statistics and Probability, vol. 1. University of California Press, Berkeley, pp. 59–82.

Firpo, S., 2007. Efficient semiparametric estimation of quantile treatment effects. Econometrica 75 (1), 259–276.

Fisher, R.A., 1925. Statistical Methods for Research Workers, first ed. Oliver and Boyd, London.

Fisher, R.A., 1935. Design of Experiments. Oliver and Boyd.

Fisher, L., et al., 1990. Intention-to-treat in clinical trials. In: Peace, K.E. (Ed.), Statistical Issues in Drug Research and Development. Marcel Dekker, New York.

Fithian, W., Sun, C., Taylor, J., 2015. Optimal Inference after Model Selection. http://arxiv.org/abs/1410.2597.

Foster, J., Taylor, J., Ruberg, S., 2011. Subgroup identification from randomized clinical trial data. Stat. Med. 30 (24), 2867–2880.

Frangakis, C., Rubin, D., 2002. Principal stratification. Biometrics (1), 21–29.

Freedman, D., 2006. Statistical models for causality: what leverage do they provide. Eval. Rev. 30, 691–713.

Freedman, D., 2008. On regression adjustments to experimental data. Adv. Appl. Math. 30 (6), 180–193.

Gail, M., Tian, W., Piantadosi, S., 1988. Tests for no treatment effect in randomized clinical trials. Biometrika 75 (3), 57–64.

Gail, M., Mark, S., Carroll, R., Green, S., Pee, D., 1996. On design considerations and randomization-based inference for community intervention trials. Stat. Med. 15, 1069–1092.

Glennerster, R., 2016. The practicalities of running randomized evaluations: partnerships, measurement, ethics, and transparency. In: Banerjee, Duflo (Eds.), Handbook of Development Economics. Elsevier, North Holland.

Glennerster, R., Takavarasha, K., 2013. Running Randomized Evaluations: A Practical Guide. Princeton University Press.

Graham, B., Imbens, G., Ridder, G., 2014. Complementarity and aggregate implications of assortative matching: a nonparametric analysis. Quant. Econ. 5 (1), 29–66.

Green, D., Kern, H., 2012. Detecting heterogeneous treatment effects in large-scale experiments using Bayesian additive regression trees. Public Opin. Q. 76 (3), 491–511.

Härdle, W., 2002. Applied Nonparametric Regression Analysis. Cambridge University Press.

Hausman, J.A., 1983. Specification and estimation of simultaneous equation models. Handbook Econ 1, 391–448.

Hill, J., 2011. Bayesian nonparametric modeling for causal inference. J. Comput. Graph. Stat. 20 (1).

Hinkelmann, K., Kempthorne, O., 2008. Design and analysis of experiments. In: Introduction to Experimental Design, vol. 1. Wiley.

Hinkelmann, K., Kempthorne, O., 2005. Design and analysis of experiments. In: Advance Experimental Design, vol. 2. Wiley.

Hirano, K., Imbens, G., Rubin, D., Zhou, A., 2000. Estimating the effect of flu shots in a randomized encouragement design. Biostatistics 1 (1), 69–88.

Hirano, K., Porter, J., 2009. Asymptotics for statistical treatment rules. Econometrica 77 (5), 1683–1701.

Hodges, J.L., Lehmann, E., 1970. Basic Concepts of Probability and Statistics, second ed. Holden-Day, San Francisco.

Holland, P., 1986. Statistics and causal inference. J. Am. Stat. Assoc. 81, 945–970 with discussion.

Hotz, J., Imbens, G., Mortimer, J., 2005. Predicting the efficacy of future training programs using past experiences. J. Econ. 125, 241–270.

Huber, P., 1967. The behavior of maximum likelihood estimates under nonstandard conditions. In: Proceedings of the Fifth Berkeley Symposium on Mathematical Statistics and Probability, vol. 1. University of California Press, Berkeley, pp. 221–233.

Hudgens, M., Halloran, M., 2008. Toward causal inference with interference. J. Am. Stat. Assoc. 103 (482), 832–842.

Imai, K., Ratkovic, M., 2013. Estimating treatment effect heterogeneity in randomized program evaluation. Ann. Appl. Stat. 7 (1), 443–470.

Imbens, G., 2010. Better LATE than nothing: some comments on Deaton (2009) and Heckman and Urzua (2009). J. Econ. Lit. 399–423.

Imbens, G., Angrist, J., 1994. Identification and estimation of local average treatment effects. Econometrica 61 (2), 467–476.

Imbens, G.W., Kolesár, M., 2016. Robust standard errors in small samples: some practical advice full access. Rev. Econ. Stat. 98 (4), 701–712.

Imbens, G., Rosenbaum, P., 2005. Randomization inference with an instrumental variable. J. R. Stat. Soc. Ser. A 168 (1), 109–126.

Imbens, G., Rubin, D., 1997. Estimating outcome distributions for compliers in instrumental variable models. Rev. Econ. Stud. 64 (3), 555–574.

Imbens, G., Rubin, D., 1997. Bayesian inference for causal effects in randomized experiments with noncompliance. Ann. Stat. 25 (1), 305–327.

Imbens, G., Rubin, D., 2015. Causal Inference in Statistics, Social, and Biomedical Sciences: An Introduction. Cambridge University Press.

Kagel, J.H., Roth, A.E., Hey, J.D., 1995. The Handbook of Experimental Economics. Princeton university press, Princeton.

Kempthorne, O., 1952. The Design and Analysis of Experiments. Robert Krieger Publishing Company, Malabar, Florida.

Kempthorne, O., 1955. The randomization theory of experimental inference. J. Am. Stat. Assoc. 50, 946–967.

Lalonde, R.J., 1986. Evaluating the econometric evaluations of training programs with experimental data. Am. Econ. Rev. 76, 604–620.

Lee, M.-J., 2005. Micro-econometrics for Policy, Program, and Treatment Effects. Oxford University Press, Oxford.

Lehman, E., 1974. Nonparametrics: Statistical Methods Based on Ranks. Holden-Day, San Francisco.

Lesaffre, E., Senn, S., 2003. A note on non-parametric ANCOVA for covariate adjustment in randomized clinical trials. Stat. Med. 22, 3583–3596.

Liang, K., Zeger, S., 1986. Longitudinal data analysis using generalized linear models. Biometrika 73 (1), 13–22.

Lin, W., 2013. Agnostic notes on regression adjustments for experimental data: reexamining Freedman's critique. Ann. Appl. Stat. 7 (1), 295–318.

List, J., Shaikh, A., Xu, Y., 2016. Multiple Hypothesis Testing in Experimental Economics. NBER working paper no. 21875.

Liu, L., Hudgens, M., 2013. Large sample randomization inference of causal effects in the presence of interference. J. Am. Stat. Assoc. 288–301.

Lui, K., 2011. Binary Data Analysis of Randomized Clinical Trials with Noncompliance. Wiley. Statistics in Practice.

Lynn, H., McCulloch, C., 1992. When does it pay to break the matches for analysis of a matched-pair design. Biometrics 48, 397–409.

Manning, W., Newhouse, J., Duan, N., Keeler, E., Leibowitz, A., 1987. Health insurance and the demand for medical care: evidence from a randomized experiment. Am. Econ. Rev. 77 (3), 251–277.

Manski, C., 1990. Nonparametric bounds on treatment effects. Am. Econ. Rev. Pap. Proc. 80, 319–323.

Manski, C., 1993. Identification of endogenous ocial effects: the reflection problem. Rev. Econ. Stud. 60 (3), 531–542.

Manski, C., 1996. Learning about treatment effects from experiments with random assignment of treatments. J. Hum. Resour. 31 (4), 709–773.

Manski, C., 2003a. Partial Identification of Probability Distributions. Springer-Verlag, New York.

Manski, C., 2003b. Statistical treatment rules for heterogeneous populations. Econometrica 72 (4), 1221–1246.

Manski, C., 2013. Public Policy in an Uncertain World. Harvard University Press, Cambridge.

Meager, R., 2015. Understanding the Impact of Microcredit Expansions: A Bayesian Hierarchical Analysis of 7 Randomised Experiments. MIT, Department of Economics.

McNamee, R., 2009. Intention to treat, per protocol, as treated and instrumental variable estimators given non-compliance and effect heterogeneity. Stat. Med. 28, 2639–2652.

Miguel, T., Kremer, M., 2004. Worms: identifying impacts on education and health in the presence of treatment externalities. Econometrica 72 (1), 159–217.

Morgan, K., Rubin, D., 2012. Rerandomization to improve covariate balance in experiments. Ann. Stat. 40 (2), 1263–1282.

Morgan, S., Winship, C., 2007. Counterfactuals and Causal Inference. Cambridge University Press, Cambridge.

Morton, R., Williams, K., 2010. Experimental Political Science and the Study of Causality. Cambridge University Press, Cambridge, MA.

Murphy, K., Myors, B., Wollach, A., 2014. Statistical Power Analysis. Routledge.

Murray, B., 2012. Clustering: A Data Recovery Approach, second ed. Chapman and Hall.

Neyman, J., 1923, 1990. On the application of probability theory to agricultural experiments. Essay on principles. Section 9. translated in Stat. Sci. 5 (4), 465–480 (with discussion).

Neyman, J., Iwaskiewicz, K., Kolodziejczyk, St, 1935. Statistical problems in agricultural experimentation. J. R. Stat. Soc. Ser. B 2, 107–180 (with discussion).

Olken, B., 2015. Promises and perils of pre-analysis plans. J. Econ. Perspect. 29 (3), 61–80.

Pearl, J., 2000, 2009. Causality: Models, Reasoning and Inference. Cambridge University Press, Cambridge.

Robins, P., 1985. A comparison of the labor supply findings from the four negative income tax experiments. J. Hum. Resour. 20 (4), 567–582.

Romano, J., Shaikh, A., Wolf, M., 2010. Hypothesis testing in econometrics. Annu. Rev. Econ. 2, 75–104.

Romer, C.D., Romer, D.H., 2004. A new measure of monetary shocks: derivation and implications. Am. Econ. Rev. 94 (4), 1055–1084.

Rosenbaum, P., 2009. Design of Observational Studies. Springer Verlag, New York.

Rosenbaum, P., 1995, 2002. Observational Studies. Springer Verlag, New York.

Rosenbaum, P., 2002. Covariance adjustment in randomized experiments and observational studies. Stat. Sci. 17 (3), 286–304.

Rothstein, J., von Wachter, T., 2016. Social experiments in the labor market. In: Handbook of Experimental Economics.

Rubin, D., 1974. Estimating causal effects of treatments in randomized and non-randomized studies. J. Educ. Psychol. 66, 688–701.

Rubin, D., 1975. Bayesian inference for causality: the importance of randomization. In: Proceedings of the Social Statistics Section of the American Statistical Association, pp. 233–239.

Rubin, D.B., 1978. Bayesian inference for causal effects: the role of randomization. Ann. Stat. 6, 34–58.

Rubin, D., 2006. Matched Sampling for Causal Effects. Cambridge University Press, Cambridge.

Rubin, D., 2007. The design versus the analysis of observational studies for causal effects: parallels with the design of randomized trials. Stat. Med. 26 (1), 20–30.

Samii, C., Aronow, P., 2012. On equivalencies between design-based and regression-based variance estimators for randomized experiments. Stat. Probab. Lett. 82, 365–370.

Sacerdote, B., 2001. Peer effects with random assignment: results for Dartmouth roommates. Q. J. Econ. 116 (2), 681–704.

Schochet, P., 2010. Is regression adjustment supported by the Neyman model for causal inference? J. Stat. Plan. Inference 140, 246–259.

Senn, S., 1994. Testing for baseline balance in clinical trials. Stat. Med. 13, 1715–1726.

Shadish, W., Cook, T., Campbell, D., 2002. Experimental and Quasi-experimental Designs for Generalized Causal Inference. Houghton Mifflin.

Signovitch, J., 2007. Identifying Informative Biological Markers in High-dimensional Genomic Data and Clinical Trials (Ph.D. thesis). Department of Biostatistics, Harvard University.

Snedecor, G., Cochran, W., 1967. Statistical Methods. Iowa State University Press, Ames, Iowa.

Snedecor, G., Cochran, W., 1989. Statistical Methods. Iowa State University Press, Ames, Iowa.

Su, X., Tsai, C., Wang, H., Nickerson, D., Li, B., 2009. Subgroup analysis via recursive partitioning. J. Mach. Learn. Res. 10, 141–158.

Taddy, M., Gardner, M., Chen, L., Draper, D., 2015. Heterogeneous Treatment Effects in Digital Experimentation. Unpublished manuscript, arXiv:1412.8563.

Tian, L., Alizadeh, A., Gentles, A., Tibshirani, R., 2014. A simple method for estimating interactions between a treatment and a large number of covariates. J. Am. Stat. Assoc. 109 (508), 1517–1532.

Ugander, J., Karrer, B., Backstrom, L., Kleinberg, J., 2013. Graph cluster randomization: network exposure to multiple universes. In: Proceedings of KDD. ACM.

Wager, S., Athey, S., 2015. Estimation and Inference of Heterogeneous Treatment Effects using Random Forests. arxiv.org:1510.04342.

Wager, S., Walther, G., 2015. Uniform Convergence of Random Forests via Adaptive Concentration. arXiv:1503.06388.

Wager, S., Du, W., Taylor, J., Tibshirani, R.J., 2016. High-dimensional regression adjustments in randomized experiments. Proc. Nat. Acad. Sci. 113 (45), 12673–12678.

Weisburg, H., Pontes, V., June 2015. Post hoc subgroups in clinical trials: anathema or analytics? Clin. Trials.

White, H., 1980. A heteroskedasticity-consistent covariance matrix estimator and a direct test for heteroskedasticity. Econometrica 48, 817–838.

Wu, J., Hamada, M., 2009. Experiments, Planning, Analysis and Optimization, Wiley Series in Probability and Statistics.

Young, A., 2016. Channelling Fisher: Randomization Tests and the Statistical Insignificance of Seemingly Significant Experimental Results. London School of Economics.

Zeileis, A., Hothorn, T., Hornik, K., 2008. Model-based recursive partitioning. J. Comput. Graph. Stat. 17 (2), 492–514.

Zelen, M., 1979. A new design for randomized clinical trials. N. Engl. J. Med. 300, 1242–1245.

Zelen, M., 1990. Randomized consent designs for clinical trials: an update. Stat. Med. 9, 645–656.

CHAPTER 4

Decision Theoretic Approaches to Experiment Design and External Validity[a]

A.V. Banerjee[*,||], S. Chassang[§,1], E. Snowberg[¶,||]
*Massachusetts Institute of Technology, Cambridge, MA, United States
§New York University, New York, NY, United States
¶California Institute of Technology, Pasadena, CA, United States
||NBER (National Bureau of Economic Research), Cambridge, MA, United States
[1]Corresponding author: E-mail: chassang@nyu.edu

Contents

[a] We thank Esther Duflo for her leadership on the handbook and for extensive comments on earlier drafts. Chassang and Snowberg gratefully acknowledge the support of NSF grant SES-1156154.

Abstract

A modern, decision-theoretic framework can help clarify important practical questions of experimental design. Building on our recent work, this chapter begins by summarizing our framework for understanding the goals of experimenters and applying this to rerandomization. We then use this framework to shed light on questions related to experimental registries, preanalysis plans, and most importantly, external validity. Our framework implies that even when large samples can be collected, external decision-making remains inherently subjective. We embrace this conclusion and argue that in order to improve external validity, experimental research needs to create a space for structured speculation.

Keywords

Ambiguity aversion; External validity; Non-Bayesian decision-making; Randomization; Self-selection

JEL Codes

C93; D70; D80

1. INTRODUCTION

1.1 Motivation

In the last couple of decades, two of the most successful areas of economic research have been decision theory—and its close cousins, behavioral, and experimental economics—and empirical microeconomics. Despite the fact that both emphasize experimentation as a method of investigation, there is almost no connection between the two literature.[1] Indeed, there are good reasons why such a dialog is difficult: an experiment designed according to the prescriptions of mainstream economic theory would get rejected by even the most benevolent referees; conversely, experimentation as it is practiced fails the standard axioms of subjective rationality.

Building on our work in Banerjee et al. (2014), this chapter seeks to establish such a dialog. We believe that modern decision theory can provide a much needed framework for experiment design, at a time when experimenters seek to codify their practice. In turn, we believe that the issues facing the experimental community present

---

[1] See Chassang et al. (2012), Kasy (2013), and Banerjee et al. (2014) for recent exceptions. This lack of connection despite the fact that economic theorists have extensively studied experimentation (Grossman and Stiglitz, 1980; Milgrom, 1981; Banerjee, 1992; Persico, 2000; Bergemann and Välimäki, 2002). Bandit problems have been a particular focus of this literature (Robbins, 1952; Bellman, 1956; Rothschild, 1974; Gittins, 1979; Aghion et al., 1991; Bergemann and Välimäki, 1996, 2006).

a rich and useful set of challenges for decision theory. It is a rare opportunity for theorists to write models that could impact the practice of their colleagues down the hall.

1.2 Overview

We believe the main difficulty in finding a good theoretical framework for understanding experimental design stems from inconsistencies between the preferences of experimenters as individuals and as a group. As individuals, experimenters behave more or less like Bayesians. As a group however, experimenters behave like extremely ambiguity averse decision makers, believing it is unwise to settle on a specific prior by which to evaluate new information.

Our framework considers the problem of a decision maker choosing both an experimental design and a decision rule—that is a mapping from experimental results into policy—who seeks to maximize her own subjective utility, while also satisfying an adversarial audience who may be able to veto her choices. We describe this framework and then summarize the results in Banerjee et al. (2014): first, it unifies the Bayesian and frequentist perspectives. For small sample sizes, or if the decision maker places little weight on convincing her audience, optimal experimentation is deterministic and maximizes subjective utility. If instead the sample size is large, then randomized experiments allowing for prior-free inference become optimal. Second, the framework sheds light on the tradeoffs involved in rerandomization. It always improves the subjective value of experiments but reduces the robustness of policy inferences. However, provided the number of rerandomizations is not terribly large (compared to the sample size), the robustness cost of rerandomization is negligible.

Having a model of experimenters also provides a useful perspective on preregistration and preanalysis. Bayesian decision makers do not need or desire either. On the other hand, a decision maker worried about an adversarial audience will value both. The important observation is that there is no need for the two perspectives to be seen as in opposition. Provided ex ante hypotheses are clearly labeled, there is no reason to constrain the dynamic updating of experiments as they are being run. Some decision makers will value knowing the ex ante hypotheses formulated by the experimenter, while Bayesian decision makers, who care only about the data collected, will value getting the most informative experiment possible. Reporting both, as "ex ante questions of interest," and "interim questions of interest" can satisfy both types.

The final sections are dedicated to the question of external validity. While there are ways to satisfy both the Bayesian and adversarial perspective in (policy) decision problems internal to the experimental environment, we argue that decision-making in external environments is necessarily subjective—things may just be different in different circumstances. However, this does not mean that external inferences need to be vague or uninformative. We embrace the idea that external inference is necessarily speculative and that it should be thought of and reported as such as part of experimental research.

We formulate a framework for structured speculation that builds on two main observations. First, the manner of speculation, whether it is through a structural model or a reduced-form set of empirical predictions, is unimportant. What is important is for speculation to be stated as crisp hypotheses that can be falsified by further data. The advantage of structural modeling is that it automatically leads to a fully specified set of falsifiable predictions. However, model parameters are no less speculative than hypotheses formulated in natural language by experienced field researchers. While models have value in systematizing and clarifying thought, there is no formal reason to rule out any format of speculation experimenters are comfortable with, provided that predictions are made is a precise, falsifiable way.

The second observation is that creating space for structured speculation may have an important effect on how experiments are designed, run, and reported. Indeed, we believe it may result in a more effective and informative process of experimentation. We argue that the need for "better" speculation will lead experimenters to collect data that are ignored, unreported, or viewed as unconstructive to reported research: for instance, data on participant preferences and beliefs, the participants' place in a broader economic system, the role that values and norms play in the outcomes we measure, and so on. We illustrate this point by providing explicit examples of interesting topics for structured speculation.

The rest of this section very briefly discusses the history of experimental design, highlighting the interplay of theory and practice.

1.3 A brief history

The first documented controlled experiment is found in the biblical book of Daniel, a story set around 605 BC comparing the health effects of a vegetarian diet with the Babylon court diet of meat and wine.

> *Then Daniel asked the guard whom the palace master had appointed over Daniel, Hananiah, Mishael, and Azariah: "Please test your servants for 10 days. Let us be given vegetables to eat and water to drink. You can then compare our appearance with the appearance of the young men who eat the royal rations, and deal with your servants according to what you observe." So he agreed to this proposal and tested them for 10 days. At the end of 10 days, it was observed that they appeared better and fatter than all the young men who had been eating the royal rations (Daniel 1:11–14, NRSV).*

Despite the early emergence of controlled trials, it took millennia for randomization to be inserted into the process—by statistical theorists well versed in field experiments. Simpson and Pearson (1904) argues for a crude form of randomization in the testing of inoculants (while at the same time performing the first meta-analysis, see

Egger et al., 2001) in order to establish a true control group. Over the years that followed, Pearson would formulate stronger and stronger defenses of randomization, emphasizing the need to draw controls from the same population as those that are treated (culminating in Maynard, 1909). Fisher (1926) was the first to provide a detailed program for randomization, which he expanded into his classic text on experimental design (Fisher, 1935).

Randomization became a mainstay of experimental design thanks to two factors. The first was medical practitioners looking for a way to evaluate treatments in a way that would prevent manipulation from the manufacturers of those treatments. Randomization alone proved insufficient to this task, which leads to the development of many tools, such as preregistration and preanalysis plans for trials, that we discuss in this chapter. These tools have had success in medicine, but their costs and benefits are likely to vary by field. As such, we have tried to identify, as abstractly as possible the factors that may make them more or less appealing, depending on the circumstances.

The second factor was a desire in many other fields of social science to identify the causal effects of interventions. Randomization was put at the center of frameworks for causal analysis leading, after some delay, to an explosion of randomized controlled field trials in several disciplines of the social sciences (Rubin, 1974; Pearl, 2000). Once again, however, randomization alone has not been sufficient to the task. Practical difficulties, such as treated participants being unwilling to receive treatment, have interfered. A number of statistical tools have been created to address these issues. However, as decision theory has little to say about the choice of statistical techniques, we do not discuss them here.

Finally, there is also work on experimental design that takes a Bayesian, rather than classical, perspective. However, like in econometrics, its presence is somewhat marginal. Even the proponents of Bayesian experimental design note that despite its strong normative appeal, it remains rarely, if ever, used (Chaloner and Verdinelli, 1995).

2. THE FRAMEWORK

We take the point of view of a decision maker who can inform her policy choice by running an experiment. She could be a scholar who is trying to come up with a policy recommendation or a political entrepreneur trying to shape policy for the better. The decision problem can be internal, if the ultimate policy decision affects the population targeted by the experiment, or external, if it applies to a population different from that involved in the experiment (hence external validity).[2]

Our discussion and modeling follows Banerjee et al. (2014) but is more informal. The interested reader may consult the original paper for more details.

---

[2] Note that the decision problem may differ because the population has changed—e.g., it consists of different people, or the same people with different beliefs, or in a different context—or because the treatment differs in some way—e.g., it is delivered at a different time, through a different distribution channel.

Actions and preferences. A decision maker needs to decide whether to implement some policy $a \in \{0, 1\}$, that provides a treatment $\tau \in \{0, 1\}$ to a unit mass population—which may be composed of people, districts, cities, schools, and so on—indexed by $i \in [0, 1]$ for individuals.[3] To inform her judgment, the decision maker is able to run experiments assigning a given number N of subjects to treatment or control.

Potential outcomes for subject i, given treatment τ, are denoted by $Y_i^\tau \in \{0, 1\}$. $Y = 1$ is referred to as a success. Each individual i is associated with covariates $x_i \in X$, where the set X is finite. Covariates $x \in X$ are observable and affect the distribution of outcomes Y. The distribution $q \in \Delta(X)$ of covariates in the population is known and has full support. Outcomes Y_i are i.i.d. conditional on covariates. The success probabilities, conditional on treatment τ, and covariates x are denoted by $p_x^\tau \equiv \text{prob}(Y_i^\tau = 1 | x_i = x)$.

Environments and decision problems. To specify the decision problem, and the distinction between internal and external problems, we define environments z, which are described by the finite-dimensional vector p of success probabilities conditional on covariates and treatment status

$$p = \left(p_x^0, p_x^1 \right)_{x \in X} \in \left([0, 1]^2 \right)^X \equiv \mathscr{P}.$$

For the first half of this chapter, we consider internal decision problems in which the environment is the same in both the experimental and policy-relevant population. The second half puts more attention on external decision problems and external validity, in which the two environments may differ.

Given a known environment p and a policy decision $a \in \{0, 1\}$, the decision maker's payoff $u(a, p)$ can be written as

$$u(a, p) \equiv \mathbb{E}_p Y^a = \sum_{x \in X} q(x) p_x^a.$$

This formulation does not explicitly recognize unobservables, although it allows p_x^τ to vary in arbitrary ways as x varies, which is effectively the consequence of unobservables.

Experiments and decision rules. An experiment is a realized assignment of treatment to individuals represented by a tuple $e = (x_i, \tau_i)_{i \in \{1, \dots, N\}} \in (X \times \{0, 1\})^N \equiv E$. Experiments generate outcome data $y = (y_i)_{i \in \{1, \dots, N\}} \in \{0, 1\}^N \equiv \mathscr{Y}$, with each y_i an independent realization of $Y_i^{\tau_i}$ given (x_i, τ_i).

The decision maker's strategy consists of both a (possibly randomized) experimental design $\mathscr{E} \in \Delta(E)$ and a decision rule $\alpha : E \times \mathscr{Y} \to \Delta(\{0, 1\})$ which maps experimental data—including the realized design e and outcomes y—to a policy decision a. We denote by $\mathscr{A}$ the set of possible decision rules. Since $\mathscr{E}$ is the set of possible probability

---

[3] For simplicity, we focus on policies that assign the same treatment status to all $i \in [0, 1]$.

distributions over the realized assignments of treatment, this framework allows for randomized experiments.

We assume that subjects are exchangeable conditional on covariates, so that experiments identical up to a permutation of labels are equivalent from the perspective of the experimenter (De Finetti, 1937).[4]

3. PERSPECTIVES ON EXPERIMENTAL DESIGN

3.1 Bayesian experimentation

Much of economic theory proceeds under the assumption that decision makers are subjective expected utility maximizers. As this implies Bayesian updating, we refer to such decision makers as Bayesians. While subjective expected utility maximization has been an incredibly useful framework, it leads to theoretical prescriptions at odds with experimental practice.[5]

Formally, let the decision maker start from a prior $h_0 \in \Delta(\mathscr{P})$ over treatment effects. In the context of our experimentation problem, optimal experiments $\mathscr{E}$ and decision rules α must solve,

$$\max_{\mathscr{E}, \alpha} \mathbb{E}_{h_0}[u(\alpha(e, \gamma), p)]. \tag{1}$$

An immediate implication of the subjective expected utility framework is that randomization is never strictly optimal and for generic priors it is strictly suboptimal.

Proposition 1 (Banerjee et al. (2014), Bayesians do not Randomize).

Assume that the decision maker is Bayesian, i.e., designs experiments according to (1). Then, there exist deterministic solutions $e \in E$ to (1). A mixed strategy (randomization) $\mathscr{E} \in \Delta(E)$ solves (1) if and only if for all $e \in$ supp $\mathscr{E}$, e solves (1).[6]

The intuition of the result is straightforward. Mixed strategies are never strictly optimal for subjective expected utility maximizers when a pure strategy equilibrium exists, and an randomized controlled trial (RCT) is a mixed strategy in the decision problem described above. Kasy (2013) uses a result similar to Proposition 1 to argue that randomized controlled trials are suboptimal. Specifically, it emphasizes that if the goal is to achieve balance between the treatment and control samples, this is more efficiently

---

[4] The framework here is not particularly general. The goal is to provide us with just enough flexibility to illustrate specific issues. For example, we consider coarse policy decisions between treating the entire population or no one. In practice, one may consider more sophisticated policy decisions indexed on observable covariates. We also assume that the number of treatment and control observations are freely chosen under an aggregate constraint. In practice, the cost of treatment and control data points may differ. These simplifications do not affect our results.

[5] It is normatively appealing as well, and the "as if" axiomatization proposed by Savage (1954) seems so natural that subjective expected utility maximization is sometimes considered an expression of rationality.

[6] See Banerjee et al. (2014) for precise definitions and a proof.

done by purposefully assigning participants to treatment and control based on their observables, so as to eliminate any chance of ending up with an unbalanced sample purely because of bad luck in the randomization process.

Proposition 1 is obviously at odds with experimental practice. Real-life experimenters go through nontrivial expense in order to assign treatment and control randomly. We interpret this mismatch as an indication that the Bayesian paradigm provides a poor description of the objectives of actual experimenters. However, we also believe there is insight into experimental practice that can be gained by carefully considering Proposition 1. We do this in the following example, before turning to the adversarial perspective discussed in the introduction.

3.1.1 Example: the logic of Bayesian experimentation

Consider an experiment evaluating educational vouchers. This experiment will influence a school superintendent's decision of whether or not to introduce vouchers in her district. The superintendent has dismissed vouchers in the past, believing that by far the most important determinant of academic outcomes is whether a student is from a poor or privileged background. She has used this belief to explain the superior performance of private schools in her district, as they are a bastion for privileged students. However, in recent years, she has become open to the radical opposite of her belief: Schooling is the sole determinant of academic success. That is, even a poor student would do better at a private school. To test this hypothesis, she has convinced a private school to let her assign, however she likes, a single student to enroll there.

Faced with an experiment with a single observation, most academic experimenters would give up. How could anyone ever learn from such an experiment? What is the comparison group? Yet designing an informative experiment is easy: a Bayesian decision maker always has a prior, and she can compare the outcome of the child to that. Suppose the superintendent believes that a poor child can never score higher than the 70th percentile on a standardized test. She would then clearly find it informative if a poor child were given the lone spot in the private school and then scored in the 90th percentile.

Adding a second child to the experiment brings new questions and new insights. In particular, suppose that a slot in a public school is also allocated to this experiment. Should the child in the public school have an identical or different background to the student assigned to the private school? Should we allocate the private-school spot by lottery?

Once we recognize the role of the prior in setting the benchmark, these questions become easy to answer. Our superintendent starts from the theory that only background matters. Under that theory, the most surprising outcome, and therefore the one likely to move her prior the most, is one in which a poor child who goes to a private school significantly outperforms a privileged child who goes to a public school. If this occurs, she would strongly update toward the alternative explanation that schooling is all that matters. Thus, the optimal design involves giving the private school slot to a poor child and sending a privileged child to a public school. In particular, she is more likely to be impressed by the outcome of this experiment than one where both students are from the same background.

Strikingly, this example falsifies the idea that balanced treatment and control groups are intrinsically appealing. Moreover, we are arguing for a deterministic, rather than random, assignment of the students. Indeed, a lottery only moves us away from the ideal design: If the privileged child is assigned to the private school, very little can be learned.

Proposition 1 shows that this result applies for all sample sizes. The limits of this line of reasoning are only met if multiple decision makers with different priors (or a single decision maker unable to commit to a single prior) are involved. Introduce another school official with a slightly different prior beliefs about the effect of economic background: she believes that while a poor student would not benefit from a move to a private school, a privileged student would be harmed by moving to a public school. In this case, the design suggested previously is much less attractive. If we observe that the poor child does better, it could be either because the private school helps him to do better or because the public school hurts the richer child (or both!).

When the experimenter wants to convince other decision makers, she will design an experiment that not only informs her but also informs members of her audience with arbitrary priors. This is the perspective that Banerjee et al. (2014) seeks to capture. In this setting, randomized experiments emerge as the only ones that successfully defend against all priors, i.e., the only experiments whose interpretation cannot be challenged even by a devil's advocate.

3.2 Ambiguity or an audience

Although Bayesian decision-making is the default framework of economic theory, it is by no means a consensus. First, a decision maker may not trust her prior, exhibiting ambiguity aversion (Ellsberg, 1961; Schmeidler, 1989; Gilboa and Schmeidler, 1989; Klibanoff et al., 2005). Second, she may simply not be able to think through all possible implications of holding a particular prior, in effect violating Savage's completeness axiom (Gilboa et al., 2009; Bewley, 1998). Third, she may recognize that she needs to convince others whose priors may diverge from her own.[7]

The model we propose in Banerjee et al. (2014) takes seriously the idea that experimenters care about convincing such an audience. This "audience" may actually reflect the experimenter's own self-doubts and internal critics, or a real audience of stakeholders

---

[7] A related concern is that she may be accused of fraudulent manipulation of the evidence by those who disagree with her a priori. However, if outright fraud is a concern, verifiable procedures, more than randomization, become necessary.

with veto power (e.g., referees).[8] The decision maker chooses the experimental design $\mathscr{E}$ and decision rule α that solve

$$\max_{\mathscr{E},\alpha} U(\mathscr{E},\alpha) \equiv \lambda \underbrace{\mathbb{E}_{h_0,\mathscr{E}}[u(\alpha(e,\gamma),p)]}_{\text{subjective effectiveness}} + (1-\lambda) \underbrace{\min_{h\in H} \mathbb{E}_{h,\mathscr{E}}[u(\alpha(e,\gamma),p)]}_{\text{robust effectiveness}} \qquad (2)$$

where $\lambda \in [0,1]$. Here, h_0 is a fixed reference prior, while H is a convex set of alternative priors $h \in \Delta(P)$. A decision maker with these preferences can be interpreted as maximizing its usefulness under reference prior h_0, while also satisfying an adversarial audience with priors $h \in H$.[9] The first term captures a desire for informativeness from the point of view of the experimenter, and the second captures a desire for robustness.

Ambiguity averse experimentation. Banerjee et al. (2014) study optimal experimentation by ambiguity-averse decision makers under one additional assumption.

Assumption 1

We assume that there exists $\nu > 0$ such that, for all $X_0 \subset X$ with $|X_0 \le N/2|$, there exists a prior $h \in \arg\min_{h\in H} \mathbb{E}_h(\max_{a\in\{0,1\}} p^a)$ such that for almost every $p_{X_0} \equiv (p_x^0, p_x^1)_{x\in X_0}$,

$$\min\left\{ \mathbb{E}_h\left[\max_{a\in\{0,1\}} \overline{p}^a - \overline{p}^0 \big| p_{X_0}\right], \mathbb{E}_h\left[\max_{a\in\{0,1\}} \overline{p}^a - \overline{p}^1 \big| p_{X_0}\right] \right\} > \nu.$$

The condition says that even if an experiment was to reveal the probability of success at every value of the covariate x in X_0, there is still at least one prior in the set H under which the conditional likelihood of making a wrong policy decision is bounded away from zero.[10]

Proposition 2. For $\lambda \in (0,1)$:

1. Take sample size N as given. For generically every prior h_0, there exists $\underline{\lambda} \in (0,1)$ such that for all $\lambda \ge \underline{\lambda}$, the solution $\mathscr{E}^*$ to (2) is unique, deterministic, and Bayesian-optimal for $\lambda = 1$.

2. Take weight λ as given. There exists $\underline{N}$ such that for all $N \ge \underline{N}$, the optimal experiment $\mathscr{E}^*$ is randomized. As N goes to infinity, the optimal experiment allows for correct policy decisions with probability going to one, uniformly over priors $h \in H$.

---

[8] The model belongs to the class of maximin preferences axiomatized in Gilboa and Schmeidler (1989).

[9] Note that if $\lambda = 1$, we recover (1), so that this model nests standard Bayesian expected utility maximization. If satisfying audience members was introduced as a hard constraint, then the weight ratio $\frac{1-\lambda}{\lambda}$ would be interpreted as an appropriate Lagrange multiplier for that constraint.

[10] The way this condition is specified implies that $N < 2|X|$. It also implies the existence of priors in H that place some weight on the possibility that the function p_x^τ is not smooth with respect to x. This lack of smoothness conditional on observables can be microfounded using unobservables although success rates conditional on observed and unobserved variables are smooth, sharp changes in variation of unobserved variables correlated with small changes in the value of observables x generates the lack of smoothness in x.

Proposition 2 shows that the optimal experimental design depends on the number of available data points (or participants), and the weight the decision maker puts on her own prior versus those of the audience. Part (1) of the result shows that when sample points are scarce, or when the decision maker does not put much weight on satisfying anyone else (λ close to 1), optimal experimentation will be Bayesian. That is, the experimenter will focus on assigning treatment and control observations to the subjects from whom she expects to learn the most. Part (2) shows that when sample points are plentiful and/or the decision maker cares about satisfying an adversarial audience, she will use randomized trials that allow for prior-free identification of correct policies.[11]

To build intuition for the result, and Assumption 1, it is useful to think of the decision maker as playing a zero-sum game against nature (with probably $1 - \lambda$). After the decision maker picks an experiment, nature picks the prior which maximizes the chance of picking the wrong policy, given that experimental design. If there is any clear pattern in the decision maker's assignment of treatment, nature can exploit these due to Assumption 1. Randomization eliminates patterns for nature to exploit.

3.2.1 A theory of experimenters

Although randomization prevents nature from exploiting patterns in an experimental design, it is not always the optimal solution. There are two possible reasons for this. First, the decision maker may care so little about the audience (λ is close to 1), that preparing for the worst is of little use. Second, with small samples, the loss of power from randomization (relative to the optimal deterministic experiment) is so large that it offsets the benefit of reducing nature's ability to exploit a deterministic assignment. As the sample becomes large, the loss of power from randomizing shrinks to nothing, while the gains from robustness against challenging priors remain positive and bounded away from zero.[12]

Fig. 1 maps out implications of Proposition 2 for practical experiment design. In scientific research, when an experimenter faces a skeptical audience, she randomizes. In contrast, a firm implementing a costly new process in a handful of production sites will not try it on random teams. The firm will focus on a few teams where it can learn

---

[11] Kasy (2013) reports a result that seems to directly contradict ours: that randomized experiments can never do better than a deterministic one, even with a maximin objective. The difference in the results comes from the fact that in Kasy's framework the audience sets its prior after randomization occurs, rather than between the revelation of the design and the actual randomization, as in our framework. In Kasy's framework, the audience will obviously pick a prior that means, in effect, that they can learn nothing from the actual treatment assignment. Taking journal referees as an example of a skeptical audience, we believe our assumption is more realistic: Referees do show a fair amount of forbearance, even when faced with imbalance in covariates generated by a randomized control trial, although there are instances where they are sufficiently troubled by a particular case of imbalance to recommend rejection.

[12] As pointed out by Kasy (2013), the decision maker may also be able to limit the set of possible interpretations by deterministically choosing the right set of xs if there is enough continuity in p_x. Too much continuity is ruled out by Assumption 1.

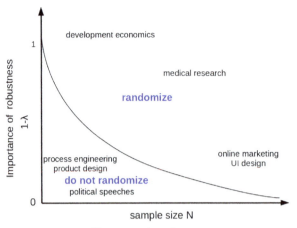

Figure 1 Different modes of experimentation.

the most.[13] Yet when the available sample is large, firms do randomize. This is the case for firms dealing online with many end users: although the firm only needs to convince itself of the effectiveness of a particular ad or user interface design, observations are plentiful and randomization is cheap and used.

The logic of Proposition 2 applies at all stages of the decision-making tree that leads to the evaluation of a particular technology. When scientists want to convince others, they run detailed randomized experiments. At earlier stages however, when a scientist decides what to experiment on, they do not just randomly pick a hypothesis. Instead, they develop a subjective prior on the technologies most likely to be worth exploring in detail. This fits well with our result: the number of experiments a scientist can run is limited, and each one of them is very costly, so it makes sense to subjectively refine the set under consideration. In online marketing, where experiments can be run at very little cost, there is much less need to use a subjective prior to refine the set of possible ads with which to experiment.

Additional implications of Proposition 2 refine our understanding of experimental practice. Part (2) implies that a decision maker who randomizes even without understanding all its ramifications—why she is randomizing, what audience the experiment is meant to satisfy—will nevertheless produce an almost-optimal experiment for large values of N. Even if someone (or her own doubts) produces a particularly challenging prior, the decision rule is still likely to be close to optimal. In this sense,

---

[13] Similarly, a politician trying out platforms will do so at a few carefully chosen venues in front of carefully chosen audiences.

our approach addresses the concern that decision makers may violate Savage's completeness axiom.[14]

Proposition 2 also highlights the importance of actually randomizing. An experiment that adopts a protocol where assignment is only "nearly" random, such as assignment based on time of day of an experimental session (see Green and Tusicisny, 2012; for a critique), or the first letter of an experimental subject's name (as was the case in the deworming study of Miguel and Kremer, 2004; see Deaton, 2010 for a critique), will tend to find a skeptical prior in its audience. Randomization provides a defense against the most skeptical priors, but near-randomization offers no such protection.

4. RERANDOMIZATION, REGISTRATION, AND PREANALYSIS

Proposition 2 suggests that the adversarial experimentation framework described by (2) may be useful for capturing the objectives of real-life experimenters. We now highlight ways in which having such a model can shed light on questions of current importance to the experimental community.

4.1 Rerandomization

Banerjee et al. (2014) brings the adversarial framework of (2) to bear on the question of rerandomization. A well-known problem with randomization is that it sometimes results in observable characteristics being poorly balanced across treatment and control groups (see Morgan and Rubin, 2012, and references therein).[15] Of course, stratification, blocking, and matching methods can be used to improve balance while maintaining randomization.[16] However, as any researcher who has tried to simultaneously stratify on multiple continuous variables knows, this can be quite difficult in practice. Moreover, these techniques have issues of their own (Athey and Imbens, 2016).

Rerandomization is a simple and intuitively attractive alternative: if a sample "looks" unbalanced, simply randomize again, and keep doing so until the sample looks balanced. While many authors caution against the use of rerandomization because it may have large

---

[14] A similar results hold for more complex policies that vary treatment with covariate x, provided the complexity of possible policies is limited. See Vapnik (1999) for operational definitions of "complexity."

[15] Balance is important because it limits the possible set of alternative interpretations of the evidence, as described previously. It also seems to serve as a rule of thumb for the experiment being competently executed, although this may not be warranted.

[16] Stratifying on several continuous variables is usually impractical for reasons related to the "curse of dimensionality." Consider an experiment with one treatment, one control, and four (continuous) variables describing participant heterogeneity. The natural strategy would be to bin subject characterizations along each dimension. In this example, we suppose each variable is split into five bins. Then there are $4^5 = 1,024$ cells in which to stratify, with each cell requiring two observations: one treatment, and one control. Unless the sample size is significantly greater than 2,048, with high likelihood there will be many cells with only one, unmatched, observation.

statistical and internal validity costs (see Bruhn and McKenzie, 2009, and references therein), our framework can be used to precisely those costs.

From a purely Bayesian perspective, rerandomization does not create any concerns and, indeed, may be beneficial because it may select an experiment closer to the optimal deterministic experiment from a particular subjective point of view. That is, why should a Bayesian learn differently from the same balanced sample if it is reached by a single lucky randomization, or by choosing among many?

In Banerjee et al. (2014), we show that the concerns brought up by Bruhn and McKenzie (2009) make sense in our adversarial framework. Rerandomization does have a cost in terms of robustness. Indeed, sufficiently many rerandomizations lead to an essentially deterministic allocation, which, we show, results in losses bounded away from zero for the adversarial audience. However, we also show that this cost is negligible, provided the number of rerandomizations is not exponential in the sample size.

We can make these costs and benefits precise, if K randomizations occur ($K = 1$ being a standard RCT), frequentist decision-making—i.e., assigning the treatment that performs best empirically—is optimal up to a loss bounded by $\sqrt{\frac{\max\{1, \log(K)\}}{N}}$. Importantly, $\sqrt{\log(N)}$ is a number between 1.5 and 3 for sample sizes between 10 and 10,000, which suggests that setting $K \leq N$ results in minimal losses of robustness. In turn, K randomizations guarantee that the final sample will be within the group of 5% most balanced samples with probability $1 - 0.95^K$. Observing that $1 - 0.95^{100} > 0.99$, this suggests the following rule of thumb for rerandomization.

Rule of Thumb:

Use the most balanced sample out of K randomizations, where $K = \min\{N, 100\}$.

Note that the balance criteria need not be defined ex ante. That is, the researcher can rerandomize K times and select the assignment of treatment and control, however, they like even after seeing the set of possible assignments.[17]

We believe our proposal for rerandomization has several benefits. First, it provides simple, effective guidelines under which rerandomization is not problematic. Second, by doing so, it may help bring rerandomization out in the open. As discussed in Bruhn and McKenzie (2009), many authors who employ rerandomization fail to disclose it, possibly because of the stigma attached to the practice. However, as long as rerandomization is done in a way that explicitly takes into account its costs and benefits, there is no reason for such a stigma.

---

[17] Two important notes are in order here. First, when clustered randomization is done, e.g., at the village level, then the number of rerandomizations should equal the number of clusters, not observations. Second, one can both stratify and rerandomize. That is, an experimenter can choose simple variables on which to stratify, and then rerandomize to achieve better balance on the more complex or continuous variables.

Finally, rerandomization may help experimenters find compromises with governments or research partners uncomfortable with randomization. In some cases, experimenters negotiate a near-random treatment assignment scheme, as in the deworming example discussed previously. Our proposal is a middle ground: experimenters could produce a list of K randomizations to give to their implementation partner, and the partner could choose from that list. The criteria the implementing partner uses to choose a particular randomization could be anything they like it to be: from the one that "looks" the fairest to them, to more cynical ones that values having a particular village or person in the treatment group. Hybrids are possible as well: an experimenter could generate 100 randomization schemes and allow the implementing partner to choose, however they want, from among the five most balanced.

4.2 Registration

Registration, enabled by platforms such as the American Economic Association's Randomized Controlled Trials Registry, is being embraced by a growing proportion of the experimental community. It has two effects. First, it creates a centralized and thorough database of experimental designs and outcomes that does not suffer from publication bias, file drawer bias, and so on. Second, it often leads researchers to commit to a particular experiment and not change the experimental design during the course of the experiment. It should be noted that the latter is not a primary intention of registries or their designers.

Within the framework described by (2), the first aspect of registration is unambiguously good. More information is always beneficial, simply because it can be ignored.[18]

The commitment value of registration is much less obvious. In a dynamic setting, where experimental designs can be updated after the arrival of new information, Bayesians have no value for commitment, as they are time consistent. Indeed, if the decision maker is limited in her ability to specify complex contingency plans, then commitment has negative value. The value is even more negative when one considers the fact that updating a design may produce more useful information.

4.2.1 Good commitment

Although registries are imperfect commitment devices, they are often used that way by experimenters. Commitment is valuable for the ambiguity-averse decision maker described by (2). Indeed, as Machina (1989) highlights, nonexpected utility maximizers are not dynamically consistent. In other words, an ambiguity-averse decision maker who

---

[18] Note that decision makers exhibiting self-control problems (Gul and Pesendorfer, 2001), or decision makers with preferences over the revelation of uncertainty (Kreps and Porteus, 1978), may prefer to restrict the information available. Players involved in a strategic game may also have this preference.

likes a particular design ex ante may be unsatisfied with the resulting experiment ex post and try to alter its design.

The kind of temptation against which a decision maker may want to commit amounts to either: (1) tampering with realized random assignments or (2) reneging from implementing a policy proven to be effective according to a burden of proof specified ex ante. Indeed, once a random assignment is drawn, there always exist priors under which the realized sample assignment and/or the policy conclusions are unsatisfactory. Commitment allows the experimenter follow through with the original plan. A plan, it should be remembered, that was ex ante satisfactory to both the experimenter and her adversarial audience.

The idea that registries allow various parties to commit to both an experiment and an action plan is plausible. Research partners may sometimes want to redraw assignments, shut down all or part of the experiment, or suppress parts of the data because they find the results misleading. Such hiding of information is likely to be undesirable in itself, in addition to its potentially harmful effects on the incentives of the experimenter (Aghion and Tirole, 1994). Registration can reduce this risk.

4.2.2 Bad commitment

There is, however, scope for excessive commitment. Indeed, while it is important for experimenters to commit to a randomized assignment, they need not commit to a specific treatment to guarantee robust inferences. For instance, after gaining experience with a treatment A, the experimenter may subjectively decide that a variant A' is likely to be much more useful. Experimenting with A' does not preclude robust inference about the value of A' versus the default alternative. In fact, data from experimenting with A and A' can be aggregated, corresponding to a mixture treatment A/A'.

In principle, if there are finite possible treatments, an ambiguity-averse decision maker may wish to randomize the treatments with which she experiments. In practice, however, experimenters do not randomize the treatments they evaluate. The space of possible treatments is simply too large for such random exploration to be useful. Instead, the experimenter's subjective prior ends up driving the choice of intervention to evaluate. Randomized assignment after the treatment is chosen allows the experimenter to convince her audience to take the data seriously, although this may create a loss of valuable information.

If experimenters are bounded in terms of the number of possibilities they can imagine (as we definitely were), committing to a very detailed design once and for all makes little sense. It is costly to do, and it limits flexibility in ways that do not improve robustness. There is little reason not to update experiments, provided that these updates are registered, as is allowed (and tracked) by most registration platforms.[19]

---

[19] Of course, experimenters should not be allowed to first collect data and then register a design that speaks only to a selected portion of this data.

4.2.3 Examples

An insider's perspective into Alatas et al. (2012) illustrates the cost of excessive commitment. Alatas et al. (2012) describe a field experiment in Indonesia where communities were asked to rank their members from poor to rich. The order in which households were considered for ranking was chosen randomly, driven by some concern for fairness. Households that were ranked earlier were ranked much more accurately, presumably because the rankers got tired or bored as the ranking meeting progressed. This was not something the authors had set out to learn. However, it might have made sense to change the protocol to guard against the inefficiency of late rankings—perhaps the ranking could have been done in batches, with breaks in between. But, the fact that the experiment was registered gave us a false sense that we were could not alter the design, although such an update could have been reflected in the registry and may have allowed for more learning.

Another example can be found in Andreoni et al. (2016), which used incentived choices to estimate time-discounting parameters of polio vaccinators in Pakistan. These parameters were then used to construct optimal contracts, which were tested against a standard piece rate. Unfortunately, the authors had preregistered and thus felt committed to, a model of time preferences that the data showed to be misspecified. This was a potentially fatal decision as the paper is a "proof of concept" of using preference estimation to design personalized contracts and had the misspecification been severe enough, it would have resulted in a failure to generate a significant improvement. Luckily, this was not the case, but it illustrates the dangers of "too much" commitment.

4.3 Preanalysis plans

A preanalysis plan lists all outcomes of interest, and the ways in which data will be analyzed when the experiment is complete. Formally, it may be thought of as a subset of statistics S of the data.

4.3.1 Preanalysis and bounded rationality

Interestingly, neither Bayesian nor ambiguity-averse decision makers find it beneficial to register a preanalysis plan, nor would her audience care if she did. This follows from two implicit assumptions: (1) all data are disclosed and (2) the decision maker and audience members have unbounded cognitive capacity. If an audience member is suspicious that the experimenter cherry-picked results, she can just run her own analyses. This seems appropriate when the experimenter faces a sophisticated professional audience (i.e., referees, editors, seminar participants). However, in practice, there is demand for preanalysis and thus, a careful, decision-theoretic foundation for preanalysis plans is likely worthwhile.

While such a foundation is beyond the scope of this chapter, we can hint at a setup in which preanalysis, i.e., preselecting a subset S of statistics to be reported, becomes relevant. We believe this reflects the bounded rationality constraints of the decision maker or audience members. Indeed, if the decision maker can only process a subset of information S, she may be rightfully concerned about the way this set is selected. Formulating a pre-analysis plan can reassure the stakeholders and facilitate actionable inference. Of course, if cognitive capacity is the issue, then preanalysis plans cannot be excessively complicated: The goal is not for authors to anticipate all possible interesting inquiries into the data. This would defeat the purpose of preanalysis plans by making them inaccessible to time-constrained decision makers.

In practice, experimenters are likely to speak to various audiences, each warranting different attitudes toward preanalysis plans. A scholarly audience might reason that by demanding robustness checks, it is, in effect, forcing the reporting of all relevant dimensions of the data. Such an audience may prefer to ignore preanalysis plans. However, an audience of time-constrained policymakers may behave differently, and only update from experiments with simple, clearly stated preanalysis plans.

We see no need to view these perspectives as oppositional. Given the variety of audiences, the best response to us seems to allow for both ex ante and ex post analyses of the data within clearly defined "ex ante analysis" and "ex post analysis" sections. Ex ante—specified hypotheses will be useful to time-constrained audiences lacking the desire to really delve into the data. Ex post analysis of the data will allow experimenters to report insights that were hard to anticipate without the help of data.

4.3.2 Caveats

The previous discussion does not touch on moral hazard concerns.[20] In this respect, two questions seem relevant: Is misbehavior by experimenters is prevalent in economics? Are the mechanisms of registration and preanalysis a long-term solution to this potential issue? The data at this point suggest that the answers are respectively "not very" and "maybe not". In particular, Brodeur et al. (2016), find very little evidence of nefarious conduct in articles in top economics journals and detect none in the reporting of results from randomized experiments. Moreover, in medicine, where norms of preregistration and pre-analysis are often enforced by journals, a recent study by the Center for Evidence Based Medicine at Oxford University found that 58/67 of the articles examined contain misreporting—i.e., failure to report prespecified outcomes.[21] Response to these results has been quite varied, with at least one prestigious journal issuing corrections to all implicated articles, and another releasing an editorial defending aspects of misreporting.

---

[20] Humphreys et al. (2013) also emphasizes a communication role for preanalysis plans. However, this should not detract from the very real commitment dimensions of registration and preanalysis plans, and the fact that in order to make them successful, one needs to pay attention to how this commitment gives authors incentives to comply, or not.

[21] See http://compare-trials.org/blog/post-hoc-pre-specification-and-undeclared-separation-of-results-a-broken-record-in-the-making/.

A valuable aspect of preanalysis plans that we do not account for is that they serve as contractual devices with research partners heavily invested in the outcome of an experiment (Casey et al., 2012; Olken, 2015). In these environments, a preanalysis plan may prevent a research partner from shifting definitions after the data are collected. In addition, specifying table formats, and the analyses therein, ahead of time, is useful in identifying and eliminating disagreement between co-authors and translating intentions into clear instructions for research assistants.

4.3.3 Theory

Prespecified theories are potentially a way to protect against the accusation (and temptation) of motivated choices in analysis, while still preserving some analytical flexibility. This is in contrast with current common practice, which is to announce the theory in the same paper that shows the results of empirical analyses. Instead, a prespecified theory should be "published" prior to empirical analysis, and, ideally prior to running the experiment.

An explicit, prespecified theory preserves some flexibility of analysis, while restricting interpretation. It can be used to justify running regressions that were not prespecified—those that are natural implications of the theory—without opening the door to full-scale specification searchers. Moreover, prespecifying theory has the effect of making the experimenter's priors public, thereby allowing the audience to challenge an experimenter's interpretation of data on the grounds that it is inconsistent with the experimenter's prior theory. Of course some elements of an analysis cannot be derived from an abstract theory, e.g., the level of clustering. Therefore, it may make sense to combine some ex ante restrictions on specifications with a prespecified theory.

It is worth emphasizing that even a theory that is developed ex post can impose useful restrictions on the analysis and reporting of results. In particular, given the implications of a theory, an audience can enquire why some are tested and others are not. While, in some cases, an ex post theory may turn out to be fully jury-rigged, it at least makes clear the author's assumptions, which then can be challenged.

In a sense, a preanalysis plan is often just a reflection of an implicit theory, thus a prespecified theory has some of the same drawbacks as a preanalysis plan, but additional benefits. Like preanalysis plans, theory will not change the beliefs of a skeptical audience that wants to examine the entire data set. In addition, if the theory turns out, ex post, to be irrelevant it may distract from useful features of the data (just as with preanalysis plans). However, theory has the added benefit of making external extrapolation easier and more transparent, as we develop further in the next section.

5. EXTERNAL VALIDITY

So far we have focused on internal decision problems, where treatment effects in the population enrolled in the experiment are the same as in the population a policy will be implemented upon. We now bring our framework to bear on external decision problems, in which treatment effects may differ between these two populations.

Formally, we allow the effectiveness of the treatment, described by vector p, to vary with the environment, denoted $z \in \{z_e, z_p\}$ (for experimental and policy-relevant):

$$p_z = \left(p_{x,z}^0, p_{x,z}^1\right)_{x \in X} \in \left([0,1]^2\right)^X \equiv \mathscr{P}.$$

While randomization is robustly optimal in internal decision problems ($z_e = z_p$)—provided the sample size is large enough—we now show that policy advice for external environments remains Bayesian even for arbitrarily large sample sizes. Under plausible assumptions, the best guess about which policy to choose in an environment or population that has not been studied is the experimenter's posterior after seeing experimental results in a related setting.

Let $H_{|p_z}$ denote the set of marginal distributions $h_{|p_z}$ over treatment effects p_z for priors $h \in H$ entertained by the audience. While information about environment z_e will likely affect the posterior over p_{z_p} for any given prior, it need not restrict the set of *possible* priors over p_{z_p}. This is captured by the following formal assumption.

Assumption 2

$$H_{|p_{z_p}} \times H_{|p_{z_e}} \subset H.^{22}$$

External validity can be thought of as the following problem: after running an experiment in environment z_e, the experimenter is asked to make a recommendation for the external environment z_p. She thus chooses $\mathscr{E}$ and α to solve

$$\max_{\mathscr{E} \sim p_{z_e}, \alpha} \left\{ \lambda \mathbb{E}_{h_e}\left[u\left(\alpha, p_{z_p}\right)\right] + (1 - \lambda) \min_{h \in H} \mathbb{E}_h\left[u\left(\alpha, p_{z_p}\right)\right] \right\}. \tag{3}$$

Proposition 3 (external policy advice is Bayesian).

The optimal recommendation rule α^* in (3) depends only on the experimenter's posterior belief $h_e(p_{z_p}|e)$ given experimental realization e. The optimal experiment $\mathscr{E}^*$ is Bayesian optimal under prior h_e.

That is, external recommendations only reflect the beliefs held by the experimenter, not by the audience. This occurs because, under Assumption 2, evidence accumulated in environment z_e does not change the set of priors entertained by the audience in environment $z_p z_p$, i.e., it does not reduce the ambiguity in environment z_p. This further implies that the most information one can hope to obtain is the experimenter's subjective posterior belief over state p_{z_p}.

---

[22] While this assumption is clearly stylized, our results generalize, provided there remains sufficient ambiguity about environment z_p, even conditional on knowing environment z_e very well.

6. STRUCTURED SPECULATION

Proposition 3 formalizes the natural intuition that external policy advice is unavoidably subjective. This does not mean that it needs to be uninformed by experimental evidence, rather, judgment will unavoidably color it.

This also does not imply that subjective recommendations by experimenters cannot be used to inform policymakers. In many (most?) cases, the policymaker will have to make a call without a randomized controlled trial tailored to the particular environment. As such, the decision maker's most useful repository of information is likely to be the experimenter, because she is likely to deeply understand the experimental environment, previous results and evaluations, and how a policy environment may differ from experimental environments.

Proposition 3 also does not mean that external policy advice is cheap talk. Indeed, further evidence may be collected, and, provided that advice is precise, it may be proven to be right or wrong. What we should aim to do is extract the experimenter's honest beliefs about the efficacy of treatment in different environments. While this is not an entirely obvious exercise, we know from the literature on incentivizing experts that it is possible (see, e.g., Olszewski and Peski, 2011; Chassang, 2013).

Practically, we do not think formal incentives are necessary to ensure truthful revelation. Instead, we believe a clear set of systematic guidelines for structured speculation may go a long way.

Guidelines for structured speculation:

1. Experimenters should systematically speculate about the external validity of their findings.
2. Such speculation should be clearly and cleanly separated from the rest of the paper; maybe in a section called "Speculation".
3. Speculation should be precise and falsifiable.

The core requirements here are for speculative statements to be labeled as such and be falsifiable. Practically, this means predictions need to be sufficiently precise that the experiment to validate or falsify them is unambiguous. This will allow testing by subsequent experimenters. By a reputational argument, this implies that speculative statements will not be cheap talk.

6.1 The Value of Structured Speculation

We believe that creating space for structured speculation is important and useful for several reasons.

First, providing a dedicated space for speculation will produce information that would not otherwise be transmitted. When assessing external questions, experimenters will bring to bear the full range of their practical knowledge built in the field. This includes an intuitive understanding of the mechanisms at work, of the underlying heterogeneity in treatment effects, how these correlates with observable characteristics, and so on.

Second, enforcing the format of speculative statements—i.e., ensuring statements are precise and falsifiable—will facilitate and encourage follow-up tests, as well as interaction with closely related work.

Finally, to us, the most important side effect of asking experimenters to speculate about external validity is the creation of incentives to produce experimental designs that maximize the ability to address external questions. To address scalability, experimenters may structure local pilot studies for easy comparison with their main experiments. To identify the right subpopulations for generalizing to other environments, experimenters can identify ahead of time the characteristics of groups that can be generalized and stratify on those. To extend the results to populations with a different distribution of unobserved characteristics, experimenters may elicit the former using the selective trial techniques discussed in Chassang et al. (2012) and run the experiment separately for each of the groups so identified.

While these benefits are speculative (and difficult to falsify!), it is our belief that creating a rigorous framework for external validity is an important step in completing an ecosystem for social science field experiments and a complement to many other aspects of experimentation.

In the next subsections, we describe an operational framework for structured speculation that can be used today. We begin by providing concrete examples of what structured speculation may look like, and how it may be useful. We then propose a baseline set of external validity issues that should be systematically addressed. We conclude by discussing possible formats for structured speculation: qualitative, reduced form, and structural.

6.2 Examples

To flesh out what we mean by structured speculation, we describe the form it may take in the context of a few papers.

Dupas (2014). Dupas (2014) studies the effect of short-term subsidies on long-run adoption and reports that short-term subsidies had a significant impact on the adoption of a more effective and comfortable class of bed nets. In its Section 5, the paper provides an extraordinary discussion of external validity.

It first spells out a simple and transparent argument relating the effectiveness of short-run subsidies to: (1) the speed at which various forms of uncertainty are resolved and (2) the timing of user's costs and benefits. If the uncertainty over benefits is resolved quickly, short-run subsidies can have a long-term effect. If uncertainty over benefits is resolved slowly, and adoption costs are incurred early on, short-run subsidies are unlikely to have a long-term effect.

It then answers the question, "For what types of health products and contexts would we expect the same results to obtain?" It does so by classifying potential technologies into three categories based on how short-run (or one-time) subsidies would change adoption patterns:

1. **Increased**: cookstoves, water filters;
2. **Unaffected**: water disinfectant;
3. **Decreased**: deworming drugs.

While very simple, these statements are perfect examples of what structured speculation might look like. They attack a relevant policy question—the extension of one-time subsidies to other technologies—and make clear predictions that could be falsified through new experiments.

Banerjee et al. (2015a). This paper does not engage in speculation but can illustrate the potential value of structured speculation for experimenters and their audiences. In particular, it reports on seven separate field trials, in seven different countries, of a program designed to help the ultra poor. The basic intervention was the same in all countries, was funded out of the same pool, and the evaluations were all coordinated by Dean Karlan of Yale University.

Within the study, there were two options for external speculation. First, different countries were evaluated at different times. Second, there were multiple rounds of results for each location. Results from countries evaluated early in the experiment could have been used to speculate about the results from those evaluated later. Within a country, earlier rounds could have been used to speculate about later rounds. But what would have been the benefit of doing so? And how would we go about it, in hindsight?

There were many common questions that came up about this research: How long did we expect the effects to last? Was there any point in carrying out this program in rich or middle-income countries? Formally speculating about these questions in earlier rounds and countries would have provided a structure for answering those multiple queries and justified elements of our experimental design that readers and reviewers had some reason to criticize. In addition, making public predictions would have provided an opportunity for the authors—and other scholars—to learn about what kinds of predictions tend to be trustworthy.

Even directional predictions—a speculation that this effect will be larger than that one, or that it will be bigger or smaller than some number, possibly zero—would have been of some use. The point estimates of the program impact are smaller in richer countries. Does this mean the program needs to be rethought for richer countries? We could have informed this decision by aggregating all we knew about the program, including the quantile results and results for certain subpopulations, to declare whether we believe the effects shrink with a country's gross domestic product. We could have done this at different points in time, as the results came in from different countries and rounds, to see how good we are at making these sorts of predictions, and thus, how strongly we should advocate for our predictions at the end of the study. A similar exercise could have also been carried to predict the change in impact over time, which is key to understanding whether the intervention actually frees people from a poverty trap.

Banerjee et al. (2015b). Directional predictions would have also been very useful in maximizing the information from a series of so-called Teaching at the Right Level (**TaRL**) interventions described in Banerjee et al. (2015b). These interventions seek to teach children basic skills they lack, even when they are in a grade that presumes they have mastered those skills. This does not happen as a matter of course in most schools in the developing world (Banerjee and Duflo, 2011). As this intervention had already been shown to work on the margins of the school system, each experiment (RCT) focused on a different way of integrating this practice into government schools. The interventions varied from training teachers, to giving them the materials to use for TaRL, to implementing TaRL during the summer break (when teachers are not required to follow the set curriculum), to integrating TaRL directly into the curriculum, and so on. Each intervention built on the successes and failures of the previous interventions, culminating in two different, but successful, models. Yet without recording the predictions made along the way, this would look like an ex post rationalization of shooting in the dark. Even minimal public predictions—this approach is likely to work better than that—would have helped at lot.

Duflo et al. (2008). Another innovation that would have been useful is our call to record structured speculation at the end of each paper (in addition to in a repository, as we describe in the following section). This would allow for a clear demarcation of results that are speculative—which will tend to arise in papers with preregistration and preanalysis plans—and those that are not. Such a demarcation would have clearly helped in dealing with Deaton's (2010, pp. 441—442) critique of the first TaRL paper (Banerjee et al., 2007).

When two independent but identical randomized controlled trials in two cities in India find that children's scores improved less in Mumbai than in Vadodara, the authors state "this is likely related to the fact that over 80 percent of the children in Mumbai had already mastered the basic language skills the program was covering" (Duflo et al., 2008). It is not clear how "likely" is established here, and there is certainly no evidence that conforms to the "gold standard" that is seen as one of the central justifications for (randomized controlled trials). For the same reason, repeated successful replications of a "what works" experiment, i.e., one that is unrelated to some underlying or guiding mechanism, are both unlikely and unlikely to be persuasive.

Our proposal would have helped with such criticism by establishing a place within the paper where it was clear that this assertion was based on our own knowledge and intuitions, rather than a part of the experimental design.

6.2.1 A Post hoc evaluation

In summary, our proposal would have helped with criticisms of prior research in three ways. First, it would establish a place within research where such speculation is both expected and encouraged. Second, by attaching reputational incentives to such speculation, the reader can be assured that it is not just idle chatter intended to explain away an uncomfortable discrepancy. Third, because experimenters will be encouraged to speculate about the outcomes of replications before they happen, replications that are close to their predictions should increase, at least slightly, the credibility of the experimenter's preferred underlying mechanism.

An alternative approach, being pioneered by Stefano DellaVigna, of the University of California, and Devin Pope, of the University of Chicago, is to elicit priors on a specific research question from a wide range of experts (Della Vigna and Pope, 2016a,b). This has the benefit of forcing the audience to think about their priors before research is carried out, and identifying the places in which research can make the largest contribution by shifting the average prior, or collapsing the distribution of priors. However, it is unlikely to protect against the most skeptical members of an audience, who may not be in any given surveyed panel of experts. Moreover, it lacks many of the side benefits of our proposal.

On the other hand, the DellaVigna and Pope approach is being implemented today, while, with the exception of Dupas (2014), none of the papers above contained structured speculation. Why not? This was, of course, in part because it was not on the agenda. But there are deeper reasons: we, like many other researchers, focused on the reduced form local average treatment effect estimates, which tell us very little directly about how they would translate to other environments. A more natural basis for speculation would be to estimate a structural model and use the estimated parameters—which can be made to directly depend on features of the environment—to predict out of sample. But, we must recognize that the choice of a model is itself subjective, so providing a model that rationalizes some prediction is not, in itself, completely reassuring.

However, the alternative may be worse. With different (Bayesian) readers having different priors and models of the world, even well-structured speculation without a model could be interpreted in multiple ways. The model serves as a currency for reducing, to a single number, the many disparate pieces of information that the author has. Without the prop of a model that exercise seems too hard to carry out with any accuracy.

To reduce the space of possible models, it would be helpful to demarcate the set of environments where structured speculation would be particularly useful, and the challenges likely to be encountered there. This is what the next subsection attempts to do.

7. ISSUES OF PARTICULAR INTEREST

While our proposal could apply to any element of external validity, it is perhaps useful to outline a number of external validity issues that are focal for economists.

Focal external validity issues:
1. How scalable is the intervention?
2. What are treatment effects on a different population?
3. What are treatment effects on the same population in different circumstances?

Another important question that we do not discuss further is the one addressed by Dupas (2014): What is the effect of a different, but related, technology?

7.1 Scalability

A central concern in many development environments is how an intervention might *scale*, i.e., how might the treatment effects measured in an experiment change if the intervention was rolled out across a province, country, or region? This concern is often composed of two interrelated issues: how spillover effects might enhance or reduce the benefits of a particular treatment, and how the incentives of an organization capable of implementing large-scale interventions might affect outcomes.

Spillovers. Spillovers encompass both general equilibrium effects and externalities. Consider an intervention that gives scholarships for top-performing students in local schools to attend provincial schools. As an experimental intervention, this policy may have large positive effects on a locality because several students from the local school would be able to get an improved education. However, if rolled out nationally, the returns on human capital may diminish, possibly diminishing the treatment effect on outcomes such as wealth, savings, and consumption. There may, however, be positive general equilibrium effects. For instance, a more educated available workforce may increase foreign direct investment and lead to the creation of new types of jobs. General equilibrium effects are difficult to apprehend through purely experimental methods, but it is possible to draw on different sources of information to inform speculation. For instance, one may use regional heterogeneity in average human capital to map out what the effect may be should the program get rolled out.

Direct externalities (e.g., physical interaction, information, contagion, and so on) may be more easily captured, as they tend to be more localized. Experimental designs that at least partially capture local externalities are now quite standard (Baird et al., 2014; CrYPER et al., 2013; Muralidharan and Sundararaman, 2015). The difficult external validity question relates to the effect of scaling on adoption rates. In some cases, such as those of deworming drugs or vaccines, private returns are a diminishing function of aggregate adoption. This may be addressed by variation in the intensity of the program across locations. While this variation is likely to not result in sufficient power to become a main finding of a paper, it would be useful for guiding speculation about external validity.

Implementation by others. Informed speculation about implementing agencies is inherently difficult. Three environments seem relevant: implementations by other researchers, implementations by non-governmental organizations (NGOs) or international agencies, and implementations by provincial or country governments (Bold et al., 2013). The difficulty is that in order to make her speculation meaningful, the experimenter would need to specify the precise governments or NGOs that her projections apply to. This might expose the experimenter to political risk and hamper her ability to conduct future experiments.[23] At the very least, it should be possible for the experimenter to highlight the specific aspects of the intervention that may make it difficult to be implemented by others.

One aspect of implementation that can possibly be controlled by experimenters is the reputational capital they have when they interact with the target population. They may be able to control for this by running initial perception surveys regarding their potential implementation partners, as well as by varying the way they present themselves. Having an official present at a meeting may significantly affect the way people engage with an experiment.

Again, an experiment may not be sufficiently well powered for variation in implementation to lead to significant findings. However, that data would clearly help informed speculation. In some cases, the experimenter may just have an intuitive understanding of how things would play out in different settings. Such intuitive understandings would be of great value to the next experimenter(s) who tried similar experiments. As such, it would be a useful contribution to speculate about the role of implementing agencies on outcomes.

7.2 Effect on other populations

If a program is effective in one region, or one country, is it effective in another? If a program is effective for a specific social group, would it be effective for different groups in the same country? For comparable groups in a different country? Answering such questions is inherently a speculative exercise, and yet it is useful for experimenters to do so. Experimenters have detailed intuitive knowledge of local mechanisms that can help clarify what matters for results to extend or not.

For example, suppose a program was found to be effective in India, and the experimenter tried to speculate about its effectiveness in Kenya. The experimenter may first assess the underlying heterogeneity in treatment effects and decide the program is principally effective in helping members of Scheduled Castes. If this is the case, one may reason that the program could be effective for historically discriminated populations of Kenya, say Muslims. However, by spelling this hypothesis out clearly, another experimenter may question its relevance if she believed affirmative action for Scheduled Castes appears essential for the treatment to be effective.

Subgroups and selective trials. We believe that subgroup analysis, which is often instructive but poorly identified, has an important role to play in formulating successful speculative hypotheses. Reweighting treatment effects by subgroups provides a natural way to project findings to different environments. This obviously includes groups formed

---

[23] This concern may be mitigated in practice by the fact that the employees of many organizations are more aware of their limited implementation abilities than researchers themselves.

on observable characteristics, say income, education, religion, and so on. Interestingly, this also includes unobservable characteristics elicited through mechanisms.

A recent strand of the experimental literature, illustrated by Ashraf et al. (2010), Berry et al. (2012), Cohen and Dupas (2010), Jack et al. (2013), and Karlan and Zinman (2009) and formalized in Chassang et al. (2012), combines randomization with self-selection in order to "observe unobservables." The idea is as follows: randomized trials are lotteries over treatment. Many trials consist of a single lottery. By having multiple lotteries with different winning rates and assigning costs to these lotteries, it becomes possible to elicit participants' values for the treatment, and estimate treatment effects conditional on values. This provides additional information helpful to project treatment effects on different populations.

For instance, as selective trials recover marginal treatment effects, Heckman and Vytlacil (2005), they allow the experimenter to figure out the effect of the program on populations selected through prices, by reduced availability, and so on. An experimenter will also make very different predictions about external treatment effects depending on whether it is effective for everybody, or only for highly motivated participants.

It is important to note that the "cost" of a lottery does not need to be monetary. Indeed, effort, more than money, seems to be a metric more easily comparable across locations. Alatas et al. (2016) varies whether a participant has to travel for an interview, or can stay at home, to see if they qualify for a cash-transfer program for the poor. They find that those who travel are significantly more likely to actually be qualified for the program and that interviewer coding of them is significantly more reliable. Randomizing the treatment (the cash-transfer program) conditional on whether or not the participant is judged to be qualified would have allowed this work to estimate returns for the motivated and for the less motivated. More generally, the variety of information that can be elicited through mechanisms is very large, and it frequently comes with a natural structural interpretation. We believe that collecting such information will prove helpful in formulating speculative hypotheses.

7.3 Same population, different circumstances

The same population may react differently to treatment in different circumstances. For instance, if an intervention helps people save more, one may ask whether it will continue to be effective as people accumulate savings. Similarly, one may ask about the effectiveness of subsidies for technology adoption as information about the new technology spreads, and so on.

As before, subgroup analysis is likely to be helpful in forming opinions about the way effects will pan out as the population evolves. Richer participants or more informed communities may be used to proxy for future populations. As such, innovations in

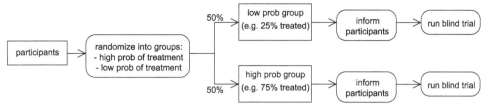

Figure 2 A two-by-two blind trial. The figure shows the two stages of randomization, with participants first allocated to either a high- or low-probability treatment group, then informed of this probability (thus generating the corresponding placebo effect) and then receiving either treatment or nontreatment in a standard, blinded manner. *(Reproduced from Chassang, S., Snowberg, E., Seymour, B. and Bowles, C., 2015. Accounting for behavior in treatment effects: new applications for blind trials, PLoS One 10 (6), e0127227.)*

experimental design may also be helpful in this respect. Chassang et al. (2012) emphasizes that by either varying incentives or by varying the participants' beliefs that they are being treated, it is possible to identify purely behavioral dimensions of treatment effects, i.e., treatment effects that are due to participant's behavioral changes accompanying (the expectation of) treatment. For instance, a small business owner participating in an experiment in which she receives accounting training may decide to work longer hours because she believes the training is making her more productive. This could result in finding positive effects to training even when accounting itself is not useful. These effects, however, may not persist, the treatment effect for an informed participant, aware that accounting is of limited use, may be much smaller.

This observation is useful in medicine, where isolating treatment effects due to the interaction of a new drug with patient behavior is essential for understanding the true value add of that drug. In the context of medical trials, Chassang et al. (2015) proposes 2 × 2 blind trials (Fig. 2) able to isolate both the pure effect of treatment and the interaction of treatment and behavior. In a 2 × 2 trial, participants are randomly split into two arms. In one arm, the participants are told they will have a high probability of treatment, and in the other, they are told they will have a low probability of treatment. The trial within each arm is then run accordingly. Under the assumption that participant behavior will change with the probability of treatment, the trial independently randomizes both behavior and treatment. This is sufficient to isolate the pure effect of treatment, the pure effect of behavior, and the interaction of treatment and behavior.

Bulte et al. (2014) implements a version of a 2 × 2 trial in a development context using seed varieties as its technology. Its findings suggest that purely behavioral responses, i.e., mediated by expectations of change—to treatment are significant. This, in turn, suggests that participants may change their response over time, as they learn the true effectiveness of a treatment. Practically, running the complex mechanisms described in Chassang et al. (2012), or using blind treatments as in Bulte et al. (2014) may not always be feasible. However, it should always be possible to survey participants about their expectations for the technology, and about how they are changing their practice in response to treatment. These survey measures, which in many cases would not naturally be reported as hard evidence, may prove quite useful in shaping speculative hypotheses.

7.4 Formats for structured speculation

We conclude our discussion of structured speculation with a brief discussion of the formats in which structured speculation may be expressed. We argue that, at this stage, there is no wrong way to formulate hypotheses about external validity, provided the hypotheses are formulated in a clear and falsifiable way.

Qualitative predictions. Simple qualitative statements are not necessarily less rigorous than analytical ones. For instance, Dupas (2014) describes environments in which treatment effects are likely to larger or smaller. These descriptions are simple, yet precise and falsifiable.

Experimenters often produce reduced form estimates for multiple subpopulations and/or quantile treatment effects—although they may not report all of them—and these, along with some intuitive understanding of which environments are similar, make it possible for them to predict the direction of change in the treatment effect, although perhaps not the magnitude of the change. Such speculation is naturally expressed qualitatively, as in, "This treatment effect is likely to be larger than that."

Predictive models. If sufficient data about subgroups are available, experimenters may feel comfortable producing statistical models predicting treatment effects in other environments conditional on observables. Multiperiod, multicountry trials such as Alatas et al. (2012), or multitrial meta-analyses offer natural starting points. The main advantage of producing a fully specified, predictive model is that it is unambiguous, and by construction, clear and falsifiable. It is therefore a better starting point for further analysis than purely qualitative predictions. Note that the model need not necessarily predict point estimates. A model predicting ranges of estimates would be equally well specified.

Theory and structural models. Theory has an important role to play in formulating useful speculative hypotheses. If an experimenter lays out a theoretical model, she thinks best, summarizes the facts she sees, and the theory is rich enough to cover environments beyond what is in her experiment, she is effectively making a directional prediction for other environments.[24]

This is already happening to some degree. For example, Karlan et al. (2012) evaluate two interventions to improve business for tailors in Ghana. In one intervention, the tailors were provided with a cash grant; in the other, they were given training. Both changed the way the tailors practiced business (at least briefly) but neither increased profits over the long term. The authors develop a model in which this occurs because

---

[24] Some predictions may be ambiguous, which is both a benefit and a drawback of formal models.

tailors treat these interventions as opportunities to explore new opportunities. While most of these fail, the option value of experimentation is likely still positive. This implies that there should be some tailors who experience very large gains from these interventions, but that, on average, the effect will be small and difficult to detect. To test this prediction, the authors look at other studies of similar interventions that are powered to detect differential changes in the right tail of the distribution. They find some support for their theory.

Identified structural models, just as predictive statistical models, are attractive because they make fully-specified predictions in external environments. An advantage they have over purely statistical models is that they can make the process of external extrapolation more transparent. We emphasize, however, the cautionary implications of Proposition 3. In all external decision-making problems, inference is unavoidably subjective. In structural modeling, the source of subjectivity is the model itself.

8. CONCLUSION

This chapter has ranged from models of experimentation, to prescriptions for experimental design, all the way to external validity. Hopefully, the wide range of (potential) applications of decision theory to experimental practice is enough to convince theorists and practitioners alike that this is a fruitful area for further discovery.

REFERENCES

Aghion, P., Tirole, J., 1994. The management of innovation. Q. J. Econ. 109 (4), 1185–1209.

Aghion, P., Bolton, P., Harris, C., Jullien, B., 1991. Optimal learning by experimentation. Rev. Econ. Stud. 58 (4), 621–654.

Alatas, V., Abhijit, B., Hanna, R., Olken, B.A., Tobias, J., 2012. Targeting the poor: evidence from a field experiment in Indonesia. Am. Econ. Rev. 102 (4), 1206–1240.

Alatas, V., Purnamasari, R., Wai-Poi, M., Banerjee, A., Olken, B.A., Hanna, R., 2016. Self-targeting: evidence from a field experiment in Indonesia. J. Polit. Econ. 124 (2), 371–427.

Andreoni, J., Callen, M., Khan, Y., Jaffar, K., Sprenger, C., 2016. Using Preference Estimates to Customize Incentives: An Application to Polio Vaccination Drives in Pakistan. NBER Working Paper Series # 22019.

Ashraf, N., Berry, J., Shapiro, J.M., December 2010. Can higher prices stimulate product use? Evidence from a field experiment in Zambia. Am. Econ. Rev. 100 (6), 2383–2413.

Athey, S., Imbens, G.W., 2016. The econometrics of randomized experiments. In: Esther, D., Banerjee, A. (Eds.), Handbook of Field Experiments, vol.1, pp. 73–140.

Baird, S., Aislinn Bohren, J., McIntosh, C., Berk, O., 2014. Designing Experiments to Measure Spillover Effects. PIER Working Paper #14-032.

Banerjee, A., August 1992. A simple model of herd behavior. Q. J. Econ. 107 (3), 797–817.

Banerjee, A., Duflo, E., 2011. Poor Economics: A Radical Rethinking of the Way to Fight Global Poverty. PublicAffairs.

Banerjee, A., Duflo, E., Goldberg, N., Karlan, D., Osei, R., Parienté, W., Shapiro, J., Thuysbaert, B., Udry, C., 2015a. A multifaceted program causes lasting progress for the very poor: evidence from six countries. Science 348 (6236), 1260799.

Banerjee, A., Banerji, R., Berry, J., Duflo, E., Kannan, H., Mukherji, S., Walton, M., 2015b. Teaching at the Right Level: Evidence From Randomized Evaluations in India. MIT Working paper.

Banerjee, A., Cole, S., Duflo, E., Linden, L., August 2007. Remedying education: evidence from two randomized experiments in India. Q. J. Econ. 122 (3), 1236–1264.

Banerjee, A., Chassang, S., Montero, S., Snowberg, E., 2014. A Theory of Experimenters. Princeton University, Mimeo.

Bellman, R., April 1956. A problem in the sequential design of experiments. Sankhyā Indian J. Statistics 16 (3/4), 221–229.

Bergemann, D., Välimäki, J., September 1996. Learning and strategic pricing. Econometrica 64 (5), 1125–1149.

Bergemann, D., Välimäki, J., 2002. Information acquisition and efficient mechanism design. Econometrica 70 (3), 1007–1033.

Bergemann, D., Välimäki, J., 2006. Bandit Problems. Cowles Foundation discussion paper.

Berry, J., Fischer, G., Guiteras, R., 2012. Eliciting and Utilizing Willingness to Pay: Evidence from Field Trials in Northern Ghana. Cornell University, mimeo.

Bewley, T.F., 1998. Knightian uncertainty. In: Jacobs, D.P., Kalai, E., Kamien, M.I. (Eds.), Frontiers of Research in Economic Theory: The Nancy L. Schwartz Memorial Lectures 1983–1997. Cambridge University Press: Econometric Society Monographs, pp. 71–81.

Bold, T., Kimenyi, M., Mwabu, G., Ng'ang'a, A., Sandefur, J., 2013. Scaling up What Works: Experimental Evidence on External Validity in Kenyan Education. Center for Global Development Working Paper #321.

Brodeur, A., Lé, M., Sangnier, M., Zylberberg, Y., 2016. Star wars: the empirics strike back. Am. Econ. J. Appl. Econ. 8 (1), 1–32.

Bruhn, M., McKenzie, D., 2009. In pursuit of balance: randomization in practice in development field experiments. Am. Econ. J. Appl. Econ. 1 (4), 200–232.

Bulte, E., Beekman, G., Di Falco, S., Hella, J., Lei, P., 2014. Behavioral responses and the impact of new agricultural technologies: evidence from a double-blind field experiment in Tanzania. Am. J. Agric. Econ. 96 (3), 813–830.

Casey, K., Glennerster, R., Miguel, E., 2012. Reashaping institutions: evidence on aid impacts using a preanalysis plan. Q. J. Econ. 127 (4), 1755–1812.

Chaloner, K., Verdinelli, I., August 1995. Bayesian experimental design: a review. Stat. Sci. 10 (3), 273–304.

Chassang, S., 2013. Calibrated incentive contracts. Econometrica 81 (5), 1935–1971.

Chassang, S., Snowberg, E., Seymour, B., Bowles, C., 2015. Accounting for behavior in treatment effects: new applications for blind trials. PLoS One 10 (6), e0127227.

Chassang, S., Padró i Miquel, G., Snowberg, E., June 2012. Selective trials: a principal-agent approach to randomized controlled experiments. Am. Econ. Rev. 102 (4), 1279–1309.

Cohen, J., Dupas, P., 2010. Free distribution or cost-sharing? Evidence from a randomized malaria prevention experiment. Q. J. Econ. 125 (1), 1–45.

Crépon, B., Duflo, E., Gurgand, M., Rathelot, R., Zamora, P., 2013. Do labor market policies have displacement effects? Evidence from a clustered randomized experiment. Q. J. Econ. 128 (2), 531–580.

De Finetti, B., 1937. La Prévision: ses lois Logiques, ses sources subjectives. Ann. l'institut Henri Poincaré 7 (1), 1–68.

Deaton, A., June 2010. Instruments, randomization, and learning about development. J. Econ. Literature 48 (2), 424–455.

Della Vigna, S., Pope, D., 2016a. What Motivates Effort? Evidence and Expert Forecasts. University of California, mimeo.

Della Vigna, S., Pope, D., 2016b. Run This Treament, Not that: What Experts Know. University of California, Mimeo.

Duflo, E., Glennerster, R., Kremer, M., 2008. Using randomization in development economics research: a tool kit. In: Paul Schultz, T., Strauss, J. (Eds.), Handbook of Development Economics, vol. 4. Elsevier, Amsterdam, pp. 3895–3962.

Dupas, P., 2014. Short-run subsidies and long-run adoption of new health products: evidence from a field experiment. Econometrica 82 (1), 197–228.

Egger, M., Davey Smith, G., Sterne, J.A.C., 2001. Uses and abuses of meta-analysis. Clin. Med. 1 (6), 478—484.

Ellsberg, D., 1961. Risk, ambiguity, and the savage axioms. Q. J. Econ. 75 (4), 643—669.

Fisher, R.A., 1926. The arrangement of field experiments. J. Ministry Agric. G. B. 33, 503—513.

Fisher, R.A., 1935. The Design of Experiments. Oliver & Boyd, Edinburgh and London.

Gilboa, I., Schmeidler, D., 1989. Maxmin expected utility with a non-unique prior. J. Math. Econ. 18 (2), 141—153.

Gilboa, I., Postlewaite, A., Schmeidler, D., 2009. Is it always rational to satisfy Savage's axioms? Econ. Philosophy 25 (3), 285—296.

Gittins, J.C., 1979. Bandit processes and dynamic allocation indices. J. R. Stat. Soc. Ser. B Methodol. 41 (2), 148—177.

Green, D.P., Tusicisny, A., 2012. Statistical Analysis of Results from Laboratory Studies in Experimental Economics: A Critique of Current Practice. Columbia University, mimeo.

Grossman, S.J., Stiglitz, J.E., June 1980. On the impossibility of informationally efficient markets. Am. Econ. Rev. 70 (3), 393—408.

Gul, F., Pesendorfer, W., 2001. Temptation and self-control. Econometrica 69 (6), 1403—1435.

Heckman, J.J., Vytlacil, E., May 2005. Structural equations, treatment effects, and econometric policy evaluation. Econometrica 73 (3), 669—738.

Humphreys, M., de la Sierra, R.S., Van der Windt, P., 2013. Fishing, commitment, and communication: a proposal for comprehensive nonbinding research registration. Polit. Anal. 21 (1), 1—20.

Jack, B.K., et al., 2013. Private information and the allocation of land use subsidies in Malawi. Am. Econ. J. Appl. Econ. 5 (3), 113—135.

Karlan, D., Knight, R., Udry, C., 2012. Hoping to Win, Expected to Lose: Theory and Lessons on Micro Enterprise Development. NBER Working Paper Series # 18325.

Karlan, D.S., Zinman, J., 2009. Observing unobservables: identifying information asymmetries with a consumer credit field experiment. Econometrica 77 (6), 1993—2008.

Kasy, M., 2013. Why Experimenters Should Not Randomize, and What They Should Do Instead. Harvard University, Mimeo.

Klibanoff, P., Marinacci, M., Mukerji, S., 2005. A smooth model of decision making under ambiguity. Econometrica 73 (6), 1849—1892.

Kreps, D.M., Porteus, E.L., 1978. Temporal resolution of uncertainty and dynamic choice theory. Econometrica 46 (1), 185—200.

Machina, M.J., 1989. Dynamic consistency and non-expected utility models of choice under uncertainty. J. Econ. Literature 27 (4), 1622—1668.

Maynard, G.D., March 1909. Statistical study of anti-typhoid inoculation. Biometrika 6 (4), 366—375.

Miguel, E., Kremer, M., January 2004. Worms: identifying impacts on education and health in the presence of treatment externalities. Econometrica 72 (1), 159—217.

Milgrom, P.R., July 1981. Rational expectations, information acquisition, and competitive bidding. Econometrica 89 (4), 921—943.

Morgan, K.L., Rubin, D.B., 2012. Rerandomization to improve covariate balance in experiments. Ann. Statistics 40 (2), 1263—1282.

Muralidharan, K., Sundararaman, V., 2015. The aggregate effects of school choice: evidence from a two-stage experiment. Q. J. Econ. 130 (3), 1011—1066.

Olken, B.A., 2015. Promises and perils of pre-analysis plans. J. Econ. Perspect. 29 (3), 61—80.

Olszewski, W., Peski, M., 2011. The principal-agent approach to testing experts. Am. Econ. J. Microeconomics 3 (2), 89—113.

Pearl, J., 2000. Causality: Models, Reasoning, and Inference. Cambridge University Press, New York.

Persico, N., 2000. Information acquisition in auctions. Econometrica 68 (1), 135—148.

Robbins, H., September 1952. Some aspects of the sequential design of experiments. Bull. Am. Math. Soc. 58 (5), 527—535.

Rothschild, M., 1974. A two-armed bandit theory of market pricing. J. Econ. Theory 9 (2), 185—202.

Rubin, D.B., 1974. Estimating causal effects of treatments in randomized and nonrandomized studies. J. Educ. Psychol. 66 (5), 688–701.

Savage, L.J., 1954. The Foundations of Statistics. Courier Corporation.

Schmeidler, D., July 1989. Subjective probability and expected utility without additivity. Econometrica 57 (3), 571–587.

Simpson, R.J.S., Pearson, K., 1904. Report on certain enteric fever inoculation statistics. Br. Med. J. 2 (2288), 1243–1246.

Vapnik, V., 1999. The Nature of Statistical Learning Theory, second ed. Springer.

CHAPTER 5

The Practicalities of Running Randomized Evaluations: Partnerships, Measurement, Ethics, and Transparency

R. Glennerster
Massachusetts Institute of Technology, J-PAL, Cambridge, MA, United States
E-mail: rglenner@mit.edu

Contents

Handbook of Economic Field Experiments, Volume 1
ISSN 2214-658X, http://dx.doi.org/10.1016/bs.hefe.2016.10.002

Abstract

A number of critical innovations spurred the rapid expansion in the use of field experiments by academics. Some of these were econometric but many were intensely practical. Researchers learned how to work with a wide range of implementing organizations from small, local nongovernmental organizations to large government bureaucracies. They improved data collection techniques and switched to digital data collection. As researchers got more involved in the design and implementation of the interventions they tested, new ethical issues arose. Finally, the dramatic rise in the use of experiments increased the benefits associated with research transparency. This chapter records some of these practical innovations. It focuses on how to select and effectively work with the organization running an intervention which is being evaluated; ways to minimize attrition, monitor enumerators, and ensure data are collected consistently in treatment and comparison areas; practical ethical issues such as when to start the ethics approval process; and research transparency, including how to prevent publication bias and data mining and the role of experimental registries, preanalysis plans, data publication reanalysis, and replication efforts.

Keywords

Data collection; Ethics; Field experiments; Partnerships; Research transparency

JEL Codes

C81; C93; O10; O12; O22

Economists have known for a long time that randomization could help identify causal connections by solving the problem of selection bias. In chapter "The Politics and Practice of Social Experiments: Seeds of a Revolution" by Gueron (2017) and Gueron and Rolston (2013) describe the effort in the United States to move experiments out of the laboratory into the policy world in the 1960s and 1970s. This experience was critical in proving the feasibility of field experiments, working through some of the important ethical questions involved, showing how researchers and practitioners could work together, and demonstrating that the results of field experiments were often very different from those generated by observational studies. Interestingly, there was relatively limited academic support for this first wave of field experiments (Gueron and Rolston, 2013), most of which were carried out by research groups such as MDRC, Abt, and Mathematica, to evaluate US government programs, and they primarily used individual-level randomization. In contrast, a more recent wave of field experiments started in the mid-1990s was driven by academics, initially focused on developing countries, often worked with nongovernmental organizations, and frequently used clustered designs.

A number of critical innovations spurred the take-off of field experiments, particularly in academic circles. Some of these were theoretical: They included understanding how to maximize power from limited sample sizes (Imbens, 2011; Bruhn and McKenzie, 2009); how to use randomized control trials (RCTs) to measure externalities (Miguel and Kremer, 2004); the diffusion of information (Duflo and Saez, 2002; Kremer and Miguel, 2007); equilibrium effects (Crépon et al., 2012; Mobarak and Rosenzweig, 2014); and parameters in network theory (Chandrasekhar et al., 2015; Beaman et al., 2013).

Many of the innovations that powered the growth of field experiments, however, were intensely practical. Researchers learned how to work with a wide range of implementing organizations including local nongovernmental organizations, private companies, and social entrepreneurs. Unlike governments, with whom most early RCTs were conducted, these new partners tended to be more open to trying new approaches to solving problems and were more willing to test different aspects of their programs separately and in combination. Logistical and financial constraints meant they could not reach everyone they wanted to, making randomization a natural method for allocating rationed resources. There were also important practical innovations in measurement which opened up new subject areas to field experiments. With these new partners and new subject areas for experiments came a range of new ethical questions, including how to define the boundary between practice and research and how to regulate activity across that boundary as researchers got more and more involved in the design and implementation of the interventions they tested. Finally, the dramatic rise in the use of experiments increased the benefits associated with research transparency.

This chapter seeks to record some of these practical innovations that have accompanied and enabled the expansion in the use of field experiments. It is impossible to be comprehensive, so we focus on four discrete and important issues. Section 1 discusses how to select and work with a partner organization that will implement the program to be evaluated by an RCT, as well the conditions under which it makes sense for a researcher to be both the implementer and the evaluator of a program. Section 2 discusses practical challenges in data collection and strategies to combat them, including minimizing attrition, monitoring enumerators, and ensuring that data are collected consistently in treatment and comparison areas. Section 3 covers the practical ethical issues a researcher conducting randomized evaluations must take into account when designing and carrying out their research. Section 4 covers topics in research transparency, including publication bias, data mining, experimental registries, preanalysis plans (PAPs), data publication reanalysis, and replication.

1. COLLABORATION BETWEEN RESEARCHERS AND IMPLEMENTERS

Unlike most academic economic research, running field-based RCTs often involves intense collaboration between researchers and the organization or individuals who are implementing the intervention that is being evaluated. This collaboration can be the best thing about working on a field experiment or the worst. If the collaboration goes well, the researcher can learn an enormous amount from the implementing partner about how local formal and informal institutions work, how to measure outcomes in the local context, and how to interpret the results of the study. If the partnership is going badly it is almost impossible to run a high-quality field experiment. In this section we discuss practical ways to develop and maintain a good collaboration with an implementing partner.

We start with tips on how to find the right implementer and what to do to make the researcher—implementer partnership as effective as possible. We then examine whether and when it is worth attempting to "self-implement," i.e., be both implementer and evaluator.

1.1 Developing a good researcher—implementer partnership

Researcher and implementer partnerships, like any other relationship, require listening to and understanding the other partner, being flexible to their needs, respecting the other's contribution, and being honest. During an initial "courtship" phase, the two groups seek to understand whether they want to enter into an evaluation partnership. What should a researcher be looking for in an implementer during this phase? What can a researcher do to make themselves useful to, and thus support a good relationship with, an implementing organization?

1.2 What makes a good implementing partner?

1. **Sufficient scale**

    A first and easy-to-determine filter for a good implementing partner is whether an organization is working at a big enough scale to be able to generate a sample size that will provide enough power for the experiment. How big is sufficient depends on the level at which the randomization is going to take place (see chapter: The Econometrics of Randomized Experiments by Athey and Imbens (2017), as well as the number of variants of the program that are going to be compared, and the outcome of interest. Thus a lot of detailed discussion needs to take place about what a potential evaluation would look like before it is possible to say if an evaluation is feasible. It is surprising how many potential partnerships can be ruled out quite early on because the implementer is just not working at a big enough scale to make a decent evaluation possible.

2. **Flexibility**

    A willingness to try different versions of the program and adapt elements in response to discussions with researchers is an important attribute of an implementing partner. We can learn a lot by testing different parts of a program together and separately or by comparing different approaches to the same problem against each other, but doing this type of testing requires a very flexible partner. The best partnerships are the ones in which researcher and implementer work together to decide the most interesting versions of the program to test.

3. **Technical programmatic expertise and a representative program**

    There is a risk of testing a program run by an inexperienced implementer, finding a null result, and generating the response, "Of course there was no impact, you worked with an inexperienced implementer." The researcher also has less to learn about how good programs are run from an inexperienced implementer and the partnership risks becoming one sided. At the other end of the spectrum, we may not want to work with a gold-plated implementer unless we want to test proof of concept. There are two risks here: that the program is so expensive that it will never be cost-effective even if it is effective; and that it relies on unusual and difficult-to-reproduce resources. For example, a program that relies on a few very dynamic teachers or mentors might be hard to replicate. An implementer working at a very big scale is unlikely to run a gold-plated program and has already shown the program can be scaled. It is also possible to work with a smaller implementer, but one that closely follows a model used by others. The microcredit organization Spandana was a perfect implementation partner for our evaluation of the impact of microcredit (Banerjee et al., 2015a). They operated at a large scale and their credit product was close to that of many other microcredit organizations. We tested their impact as they expanded into a large Indian city, a popular type of location for microcredit organizations.

4. Local expertise and reputation

Implementers who have been working with a population for many years have in-depth knowledge of local formal and informal institutions, population characteristics, and geography that is invaluable in designing and implementing an evaluation. They can answer questions, such as what messages are likely to resonate with this population? what does success look like and how can we measure it? When I started working in Sierra Leone I spent a long time traveling round the country with staff from Statistics Sierra Leone, Care, and the Institutional Reform and Capacity Building Project. One had worked with Paul Richards, an important anthropologist in Sierra Leone. Our final measures of trust, group membership, and collective action relied heavily on their suggestions and input. I learned that it was socially acceptable to ask about the bloody civil war that had just ended but that asking about marital disputes could get us thrown out of the village. From Tejan Rogers I learned that every rural (and some urban) communities in Sierra Leone come together for "road brushing" where they clear encroaching vegetation from the dirt road that links their community to the next and even build the common palm-log bridges over rivers. How often this activity took place and the proportion of the community that took part became our preferred measure of collective action and has been used by many other authors since.

Just as importantly, an implementer who has been working locally has a reputation in local communities that would take a researcher years to build. This reputation can be vital. We learn little about the impact of a program if suspicion of the implementer means that few take up the program. The reputation of the implementing organization can also be critical to the research team being permitted to operate in the community and to getting a high response rate to surveys.

Researchers need to understand how valuable this reputational capital is to the implementer. What may seem like reluctance on the part of the implementing partner to try new ideas may be a fully justified caution to put their hard-won reputation on the line.

5. Low staff turnover

Evaluation is a partnership of trust and understanding and this takes time to build. All too often a key counterpart in the implementing organization will move on just as an evaluation is reaching a critical stage. Their successor may be less open to evaluation, want to test a different question, be against randomization, or just uninterested. High turnover can happen in any organization, but governments and organizations with foreign staff are particularly likely to have high turnover. NGOs that draw their staff from the local community tend to experience less staff turnover. The only way a researcher can protect the evaluation is to try and build relationships at many levels of the implementing organization, so that the loss of one champion does not doom the entire project.

6. Desire to know the truth and willingness to invest in uncovering it

The most important quality of an implementing partner is the desire to know the true impact of an intervention and a willingness to devote time and energy to helping the researcher uncover the truth. Many organizations start off enthusiastic about the idea of an evaluation: they want an expert to certify that their program is very successful. At some point these organizations realize that it is possible that a rigorous evaluation may conclude that their program does not have a positive impact. At this point, two reactions are possible: a sudden realization of all the practical constraints that will make an evaluation impossible or a renewed commitment to learn.

In Glennerster and Takaravasha (2013, p. 20), we quote Rukmini Banerji of Pratham at the launch of an evaluation of Pratham's flagship "Read India" program:

And of course [the researchers] may find that it doesn't work. But if it doesn't work, we need to know that. We owe it to ourselves and the communities we work with not to waste their and our time and resources on a program that does not help children learn. If we find that this program isn't working, we will go and develop something that will.[1]

This is the kind of commitment that makes an ideal partner. It is not just that an unwilling partner can throw obstacles in the path of an effective evaluation. An implementation partner needs to be an active and committed member of the evaluation team. There will inevitably be problems that come up during the evaluation process that the implementer will have to help solve, often at a financial or time cost to themselves. The baseline may run behind schedule and implementation will need to be delayed until it is complete; transport costs of the program might be higher

---

[1] This quote reflects my memory of Rukmini's speech.

as implementation communities end up being further apart than they otherwise would be to allow for controls; when and where a program is to be rolled out may need to be set further in advance because of the evaluation; selection criteria must be written down and followed scrupulously to reduce the discretion of local staff in accepting people into the program; or some promising program areas may need to be left for the control group. Partners will only put up with these problems and actively help solve them if they fully appreciate the benefits of the evaluation being high quality and if they understand why these restrictions are necessary to a high-quality evaluation. Padmaja Reddy of Spandana provides a good example of this commitment. In the early stages of our evaluation of Spandana's microcredit product we became aware that credit officers from Spandana were going into some control areas to recruit microcredit clients. Only Padmaja's active intervention managed to stop this activity, which would have undermined the entire experiment if left unchecked.

Commitment to the evaluation needs to come from many levels of the organization. If the headquarters in Delhi want to do an impact evaluation but the local staff do not, it is not advisable for HQ to force the evaluation through because it is the staff at the local level who will need to be deeply involved in working through the details with the researcher. Similarly, if the local staff are committed but the HQ is not, there will not be support for the extra time and cost the local staff will need to expend to participate in the study. Worst of all is when a funder forces an unwilling implementer to do an RCT run by a researcher. My own and others' bitter experience suggests that being involved in a scenario of this kind will suck up months of a researcher's time trying to come up with evaluation designs that the implementer will find some way to object to.

If this level of commitment to discovering the unvarnished truth sounds a little optimistic, there are practical ways to make an impact evaluation less threatening to a partner. An implementer who runs many types of programs has less at stake from an impact evaluation of one of their programs than an organization with a single signature program. Another option is to test different variants of a program rather than the impact of the program itself. For example, testing the pros and cons of weekly versus monthly repayment of microcredit loans (Field et al., 2012) is less threatening than testing the impact of microcredit loans. In some cases researchers have started relationships with implementers by testing a question that is less threatening (although potentially less interesting). As the partnership has built up trust, the implementing partner has opened up more and more of their portfolio to rigorous testing.

7. Trade-offs between partner criteria

An important concern is that a partner, who is committed to knowing the truth about the effect of the program understands randomization, and has the time and expertise to invest in a serious evaluation partnership, is unlikely to be representative of other implementers. We may worry that there is a systematic bias in the programs that are evaluated. Allcott (2015) examines 111 RCTs of similar programs to encourage energy conservation across the United States. He finds that the program was more effective in the first 10 sites to adopt the program and be evaluated than those who adopted and were evaluated later. This holds true even after correcting for observable differences between sites. He suggests that utilities in areas that were particularly keen to reduce energy signed up to the program earlier and also had clients who responded more to conservation messages. Note that in this case evaluation and program adoption are a single package. Allcott's estimation of site selection bias combines two possible biases: the program is more effective for those who (1) are early adopters and (2) are willing to be evaluated. Allcott is not able to test whether those who are willing to evaluate are likely to run higher quality programs because, in his case, the programs are all run by a single operator at different sites.

Whether we want to prioritize having a representative partner or a highly committed partner depends on the objective of the research. If we are testing an underlying human behavior—such as a willingness to pay now for benefits in the future—the representativeness of the partner may be less relevant. If we want to know whether a type of program, as it is usually implemented, works, we will want to prioritize working with a representative partner. Note that "does this type of program work" is not necessarily a more policy-relevant question than a more general question about human behavior. By their nature, more general questions generalize better and can be applied to a wider range of policy questions.

1.3 What can a researcher do to foster a good partnership with an implementing organization?

We have set out a long list of characteristics a researcher wants in an implementing partner. But what does an implementer want in a research partner, and how can a researcher make him- or herself a better partner?

1. **Answer questions the partner wants to be answered**

    Start by listening. A researcher will go into a partnership with ideas about what they want to test, but it is important to understand what the implementer wants to learn from the partnership. Try to include a component of the evaluation that answers the key questions of the implementer as well as elements that answer the key researcher questions. For example, sometimes these questions do not require another arm to be added to the study, but rather some good monitoring data or quantitative descriptive data of conditions in the population to be collected.

2. **Be flexible about the evaluation design**

    The research design a researcher has in his/her head when he/she starts a partnership dialogue is almost never the design that ends up being implemented. It is critical to respond flexibly to the practical concerns raised by the implementer. One of the main reasons that randomized evaluations have taken off in development in the last 20 years is because a range of tools have been developed to introduce an element of randomization in different ways. It is important to go into a conversation with a partner with all those tools in mind and use the flexibility they provide to achieve a rigorous study that also takes into account the concerns of the implementer.

A common concern implementers have about randomization is that they will lose the ability to choose the individuals or communities that they think are most likely to benefit from their intervention. They may worry a community mobilization program will not work if the community is too large and lacks cohesiveness, or is too small to have the resources to participate fully. A training program may want to enroll students who have some education but not too much. These concerns are relatively easy to deal with: agree to drop individuals or communities that do not fit the criteria as long as there are enough remaining to randomize some into treatment and some into control. This may require expanding the geographic scope of the program. Randomization in the bubble can be a useful design in dealing with these concerns.

Randomized phase-in designs are also useful for addressing implementer concerns, although they come with important downsides (Glennerster and Takavarasha (2013) detail the pros and cons of different randomization techniques.).

There are limits to the flexibility that can and should be shown. If an implementing organization repeatedly turns down many different research designs that are carefully tailored to address concerns that have been raised in previous conversations, at some point the researcher needs to assess whether the implementer wants the evaluation to succeed. This is a very hard judgment to make and is often clouded by an unwillingness to walk away from an idea that the researcher has invested a lot of time in. The key question to focus on in this situation is whether the implementer is also trying to overcome the practical obstacles to the evaluation. If not, then it probably makes sense to walk away and let go of the sunk costs already invested. Better to walk now than be forced to walk away later when even more time and money have been invested.

3. Share expertise

Many partners are interested in learning more about impact evaluation as part of the process of engaging with a researcher on an evaluation. Take the time to explain the impact of evaluation techniques to them and involve them in every step of the process. Offer to do a training on randomized evaluations for staff at the organization or run a workshop on Stata. Having an organization-wide understanding of randomized evaluations also has important benefits for the research. In Bangladesh, employees of the Bangladesh Development Society were so well versed in the logic of RCTs that they intervened when they noticed girls attending program activities from surrounding communities. They explained to the communities (unprompted) that this could contaminate the control group and asked that only local girls attend.

Researchers often have considerable expertise in specific elements of program design, including monitoring systems and incentives, as well as knowing about potential sources of funding—all of which can be highly valued by implementers. Many researchers end up providing technical assistance on monitoring systems and program design that go well beyond the program being evaluated. The goodwill earned is invaluable when difficult issues arise later in the evaluation process.

4. **Provide intermediate products**

While implementing partners benefit from the final evaluation results, the time-scales of project funding and reporting are very different from academic timelines. Often an implementing organization will need to seek funding to keep the program going before the end line is in place and several years before the final evaluation report is complete. It is therefore very helpful to provide intermediate outputs. These can include a write-up of a needs assessment in which the researcher draws on existing data and/or qualitative work that is used in project design; a description of similar programs elsewhere; a baseline report that provides detailed descriptive data of the conditions at the start of the program; or regular monitoring reports from any ongoing monitoring of project implementation the researchers are doing. Usually researchers collect these data but do not write them up until the final paper. Being conscious of the implementers' different timescale and getting these products out early can make them much more useful.

5. **Have a local presence and keep in frequent contact**

Partnerships take work and face time. A field experiment is not something you set up, walk away from, and come back sometime later to discover the results. Things will happen, especially in developing countries: strikes, funding cuts, price rises, Ebola outbreaks. It is important to have a member of the research team on the ground to help the implementing partner think through how to deal with minor and major shocks in a way that fits the needs of both the implementer and the researcher. Even in the middle of multiyear projects I have weekly calls with my research assistants, who either sit in the offices of the implementer or visit them frequently. We always have plenty to talk about. I also visit the research site once and often twice a year. Common issues that come up during the evaluation are lower-than-expected program take-up, higher-than-expected costs of running the program, uneven implementation quality, and new ideas on how to improve the program.

1.4 Special considerations when partnering with governments

Working with government partners has particular benefits and challenges. On the benefit side, governments often have substantial resources at their disposal and their geographic reach is expansive. Thus, for example, Olken et al. (2014) were able to randomize at the level of subdistrict in Indonesia with 1.8 million target beneficiaries in treatment areas.

Governments also collect a lot of data on individuals such as test scores for children, earnings for adults, and encounters with the criminal justice system. While it may be possible to access these data even if the government is not the implementer of the program being evaluated, a formal partnership makes doing so much easier. Administrative data can enable researchers to assess impacts without extensive surveys.

This is particularly beneficial for study designs that require large samples sizes and/or long-term tracking. For example, Angrist et al. (2006) are able to follow up with winners and losers of a lottery for vouchers to attend private school in Colombia by linking winners to a centralized college entry exam seven years after the vouchers were issued. In ongoing work, Bettinger et al. link the same voucher winners and losers to government tax and earnings data, 17 years after the lottery. Governments' wide reach makes it possible to randomize on populations that are representative of large geographic units. Muralidharan and Sundararaman (2011) test the impact of teacher incentive pay in a representative sample of rural schools across the state of Andhra Pradesh, meaning their results are valid across a population of 60 million.[2]

Another benefit of working with governments is that they have the ability to scale-up a program to a large number of people if a pilot is found to be effective. If the evaluation is of a government-implemented pilot this may ease, though not necessarily erase, the concern that the scale-up will not be implemented as well as the pilot. Governments may also find the results from such a pilot more persuasive than one conducted by another organization. In 2015, Banerjee, Hanna, and Olken worked with the Government of Indonesia to test how providing individual ID cards to recipients of government-subsidized rice (which indicated the amount and price of rice they were eligible for) could reduce corruption in the distribution system. The results showed that the cards increased the subsidy received by targeted recipients by 25%, so the government scaled up the ID card program, reaching 66 million people. The time from evaluation design to scale-up was about a year.

Some issues can only be examined by working with governments: for example, manipulating how tax collectors are rewarded (Khan et al., 2014); how police are trained and rewarded (Banerjee et al., 2012); or how firms' emissions into the environment are regulated (Duflo et al., 2013).

With these benefits, however, come considerable costs. Governments can be slow moving and less able or willing to test out-of-the-box solutions than NGOs. It may be particularly difficult to run more theory-oriented field experiments with governments. They tend to be less interested in answering an abstract question, the answer to which could inform many policies but would not be scaled up as a specific program. Governments can also find it harder than NGOs to provide services only to a limited

---

[2] Andhra Pradesh has a population of 80 million and is 75% rural.

group of needy citizens. Some governments have laws requiring them to treat citizens of equivalent need equally. When the Government of France wanted to test programs using randomized trials they first had to change the constitution to make this possible (J-PAL, 2015). Additionally, staff turnover in governments can be high as civil servants are transferred regularly. This makes it even more important to build support at different levels of government: if the RCT has support from the minister but not the bureaucrats, then it is likely to die with the next cabinet reshuffle. An election can lead to a dramatic change in policy priorities and personnel at the same time. It can also lead to paralysis for a period both before and after an election, even if the program being evaluated has bipartisan support. As an example, an RCT I was involved in collapsed when none of the planned monitoring could take place because a newly elected government froze all nonessential expenditure while they thought through new priorities. In another instance a survey had to be suspended just as it was about to go into the field because of a national exchange rate crunch, which again led to a freeze. Government budget shortfalls and last minute crunches are not confined to developing countries. Finally, it is worth recognizing that governments can renege on any agreement with impunity. There is not much a researcher can do when a government decides to fill a shortfall in a program budget with money set aside for, say, the end line.

Many of the strategies discussed earlier for fostering partnerships in general are particularly important for fostering partnerships with governments. Government partners are in a powerful position vis-à-vis the researcher, so it is important to listen hard to what they want. They often work within short political timelines, so delivering intermediate products such as baseline reports can be key for keeping them engaged.

Working with governments often requires a more formal approach to partnership than working with NGOs. Governments often require a memorandum of understanding that sets out clear expectations for both parties. Discussions may be going well at the practical implementation level, but any final decision—even a relatively small one—is likely to require sign-off from someone senior. It is important to build extra time into the schedule to account for this. Government procurement rules can also cause considerable delay. For example, if we decide that an intervention needs a leaflet to explain the study to participants, the government may require a competitive bid for the printing of the leaflet, leading to several months delay. Having some independent funding that does not run through the government can be very helpful in easing some of these constraints: a researcher can come in and offer to pay for a leaflet, or for additional monitoring, etc. Independent funding can also help keep the research going if the government faces short-run liquidity constraints.

Being the first to do something might be exciting for an NGO but can make a government nervous as it exposes them to criticism. Thinking through the optics of the experiment (i.e., how it would look on the front page of a newspaper) can help alleviate concern. Another strategy is to bring in an official from another department or country who has worked on an experiment before, preferably of a similar type. It is much more reassuring for officials to talk to other officials than it is to hear from a researcher.

Policymakers often have a healthy skepticism of researchers who want to provide advice about how to measure or improve a program, especially those coming from another country, state, or region. It is important for researchers to prove their relevance and their local knowledge. A mix of humility, a desire to learn from the policymaker, and a lot of homework about local conditions can help. I have seen policymakers visibly relax and start to engage when they hear from a researcher about their on-the-ground experience. A well-placed anecdote about a conversation with a farmer in Kenema or a teacher in Pittsburgh can be critical for building credibility.

1.5 Self-implementation

The major benefit of not working with an implementing partner, but implementing the intervention as a researcher, is the high degree of flexibility to precisely test the intervention or range of interventions. To understand how and why a particular program has the impact it has, we may want to take it apart and test different elements separately and together, and it may be hard to find an implementer who is willing to do this. For example, community-driven development (CDD) is a very common development program that combines the provision of block grants for locally designed projects to communities with facilitation to encourage inclusive decision making in selecting the programs. For many years, researchers have wanted to test the marginal benefit of the facilitation, but this would involve providing some grants without facilitation, something most implementers of CDD are strongly opposed to. The result is that most studies have tested the combination of grants and facilitation (Casey et al., 2012; Fearon et al., 2009; Humphreys et al., 2012; Beath et al., 2013).

We may want to compare two very different types of programs that are designed to deliver the same outcome against each other. But individual implementers may specialize in doing program A or program B, with none willing and able to do A in some randomly determined locations and B in others. We could try and find two implementers who would cooperate on where they did their respective intervention, but this kind of tripartite collaboration is likely to be exceptionally difficult. Even if we succeed it will be impossible to disentangle the differential impact of program A versus B from the impact of differential implementation skill of the organizations running each. A good example of this is the potential comparison between any program and cash. It is often useful to compare the effectiveness of a program in achieving a given objective to providing cash in achieving the same outcome. As with the CDD example mentioned in previous paragraphs, most implementers are reluctant to simply hand out cash (an exception is GiveDirectly, which was started by academic economists with the ultimately correct view that giving out cash might be an effective way to help the poor with few downsides

(Haushofer and Shapiro, 2013)). It is sometimes possible to reach a compromise with partners to do this type of comparison. A study in Bangladesh randomized different elements of Save the Children's girls' empowerment program but also added an arm with an (noncash) incentive to delay marriage. While not part of the original program, Save the Children agreed to a hybrid arrangement where the researchers took the responsibility for designing, raising the funding for, and helping to implement the noncash delivery program, while Save the Children supported the delivery of the noncash incentive through its existing food distribution system and provided support in implementation so that this element closely resembled a Save the Children program (Buchmann et al., 2016).[3]

The flexibility of self-implementation is particularly useful when we want to test a theory of underlying human behavior through an intervention that may not have a lot of practical benefit in itself. Lab experiments are an extreme form of this. Implementing partners are unlikely to want to run a lab experiment and they do not have as much expertise to contribute as this is far removed from what they normally do. But lab experiments can be very useful in testing precise hypotheses because they isolate very specific differences between arms. Many RCTs outside the lab are effectively somewhere between lab experiments and program evaluations.

A series of RCTs on take-up of health prevention products are a good example of the continuum between program evaluation and lab experiments, and how researchers shift from working with implementers to implementing themselves through this continuum. Kremer and Miguel (2007) worked with a nongovernmental organization to randomize the price at which deworming pills were provided as part of a larger program. Ashraf et al. (2010) sought to understand whether price influenced use of health products (something that was not an issue for deworming pills) and to distinguish between a psychological commitment effect of paying for a product and a selection effect. To do this, people went door to door selling dilute chlorine at randomly selected prices. Some of those who agreed to buy the chlorine at a given price then received a discount, or were surprised to receive the chlorine for free. Even though this two-stage pricing did not much resemble a normal NGO program, the researchers were able to work with Population Services International (PSI) to implement it because of the long-run relationship between the researchers and PSI and PSI's realization of the value of understanding the underlying behavior of health consumers in designing their future programs.[4] Hoffmann et al. (2009) in contrast, implemented their own program in which they randomized the price at which people were offered bed nets. To abstract from cash constraints, they provided subjects with enough cash to purchase a net prior to the offer of sale. They also looked at loss aversion by offering to purchase nets from individuals once they had bought them. While this design was very helpful in distinguishing different theories of consumer behavior with respect to preventive health, no one would think it was a good way to run a bed-net distribution program, so working with an implementing partner was unlikely to be an option (Hoffman was also a graduate student at the time, meaning she had not developed the long-run partnerships with implementing organizations that Kremer, Miguel, and Ashraf had each developed with their respective partner organizations).

Researchers sometimes choose to work through research organizations as implementers or create new implementing organizations because their empirical and theoretical works suggest a new strategy that has the potential to be effective at scale. In these cases, researchers often work through the design of the program and the research simultaneously. Chlorine Dispensers for Safe Water and StickK are examples where researchers helped create new products and organizations to scale these products, which were also evaluated through field experiments.[5]

Offsetting these important benefits of self-implementation are important disadvantages: it takes an extraordinary amount of focused attention and work to implement a complex program well; the researcher does not benefit from the insights of the implementer who usually knows a lot about the local context; questions may be raised about the extent to which the results will generalize to a program implemented not by nonresearch organizations; and different and more complicated ethical questions arise with researcher-implemented programs. As part of nonprofit universities, academics may be restricted from political advocacy, which may limit their ability to self-implement election work. (I address these last two points in Section 3.)

It is easy for researchers to underestimate the challenges in implementing a program directly, particularly in a developing country. It is common for researchers, particularly junior ones, to look at the overhead costs that implementing organizations charge and decide it would be cheaper to implement the program themselves, only to realize halfway through the experiment why others charge high overheads. Permits are hard to get, supplies do not arrive on time, staff get sick or quit, or hurricanes happen. It is hard enough to run the RCT: running the implementation at the same time is a major headache. Nor do researchers necessarily have a comparative advantage in most implementation tasks such as logistics and human-resource management. This is another reason why it is more common for researchers to self-implement the type of RCTs that have quick turnaround, and/or

---

[5] In the case of chlorine dispensers, the program was originally implemented by ICS Africa, then by Innovations for Poverty Action where more testing with scaling was done, before being spun off to Evidence Action. More about Dispensers for Safe Water can be found at http://www.evidenceaction.org/dispensers/. For more on StickK, see http://www.stickk.com/.

involve a lab in the field: the key tasks of implementation (such as determining the precise wording of a behavioral intervention in a lab) are closer to the comparative advantage of a researcher and long-term employment of staff is not required.

To what extent can we generalize the results from researcher-led RCTs? Vivalt (2015), in a metaanalysis of field experiments in developing countries, finds that the identity of the organization running the program is the largest predictor of impact within studies of the same type of program. This suggests that the results from a researcher-implemented program may not necessarily translate into the same impact if the program were run by a government. However, whether this is a drawback to studies of researcher-implemented programs depends a lot on what type of lesson we are seeking to draw from a study and the type of intervention that is being tested. As we have discussed, the objective of researcher-led implementation is often to tease out an underlying behavior rather than to test whether a program would be effective at scale. In this case, the fact that an NGO or government might implement the program differently than a researcher is not relevant to achieving the objectives of the study. No NGO is going to implement Hoffmann et al.'s bed net distribution the way they implemented it, but that does not undermine the general lesson about loss aversion that the RCT provides. A point that is often missed is that lessons about human behavior that often come from researcher-implemented studies or studies that are not designed to test scalable interventions are, in some ways, more generalizable than lessons from evaluations of specific programs precisely because they seek to test more general and theoretical questions.

But what if the objective of an RCT is to draw lessons about whether a particular type of intervention is effective in achieving certain outcomes and whether this type of program should be scaled? How useful are evaluations of researcher-implemented programs then? To understand this we need to think through why researcher-implemented programs may be different from those implemented by others.

Some researcher-implemented programs are criticized as not being a valid test of an approach because researchers do not have the expertise to run a program properly. One possibility is to hire someone with the technical capacity the researcher does not have. In certain disciplines (such as medicine or agronomy) an expert's qualifications can be documented and their advice can be validated by independent experts. Thus Cole and Fernando (2012) evaluated a phone-based agricultural extension program. To do this they needed an agricultural expert. The advice this expert gave is easy to assess. But in other areas this external validation of the quality of implementation is harder to do. For example, if an economics researcher ran and evaluated a program on community mobilization and found no impact, this is likely to carry less weight than a null result from a program evaluation of a well-known and respected implementer of community mobilization programs.

A more common concern is that researcher-implemented programs are not representative because they are too well-implemented. Researchers tend to have a high level of education and, during the evaluation, will be focusing a lot of attention on a relatively small number of participants. It is, unfortunately, not typical to have so many highly educated people focus on the implementation of a program in a relatively small area. People of equivalent education levels in implementation organizations tend to be responsible for a very large number of programs often covering hundreds of thousands of people. This is not just an issue for researcher-implemented programs. Programs that are evaluated often get greater scrutiny than those that are not being evaluated. Again, however, the extent to which this is a problem depends on the objective of the study.

If a study is designed to test proof of concept, then researcher focus (as an implementer or just as an engaged partner) is not a problem. A proof-of-concept study asks the question, "What is the impact of an intervention if it is implemented as well as it could be?" Medical and public-health trials are often proof-of-concept studies. For example, it is useful to know whether addressing anemia increases productivity, even if this involves an intensive intervention in which households are given iron pills and are visited regularly to make sure there is high compliance (Thomas et al., 2003). If the study finds such a link, the question remains how best to increase iron uptake in a sustainable way. Studies of researcher-implemented programs are often proof-of-concept studies.

An alternative approach for ensuring that wider lessons can be learned from researcher-implemented studies is for the researcher to very carefully document implementation steps so that it is clear what the implementation was that was tested, and how others could replicate it. This sort of monitoring can be used to assess whether implementation quality declines as the program is scaled. This approach works best when quality is easy to measure. For example, it is possible to objectively monitor how often a chlorine dispenser is empty and therefore judge the extent to which program quality deteriorates as it is scaled and less attention is paid to each community. It is much harder to judge how the quality of a mentoring program changes as it is scaled. This point is not only relevant to researcher-implemented programs, but it is particularly relevant for them.

In summary, then, when deciding whether to implement a program as a researcher it is important to think through the objectives of the study. If it is a short lived, small-scale experiment with quite theoretical objectives where subtle differences in implementation are crucial to the design, self-implementation may be a good approach. If the objective is to test a proof of concept, and there are objective ways to measure the quality of implementation, then self-implementation may be possible—but not necessarily advisable—given the work involved. But for the vast majority of field experiments, the benefits of self-implementation do not outweigh the costs. In particular, researchers isolate themselves from potentially useful partners.

Some commentators have concluded that the involvement of researchers in the implementation of programs raises important ethical issues. The issue has arisen mainly in the context of field experiments around elections.[6] We discuss this in Section 3.

2. PREPARING FOR PRACTICAL PITFALLS IN FIELD EXPERIMENTS

When running a field experiment it is best to prepare for the worst. Some crises cannot be foreseen: in one 12-month period my field experiments were hit by Ebola, riots, a national strike, and a coup. The likelihood of unforeseen shocks makes it more critical to prepare for challenges that can be foreseen. Even with the best implementing partner, there will be issues of compliance with the randomization protocol and take-up will be lower than you expect. Even with a team of experienced and well-trained enumerators, someone will try to make up the data and attrition will have to be addressed. In this section we discuss strategies to combat these challenges.

2.1 Noncompliance

Despite our best efforts, there will always be people randomized to receive treatment who do not access the program and those who are randomized to the comparison group who manage to get access. Intention-to-treat estimates are still valid if there is a low level of noncompliance, but by reducing the contrast between treatment and comparison, noncompliance dramatically reduces power.[7] Choosing the right partner, as discussed earlier, is key to compliance but so is designing a randomization protocol that is easy to follow. Program implementers have enough to deal with in making the program run smoothly. In the best designs they have no decisions to make related to the randomization protocol. Often the best strategy is to ensure that any front-line implementer works entirely with either treatment or control people, but never implements differently across arms. For example, Buchmann et al. (2016) compared two different versions of an empowerment program, but field supervisors who supervised many villages were always given villages running the same version of the program. The one case where it is sometimes possible to have front-line staff implement differently with different people is if they are following a script on a computer and the computer randomizes the script (Duflo et al., 2005). Karlan and Appel (2016) have many examples of field experiments gone wrong, many of which involved noncompliance. There are several cases of attempts

---

[6] A get-out-the-vote field experiment in Montana caused considerable debate about research ethics when the fliers used in the experiment inappropriately used the Montana State seal. However, questions were also raised about whether it was ethical to conduct research that might influence the outcome of an election. For further discussion see, for example: https://thewpsa.wordpress.com/2014/10/25/messing-with-montana-get-out-the-vote-experiment-raises-ethics-questions/.

[7] The minimum detectable effect (MDE) size is squared when it enters the power equation, so power is particularly sensitive to changes in the MDE.

to evaluate layering an additional element onto an existing program. The new element was simply added to the work load of existing program staff, was not their main focus nor expertise, and as a result the new element was implemented poorly and inconsistently.

Even if program staff are implementing the program well and in line with the randomization protocol, take-up of the program may be disappointing. In Banerjee et al. (2015a), Spandana predicted that 80% of eligible women would take up their microcredit product. In planning the study we assumed this was an overestimate and predicted take-up of 60%. The actual take-up was less than 20%. Take-up is critical to power, so it is important to get right. If the program is being run elsewhere, one approach is to collect data on actual take-up in the other location. Alternatively, running a pilot on a small scale prior to the evaluation is useful for estimating take-up as well as to sort out the details of program and research implementation. Even then, take-up is likely to be lower in the main study than in the pilot as pilots often get a particularly high level of attention.

Another driver of noncompliance is that randomization units which appear separable on paper are much messier on the ground. The clear clinic catchment areas delineated on maps by the ministry of health may bear little relationship to who actually attends which clinic. Government-imposed political boundaries such as towns, villages, or states do not always correspond to the patterns of daily interaction that are likely to drive program implementation and spillovers. Even the definition of household is not always straight-forward: households are usually defined as those who eat together, but it may be hard to treat one part of a family and not the other part if they live in the same dwelling, even if they do not eat together. To prevent this type of noncompliance it is critical to establish natural randomization units that are informed by how people actually interact—not how they are meant to interact according to some government plan (Chapter 4 of Glennerster and Takavarasha (2013) covers this issue in greater depth).

The most problematic form of noncompliance is the defier: people who take up treatment because they were randomized to control, or who do not take it up because they were randomized to treatment. Unlike other forms of noncompliance, which just reduce power, defiers can bias results. Defiers are most likely to occur in information interventions because of the interaction of information provision with previous priors.[8] If we are concerned about defiers we need to identify groups where they may be an issue (for example, by collecting baseline data on existing priors) and calculating heterogeneous effects. We can separately examine the effects of an information program on those where

---

[8] For example, we might tell people about the benefits of wearing a seat belt as a way of increasing the use of seat belts, and thus further measuring their effectiveness. However, if some people previously had an overinflated view of the benefits of seat belts, the information might actually make them less likely to use seat belts. Our estimate of the information program would be valid, but the estimate of the effect of seat belts would be incorrect if defiers are different from nondefiers in other aspects of their behavior.

the information was in line with previous priors, was higher than previous priors, or lower than priors (see Glennerster and Takavarasha (2013) for more details on this subject).

Even with the best preparation possible, things will go wrong. It is therefore essential to monitor compliance and take-up throughout the implementation phase and provide feedback to the implementer so that they can fix any issues with implementing staff and redouble efforts at take-up. Data on who is not taking up the program can be very helpful to implementers in focusing their take-up promotion strategies. Collecting data in the end line about who took up the program will be important in interpreting the results; for example, distinguishing between limited impact being driven by low take-up or by low impact among those who took up. These data are also needed for calculating treatment-on the-treated estimates where appropriate.

2.2 Attrition

A high attrition rate can ruin an otherwise well-designed and implemented RCT. Most RCTs involve collecting panel data on the same people before and after the start of the intervention. While it is possible to account for attrition in these studies by placing bounds on the estimated coefficient, unless attrition is very small, these bounds will be large, making it hard to draw precise conclusions from the results. Even RCTs that do not collect panel data still have to worry about attrition from the selected sample: if we randomly select people who were subject to a natural field experiment to measure its effects, but only reach a portion of those we sought to interview, our results could be biased.

The following are some tips for keeping attrition low:

1. **Plan for more than one visit**

    Whether the surveys are conducted in people's homes, schools, or workplaces, some people will be absent on the day the enumerators come for the survey even when they have been warned in advance. Up to three separate visits may be needed to ensure that a high proportion of people are reached.

2. **Track people where they are**

    Simply returning to the same location repeatedly may not be sufficient if the respondent has moved. If children have dropped out of school, the enumerator needs to go to the child's home, and if the outcome is child test scores, the test will need to be administered at home. If families have moved it may be necessary to track and interview people in their new locations. Baird et al., (2008) provide detail on the work of the Kenya Life Panel Survey, which has successfully tracked adolescents (a particularly hard age group to track) from 1998 to 2011 as they completed their education, married, and moved into the workforce. In the first round, 19% had moved out of the district, and the team tracked respondents across Kenya as well as in Uganda, Tanzania, and even the UK.

3. **Think carefully about the timing of data collection**

People are more or less willing or able to talk to enumerators depending on the time of day or year. Turn up in the middle of a work day and most people will not be at home. Call during dinner and they may not want to talk. Choosing the right time to collect data requires knowing your population well. It may also require paying enumerators extra to work outside normal working hours. Studies done at schools or workplaces have the advantage of keeping attrition down at relatively low cost as respondents are conveniently brought together in one location at specific times. Late afternoon or evening, when people have returned from work, is often a good time to interview people at their home. In rural Sierra Leone, enumerators stay in communities during surveys. This allows them to warn people the night before that they will want to interview them and arrange a mutually convenient time. It also means they are in the community at all times of the day, making it easier to find a time when people can be reached.

Usually it is good to avoid doing a survey in traditionally high-travel months. August would be a terrible time to interview professionals in Paris, for example. The exception is if the study is tracking adolescents who may return to their parents' house during specific periods, such as Thanksgiving in the United States. When trying to track girls for our study in Bangladesh, we reduced our attrition by having a final round during Eid, a time when girls who are working in factories in Dhaka or have left for marriage traditionally return to their parents' houses.

4. **Collect tracking data at baseline**

The baseline questionnaire should include a "tracking module" which asks questions like, "If you moved, who in the local community would know where you moved to, but would not move with you?" The tracking module should ask for phone numbers of the respondent and their relations.

5. **Can data be collected from people other than the participant?**

Even if people have moved, or children have dropped out of school, it may be possible to collect some data on them from others who know them, which will minimize the costs of tracking and reduce attrition. Schools may know when a child dropped out. A child's peers may know if a girl got pregnant even if they are not still in school. Clinics may have data on when a patient stopped collecting their medicine and reporting for regular checkups (but note that the respondent's permission to get these data must be collected at baseline). Parents may know a lot about their grown children and parents often move less than their children.

6. **Make the survey as costless to answer as possible**

Long surveys that ask stressful questions are likely to get lower response rates. The appropriate length depends on the respondent and means of data collection. Even if respondents finish the baseline survey, they may deliberately make sure they are out in subsequent rounds if the survey is too long. Children have shorter attention spans so need shorter surveys. Phone surveys also need to be shorter than in-person surveys. If there are questions that might prompt someone to end the interview, such as questions on spousal abuse, these should be put at the end of the survey so that if the interview is terminated, only a limited amount of data are lost.

7. **Specify targets on attrition, not on the number of attempts made**

    It is common to specify the number of times an enumerator should attempt to reach a given respondent, but this can set up inefficient incentives. An enumerator has private information about when it is best to return to a household to maximize the chance of reaching the respondent, and it is important for them to have an incentive to utilize this (without having such a strong incentive to reduce attrition that they will fake data). Consider a phone survey where an enumerator has been given a list of people to call and told to call each at least three times. The easiest way to reach this goal is to call at a time when it is unlikely the person will be in and then call three times immediately one after each other. Attrition would be terrible in this scenario. If the enumerator is given a list of names and told to do what they can to reach as many as possible, they will learn about what times of the day seem to get high response rates, will ask when people might be available, and try the same person at different times of day.

8. **Consider compensation**

    Surveys take a lot of time and it may be appropriate to compensate people for this time. If the survey is long or a respondent needs to travel to a clinic or testing center to complete it, a small incentive may be useful in reducing the attrition rate. This is particularly true for panel surveys where the respondent knows that the survey will be long. Any incentive needs to be cleared with the institutional review board (IRB), which assesses the ethics of the study to ensure that people are not taking untoward risks because of the incentive. Compensating people for their time is usually seen as ethical by IRBs. Incentives that have been used include small backpacks for children, bars of soap, and seasoning cubes for cooking.

2.3 Poor data quality

The challenges of collecting high-quality data are not unique to field experiments, and some field experiments rely on administrative data (JPAL provides a useful guide to using administrative data in field experiments https://www.povertyactionlab.org/admindata). However, administrative data are often unavailable to researchers, not collected on all individuals, are unreliable, or not detailed enough for the researcher's needs, forcing the researcher to collect their own data. Data collection is hard and difficult to monitor which means enumerators can be tempted to take shortcuts and, in the extreme, make up data.

    An essential part of data collection is therefore monitoring the quality of data, and critical to this is the back-check process. A highly skilled enumerator (usually a supervisor) goes back and reasks a few questions from a randomly chosen subsample of respondents. The consistency between the two responses is then assessed. Many researchers do "back checks" of this kind on 10% of the sample. Because we need enough data to make this a valid comparison for larger surveys, the rate can be lower than this, and for smaller surveys it should be higher. The back-check survey does not have to be comprehensive. Indeed, the back check should be kept short to avoid respondents becoming annoyed at being asked the same questions twice. One reason for the back check is to make sure the enumerator is not making up data. Asking whether the respondent has been interviewed recently, and asking simple questions to which the respondent's answer is unlikely to change in the space of a few days are useful for achieving this. Enumerators should be warned that back checks will take place on an unannounced basis. It is good practice to make sure all enumerators have their work back checked at least once in the first few days of a survey and to discuss any important discrepancies between the two surveys with the enumerator. It should not be assumed, however, that all discrepancies are the fault of the enumerator. Respondents will often change their response depending on the day and how they are feeling, even when they are asked about slow-moving variables such as age or size of household.

Technology is providing an increasing range of options for monitoring enumerators. With paper-based surveys, monitoring has to rely on surprise visits from external monitors to check that the enumerator is in the right place at the right time. The monitor can also observe part of the interview to see if the enumerator is asking the questions well and appropriately recording answers. Paper checks can also be done: the team supervisor can pick up if certain questions are being missed or if a given enumerator has a high rate of failing to find target households. With GPS devices, enumerators can be tracked more closely. Even if we do not need to have the GPS coordinates of the interviewed household for the analysis, having enumerators record it helps ensure that they actually visited the household. Electronic data collection now allows part of or complete interviews to be recorded. Unlike having a supervisor listening over their shoulder, an enumerator does not know when the recording is on or which part of the interview recording will be checked, providing added motivation to perform well.

Electronic data collection also allows incoming data to be assessed while the survey is still in the field. By looking for patterns it is possible to find and correct errors enumerators may be making, and in worse-case scenarios to terminate employment. Warning signs include high variation between the answers collected by back checkers and enumerators, high rates of failing to find target households, and lower than average duration of interviews (measured by comparing the recorded start and end time of the interview). Surveys usually have important trigger questions in a survey which, depending on the respondent's answer, can change the survey's length. In a demographic survey there will be many questions for each pregnancy a woman has had; in an agricultural survey there will be lots of questions for each crop a famer grows. Enumerators who want to keep their workload down have an incentive to have respondents answer a smaller number to these key trigger questions. Checking to see if certain enumerators have lower than average responses to these trigger questions is a good way to spot poor-quality enumerators. These trigger questions are also important to check during the back-check process.

Back checking is not able to solve the problem of respondents, not understanding the question, systematic under- or overreporting (which may be the result of, for example, social desirability bias), not knowing the answer, or being tired and inaccurate. Many of the chapters in this book discuss good practice in measurement. But it is also important to do extensive field testing in a given location with a survey instrument because questions that work with one population may not be well understood by another. It may also be necessary to develop locally relevant indicators especially for hard to measure and culturally specific outcomes such as social capital. Prior to the launch of the baseline survey for and evaluation of CDD program in Sierra Leone, Casey spent a year working with local partners to develop locally relevant indicators of collective action, trust, and participation (Casey et al., 2012). There is a tension, however, between relying on locally relevant indicators and internationally recognized indicators that can be used to benchmark levels and impacts across countries. If every study uses a different way of measuring outcomes it is hard to compare cost-effectiveness across projects because there is no single standard of effectiveness. Therefore, it is usually a good idea to have a mix of locally tailored and internationally recognized indicators. For example, in education studies we will want a test of learning that is appropriate to the level of learning in the population where the experiment takes place. However, if we are to compare program effectiveness across sites we want to also include some benchmark questions that can be compared across studies. For more discussion, see the chapter "Field Experiments in Education in the Developing Countries" by Muralidharan (2017).

2.4 Avoiding systematic differences in data collection between treatment and comparison

Most measurement issues that a researcher conducting an RCT has to deal with are similar to those faced by researchers working on studies using other methodologies. There are, however, a few issues that an RCT researcher has to be particularly concerned about. All of these boil down to the need for data to be collected in the same way in the treatment and comparison group and to avoid the intervention interacting with the way people report data.

Programs often collect a lot of data as part of their regular monitoring processes. These monitoring data can be very useful for interpreting the results of an RCT. For example, they can help us distinguish whether a null effect was due to a poorly implemented program or due to little impact from a well-implemented program. However, these program data should usually not be used to measure outcomes. If the program is operating only in the treatment area then there is no process data in the comparison areas, making a comparison impossible. If we use program process data in the treatment area and try to collect similar data in the comparison areas, we will never know if any difference in measured outcomes is due to a real underlying difference in outcomes or due to a difference in measurement processes in treatment and comparison. For example, if data are collected by program staff in treatment areas and by professional enumerators in comparison areas, there is a risk that professional enumerators are better at probing respondents and checking inconsistent answers, and thus end up with systematically different outcomes than program staff.

In general, using program staff to collect outcome data is problematic as it can accentuate the risk of social desirability bias. Respondents may, for example, find it particularly awkward to admit to having practiced unsafe sex when asked by the person who trained them in the dangers of unsafe sexual practices. Data collection is also hard to do well, and there are considerable benefits from having it conducted by people who are highly experienced and motivated to do a good job because their future career prospects rely on them performing the tasks well.

The one exception where process data are sometimes used to measure outcomes is when the RCT takes place within a sample in which everyone participates in the program, the randomization is into different types of program participation, and process data are collected routinely on those in treatment and comparison in identical ways. For example, if different borrowers within the same credit organization are randomized to receive alternative versions of the credit contract and repayment is the outcome of interest, then the lender's information on repayment rates can be used to compare outcomes for treatment and comparison clients (Giné and Karlan, 2014) use this approach when looking at microcredit contracts, and William et al. (2016),[9] use this to look at farming cooperative contracts—although both collect survey data as well. Even in these cases, it is useful to check the validity of the data by comparing self-reported data from surveys with administrative data from the implementing organization, especially if there is subjectivity in the measurement of outcomes. The concern is that to the extent that program staff are collecting process data and know which participants have been allocated to treatment and which to comparison, this knowledge and any biases they have about outcomes may influence how they record outcomes.

Another temptation is to collect data on the treatment group at a different time than the comparison group. For example, if the partner is pushing to get the program implemented quickly they may request that baseline data are collected in the treatment area first so that the program can start, with data collection done in comparison areas later. This timing difference compromises the difference between treatment and comparison data and should be avoided.

---

[9] A description of this ongoing study can be found at: http://www.povertyactionlab.org/evaluation/encouraging-adoption-rainwater-harvesting-tanks-through-collateralized-loans-kenya.

If the program has an impact on the relationship between the underlying outcome and the measurement of the outcome—even if data are collected in the same way in treatment and comparison—the data cannot be interpreted the same way in the two groups, thus undermining the validity of the experiment.

This problem most often arises when a program provides an incentive to change a particular behavior, which also changes the incentive to misreport the behavior. We want to be able to distinguish between the incentive leading to changes in actual behavior and the incentive leading to changes in reported behavior but not actual behavior. The more objective the measurement of the outcome, the less likely this is to happen, but if the incentive is high enough it is possible that it will induce substantial cheating that can corrupt even more objective measures. This is why it is preferable to use an outcome measure separate from the measure that is used for the incentive. For example, Dhaliwal and Hanna (2014) study a program in which medical worker attendance is monitored with a threat from officials that action will be taken against those with high absence rates. To judge if the program impacted attendance, the authors use random checks that are not linked to the official monitoring. Even if a program does not change respondents' incentives to report an outcome, it may change the perceived social desirability of a behavior. For example, a program designed to encourage saving may make people more liable to report saving even if it does not change saving itself. In situations where the program may change social desirability, it is imperative to rely on more objective measures of outcome, often including nonsurvey outcomes. Glennerster and Takavarasha (2013) have a catalog of nonsurvey outcomes with the pros and cons of each.

3. ETHICS[10]

Most field experiments involve humans as subjects in their research, and in this they are no different from most empirical economic research. But the expansion in the use of field experiments has been associated with more researchers, and more junior researchers, collecting their own data, especially in developing countries. There are a host of practical challenges associated with collecting and storing confidential data, which we discuss in this section. While most of the practical and ethical issues involved in running field experiments are common across any research that involves primary data collection, the intense collaboration between researchers and implementers common in field experiments does raise specific ethical questions, particularly in relation to the boundary between practice (which is regulated by national laws as well as norms and professional ethical standards) and research (which in most countries has separate formal regulatory structures).

---

[10] This section draws on Glennerster and Powers in The Oxford Handbook of Professional Economic Ethics, edited by George DeMartino and Deirdre N. McCloskey (2016).

The basic principles underlying the US system of ethical research regulation were set out in the Belmont Report. This report was issued in 1978 by the US National Commission for the Protection of Human Subjects of Biomedical and Behavioral Research and provides the basis for decisions about the ethics of research funded by most federal departments or agencies (Code of Federal Regulations, title 45, sec. 46.101).[11] While the principles set out in the report were formulated in the United States, they are reasonably general and are similar to the principles behind institutional review structures around the world.[12] Since 1978 hundreds of thousands of research studies have been evaluated against these principles building up a considerable bank of experience in how to apply them in practice.[13] The principles explicitly cover both medical and nonmedical studies and recognize that the level of review and safeguards should be adapted to the level of risk for a given study. This is important as social science research often has lower levels of risk than many medical studies.

There are three key principles spelled out in the Belmont Report:

1. **Respect for persons**

   People should be treated as autonomous agents. They have their own goals and have the right and ability to decide the best way to pursue them. In most cases this principle requires that researchers clearly lay out the risks and benefits of the study to potential participants and let them decide if they want to participate. The principle also recognizes that there are individuals who do not have full autonomy, such as children who may not understand the full risks and benefits of the research, or prisoners, who may not have freedom of action. Where autonomy is compromised, the researcher has to take special precautions.

2. **Beneficence**

   Researchers should avoid knowingly doing harm and seek to maximize the benefits and minimize the risks to subjects from research. However, avoiding all risk of harm is unrealistic and would prevent the gains to society that come from research. Therefore, risk of harm needs to be weighed against likely benefits to society that could flow from the research.

3. **Justice**

   The justice principle focuses on the distribution of costs and benefits of research. It seeks to avoid a situation where one group of people (for example, the poor or prisoners) bears the risks associated with research while another group receives the benefits. It recognizes that the individuals who take on the risks of research may not be

---

[11] Accessed at http://www.hhs.gov/ohrp/humansubjects/guidance/45cfr46.html#46.101, August 15, 2013.

[12] For example, the Australian guidelines similarly include principles of justice, beneficence, and respect, although they also include a "research merit and integrity" principle. The three main principles underlying Canadian ethics review are respect for persons, concern for welfare, and justice.

[13] PubMed, a database of medical research, reports over 325,000 medical trials registered between 1978 and 2013.

precisely those who reap the benefits. Instead it aims to ensure that research is conducted among the types of people who will benefit from it.

The principles are a compromise between two somewhat separate ethical traditions: a rights-based approach and a utilitarian approach. The beneficence principle's emphasis on the need to weigh risks (which fall on the individual) and benefits (many of which accrue to society) is familiar to utilitarians and economists. It is modified by the right to self-determination in the respect-for-persons principle: Research that imposes risks on the individual for the sake of society is ethical, but only if the individual understands the risks and is willing to take them. But the right to be informed from the respect-for-persons principle is not absolute and is itself modified by the beneficence principle: Where the risks associated with the research are minimal and the costs of fully informing the subject are large, it is ethical to not fully inform, and in some cases even deceive, subjects. The costs in this case can be monetary or costs to the effectiveness of the research.

The justice principle explicitly addresses one of the objections to utilitarianism—that it justifies harm to some if it creates benefits to others—by saying that those who take the risks should receive the benefits. But by applying the principle to groups of people rather than individuals, it is a compromise between the two ethical traditions.

3.1 Institutional review boards

As the principles make clear, there are difficult trade-offs to make when determining the most ethical way to proceed with research. Researchers have the primary responsibility for judging these trade-offs. However, they also have an interest in moving ahead with their research, which may blur their perceptions of risks and benefits. An independent authority is therefore needed to assess the trade-offs and ensure that ethical rules are applied appropriately. IRBs fulfill this role. Most universities in the United States have IRBs with their own processes for reviewing and approving research conducted by faculty, staff, and students at the university. Research funding from most agencies of the US government requires that researchers follow a set of ethical review guidelines established by the Office for Human Research Protections (OHRP), and these guidelines have therefore become the default standard applied by universities even when a study is not funded by the US government. OHRP standards flow from the Belmont Report but are updated regularly.[14]

Some US nonuniversity research organizations maintain their own internal IRBs, which follow OHRP standards (for example, Innovations for Poverty Action and Abt Associates). Others, such as Mathematica Policy Research, use external IRBs accredited

---

[14] Available at http://www.hhs.gov/ohrp/humansubjects/commonrule/index.html. See also http://www.hhs.gov/ohrp/humansubjects/guidance/45cfr46.html#46.101.

by the Association for the Accreditation of Human Research Protection Programs, a voluntary organization.

Outside the United States, the system of ethical review for social science research that involves human subjects is quite mixed. Some countries have systems similar to the United States. Australian research guidelines, for example, include principles of justice, beneficence, and respect, although they also include a "research merit and integrity" principle (which in the Unites States is integrated into the beneficence principle). The three main principles underlying Canadian ethics review are respect for persons, concern for welfare, and justice.

A surprising number of universities outside the United States have no formal system of ethical review for research involving human subjects. Because ethical review boards have mainly been seen as the province of medical research, many universities that do not have medical schools do not have ethical research review boards. In addition, some medical review boards either do not accept nonmedical research for review or are ill equipped to review nonmedical studies.

Social scientists face three main problems when seeking review from medical review boards: these boards are unfamiliar with the type of work social scientists undertake; they have procedures that are designed for studies that impose much higher risks on subjects; and they impose medical ethics standards, which are not the same as research ethics standards. Lack of familiarity can mean that questions are raised about outcome measures that are standard in social science (I was once asked to remove a question about what assets a household owned from a survey as it was seen as too intrusive). Because medical boards are used to dealing with studies that impose substantial risks on subjects, they often have more rigorous safeguards as standard requirements than is normal in low-risk social science studies and are unwilling to approve waivers for informed consent or written informed consent, even when the risks are low and the burden very high. If a study is examining the impact of a new drug that may have dangerous side effects, it is probably appropriate to get written consent from illiterate participants by having someone they know carefully read to them the consent form that lists all the risks and have them sign. If the study simply measures their height, it may still be regarded as a "health" study but gaining oral consent from illiterate participants should be justifiable. Doctors and nurses have ethical obligations that go beyond research ethics including providing care to those in need. Thus medical ethics boards may require researchers to offer medical care to those they find are in need of care as a result of their research. For example, if anthropometric measurements reveal that a child is malnourished, a medic may be expected to refer them to care. While medical boards may require treatment of subjects that researchers find to be ill, this obligation does not flow from most research ethics principles.

Some researchers working on field experiments have responded to the lack of IRBs by working with their universities to establish such review boards. The Paris School of

Economics and the Institute for Financial Management and Research in India worked with J-PAL Europe and J-PAL South Asia, respectively, to establish IRBs in 2009. The World Bank, which currently relies on the regulations in its member countries, is actively discussing the creation of an ethical review board (Alderman et al., 2014). It is somewhat surprising that the field experiment movement should have spurred the creation of IRBs as many of these institutions (including the World Bank) collected data from human subjects long before field experiments became popular.[15]

3.2 When is ethical review required?

Researchers have to seek ethical review when they conduct research that involves human subjects. The precise definitions of "research" and "involving human subjects" can vary between jurisdictions, so a researcher needs to understand the local rules that apply to their research. In some cases multiple standards apply (for example, when a researcher at a US university conducts a study in Kenya, they may need to seek approval both from their home university and from the Kenyan Medical Research Institute (KEMRI).

In the United States, "research" is defined as systematic investigation that leads to the creation of general knowledge. Process data about the functioning of a program is not research because it is designed to inform the program, but not to generate general knowledge that is useful for other programs. Asking a few beneficiaries of a program about their experience is not research because it is not systematic (and therefore does not generate general knowledge). This is why most internal evaluations done by nongovernmental organizations and governments do not count as research and are not subject to the same rigorous ethical review.[16]

The practical implication of this definition for researchers is that the early stage work that researchers do to prepare for a field experiment does not usually count as research and thus can be done prior to ethical research approval. For example, researchers may visit the program and talk to beneficiaries and program staff. They may examine administrative data and pilot questionnaires, all before approval has been given. Indeed, much of this work is needed to prepare the paperwork for ethical review, as most reviews require a copy of the final questionnaire to be used in any primary data collection. Approval (or a waiver stating that full approval is not required) needs to be secured before the collection of any data that will be used in the study and that is collected for the purpose of the study. Data that are used in the study but are not collected for the purpose of

---

[15]   One potential spur to the creation of IRBs is the relatively new requirement instituted by the American Economic Association that papers involving the collection of data on human subjects must disclose whether they have obtained IRB approval.

[16]   This is the case even though internal evaluations often collect similar kinds of data to those collected in field experiments and the risks associated with inappropriate release of the data is similar. In some countries NGO or governmental handling of data from internal evaluations is covered by privacy regulations.

the study (including ongoing administrative data collection) can take place before approval has been received because it would have gone ahead with or without the study. However, approval may be required for the researcher to access and utilize even administrative records because these can include personal information, the release of which could cause harm to a research subject.

The second trigger for ethical review is that the research involves human subjects. (There are other guidelines for research on animals, but as social science rarely has animal subjects we ignore these regulations here.) Research counts as having human subjects if it includes interviews with human subjects, or collects physical specimens from humans (e.g., urine or blood).

If research involves use of data about humans but does not involve the collection of that data, and the researcher never has access to information that would allow them to personally identify them, then ethical approval is not required. Nor is approval required if the researcher only uses publicly available data (which usually has all personal identifying information removed before being made public). Thus a study which uses data from a Demographic and Health Survey would not require ethical approval. Much like the use of administrative data, if the researcher needs to acquire personal identifiers (such as precise geographic location) to undertake their research, then approval is required even if they do not collect the data themselves.

3.3 Practical issues in complying with respect-for-human-subjects requirements

1. Informed consent

The respect-for-persons principle requires that researchers explain any risks of harm associated with participating in the study to those involved and gain their consent before proceeding.

In the case of an experiment randomized at the individual level, complying with this requirement is usually relatively straightforward. We select the study sample and then approach the individual, inform them of any risks associated with participating in the study, and request their consent to participate. Usually this is done before randomization, in the context of collecting baseline data. If the subject does not consent they are dropped from the sample, although it is good practice to record the number of subjects who decline to participate to give a sense of the representativeness of those who do participate.[17] The precise wording of the consent and the method by which it is collected has to be approved by the IRB and depends on the circumstances of the experiment and the risk involved. In general, written consent

---

[17] Information on the number of those approached who declined to participate is a requirement under consortium guidelines, and thus usually has to be included in a paper published in a medical journal.

(i.e., having a subject sign a consent form which sets out the risks and any potential benefits) is preferred. However, when many of the subjects are illiterate, a written consent form may not be the most effective way to convey risks. It may even cause distress to ask illiterate subjects to place their mark on a written document they cannot read. Alderman et al. (2013) suggest that in India, asking an illiterate person to provide their mark on a paper as part of the interview process may give the impression that the survey is run by the government (as thumb prints are often associated with official documents) and that therefore participation is mandatory, undermining respect for persons. If the risks are high, we may nevertheless need to get written consent by finding a literate member of the community and trusted by the participant to carefully explain the written document to the participant. For the most part, however, social science experiments do not involve this high level of risk and gaining oral consent is often appropriate, especially when a high proportion of subjects are illiterate. In this case, the enumerator reads the consent language and asks if the subject provides consent, and then checks a box if this consent is given. A key part of consent language is explaining that the subject has the right to leave the experiment at any time and has the right not to answer any question during the data collection process. It is important that the consent is written in a way that subjects readily understand. Zywicki (2007) provides examples in which IRBs have made consent forms more technical and harder to understand—which makes it harder for those with limited education to make informed decisions about participation.

Collecting informed consent when randomization is at the community level is more complicated, as data are often only collected on a random sample of those in the community and thus the research team may not interact directly with all individuals in the community. There are three important issues to keep in mind when determining how to proceed in this situation: Does the program require participants to opt in? Will data be collected on community-level outcomes, in which case all members of the community are under some definitions subjects of the experiment? To what extent is the program itself standard practice, and thus those who participate in the program but from whom no data are collected are not considered part of the research?

Many of the programs that are evaluated by field experiments require participants to opt in. For example, if a program offers the chance for mothers in a given community to attend literacy classes, mothers have a chance to opt in or out of the treatment. As we discuss later, some IRBs would not consider those who take part in the program but on whom the researcher does not collect individually identifiable data, as being subjects of the experiment. However, even if these program participants are considered subjects of the experiment, the program is compliant with the principle of respect for persons if someone explains the program to potential participants, who then choose whether or not to participate.

The ethical issues become more complicated if the program provides a service to the entire community that participants cannot opt out of (Hutton, 2001). Examples include adding chlorine to the community well, erecting streetlights, modifying the rules under which the mayor is elected, or changing how teachers teach. Usually implementing organizations have ways of seeking community assent before proceeding with this type of community-level intervention, and are either governmental bodies themselves with their own processes of accountability, or are regulated by government as implementing bodies. If the risks of the intervention are low, then individual consent from all community members is not usually required: either because the IRB decides the costs of collecting it are too high given the small risks or because they consider the program implementation as practice rather than research and thus outside their purview. The exception might be if the program design were considered to be driven more by research considerations than program considerations (we discuss this issue in the next section).

In many medical clustered RCTs, informed consent is not collected from individuals because individuals are not considered the subjects of the trial, especially if the intervention works at the level of the medical practitioner. McRae et al. (2011) argues that patients are not the subjects of trials that provide different types of training or incentives to doctors. This is because researchers do not directly interact with patients, while medical professionals, who should be considered the subjects of the trial, are ethically responsible for deciding what is right for their patients.

2. **Waiving informed consent**

Research ethics rules allow the requirement for informed consent to be waived when the risks to the subject are low and the costs of collecting informed consent are high. The costs of collecting informed consent could be monetary or come in the form of damaging the integrity of the research. Imagine an experiment on the effectiveness of different forms of advertisement in reducing smoking amongst adults. The experiment randomizes the position of antismoking billboards across the United States and then measures the level of smoking from sales of cigarettes. The participants of the study include anyone who sees the billboard. The researcher has no good way of identifying the individuals who see the billboard, and data to assess the effectiveness of the intervention comes from administrative records on cigarette sales, so they have no opportunity to ask for consent during data collection. Going door to door in the area to collect consent would be prohibitively expensive and the risks of harm from seeing a billboard are low, so the research is likely to receive a waiver for informed consent. Similarly, many education field experiments in the United States are exempt from collecting consent from all parents of students, as it would be infeasible and the risks are low.

The other cost of collecting informed consent is that knowing they are part of a study, or knowing the full details of the study, could change a subject's behavior, which could undermine the validity of an experiment. We may not want to tell people, for example, that they are involved in an experiment on racial bias as this may make them more aware of potential bias and thus change their behavior during the experiment. One approach is to tell the subject they are part of a study, but not give a full explanation about what the experiment is about, or even mislead the subject about what the experiment is about. Another approach is not to tell subjects they are part of an experiment. If we do not tell people they are part of an experiment or mislead them about what the experiment is about, permission is required from an IRB before the experiment can go forward. A researcher must justify the waiver of informed consent by explaining the likely benefit of the research to society, and why the research would be undermined if the subjects knew they were part of an experiment or knew the real reason for the experiment. The IRB will then decide if the lack of full transparency is warranted. IRBs will often require researchers to debrief subjects at the end of the experiment as a condition for gaining the waiver.

Note that this is different from deception within the experiment, which is when a research tells a subject something that is untrue as part of the experiment. Perhaps the most common form of deception in field experiments is when enumerators pretend to be someone they are not: for example, pretend to have a specific set of symptoms to see whether the medical professional asks them the appropriate questions and responds to the answers with the appropriate care recommendations. One way to achieve informed consent in these situations is to warn the provider in advance that there will be mystery patients at some point and get their consent for this test. If the experiment runs over many months, this knowledge that one of many patients will be a mystery patient is unlikely to dramatically change their behavior. For more on deception and informed consent, see Alderman et al. (2013).

3. **Protecting confidentiality of information**

As part of informed consent, the subject is usually told that any information they provide will be kept confidential. This agreement with the subject must be strictly adhered to and an IRB application needs to set out the practical steps a researcher will take to comply with this agreement. Anyone in the research team who is involved in handling data—from the enumerator to the principal investigator—must be trained on proper data handling to ensure that the protocols described to the IRB are followed. Important ways to ensure the maintenance of subject confidentiality are to ensure that any information that can link the data back to an individual (i.e., personal identifiers), such as name, address, phone number, or photo, is separated from the rest of the data as rapidly as possible; that only deidentified data be used, wherever possible, during analysis (to prevent the risk of data leaks); and that data with personal identifiers are kept secure. The precise steps will depend on what the data consist of and how they were collected. For example, when data are collected through paper surveys, all personal identifiers should be put on the first one or two pages of the survey and an ID number (generated only for the purposes of the research and thus uninformative to anyone else) should be printed on all pages of the survey. This means that as soon as the survey is completed and checked by a supervisor in the field, the first pages with identifying information can be separated and stored separately from the rest of the survey. The pages with the identifying information and the codes that link that back to the answers to the survey must then be stored in a secure place (such as a locked cabinet). When data are collected electronically, the device can be encrypted so that if the phone, tablet, or PDA is stolen no one can access the data. If analysis does require some identifying information (for example, global positioning data to examine geographic spillovers), the analysis needs to take place on an encrypted computer so that if the computer is stolen the data cannot be accessed. As we discuss later, when identifying information, such as global positioning data, is an integral part of the analysis, it can be complicated to publish sufficient data to fully replicate the study while still maintaining confidentiality.

3.4 The ethics of implementation

In the discussion of informed consent, it became apparent that it is not always straightforward to identify who is the subject of research and thus from whom informed consent is required. In particular, when a field experiment is evaluating a program, are those involved in the program but on whom the researcher does not collect data, subjects of the research or not? and do research ethics thus govern the program? The Belmont Report notes that the line between research and practice, and thus the line between what requires ethical approval and what does not, is blurred. While most of the report is appropriate both for biomedical and behavioral (or social science) research, the section that deals with the distinction between research and practice is written almost entirely from a biomedical perspective. This has led to some confusion and debate about the ethical standards to be applied to the implementation of programs that goes alongside many social science field experiments. Indeed, the Belmont Report explicitly states, at the end of the section defining the separation of research and practice, that the authors do not feel equipped to define the boundary between research and practice in social science:

> *Because the problems related to social experimentation may differ substantially from those of biomedical and behavioral research, the Commission specifically declines to make any policy determination regarding such research at this time. Rather, the Commission believes that the problem ought to be addressed by one of its successor bodies.*

Subsequently, a group was established to work on this, but no additional guidelines were released. The practical question that faces researchers and IRBs evaluating research proposals from social scientists is if and when ethical approval should be sought, and research rules (including requirements for informed consent) applied to the program that is being evaluated. The discussion in following paragraphs represents my view based on a close reading of the Belmont Report and requesting ethical review for many RCTs. However, it is worth reiterating that different IRBs in the United States interpret the standards differently; different countries have different rules; and the regulation of implementation is one of the areas where standards differ most sharply across institutions.

At one end of the spectrum the answer seems obvious: in the canonical case of a medical field experiment testing a new drug, the risks associated with the drug (the intervention) need to be assessed against the benefits of learning about its effectiveness. In other words, the assessment of risks and benefits and the informed consent apply to the program being tested (the drug) as well as the data collection that surrounds it.

Yet there are also examples where it is equally obvious that ethical regulations have no jurisdiction over the intervention a researcher is evaluating. Angrist (1990) evaluates the impact of the Vietnam War, which involved a lottery to determine participation. Chattopadhyay and Duflo (2004) similarly evaluated the impact of a ruling by the Indian Supreme Court that the position of village leader (*pradhan*) had to be given to a woman in one-third of cases (allocated randomly in many Indian states). In these cases IRBs had no jurisdiction over the implementation of the program being evaluated: there was no question of insisting that those whose names were entered into the Vietnam lottery had to provide informed consent. Nor could villages decline to participate in the quota program for women's political participation.

What is the key distinction between the evaluation of a new drug and the evaluation of the Vietnam War/quotas cases that explains why implementation is part of research for the first, but not the other cases? One difference is that the drug (the intervention) was designed by the researcher, whereas in the other two cases the intervention was designed and implemented by someone else (e.g., the government or the Supreme Court). I do not think this is the *key* distinction for two reasons. First, we think the review of the drug trial should include the risks and benefits of the drug whether or not the researcher who developed the drug goes on to test it, or if someone else runs the clinical trial. Second, if the identity of the implementer determines whether the intervention should be reviewed, then we would say that if a researcher also helped run a nongovernmental organization, then everything that NGO did, whether or not it was evaluated, should be subject to ethical approval.

The Belmont Report also supports the idea that whether or not an activity falls under research guidelines should be based on what the activity is, not on who undertakes it. The report acknowledges that (for biomedical research) researchers will often practice medicine (just as social science researchers sometimes practice direct poverty-alleviation work or advise governments or NGOs on the design of policy). This "practice" is deemed to fall outside the purview of research ethics. Instead, the Belmont Report defines research as an activity that leads to generalizable knowledge.

The challenge in applying this rule in the case of field experiments is that it is a combination of two different activities that lead to generalizable knowledge. Most field experiments combine the rollout of a program with data collection, and neither on their own would create generalizable knowledge.

But this gives a useful criterion for deriving whether and what part of implementation falls under research ethics guidelines: namely any change in program implementation from normal practice (or what would have happened otherwise) that is brought about for the purpose of creating generalized knowledge. Thus if a program was to be rolled out by an NGO in a new area anyway, this would not create generalized knowledge and would not (in my view) count as research, and the program itself should be governed by the regulation of NGO activity rather than a research ethics board. The use and collection of data by researchers studying the rollout does fall under research ethics, as it is necessary to draw general lessons from the rollout. However, if to learn from the program the rollout was changed in a substantive way, then this change is covered by research ethics. Note that this is not the position that all IRBs take. KEMRI required that parents of all children who were part of a school-based deworming program in Kenya run by International Child Support provide written permission before receiving the drug because the program was being studied. If the program was not being evaluated, the NGO would not have had to collect written (or even oral) consent as deworming drugs have been shown to be extremely safe. In other words, exactly the same action by the same organization was considered research when the action was being studied, but was not considered research when not studied. Zywicki (2007) discusses an example where a study that included provision of a potentially life-saving medication was shut down because researchers were unable to get signed consent in advance—even though in the absence of a study, written consent would probably not have been required to provide the medication.

It is sometimes assumed that if a researcher implements a program, then the entire program is part of the change that is introduced with the purpose of generating knowledge. But as I have argued earlier, ethics guidelines are not based on who does the activity, but what the activity is. Thus if a researcher evaluated an NGO program that hands out bed nets at a school and the researcher interviews a random subset of children at the school, then the researcher would only have to get informed consent from the individuals who they interview. If the researcher organization is the one to hand out the bed nets, I would argue the same rules apply: research rules cover the interviews and data collection, but informed consent is not required to hand out the bed nets themselves.

Questions around researcher implementation were vividly illustrated in a controversy surrounding an election experiment conducted in Montana (Johnson, 2015). In the experiment, researchers sent voters flyers that put individual judges up for election on an ideological scale. Key complaints about the project were that (1) the flyers used the State of Montana seal, giving the impression that the document was an official state document when it was not; (2) the flyers were "express advocacy," i.e., they advocated for individual candidates rather than issues and thus fell underreporting rules which were not followed; (3) IRB approval for the study as it was carried out was not sought or received; and (4) the intervention may have changed the results of some elections. The first two are violations under Montana election law according to the report of the Commissioner of Political Practices of the State of Montana (2015) and are being dealt with as such (Motl, 2014). In other words, the researchers are being regulated as implementers and being held to those standards. This fact adds one twist: due to universities' tax status, even if the researchers had followed disclosure rules to express advocacy, any money that ran through the university could not be used for advocacy.

There is more debate about whether changing the outcome of an election is a violation of ethics. Presumably the objection applies only if researchers run the intervention, because researchers study interventions that influence elections all the time. If the view is that interventions run by researchers should not change elections, this raises the question of whether interventions run by researchers should not change other outcomes. It would be odd to say that we do not want field experiments in medicine to change peoples' health outcomes, for example.

One argument to suggest that elections are different from other interventions is that while improving one person's health does not influence another person's health, election outcomes are a zero sum gain; an intervention cannot contribute to an overall improvement in society and instead must inevitably help one group at the expense of another. But many of the interventions that researchers study have some distributional or zero sum aspects. Is it unethical for a researcher to run a study that helps some women establish small businesses, which could have a potential negative externality on existing local businesses? The truth is that social science is involved in the real world and the interventions that social scientists study will have impacts in that world. One practical call for change that has come out of the Montana case is that IRBs may be too focused on potential harm to the narrow subjects of the experiment and should be more aware of costs to society as a whole, as well as benefits to society as a whole (Humphreys, 2014; Johnson, 2015). As we conduct studies we must be aware both of research ethics and the ethics and regulations surrounding the interventions we study. But it is unclear why researchers should, when acting as implementers, have a different set of ethics standards or regulations from other implementers.

One benefit of deciding what should be covered by research ethics based on the activity and not on who undertakes the activity is that it avoids drawing a bright line about when a program is researcher implemented and when it is not. Given the close partnership between researchers and implementers in field experiments, most programs that are evaluated are a combination of the two. Even when someone who is not a researcher implements a program, the researcher often provides advice (based on their knowledge about what has worked elsewhere) about the program design. But advice about how to improve a program is not research. What counts as research is deliberately manipulating the program to produce general lessons: for example, to create a control group so that the program can be evaluated rigorously. In the next section we discuss examples of where there might be potential risks or costs associated with the changes in implementation brought about by the manipulation of a program necessary to rigorously evaluate it.

3.5 Potential harm from different forms of randomization

There are many different ways of introducing an element of randomization into a program to enable rigorous evaluation of its impact. Each approach raises its own unique ethical issues.

The research manipulation that nonresearchers often feel most uncomfortable with is the treatment lottery. In this design, some study participants are randomized to have access to the program and some never receive the program. The concern is that some potential participants in a program are "denied" access to the program in order to evaluate its impact. When assessing potential harm from a field experiment we need to consider whether the introduction of a treatment lottery changed the total number of people who receive the program or whether it changed who received the program. In most cases, the treatment lottery approach is used when there are insufficient funds to provide the policy or program to all those who could benefit from it. For example, a program provides financial literacy training to small-scale entrepreneurs in Bolivia but only has funding to cover 200 entrepreneurs, far fewer than the number of all eligible entrepreneurs. A lottery is used to decide who receives access to the program but does not change the number of people treated.

There may be cases where a program (often a government program) does have sufficient funds to provide the treatment to all those who are eligible, but a decision is made to reduce the number of people who receive the program in the first phase to evaluate it. In this case, the risk of harm is that the program is beneficial and delaying its introduction to all of the eligible delays benefits to those potential participants. Note that this is a risk of harm, not a known harm, because at this stage we do not know that the program will be beneficial. (If we did know it was beneficial and there was funding for everyone to receive it, we should not be doing the experiment.) This risk of harm needs to be offset against the potential benefits of understanding the impact of the program, including the possibility that we find the program has unanticipated negative effects and that evaluating it saves people from these harms.

If a treatment lottery does not change the number of participants in a program, it might change who participates in a program. Ravallion (2012) suggests that allocating benefits randomly treats research subjects "merely as means to some end," and thus violates the respect-for-persons principle. But all research with human subjects uses information from some individuals as a mean to the end of drawing general lessons. Especially if the risk of harm is small (for example, the time cost of filling in a survey), and even when they are large (as in some medical trials), many people are happy to contribute if they feel there are benefits from the research to society.[18] The respect-for-persons principle recognizes that people can make informed choices about whether to participate in a study that may mainly help others.

A subtler objection is that random allocation of resources is a form of mistargeting (Barrett and Carter, 2014). Imagine that a program has funds to provide warm clothing to 500 poor families in a city in the northeastern US, and the implementers have a good way to identify those most in need. Evaluating this program would require identifying 1000 needy families, some of who might not be as needy as the original 500 if the program had really identified the 500 neediest families in the city. From the 1000, half would be randomly chosen to receive the warm clothing. In this case, the evaluation imposes some risk of harm because some of those identified as the 500 most needy will end up not receiving the warm clothes, while some who are slightly less needy will receive them. Note, however, that it is only a *risk* of harm because we do not know if receiving the warm clothes is a benefit (if we did we would not be evaluating the program) and we usually do not know whether the way that the program identifies the neediest is effective. Recent field experiments that specifically look at the question of targeting (by randomizing different approaches to targeting in different communities) suggest that conventionally used targeting approaches may not necessarily be the best way to identify need (Alatas et al., 2013). Many programs do not do a comprehensive assessment of who are the neediest in a given target area. Instead they have eligibility criteria and stop recruiting to their program when it is full. In these cases, it is possible to work with implementers to continue the recruitment process until a larger number of eligible participants have been identified and then randomized among them. As the most vulnerable are often not the first to sign up to a new program, this extended recruitment period can actually help improve targeting.

When designing a field experiment it is usually possible to avoid weakening the targeting criteria of the program by expanding the geographic scope of the program. In the example stated previously, instead of expanding the potential pool of families to 1000 in the same city, it might be possible to expand the program to a second city, identify the 500 neediest families in each, and then randomly pick 250 from each to receive the program. This would allow the evaluation to go ahead without weakening the targeting. This geographic expansion to accommodate an evaluation does usually increase the logistical costs of the program implementers, and this cost needs to be set against the benefit of doing the evaluation.

---

[18] As we discuss under the respect-for-person principle, there is often a challenge of getting informed consent in clustered trials.

If none of these options are workable and there is a high risk that the evaluation will lead to poorer targeting of the program, this would not necessarily make the evaluation unethical, because this risk needs to be compared to the benefits associated with the study.

One form of field experiment where the issue of mistargeting is particularly relevant is the treatment lottery around a cutoff. Unlike a simple treatment lottery, this methodology explicitly recognizes that some potential participants may be more qualified than others and is used when programs have explicit criteria for ranking eligibility. Potential participants who are near the cutoff for eligibility are randomized into or out of the program. There are three slightly different ways to do a lottery around a cutoff. Eligibility can be expanded to those who would previously have been ineligible, and access to the program within this group can be randomized. Or the group that is to be randomized can come out of those who would previously have been just above and just below the eligibility cutoff. Or the randomization can occur only among those who would previously have been eligible, thus reducing the total access to the program. Usually the methodology does not change the number of beneficiaries, but in most cases it involves accepting some people into the program who are less qualified than some others who are not accepted.

In assessing the trade-off between costs and benefits of using a lottery around the cutoff, there are a number of issues to keep in mind. As we have said, it is unlikely that the program is known to be beneficial, or else the evaluation would not be occurring. There are degrees of uncertainty: the stronger the evidence that the program is beneficial, the greater the concern about "denying" people access. Another key question is whether the benefits of the program are likely to be higher for those who appear to be more qualified.

For example, imagine the methodology is being used to evaluate the effect of giving access to consumer loans to people in South Africa (Karlan and Zinman, 2010). The bank has a scoring system for deciding who is creditworthy. The assumption is that those who score highly will use the loan wisely and will be able to repay the bank, making both the bank and the participants better off. The scoring system is also meant to weed out those who would be a bad risk and will not be able to repay. Potentially bad risks do worse if they are given a loan and cannot repay it because they acquire a bad credit record (although if they would never otherwise have been eligible for a loan from any lender it is not clear a poor credit record hurts them). It was precisely this concern on the part of the bank about the quality of their targeting approach that led them to invite the researchers to study the cutoff and help them improve it.

But do the researchers, or the bank, know that the scoring system is good at determining who is a good risk and who is a bad risk? Maybe the system is good enough to detect the very good and the very bad risks, but does it do a good job of selecting people around the cutoff? It is also possible that the credit scoring system may be discriminating against people who are good risks but happen to live in a poorer neighborhood. In this case, using a lottery may actually reduce the harm of discrimination. If there is uncertainty about the quality of the scoring system, a lottery around the cutoff can be a very good reason to do a randomized evaluation, because it helps generate knowledge about how good the scoring system is and whether the cutoff has been placed at the right point. It was precisely this uncertainty about the appropriate scoring system and cutoff that led the South African bank in Karlan and Zinman (2010) to ask the researchers to undertake the research.

In the bank example, if the evaluation finds that those just below the cutoff do just as well as those above it, then the bank will be encouraged to extend its loans to more people, and those just below the cutoff will gain, as will the bank. There is a risk that the cutoff was at the right place and that those below the cutoff will get into debt as a result of being offered a loan they cannot repay. This risk has to be taken into account when designing the study. The risk can be ameliorated by only randomizing above the cutoff (lottery among the qualified) but this has other risks: the evaluation cannot tell if the cutoff was too high, and it reduces access among the qualified more than in other designs. It is also possible to narrow the range around the cutoff within which the randomization takes place so that the bank never lends to anyone who has a very bad score. But this also has downsides: less would be learned about where the cutoff should be and, for a given size program, there would be less statistical power and thus less precision in the impact estimate.

The better the evidence there is that the cutoff is well measured and targets the program well, the more careful researchers should be with a lottery around the cutoff. For example, there is a strong evidence base suggesting that weight-for-age and arm circumference are good criteria for judging which children need a supplemental feeding program. Researchers may therefore decide that randomizing around the cutoff for a supplemental feeding program is not appropriate.

4. TRANSPARENCY OF RESEARCH[19]

Organized skepticism is essential to the process of scientific inquiry: "Involving as it does the verifiability of results, scientific research is under the exacting scrutiny of fellow experts. … The activities of scientists are subject to rigorous policing, to a degree perhaps unparalleled in any other field of activity" (Merton, 1942, p. 276, as quoted in Miguel, 2015).

In the last few years there has been growing concern that research in the social and medical sciences does not always live up to this ideal. In 2011 an investigation of the

---

[19] In preparing this section, I learned a lot from the lecture notes of Edward Miguel's semester long course on transparency of research (http://emiguel.econ.berkeley.edu/teaching/12), although I do not always come to the same conclusions.

work of Diederik Stapel revealed at least 30 papers in peer-review psychology journals were based on made-up data (reported in Callaway, 2011). Science retracted a highly publicized field experiment on attitudes to gay marriage when concerns were raised about the authenticity of the data (McNutt, 2015). Medical trials funded entirely by for-profit sources are more likely to find positive results from new treatment compared to existing care than studies funded by nonprofit sources (Ridker and Torres, 2006). The reproducibility project asked researchers to run new experiments to attempt to replicate the results from studies published in top psychology journals in 2008. Of a 100 original studies, only 35 had statistically significant effects in the replication in the same direction as in the original study and the effect sizes in the replication studies had statistically significantly smaller effect sizes (Open Science Collaboration, 2015).

Nor has economics escaped the spotlight. Brodeur et al. (2016) examine studies from top economic journals published between 2005 and 2011 and finds a bunching of results with a p-value just below 0.05, the traditional standard for statistical significance. In chapter "The Production of Human Capital in Developed Countries: Evidence From 196 Randomized Field Experiments" by Fryer (2017) shows a relationship between the magnitude of estimated effect sizes and sample size in published papers of field experiments in education (a telltale mark of publication bias discussed later). Chang and Li (2015) in their examination of macroeconomic papers are only able to "successfully replicate the qualitative findings from 22 of 67 (33%) papers without contacting authors. Excluding the 6 papers with confidential data and 2 papers that use software we do not possess we replicate 29 of 59 papers (49%) with assistance from the authors."

Finally, there have been high-profile arguments about whether there were mistakes in data or analysis and the extent to which the conclusion of several important economics studies should be revised including (in chronological order) Hoxby (2000) (comment Rothstein, 2004, 2005; and response Hoxby, 2007); Donohue and Levitt (2001) (comments Foote and Goetz, 2008; and response Donohue and Levitt, 2006); Rogoff and Reinhart (2010) (comment Herndon et al., 2014; and response Rogoff, 2013); and Miguel and Kremer (2004) (comment Davey et al., 2015; and response Hicks et al., 2015).

It is worth distinguishing between different concerns. Research results may not be reflective of the underlying true state of the world because of the following:
1. data are made up;
2. there was a mistake in the data collection or data analysis;
3. results are not robust to alternative specifications;
4. the findings hold only in a very specific context and are not general;
5. the intervention is not described in enough detail to make it possible to test whether the results hold in a similar context; or
6. sampling variation means the results were due to chance.

One way to address (1) through (3) is to make the data behind a study publicly available. Other researchers can then check the data for signs that it was made up or manipulated (e.g., Broockman et al., 2015 whose analysis led to the Science retraction mentioned earlier). They can also check that simple mistakes in analysis were not made and that the result is robust to different specifications. Problem (4 requires findings to be tested in different contexts, while (5) requires details of implementation to be included in supplemental material, as journals usually require that this detail is not included in the main paper. Problem (4) can be reduced by adjusting for multiple hypothesis testing and PAPs (discussed in detail later) and by testing the same intervention more than once. However, none of these approaches designed to increase reliability are costless or unproblematic.

In parallel with the concerns about the reliability of original studies, there is also concern about the reliability of attempts to reproduce findings. In commenting on the International Initiative for Impact Evaluation's effort to check the replicability of key international development papers, Ozler (2014) says, "the point of robustness checks in such a replication exercise is not to rerun regressions until you convert one statistically significant result to insignificant and highlight that. ... A big part of the point of replication is to reduce p-hacking, not to proliferate it." Commenting on the discussion of the reanalysis of Miguel and Kremer (2004), Blattman in his blog, "Dear Journalists and Policymakers: What you need to know about the Worm Wars," concluded, "Whether it's a sensational photo, a sensational result, or a sensational take down of a seminal paper, everyone has incentives to exaggerate. This whole episode strikes me as a sorry day for science." Simonsohn (2015) points out that many studies that claim to find a "failure to replicate" have a smaller sample size than the original study and are not sufficiently well powered to test whether the original study replicates. Again, there are several different concerns:

1. researchers attempting to test the reliability of an original paper either by reanalyzing the data or running a new study may have incentives to find a result that contradicts the original study;
2. small errors in data or analysis do not always translate into a substantial change in the overall conclusions and it is important to distinguish between meaningful and insubstantial changes in results;
3. if a large number of different specifications are tried in an attempt to test the "robustness" of a result, selective presentation of a few of these specifications may give a misleading impression of how robust the results are;
4. authors may pursue publication only when they find a study does not replicate, giving a misleading impression of the overall reliability of a broad body of research;
5. sample variation may mean the result of a follow-up study is due to chance; and
6. the statistics involved in replication or reproducibility are not straightforward and there is no single agreed standard to judge whether a reanalysis or replication "fails to replicate" the original study.

Confusing the discussion even further is nonstandard use of terminology. Sometimes the term "replication" is used to mean taking the original data and seeing if the same data generates the tables in the published paper. Sometimes the term is used to mean testing whether the same result is found when the experiment is run on a different sample of the same underlying population. Finally, it could mean testing in a new population. Clemens (2015) provides a useful classification of the different possible options and suggests a standardization of terms. Note that while I try and use Clemens' definitions as much as possible in this chapter, when talking about papers that use different definitions I use the term as used by the author of the paper (especially when quoting papers) (Fig. 1).

4.1 The statistics of data mining, multiple hypothesis testing and publication bias

Before discussing approaches that can be used to address some of the challenges addressed earlier, it is important to be precise about these challenges and the statistics behind them. With the exception of making up data, which is simple fraud, the challenges arise from the fact that standard statistical tests of the significance of the estimated coefficients in a randomized evaluation are based on the assumption that we are testing an independent hypothesis once. In reality, researchers often use one study to test more than one related hypothesis, and one study may not be the only study to test that hypothesis. With full information it is possible to adjust the standard statistical tests to account for the fact that multiple different hypotheses have been tested within a study, or that one hypothesis has been tested multiple times across different studies.

Table 1: A Proposed Standard for Classifying Any Study as a Replication

| | Sampling distribution for parameter estimates | Sufficient conditions for discrepancy | Types | Methods in follow-up study versus methods *reported* in original: | | | Examples |
				Same specification	Same population	Same sample	
Replication	*Same*	*Random chance, error, or fraud*	Verification	*Yes*	*Yes*	*Yes*	*Fix faulty measurement, code, dataset*
			Reproduction	*Yes*	*Yes*	*No*	*Remedy sampling error, low power*
Robustness	*Different*	*Sampling distribution has changed*	Reanalysis	*No*	*Yes*	*Yes/No*	*Alter specification, recode variables*
			Extension	*Yes*	*No*	*No*	*Alter place or time; drop outliers*

The "same" specification, population, or sample means the same as *reported* in the original paper, not necessarily what was contained in the code and data used by the original paper. Thus for example if code used in the original paper contains an error such that it does not run exactly the regressions that the original paper said it does, new code that fixes the error is nevertheless using the "same" specifications (as described in the paper).

Figure 1 A proposed standard for classifying any study as a replication.

Most RCTs report both the estimated coefficient on the treatment dummy and the p-value associated with this coefficient. The p-value gives the probability that the estimated coefficient came about by chance. The uncertainty in the estimated coefficient is driven by sampling variation. We randomly sample our treatment and comparison groups from a wider population and we may by chance choose people to include in the treatment group who experience a positive (or negative) shock unrelated to the program we are evaluating. This would lead us to overestimate (or underestimate) the true program effect. If we ran a very large number of RCTs, the average estimated treatment effect would be close to the true treatment effect. An estimated treatment effect from any one trial is one random draw from a distribution of possible treatment effects, centered around the true effect. The probability that any nonzero treatment effect we observe in one particular experiment is due to chance depends on the estimated effect, the sample size, and the variance in the underlying population from which we draw our sample (which we approximate using the sample's variance). The standard calculation for the p-value of an estimated treatment effect assumes that we have made one random draw from the distribution of possible combinations of treatment and comparison groups. If we make more than one draw, we need to be transparent about this and to account for it. (See chapter: The Econometrics of Randomized Experiments by Athey and Imbens (2017) for more discussion on the econometrics behind randomized trials.)

There are two main ways in which our research may deviate from the simple one-arm, one-study assumption behind standard hypothesis testing: a single hypothesis may be tested more than once with several different studies, or multiple different and interrelated hypotheses may be tested in the same study. When we know exactly which hypotheses have been tested by which researchers, it is possible to draw valid conclusions, including by adjusting the calculation of p-values. However, lack of research transparency can lead other researchers to misinterpret the implications of a single study or combination of studies.

4.2 Publication bias

If several RCTs are run on the same population, we are taking multiple draws from the distribution of possible RCTs, and this will increase the precision of our estimate of the true effect size. We will have greater confidence in the weighted average-effect size of all the different studies than in the estimated effect size from one study on its own (where studies with larger sample sizes are given greater weight).[20]

---

[20] Economists rarely do a formal metaanalysis where coefficients are averaged in this way because we rarely see multiple RCTs of precisely the same intervention on the same population. As Meager (2015) reports, averaging coefficients is not an efficient way to use the data from many studies. Metaanalyses are more common in health, and studies of the same intervention on different populations are averaged based on an assumption that the treatment effect (and underlying population variance) is the same in the different populations. Instead, economists tend to review the studies and discuss how and why treatment effects might or might not vary between populations. Publication bias is as damaging to a metaanalysis as it is to a review of the literature.

However, if we see only a select sample of the RCTs conducted, we may not draw a correct inference about the true effect size. If we see only those realizations that fall in a particular part of the distribution of possible estimated-effect sizes, our overall estimated-effect size will be biased. This selection in the effect sizes we observe can result from researchers seeking to publish only those RCTs that have estimated-effect sizes that fall in a certain range, or if journals only publish those estimated effects that fall in a given range of effect sizes. To illustrate, we take an example where all studies have the same sample size N (and thus should be accorded the same weight) and are done on the same underlying population (and thus are all draws from the same distribution and have the same variance which we assume to be known). Fig. 2A shows the case where the true effect size is zero, and therefore the distribution of possible estimated-effect sizes from RCTs with sample size N is centered around zero. Standard hypothesis testing would give us a critical value $\pm\widehat{\beta}_{cv}$ (i.e., if the estimated effect size is larger/smaller than $\pm\widehat{\beta}_{cv}$, there is less than a 5% probability that the effect size was the result of chance if the true effect was zero). Imagine three different RCTs were run and they provide

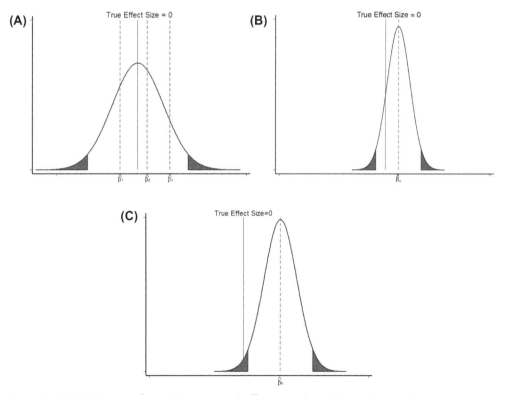

Figure 2 (A) Distribution of possible estimated-effect sizes from RCTs with sample size N centered around zero and a true effect size of zero. (B) Estimated distribution of effect sizes drawn from the results of 3 randomized studies. (C) Estimated distribution of effect sizes drawn from observing only studies 2 and 3.

estimated-effect sizes $\widehat{\beta}_1$, $\widehat{\beta}_2$, and $\widehat{\beta}_3$. If we observe all three estimates, we have a new estimated-effect size based on all three studies that has a tighter confidence band than any of the studies on their own. As this confidence band nevertheless includes zero, we correctly fail to reject the null hypothesis that the true effect is zero, and indeed we have reasonable confidence that the true effect is close to zero given our tight confidence band.

However, if those doing or funding the studies have an interest in a certain outcome and repress the results of those studies that do not have a positive coefficient (in this case $\widehat{\beta}_2$) we may reject the null hypothesis, i.e., conclude that the true effect is different from zero with greater than 95% probability. Note that our new estimate of the true effect may be within our original confidence band around zero, but not within our new confidence band, which is smaller given that we are drawing on two studies. Both our estimate of the true effect size and our new confidence band will be biased because of the deliberate exclusion of studies whose estimated effect sizes fall outside a given range. This is one form of publication bias, also known as the "file drawer problem" (Rosenthal, 1979).

Publication bias can also arise if researchers and publishers have no reason to prefer positive or negative results but are more likely to publish results that are significantly different from zero. In the illustration stated previously, only $\widehat{\beta}_3$ is, on its own, significantly different from zero. If only this study is published we might erroneously reject the null hypothesis and conclude the true effect is less than zero. Note that with a large enough set of studies, we will eventually correctly conclude that the estimated effect is indistinguishable from zero even if only studies with results significantly different from zero are published. This is because some studies will be published that have significant positive effects and some will be published with significantly negative effects, and eventually it will be possible to conclude that the correct effect is indistinguishable from zero. However, this process will take much longer than if all studies were published.[21]

Publication bias can be avoided if we know the full population of studies that have been undertaken and know the results of each. This could be achieved by a two-step process in which researchers (1) record the existence of a study and the hypothesis it intends to test before the researcher (or journal) knows the results; and (2) the researcher commits to reporting the results (preferably in the same place) even if the paper never gets accepted in a journal. A researcher doing a literature review could then observe the results of all the RCTs examining a given hypotheses. The second step is harder to police, especially as some journals will not publish a study if the results have been reported elsewhere.

---

[21] Simply having a longer gap between RCT completion and publication for studies that have results that are, on their own, not significantly different from zero at the traditional confidence levels is sufficient to cause some bias. If there is a stream of RCTs being conducted and a shorter gap between completion and publication for studies that have estimated effects within a given range than for those with estimated effects outside this range, then at any given time a review of published studies will observe a biased set of results and draw inaccurate conclusions.

Thus a researcher may spend years attempting to get a study with a zero treatment effect published and not be able to release the results during that process. Fortunately, even step 1 moves us closer to the goal of reducing publication bias by allowing a researcher undertaking a literature review to observe how many of the studies that sought to test a given hypothesis have had their results published relatively soon after the predicted end of the study. If they observe that all the published studies have positive estimated treatment effects, but that only a small proportion of those that were due to have been completed at the time of the review have been completed, this would cast some doubt on the reliability of the estimated effect of the published studies.

4.3 Current moves to address publication bias

A system of approved registries in which researchers record RCTs that involve health outcomes has been in place for many years: commonly used registries include ClinicalTrials.gov and the EU Clinical Trials Register. An international system for uniquely numbering trials, the International Standard Randomized Clinical Trial Number (ISRCTN), attempts to make it easier to track the number of unique clinical trials on a given topic: trials may have different names and be registered in different places, but they can only have one unique ISRCTN.

The American Economic Association (AEA) recently established a registry for randomized trials in the social sciences (socialscienceregistry.org). The International Initiative for Impact Evaluations (3ie) also has a Registry for International Development Impact Evaluations, which accepts evaluations that are not randomized, but does not accept evaluations of programs in advanced economies. The objective of these registries is to make it easier to track how many studies have attempted to test a given hypothesis in the social sciences. Unlike health journals, social science journals do not (yet) require authors to register their field experiments in an approved registry to be published. However, the AEA and other professional bodies strongly encourage their members to register their trials and a number of funders are now requiring their grantees to do so.

Registering a field experiment is relatively straightforward. The required fields in the AEA registry include title, country, status, trial start and end date, intervention start and end date, a brief description of the experimental design (i.e., the hypothesis to be tested), the main outcomes to be measured, keywords (to allow those doing a literature review to search for all studies that examine a given issue), whether the RCT is clustered, and if so, the number of clusters, the number of planned observations, and whether and from whom human subjects approval was obtained. All of these pieces of information are usually required to obtain human subjects approval to proceed with a field experiment, so the additional burden on researchers of registering is minimal. The registry allows researchers to report the final results on the registry or link to a final paper so that those doing a review can tell whether the results of the study were ever released and what they were.

There is no requirement to provide details on how the data will be analyzed (although it is possible to use the AEA registry to register such a plan, as discussed in the next section). Nor does registering a study mean the authors have to publicly release their data, although the AEA registry does allow for links to published data and the final paper. While it is possible to change information in the AEA registry once a trial has been registered (for example, changing the end date because of delays in program implementation), these changes are tracked so that it is possible to see the evolution of the trial over time. For example, if the sample size is changed, this can be tracked.

If registration is to help mitigate publication bias, it should be completed before the results are known. The AEA labels studies as being "preregistered" if the registration is completed before the intervention starts.

There are relatively few downsides to registration as a way to reduce publication bias. The cost is mainly the time taken to fill out the registration. The main risk is that a registration system may not be useful because it is not complete. While registries for medical studies have operated for a longer time than those in social science and medical journals provide strong incentives for registration, a very large number of studies in these registries never disclose results, even in the registry.

4.4 Data mining and correcting for multiple hypothesis testing

When two different studies test the same hypothesis, it is clear that these represent two draws from the set of possible results, but even within a single study it is possible to effectively take more than one draw.

Imagine we are running a field experiment to test the effectiveness of different health messages in encouraging people to purchase soap. Every day we stand at a grocery store and recruit shoppers into the study. Some are randomized to receive one message and others to receive another message, and we observe their purchases as they check out. Each evening we go home and analyze the data from our field experiment. At the end of the first and second day there is no significant difference in purchasing decisions between those randomized to receive different messages. After the end of the third day we see a significant difference and decide we have reached a big enough sample size to show a significant difference and thus stop the experiment and publish the result. While all three days were part of the same experiment, we are falling into exactly the same trap as described in Section 4.2. We randomly chose three different samples to run our experiment: *day 1 data, day 1 and 2 data,* and *day 1, 2, and 3 data*; we decided to show the results of only one of these three—because it produced a result we wanted to see. It is quite possible that this result came from chance variation in who was randomized into which group on day 3. If we had continued the experiment for another day, the difference between the two groups might have gone away again. The solution to this "stopping problem" is relatively simple: we need to define our sample size in advance, based on power calculations, and stop when we reach our predetermined sample size.

To be able to credibly show to others that we followed this procedure it is useful to commit publicly, in advance, to the sample size at which we intend to stop the experiment. The AEA registry is one place where such commitments can be archived. It preserves a record of the date on which the commitment was made and of any changes made to the commitment over time with relevant dates.

The decision about when to stop a rolling enrollment field experiment is only one of many potential choices that a researcher makes about how to collect and analyze data. Many of these choices are, in the case of field experiments, made before the researcher knows what implication these choices will have on the final outcome of the analysis. For example, we make the decision about where to do the study, what type of participants to survey, the sample size, what variables to collect, the time frame over which we expect the impact to become apparent, and how to phrase the questions. Critically, who falls into the treatment and who into the control group is not decided by the researcher.

Decisions over which a researcher has discretion during the analysis stage include whether or not to control for independent variables in the estimating regression; whether to drop "outliers" from the analysis sample and which observations count as outliers; which of potentially many outcome variables to consider the most important; whether to define the outcome measure in levels, logs, or changes; whether and how to combine different outcome measures into an aggregate outcome measure; and within which subgroups to test for heterogeneous treatment effects. The risk that different choices on these issues can lead to different conclusions has been accepted for some time (Leamer, 1983). However, it is important not to overstate this risk, which will vary depending on the situation. With a large enough sample size, controlling for independent variables may somewhat increase the precision of the estimated effect, but choosing different variables to add as controls rarely changes the estimated coefficient much. In most cases, results are not sensitive to whether or not outliers are dropped, and reviewers usually request authors to show that results are robust to including or excluding outliers and controls. In some cases there is also not much discretion about what the main outcome variable should be. A program designed to increase school enrollment will have school enrollment as the main outcome; one designed to improve vaccination rates will likely use percent of children fully vaccinated. While there may be slightly different ways of defining even a seemingly simple outcome measure such as vaccination rates (valid measures include number of children with any vaccinations, proportion of children aged 2–5 years fully vaccinated, proportion of children vaccinated on time, etc.), these measures are usually highly correlated with each other and reviewers will often require the author to show that the results hold for valid, alternative ways of defining the outcome.

A more serious risk of data mining arises when researchers have a concept that has a less precise and generally agreed-upon indicator of success as an outcome. Measurement of concepts such as women's empowerment or social capital may require multiple indicators, with no one indicator being obviously superior to another. In Casey et al. (2012) for example, we collected over 300 indicators to measure the impact of the GoBifo program on social capital. If we were to consider these indicators separately and run a regression of each potential outcome indicator against our treatment dummy, it is likely that by chance we would find a significant relationship between the treatment dummy and one of these indicators. Indeed, we demonstrate that it is possible to cherry-pick individual outcome indicators which (when taken in isolation) suggest the GoBifo program had positive or negative impacts on a particular aspect of social capital. The true effect from a comprehensive examination of outcome indicators suggests a precise zero impact. If we report all 300+ regressions it would be pretty clear that for the vast majority of outcomes the estimated effect size was zero, and that the few that show significant coefficients (some positive and some negative) were probably the result of chance. If, however, we ran estimating regressions for 300+ potential outcome variables and reported only those where the coefficient was positive and significantly different from zero, we could give the impression that the program was effective in changing social capital, when in fact the data do not support this conclusion. Running many regressions and only reporting those that produce a significant coefficient is often called "data mining," "phishing," or "p-hacking."

There are three basic approaches that can be used to avoid data mining when there are multiple potential ways of defining the main outcome of a study. The first is to combine many outcome variables into a few aggregate outcome variables; the second is to adjust p-values for the fact that multiple hypotheses are being tested; and the third is to commit in advance to how the data from an experiment (or other analysis) will be analyzed.

The simplest way to combine many potential outcome variables into one is to create an index. We may collect many indicators designed to measure wealth, including a series of asset dummies that take the value 1 if a household owns a radio, or bike, or TV. Rather than test the impact of a program on each individual asset dummy, we create a wealth index that is the mean of all the individual asset dummies. We then estimate the impact of the program on the overall wealth index. The same can be done for other multifaceted outcome measures. For example, we may ask a series of questions about whether a woman is involved in various household decisions. We can create a decision-making index by averaging the responses to all these questions. Indices are usually used to combine many similar dummy variables.

A mean effects approach used by Kling et al. (2007) in their evaluation of Moving to Opportunity is an alternative and increasingly popular way to combine outcome indicators that are in a similar "family" of outcomes. A family of outcomes may be ones that all ask about health or education or another similarly broad topic. To estimate mean effects, all the variables in a family need to be placed on a similar scale so that each has the same mean (zero), standard deviation, and direction (negative should be bad for all variables, and positive good). We then run a linked set of estimations on the new set of variables, and the "mean effect" is the average of all the coefficients in the set of linked estimations.

An index of mean effects can be used to reduce the number of outcome measures for which we estimate a treatment effect. Having reduced our hypotheses to a manageable number, we can adjust the p-values for the fact that we are testing several related hypotheses. The Bonferroni correction is the simplest way to do this but it suffers from low power: we may fail to reject the null even when we should. A better approach is to use the free step-down resampling method for the family-wise error rate (Westfall and Young, 1993 are credited with the approach, and Anderson, 2008 provides a good explanation of its use). One advantage of this latter approach is that it takes into account that the outcome variables may be correlated with each other.

Adjusting p-values when we present different outcome measures is not always necessary or appropriate. Some hypotheses are clearly secondary and are designed to illustrate the mechanism through which the main effect was achieved (or was not achieved). In Banerjee et al. (2010a,b,c) we evaluated a Pratham program designed to increase reading levels by providing information to parents about the poor reading levels of students and ways in which they could advocate for change. We collected outcomes on whether the information was provided to parents, whether parents changed their beliefs about how much their child was learning, whether parents put in more effort to monitor schools or advocate for more education resources, whether more resources were secured for schools, and whether test scores increased. We created families of outcomes for variables associated with each step in the process, but we did not collapse them into one family, nor did we adjust the p-values for the fact that we had several families. This is because even though we found statistically significant results for the first two outcomes (information sessions happened and parents were more informed), we did not declare the program a success because the causal chain clearly stopped at this point. Being better-informed did not lead to more effort, resources, or outcomes. In other words, results are always judged in the context of theory, and this can be an important barrier to data mining. Note that some authors fail to make this distinction between a paper's main outcome and regressions that test mechanisms. Thus Young (2016) "corrects" the significance for various RCTs by adjusting p-values for all the regressions reported in the paper whether or not these regressions tested a main outcome.

The other key area where data mining is a particular risk (and being accused of data mining is a serious risk) is subgroup testing. As with multiple outcomes, testing for differential effects among subgroups raises concerns about multiple hypotheses. If we simply test for effects in every possible subgroup, we will likely find one with a significant treatment effect. One option is to adjust p-values for the number of subgroups tested. A better approach is to have a clear motivating theory behind why some subgroups will react differently than others. For example, if we are evaluating a program that provides incentives for girls to stay in school and we find that the program had a bigger effect on girls who are within walking distance of a secondary school than those who are not, this will strengthen our confidence in the overall result.

4.5 Preanalysis plans

Perhaps the most robust way to avoid data mining, or being accused of data mining, is to commit in advance to how the data from a field experiment will be analyzed by creating a PAP. A PAP can be a useful complement to the strategies discussed earlier. For example, if we plan to create five families from 300+ outcome variables, we have a large amount of discretion about how to divide them up unless we commit in advance which variables will go into which families. It is hard to credibly adjust our p-values for the number of regressions run unless we commit in advance to exactly which regressions we intend to run (without this we could run more and only pick the ones that were significant, and then adjusting our p-values for those would be meaningless). Similarly, if we want to adjust our p-values for the number of subgroup analyses we run, it is important to state at the start which subgroups we intend to test.

There has been an increase in the use of PAPs among those doing field experiments, but they are far from the norm. Many economists feel PAPs are too constraining, that authors discover important truths in the data that they could not have predicted prior to their examination of it, and that it would be wrong not to pursue these revelations. Others worry that "following the data" in this way can lead researchers to find patterns that are there just by chance and that tying their hands in advance is useful.

Writing a PAP is not without costs. It is a time-consuming and difficult process. It is hard to think through what additional tests should be carried out under each combination of possible results, especially when a trial has multiple arms. As Olken (2015) explains, "Most research papers test a large number of hypotheses. Hypotheses themselves are often conditional on the realization of other, previous hypothesis tests: the precise statistical question a paper might test in Table 4 depends on the answer that was found in Table 3; the question posed in Table 5 might depend on the answer in Table 4, and so on."

There is nothing to stop a researcher from including results to questions that were not posed in the PAP in a paper. These can be considered exploratory rather than confirmatory. However, most readers will put less weight on these results than they would put on a result in a paper without a PAP. While the abstract scientific model would suggest that subsequent research can follow-up such exploratory results with confirmatory tests, Olken notes that such follow-up work is less common in economics than in medicine, not least because funding for economic research is a fraction of that in medicine. Olken also argues that there is an opportunity cost to researchers thinking through how they would analyze results under multiple different scenarios ahead of time and that this may come at the cost of focusing more deeply on the one scenario that is revealed once the data are analyzed. This may be less a question of the opportunity cost of time than the risk that the PAP process makes a researcher fix ideas ahead of time and is thus less flexible to seeing patterns they had not thought of prior to exploring the data. Indeed, this "fixing ideas ahead of time" is precisely the benefit of a PAP (it reduces the risk of being persuaded by patterns that are there by chance) but also the cost (maybe the patterns are not there by chance, but we miss them if we are blinded by our PAP). This is the fundamental trade-off in PAPs.[22]

Given these trade-offs, the most common use of PAPs is for field experiments in which there is no obvious single, primary outcome variable, or where the authors know that sub-group analysis will be a critical part of their paper and are nervous of being accused of data mining. Given the complexity of doing PAPs in multiarm studies, PAPs are also more common in one-arm trials. PAPs are also used by researchers to help manage relationships with partners. It can be very helpful to have a written document that clarifies what outcome the partner hopes or expects to see and would count as success. This can prevent awkward discussions later in which the partner wants to cherry-pick positive findings. These partner/researcher documents do not necessarily have to be as detailed as a full PAP to be useful (an example of a broad partner/researcher agreement followed by a detailed PAP can be found in Casey et al., 2012).

Olken (2015) provides a useful checklist for what should be included in a PAP:

Preanalysis plan checklist

Item	Brief description
Primary outcome variable	The key variable of interest for the study. If multiple variables are to be examined, one should know how the multiple hypothesis testing will be done.
Secondary outcome variable(s)	Additional variables of interest to be examined.
Variable definitions	Precise variable definitions that specify how the raw data will be transformed into the actual variables to be used for analysis.
Inclusion/Exclusion rules	Rules for including or excluding observations and procedures for dealing with missing data.
Statistical model specification	Specification of the precise statistical to be used, hyperthesis tests to be run.
Covariates	List of any covariates to be included in analysis.
Subgroup analysis	Description of any heterogeneity analysis to be performed on the data.
Other issues	Other issues include data monitoring plans, stopping rules, and interim looks at the data.

Olken, B.A., 2015. Promises and perils of pre-analysis plans. J. Econ. Perspect. 29 (3), 61–80.

---

[22] A related but different issue is that if all the regressions committed to in the PAP are reported in the main paper, this can make for a boring read. Imagine, for example, that treatments 1, 2, and 3 are different twists on a base program and the treatment effects on all three are all insignificant from zero, as is the coefficient on the pooled outcome and all subgroups. We really do not need to see all of these results; we just need to see the result from the three-pooled arms (which has the most precise estimate) and a footnote saying none are significant when run separately, and none of the subgroups are significant. Some authors put all the results specified in the PAP in an appendix but do not necessarily show them all in the main text to help with this problem.

One issue that is still debated within economics is the best time during the research process to write a PAP. A purist approach would suggest that the PAP should be written before the start of the experiment, but it is not clear that this is optimal. Casey et al., for example, argue that there are several advantages to waiting: the literature may have advanced during the trial which may raise additional hypotheses that can be tested with the data generated in the trial; observations on the ground may also generate additional hypotheses that can be tested, including unforeseen negative impacts of the intervention; and the process of baseline data collection can also inform the researcher about which outcome variables are well measured and for which outcome measures there is room for improvement.

In FDA-regulated trials, only the primary and secondary outcome variables are specified prior to the start of the trial, while the detailed data handling and analysis plan is written after the end line data are collected, but before the data are combined with information on which observations are treatment and which are comparison (Olken, 2015). This allows the researcher to determine the best-fit specification prior to including treatment status, or drop outliers before the researcher knows whether the outliers are treatment or control. Some economists have used this approach (Olken in particular recommends it), while others prefer to set the PAP before the end line is collected. Bidwell et al., (2015) use a multistage PAP for a paper that included several rounds of data collection: an initial overarching PAP was written and was then updated at prespecified times after the analysis of a given data set raised hypotheses which could then be tested in subsequent data sets.

A number of PAPs for field experiments are now publicly available and are worth examining before writing one for the first time. Some of the early PAPs in economics can be found at http://www.povertyactionlab.org/Hypothesis-Registry. These include PAPs for Targeting the Poor (published as Alatas et al., 2013), GoBifo (published as Casey et al., 2012), and the Oregon Health Insurance Experiment (published as Finkelstein et al., 2012). Since the opening of the AEA Registry, new PAPs in economics have been published at https://www.socialscienceregistry.org/.

4.6 Evidence on the magnitude of the problem

Increasing the transparency and reproducibility of research results is not costless. Preparing data for publication takes time that could be devoted to doing new studies. The same is true of reanalyzing data and running reproduction and extension studies. Whether these costs are worth incurring depends in part on how big the problems are compared to the costs. Estimating the magnitude of the problem is not easy. We cannot judge the magnitude of the problem by examining published studies of replication or reanalyses and asking how many of these published articles find the study replicates and how many claim to have found a failure to replicate. Replication or reproducibility efforts can be subject to the same issues of publication bias and data mining. If anything, the incentives for publication bias and data mining may be worse for reproduction studies than for original studies. A zero effect in an original study may not be as exciting as a large positive or negative impact, but it is at least a new finding. If a replication study finds exactly the same effect as the original study it does not even have the benefit of being news and an author may well not put a lot of effort into trying to get it published, or worse may attempt to manipulate the results to show that the original finding is not robust. In other cases, replication studies have been much less well powered than the original study. Failing to find a significant effect in a low-powered study when the original study found a significant effect is not a "failure to replicate" as is too often claimed. Simonsohn (2015) also points out that testing whether the two estimated-effect sizes in the different papers are significantly different from each other may also not be a good way to judge if the new study fails to replicate the first study. He suggests that the appropriate standard is whether the replication results are consistent, i.e., that there is an effect size that is large enough to be detectable by the original study. Simonsohn argues that much of the evidence for bias in the psychology literature is based on inappropriate tests. For example, all 10 of the most cited studies in psychology that use "failure to replicate" in their title use as their test whether the replication study is significantly different from zero even though the replication studies often have substantially smaller samples than the original study.

A way round this publication bias in replications is to define a specific set of studies that are to be reanalyzed or reproduced and set clear standards in advance about how the reanalysis or reproducibility is to be judged. An additional benefit of this approach is that there is little incentive among the reproducers to either confirm or undermine the initial result: the result will surprise some people whether the finding is that many studies can be reproduced or few can be reproduced.

Two large initiatives to reproduce findings from psychology studies have recently concluded. Klein et al. (2014) had multiple labs retest important findings in psychology. Some of the labs were in the same country as the original experiment (i.e., were reproductions, in Clemens' parlance) and some were on new populations (extensions, according to Clemens' definition). Of the 13 original findings, similar results were found for 10, reasonably similar results were found for one, and in 2 cases there was little evidence of a consistent result holding either in the original or new population. The effect sizes in the replications were sometimes larger and sometimes smaller than the original. Combined, these results are rather encouraging.

A second initiative in psychology looked at a larger number of studies (100) but attempted to reproduce them only once and mostly on similar populations (Open Science Collaboration, 2015). With one original study and one reproduction where the results are not consistent, it is not possible to say which is the correct result. However, it is possible to examine patterns across the many pairs of original and reproduction studies. As shown in the figure of a study by Open Science Collaboration (2015) it is possible for a replication to find an effect size of similar magnitude to the original study but not be significantly different from zero. It is also possible for the replication to generate an effect size that is significantly different from zero but not be of similar magnitude. Neither is a good measure of reproducibility on its own. However, what the figure in the study by Open Science Collaboration (2015) also shows is that, on average, replication studies had substantially lower estimated effect sizes than original studies and had substantially lower significance. This is true even if we look just at the studies with high power. Combined, these results raise important concerns about reproducibility. What explains the difference between the findings of these two initiatives is unclear. One possible theory is that Klein et al. looked at more famous results, and that these results are famous for a reason. This contention is supported by Dreber et al. (2015), which shows psychology researchers are able to predict reasonably well which of the 100 studies would replicate.

No such well-structured, systematic attempt to reproduce economics studies has been undertaken. Instead, Brodeur et al. (2016) use a different approach to estimating the bias in field experiments in economics. If researchers' data mine to tip their results just above a critical significance level of 5% or 10%, or if studies with results under these levels are less likely to be published, there will be few published results just below these cutoffs. By examining empirical studies from three top journals (*AER*, *JEP*, and *QJE*) between 2005 and 2011, Brodeur et al. find evidence of this "missing mass" just below conventional significance levels in nonrandomized studies in economics, but not in field experiments. Olken (2015) argues that even the level of manipulation observed in nonrandomized studies in economics suggested by the missing mass is not substantial. Brodeur et al. estimate that 10–20% of p-values below 0.05 should in fact be between 0.10 and 0.25. Olken points out that this means that of a 100 studies, instead of having 5 false rejections, we would have 7.25 false rejections. He argues that while this is not an ideal outcome, it suggests that actions to address publication bias and data mining should only be taken if they do not impose a large cost on research.

Why do we not see more evidence of p-hacking? One explanation is that the long process economics papers go through prior to publication helps reduce the ability to p-hack. Papers are typically presented many times with robust discussion and criticism. During this and the referee process, if an obvious specification is not included in robustness checks, seminar participants and referees will usually ask to see it. Authors are not just motivated by how many publications they have but by the respect of their peers, and any appearance of twisting the data to get a certain result loses an author the respect of their peers. Now that data are more commonly published alongside the article, authors may be conscious that others will try different robustness checks, and that they will be criticized if the results are not found to be robust. Finally, financial stakes are not as high in economics as they are in medicine, where multimillion dollar revenue streams rest on a drug or device being found effective. This does not mean there is no p-hacking in economics or that the referee system works perfectly; only that we need to keep the magnitude of the problem in perspective.

While Brodeur et al.'s results and similar analyses of the distribution of p-values can tell us about p-hacking as well as possible publication bias around specific cutoffs like 0.05, they are not very informative of the overall magnitude of publication bias. While Brodeur et al. find fewer studies with p-value of 80% than 4%, this does not necessarily signify publication bias; it may signify that authors are more likely to test for plausible relationships than implausible relationships. If we want to test the magnitude of publication bias, we need to find a defined sample of studies of similar quality when they are started and follow up which ones make it to publication.

Franco et al. (2014) do exactly this: they follow up all 221 research proposals that won a competitive award to get access to a representative sample of the US population with the objective of running an experiment under the Time-sharing Experiments in the Social Sciences initiative. Of 49 studies that produced null results, only 10 were published in journals and 1 as a book chapter. Of 93 studies with strong results, 56 were published as journal articles and 1 as a book chapter. Much of the difference between the two groups can be explained by whether the authors wrote up the results. For example, only 7 of the 38 unpublished studies with null results were even written up. The last finding may simply be authors internalizing that journals are unlikely to publish the study if it was written up. It may also reflect some unobserved heterogeneity in quality of study, although the authors argue this is less of a concern given the tough competition to get these grants.

It is also the case that some findings are less interesting than others, and researchers and journals should place more emphasis on important and interesting results. An out-of-the-box idea may be interesting if it has a significant impact effect, but not if it has zero effect. This opportunity cost of time and journal space has to be set against the costs of publication bias.

4.7 Incentives for replication and transparency

In this section we discuss the extent to which there are sufficient incentives for researchers undertaking field experiments in the social sciences to be transparent, and what, if any, additional incentives should be put in place to encourage transparency, reanalysis, robustness testing, reproduction, and extension work.

Of all the strategies for creating greater transparency, registration of field experiments is probably the least costly: it takes little time and is unlikely to distort research.[23] Because it is not hard, it may not require large incentives. However, as the benefits are public, a nudge is appropriate, especially to get experiments registered early. Increasingly, funders and research-implementing organizations are requiring registration.

As discussed earlier, PAPs are hard and costly, and there is little evidence of statistical data mining in field experiments in economics. The main incentive to do a PAP is for the author to protect themselves from accusations of data mining. Further incentives at this stage are unlikely to be warranted.

The benefits of data publication are potentially larger, as it allows for checks of robustness and fraud, and allows others to do research on related issues. The costs to researchers are reasonably high, but are one-time costs. Publication does not distort research inappropriately. It is here that incentives should be focused.

Twenty or even ten years ago there was little expectation among economists that the data behind a paper would be made available at the time of publication. There were exceptions. For example, the MacArthur Foundation Network on Inequality in the late 1990s funded a series of studies in development, including some of the early field experiments, and required that data from all the studies were published (Research Network on Economic Equality & Social Interactions). It was also the case that many economists in development felt obliged to make their data available when others requested it.

The incentives to make data publicly available have increased rapidly. In 2004, the *American Economic Review* started requiring authors to make public the data and replication code in support of the tables in the published paper. Most top journals followed, as well as applied field journals such as the *Journal of Labor Economics* and the *Journal of Development Economics*. Knowing data publication will be required if the paper does well can encourage good data management and documentation along the way, which then makes the task of publication easier. Many funders, including the International Initiative on Impact Evaluation, the Arnold Foundation, and the Abdul Latif Jameel Poverty Action Lab, require studies they fund to publish their data.

Exactly what counts as data publication is still debated. Most economics journals only require authors to post the part of the data set that is necessary to replicate the tables in the paper. Nor do they require the original raw data to be posted. This means that some robustness checks cannot be carried out (for example, whether the result holds when controlling for a variable that is collected but not included in the controls and thus not published). It also means that some manipulation can happen during the creation

---

[23] Coffman and Niederle (2015) suggest that a possible cost of registries is that authors may not want to share their research designs before the paper is published. However, the AEA registry allows authors to hide details of design until the paper is published.

of aggregate variables or in "cleaning" the data. But it is not clear that posting raw data is in fact more transparent. Most raw data requires so much work that it is impenetrable to anyone not involved in the study. Even if the raw data and the code to turn it into clean data are posted, the cleaning files will be so long and tedious that it is unlikely anyone will learn anything useful from them. As an example, in a nationally representative survey of smallholder agriculture in Sierra Leone, cleaning involved thousands of manual corrects for double-entry reconciliation errors, as well as turning a dozen different local ways of measuring output into a common standard. It would be hard for another researcher to comment on how much bigger a Kenema buttercup is than a Bo buttercup and how many there are in a bushel. In psychology, authors have pointed out that some raw data consist of brain scans and posting all the brain scans in a study would be infeasible.

More concerning is the finding from Chang and Li (2015) detailed earlier that many studies published in journals with data publication requirements do not have sufficient information posted to allow authors to reproduce the results in the paper. In addition, many data sets sit unpublished for lack of a few days additional work, even though this is a tiny proportion of the work that went into collecting, cleaning, and analyzing data. These data represent an important public good: in addition to being useful in checking the validity of published findings, they can be used by other researchers to calculate intracluster correlations for power calculations, combine with other data to do new analysis, publish descriptive studies, or explore relationships not explored by the original authors. An effort is now underway by various institutions, including the Berkeley Initiative for Transparency in Social Sciences, Innovations for Poverty Action, and the Abdul Latif Jameel Poverty Action Lab, to provide assistance and financial incentives to get more data published. Papers such as Chang and Li, which audit journals' implementation of publication rules, are also useful.

Should anything be done to incentivize the researchers to use data that are published to check the validity of existing studies? One position is that academic incentives are skewed toward producing new studies and thus there is not enough checking of existing studies. This was one reason that 3ie launched their project to fund researchers to attempt to verify existing studies. As we discussed earlier, however, many criticized this attempt: the incentives were for those doing the verification and robustness checks to find problems and the results were published on the 3ie Website without going through peer review; verification attempts that found no problems appear to be less likely to be published; and there were accusations that verification authors departed from their PAPs. (In the interests of full disclosure I am married to Michael Kremer whose paper was part of this process and the comment on which started the worm wars.)

PhD students undertaking verification as part of their studies is a process widely regarded as less subject to incentive problems. Students learn a lot from the process and will do as well in the class if they achieve verification as if they find an error. The only disadvantage is that there is no public record of what papers are verified in this way: The profession has a sense that many papers are tested and only a few headline errors have come out, but no one knows for sure how many have been tested. This lack of a record also means that different classes may be verifying the same paper again and again while others go unverified. Professors teaching these classes have expressed concern in going public with the results of all their students' work, explaining that students do not always have the time or the ability to do a thorough verification job. Nevertheless, a simple record of which papers have been the subject of scrutiny in a given class, without indicating the results, could be a useful step toward transparency. If a paper has been examined in multiple classes without any published comment about potential errors, this could help increase confidence in the result even if no one student paper should be taken as meaning a clean bill of health.

An even lower pressure, incentive-aligned strategy is to have the verification take place before publication. Authors could submit data and code to an independent team that attempts to verify the analysis prior to publication. This could be done through journals themselves or through independent groups. Again, PhD students or postdocs might be happy to do this work if it was as well paid as teaching assistant jobs providing them with the income they need to pursue their own research. JPAL is now undertaking pre-publication verification of selected papers.

This leaves the more complex and expensive problem of encouraging reproductions or extensions, i.e., running a new experiment in either the same/similar or a different population. Coffman and Niederle (2015) conclude that reproductions are particularly helpful. They address issues of p-hacking, errors in data and analysis, and the risk that a result is due to chance. They consider them less distortionary to the research process than PAPs, which they argue have considerable costs in preventing flexibility in analysis. They recognize, however, that large field experiments may be too expensive and hard to undertake multiple times. Additionally, academics may not have the incentive to do the second, third, or fourth study on a given issue. One approach is to fund well-coordinated efforts that test an approach in many different contexts at once. The resulting collection of results may well attract significant attention and academic reward. For example, the coordinated series of studies on the graduation approach pioneer by BRAC was published in *Science* (Banerjee et al., 2015b). These coordinated approaches are expensive and hard. They face the constant tension between the goal of testing a very standardized program across contexts and allowing the program to be adapted to local needs and preferences. Coffman and Niederle (2015) propose having a new journal that only publishes reproductions and possibly extensions. This has the advantage that the new studies are peer reviewed for quality and authors know there is an academic outlet for their reproduction studies.

A particularly interesting part of their suggestion is that any subsequent citation of the original study could be followed with notation indicating whether the result has been reproduced (R+ for one that has been successfully reproduced; R− for one that has been unsuccessfully reproduced). This means there are some upsides for the original author in having their study reproduced. They admit there are many issues to sort out, such as what counts as a successful reproduction. They also note that reproductions are likely to be more common for studies that are cheap to run. We would add this approach is more useful when the intervention is very clearly defined, as this is the only way to ensure that exactly the same intervention is being tested in the original and the reproduction. Very large, complex, and expensive studies may never, or rarely, have an attempted reproduction. Another, decentralized approach, which is currently more typical in economics, is for different researchers to test the predictions of a single theory in different ways in different contexts. The theory-driven approach is less useful for testing programs with complex interdependent components, as in the graduation program, where multisite studies may be more useful. The decentralized theory-driven testing is more likely to remain more prevalent, and academics continue to have strong incentives to test theories posed in one paper in similar and different contexts.

The debate about increased transparency and reproducibility in economics too often fails to apply this more theoretical lens, and in doing so can give the impression that we know less than we do. For example, we may have few exact replicas testing whether the incentives for immunization program in India tested by Banerjee et al. (2010c) "works" in other countries. But we do have multiple studies from different countries testing the same underlying hypothesis that small changes in price (both positive and negative) can have surprisingly large impacts on the take-up of health prevention products (for a summary, see Kremer and Holla, 2008; Kremer and Glennerster, 2011). Similarly, the recent series of studies on the impact of providing voters information about candidates prior to elections all test whether voting is purely clientalistic (Fujiwara and Wantchekon, 2013; Bidwell et al., 2015; Ferraz and Finan, 2007; Banerjee et al., 2010a,b,c). We would not want to provide exactly the same information to voters in the same way in different countries. Nor would we want to test whether the coefficient found in later ("replication") studies were significantly lower than those in earlier ("original") studies, or test if one study is within the margin of error of that found in another study. However, the fact that studies in different developing countries have consistently found information provision changes how people vote provides us with more confidence in the reliability of the finding than one study on its own.

The classic approach in economics is, instead of testing whether a program "works" across contexts, to test whether theories hold in a variety of situations.

5. CONCLUSION

Field experiments are hard to do well, and the majority of blood, sweat, and tears come in the details of research implementation. Poor judgment during any one of the thousands of small decisions can undermine the entire venture. Attention to detail is critical. A miscommunication with a partner can lead to the randomization protocol not being followed, an underestimated budget will mean the project cannot be completed as envisaged, a badly worded survey question can lead to an ambiguous outcome measure, low take-up can cause the experiment to be underpowered, or a survey conducted at the wrong time of year can lead to high attrition rate. The role of the researcher is not just to design the evaluation, but to be on top of these practical decisions throughout the process, from design to data publication.

REFERENCES

Alatas, V., Banerjee, A., Hanna, R., Olken, B.A., Purnamasari, R., Wai-Poi, M., 2013. Ordeal mechanisms in targeting: theory and evidence from a field experiment in Indonesia. Natl. Bur. Econ. Res.

Alderman, H., Das, J., Rao, V., 2013. Conducting Ethical Economic Research: Complications from the Field. World Bank Policy Research Working Paper, No. 6446.

Aldermanet, H., Das, J., Rao, V., 2014. Conducting Ethical Economic Research: Complications from the Field. The Oxford Handbook of Professional Economic Ethics, Oxford, UK. http://www.oxfordhandbooks.com/view/10.1093/oxfordhb/9780199766635.001.0001/oxfordhb-9780199766635-e-018.

Allcott, H., 2015. Site selection bias in program evaluation. Q. J. Econ. 130 (3), 1117–1165. http://dx.doi.org/10.1093/qje/qjv015.

Anderson, M.L., 2008. Multiple inference and gender differences in the effects of early intervention: a reevaluation of the abecedarian, Perry preschool, and early training projects. J. Am. Stat. Assoc. 103 (484).

Angrist, J., Bettinger, E., Kremer, M., 2006. Long-term educational consequences of secondary school vouchers: evidence from administrative records in Colombia. Am. Econ. Rev. 847–862.

Angrist, J.D., 1990. Lifetime earnings and the Vietnam era draft lottery: evidence from social security administrative records. Am. Econ. Rev. 313–336.

Ashraf, N., Berry, J., Shapiro, J.M., 2010. Can higher prices stimulate product use? Evidence from a field experiment in Zambia. Am. Econ. Rev. 100 (5), 2383–2413. http://dx.doi.org/10.1257/aer.100.5.2383.

Athey, S., Imbens, G.W., 2017. The econometrics of randomized experiments. In: Duflo, E., Banerjee, A. (Eds.), Handbook of Field Experiments, vol. 1, pp. 73–140.

Baird, S., Hamory, J., Miguel, E., 2008. Tracking, attrition and data quality in the kenyan life panel survey round 1 (KLPS-1). Cent. Int. Dev. Econ. Res.

Banerjee, A., Chattopadhyay, R., Duflo, E., Keniston, D., Singh, N., 2012. Improving Police Performance in Rajasthan, India: Experimental Evidence on Incentives, Managerial Autonomy and Training. w17912. National Bureau of Economic Research, Cambridge, MA. http://www.nber.org/papers/w17912.pdf.

Banerjee, A., Duflo, E., Glennerster, R., Kinnan, C., 2015a. The miracle of microfinance? Evidence from a randomized evaluation. Am. Econ. J. Appl. Econ. 7 (1), 22–53. http://dx.doi.org/10.1257/app.20130533.

Banerjee, A., Duflo, E., Goldberg, N., Karlan, D., Osei, R., Parienté, W., Shapiro, J., Thuysbaert, B., Udry, C., 2015b. A multifaceted program causes lasting progress for the very poor: evidence from six countries. Science 348 (6236), 1260799.

Banerjee, A., Hanna, R., Kyle, J.C., Olken, B.A., Sumarto, S., 2015. Contracting Out the Last-Mile of Service Delivery: Subsidized Food Distribution in Indonesia, w218372015. National Bureau of Economic

Research, Cambridge, MA. https://www.povertyactionlab.org/sites/default/files/publications/553% 20Raskin%20Contracting%20Last%20Mile%20NBER%20Dec2015.pdf.

Banerjee, A., Kumar, S., Pande, R., Su, F., 2010a. Do Informed Voters Make Better Choices? Experimental Evidence from Urban India. Unpublished Manuscript. http://www.Povertyactionlab.org/node/2764.

Banerjee, A.V., Banerji, R., Duflo, E., Glennerster, R., Khemani, S., 2010b. Pitfalls of participatory programs: evidence from a randomized evaluation in education in India. Am. Econ. J. Econ. Policy 1–30.

Banerjee, A.V., Duflo, E., Glennerster, R., Kothari, D., May 17, 2010c. Improving immunisation coverage in rural India: clustered randomised controlled evaluation of immunisation campaigns with and without incentives. BMJ 340 (1), c2220. http://dx.doi.org/10.1136/bmj.c2220.

Barrett, C.B., Carter, M.R., 2014. Retreat from radical skepticism: rebalancing theory, observational data and randomization in development economics. In: Field Experiments and Their Critics: Essays on the Uses and Abuses of Experimentation in the Social Sciences, pp. 58–77.

Beaman, L., Keleher, N., Magruder, J., 2013. Do Job Networks Disadvantage Women? Evidence from a Recruitment Experiment in Malawi. Working Paper. Department of Economics, Northwestern University.

Beath, A., Christia, F., Enikolopov, R., 2013. Winning hearts and minds through development: evidence from a field experiment in Afghanistan.

Bidwell, K., Casey, K., Glennerster, R., June 2015. Debates: The Impact of Voter Knowledge Initiatives in Sierra Leone. Abdul Latif Jameel Poverty Action Lab Working Paper. http://www.povertyactionlab. org/publication/debates-impact-voter-knowledge-initiatives-sierra-leone.

Blattman, C., October 23, 2015. Dear Journalists and Policymakers: What You Need to Know about the Worm Wars. Chris Blattman Blog. http://chrisblattman.com/2015/07/23/dear-journalists-and-policymakers-what-you-need-to-know-about-the-worm-wars/.

Board of Governors of the Federal Reserve System, Chang, A.C., Li, P., 2015. Is Economics Research Replicable? Sixty Published Papers from Thirteen Journals Say 'Usually Not'. Finance and Economics Discussion Series 2015 (83), pp. 1–26. http://dx.doi.org/10.17016/FEDS.2015.083.

Brodeur, A., Lé, M., Sangnier, M., Zylberberg, Y., 2016. Star wars: the empirics strike back. Am. Econ. J. Appl. Econ. 8 (1), 1–32. http://dx.doi.org/10.1257/app.20150044.

Broockman, D., Kalla, J., Aronow, P., 2015. Irregularities in LaCour. https://web.stanford.edu/~dbroock/ broockman_kalla_aronow_lg_irregularities.pdf.

Bruhn, M., McKenzie, D., 2009. In pursuit of balance: randomization in practice in development field experiments. Am. Econ. J. Appl. Econ. 1 (4), 200–232. http://dx.doi.org/10.1257/app.1.4.200.

Buchmann, N., Field, E., Glennerster, R., Nazneen, S., Pimkina, S., Sen, I., 2016. The effect of conditional incentives and a girls' empowerment curriculum on adolescent marriage, childbearing and education in rural Bangladesh: a community clustered randomized controlled trial. Abdul Latif Jameel Poverty Action Lab Working Paper December 2016. https://www.povertyactionlab.org/sites/default/files/KK_ empowerment_Bangladesh_Dec2016%20%281%29.pdf.

Callaway, E., 2011. Report finds massive fraud at Dutch universities. Nature 479 (7371), 15. http:// dx.doi.org/10.1038/479015a.

Casey, K., Glennerster, R., Miguel, E., 2012. Reshaping institutions: evidence on aid impacts using a pre-analysis plan. Q. J. Econ. 127 (4), 1755–1812. http://dx.doi.org/10.1093/qje/qje027.

Chandrasekhar, A., Kinnan, C., Larreguy, H., 2015. Social Networks as Contract Enforcement: Evidence from a Lab Experiment in the Field. Working Paper. http://faculty.wcas.northwestern.edu/ ~cgk281/SaI.pdf.

Chattopadhyay, R., Duflo, E., 2004. Women as policy makers: evidence from a randomized policy experiment in India. Econometrica 72 (5), 1409–1443.

Clemens, M.A., 2015. The Meaning of Failed Replications: a Review and Proposal. Institute for the Study of Labor (IZA).

Coffman, L.C., Niederle, M., 2015. Pre-analysis plans have limited upside, especially where replications are feasible. J. Econ. Perspect. 29 (3), 81–98. http://dx.doi.org/10.1257/jep.29.3.81.

Cohen, J., Dupas, P., 2010. Free distribution or cost-sharing? Evidence from a randomized malaria prevention experiment. Q. J. Econ. 125 (1), 1–45. http://dx.doi.org/10.1162/qjec.2010.125.1.1.

Cole, S.A., Fernando, A.N., 2012. The value of advice: evidence from mobile phone-based agricultural extension. SSRN Electron. J. http://dx.doi.org/10.2139/ssrn.2179008.

Crépon, B., Duflo, E., Gurgand, M., Rathelot, R., Zamora, P., 2012. Do Labor Market Policies Have Displacement Effects? Evidence from a Clustered Randomized Experiment. w18597. National Bureau of Economic Research, Cambridge, MA. http://www.nber.org/papers/w18597.pdf.

Davey, C., Aiken, A.M., Hayes, R.J., Hargreaves, J.R., July 2015. Re-analysis of health and educational impacts of a school-based deworming programme in western Kenya: a statistical replication of a cluster quasi-randomized stepped-wedge trial. Int. J. Epidemiol. http://dx.doi.org/10.1093/ije/dyv128 pii:dyv128.

Dhaliwal, I., Hanna, R., 2014. Deal with the devil: the successes and limitations of bureaucratic reform in India. Natl. Bur. Econ. Res.

Donohue, J.J., Levitt, S.D., 2001. The impact of legalized abortion on crime. Q. J. Econ. 116 (2), 379—420. http://dx.doi.org/10.1162/00335530151144050.

Donohue, J., Levitt, S., 2006. Measurement Error, Legalized Abortion, and the Decline in Crime: a Response to Foote and Goetz (2005). w11987. National Bureau of Economic Research, Cambridge, MA. http://www.nber.org/papers/w11987.pdf.

Dreber, A., Pfeiffer, T., Almenberg, J., Isaksson, S., Wilson, B., Chen, Y., Nosek, B.A., Johannesson, M., November 2015. Using prediction markets to estimate the reproducibility of scientific research. Proc. Natl. Acad. Sci. http://dx.doi.org/10.1073/pnas.1516179112.

Duflo, E., Gale, W., Liebman, J., Orszag, P., Saez, E., 2005. Saving incentives for low-and middle-income families: evidence from a field experiment with H&R block. Natl. Bur. Econ. Res.

Duflo, E., Saez, E., 2002. Participation and investment decisions in a retirement plan: the influence of colleagues' choices. J. Public Econ. 85 (1), 121—148. http://dx.doi.org/10.1016/S0047-2727(01)00098-6.

Duflo, E., Greenstone, M., Pande, R., Ryan, N., 2013. Truth-Telling by Third-Party Auditors and the Response of Polluting Firms: Experimental Evidence from India, w192592013. National Bureau of Economic Research, Cambridge, MA. http://www.nber.org/papers/w19259.pdf.

Fearon, J.D., Humphreys, M., Weinstein, J.M., 2009. Can development aid contribute to social cohesion after civil war? Evidence from a field experiment in post-conflict Liberia. Am. Econ. Rev. 287—291.

Ferraz, C., Finan, F., 2007. Exposing Corrupt Politicians: The Effects of Brazil's Publicly Released Audits on Electoral Outcomes.

Field, E., Pande, R., Papp, J., Park, Y.J., 2012. Repayment flexibility can reduce financial stress: a randomized control trial with microfinance clients in India. Edited by Tiziana Leone PLoS One 7 (9), e45679. http://dx.doi.org/10.1371/journal.pone.0045679.

Finkelstein, A., Taubman, S., Wright, B., Bernstein, M., Gruber, J., Newhouse, J.P., Allen, H., Baicker, K., Oregon Health Study Group, 2012. The Oregon health insurance experiment: evidence from the first year. Q. J. Econ. 127 (3), 1057—1106. http://dx.doi.org/10.1093/qje/qjs020.

Foote, C.L., Goetz, C.F., 2008. The impact of legalized abortion on crime: comment. Q. J. Econ. 123 (1), 407—423.

Franco, A., Malhotra, N., Simonovits, G., 2014. Publication bias in the social sciences: unlocking the file drawer. Science 345 (6203), 1502—1505. http://dx.doi.org/10.1126/science.1255484.

Fryer Jr., R., 2017. The production of human capital in developed countries: evidence from 196 randomized field experiments. In: Duflo, E., Banerjee, A. (Eds.), Handbook of Field Experiments, vol. 2, pp. 95—322.

Fujiwara, T., Wantchekon, L., 2013. Can informed public deliberation overcome Clientelism? Experimental evidence from Benin. Am. Econ. J. Appl. Econ. 5 (4), 241—255.

Giné, X., Karlan, D.S., 2014. Group versus individual liability: short and long term evidence from Philippine microcredit lending groups. J. Dev. Econ. 107, 65—83.

Glennerster, R., Powers, S., 2016. Balancing risk and benefit: ethical tradeoffs in running randomized evaluations. In: DeMartino, G.F., McCloskey, D.N. (Eds.), The Oxford Handbook of Professional Economic Ethics. Oxford University Press, Oxford, UK.

Glennerster, R., Takavarasha, K., 2013. Running Randomized Evaluations: a Practical Guide. Princeton University Press, Princeton, NJ.

Gueron, J.M., 2017. The politics and practice of social experiments: seeds of a revolution. In: Duflo, E., Banerjee, A. (Eds.), Handbook of Field Experiments, vol. 1, pp. 27—70.

Gueron, J.M., Rolston, H., 2013. Fighting for Reliable Evidence. Russell Sage Foundation, New York, pp. 1—22.

Haushofer, J., Shapiro, J., 2013. Household response to income changes: evidence from an unconditional cash transfer program in Kenya. Mass. Inst. Technol.

Herndon, T., Ash, M., Pollin, R., 2014. Does high public debt consistently stifle economic growth? A critique of Reinhart and Rogoff. Camb. J. Econ. 38 (2), 257—279.

Hicks, J.H., Kremer, M., Miguel, E., July 2015. Commentary: deworming externalities and schooling impacts in Kenya: a comment on Aiken et al. (2015) and Davey et al. (2015). Int. J. Epidemiol. http://dx.doi.org/10.1093/ije/dyv129 pii:dyv129.

Hoffmann, V., Barrett, C.B., Just, D.R., 2009. Do free goods stick to poor households? Experimental evidence on insecticide treated bednets. World Dev. 37 (3), 607—617.

Hoxby, C.M., 2000. "Does competition among public schools benefit students and taxpayers?". Am. Econ. Rev. 90 (5), 1209—1238. http://dx.doi.org/10.1257/aer.90.5.1209.

Hoxby, C.M., 2007. Does competition among public schools benefit students and taxpayers? reply. Am. Econ. Rev. 97 (5), 2038—2055. http://dx.doi.org/10.1257/aer.97.5.2038.

Humphreys, M., November 2, 2014. How to Make Field Experiments More Ethical. The Monkey Cage. https://www.washingtonpost.com/blogs/monkey-cage/wp/2014/11/02/how-to-make-field-experiments-more-ethical/.

Humphreys, M., Sanchez De La Sierra, R., Van Der Windt, P., 2012. Social and Economic Impacts of Tuungane: Final Report on the Effects of a Community Driven Reconstruction Program in Eastern Democratic Republic of Congo. Unpublished, Department of Political Science, Columbia University.

Hutton, J.L., 2001. Are distinctive ethical principles required for cluster randomized controlled trials? Stat. Med. 20 (3), 473—488. http://dx.doi.org/10.1002/1097-0258(20010215)20:3<473::AID-SIM805>3.0.CO;2-D.

Imbens, G., 2011. Experimental Design for Unit and Cluster Randomized Trials. International Initiative for Impact Evaluation (3ie), Washington, DC. http://cyrussamii.com/wp-content/uploads/2011/06/Imbens_June_8_paper.pdf.

Johnson, J., May 13, 2015. Campaign Experiment Found to Be in Violation of Montana Law. The Monkey Cage. https://www.washingtonpost.com/blogs/monkey-cage/wp/2015/05/13/campaign-experiment-found-to-be-in-violation-of-montana-law/.

J-PAL, 2015. Martin Hirsch/Government Panel: Creating Space for Evidence in Policymaking in France. https://www.youtube.com/watch?v=gCi60Dyxgws&list=PL5Dr5MK6NSso3iEqn6BDu8OzyMFyLwiNE&index=19.

Karlan, D., Appel, J., 2016. Failing in the Field: What We Can Learn When Field Experiments Go Wrong. Princeton University Press, Princeton, NJ.

Karlan, D., Zinman, J., 2010. Expanding credit access: using randomized supply decisions to estimate the impacts. Rev. Financ. Stud. 23 (1), 433—464. http://dx.doi.org/10.1093/rfs/hhp092.

Khan, A.Q., Khwaja, A.I., Olken, B.A., 2014. Tax Farming Redux: Experimental Evidence on Performance Pay for Tax Collectors, w206272014. National Bureau of Economic Research, Cambridge, MA. http://www.nber.org/papers/w20627.pdf.

Klein, R.A., Ratliff, K.A., Vianello, M., Adams, R.B., Bahník, Š., Bernstein, M.J., Bocian, K., et al., 2014. Investigating variation in replicability: a 'many labs' replication project. Soc. Psychol. 45 (3), 142—152. http://dx.doi.org/10.1027/1864-9335/a000178.

Kling, J.R., Liebman, J.B., Katz, L.F., 2007. Experimental analysis of neighborhood effects. Econometrica 75 (1), 83—119.

Kremer, M., Glennerster, R., 2011. Improving health in developing countries. In: Handbook of Health Economics, vol. 2. Elsevier, pp. 201—315. http://linkinghub.elsevier.com/retrieve/pii/B9780444535924000049.

Kremer, M., Holla, A., 2008. Pricing and Access: Lessons from Randomized Evaluation in Education and Health. Citeseer.

Kremer, M., Miguel, E., 2007. The illusion of sustainability. Q. J. Econ. 122 (3), 1007–1065. http://dx.doi.org/10.1162/qjec.122.3.1007.

Leamer, E.E., 1983. Let's take the con out of econometrics. Am. Econ. Rev. 31–43.

McNutt, M., 2015. Editorial retraction. Science 348 (6239), 1100. http://dx.doi.org/10.1126/science.aac6638.

McRae, A.D., Weijer, C., Binik, A., Angela White, Grimshaw, J.M., Boruch, R., Brehaut, J.C., et al., 2011. Who is the research subject in cluster randomized trials in health research? Trials 12 (1), 183. http://dx.doi.org/10.1186/1745-6215-12-183.

Meager, R., August 2015. Understanding the Impact of Microcredit Expansions: a Bayesian Hierarchical Analysis of 7 Randomised Experiments. MIT Working Paper. http://economics.mit.edu/files/10595.

Miguel, E., Kremer, M., 2004. Worms: identifying impacts on education and health in the presence of treatment externalities. Econometrica 72 (1), 159–217. http://dx.doi.org/10.1111/j.1468-0262.2004.00481.x.

Miguel, T., 2015. "Introduction to Economics 270D." Presented at the Econ 270D: Research Transparency in the Social Sciences. University of California, Berkeley. http://emiguel.econ.berkeley.edu/assets/miguel_courses/12/Lectures-PDF.zip.

Mobarak, A.M., Rosenzweig, M., 2014. "Risk, insurance and wages in general equilibrium. Natl. Bur. Econ. Res.

Motl, J., 2014. Decision Finding Sufficient Facts to Demonstrate a Violation of Montana's Campaign Practice Laws. Commissioner of Political Practices of the State of Montana.

Muralidharan, K., 2017. Field experiments in education in the developing countries. In: Duflo, E., Banerjee, A. (Eds.), Handbook of Field Experiments, vol. 2, pp. 323–386.

Muralidharan, K., Sundararaman, V., 2011. Teacher performance pay: experimental evidence from India. J. Polit. Econ 111 (1), 39–77.

Olken, B.A., 2015. Promises and perils of pre-analysis plans. J. Econ. Perspect. 29 (3), 61–80.

Olken, B.A., Onishi, J., Wong, S., 2014. "Should aid reward Performance? Evidence from a field experiment on health and education in Indonesia. Am. Econ. J. Appl. Econ. 6 (4), 1–34. http://dx.doi.org/10.1257/app.6.4.1.

Open Science Collaboration, 2015. Estimating the reproducibility of psychological science. Science 349 (6251), aac4716. http://dx.doi.org/10.1126/science.aac4716.

Ozler, B., October 15, 2014. How Scientific Are Scientific Replications? World Bank Blog. http://blogs.worldbank.org/impactevaluations/how-scientific-are-scientific-replications.

Ravallion, M., 2012. Fighting poverty one experiment at a time: a review of Abhijit Banerjee and Esther Duflo's *poor economics*: a Radical Rethinking of the Way to Fight global poverty. J. Econ. Lit. 50 (1), 103–114. http://dx.doi.org/10.1257/jel.50.1.103.

Research Network on Economic Equality & Social Interactions. MacArthur Foundation, n.d.

Ridker, P.M., Torres, J., 2006. Reported outcomes in major cardiovascular clinical trials funded by for-profit and not-for-profit organizations: 2000–2005. JAMA 295 (19), 2270. http://dx.doi.org/10.1001/jama.295.19.2270.

Rogoff, K., October 2013. FAQ on Herndon, Ash and Pollin's Critique of 'Growth in a Time of Debt'. Technical report. Unpublished Mimeo available on Rogoff's website at: http://tinyurl.com/ot8h53e.

Rogoff, K., Reinhart, C., 2010. "Growth in a time of debt. Am. Econ. Rev. 100 (2), 573–578.

Rosenthal, R., 1979. The file drawer problem and tolerance for null results. Psychol. Bull. 86 (3), 638–641. http://dx.doi.org/10.1037//0033-2909.86.3.638.

Rothstein, J., 2004. Does competition among public schools benefit students and taxpayers? A comment on Hoxby (2000). SSRN Electron. J. http://dx.doi.org/10.2139/ssrn.692582.

Rothstein, J., 2005. http://www.nber.org/papers/w11215.

Simonsohn, U., 2015. Small telescopes detectability and the evaluation of replication results. Psychol. Sci. 0956797614567341.

Thomas, D., E. Frankenberg, J. Friedman, J.-P. Habicht, M. Hakimi, N.J. Jaswadi, G. Pelto, B. Sikoki, T. Seeman, and J.P Smith. 2003. "Iron deficiency and the well-being of older adults: early results from a randomized nutrition intervention." In.

Vivalt, E., 2015. How Much Can We Generalize from Impact Evaluations? Unpublished Manuscript New York University.

Westfall, P.H., Young, S.S., 1993. Resampling-Based Multiple Testing: Examples and Methods for P-value Adjustment. Wiley Series in Probability and Mathematical Statistics. Wiley, New York.

William, J., Kremer, M., de Laat, J., Tavneet, S., 2016. Borrowing Requirements, Credit Access, and Adverse Selection: Evidence from Kenya (in press).

Zywicki, T.J., 2007. Institutional review boards as academic bureaucracies: an economic and experiential analysis. Northwestern Univ. Law Rev. 101, 861.

CHAPTER 6

The Psychology of Construal in the Design of Field Experiments[a]

E.L. Paluck[1], E. Shafir[1]

Princeton University, Princeton, NJ, United States
[1]Corresponding authors: E-mail: epaluck@princeton.edu; shafir@princeton.edu

Contents

Abstract

In this chapter, we argue that good experimental design and analysis accounts for the notion of construal, a person's subjective interpretation of a stimulus, a situation, or an experimental intervention. Researchers have long been aware of motivations, such as self-presentation, profit seeking, or distrust, that can influence experimental participants' behavior. Other drivers of behavior include consistency, identity, social norms, perceptions of justice, and fairness—all factors that shape individuals' construal of the immediate situation. Experimental tools and interventions are similarly "construed" in ways that shape what participants are responding to. We review the logic and findings around the notion of construal and the ways in which considerations of construal should affect how experiments are designed and deployed so as to achieve a shared construal between participants and investigators. These considerations also apply to the replication and scale-up of experimental studies. We finally discuss how construals of the experimental hypotheses can influence investigators' construal of the data.

[a] Revised version, prepared following the NBER Conference on Economics of Field Experiments, organized by Esther Duflo & Abhijit Banerjee. Thank you to Robin Gomila, Sachin Banker, Peter Aronow, and Ruth Ditlmann for helpful comments. Address correspondence to epaluck@princeton.edu and eshafir@princeton.edu.

Keywords
Behavioral science; Construal; Field experimental design; Measurement; Psychology; Scale-up; Survey design

JEL Codes
C930; C830

1. INTRODUCTION

Why might you be interested in this chapter? A fair assumption is that you are reading because you care about good experimental design. To create strong experimental designs that test people's responses to an intervention, researchers typically consider the classically recognized motivations presumed to drive human behavior. It does not take extensive psychological training to recognize that several types of motivations could affect an individual's engagement with and honesty during your experimental paradigm. Such motivations include strategic self-presentation, suspicion, lack of trust, level of education or mastery, and simple utilitarian motives such as least effort and optimization. For example, minimizing the extent to which your findings are attributable to high levels of suspicion among participants, or to their decision to do the least amount possible, is important for increasing the generalizability and reliability of your results.

Psychologists agree that these motivations are important to consider when designing experiments, but they rank other behavioral drivers higher. Some drivers of individual behavior often ignored by other experimental researchers, which psychologists consider critical, include the following: consistency, identity, emotional states such as pride, depression, and hunger, social norms, and the perception of notions such as justice and fairness. Moreover, psychologists are keenly aware of features of the immediate situation that promote or diminish these behavioral drivers. The question for any experimenter is: how do we figure out which behavioral drivers matter in any one particular experiment, and how they matter?

In this chapter, we focus on the notion of construal, an underappreciated concept that psychologists employ to understand behavior and to design experiments that can better approximate and help isolate the causal dynamics that lead to the behavior of interest. Construal is defined as an individual's subjective interpretation of a stimulus, whether the stimulus is a choice set, a situation, another person or group or people, a survey, or an experimental intervention (Ross and Nisbett, 1991). Thus, for example, an individual's construal of various items in a survey will depend on the subjective meaning that he or she attaches to the survey as a whole. He or she may interpret a survey about risk preferences as a "survey about whether I would be a good investor," even if that is not how the survey is introduced by the investigator, nor what the investigator is really trying to understand.

In the last two decades, psychological insights have been integrated into the study of economic perception and behavior, creating a subdiscipline called behavioral economics or applied behavioral science (Kahneman, 2013). One result is that many economists interested in behavior have a greater appreciation for the seemingly mundane immediate situational features that can promote or diminish behavioral drivers and thus the behaviors themselves. Most behaviorally informed scientists from a range of disciplines can now tell you that the "situation matters." For example, removing small demands on a person's time, such as signing a form or altering defaults, can dramatically increase take-up rates, such as signing up for 401K plans or becoming an organ donor (Thaler and Sunstein, 2008).

The interdisciplinary behavioral science literature has generated a great deal of advice on how to design an intervention, given that the situation matters—advice to the effect that individuals are sensitive to the timing, physical location, milieu, and framing of an intervention (Datta and Mullainathan, 2014; Shafir, 2013). And while psychology has been merged with economics to create a more "behaviorally informed science," psychologists have pointed out that this field would never be fully "behavioralized" (Ross and Nisbett, 1991). In other words, when studying behavior we cannot ignore individuals' subjective thoughts about the behavior, much as the early psychologists tried to do when studying Stimulus—Behavior response patterns by training rats and pigeons to respond to lights and sounds (Skinner, 1960; Seligman, 1970). This is because the interventions and research designs we create are never interpreted directly—as they are—or as the experimenter might have intended. Instead, our interventions and research tools are "construed" in ways that must be understood to know what participants are actually responding to.

There is, in this sense, a presumption in standard economic thinking that is really quite radical from the point of view of a psychologist. Economic theorizing posits that people choose between options in the world: Job A versus Job B, or, if one is looking to buy a car, Cars A, B, or C, where the decision maker takes into consideration the information at their disposal. As it turns out, what people actually decide about are not options as they appear in the world but, rather, as they are mentally represented. When a person is presented with a choice between options A and B, he or she chooses not between A and B as they are in the world, but rather as they are represented by the 3-pound machine behind his or her eyes and between his or her ears. And that representation is not a complete and neutral summary but rather a specific and constructed rendering—a construal.

Building on previous work that discusses how to design interventions based on an understanding of situational pressures and individuals' construal of those pressures (Datta and Mullainathan, 2014; Ross and Nisbett, 1991; Shafir, 2013), this chapter points out ways in which participants' construal of your experiment—everything from the behavior in question to the setting, the intervention, the deployment of the intervention, and the measurement tools—should affect the way you design and deploy your experiment.

Acknowledging subjective interpretation of the experiment is not the same as claiming to have no knowledge of participants' construction of reality. Psychologists can provide many ways in which construal processes might be systematic and predictable. Nonetheless, one deep message is that experimenters need to be modest about and to explicitly test assumptions concerning how participants view experimental interventions. Being aware of and taking steps to understand participants' construal in advance can help you to design and deploy the kind of field experiment that will shed light on the causal processes leading to the behavior in which you are interested.

You as the investigator, furthermore, are not excluded from the forces of construal. Toward the end of this chapter, we will also explore how your own construal of your experiment and of the data can affect the way you interpret your results, conduct replications, and recommend elements of your intervention for scaling up or for institutional policies. We begin by providing an overview of construal: its definitions, functions, and some illustrative examples.

1.1 Principle of construal

At the turn of the 20th century and particularly during the two world wars, psychologists were moving away from a Freudian focus on personal histories and individual differences driving behavior and behavioral disorders. Kurt Lewin, a German psychologist and an èmigrè who eventually directed the Center for Group Dynamics at MIT, developed a situationally driven alternative to Freud's claim that conflicting forces within the individual (the id, the ego, and superego), only available through the introspection of the individual and his or her therapist, could explain behavior and individual decision-making. To facilitate the scientific study of behavior, Lewin proposed, we should look for conflicting forces in the environment surrounding the individual, such as laws, family pressures, social norms, peers, and even the physical environment, and analyze how those forces push an individual and his or her self-proclaimed beliefs and desires into particular behavior choices.

Lewin called these conflicting forces in the environment, pushing and pulling an individual's behavioral choices, a tension system. The tensions he mapped were between individual motivations and environmental forces. Through a series of field experiments, Lewin showed how leaders, workplace hierarchies, peers' public behavior, and the physical proximity of particular resources could promote or inhibit a person's personal desires and beliefs and change behavior in predictable ways (Lewin and Gold, 1999). His early theorizing formed the foundation of modern social and cognitive psychology, and today it guides the assumptions that psychologists make as they design and evaluate of behavior change and decision-making experiments.

As Lewin was exploring the importance of situational pressures on behavior, some psychologists took this view to the extreme, including radical behaviorists such as B.F. Skinner who felt that all behavior was no more than a response to objective environmental forces learned over time. This view, while at first popular, proved profoundly insufficient. Particularly glaring was the absence of a principle of human thought that Lewin proposed as a critical part of the tension system analysis: construal. Environmental forces were not directly and objectively perceived by the individuals inhabiting a tension system, Lewin reasoned. Perception is a subjective process, which can happen in a considered, deliberate fashion or in a fast and less conscious manner. Construal, the act of interpreting and attaching subjective meaning to forces such as one's peers, leaders, workspace, group identities, choices, and the like, is also inherently variable—a stimulus may be interpreted by the same person one way at a certain time or in a certain situation, and differently in the next situation. Similarly, two people experiencing the same stimulus can construe it in different ways.

Some classic examples of how construal can affect judgments and behavior include the following:

- Judgments of a stimulus depend on how you construe the judgment relative to similar stimuli you have adapted to in your environment: A rule is perceived as strict when you are used to lax rules, and as lax when you are coming from a stricter rule environment. This is intuitive, and easily demonstrated through a comparable physical experience, that of judging water temperature with your hand, just after you have plunged your hand first in a cold or a hot bucket of water. Judgment will be relative and not reflective of an absolute physical (or social) property (Weber et al., 1996).
- Framing affects construal: Framing a monetary amount as a loss or a gain changes its construal, and the risk attitude it elicits (Tversky and Kahneman, 1981). More generally, any frame depicting a stimulus (an idea, choice, or behavior) as consistent with or as a departure from a perceived reference point shifts an individual's reception of the stimulus (Kahneman and Miller, 1986).
- Self-appraisal is made through social comparisons: Judgments about the self, including accomplishments, motivations, the strength of particular identities, and ideologies, are often made relative to other individuals present in the situation or other individuals mentioned in the question (Markus and Kunda, 1986; Morse and Gergen, 1970).
- Taxes and subsidies provoke unintended reactions, depending on individuals' construal of the behaviors they target: Individuals may construe economic incentives as psychological taxes (i.e., demotivating) when the incentives subsidize behavior that is self-motivated—the small economic reward replaces what before was a substantial psychological boost. Likewise, economic taxes may be interpreted as psychological subsidies (motivating) when they are imposed on behavior that individuals have mixed feelings about or are trying to stop—the original feeling of guilt is alleviated through the fine (Miller and Prentice, 2013).
- Peer pressure is effective not just because of conformity but because peers redefine the behavior in question: Individuals do not just adopt peer behavior but also their peers' construal of the behavior or the situation. For example, when individuals observe peers ranking "politician" very positively versus very negatively as a profession, the individual's own ranking of the term politician changes, not out of mimicry but

because the individual has a different kind of politician in mind as a result of their peers' ranking (Asch, 1940).

- Global judgments color more specific ones and earlier information changes the meaning of later information: For example, global traits such as warmth can change the construal of a more specific trait like intelligence: the latter is interpreted as wisdom when a person is globally judged to be warm but as cunning when the person is thought of as cold. Along similar lines, learning about a teacher's argument with a student is interpreted differently if it is first versus later revealed that the teacher was voted teacher of the year by his or her students (Ross and Nisbett, 1991).
- The source of a message colors the meaning of the message: Asch (1948) showed in a classic study that the quote "a little rebellion now and then is a good thing" was interpreted significantly differently by students when it was attributed to Thomas Jefferson versus Lenin. Moreover, the words in a message can color the message. When asked about the wisdom of potential US intervention in a foreign crisis, Americans report significantly different levels of endorsement depending on whether the situation—otherwise described in identical terms—uses a few words (blitzkrieg invasion, troop transports) associated with WWII, or else words (quickstrike invasion, Chinook helicopters) reminiscent of the Vietnam War (Gilovich, 1981).
- Ideology changes which facts are noticed, believed, and remembered: Partisanship determines which facts individuals attend to, believe, remember, and understand when consuming news or other kinds of fact-based reports (Vallone et al., 1985).
- Construal affects how individuals assess the relative importance of various causal factors. While lay people (and researchers) reasonably search out various types of "data" to understand the causes of behavior in the world, including observations of distinctiveness (how specific is the behavior to this instance or individual), consistency (over time, is this behavior observed in this situation or for this individual), and consensus (how many other people behave this way or in this situation), people are often biased toward dispositional explanations of behavior that focus on a person's character, over situational explanations of that behavior that rely on the pressures of the environment (Kelley, 1973; Ross and Nisbett, 1991).

In the words of the cognitive psychologist Jerome Bruner (1957), individuals who construe stimuli differently according to current levels of adaptation, frames, social comparisons, and present desires are "going beyond the information given". Psychologists see this subjective interpretation as a normal feature of human cognition, which can happen deliberately and consciously as well as spontaneously and unconsciously. That construal can be an automatic and unconscious process troubles our ability as investigators to ask directly about how an individual's interpretation might depend on their current circumstance. Indeed, individuals do not usually have insight into the ways in which problem presentation, peers, and other Lewinian environmental pressures affect their own construal.

The elements that influence the construal of social circumstances can be subjective and subtle. Let us provide, therefore, one final example from visual perception, where the elements are more objective and clear. Consider the picture below (Fig. 1). If you the experimenter were to present this picture to a person in a study, you would be showing them heads of identical size (on paper), but the person would be construing heads of very different sizes. If you asked the participant how much Magic Marker would be needed to cover each head in the picture, you would get different estimates, despite the fact that they are identical in size. Here, of course, cues of depth and perspective generate—imperceptibly, effortlessly, universally—a construal of different head sizes. (In fact, in this example, you the experimenter, if you did not know better, might rely on those cues too.) The factors underlying the construal of social contexts are more varied and less obvious, but they similarly generate subjective representations that depart from what was "objectively presented."

Fortunately, psychologists have identified some "systematic factors [that contribute] to variability and instability of meaning" in people's construal processes (Ross and Nisbett, 1991, p. 69). Ross and Nisbett (1991) review the classic literature on various "tools of construal," which include knowledge structures such as scripts, schemas, models, and various heuristics that help individuals to quickly and with minimal effort make sense of other people, situations, choices, and assorted stimuli.

Figure 1 A visual illusion.

Schemas, for example, are mental constructs representing knowledge about a group of related topics. Once a schema is activated, subsequent stimuli are interpreted along the lines suggested by that schema, with consequences for memory, decision-making, judgment, and behavior. A schema for "farm," for example, will influence an individual's attention when considering a farm environment; he or she would spend more time paying attention to aspects of the farm that do not fit with his or her farm schema, such as the appearance of an octopus. In this case, his or her schema will predict what she expects to see, what piece of information about the farm he or she spends the most time considering, as well as what he or she remembers about the farm (Loftus and Mackworth, 1978). Scripts, such as a script for how to behave at an academic conference, contain even more specific knowledge structures about the order in which certain events should unfold and how an individual is expected to behave during each event, such as a discussion section, a coffee break, or an evening dinner with colleagues (Schank and Abelson, 2013).

Scripts, schemas, and heuristics (Gilovich et al., 2002) may be investigated as local tools of construal that exist within certain populations (such as among people in farms or at academic conferences), or as tools of construal that apply to most people [such as the status quo bias against change, which manifests itself in many different populations (Eidelman and Crandall, 2009; Kahneman et al., 1991)]. These various tools of construal improve individuals' ability to interpret novel situations, and even if they sometimes guide behavior and judgments in directions that deviate from the predictions of rational actor models, they help to make resulting behaviors and judgments more fluid and more predictable.

Laypeople and social science researchers often fail to appreciate the role of construal in guiding people's responses; instead, they tend to attribute choices that deviate from some rational prediction or norm to individuals' dispensational characteristics such as intelligence, personality, or ideology. The literature on construal encourages the view that behavior is not necessarily a product of a person's character, but rather a window into how the person construes their choices or environment. "Where standard intuition would hold the primary cause of a problem to be human frailty, or the particular weakness of a group of individuals, the social psychologist would often look to situational barriers and to ways to overcome them" (Ross and Nisbett, 1991).

For experimenters (and for policy makers, the consumers of much of this research) this insight should be of great importance. Behavior in experiments, and its interpretation, is determined not simply by the objective building blocks of the experiment, but by what participants know, want, attend to, perceive, understand, remember, and the like. Thus, experiments that are otherwise well designed, including well-intentioned interventions, can fail because of the way they are construed by the participants or by the investigators themselves. The difference between success and failure can sometimes boil down to a relatively benign and supposedly immaterial change in presentation and subsequent construal, rather than a complex and costly rearrangement of experimental logic or procedure.

In the following pages, we show how psychologists understand construal as important to the design of an effective experiment. We offer a number of suggestions for how you as an investigator can attempt to understand your participants' construal of the stimuli in your experiment, or how you might reach what we term *shared construal* with your participants. The goal is to design and deploy a stimulus (intervention) in a field setting that participants will construe the way you intend them to.

By shared construal we do not mean that investigators and participants understand a behavioral problem or a choice set in the same way. Naturally, the experimenter (say, a professor studying children's candy preferences) may view the options very differently than do the subjects. The experimenter will also know things that the participant does not, and might arrange things in ways that escape the participant's attention. What we mean by shared construal is that the investigator inhabits participants' perspective as best they can, as they are designing the experiment. When Mischel (Mischel et al., 1972) designed his famous marshmallow experiments, he needed to know that kids found those strange, almost nonfood-like treats, which he may have detested, irresistible.

Psychologists think of designing experiments as a way of creating different counterfactual worlds for their participants to inhabit and respond to. As the saying goes, "I can explain it for you, but I can't understand it for you." The point, then, is to design a world in which a participant understands the world in the way the experimenter intended, and without him or her having to explain too much of it. How to do this is no easy feat, and there is no foolproof recipe to follow. In the following sections, we offer suggestions for understanding participants' construal, as well as your own, as you conceptualize your intervention and experiment (piloting phase), as you design and deploy your intervention and measurement (design phase), and as you interpret your results and plan follow-up experiments or scale-ups (interpretation phase).

2. PILOT: SEEK SHARED CONSTRUAL OF BEHAVIOR AND THE SITUATION BETWEEN INVESTIGATORS AND PARTICIPANTS

Piloting often means testing out an experimental paradigm before the actual trial. But piloting can also be time set aside to understand a participant population's construal of the behavior in question and of the situations involved in your experimental paradigm prior to designing the full experiment. In this sense, piloting is an investigation and discovery stage about construal. It requires a high level of modesty, curiosity, and openness on the part of the experimenter, to better understand what is driving people, how they see the problem in question, before crafting an intervention to test their behavior.

Before designing the intervention or the experimental paradigm (i.e., the content or the setup and deployment of the manipulation and measurement), it is important to first understand the underlying drivers of the behavior in question in the particular setting of interest. What are the "restraining forces" that cause the behavior not to be enacted, or the "compelling forces" that drive the behavior at particular times or among particular people?

Redelmeier et al. (1995) were interested in why homeless adults in a southeast region of Toronto, Canada, repeatedly visited the emergency room (ER) for care of nonlife-threatening ailments, up to 60 times per year, even when they were not given everything they needed. A common construal among medical professionals and researchers was that the behavior was driven by the homeless adults' neediness and the appeal of a warm place of shelter, and that if hospitals provided more care, this would only increase demand. The authors used survey data to understand the construal among homeless adults who attended the hospital's ER: many reported being treated rudely by hospital staff, and nearly half reported that their needs were not met at the time of their visit. Crucially, 42% reported that they returned to the ER because of an unmet medical need.

Based on this alternate construal, Redelmeier et al. (1995) hypothesized that increased care might address homeless adults' perceived satisfaction with their care experience and lessen the number of return visits. This informed their experimental design: a compassionate care condition run by volunteers who provided randomly assigned homeless adults with extra (though nonclinical) attention during their visit through friendly conversations and other kinds of rapport building, and a baseline condition in which the other half of the selected sample were treated as per ER policy. In this case, the compassionate treatment, which directly addressed participants' construal of the situation, led to a 30% drop in repeated visits to the ER.

It is notable that the experiment excluded homeless adults, who might be unresponsive to changes in treatment, including those who were acutely psychotic, unable to speak English, or intoxicated or extremely ill. These choices, along with the insights regarding participants' versus the medical professionals' understanding of the triggers of repeated visits to the hospital, were won through familiarity with the context of the experiment, a willingness to admit uncertainty in the standard interpretation of the observed behaviors, along with some data collection regarding the participants' own construal.

Investigating participants' construal of the behaviors of interest ahead of the experiment may shift the intervention design, helping you to reconceptualize what is at issue for your experiment. The ER experiment is one in which individuals with a "big picture" view of the situation, the hospital administration and medical professionals, had the wrong construal. Piloting helped to uncover a different insight into the behavior, a point that is also made by the literature on intervention design (Datta and Mullainathan, 2014). The lesson of the ER study is not only that the intervention achieved the right construal, but, more importantly, that highly experienced hospital professionals had the wrong construal all along. This is remarkable also because of what was needed for the revision of construals: ask the clients what they thought and felt.

Piloting to understand local construals can help craft the most effective control or comparison conditions. It can help create the most salient contrast that draws out the causal factor believed to be responsible for the behavior under investigation. In the Redelmeier et al. (1995) experiment, experimenters did not offer financial incentives, for example, but rather focused on the way clinical treatment was delivered—with compassion.

Piloting can also help you to understand more about participants' construal of the environments where you plan to conduct your experimental manipulations or measurements. The choice of an intervention site ought not to be guided by logistical convenience alone (though this is often critical to the successful deployment of a field experiment). Psychological research on context effects suggests that the site of the experiment can often drive some aspect of the experimental results, a point often less appreciated compared to other concerns. Obviously, you spend lots of time designing the form of your experimental intervention—say, a community meeting, versus a phone call, or a letter. Once designed, will you convene your community meeting in a church, in an old school, or in a restaurant? Will you send your thoughtfully crafted letter, or make the phone call, to a person's home, or to his or her workplace? At the beginning or the end of the month?

By this point, it will not surprise you that psychologists believe these choices matter deeply for how your participants will construe your intervention and the issues addressed by it. In the famous Milgram obedience study, participants were ordered by an experimenter to apply (ultimately fake) electric shocks to another study participant when he or she failed at a memory task. In the version of the study run at Yale University, 65% of participants were fully obedient to the experimenter's commands in delivering the maximum level of shock; 48% of participants were fully obedient when the study was run at a nondescript office building in the nearby city of Bridgeport without a visible university affiliation (and nearly nobody obeyed when the instructions were conveyed by phone) (Milgram, 1974).

Consider also a study of context and behavior by Berger et al. (2008), who examined voting outcomes when voters were assigned to vote in churches versus schools. First, using observational data, they estimated that voters were approximately 0.5 percentage points more likely to vote in favor of increasing education spending (by raising the state sales tax from 5.0% to 5.6%) when they had been assigned to vote in a school versus a church. Second, using an experiment in which participants were initially shown images of either schools or office buildings before stating their policy preference, the authors suggested that the school context primed participants to think positively about education and to vote in its favor. This effect held even though none of the participants believed that exposure to school images boosted their support for the increased sales tax to support education, "suggesting environmental stimuli can influence voting choice outside of awareness" (p. 8847).

This study highlights an important tension. An experiment's piloting stage is the right time to worry about things like the unintended effects of the context, or the underappreciated perspectives participants bring with them as one aims to achieve shared construal. At the same time, it is important to keep in mind that participants are unlikely often to be the most useful informants. After all, if participants had good insight into what drives their behaviors, we could simply ask them—no need to run expensive studies. As it turns out, construal processes are mostly out of contact with conscious awareness. By running carefully controlled studies, we can find regularities in people's construal, of which the participants themselves are largely unaware.

3. DESIGN: ENSURE THE INTERVENTION DESIGN, MEASUREMENT, AND DEPLOYMENT ACHIEVE SHARED CONSTRUAL BETWEEN INVESTIGATORS AND PARTICIPANTS

3.1 Intervention design and deployment

Do participants in your field experiment understand the content of your intervention in the same way that you do as the investigator? In a now classic study, Gneezy and Rustichini (2000) introduced fines for picking up children late from day care in a random subset of a sample of day care centers in Israel. A fine is normally understood as a deterrent to action, and we might predict that parents in the treatment day cares would be motivated to show up on time, given the increased economic costs to their delay.

Instead, it appears that parents perceived the fines to be what some psychologists have termed an "economic tax but a psychological subsidy" (Miller and Prentice, 2013). Parents in day cares where fines were implemented were significantly *more* likely to pick up their children late, an effect that persisted even after the fine was removed 17 weeks later. Gneezy and Rustichini (2000) and others have reasoned that the fine reshaped the parents' understanding of their environment. In particular, the contract between parents and day care providers changed regarding pickups. The fine clarified the contract—picking up your child late "costs" this amount of money. So parents willing to pay the price came late. Another way of stating these results is that parents initially construed on-time pickups as a moral imperative; being late meant you were violating it. The fine was thus construed as a psychological subsidy, a release from this moral guilt. Parents released from this moral obligation now felt they only had to pay, and no longer experienced guilt about a late pickup.

What about community members and other bystanders to your experimental intervention? One negative externality of a field experiment might be that other (non-targeted) people in your participants' social networks may construe the intervention in unintended ways, and influence your participants. Ross and Nisbett (1991) describe the surprising results of the Cambridge Somerville Study, in which at-risk boys were randomly assigned to receive or not to receive a bucket of treatments for an extended period of time during early adolescence, including after school and summer programming, tutoring, home visits, and more. In the forty-year follow-up to the experiment, investigators found that treatment participants had no better outcomes than control participants, and in some aspects including adult arrests and mortality, treatment participants looked somewhat worse.

Ross and Nisbett (1991) reason that one potential explanation for this lack of observed response to treatment rests in the community's construal of and response to the intervention. For example, community members such as coaches and ministers who might have naturally reached out to the at-risk boys may have perceived that the treated boys no longer needed the help of the community, and withdrew crucial support. Another possibility is that community members construed the treated boys as much worse "troublemakers" due to all the outside attention that they received, and treated them as such. These are post hoc proposals, but plausible ones that remind us of the importance of understanding the community's construal—even when the community is not directly implicated in the experimental manipulation, particularly because they might affect the actual findings.

Anticipating different construals, and achieving shared construal of your intervention design and the way it is deployed[1] in the participant population and the surrounding community is no small task. The examples we used point to the necessity of running a small-scale version of the intervention to invite reactions and reported construals of the intervention that are not merely hypothetical in nature. In cases like the ER, interview those experiencing the treatment. Or, as in the case of the day care experiment, interview parents to see how they understand their current "contract" with the day care—what drives them to come late, and how do they think the day care feels about late pickups. Only when parents' construal of the late fee was understood could researchers explore an intervention predicated on a shared construal, which would yield the desired reduction as opposed to increase in late arrivals.

Finally, although it arrives after the implementation of the intervention, all experiments should involve some form of a manipulation check, which assesses whether and what the participant understood and noticed about the intervention. Manipulation checks are used all the time in psychological experiments, for descriptively understanding how participants perceived the intervention, but they are relatively rare outside of psychology. Manipulation checks can be much more than a simple determination of treatment delivery, for generating the estimated LATE given randomized intention to treat. They can give a picture of the participants' construal of the intervention, through questions like "what did the letter tell you?" or "who sent that letter, and why do you think they sent it?" after

---

[1] See also recent work by Haushofer and Shapiro (2013) on participant construal of the fairness of the process of random assignment.

participants are sent letters about, say, an opportunity for financial literacy training. When we run "deception-free" studies, we might want to inquire whether participants actually fully believe it. And when we tell them a treatment assignment is "random," might participants suspect it is actually rigged? We have encountered cases where participants were convinced an attractive experimenter was "part of the study." And others where parts of the study—claims such as "we are genuinely interested in your beliefs and preferences"—were dismissed. More intrusive manipulation checks via surveys or interviews can happen for a small subsample of the target population, or during piloting.

3.2 Measurement of outcomes and processes

How do participants construe your measurement tools? Do they understand your survey questions the way they were meant to be understood? Do community members assisting with an archival data collection (e.g., photos of a neighborhood over time) perceive the data collection to be appropriate, and do they share the investigator's belief that the records of interest represent accurate traces of the behaviors under study?

Although survey measures are considered second-best to unobtrusively measured behavioral outcomes, they are often desirable additional pieces of information or the only source of outcome measurement in institutionally weak or disorganized settings without good records of behavior. Fortunately, an enormous literature in psychology on psychometrics, heuristics, and biases provides a framework for thinking about when participants' construal of survey questions may differ from that of the investigator's.

When participants read or listen to a series of questions, they often engage in active acts of interpretation, or misinterpretation. They do not merely listen, or read, and then respond. Rather, they try, often quite innocently, to interpret what it is the investigator is looking for, what is meant by each question in light of the previous question. Questions are not handled in isolation, and a general attempt is made to make global sense of the questionnaire, assessing its general purpose and its broad themes. For a striking example, one of the most widely used questionnaires in psychology is the Rosenberg Self-Esteem Scale, which features a series of survey items aimed at assessing an individual's self-esteem—none of which include the term *self-esteem*. Participants rate their agreement with items such as "On the whole, I am satisfied with myself," and "All in all, I am inclined to feel that I am a failure" (reverse scored).

Robins et al. (2001) intuited that participants taking this scale would quickly construe the purpose of the scale to be the measurement self-esteem and that a response to a direct question about self-esteem would be equally valid. They constructed an alternative questionnaire consisting of one item: "I have high self-esteem." Ratings of this single item correlated to the same degree as did the multiitem self-esteem questionnaire with a broad number of criterion measurements, including other self-evaluations and biases, mental and physical health, and peer ratings of the participant. The single-item survey also cut down on the number of complaints from participants about answering the same question multiple times, and reduced the number of skipped questions or random responses and other problems with the multiitem survey protocol.

To be fair, in many cases a more complex topic necessitates multiple items; our point here is not that surveys must be short but that participants are not passive recipients of each survey item. Their interpretations, of course, may overlap to various degrees with the investigator's own understanding. Many psychologists use the technique of "cognitive interviewing" (Willis, 2004) to test participants' understanding of a questionnaire before broader deployment. This technique involves asking the participant to react aloud to each question, talking through their reaction to the question, also in light of responses to preceding questions, and why they are providing the responses they provide.

Participants can also construe certain questions in meaningfully different ways, simply as a result of what comes to mind as a function, for example, of the ordering of questions. Schwarz and Xu (2011) inquired about drivers' enjoyment commuting to work in luxury as opposed to economy cars. In one study, they asked University of Michigan faculty and staff which car they drove (brand, model, and year) and subsequently, how they "usually" feel while commuting. Consistent with common intuition, drivers reported more positive emotions when they drove more luxury cars. Thus, estimated mean scores for drivers' positive affect while commuting was significantly higher while driving cars corresponding to the Bluebook values of a BMW than that of a Honda Accord.

A reversed order of questioning, however, paints a different picture. In this ordering, university faculty and staff were first asked to report how they felt during their most recent episode of driving to work, and only then after they had reported their feelings, were they asked what car they drove. In this condition, the quality of the car driven, as indexed by (the natural log of) its Bluebook value, was thoroughly unrelated to the drivers' affective experience.

These and similar findings make a simple but important point: What is momentarily on people's mind can influence their construal. The car matters to reported judgments of enjoyment when it is on the driver's mind, but not otherwise. When asked to report how they usually feel while commuting, drivers who are led to think about their car, arrive at answers that correlate with its value. But when the car goes unmentioned, its value figures not at all.

In other cases, participants respond to a slightly different question, or perform a slightly different computation, than that requested by the investigator, particularly when the concepts involved are only superficially understood by the participants. Item substitution is a phenomenon that was observed in the classic Linda-type problems. Tversky and Kahneman (1973) [2] gave participants a description of a

---

[2] See also Kahneman and Frederick (2002), for further discussion.

fictitious graduate student shown along with a list of nine fields of graduate specialization. Here is a description:

Tom W. is of high intelligence, although lacking in true creativity. He has a need for order and clarity, and for neat and tidy systems in which every detail finds its appropriate place. His writing is rather dull and mechanical, occasionally enlivened by somewhat corny puns and by flashes of imagination of the sci-fi type. He has a strong drive for competence. He seems to have little feel and little sympathy for other people and does not enjoy interacting with others. Self-centered, he nonetheless has a deep moral sense.

One group of participants was given a representativeness (or similarity) question; others were given a probability question. Participants in a representativeness group ranked the nine fields of specialization by the degree to which Tom W. "resembles a typical graduate student" in each of those fields. Participants in the probability group ranked the nine fields according to the likelihood of Tom W. specializing in each. The correlation between reported representativeness and probability is nearly perfect (0.97), showing near-perfect attribute substitution. Representativeness judgments—which are natural and automatic—are more accessible than probability judgments, which are not intuitive and can be rather difficult. (And there is no third attribute that could easily explain both judgments.) When asked about probability, a concept at once subtle yet familiar enough not to require further clarification, people substitute similarity judgments for their response. This, of course, can lead to actual error, where things that are more similar, but less likely, are rated higher in likelihood. (The study also showed that participants' probability judgments correlated highly negatively with their own estimated base rates of the graduate fields of specialization.)

Probability is an example of a concept that feels familiar and straightforward, yet generates responses based on other considerations, such as similarity or fear, which have little to do with actual probability. Along similar lines, one needs to worry about what it is exactly that respondents are responding to, what precisely are they computing, when asked about concepts such as anger, or depression, or wellbeing. Many investigators who work with less educated populations, for example, use pictures to help with participant construal of the questionnaire—quite literally, pictures to illustrate the point. Naturally, participants use subjective interpretation with pictures as well as with words, so it is important to pilot how well those pictures are able to communicate the intended question or response options. One of us used a pictorial scale of depression for a field experiment conducted in Rwanda. The scale had been previously used in published work in the same country and more broadly in the Great Lakes region of Africa. It asked participants to answer the question "how have you been feeling in the past few weeks" by pointing to one of a series of pictures featuring a person carrying a stone. From picture to picture, the stone increased in size: on one end of the scale, the person held a small stone in his hand, and at the other end of the scale, the person was bent in half as they held up the weight of an enormous boulder on their shoulders.

Because the scale had been used successfully in previous studies in the area, we brought the scale directly into the field without a pilot. At one site, a participant was asked how they were currently feeling and was shown the pictorial scale. The participant waited, and then left the interview to confer with others nearby. When he returned, he informed the interviewer that he was willing to carry some of the smaller stones for him, but not some of the larger ones. The misunderstanding of the scale ran even deeper. The scale caused active discussions in this community, and we were informed that during the recent civil conflict a military group asked a group of young men from the community to help carry supplies for them, and the young men were never seen again. A scale to measure depressive reactions to trauma was construed by the community as related to one of their original sources of trauma. We took care to clarify our intentions and to repair the situation, threw out the scale from our study, and resolved never again to use a scale without a pilot.

3.3 Investigator presence

How do participants construe who you are, as an investigator, and what your presence in their community means for them and for their participation in the experiment? Some ethical discussions encourage investigators to stay away from certain data collections or intervention deployments because participants' respect for or fear of scientists may lead them to construe participation or responses to certain types of questions as mandatory (Orne, 1962; Rosnow and Rosenthal, 1997).

Paluck (2009) reports that varying levels of government scrutiny and physical security in the postconflict countries where she has deployed field experiments has led to different self-presentation strategies for interviewers and other representatives of the experiment. For example, in Rwanda, where security was excellent and government scrutiny was extremely high, research staff identified themselves strongly with the university supporting the investigator and the study. However, just across the border in the Democratic Republic of Congo (DRC) where security and government surveillance were low, staff wore T-shirts featuring the local NGO that was collaborating with the university. In Rwanda, participants would have construed the emphasis on the NGO to mean that their responses were subject to government surveillance, as were most NGOs in the country during the experiment. However, in DRC, participants needed reassurance of legitimacy from a known local source, the NGO, due to the lack of security, and did not construe the NGO as an actor that would share their answers with the government.

Many other examples are possible, but our bottom line is that the perceived source of the experiment will affect participants' construal of their choice to participate or not, the confidentiality of their responses, and the overall meaning of the experiment, among other things. Of course, a "social desirability bias"—the tendency to answer questions in a manner that will be viewed favorably by others, in this case by the experimenters—is a serious risk as well. (Social desirability bias can be somewhat alleviated via the use of self-administered computer surveys, and an attempt at highly neutral question wording.) We may even use the analogy of your own construal of the source of information in this chapter: as an economist reading this chapter, might you find certain aspects of it more or less authoritative if you knew they were coming from two economists, sociologists, psychologists?

4. INTERPRET: HOW DO INVESTIGATORS CONSTRUE WHAT MATTERS IN THE DATA?

Thus far, our focus has been on participants' construal. But investigators use the same tools of construal as participants: we construe what participants do and what they tell us in ways that may or may not match up with their actual actions or meanings. Construing participants' self-reports is not the only way that construal processes operate for investigators and can shape the way they understand experimental outcomes. Construal can also affect the ways in which we conduct data analysis, and the factors we interpret to be important for a replication or for scaling up an intervention.

Recently, social scientists have laid out a rationale and evidence for the advantages of preregistration of analyses prior to the deployment of a field experiment or to the commencement of analysis (Casey et al., 2011; Olken, 2015; Committee, 2015). Just as (Vallone et al., 1985) pointed out that partisanship can affect what individuals see in a factual news article, so too can researchers selectively pick analyses that support their preferred hypothesis in a large dataset (Casey et al., 2011). As Olken puts it, "Even researchers who have the noblest of intentions may end up succumbing to the same sorts of biases when trying to figure out how, ex-post, to make sense of a complex set of results" (p. 1).

Psychologists understand this practice as a result of the ordinary and sometimes inevitable process of construal: what you understand to be the most important test at the design stage can change as you observe the process of data collection, as you analyze your data, and as you form, or perhaps slightly revise, a working hypothesis about the study results. While there are nonnegligible costs to preregistering all of your analyses in advance (Olken, 2015) there are also clear advantages. In addition to publicly committing to a priori predictions, preregistration can help investigators think more carefully about their hypotheses as they design and modify the experimental protocol. A similar practice that can help the post hoc downweighting of experimental hypotheses is preregistering a field experiment. This practice helps to prevent the selective reporting of entire trials that do not yield the results expected by investigators (using, for example, http://www.socialscienceregistry.org/ or the newly instantiated Open Science Framework).

Construal can also influence which factors investigators take to be the generalizable lesson of the overall experiment: i.e., it can shape what is seen as the causal driver of the results. At first blush, this may seem counterintuitive. Randomization of an independent variable, after all, allows for the estimation of a causal relationship. But how do investigators interpret what exactly was the important feature of the independent variable, to replicate or to scale up their study?

Consider the field experiment conducted in South Africa, in which Bertrand et al. (2010) manipulated information a bank provided about loans in letters to their clients manipulated the information a loan provider included in letters sent to their clients offering financial loans. Some of the information was central to what clients should want to know about the loan terms, including size of loan, duration, and interest rates. Other "information" was peripheral, such as various examples of possible loans one could take, or a picture of a man's versus a woman's face, embedded in the letter's graphic design. As predicted, the researchers found that some peripheral features in the letter had substantial impact on loan take-up. For example, for male customers, having a picture of a woman on the letter significantly increased demand for the loan, about as much as dropping the interest rate to 4.5 percentage points, a reduction of about 25% of the loan interest rate.

How to interpret this experiment? What precisely does it show? Does it show that pictures of women especially increase take-up of loans? Should we always expect pictures of women's faces to increase the take-up of financial products? Would pictures of women be equally effective in Belgium, or would other kinds of pictures prove more effective there? How investigators construe the role played by the woman's picture as the causal driver of loan take-up in their experiment determines how they might try to replicate the experiment in other contexts, or how they might want to institutionalize or scale up their results for the specific bank or other banks with which they work in South Africa or elsewhere. Replicating experiments in slightly different contexts, such as different banks or governments or other firms, introduces the possibility that participants will construe the intervention differently. This is particularly relevant when the intervention might be perceived as originating from a very different source or might be associated with slightly different constructs. "Women," after all, like many other possible peripheral cues may play different roles, carry different symbolic connotations, and have different association with financial markets in different places.

4.1 Replicating experiments

At its most general level, the South Africa loan experiment teaches us that simple, seemingly peripheral tweaks to advertisements of financial products can make a big difference. Beyond that, it may be unclear how to construe the specifics of the manipulation, for example, regarding the role played by the woman's photo. It is the investigator's challenge to attempt to distill what was most important—and likely to remain stable—about the original significant result for the attempt at replication or scale-up.

Our advice is to think about the conversion of specific manipulations in an experiment like you would about the conversion of currency. Shekels will work well for you in Israel, both in Tel Aviv and in Jerusalem, but it would be a mistake to try to "replicate" that in Japan. Similarly, a manipulation that has worked well in one place ought to work well in another that shares the necessary common features, but it may well fail when transported to a context that differs in some important ways. Because of construal, this advice may be a bit less obvious, or easy to apply, than might first seem. Both field and lab experimental replications are often based on replicating the surface structure—the Shekels—without replicating the deeper structure—their purchasing power. This is related to the concern with functional or methodological equivalence discussed by cross-cultural researchers (Alasuutari et al., 2008), and it should give pause to any investigator engaged in a "direct replication" of a study. A replication needs to replicate the "deep," not the surface, structure of the original. It needs to replicate participants' construal from the original study, which, paradoxically, may require some reconfiguring of the original, particularly when construal processes in the new context obey a somewhat different logic from the original. Indeed, however faithful to the original on the surface, failure to reproduce the features that truly matter may cause failures to replicate. For recent discussions on conceptual replication from psychology, see Monin et al. (2014).

4.2 Institutionalizing and scaling up experimental results

In fact, discerning how to construe the causal drivers of your effect for a replication presents similar challenges to those encountered when attempting to identify which factors should be "scaled-up." By scale-up, we mean either a large-scale replication of your experiment or the installation of your experimental manipulation as part of a public or private institution's regular operating procedure. Among the potential complications involved in scaling up, an experimental manipulation is that the targeted population will most likely receive the intervention from a source that is different from that used in the original experimental evaluation. And that source (e.g., university, nongovernmental organization or government) can matter a great deal for participants' construal of the intervention. Furthermore, the very fact that an intervention is no longer presented as a trial, or as merely "experimental," but, rather as an established policy, may itself generate significantly different construal.

To our knowledge, one of the most striking and sobering examples of a shift in participant's construal from an experimental to an institutionalized policy is the domestic violence experiment led by the National Institute of Justice (Garner et al., 1995). The experiment used an encouragement design for police officers responding to a call reporting a domestic incident. Officers were randomly assigned to arrest, mediate, or separate upon arrival at the scene through a color-coded notepad (though they could break with the randomization in the case of an emergency). The estimated effect of this experiment revealed the importance of arrests for preventing recidivism in domestic abuse—arrests were found to reduce estimated future violence by more than 50%. The results were subsequently used to support laws promoting arrests of individuals believed to be responsible for spousal abuse. Follow-up estimates (Iyengar, 2010), however, found that these laws had *increased* the number of intimate partner homicides where they had been implemented.

Setting aside debates about the methods and findings from Iyengar (2010) versus those from the National Institute of Justice experiments, we can ask how laws mandating arrest of abusive spouses could increase homicides. A plausible explanation boils down to violence victims' construal of a call to the police for help. During the National Institute of Justice's experiment, a call to the police was understood as just that—a call for help. The exact repercussions, what the police officer might do once on the scene, was uncertain. Clearly, abusive partners would never construe a call to the police as a welcome action; however, prior to laws mandating immediate arrest, these calls were not understood as requesting an arrest. Once inscribed into law, a call to the police meant a call to arrest the partner. Both partners in a domestic dispute presumably shared this new construal, which rendered it more consequential at least for the abuser, if not also for the abused. Certainty of arrest was a different construal from that which predominated the earlier "experimental" phases, and could explain why homicides rose following the introduction of the laws.

In sum, a target population's understanding of an intervention may change as the intervention scales-up, comes from a different source, slightly changes form, or is no longer novel. Thinking about participants' construal in this way is also a means of understanding and anticipating negative externalities. As the scaled-up intervention misaligns with participants' construal, losses—fewer abused women saved, fewer plastic bags recycled—are thereby imposed on society at large.

5. CONCLUDING THOUGHTS

A fundamental tension in the behavioral sciences has long pitted the study of overt behavior, most blatantly represented by behaviorism, with that of covert mental processes, studied by the cognitive sciences. This tension is central to field experiments, where the ultimate goal is to change and measure actual behaviors, but where the design of the intervention rests heavily on participants' mental lives. In this chapter, we have focused on one fundamental aspect of mental life, namely construal.

Construal is how people come to represent everyday experiences. Some of it can be natural, immediate, and effortless, other parts can be conscious and effortful—the outcomes of both "System 1" and "System 2" thinking, respectively (Kahneman, 2011). This presents a significant challenge to researchers, because the resulting behavior, which ultimately is the thing of interest, will have been shaped by processes that are always difficult to observe, often hard to control, and ever-sensitive to minor nuance.

This chapter should have convinced you that field experiments are not off-the-shelf type instruments. They need to build shared construals in contexts where nuance really matters. Even in simple behavioral laboratory "games" that measure behavior in response to differing incentives, where moves and payoffs are all well defined, a mere alteration of the name of the game can significantly change participants' chosen strategies. In one study, participants (American college students as well as Israeli pilots) played an N-move Prisoner's Dilemma game, referred to as either the Wall Street or the Community game (Liberman et al., 2004). The results showed that labeling exerted far greater impact on the players' choice to cooperate versus defect—both in the first round and overall—than anticipated by predictions of their peers based on the players' reputation.

Let's eat, Grandma!

Let's eat Grandma!

Small nuances can save lives. They can change strategic behaviors. And they can change the way that your experimental stimuli are construed during an experiment, or in an attempt at replication.

While we have no surefire method for managing construal, our advice is to think about and explore the various facets that might impact how your study might be construed. Rather than merely "delivering" the relevant information, think about the terms—community, Wall Street—used in the delivery, the context—church, school—in which it is being delivered, and who—woman, man, child—delivers the message as well as their potential role in this particular milieu. Similarly, when you attempt to replicate, worry about the participants' construal in the original study, not just the original stimuli or procedures. Repeat the psychologically important, not the superficial structure, of an experiment.

There is a famous anecdote about three baseball umpires talking about how they call balls and strikes. The first umpire calls them as he sees them, and the second umpire calls them as they are. The third umpire says they are nothing until he calls them. We think about construal that way. You might think participants simply construe based on what they see, or you might think they construe what is really there. But the fact is that there is nothing much happening in your study until participants have construed it. And the challenge is to handle that construal with great care.

REFERENCES

Alasuutari, P., Bickman, L., Brannen, J., 2008. The SAGE Handbook of Social Research Methods. Sage.
Asch, S.E., 1940. Studies in the principles of judgments and attitudes: II. Determination of judgments by group and by ego standards. J. Soc. Psychol. 12, 433–465.

Asch, S.E., 1948. The doctrine of suggestion, prestige and imitation in social psychology. Psychol. Rev. 55, 250.

Berger, J., Meredith, M., Christian Wheeler, S., 2008. Contextual priming: where people vote affects how they vote. Proc. Natl. Acad. Sci. U.S.A. 105, 8846—8849.

Bertrand, M., Karlan, D.S., Mullainathan, S., Shafir, E., Zinman, J., 2010. What's advertising content worth? Evidence from a consumer credit marketing field experiment. Q. J. Econ. 125, 263—306.

Bruner, J.S., 1957. Going beyond the information given. Contemp. Approaches Cogn. 1, 119—160.

Casey, K., Glennerster, R., Miguel, E., 2011. Reshaping Institutions: Evidence on Aid Impacts Using a Pre-analysis Plan. Technical report. National Bureau of Economic Research.

Committee, The TOP Guidelines, 2015. Promoting an open research culture: the top guidelines for journals. Work. Pap. 1, 1—2.

Datta, S., Mullainathan, S., 2014. Behavioral design: a new approach to development policy. Rev. Income Wealth 60, 7—35.

Eidelman, S., Crandall, C.S., 2009. A psychological advantage for the status quo. In: Social and Psychological Bases of Ideology and System Justification, pp. 85—106.

Garner, J., Fagan, J., Maxwell, C., 1995. Published findings from the spouse assault replication program: a critical review. J. Quant. Criminol. 11, 3—28.

Gilovich, T., 1981. Seeing the past in the present: the effect of associations to familiar events on judgments and decisions. J. Pers. Soc. Psychol. 40, 797.

Gilovich, T., Griffin, D., Kahneman, D., 2002. Heuristics and Biases: The Psychology of Intuitive Judgment. Cambridge University Press.

Gneezy, U., Rustichini, A., 2000. A fine is a price. J. Leg. Stud. 29, 1—18.

Haushofer, J., Shapiro, J., 2013. The Social Costs of Randomization.

Iyengar, R., 2010. Does arrest deter violence? Comparing experimental and nonexperimental evidence on mandatory arrest laws. In: Di Tella, R., Edwards, S., Schargrodsky, E. (Eds.), The Economics of Crime: Lessons for and from Latin America. NBER/University of Chicago Press, pp. 421—452.

Kahneman, D., 2011. Thinking, Fast and Slow. Macmillan.

Kahneman, D., 2013. Foreword. In: Shafir, E. (Ed.), The Behavioral Foundations of Public Policy. Princeton University Press, pp. 7—9.

Kahneman, D., Frederick, S., 2002. Representativeness revisited: attribute substitution in intuitive judgment. In: Heuristics and Biases: The Psychology of Intuitive Judgment, 49.

Kahneman, D., Knetsch, J.L., Thaler, R.H., 1991. Anomalies: the endowment effect, loss aversion, and status quo bias. J. Econ. Perspect. 193—206.

Kahneman, D., Miller, D.T., 1986. Norm theory: comparing reality to its alternatives. Psychol. Rev. 93, 136—153.

Kelley, H.H., 1973. The processes of causal attribution. Am. Psychol. 28, 107.

Lewin, K., Gold, M.E., 1999. The Complete Social Scientist: A Kurt Lewin Reader. American Psychological Association.

Liberman, V., Samuels, S.M., Ross, L., 2004. The name of the game: predictive power of reputations versus situational labels in determining prisoner's dilemma game moves. Pers. Soc. Psychol. Bull. 30, 1175—1185.

Loftus, G.R., Mackworth, N.H., 1978. Cognitive determinants of fixation location during picture viewing. J. Exp. Psychol. Hum. Percept. Perform. 4, 565.

Markus, H., Kunda, Z., 1986. Stability and malleability of the self-concept. J. Pers. Soc. Psychol. 51, 858.

Milgram, S., 1974. Obedience to Authority.

Miller, D.T., Prentice, D.A., 2013. Psychological levers of behavior change. In: Shafir, E. (Ed.), The Behavioral Foundations of Public Policy. Princeton University Press, pp. 301—309.

Mischel, W., Ebbesen, E.B., Zeiss, A.R., 1972. Cognitive and attentional mechanisms in delay of gratification. J. Pers. Soc. Psychol. 21, 204.

Monin, B., Oppenheimer, D.M., Ferguson, M.J., Carter, T.J., Hassin, R.R., Crisp, R.J., Miles, E., Husnu, S., Schwarz, N., Strack, F., et al., 2014. Commentaries and Rejoinder on Klein et al. (2014).

Morse, S., Gergen, K.J., 1970. Social comparison, self-consistency, and the concept of self. J. Pers. Soc. Psychol. 16, 148.

Olken, B., 2015. Pre-analysis plans in economics. J. Econ. Perspect. 29 (3), 61—80.

Orne, M.T., 1962. On the social psychology of the psychological experiment: with particular reference to demand characteristics and their implications. Am. Psychol. 17, 776.

Paluck, E.L., 2009. Methods and ethics with research teams and NGOs: comparing experiences across the border of Rwanda and Democratic Republic of Congo. In: Surviving Field Research: Working in Violent and Difficult Situations, pp. 38—56.

Redelmeier, D.A., Molin, J.-P., Tibshirani, R.J., 1995. A randomised trial of compassionate care for the homeless in an emergency department. Lancet 345, 1131—1134.

Robins, R.W., Hendin, H.M., Trzesniewski, K.H., 2001. Measuring global self-esteem: construct validation of a single-item measure and the Rosenberg self-esteem scale. Pers. Soc. Psychol. Bull. 27, 151—161.

Rosnow, R.L., Rosenthal, R., 1997. People Studying People: Artifacts and Ethics in Behavioral Research. WH Freeman, New York.

Ross, L., Nisbett, R.E., 1991. The Person and the Situation: Perspectives of Social Psychology. Mcgraw-Hill Book Company.

Schank, R.C., Abelson, R.P., 2013. Scripts, Plans, Goals, and Understanding: An Inquiry into Human Knowledge Structures. Psychology Press.

Schwarz, N., Xu, J., 2011. Why don't we learn from poor choices? the consistency of expectation, choice, and memory clouds the lessons of experience. J. Consum. Psychol. 21, 142—145.

Seligman, M.E., 1970. On the generality of the laws of learning. Psychol. Rev. 77, 406.

Shafir, E., 2013. The Behavioral Foundations of Public Policy. Princeton University Press.

Skinner, B.F., 1960. Pigeons in a pelican. Am. Psychol. 15, 28.

Thaler, R.H., Sunstein, C.R., 2008. Nudge. Yale University Press.

Tversky, A., Kahneman, D., 1973. Availability: a heuristic for judging frequency and probability. Cogn. Psychol. 5, 207—232.

Tversky, A., Kahneman, D., 1981. The framing of decisions and the psychology of choice. Science 211, 453—458.

Vallone, R.P., Ross, L., Lepper, M.R., 1985. The hostile media phenomenon: biased perception and perceptions of media bias in coverage of the Beirut massacre. J. Pers. Soc. Psychol. 49, 577.

Weber, Heinrich, E., Elizabeth Ross, H., Murray, D.J., 1996. EH Weber on the Tactile Senses. Psychology Press.

Willis, G.B., 2004. Cognitive Interviewing: A Tool for Improving Questionnaire Design. Sage Publications.

Understanding Preferences and Preference Change

CHAPTER 7

Field Experiments in Markets

O. Al-Ubaydli*[,§,¶,1], J.A. List[‖,#,a]

*Bahrain Center for Strategic, International and Energy Studies, Manama, Bahrain
§George Mason University, Fairfax, VA, United States
¶Mercatus Center, Arlington, VA, United States
‖University of Chicago, Chicago, IL, United States
#NBER (National Bureau of Economic Research), Cambridge, MA, United States
[1]Corresponding author: E-mail: omar@omar.ec

Contents

Abstract

This is a review of the literature of field experimental studies of markets. The main results covered by the review are as follows: (1) Generally speaking, markets organize the efficient exchange of commodities; (2) There are some behavioral anomalies that impede efficient exchange; (3) Many behavioral anomalies disappear when traders are experienced.

Keywords

Behavioral economics; Field experiment; Markets; Welfare theorems

JEL Codes

B21; B53; C93; D41; D51; D61

[a] We would like to thank Andrew Simon for excellent research assistance.

Handbook of Economic Field Experiments, Volume 1
ISSN 2214-658X, http://dx.doi.org/10.1016/bs.hefe.2016.09.001

1. INTRODUCTION

Traditionally, the study of economics is virtually synonymous with the study of markets, with the most notable illustration being Adam Smith's *Wealth of Nations*—arguably the discipline's inaugural contribution. The Scottish economist's treatise was followed by seminal contributions from numerous luminaries such as Alfred Marshall, John Maynard Keynes, Friedrich Von Hayek, Kenneth Arrow, Gary Becker, and Robert Lucas. While the range of topics studied by economists has undoubtedly expanded in the years following the *Freakonomics* revolution, markets remain the centerpiece of the discipline's intellectual mission. For example, in the 14 years since 2001, eight Nobel prizes in economics have been explicitly for research on markets, and of the remaining six, two were for econometric methods that are most frequently applied to the study of markets.

The methodological tools deployed by economists have evolved from the narrative and deductive arguments of the likes of John Stuart Mill, going on to introduction of elementary mathematical methods by the likes of Leon Walras, followed by the formal decision-theoretic mathematical machinery used by the likes of John Hicks and Gerard Debreu, the game-theoretic analysis of scholars such as James Mirrlees and George Akerlof, and most recently, the arrival of agent-based modeling. These theoretical contributions have been complemented by a huge volume of empirical work, with some of the most notable studies relating to international trade and financial markets. Without doubt, our understanding of how markets function has advanced immeasurably due to the efforts of the aforementioned scholars.

Until the 2002 Nobel prize, one of the most important contributions to our understanding of markets—Vernon Smith's (1962, 1965) real-stakes double oral auctions—remained under the radar of most mainstream economists. Smith's experiments, which followed in the footsteps of Chamberlin (1948), spawned a massive experimental literature investigating market processes. Subsequent scholars have examined alternative institutions, such as conventional auctions (Coppinger et al., 1980), decentralized bilateral bargaining (Hong and Plott, 1982), and posted prices (Plott, 1986). They have also varied the information structure to study important phenomena such as asset bubbles (Smith et al., 1988), while other studies have examined the possibility of social preferences interfering with the market-clearing process (Fehr et al., 1993). The single most important conclusion emerging from the early experimental literature was one that no theoretical or nonexperimental study had ever convincingly demonstrated: markets lead to the efficient exchange of commodities, and that this occurs even when many of the traditional assumptions of "perfect markets" break down, that is, when there is a small number of price-setting traders who have incomplete information, and in the absence of a centralized orchestrator such as the nebulous "Walrasian auctioneer" (Hayek, 1945; Smith, 1982).

Compared to conventional naturally occurring data, the key advantage offered by the laboratory experimental methods pioneered by Vernon Smith was the ability to artificially control how much traders valued the commodities being traded (known as inducing values), as this allowed researchers to accurately estimate demand-and-supply schedules, thereby permitting a precise welfare analysis. This point should not be understated: while mainstream economics embraced Adam Smith's theory of the "invisible hand," it took almost 200 years for economists to present plausible evidence of the phenomenon. Despite the fundamental importance of this result, laboratory experiments in general (let alone ones used to study markets) remained a niche tool. One of the reasons for the relative lack of enthusiasm among many mainstream economists was the perceived artificiality of laboratory experiments; many scholars were concerned that the small stakes, the restricted strategy space, the inexperience of subjects, and the scrutiny of the experimenter all contributed to empirical insights that were of limited value to understanding naturally occurring markets (Levitt and List, 2007). In particular, many behavioral anomalies that were regularly detected in laboratory experiments, such as the endowment effect (Knetsch, 1989) and reciprocity in zero-reputation environments (Fehr and Gachter, 2002), were inconsistent with both the premises and the conclusions of the neoclassical model, and were being used as an intellectual platform to challenge mainstream economics.

Just as the theoretical and empirical literature on markets developed in line with the advancement of the available methodological tools, so too did the subliterature on experimental studies of markets with the advent of field experimental techniques in the early 2000s. This change was a fundamental step toward unifying empirical methods as in many situations, field experimental techniques offered the advantages of both conventional naturally occurring data and laboratory experimental data with neither set of disadvantages. Empirical economists who would previously reject laboratory experimental data due to a perceived lack of realism embraced natural field experiments as an elixir for the endogeneity problem associated with naturally occurring data.

In particular, field experiments allowed researchers to investigate real traders operating in real markets without the researcher having to surrender control over the environment. Consequently, the literature offered more sophisticated answers to questions such as: "how prevalent is ethnic discrimination in rental markets?," (Ahmed and Hammarstedt, 2008), "what are the productivity consequences of increasing wage rates?," (Gneezy and List, 2006), and "what is the impact of business training on the microfinance market?" (Karlan and Valdivia, 2011).

Markets are a large and extremely diverse area of research, and many of the other studies in this volume cover important components of the literature. In this review, we focus on the overarching conclusions. Moreover, in the light of the literature's relative youth, we also discuss some of methodological issues associated with the literature.

In our review of the literature on field experimental studies of markets, we present three main conclusions: First is the most important one as, generally speaking, markets organize the efficient exchange of commodities; second, consistent with much of the laboratory experimental literature, there exist behavioral anomalies that impede markets' ability to organize the efficient exchange of commodities; and third, many behavioral anomalies disappear when traders are sufficiently experienced in their roles, rehabilitating markets' ability to organize the efficient exchange of commodities.

This review is organized as follows:Section 2 is the preamble, where we discuss how markets are defined, the studies that will be covered by this review, the classification of field experimental studies of markets, and the advantages and disadvantages of field experiments when studying markets;Section 3 is a presentation of the main results in the literature;Section 4 is a discussion of the key methodological insights for scholars considering the use of field experiments in an empirical market study; and Section 5 provides closing remarks, including a discussion of possible future field experimental studies of markets.

2. PREAMBLE

The importance of markets to academic economics is self-evident, and many of the earliest contributions to the experimental literature in general (Chamberlin, 1948; Smith, 1965) and to the field-experimental subliterature in particular (List, 2004a) were studies of markets. Accordingly, when the editors of this volume approached us with the idea of writing a literature review on field experiments in markets, in addition to being delighted and honored by the proposal, we regarded it as a very logical component of a volume dedicated to field experiments.

As any author of a literature review is well aware, deciding on which studies to include can be somewhat problematic as one attempts to balance the desire for parsimony with efforts at being comprehensive. In addition to this conventional challenge, we encountered an unexpected difficulty—finding an operationally suitable definition of a "market."

2.1 Defining markets

Somewhat perversely for a concept so central to the discipline of economics, economists scarcely provide a definition of a market (Hodgson, 2008). As an illustration of this bizarre lacuna, the otherwise comprehensive 1987 edition of the *New Palgrave Dictionary of Economics* does not even contain an entry on "markets"! (This omission is corrected in the second edition published in 2008.) As we will see, a serious challenge for a review article is that given any reasonable definition of a market, an overwhelmingly large number of research contributions can be classified as studies of a market.

In the light of the absence of a textbook definition, the layperson's dictionary definition is an obvious starting point. According to Merriam-Webster, a market is: "The course of commercial activity by which the exchange of commodities is effected," or, alternatively: "A meeting together of people for the purpose of trade by private purchase and sale and usually not by auction." This concurs with the broad, Austrian-inspired definition offered by the second edition of the *New Palgrave Dictionary of Economics*: "All forms of trade or exchange that involve private property, defined loosely as assets under private control," (Hodgson, 2008).

In an effort to deploy specialist concepts and to narrow the characterization, the *New Palgrave Dictionary of Economics* offers a different definition along the following lines: "Markets involve multiple exchanges, multiple buyers or multiple sellers, and thereby a degree of competition. A market is defined as an institution through which multiple buyers or multiple sellers recurrently exchange a substantial number of commodities of a particular type. Exchanges themselves take place in a framework of law and contract enforceability. Markets involve legal and other rules that help to structure, organize and legitimize exchange transactions. They involve pricing and trading routines that help to establish a consensus over prices, and often help by communicating information regarding products, prices, quantities potential buyers or potential sellers. Markets, in short, are organized and institutionalized recurrent exchange." (Hodgson, 2008).

According to the broadest definition, markets cover the organized exchange one would encounter in a stock exchange, the relational exchange that is commonplace between two firms with a repeating supply arrangement, the one-off, haphazard exchange that may be observed under Craigslist, and the completely informal transaction whereby a teenager shovels snow from a neighbor's driveway in exchange for $20. If one switches to the narrower definition, one could make an argument for excluding all but the stock exchange example. However, the specter of *potential* or *latent* competition combined with the existence of a legal system that permits civil lawsuits together ensure that one could make a perfectly legitimate argument for classifying all four of the examples as market transactions according to *both* the broad *and* narrow definitions. This complicates the process of selecting which studies to include in the literature review.

2.2 Studies covered by the literature review

As indicated above, starting with a broad definition of markets leaves us struggling to exclude studies from our literature review. After all, the industrial organization literature—a huge literature—is automatically subsumed into the market's literature. As an illustration, if one examines the latest (at the time of writing) issue of the *American Economic Review* (105:2), there are 14 papers, of which we regard 10 as being about markets. Informally browsing other issues of the same and other leading journals confirms that a majority of economics papers can be classified as a market study of some sort.

Field experiments constitute a small minority of papers published in journals such as the *American Economic Review*; thus, perhaps restricting our attention to field experimental studies of markets will make the coverage manageable. At this point, we note that we are employing the Harrison and List (2004) definition of field experiments, which means the union of artefactual, framed, and natural field experiments, to the exclusion of conventional laboratory experiments.

• *Conventional laboratory experiments* employ a standard subject pool of students, an abstract framing, and an imposed set of rules.
• An *artefactual field experiment* is the same as a conventional laboratory experiments, but with a nonstandard subject pool.
• A *framed field experiment* is the same as an artefactual field experiment but with field context in either the commodity, task, or information set that the subjects can use.
• A *natural field experiment* is the same as a framed field experiment but where the environment is one where the subjects naturally undertake these tasks and where the subjects do not know that they are in an experiment.

The easiest way to restrict our attention to field experiments is to use the electronic paper repository www.fieldexperiments.com (note that this is a highly incomplete database but it is accurate in the sense that any included paper is definitely a field experiment). Again, somewhat informally, we look at the first 50 of the approximately 350 listed papers in alphabetical order, and we find 25 papers that can reasonably be classified as studies of markets, covering topics as diverse as the returns to education, large-scale blood donation, ethnic discrimination in rental markets, behavior in sealed-bid auctions, real versus hypothetical willingness-to-pay for consumer goods, and the manipulation of betting markets.

As an alternative, we also conducted a JSTOR search of articles containing the words "field experiment" in the title sorted in reverse chronological order. Again, out of the first 50 papers, we found 25 that can reasonably be classified as studies of markets, also covering a wide array of topics such as the demand for insurance, vote buying in West Africa, microfinance in Guatemala, skilled immigrants in labor markets, pricing health products, female entrepreneurship, and product customization.

The main conclusion that we draw from this informal search and classification exercise is that an exhaustive review of field experiments on markets is impossible. Moreover, even if one were to make it feasible by reviewing a randomly selected sample of the papers, it is not clear that such a review would be of much scientific value given the diversity of topics covered by field experiments on markets.

In light of the above, this review will deliver extra focus on methodological issues. We will survey a broad range of field experiments with the goal of giving insight on recurring methodological issues that arise.

Another factor to consider is the other contributions in this volume, as many of them cover topics that overlap significantly with "markets". To avoid needless replication, we will cover the following topics minimally at most: marketing; issues specifically relating to developing countries and antipoverty interventions; discrimination; education; and labor markets.

2.3 Classifying the field experiments in markets

Our review will cover the overarching results in field experimental studies of markets without structuring the results around a classification of the studies. However, in the background, it is instructive to keep the following classification in mind as it helps organize the types of contribution. We classify the literature along three primary dimensions.

First: studies that investigate a specific market institution with the aim of gaining a better understanding regarding how it functions, versus studies that do not. Thus, for example, Lucking-Reiley (1999) uses a framed field experiment to test the revenue equivalence of first-price sealed bid and Dutch auctions; this clearly constitutes an investigation of a specific market institution. On the other hand, Bertrand et al. (2010) study the effect of advertising content on demand for the advertised product; the highly context-specific nature of the investigation combined with the lack of focus on the rules of the exchange process render this study as *not* an investigation of a specific market institution.

Second: studies where the empirical modeling is structural versus reduced-form (consider them as the two end-points of a spectrum). We define structural modeling as an econometric specification derived from explicit modeling of the optimization problems faced by the different decision makers. Typically, this includes an equilibrium concept to reconcile the decision-makers' optimization as a step toward developing an econometric specification. Such models are primarily *deductive* methods of building knowledge. In contrast, in a reduced-form model, the econometric specification can be interpreted at face value rather than the end point of a series of optimization problems by agents. Reduced-form modeling corresponds to an *inductive* approach toward building the knowledge.

The choice of structural versus reduced-form modeling in field experimental studies of markets is more noteworthy than in typical economics research. For most fields, the researcher makes a largely unrestricted choice between the two techniques on the basis of the standard pros and cons: on the one hand, structural models involve more arbitrary assumptions (thereby risking serious specification errors) and they can be particularly data hungry; on the other hand, structural models can help inform more statistically efficient econometric specifications (including superior extrapolation), and they permit welfare and counterfactual analysis.

In empirical studies of markets, researchers face an additional hurdle when considering structural models: in markets with large numbers of buyers and sellers interacting physically and verbally, it may be very difficult to model the strategy space in a way that is both tractable enough to permit the derivation of an estimable econometric specification, and complex enough to capture the institution's essence. For example, despite well over a century of seasoned effort by the profession's biggest names, economists are yet to offer a substantive advance over the basic Walrasian model of demand and supply using modern game-theoretic techniques, and this is primarily the result of the environment's intractability (Al-Ubaydli et al., 2012). (An alternative route taken by some studies, such as Gjerstad and Dickhaut (1998), is to relax the strict rationality assumption and use agent-based modeling to derive testable predictions.) Thus, in the context of the literature on field experimental studies of markets, in many institutions, we find an extraordinary dearth of structural models because of their infeasibility. The consequent abundance of reduced-form models reflects researchers' efforts at inductively learning about markets with any method that comes to hand. There is much to be gained from filling this gap in the literature since markets that are difficult to model are the heartbeat of modern economies, and concrete welfare analysis of real markets is the holy grail.

Third: studies where all theoretical and empirical modeling conforms to the neoclassical blueprint, versus studies where explicit consideration is given to behavioral alternatives to the neoclassical model. A useful operational definition of neoclassical models is one where each decision maker maximizes expected utility over her own money outcomes, and where uncertainty is modeled according to rational expectations. The most frequent behavioral alternatives to the neoclassical model correspond to a breakdown of egoism (e.g., inequity aversion, reciprocity in one-shot environments) or a breakdown of expected utility (e.g., loss aversion, ambiguity aversion).

As in the case of the structural- versus reduced-form dimension, the neoclassical- versus behavioral dimension is noteworthy in the empirical studies of the market's literature. Ever since the days of Adam Smith, there has been a vibrant debate over whether unregulated markets can deliver efficient outcomes. The debate crosses over disciplines and remains a highly politicized issue. According to the first welfare theorem, a market operating under the conditions of the neoclassical model will operate efficiently. As such, when researchers posit behavioral alternatives to the neoclassical model as being superior, in many cases, they are not merely attempting to refine the predictive accuracy of the narrow model at hand; rather, they are attacking the first welfare theorem by undermining its tenets. Conversely, when a study rejects a behavioral alternative to the neoclassical model, it is often attempting to rehabilitate the first welfare theorem. Naturally, these trends are not absolute, and many insightful contributions to the behavioral versus neoclassical debate reflect attempts at refining our understanding of a specific market scenario only. However, in general, consumers of the literature on empirical studies of markets should bear in mind that studies that empirically investigate behavioral preferences are often trying to make a much more significant point about the efficiency of unregulated markets and the desirability of corrective government intervention. Accordingly, such studies are associated with a political and/or sociological undercurrent that emotionally inflames the debate.

In summary, similar to most literature, the field experimental studies of the market's literature involves a mixture of studies that focus on general principles as well as those that drill deeper into specific cases (i.e., specific market institutions). However, *unlike* most literature, structural modeling is underrepresented in the field experimental studies of the market's literature due to the difficulty of tractably modeling even the simplest markets. Further, in the context of behavioral versus neoclassical modeling, the field experimental studies of the market's literature is an intellectual battleground for a much larger and more significant debate over the first welfare theorem and the desirability of government intervention in markets. As such, even somewhat mundane issues such as the existence of the endowment effect (List, 2003) can become flashpoints.

2.4 What are the advantages and disadvantages of field experiments?

Most types of data can be classified into one of the three categories: naturally occurring data, laboratory experimental data, and field experimental data. The merits of experimental data as a whole compared to naturally occurring data are well understood (Kagel and Roth, 1997), and more recently, economists have extensively debated the pros and cons of laboratory- and field experimental data (Levitt and List, 2007; Falk and Heckman, 2009; Frechette and Schotter, 2015). While the general principles presented in those debates apply well to empirical studies of markets, there are some idiosyncratic factors that are worth mentioning.

As discussed above, markets are especially interesting because economists are constantly searching for evidence of their ability to deliver efficient outcomes. Assessing the efficiency requires knowledge of the agent's preferences over different outcomes; most commonly, this refers to buyers' (sellers') values (costs) of the commodities being traded. Generally speaking, this is very difficult because the values are homegrown (meaning that they are assigned organically rather than explicitly by an experimenter), and so the information has to be extracted from the traders. Further, in most market institutions, traders are faced with strong incentives to *misrepresent* their true valuations over commodities—specifically to gain a bargaining advantage. (In studies of discrimination in the marketplace, there is an added incentive to conceal true valuations: not wanting to be perceived as a bigot due to, for example, harboring animosity toward people of a certain race.) One of the most commonly used methods for eliciting trader values is surveys (also known as contingent valuation); in spite of the deployment of a variety of complex schemes, they remain costly, unwieldy, and unreliable methods of estimating values (Diamond and Hausman, 1994).

Experiments offer researchers a way of assessing efficiency: researchers can induce values rather than relying on homegrown values that are extremely difficult to recover. Note that this is distinct from the most commonly cited advantage of experiments, which is that they permit randomization. This is why Vernon Smith's real stakes experiments (Smith, 1962, 1965) are retrospectively considered so path-breaking; they were the first systematic and transparent demonstrations of a "regular" market equilibrating according to Walrasian dynamics.

To a large extent, the virtue of being able to induce values is restricted to laboratory experiments. In natural field experiments, researchers can easily *influence* homegrown values, but only in limited circumstances can they *induce* values, and full-information is usually required for assessing the efficiency. One intelligent workaround is for a researcher to use confederates whose values are induced and whose behaviors are strictly controlled by the researcher, and to have the confederates interact covertly with a regular trader who is unaware of the experiment (List, 2006a). While the regular trader's values are homegrown and unknown, knowledge of the confederate's value only can be sufficient for assessing some issues pertaining to efficiency.

Efficiency is not the be-all and end-all of market studies; however, there are a wide range of intellectually valuable questions that do not relate to efficiency and, more importantly, do not require knowledge of values. The literature on discrimination in the market place is a good example as techniques can be deployed to detect and evaluate discrimination without necessarily knowing the values of the commodities being traded. Auction studies that focus on comparing the revenue-generating properties of different schemes (rather than the efficiency of the allocation) also fall into this category. In these situations, the usual pros and cons associated with natural, laboratory, and field-experimental data apply.

3. MAIN RESULTS

3.1 Conventional commodity markets

In our opinion, the most important result in field experiments in general (let alone field experimental studies of markets) is no more than a replication of the most important result in laboratory experiments in general. We therefore regard the result as being the most important result in experimental economics, and certainly one of the most important results in empirical economics (if not *the* most important).

Result 1.1: Markets based on decentralized trade successfully organize the efficient exchange of commodities.

The flagship paper for this result is List (2004a). To properly understand this paper, one needs to first cover two of its pivotal antecedents, Chamberlin (1948) and Smith (1962), both of which were conventional laboratory experiments.

In Chamberlin (1948), subjects were divided into buyers and sellers and assigned a value v that was private information (the induced value). The traders participated in a market for a fictitious commodity where buyers were seeking to purchase one unit and sellers were seeking to sell one unit. In the event of a successful trade at price p, the buyer would earn $v - p$, and the seller would earn $p - v$; failure to trade would result in earnings of zero. Thus, the value operated as a reserve price for traders. This payoff structure allows the experimenter to draw a stepwise demand and supply schedule, which in turn permits the prediction of an equilibrium price, and the designation of intramarginal and extramarginal traders. For full efficiency, all intramarginal traders should trade, and none of the extramarginal traders should.

The Chamberlin trading environment operated according to the following rules:

- During the trading round, traders had the opportunity to mill around and try to secure a trade via unrestricted verbal negotiations, within earshot of other traders.
- Upon successfully negotiating a trade, the two traders would notify the experimenter, at which point the trade price would be publicly declared.

A crucial feature of Chamberlin's experiment was that the earnings were entirely hypothetical; subjects were instructed to behave *as if* they were earning real money.

The primary variable of interest (retrospectively) was that actual rents realized as a proportion of potential rents, known as the efficiency. This is equivalent to examining the extent to which intramarginal traders managed to trade vis-à-vis extramarginal ones. Almost equivalent is examining the extent to which, and speed with which, trading prices converged to the predicted equilibrium price.

Chamberlin found that prices were volatile, and that they converged to a below-equilibrium price, implying less-than-fully-efficient exchange. He ascribed this to the possibility that in his experiments, buyers were better bargainers than sellers because most subjects only had real-life experience being buyers.

Vernon Smith reasoned otherwise, positing three potential reasons for the failure of the Chamberlin market to equilibrate in the predicted fashion. First, the lack of financial incentives; second, the lack of experience (subjects would play a very limited number of rounds); and third, the limited circulation of information; in particular, only trade prices were truly public, and regular bids and offers were usually known only by the pair of traders involved.

Smith (1962, 1965) tested his hypotheses by introducing financial incentives, giving the subjects more experience in trading, and by changing the trading rules from Chamberlin's decentralized bilateral bargaining with public prices to a double oral auction. In Smith's setup, which resembles a traditional trading pit, all bids and offers were public information, including those that actually led to trades. As a result, prices rapidly converged to the Walrasian equilibrium, and extremely high levels of efficiency were observed. A huge subsequent literature confirmed the robustness of these findings.

As remarked earlier, Smith's work was the first convincing demonstration of Walrasian dynamics and of the invisible hand, and this was possible because of induced preferences (values). Despite the magnitude of the intellectual leap taken by Smith, there was still an intellectual gap between Smith's results and real, non-artificial markets due to his reliance on conventional laboratory experiments. Decades of research in social psychology had demonstrated that the unusual conditions associated with conventional laboratory experiments could generate behaviors that were unreflective of behaviors outside the laboratory (Levitt and List, 2007). Thus, the challenge for subsequent scholars was to see if there was some way to make use of Chamberlin's and Smith's innovations in the field.

This brings us to List (2004a), which was nominally a field-based mélange of Chamberlin (1948) and Smith (1962, 1965). Ideally, List would have run a natural field experiment. However, scholars are yet to discover a way of inducing values in a manner that is compatible with natural field experiments' defining characteristic, namely, the subject being unaware of their participation in an experiment. Certainly, an experimenter can covertly *influence* a subject's homegrown value via, for example, advertising; however, constructing precise demand and supply schedules requires knowledge of the exact value.

Survey methods could, in principle, allow the research to bypass the need to induce values. However, they are yet to provide the solution for several reasons. First, there remains significant controversy over survey method's ability to deliver accurate estimates of homegrown values (Diamond and Hausman, 1994). Second, constructing demand and supply schedules that can be tractably analyzed requires a small, contained market and a short time horizon. Such markets are quite difficult to come by in practice, and if they are covertly constructed by an experimenter, adding something as unusual as contingent-value surveys would surely undermine the experimenter's efforts at maintaining the subjects' ignorance of the experiment.

Thus, List conceded that with the tools available at the time (and still today, to the best of our knowledge), the closest he could come to a natural field experiment of a market with a known demand and supply schedule was a framed field experiment. List's task was therefore to find a real market with the following two features: First, it would be a market where a representative sample of traders would be willing to participate in an experiment; Second, it would be a market that could be effectively mimicked in a laboratory environment with a small number of traders.

In the end, List chose the decentralized bilateral bargaining market that was selected by Chamberlin, and that is currently deployed in the trading of sports paraphernalia and collector pins. Why did List choose a Chamberlin market rather than a double oral auction, such as those that can be found in the Chicago Board of Trade, a double electronic auction similar to those operating in modern stock exchanges, or any one of the numerous alternatives? For sure, the primary motivation was feasibility rather than the belief that these two markets were in some way systematically more interesting or representative than other markets. In particular, being a keen trader in the markets afforded List the knowledge and the contact network necessary to formulate and run the experiments. See List (2011b) for more advice on executing natural field experiments.

List's (2004a) Chamberlin market differed slightly from its progenitor in that the sellers worked from fixed trading desks, and the ability to move around the trading area was restricted to the buyers. This was to more closely mimic the markets being studied: sports paraphernalia exhibitions look similar to farmer's markets, whereby sellers display their wares at fixed installations and in the immediate proximity of other sellers. Also, the commodity being traded was less abstract than the completely fictitious commodity in Chamberlin (1948) and Smith (1962, 1965): it was a real item from the market being studied, but damaged so that it would have no intrinsic value, and so that the experimenter was free to induce values as required. The induced demand and supply schedules for some of the rounds can be seen in Fig. 1 below, where the equilibrium price is predicted to lie in the range $13–$14.

These differences were largely cosmetic. From a scientific viewpoint, the key differences were those that rendered List (2004a) a framed field experiment: the subjects were real buyers and sellers from sports paraphernalia and commemorative pin markets, and each occupied its natural role with a natural level of experience, and the stakes (induced values) were calibrated to natural levels.

List (2004a) experimented with different genders and ages of participants, and, more importantly, with different-shaped demand and supply schedules, including some highly asymmetric systems where one out of demand or supply was perfectly elastic. Overall, he found consistent convergence of prices to equilibrium (average trade prices were always in the range $13–$14), and consequently, high levels of efficiency (95% on average for the later trading rounds). The efficiency was achieved without requiring bids and offers to be public information, as in a double oral auction. This is notable because at a casual level, most markets are not typified by public bids and offers, and so it would be concerning for economists if their flagship model for predicting prices depended on institutional features rarely seen in practice.

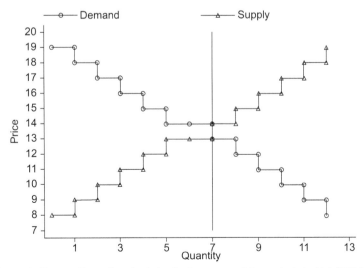

Figure 1 Demand/supply schedules in the symmetric markets in List (2004a).

List and Price (2006) repeat List (2004a), but they had a smaller number of sellers each of whom could sell multiple units. They also observed efficiency levels of the order of 95%.

Relatedly, Haushofer and Zurlinden (2013) stage a double auction game with 220 residents of the informal settlement of Kibera in Nairobi, Kenya. Each participant is assigned the role of buyer or seller and given a reservation price of 20 or 10 KES, respectively. Transaction prices converge rapidly to slightly over 11 (but less than 12) within four rounds, and the rate of convergence is strongly associated with mathematical ability in both buyers and sellers. When roles were switched, offered prices dropped more rapidly, suggesting that observational learning plays a role in the development of market behavior. In general, the paper finds evidence that neoclassical price theory can accurately predict market behavior with nonstandard subjects.

Likewise, Waichman and Ness (2012) run an artefactual field experiment in which 45 German farmers and 45 students participate in one of three decentralized bargaining markets, differing only in market size. Subjects are randomly assigned a reservation value and the role of buyer or seller. The allocative efficiency ratio is, on average, higher than 80% in all treatments, though statistically significantly lower than 100%. There are no significant differences between the farmers' and students' trading volumes and prices; however, in two pairs of treatments and in the pooled data, farmers create surpluses that significantly exceed those of students and those predicted by market equilibrium. Waichman and Ness's results confirm that neoclassical competitive theory predicts the allocative efficiency outcome of this type of market well. Both studies are at odds with Chamberlin (1948), but lend support to List's (2004a) results.

To add theoretical structure to these empirical insights, Miller (2013) presents a *General Convergence Theorem* explaining the convergence of markets to the competitive equilibrium (CE). This theory posits that if prices converge in a market in which there are no loss-generating trades or profitable units left untraded, the prices and quantities must converge to a CE. To demonstrate this model, Miller modifies Gode and Sunder's (1993) zero-intelligence agent (ZIA) market simulations by adding status consciousness to the agents and running both Smith and Chamberlin market treatments. He finds that all experiments converge to the CE according to the General Convergence Theorem.

To the best of our knowledge, other than a handful of experiments (a few of which we just mentioned), List (2004a) did not spawn a wave of induced-value framed field experiments in a manner similar to Smith (1962, 1965), and so there are few other studies to report. For the reasons discussed in Section 2.3—the difficulty of developing a tractable model—few studies that do investigate Walrasian dynamics do not employ any structural modeling. Thus, while papers such as List (2004a) add significantly to our understanding of the market process, there remains a large theoretical gap that economists need to fill.

Before discussing some of the other market institutions studied in the literature, we briefly take a detour relating to the work of Friedrich Von Hayek. The general equilibrium version of the Walrasian model that was advanced by Kenneth Arrow and Gerard Debreu is tractable because it is a decision-theoretic model rather than a game-theoretic one: agents are price-takers and nobody in the model actively sets prices. The model is associated with the list of "perfect market" assumptions that is familiar to undergraduate economics students and often derided by non-economists for their implausibility—perfect information (of all prices), no externalities, price-taking behavior (possibly justified by having a continuum of traders), and rational expectations.

Employing a narrative mode of argument rather than the mathematical modeling techniques now considered mainstream, Hayek (1945) regarded these assumptions as unnecessary for markets to serve their most important function—facilitating the efficient exchange of commodities. Rather than the static and certainty-filled markets of the Arrow—Debreu universe, Hayek regarded markets as being inherently dynamic and unpredictable. He characterized the environment as being driven by price-setting, risk-taking entrepreneurs who would make new markets and eliminate existing ones through a process of creative destruction. Insofar as an equilibrium price even exists, a Hayekian economist believes that the path *to* the equilibrium is where the market creates value; in contrast, a traditional neoclassical economist regards the out-of-equilibrium activity as a nuisance, and the equilibrium as being where the rubber meets the road.

Vernon Smith attached the name the "Hayek hypothesis" to the idea that none of the perfect market's assumptions was necessary for the efficient functioning of a market (Smith, 1982). Smith's laboratory experiments provided strong evidence to support this view: the double oral auctions led to efficient exchange even though the number of traders was small (around 20), the traders set prices, information was incomplete and imperfect, expectations were not necessarily rational, and there was no centralized orchestrator. Al-Ubaydli and Boettke (2012) reviewed the field experimental literature—including the studies considered in this paper—and they also found strong support.

Result 1.2: Result 1.1 holds even when many of the conditions of the standard neoclassical model break down, specifically when the number of traders are small, traders are price setters, information is incomplete and/or imperfect, expectations are not rational, and there is no centralized orchestrator (Al-Ubaydli and Boettke, 2012).

The environments in List (2004a) and List and Price (2006) clearly violate the standard perfect market assumptions and look much closer to the sort of market that Hayek envisaged (see Joyce (1984) for an experiment with an actual Walrasian auctioneer). We urge scholars to more seriously consider the Hayekian approach as they design future field experiments since neoclassical modeling techniques have yielded essentially no testable predictions since Walras (1874). For more on Hayek's work, see Boettke (2012), Boettke and O'Donnell (2013), Boettke and Candela (2014), and Boettke et al. (2014).

3.2 Financial markets

In conventional markets, traders are certain of the value *to themselves* of the commodities being traded, and they are imperfectly informed about the commodities' values to other traders. Job of prices is to give each trader information about how much the other traders value the different commodities, thereby helping each trader to decide how to allocate his or her resources across the available commodities. Efficiency is gauged by the extent to which commodities end up being consumed by those who value them the most. Equivalently, inefficiency is indicated by prices that result in sub-optimal consumption.

In classically conceived financial markets, each commodity being traded is valued equally by all traders (apart from risk preferences), but the traders are imperfectly informed about what that value is. If traders are heterogeneously imperfectly informed about the common value, then the job of the price is to disseminate information about the commodity's fundamental value. Inefficiency is indicated by prices that depart significantly and persistently from the commodity's fundamental value. The most common illustration is an asset bubble.

Financial market experiments are attractive for the same reason that conventional market experiments are: in real financial markets, we are rarely aware of the fundamental value of the asset, primarily due to incomplete information about the underlying probability distribution. (A good example of an exception is mechanized gambling, such as a roulette wheel.) A laboratory experiment, such as Smith et al. (1988), affords researchers the opportunity to manipulate the information available to traders while retaining full information about the true value of all the commodities.

An additional analogy with conventional market experiments is that natural field experiments in financial markets are relatively uninformative because the commodities' fundamental values are unknown. Consequently, when we are looking to make definitive statements about efficiency in financial markets, framed field experiments are the closest that we can get to natural field experiments.

A key difference between studies of financial and conventional markets is that the additional structure makes theoretical modeling easier. While models still fail to capture the process of making bids and offers in a fully satisfactory way, the literature has delivered highly sophisticated structural models of how rational expectations of asset values are formed, and how traders respond to the flurry of information released continuously in such markets (Bikchandani et al., 1992; Celen and Kariv, 2004).

Result 1.3: Evidence on the efficiency of financial markets is mixed; while the general tendency is toward efficient prices, systematic deviations of limited magnitude are regularly detected.

One method that researchers have employed to investigate the efficiency of financial markets is experiments that measure the incidence of Bayesian decision-making in strategic settings: if everyone behaves in a Bayesian way, then information is aggregated efficiently and, in the context of asset markets, asset prices will approach their fundamental value as quickly as possible. In Alevy et al. (2007), professional traders are placed in a common state of the world and each is given a private, independently drawn signal about the true state of the world. Each has to declare the state of the world he or she believes that the traders are in based on all of the available information, and in a randomly determined sequence. Thus, the first trader can base his or her decision purely on his or her private signal, but the second one can also make use of the first trader's statement, and the third trader can make use of the first two traders' statements, and so on. Professional traders are found to be Bayesian 76% of the time. Superficially, this suggests that in a parallel market setting, asset prices would bear some reflection of the fundamental value, but that they may also stray. Alevy et al.'s (2007) data offered some support for this view, with traders entering reverse information cascades (herding on the wrong state) 3% of the time.

Cipriani and Guarino (2009) modify the Alevy et al. (2007) design to allow traders to trade assets, where the returns to holding the assets depend upon the real state of the world. Similar to Alevy et al. (2007), the authors find that decision making is largely rational, but with a small percentage of traders engaging in anomalous behavior, including irrational abstention, contrarianism, and herding. Drehmann et al. (2007) conduct a similar framed field experiment, but with the addition of positive and negative externalities in some of the treatments. Similar to the other two papers, they also find a moderate level of rational (Bayesian) decision-making.

Drehmann et al. (2004) have a framed field experiment where the theoretical model predicts no rational herding because the price performs its function—aggregating market information. In support of the model's predictions, the authors fail to detect any significant herding. However, prices deviate systematically from the theoretically predicted levels, and they attribute this to contrarian behavior among a subset of traders.

List and Haigh (2010) examine a model of options trading that makes sharp predictions about how traders should respond to the potential for future upside investment news versus downside investment news. In their framed field experiment, they find that professional traders largely adhere to the model's predictions.

A separate strand of the literature on field experiments in financial markets examines trading behavior without necessarily tying it to efficiency, and without requiring full information of assets' fundamental values. This includes many studies that investigate the susceptibility of professional traders to behavioral anomalies (Haigh and List, 2005). Note that when such studies are used to draw conclusions about efficiency, then the evidence should be considered indirect: theoretical models present sufficient rather than necessary conditions for efficiency, and so a breakdown of the initial conditions or any intermediate step does not alone imply inefficiency. We defer our discussion of these behavioral anomalies studies to Section 3.4 below.

Overall, the number of framed field experiments of financial markets that permit a direct assessment of efficiency is small, and it is miniscule when compared to the vibrant laboratory experimental literature that was inspired by Smith et al. (1988). This is understandable because the chief protagonists in financial markets are people whose time is relatively expensive. For example, Drehmann et al. (2004, 2007) use McKinsey consultants. Conventional markets are typically populated by traders whose time can be purchased for amounts that fall within most research budgets, such as the flea market traders in List (2004a), meaning that framed field experiments are feasible. Nevertheless, we urge the profession to try to conduct more such experiments, especially in the light of the limited usefulness of natural field experiments for the assessment of issues pertaining to efficiency.

3.3 Single auctions

Auctions are considerably easier to model theoretically than most market institutions for two reasons. First, once the opening bell rings, only one side of the market (the buyers) is active. Second, there are a lot more restrictions on the strategy space of the active side. For example, in a sealed bid auction, conditional on their value, a buyer has no decision to make beyond selecting one number. While sealed bid single auctions are very common in practice, we are unaware of any naturally occurring sealed bid double auctions.

As a result of the elevated tractability, models of auctions are able to produce a much richer variety of testable predictions than models of standard markets, which have barely gone beyond the predictions posited by Walras in the 19th century. Structural modeling becomes an option (Brown and Morgan, 2009; Ely and Hossain, 2009). This is particularly exciting for field experimentalists, because in the case of conventional markets, scholars require knowledge of the values of market participants to be able to investigate the limited range of testable predictions. Thus, while field experimental investigations of conventional markets are typically restricted to being framed field experiments, with natural field experiments being incompatible with induced values, field experiments of *auctions* can easily be natural field experiments.

A further reason for the comparative ease of field experimentation with auctions is that auctions are inherently one-off exercises, meaning that the researcher can oversee and potentially control the entirety of the process. In contrast, conventional markets are fluid entities that sometimes have no perceivable starting or ending point (such as purchasing a good on Amazon), and they entertain much larger numbers of buyers and sellers.

Due to the expanded opportunity for generating testable hypotheses, and the relative youth of the literature on field experiments, in our opinion, the literature is yet to produce the sort of overarching conclusions that we are interested in for the purposes of this paper. We are particularly interested in results pertaining to efficiency, yet, to the best of our knowledge, these have not attracted anywhere near the research effort that they receive in laboratory experiments on auctions (Kagel and Levin, 2014).

Instead, the literature on field experiments in auctions is more focused on the issue of revenue maximization from the seller's perspective as a function of factors that can be manipulated easily in a theoretical model and in practice, such as the seller's stated reserve price (Ostrovsky and Schwarz, 2011) or the auction type (Lucking-Reiley, 1999). Accordingly, in this section, we give a brief overview of some of the most important papers, with an emphasis on those that contain methodological lessons.

An auction's field experimental paper that contains an instructive blend of theory and empirics is Hossain and Morgan (2006). They use a 2 × 2 natural field experiment whereby they sell matched pairs of CDs and Xbox games on EBay. Their key treatment variable is shipping costs: they compare bidding patterns across a high shipping cost treatment versus a low shipping cost treatment. To complete the design, they cross that treatment with a high total minimum bid versus low total minimum bid treatment. Together, the design allows them to verify several basic predictions of auction theory. They report that increasing the total minimum bid decreases the number of bidders and the probability of sale, but it increases the expected revenue conditional on sale. These results accord well with standard auction theory.

As such, increasing the shipping costs while decreasing the minimum bid tends to increase the overall revenues (including shipping) obtained by the seller. This result holds true for both Xbox games and audio CDs, as long as the total minimum bid is less than 30% of the retail price of the object. Interestingly, this effect disappears when the total minimum bid is more than half the retail price, achieved in this experiment when an $8 total minimum bid was applied to CDs. Though surprising from the point of view of rational bidding theory, the authors point out that this result can be explained with a simple model that involves bidders tending to ignore the size of shipping costs in an auction unless shipping costs become unusually large.

Related to this research are the innovative framed field experiments of Lucking-Reiley (1999) and Katkar and Reiley (2006). The first study, as noted above, represents an early example of how the internet can be used to test economic theory. Lucking-Reiley (1999) uses Internet-based auctions in a preexisting market with an unknown number of participating bidders to test the theory of revenue equivalence between the four major auction formats. Katkar and Reiley (2006) tests the auction theory related to reserve prices, and in this way is in the spirit of Hossain and Morgan (2006). More specifically, Katkar and Reiley (2006) designs a natural field experiment to compare outcomes in auctions with secret versus public reserve prices. Katkar and Reiley (2006) auctioned 50 matched pairs of Pokeman trading cards on eBay. To gain identification, each card was auctioned twice, once with a minimum bid of 30% of the card's book value and once with a minimum bid of $0.05 and a secret reserve price equal to 30% of the card's book value. The use of a secret reserve price resulted in lower earnings for the sellers than did making the reserve price known. Interestingly, keeping the reserve price secret reduced: (1) the probability of selling the card, (2) the number of serious bidders in an auction, and (3) the winning bid. Thus, contrary to the beliefs of many eBay sellers and to the predictions of models of rational bidder behavior, using secret reserve prices instead of public reserve prices actually lowers a seller's expected returns, by lowering both the probability that the auction will result in a sale, and the price received if it does result in a sale. We consider these types of studies as ripe for replication and further study, as the internet remains a useful, though underutilized experimental laboratory.

List and Lucking-Reiley (2000) test predictions associated with multiunit Vickrey auctions using a sports card field experiment. Theoretically, there should be a demand reduction in uniform price auctions compared to Vickrey ones, and the authors find evidence of this. Moreover, consonant with theory, the demand reduction is shown to be inefficient, and switching to Vickrey auctions to eliminate the inefficiency does not adversely affect the seller's revenues.

Online auction websites also offer researchers the opportunity to test the effects of reputations. Modeling the effect of online reputations is more challenging than modeling more basic features, such as the effect of a reserve price or auction type, and so the associated field experiments rely on reduced-form econometric methods. Both Jin and Kato (2006) and Resnick et al. (2006) manipulate seller reputations and find, as expected, evidence that superior reputations lead to superior outcomes.

As explained above, an advantage of field experiments is the expanded strategy space compared to laboratory experiments. Grether et al. (2015) exploit this to find evidence of cyber-shilling in online automobile auctions: groups of buyers are found to behave in a peculiar manner that suggests that they have been enlisted by sellers to work on their behalf.

Finally, another strand of the literature examines charity auctions. Carpenter et al. (2008) repeat Lucking-Reiley's (1999) investigation of revenue differences, but in the context of an auction that is designed to raise money for a charitable cause. This paper again displays the advantages of using single auctions rather than double ones: the environment can be tractably modeled and sharp predictions derived. They find that, contrary to theory and previous laboratory experiments, first price auctions outperform second price auctions and all pay-ones. They speculate that familiarity with the first price format is a key factor in explaining the results.

3.4 Behavioral anomalies

Behavioral economics has substantially enhanced the profession's intellectual toolkit. Early on, laboratory experiments were the field's dominant empirical method. The precision and ease of replication associated with laboratory experiments allowed researchers to produce a laundry list of robust (in the laboratory, at least) deviations from the neoclassical model, such as the endowment effect, bounded rationality, and altruism. However, many mainstream economists have expressed reluctance to accept these findings due to their dependence upon laboratory experiments, which they regard as an ungeneralizable source of data. Further, the field's conclusions are often deployed as a means of attacking the first welfare theorem, thereby politicizing the debate (intentionally or otherwise), and attracting criticism unrelated to the generalizability of the supporting data.

For those with an exclusively methodological qualm with the flagship results of behavioral economics, field experiments present an avenue for potentially resolving the controversy. In fact, numerous attempts at exploring behavioral biases in a field setting have found the initial, laboratory-based conclusions to be robust, with important implications for markets.

A welcome feature of the behavioral experimental literature is that a researcher's choice between structural and reduced-form modeling is not restricted by the intractability of structural models. Similar to auctions, the environment can be simplified in a manner that permits the construction of insightful models.

The first behavioral anomaly that we discuss is a derivative of the huge literature on prospect theory, which is a refinement of the expected utility theory.

Result 2.1: The endowment effect and loss aversion are observed in real markets and impede efficient exchange.

The following draws heavily from the literature review by Ericson and Fuster (2014). The endowment effect is defined as the observation that people seem to attach additional value to things they own simply because they belong to them.

The typical laboratory demonstration (Knetsch, 1989) involves randomly assigning subjects one of two commodities with similar values (such as a mug and a candy bar). The experimenter then offers the subject the opportunity to trade the assigned commodity for the other one. If the observed likelihood of ending up with good 1 (e.g., the mug) statistically depends (positively) upon the initial assignment, then this is evidence of the endowment effect. It is often explained by appealing to loss aversion: the loss in utility associated with giving up a good exceeds the gain associated with its acquisition.

If the endowment effect is strong and widespread, then it impedes the market's ability to allocate goods efficiently, as it makes people "irrationally" reluctant to trade. The first welfare theorem requires that, conditional on the market value of initial endowments, final consumption be independent of initial endowments, which is inconsistent with the endowment effect.

The laboratory evidence of the endowment effect is strong, though it is not absolute (Plott and Zeiler, 2005, 2007). In the field, the evidence is more mixed. List (2003) mimics Knetsch's (1989) design, but covertly to ensure that the experiment is a natural field one. In a sports paraphernalia exhibition, he recruits participants for the completion of a survey in exchange for a small amount of money and a sports card. The sports card is one of the two comparably valued ones, and the assignment is randomized. After being assigned the card and completing the survey (allowing time for the subject to build a sense of attachment to the initially assigned card), the subject is offered the opportunity to exchange it for the remaining card. List detects the endowment effect, albeit primarily in the case of inexperienced traders (we will discuss experienced ones below): 20% of those randomly assigned card 1 traded it for card 2, and 26% those randomly assigned card 2 traded it for card 1 (these figures should sum to 100% if subjects do not suffer from the endowment effect). List (2003) also finds similar results, also in a field setting, as do Englenmann and Hollard (2010). Inexperienced traders are present in most markets, including sports paraphernalia markets, and so these experiments suggest that the endowment effect may well impede efficient exchange in real markets. Apicella et al. (2014) runs an endowment effect experiment with an isolated tribe of hunter-gathers, finding that only those that have increased exposure to modern society display the endowment effect.

In the context of financial markets, Haigh and List (2005) found indirect evidence of the endowment effect in a field experiment where the participants are professional traders from the Chicago Board of Trade. Subjects are asked to bet on lotteries designed to detect—among other things—the presence of loss aversion. Previous laboratory experiments with standard student subject pools had demonstrated the prevalence of loss aversion; contrary to what was detected in sports paraphernalia markets, Haigh and List (2005) found that loss aversion was even stronger among professional traders, confirming the possibility of the loss aversion (and hence the endowment effect) interfering with efficient exchange.

Labor markets are another setting where loss aversion has been shown to drive supply-side behavior. Hossain and List (2012) find that workers in a high-tech Chinese manufacturing facility supply more effort when an incentive is framed as a loss instead of a gain. Fryer et al. (2012) find the same result with urban teachers. Tests of loss aversion when the experimenter does not control the reference point have proven more mixed with Goette et al. (2004) and Fehr and Goette (2007) finding evidence in favor and Andersen et al. (2014) finding evidence against.

The second behavioral anomaly that we will cover is bounded rationality, that is, limits to a decision maker's ability to optimize. Many different forms of bounded rationality have been investigated by economists. In the context of field experiments, the opportunities are more difficult because preferences are almost always homegrown rather than induced.

Result 2.2: Bounded rationality is observed in real markets and impedes efficient exchange.

The winner's curse is a form of bounded rationality that has been observed in field experiments. It is defined as the tendency for winning bids to systematically exceed the value of an auctioned item in common value actions under uncertainty. The winner's curse is an impediment to efficient exchange because it can lead to a winning bid from a buyer who—unbeknownst to him or her—values the item less than the seller does.

In laboratory experiments, testing for its presence is straightforward: an item is assigned a common value and subjects are randomly assigned independently and identically distributed signals of the common value drawn from a distribution that is common knowledge. Bidding then proceeds according to English auction rules, and the winning bid is compared to the induced, common value. Laboratory experiments regularly detect the winner's curse (Kagel and Levin, 1986).

Harrison and List (2008) used framed field experiments to test for the winner's curse's presence when the bidders are professional auction participants drawn from sports paraphernalia exhibitions. They find that professionals successfully avoid the winner's curse unless they adopt unfamiliar roles.

Hou et al. (2009) investigate the winner's curse using a natural field experiment on eBay. They purchase collector coins that have been professionally certified, and then they advertise them for auction without full information about the degree of certification, thereby manipulating the degree of uncertainty about the common component of the coins' values. In this natural setting, they find that for coins posted as uncertified, 83% of the 60 auctions that they arranged resulted in a winner paying more for the coin than its purchase value.

Another form of bounded rationality is a limited mental-accounting ability. As noted above, Hossain and Morgan (2006) investigate the sensitivity of online shoppers to the breakdown of an item's price between its direct cost and the shipping and handling cost. Rational shoppers should be indifferent to the breakdown conditional on the total cost. By randomly varying the components in a natural online auction setting, the authors demonstrate that charging a larger shipping cost leads to greater revenues for the seller. They also show how this case of bounded rationality can be partially attributed to loss aversion.

List and Haigh (2005) employ a framed field experiment to investigate the prevalence of the Allais paradox among professional traders at the Chicago Board of Trade. They find that professionals do indeed exhibit behavior consistent with the Allais paradox. Anomalies such as this and Hossain and Morgan (2006) imply the availability of unrealized arbitrage earnings and hence the potential inefficiency of the market process.

List and Millimet (2008) also employ a framed field experiment to study the prevalence of consistent preferences in a sports card market populated by children. They find that among children with experience trading, 38% exhibit preferences that violate the generalized axiom of revealed preference (GARP).

Another example of such bounded rationality in markets can be found in Anderson and Simester (2003), who explore consumer reactions to $9 endings on prices. They use a natural field experiment to partner with a retail catalog merchant by randomly selecting customers to receive one of three catalog versions that show different prices for the same product. By systematically changing a product's price by varying the presence or absence of a $9 price ending, they can explore various features of neoclassical theory. For example, a baseball bat may be offered to all consumers, but at prices of $39, $34, and $47 in each catalog version. Anderson and Simester (2003) find a positive effect of a $9 price on quantity demanded, large enough that a price of $39 actually produced higher quantities than a price of $34. This finding is puzzling in that their data can reject the theory that consumers turn a price of $34 into $30 by either truncation or rounding. This finding gives hard evidence on an interesting topic and demonstrates the need for a better theory of how consumers process prices, and more specifically, price endings.

The third deviation from the neoclassical model that we consider is social preferences, whereby decision-makers have preferences over the outcomes of others, conditional on their own outcomes. There are so many varieties of social preferences that the literature is yet to offer a unified model. However, the models that have been studied have generated a wide range of structural and reduced-form insights. These include pure altruism, warm glow (Andreoni, 1990), inequity aversion (Fehr and Schmidt, 2001), reciprocity (Dufwenberg and Kirchsteiger, 2004), guilt aversion (Battigalli and Dufwenberg, 2007), and others.

Similar to the other behavioral anomalies, social preferences represent a breakdown of the premises of the first welfare theorem, and so in principle, they impede the ability of the market to allocate resources efficiently. However, among the behavioral anomalies, a distinguishing feature of social preferences is that in practice, they often offer a potential solution to a coincidental market failure. For example, in a one-shot market setting in the absence of external enforcement, a fear of fraud may prevent an efficient exchange from taking place; however, if both parties have a concern for fairness or justice, then the efficient exchange may yet occur. This is an example of the theory of the second best (Lipsey and Lancaster, 1956).

Result 2.3: A concern for fairness and other forms of social preferences are observed in real markets though it is unclear whether it enhances or impedes the prospects for efficient exchange.

One particularly rich vein of market field experiments is studies of the gift exchange hypothesis. Akerlof (1982) suggested that problems of asymmetric information, namely managers' inability to specify worker effort in contracts in a perfectly enforceable way, can be attenuated by social preferences. By giving workers a "fair" wage in excess of the market wage, managers can induce a "fair" level of effort, which exceeds the minimum enforceable level of effort, hence the expression "gift exchange." While the original context is labor markets, the mechanism applies in many isomorphic settings, such as the investment game (trust game; Berg et al., 1995).

Fehr et al. (1993) was the first laboratory demonstration. Managers are paired anonymously with workers for one-shot interactions. Managers select the wage, it is reported to their partners, and the workers complete the play by selecting effort. The efficient outcome is high wage, high effort, but the Nash equilibrium (by backward induction) is minimum wage, minimum effort. The authors detected a strong, positive relationship between wages and effort, and they also observed average wages and effort well in excess of their permissible minima. They attributed this to a combination of positive reciprocity and inequity aversion.

Investigating social preferences in a field experiment is challenging because, in the presence of repeated interactions, it is difficult to design an experiment that allows researchers to distinguish between reputational concerns and social preferences as explanations of behavior (List, 2006a). In the laboratory, the high levels of experimenter control over the environment make it easy to circumvent the problem as the experimenter can create a one-shot environment, as in Fehr et al. (1993).

Gneezy and List (2006) offer one practical solution: focus on jobs where it is natural to employ people once and for a short time period, and where the job differs sufficiently from the workers' long-term career plans that it is unlikely that they would seek a recommendation from the manager. The two jobs were library cataloguing and door-to-door fundraising, and the recruitment pool was college students. The authors found results that initially confirmed Fehr et al.'s (1993) lab findings—worker effort responding positively to above-market wages—but that, over time, productivity reverted to the baseline level associated with the market wage.

Other contributions to this volume (von Wachter) cover this literature in detail, as Gneezy and List (2006) spawned numerous gift-exchange field experiments. The review by Fehr et al. (2009) confirms that there is robust evidence of the presence of social preferences in labor markets, especially reciprocity. In some cases, the social preferences clearly promote efficient exchange by helping combat the problems arising from asymmetric information. In other cases, social preferences impede efficient exchange. For example Kube et al. (2013) mimic the design in Gneezy and List (2006) but they introduce an arbitrary wage cut. They find that it leads to a persistent diminution of productivity due to a revenge motive. As Akerlof and Yellen (1990) speculated, and in the spirit of Keynes (1936), this could be a source of involuntary unemployment at the macroeconomic level.

Anderson and Simester (2008) is a study of social preferences that is tangentially related to the gift exchange literature. The authors collaborate with a mail-order catalog firm to study the effect of allowing for the price of larger sizes of clothes to exceed that of smaller sizes. They find that a subset of customers regard such a pricing system as "unfair" and react by substantially decreasing their purchases, a manifestation of negative reciprocity. Like Kube et al. (2013), this is an example of social preferences impeding an efficient exchange.

Perhaps somewhat further removed from the gift exchange literature is the work that explores identity and trading patterns in markets. For example, Bramoulle et al. (2010) investigate the effect of relationship formation—that is, of agents preferring to trade with specific agents—on market outcomes. In a series of simulations with agents of two different types, they find that more relationships develop in a model where agents learn from round to round than in a model of random trading partner selection, that relationships make participants more likely to trade, and that relationships reduce overall surplus by encouraging inefficient trades. In experiments set at a sports paraphernalia exhibition and at a flea market, the authors find statistically significant spontaneous (unprompted) relationship formation, increased likelihood of extra-marginal buyers executing trades (and a corresponding efficiency loss), and evidence of lower overall surplus for repeated trades (i.e., trades within relationships).

Relatedly, Bulte et al. (2015) conduct Hawthorne markets with subjects in Sierra Leone that have extraordinarily limited market experience (43% of subjects reported buying or selling something more than once a week). The first set of results looks at market outcomes when subjects engage with members of their village versus other villages. Across these two treatments the authors find lower levels of economic efficiency than earlier work (measured as a percentage of predicted surplus). The second set of results look at the variation in efficiency induced by the introduction of a middleman to act as a negotiator for the buyer. The results show that efficiency rises when the middleman is introduced, suggesting social norms around haggling are important for determining market behavior in the sample.

Also along the lines of negative social preferences engendering inefficient outcomes, there exists a large field experimental literature on discrimination, and it is the subject of a chapter in this volume (Bertrand and Duflo). The deployment of field experiments for studying such phenomena is particularly instructive due to the socially unacceptable nature of discrimination; the scrutiny of an overt experiment would motivate subjects to try extra hard to avoid appearing as if they discriminate, even if they do actually discriminate in their day-to-day lives (Al-Ubaydli and List, 2015).

Although the excellent chapter by (Bertrand and Duflo) catalogues a variety of field experiments that test for discrimination in the marketplace, a brief overview of the empirical approach is worthwhile to provide a useful benchmark (see also Riach and Rich, 2002; List, 2006b). The work in this area can be parsed into two distinct investigation techniques: personal approaches and written applications. Personal approaches include studies that have individuals either attend job interviews or apply for employment over the telephone. In these studies, the researcher matches two testers who are identical along all relevant employment characteristics except the comparative static of interest (e.g., race, gender, age). Then, after appropriate training, the testers approach potential employers who have advertised a job opening. Using various outcome measures, the researcher then reports differences based on the variable(s) of interest.

Under the written application approach, which can be traced to Jowell and Prescott-Clarke (1970), carefully prepared written job applications are sent to employers who have advertised vacancies. The usual approach is to choose advertisements in daily newspapers within some geographic area to test for discrimination. Similar to the personal approach tests, care is taken to ensure that the applications are similar across several dimensions except the variable of interest. One recent study that uses the written approach is due to Bertrand and Mullainathan (2004b), who manipulate perception of race by randomly assigning white-sounding or black-sounding names to resumes sent to various prospective employers in Boston and Chicago. They find that the simple name manipulation makes a large difference: the "white" applicant garners an interview request for every eight resumes sent whereas the "black" applicant must send out 14 resumes to gain one interview. Adding positive background information to both resumes exacerbates, rather than attenuates, this difference.

More recently, when designing discrimination field experiments, researchers often seek to distinguish between the two major economic theories of discrimination: statistical and animus. In the former, preferences remain neoclassical, and behavioral responds to category (race, gender, sexual orientation, etc.) as the category carries statistically useful information about factors that do directly affect profits/utility, such as productivity, criminality, and so on. Setting aside moral considerations, this type of discrimination can help grease the wheels of the market process as it denudes the difficulties associated with imperfect information. In contrast, animus reflects negative social preferences, and so it likely impedes efficient exchange. Thus, for example, if bigotry prevents people with long hair from entering the labor market, and 30% of the population has long hair, then the foregone output is highly significant.

Discrimination field experiments therefore gauge subject responses to a vector of observable attributes, where one dimension—the category being studied (race, gender, etc.)—is varied randomly. To isolate animus, the vector of the remaining observable attributes includes the variables that the category is most plausibly proxying for, thereby eliminating the category's role as a statistical tool (List, 2004b). For example, if, hypothetically, employers discriminate against people with bushy eyebrows because they tend to drive red cars, and driving a red car is bad for business, the researcher will present employers in the experiment with people who have bushy eyebrows and that manifestly do not drive red cars, meaning that any residual discrimination toward them is the result of animosity.

This kind of design is not perfect. First, it requires that the researcher can capture all the statistical channels linking the category to pay off relevant information. In the bushy-eyebrows example, perhaps the employer is worried about the potential employee having a second car. Second, it requires that the subjects are carefully considering all available informations when making decisions. If they are boundedly rational and overwhelmed with information (or are not paying attention), they may resort to statistically motivated discriminatory heuristics even in the presence of information that renders the heuristic redundant. Thus, in the bushy-eyebrows example, the employer may not notice that the bushy-eyebrowed job candidate is driving a red car.

Studies employing the above technique have been used to study a wide array of phenomena, such as employment (Bertrand and Mullainathan, 2004), vehicle sales (List, 2004b), housing sales (Ahmed and Hammarstedt, 2009), and taxi rentals (Castillo et al., 2012). While some, such as List (2004b), find that observed discrimination in a particular context is primarily statistical, whereas others, such as (Gneezy et al., 2012), produce convincing evidence of animus. Hence, the discrimination literature contributes to the broadly mixed conclusions on social preferences: they exist in the marketplace, and they sometimes facilitate and sometimes impede efficient exchange.

Finally, an extensive body of field experimental evidence on social preferences in a context slightly removed from conventional market scenarios is the literature on charitable contributions (List, 2009). For example, efforts at soliciting financial donations in a natural field setting have consistently resulted in non-zero donations that cannot be plausibly reconciled with reputational concerns masquerading as social preferences. See, for example, List and Lucking-Reiley (2002), Landry et al. (2006), and Karlan and List (2007).

The behavioral anomalies discussed above are by no means exhaustive; in the interests of parsimony, we have examined the subset that we feel provide the best exposition of the main results and that is most instructive.

3.5 Experience and behavioral anomalies

Laboratory experiments have amassed huge amounts of evidence of behavioral anomalies within laboratory environments. The previous section surveys market field experiments and finds that there is considerable evidence of behavioral anomalies in field settings too, some of which impede the ability of markets to allocate goods efficiently. However, the field prevalence is certainly weaker than that found in the laboratory, and a closer examination suggests that this is at least partially systematic.

Result 3: There is evidence that some behavioral anomalies that impede efficient exchange and can be observed in real markets diminish and potentially disappear with market experience.

This conclusion remains a considerable source of controversy because it falls into a larger methodological debate about the desirability of laboratory versus field experiments (Levitt and List, 2007; Falk and Heckman, 2009; Al-Ubaydli and List, 2015), and, to some extent, the even larger—and highly politicized—debate over the efficacy of decentralized markets as a mechanism for allocating resources.

As mentioned above briefly, in his investigation of the endowment effect, List (2003) found that its strength diminished with the market experience of the subject, and was absent for the most experienced market professionals. List (2003) presents nonexperimental evidence that this is more likely due to treatment rather than selection, and this is supported by the experimental evidence in List (2011a). Further evidence that professionals are systematically less loss-averse than college students is presented in List and Haigh (2010), which is a test of options' models. Notably, however, in Haigh and List (2005), the same authors found that myopic loss aversion was more prevalent for professional traders than for college students participating in the same experiment, indicating that the effect of market experience does not uniformly reduced the incidence of behavioral anomalies.

Despite detecting the Allais paradox among professional traders, using parallel experiments with college students, List and Haigh (2005) find that it is weaker for professionals.

In their study of Bayesian decision-making in financial markets, Alevy et al. (2007) found that professionals were *less* likely to be Bayesian than college students, though it did not affect their earnings. However, in certain settings, professionals exhibited a lower propensity to be drawn into reverse cascades, which the researchers were able to attribute to superior inferential capabilities. Moreover, unlike college students, Bayesianism among professionals did not differ as the domain switched from gains to losses. Lending credence to the causal role of experience in improving performance, in later rounds, like professionals, college students began to harmonize behavior across gain/loss domains. Further, the degree of Bayesian decision-making among professionals was also positively correlated with the reported intensity of the professionals' trading activity.

Along similar lines, in List and Millimet's (2008) study of GARP violations among children participating in sports card markets, the authors found that GARP violations were significantly lower among experienced traders, including experience that was randomly assigned via a treatment that caused subjects to increase their trading activity.

In their study of the winner's curse, as mentioned above, Harrison and List (2008) find that experienced traders assuming natural roles did not suffer from the winner's curse.

These field experimental findings follow in the footsteps of a large number of laboratory studies that find that even within the laboratory, behavioral anomalies diminish with the controlled experience that the subject is exposed to during their brief participation. For example, in their investigation of the endowment effect, Plott and Zeiler (2005) discover that it disappears once paid practice rounds and feedback on elicitation methods are introduced. They conclude that the previously observed endowment was more likely the result of subject misconceptions rather than fundamental features of human preferences. Similarly, as mentioned above, Vernon Smith (1962) attributed the successful equilibration of his double oral auctions, as compared to the failed equilibration of Chamberlin's (1948) decentralized markets, partially to the fact that subjects were able to amass significant experience on how to operate in a double oral auction.

The difficulty of running field experiments in general, and in particular of mimicking the precise structure of a specific laboratory experiment in the field, means that the evidence on the interaction between experience and the incidence of behavioral anomalies is limited. However, the conclusion that the majority of studies support—that professional experience diminishes the incidence of (and sometimes eliminates) behavioral anomalies that impede efficient exchange—should not come as a surprise. After all, impeding efficient exchange is tantamount to leaving money on the table, either at the individual or collective level. As such, all parties have an intrinsic incentive to actively seek to rid themselves of their behavioral anomalies. One imagines that a stock trader afflicted by the endowment effect will suffer below average earnings until they remedy the situation.

Even if people are ignorant of their biases, or find that they are incapable of doing anything about them, the market imposes a selection force that will tend to weed out the sufferers since they will have inferior trading performance. There is a rich mainstream (Witt, 1986; Blume and Easley, 2002) and heterodox (Hayek, 1945) literature that argues this point.

4. METHODOLOGICAL INSIGHTS

Due the inescapable breadth of the definition of a market, we have provided a necessarily cursory review of the literature on field experimental studies of markets. Despite the disparateness of the studies considered, we believe that there are some central methodological insights that can be garnered.

Conclusion 1: Inducing preferences for all participants in a natural field experiment is currently impossible.

The leading insight that we take away from the literature is that at the moment, nobody has developed a way of truly inducing preferences (values) for all participants in a natural field experiment. If one relaxes the requirement that the preferences of *all* participants be induced, then confederates can provide a partial workaround. For example, in List (2006a) and Castillo et al. (2012), a confederate with induced preferences is given strict instructions on how to behave in the market, and remaining participants who are unaware that they are participating have homegrown preferences. This allows the researcher to study parts of the market process. However, the equilibrium and welfare properties of the market cannot be studied due to the incomplete information on preferences.

This means that while field experiments such as List (2004a) represent a significant addition to the foundational work of Smith (1962, 1965), we are yet to open the black box of demand and supply in a naturally occurring market and definitively observe what is happening to demand, supply, actual prices, equilibrium prices, and surplus. The extensive literature on psychological priming (Bargh and Chartrand, 2000) gives us many suggestions on how to influence homegrown preferences covertly, thereby retaining the key feature of a natural field experiment, but the informational bar for testing the most important theories of market economics require more than this. As such, we believe that if scholars were to develop ways of precisely inducing preferences covertly in naturally occurring markets, then the intellectual returns would be massive.

Accordingly, until such an advance is made, there remains a fundamental trade-off when choosing between framed field experiments and natural field experiments to study markets.

Conclusion 2: Scholars must be particularly careful when considering generalizing laboratory experimental evidence on behavioral anomalies to natural market settings.

The generalizability debate is large enough to be studied separately (see the symposium at the end of Frechette and Schotter, 2015). One point that is worth making without wading too deep into the broader debate concerns behavioral anomalies and the market. By their very nature, markets are natural settings with enhanced financial incentives, and they are characterized by evolutionary forces that aggrandize the influence of actors who optimize well and generate surplus for themselves and others. Moreover, the same forces diminish the influence of those that optimize poorly and fail to realize surplus for themselves and others.

Consequently, scholars need to be very careful when they want to extrapolate behavioral anomalies from laboratory settings to field ones. It is in professional trader's interests to avoid suffering from behavioral biases, meaning that we should be unsurprised to find that they suffer from them less than college students operating in low stakes, and low experience laboratory experiments.

Social preferences are an exception to this very specific line of argument (though not to the broader laboratory vs. field debate) because they do not necessarily impede efficient exchange, and in fact, they may promote it by compensating for the market's failings.

Conclusion 3: Distinguishing between social preferences and reputational concerns in natural markets can be extremely challenging because of the difficulty of constructing environments with zero reputational concerns.

As discussed above, depending upon the circumstances, social preferences can both facilitate and impede efficient exchange, meaning that there is much to be gained from studying their prevalence in the marketplace. Researchers designing experiments must be cautious when interpreting data as being supportive of the existence of social preferences due to the specter of the Folk theorem: often, behavior that can be attributed to social preferences can also be explained by reputational concerns.

Laboratory experiments can eliminate reputational concerns between subjects by employing anonymity and perfect stranger designs. Such techniques are scarcely available to field experimentalists. Moreover, as List (2006a) demonstrates, seemingly innocuous changes in background variables can have a big impact on the prevalence of reputational concerns. In his study of the trust game in a natural field experiment conducted at a sports paraphernalia exhibition (executed with the assistance of confederates), List found that whether or not traders were locally based, and whether or not there had been an announcement and/or an implementation of third-party quality certification, all had a profound impact on the observed trustworthiness of traders. Examining the pooled data suggests the presence of either weak social preferences or weak reputational concerns; parsing the data according to sources of reputational concerns that are obvious to an industry-insider like List—and not so obvious to a layperson—suggests the absence of social preferences.

As a reminder, we know from the huge charitable contributions' literature that social preferences exist, and have a significant impact upon the economy. Conclusion 3 is not about disavowing the existing of social preferences; rather it is about how careful one has to be when attributing market behavior to them.

Conclusion 4: Researchers should make use of agent-based models to inform designs for market field experiments, and to generate welfare prescriptions.

Theoretical models of conventional markets are currently significantly less informative than theoretical models in other fields due to the difficulty of constructing a tractable model. This is not for lack of trying—a substantial literature emerged in the 1980s applying game theory tools to conventional markets in an effort to build upon the foundational analysis of Walras, and its contributors included some of the most illustrious names in economic theory. Unfortunately, testable predictions could only be produced in the most abstract of environments, meaning that empirically minded economists are forced to rely on inductive methods to learn about markets, and econometric specifications are almost always in reduced-form. This is contrast to, for example, the auctions literature, where rich structural models can be estimated, and sophisticated theories tested.

With the advent of powerful personal computers, agent-based modeling has been expanding in economics. However, to the best of our knowledge, it has been seldom deployed for improving our understanding of conventional markets. Gjerstad and Dickhaut (1998) is an example of how agent-based modeling can plug some of the holes resulting from the analytical intractability of conventional markets: the authors are able to produce a model that better captures the price dynamics of double oral auctions than previous efforts based purely on the Walrasian model.

Puzzlingly (to us), Gjerstad and Dickhaut (1998) have not led to a flurry of follow-up studies in spite of the rich intellectual returns that we associate with improving our understanding of markets. Their contribution predated the recent proliferation of field experiments; as such, we regard building upon their work by combining agent-based models with field experimental methods as even more fruitful, and we encourage scholars to make use of the available tools.

5. CLOSING REMARKS

Markets are the heartbeat of the economics profession yet we still know so little about them. The best way for scholars to improve our knowledge of markets and the market process is for us to combine the insights that can be garnered from all available sources:

neoclassical theory, agent-based modeling, narrative—deductive reasoning, laboratory experiments, field experiments, and naturally occurring data. In this regard, the study of auctions is exemplary: all types of theoretical and econometric modeling, and all types of data, have combined to deepen our understanding.

The difficulty of producing tractable theoretical models of markets means that we have to squeeze the alternative sources of knowledge even harder. Accordingly, field experiments have an enhanced role in developing our understanding of markets, and it is a role that has been seized upon by the profession during the last 15 years.

In our review of the literature, we have arrived at three main conclusions:

1. Generally speaking, markets organize the efficient exchange of commodities;
2. There exist behavioral anomalies that impede markets' ability to organize efficient exchange; and
3. Many behavioral anomalies diminish and sometimes disappear when traders are sufficiently experienced, rehabilitating markets' ability to organize the efficient exchange of commodities.

If scholars were able to produce a structural model of a market in disequilibrium and to estimate using field experimental data, thereby permitting welfare analysis of a market in disequilibrium, we would regard this as a huge intellectual leap for the profession. At the moment, this does not seem possible; we therefore urge the profession to more seriously consider agent-based models combined with field experiments as an intermediate step.

A final remark concerns financial markets. The small number framed field experiments that have been conducted so far provide mixed evidence on the ability of financial markets to operate efficiently. Given the manifest importance of such markets to the global economy, we urge the profession to forge greater links with professional traders in order to facilitate more research in this vein.

REFERENCES

Ahmed, A.M., Hammarstedt, M., 2008. Discrimination in the rental housing market: a field experiment on the internet. J. Urban Econ. 64 (2), 362—372.

Ahmed, A.M., Hammarstedt, M., 2009. Detecting discrimination against homosexuals: evidence from a field experiment on the internet. Economica 76 (303), 588—597.

Akerlof, G.A., 1982. Labor contracts as partial gift exchange. Q. J. Econ. 97 (4), 543—569.

Akerlof, G.A., Yellen, J.L., 1990. The fair wage-effort hypothesis and unemployment. Q. J. Econ. 105 (2), 255—283.

Al-Ubaydli, O.A., Boettke, P.J., 2012. Markets as Economizers of Information: Field Experimental Examination of the 'Hayek Hypothesis'. George Mason University Working Paper.

Al-Ubaydli, O., List, J.A., 2015. Do natural field experiments afford researchers more or less control than laboratory experiments? Am. Econ. Rev. 105 (5), 462—466.

Al-Ubaydli, O., Houser, D., Nye, J., Paganelli, M.P., Pan, X.S., 2012. The causal effect of market priming on trust: an experimental investigation using randomized control. PLoS One 8 (3), e55968.

Alevy, J.E., Haigh, M.S., List, J.A., 2007. Information cascades: evidence from a field experiment with financial market professionals. J. Finance 62 (1), 151—180.

Andersen, S., Brandon, A., List, J.A., Gneezy, U., 2014. Toward an Understanding of Reference-Dependent Labor Supply: Theory and Evidence from a Field Experiment. NBER Working Paper No. 20695.

Anderson, E.T., Simester, D.I., 2008. Does demand fall when customers perceive that prices are unfair? The case of premium pricing for large sizes. Mark. Sci. 27 (3), 492−500.

Anderson, E.T., Simester, D., 2003. Effects of $9 price endings on retail sales: evidence from field experiments. Quantitative Mark. Econ. 1 (1), 93−110.

Andreoni, J., 1990. Impure altruism and donations to public goods: a theory of warm-glow giving. Econ. J. 100 (401), 464−477.

Apicella, C.L., Azevedo, E.M., Christakis, N.A., Fowler, J.H., 2014. Evolutionary origins of the endowment effect: evidence from hunter-gathers. Am. Econ. Rev. 104 (6), 1793−1805.

Bargh, J.A., Chartrand, T.L., 2000. The mind in the middle. In: Handbook of Research Methods in Social and Personality Psychology, pp. 253−285.

Battigalli, P., Dufwenberg, M., 2007. Guilt in games. Am. Econ. Rev. 97 (2), 170−176.

Berg, J., Dickhaut, J., McCabe, K., 1995. Trust, reciprocity, and social history. Games Econ. Behav. 10 (1), 122−142.

Bertrand, M., Mullainathan, S., 2004a. Are Emily and Brendan more employable than Latoya and Tyrone? Evidence on racial discrimination in the labor market from a large randomized experiment. Am. Econ. Rev. 94 (4), 991−1013.

Bertrand, M., Mullainathan, S, 2004b. Are Emily and Greg more employable than Lakisha and Jamal? A field experiment on labor market discrimination. Am. Econ. Rev. 94 (4), 991−1013.

Bertrand, M., Karlan, D.S., Mullainathan, S., Shafir, E., Zinman, J., 2010. What's advertising content worth? Evidence from a consumer credit marketing field experiment. Q. J. Econ. 125 (1), 263−306.

Bikchandani, S., Hirshleifer, D., Welch, I., 1992. A theory of fads, fashion, custom, and cultural change as information cascades. J. Political Econ. 100 (5), 992−1026.

Blume, L., Easley, D., 2002. Optimality and natural selection in markets. J. Econ. Theory 107 (1), 95−135.

Boettke, P.J., 2012. Living Economics. The Independent Institute, Oakland, CA.

Boettke, P.J., Candela, R., 2014. Hayek, Leoni, and Law as the fifth factor of production. Atl. Econ. J. 42 (2), 123−131.

Boettke, P.J., O'Donnell, K.W., 2013. The failed appropriation of F.A. Hayek by formalist economics. Crit. Rev. A J. Polit. Soc. 25 (3−4), 305−341.

Boettke, P.J., Coyne, C.J., Leeson, P.T., 2014. 12. Hayek versus the neoclassicists: lessons from the socialist calculation debate. In: Elgar Companion to Hayekian Economics, 278.

Bramoulle, Y., List, J.A., Price, M.K., 2010. Buyer-Seller Relationships under Perfect Information. University of Tennessee Working Paper.

Brown, J., Morgan, J., 2009. How much is a dollar worth? Tipping versus equilibrium coexistence on competing online auction sites. J. Political Econ. 117 (4), 668−700.

Bulte, E., Andreas, K., List, J.A., Turley, T., Voors, M., 2015. From Personalized Exchange towards Anonymous Trade: A Field Experiment on the Workings of the Invisible Hand. BYU Working Paper.

Carpenter, J., Holmes, J., Matthews, P., 2008. Charity auctions: a field experiment. Econ. J. 118 (1), 92−113.

Castillo, M., Petrie, R., Torero, M., Vesterlund, L., 2012. Gender Differences in Bargaining Outcomes: A Field Experiment on Discrimination. National Bureau of Economic Research No. 18093.

Celen, B., Kariv, S., 2004. Observational learning under imperfect information. Games Econ. Behav. 47, 72−86.

Chamberlin, E.H., 1948. An experimental imperfect market. J. Political Econ. 56 (2), 95−108.

Cipriani, M., Guarino, A., 2009. Herd behavior in financial markets: an experiment with financial market professionals. J. Eur. Econ. Assoc. 7 (1), 206−233.

Coppinger, V.M., Smith, V.L., Titus, J.A., 1980. Incentive behavior in English, Dutch and sealed-bid auctions. Econ. Inq. 18 (1), 1−22.

Diamond, P.A., Hausman, J.A., 1994. Contingent valuation: is some number better than no number? J. Econ. Perspect. 8 (4), 45−64.

Drehmann, M., Oechssler, J., Roider, A., 2004. Herding and contrarian behavior in financial markets: an internet experiment. Am. Econ. Rev. 95 (5), 1403−1426.

Drehmann, M., Oechssler, J., Roider, A., 2007. Herding with and without payoff externalities—an internet experiment. Int. J. Industrial Organ. 25 (2), 391—415.

Dufwenberg, M., Kirchsteiger, G., 2004. A theory of sequential reciprocity. Games Econ. Behav. 47 (2), 268—298.

Ely, J., Hossain, T., 2009. Sniping and squatting in auction markets. Am. Econ. J. Microeconomics 1 (2), 68—94.

Engelmann, D., Hollard, G., 2010. Reconsidering the effect of market experience on the 'endowment effect'. Econometrica 78 (6), 2005—2019.

Ericson, K.M.M., Fuster, A., 2014. The endowment effect. Annu. Rev. Econ. 6 (1), 555—579.

Falk, A., Heckman, J.J., 2009. Lab experiments are a major source of knowledge in the social sciences. Science 326 (5952), 535—538.

Fehr, E., Gachter, S., 2002. Altruistic punishment in humans. Nature 415, 137—140.

Fehr, E., Goette, L., 2007. Do workers work more if wages are high? Evidence from a randomized field experiment. Am. Econ. Rev. 97 (1), 298—317.

Fehr, E., Schmidt, K.M., 2001. Theories of Fairness and Reciprocity — Evidence and Economic Applications. CEPR Discussion Paper No. 2703.

Fehr, E., Goette, L., Zehnder, C., 2009. A behavioral account of the labor market: the role of fairness concerns. Annu. Rev. Econ. 1, 355—384.

Fehr, E., Kirchsteiger, G., Riedl, A., 1993. Does fairness prevent market clearing? An experimental investigation. Q. J. Econ. 108 (2), 437—459.

Fréchette, G.R., Schotter, A., 2015. Handbook of Experimental Economic Methodology. Oxford University Press.

Fryer, R.G., Levitt, S.D., List, J., Sadoff, S., 2012. Enhancing the Efficacy of Teacher Incentives Through Loss Aversion: a Field Experiment. NBER Working Paper No. 18237.

Gjerstad, S., Dickhaut, J., 1998. Price formation in double auctions. Games Econ. Behav. 22 (1), 1—29.

Gneezy, U., List, J.A., 2006. Putting behavioral economics to work: testing for gift exchange in labor markets using field experiments. Econometrica 74 (5), 1365—1384.

Gneezy, U., List, J., Price, M., 2012. Toward an Understanding of Why People Discriminate: Evidence from a Series of Field Experiments. NBER working paper.

Gode, D.K., Sunder, S., 1993. Allocative efficiency of markets with zero-intelligence traders: market as a partial substitute for individual rationality. J. Political Econ. 119—137.

Goette, L., Huffman, D., Fehr, E., 2004. Loss aversion and labor supply. J. Eur. Econ. Assoc. 2 (2—3), 216—228.

Grether, D., Porter, D., Shum, M., 2015. Cyber-shilling in automobile auctions: evidence from a field experiment. Am. Econ. J. Microeconomics 7 (3), 85—103.

Haigh, M.S., List, J.A., 2005. Do professional traders exhibit myopic loss Aversion? And experimental analysis. J. Finance 60 (1), 523—534.

Harrison, G.W., List, J.A., 2008. Naturally occurring markets and exogenous laboratory experiments: a case study of the winner's curse. Econ. J. 118 (528), 822—843.

Harrison, G.W., List, J.A., 2004. Field experiments. J. Econ. Literature 42 (4), 1009—1055.

Haushofer, J., Zurlinden, N., 2013. Market Convergence and Equilibrium in a Kenyan Information Settlement. Princeton Working Paper.

Hayek, F.A., 1945. The use of knowledge of society. Am. Econ. Rev. 35 (4), 519—530.

Hodgson, G.M., 2008. Markets. In: The Elgar Companion to Social Economics.

Hong, J.T., Plott, C.R., 1982. Rate filing policies for inland water transportation: an experimental approach. Bell J. Econ. 13 (1), 1—19.

Hossain, T., List, J.A., 2012. The behavioralist visits the factory: increasing productivity using simple framing manipulations. Manag. Sci. 58 (12), 21—51.

Hossain, T., Morgan, J., 2006. Plus shipping and handling: revenue (non) equivalence in field experiments on eBay. The B.E. J. Econ. Analysis Policy 5 (2), 1—30.

Hou, J., Kuzma, A., Kuzma, J., 2009. Winner's curse or adverse selection in online auctions: the role of quality uncertainty and information disclosure. J. Electron. Commer. Res. 10 (3), 144—154.

Jin, G., Kato, A., 2006. Price, quality, and reputation: evidence from an online field experiment. RAND J. Econ. 37 (4), 983—1005.

Jowell, R., Prescott-Clarke, P., 1970. Racial discrimination and white-collar workers in Britain. Race 11, 397–417.

Joyce, P., 1984. The Walrasian tantonnement mechanism and information. RAND J. Econ. 15 (3), 416–425.

Kagel, J.H., Levin, D., 1986. The winner's curse and public information in common value auctions. Am. Econ. Rev. 76 (5), 894–920.

Kagel, J., Levin, D., 2014. Auctions: A Survey of Experimental Research (working paper).

Kagel, J.H., Roth, A.E., 1997. Handbook of Experimental Economics. Princeton University Press, Princeton, NJ.

Karlan, D., List, J.A., 2007. Does price matter in charitable giving? Evidence from a large-scale natural field experiment. Am. Econ. Rev. 97 (5), 1774–1793.

Karlan, D., Valdivia, M., 2011. Teaching entrepreneurship: impact of business training on microfinance clients and institutions. Rev. Econ. Statistics 93 (2), 510–527.

Katkar, R., Reiley, D.H., 2006. Public versus secret reserve prices in eBay auctions: results from a Pokémon field experiment. B.E. J. Econ. Analysis Policy 6 (2). Advances Article 7. http://www.bepress.com/bejeap/advances/vol6/iss2/art7.

Keynes, J.M., 1936. The General Theory of Interest, Employment and Money. Palgrave Macmillan, London, UK.

Knetsch, J.L., 1989. The endowment effect and evidence of nonreversible indifference curves. Am. Econ. Rev. 79 (5), 1277–1284.

Kube, S., Marechal, M.A., Puppe, C., 2013. Do wage cuts damage work morale? Evidence from a natural field experiment. J. Eur. Econ. Assoc. 11 (4), 853–870.

Landry, C.E., Lange, A., List, J.A., Price, M.K., Rupp, N.G., 2006. Toward an understanding of the economics of charity: evidence from a field experiment. Q. J. Econ. 121 (2), 747–782.

Levitt, S.D., List, J.A., 2007. What do laboratory experiments measuring social preferences reveal about the real world? J. Econ. Perspect. 21 (2), 153–174.

Lipsey, R.G., Lancaster, K., 1956. The general theory of second best. Rev. Econ. Stud. 24 (1), 11–32.

List, J.A., 2003. Does market experience eliminate market anomalies? Q. J. Econ. 118, 47–71.

List, J.A., 2004a. Neoclassical theory versus prospect theory: evidence from the marketplace. Econometrica 72 (2), 615–625.

List, J.A., 2004b. The nature and extent of discrimination in the marketplace: evidence from the field. Q. J. Econ. 119 (1), 49–89.

List, J.A., 2006a. The behavioralist meets the market: measuring social preferences and reputation effects in actual transactions. J. Political Econ. 114 (1), 1–37.

List, J.A., 2006b. Field experiments: a bridge between lab and naturally occurring data. Adv. Econ. Analysis Policy 6 (2). Article 2.

List, J.A., 2009. Social preferences: some thoughts from the field. Annu. Rev. Econ. 1, 563–579.

List, J.A., 2011a. Does market experience eliminate market anomalies? The case of exogenous market experience. Am. Econ. Rev. 101 (3), 313–317.

List, J.A., 2011b. Why economists should conduct field experiments and 14 tips for pulling one off. J. Econ. Perspect. 25 (3), 3–15.

List, J.A., Haigh, M.S., 2005. A simple test of expected utility theory using professional traders. Proc. Natl. Acad. Sci. U.S.A. 102 (3), 945–948.

List, J.A., Haigh, M.S., 2010. Investment under uncertainty: testing the options model with professional traders. Rev. Econ. Statistics 92 (4), 974–984.

List, J., Lucking-Reiley, D., 2000. Demand reduction in multiunit auctions: evidence from a sportscard field experiment. Am. Econ. Rev. 90 (4), 961–972.

List, J.A., Lucking-Reiley, D., 2002. The effects of seed money and refunds on charitable giving: experimental evidence from a university capital campaign. J. Political Econ. 110 (1), 215–233.

List, J.A., Millimet, D.L., 2008. The market: catalyst for rationality and filter of irrationality. B.E. J. Econ. Analysis Policy 8 (1), 1–55.

List, J.A., Price, M.K., 2006. On the Fragility of Collusive Arrangements: Evidence from Field Experiments. University of Nevada Reno Working Paper.

Lucking-Reiley, D., 1999. Using field experiments to test equivalence between auction formats: magic on the internet. Am. Econ. Rev. 89 (5), 1063–1080.

Miller, R.M., 2013. A General Model of Convergence for Competitive Markets. State University of New York at Albany Working Paper.

Ostrovsky, M., Schwarz, M., 2011. Reserve prices in internet advertising auctions: a field experiment. In: ACM Conference on Electronic Commerce, pp. 59–60.

Plott, C.R., 1986. Rational choice and experimental markets. J. Business 59 (4), S301–S327.

Plott, C.R., Zeiler, K., 2005. The willingness to pay-willingness to accept gap, the "endowment effect," subject misconceptions, and experimental procedures for eliciting valuations. Am. Econ. Rev. 95 (3), 530–545.

Plott, C.R., Zeiler, K., 2007. Asymmetries in exchange behavior incorrectly interpreted as evidence of prospect theory. Am. Econ. Rev. 97 (4), 1449–1466.

Resnick, P., Zeckhauser, R., Swanson, J., Lockwood, K., 2006. The value of a reputation on eBay: a controlled experiment. Exp. Econ. 9, 79–101.

Riach, P.A., Rich, J., 2002. Field experiments of discrimination in the market place. Econ. J. 112, F480–F518.

Smith, V.L., 1962. An experimental study of competitive market behavior. J. Political Econ. 70 (2), 111–137.

Smith, V.L., 1965. Experimental auction markets and the Walrasian hypothesis. J. Political Econ. 73 (4), 387–393.

Smith, V.L., 1982. Microeconomic systems as an experimental science. Am. Econ. Rev. 72 (5), 923–955.

Smith, V.L., Suchanek, G.L., Williams, A.W., 1988. Bubbles, crashes, and endogenous expectations in experimental spot asset markets. Econometrica 56 (5), 1119–1151.

Waichman, I., Ness, C., 2012. Farmers' performance and subject pool effect in decentralized bargaining markets. Econ. Lett. 115 (3), 366–368.

Walras, L., 1874. Elements D'Economie Politique Pure. Rouge, Lausanne.

Witt, U., 1986. Firms' market behavior under imperfect information and economic natural selection. J. Econ. Behav. Organ. 7, 265–290.

CHAPTER 8

Field Experiments on Discrimination[a]

M. Bertrand[*,1], E. Duflo[§]

*University of Chicago Booth School of Business, Chicago, IL, United States
§Massachusetts Institute of Technology, Cambridge, MA, United States
1Corresponding author: E-mail: Marianne.Bertrand@chicagobooth.edu

Contents

[a] Laura Stilwell and Jan Zilinsky provided excellent research assistance. We thank Abhijit Banerjee for comments. We are particularly grateful to Betsy Levy Paluck, our discussant, for her detailed and thoughtful review of an earlier draft.

Handbook of Economic Field Experiments, Volume 1
ISSN 2214-658X, http://dx.doi.org/10.1016/bs.hefe.2016.08.004

Abstract

This article reviews the existing field experimentation literature on the prevalence of discrimination, the consequences of such discrimination, and possible approaches to undermine it. We highlight key gaps in the literature and ripe opportunities for future field work. Section 2 reviews the various experimental methods that have been employed to measure the prevalence of discrimination, most notably audit and correspondence studies; it also describes several other measurement tools commonly used in lab-based work that deserve greater consideration in field research. Section 3 provides an overview of the literature on the costs of being stereotyped or discriminated against, with a focus on self-expectancy effects and self-fulfilling prophecies; Section 4 also discusses the thin field-based literature on the consequences of limited diversity in organizations and groups. The final section of the paper, Section 4, reviews the evidence for policies and interventions aimed at weakening discrimination, covering role model and intergroup contact effects, as well as sociocognitive and technological debiasing strategies.

Keywords

Audit studies; Contact hypothesis; Correspondence studies; Costs of discrimination; Psychology and economics

JEL Codes

A33: Handbooks; J15: Economics of Minorities, Races, Indigenous Peoples, and Immigrants — Non-labor Discrimination; J16: Economics of Gender — Non-labor Discrimination; J71: Labor Discrimination

1. INTRODUCTION

Black people are less likely to be employed, more likely to be arrested by the police, and more likely to be incarcerated. Women are very scarce at the top echelon of the corporate, academic, and political ladders despite the fact that (in rich countries at least) they get better grades in school and are more likely to graduate from college. While many in the media and public opinion circles argue that discrimination is a key force in driving these patterns, showing that it is actually the case is not simple. Indeed, it has proven elusive to produce convincing evidence of discrimination using standard regression analysis methods and observational data, in the sense in which we define discrimination throughout this chapter: members of a minority group (women, blacks, Muslims, immigrants, etc.) are treated differentially (less favorably) than members of a majority group with otherwise identical characteristics in similar circumstances.

However, over the last couple of decades, a rich literature in economics, sociology, political science, and psychology has leveraged experiments (in the lab and in the field)

to provide convincing evidence that discrimination, thus defined, indeed exists. We begin this chapter by describing the various experimental methods that have been used to measure discrimination in the field. Overall, this literature offers staggering evidence of pervasive discrimination against minority or underrepresented groups all around the world. We summarize this research and discuss some of its key limitations.

If discrimination is as pervasive as the evidence suggests, what do existing theories tell us about the costs to minority groups and to society overall? The two workhorse models of discrimination in the economic literature give drastically different answers, particularly with respect to the societal consequences. In the first model, developed by Becker (1957) for the context of the labor market, some employers have a distaste for hiring members of the minority group. They may indulge this distaste by refusing to hire, say, blacks or, if they do hire them, paying them less than other employees for the same level of productivity. If the fraction of discriminating employers in the economy is sufficiently large, a wage differential will emerge in equilibrium between otherwise identically productive minority and majority employees, and this wage differential will be a reflection of the distaste parameter of the marginal employer for minority workers (Becker, 1957; Charles and Guryan, 2008). By electing to not hire minority workers, inframargin racist employers will experience lower profits. In fact, if the conditions of perfect competition were satisfied, discriminating employers would be wiped away and taste-based discrimination would disappear.[1]

This "taste-based" explanation for discrimination stands in contrast with what many economists would view as a more disciplined explanation, which does not involve an ad hoc (even if intuitive) addition to the utility function (animus toward certain groups) to help rationalize a puzzling behavior. In a "statistical discrimination" model (Phelps, 1972; Arrow, 1973; Aigner and Cain, 1977), the differential treatment of members of the minority group is due to imperfect information, and discrimination is the result of a signal extraction problem. As a profit-maximizing prospective employer, renter, or car salesman, tries to infer the characteristics of a person that are relevant to the market transaction they are considering to complete with that person, they use all the information available to them. When the person-specific information is limited, group-specific membership may provide additional valuable information about expected productivity. For example, again using the labor market scenario, it may be known to employers that minority applicants are on average less productive than majority applicants. In this case, an employer who sees two applicants with similar noisy but unbiased signals of productivity should rationally favor the majority applicant to the minority one as her expected productivity is higher. While expected productivity will equal true productivity on average

---

[1] Refusing to hire black people could be efficient if the employer knows he cannot work well with them due to his animus, but this does not take away from the fact that businesses that do this should not survive.

within each group, statistical discrimination will result in some minority workers being treated less favorably than nonminority workers of the same true productivity, that is, will result in discrimination as defined previously. In the extreme case where individual signals of productivity are totally uninformative, an employer may rationally decide to make offers only to whites if the mean productivity among blacks does not exceed the required threshold.

While taste-based discrimination is clearly inefficient (simply consider how it constrains the allocation of talent), statistical discrimination is theoretically efficient and, hence, more easily defendable in ethical terms under the utilitarian argument. Moreover, statistical discrimination can also be argued to be "fair" in that it treats identical people with the same expected productivity (even if not with the same actual productivity) and is not motivated by animus. In fact, many economists would most likely support allowing statistical discrimination as a good policy, even where it is now illegal (as it is, e.g., in the US labor market and real-estate market contexts).

Unfortunately, as we discuss in the following section, while field experiments have been overall successful at documenting that discrimination exists, they have (with a few exceptions) struggled with linking the patterns of discrimination to a specific theory.

Meanwhile, psychologists have made considerable progress in their own understanding of the roots of discrimination, on a largely parallel track. The theories they have advanced and the (mainly lab) experiments they have conducted have been helpful in better nailing the microfoundations of discrimination. We believe this body of work blurs the sharp line economists tend to draw between taste-based and statistical explanations.

Psychologists' work on discrimination is embedded in an immense literature that attempts to understand the roots of prejudice, widely characterized as negative evaluation of others made on the basis of their group membership. This literature has looked for the microfoundations of such negative evaluation in a wide variety of areas, including personality development, socialization, social cognition, evolutionary psychology, and neuroscience.

Early scholarship in psychology viewed prejudice as a form of abnormal thinking and equated it to a psychopathology (think Adolf Hitler) that could be treated by addressing the personality disorders of subset of the population that was "diseased." It was only in the second half of the 20th century that the prevalent view of prejudice among psychologists became rooted in normal thinking processes (Dovidio, 2001), with socialization and social norms being viewed as dominant drivers. Influential work by Tajfel (1970) and Tajfel and Turner (1979) demonstrated the key role social identity plays in the process underlying prejudice. Experimental evidence has shown that the assignment of people to groups, even if totally arbitrary ones and even if they do not last, is sufficient to produce favoritism for in-group members and negativity toward out-group members. At the same time, evolutionary psychology has stressed the importance of social differentiation and the delineation of clear group boundaries as a way to achieve the benefits of cooperation between human beings without the risk of excessive costs, with group membership and group identity emerging as a form of contingent altruism (Brewer, 1981). While in-group love might not necessarily imply out-group hate, the same factors that make allegiance with group members important provide grounds for antagonism and distrust of outsiders.

In addition, more recent advances in the psychology literature have demonstrated the existence of unconscious, unintentional forms of bias. Modern social psychologists believe that attitudes can occur in implicit modes and that people can behave in ways that are unrelated or even sometimes opposed to their explicit views or self-interests (Banaji and Greenwald, 1995; Bertrand et al., 2005; Dovidio et al., 1998a,b; Greenwald and Banaji, 1995). Neuroscience studies have shown that different regions of the brain are activated in conscious versus unconscious processing, suggesting that unconscious processes are distinct mental activities. For example, the unconscious processing of black faces has been associated with activations of area of the brain associated with emotions and fear while the conscious processing of the same faces increases brain activity in areas related to control and regulation. Implicit biases are more likely to drive behavior under conditions of ambiguity, high time pressures and cognitive loads, or inattentiveness to the task.

Both of these dominant views of prejudice in the psychology literature—as an evolutionary phenomenon making group membership an important component of one's social identity or as an unconscious automatic negative association triggered by exposure to out-group members—could serve as microfoundations to what the more reduced form "animus-based" models' economists have worked with. More importantly, these psychological models make clear that the limited information and decision-making model that drives statistical discrimination might itself be endogenous to conscious or unconscious prejudice against the out-group members. If a social need to positively associate with one's own group also makes the out-group members feel more distant and unknowable (Brewer, 1988), an employer may not invest in collecting information on an out-group member or decide that the individual signals of productivity for minority group members are totally uninformative, resulting in all minority group members being equally treated as unhirable. Limited de facto contact between in-group and out-group members will imply that majority employees or coworkers will be fairly ignorant about the quality of minorities; this would mean that employing, electing, or renting to them may seem riskier which, in the presence of risk aversion, will also trigger more statistical discrimination (Aigner and Cain, 1977). Unconscious bias may influence the specific criteria or formulae that are used to assess expected productivity (Uhlmann and Cohen, 2005): for example, the sense of danger that is implicitly triggered by seeing a black face or reading a black name on a résumé may lead an employer to put too great a weight on docility as a work quality than would be warranted for maximum productivity. Recently, the emphasis on "fit" between a prospective employee and the company as a hiring criterion in technology jobs has raised the spectrum of a new form of subtle discrimination. Similarly, unconscious stereotypes may influence our judgment of the inputs into productivity, with the same level of assertiveness being deemed as good for productivity when coming from men but bad when coming from women (Rudman and Glick, 2001).

Perhaps most importantly, whether discrimination is taste based or statistical, it may ultimately result in genuine difference between groups, through self-fulfilling prophecies. If the stereotypical woman is not good at math, talented girls may become discouraged and ultimately not become good at math. If teachers or employers assume that students of a particular color are less smart, they will invest less in them. Thus, discrimination, whether it is taste based or statistical, can create or exacerbate existing differences between groups. Discrimination that starts as taste based and inefficient can easily morph into the more "justifiable" form. "Valid" stereotypes today could be the product of ambient animus, very much complicating the division between the different theories of discrimination.

The chapter proceeds as follows. Section 2 is devoted to the various experimental methods that have been used in the field to measure discrimination, in particular, audit and correspondence studies. Audit studies send out individuals who are matched in all observable characteristics except for the one in question (race, criminal record, etc.) to apply for jobs or make purchases, then researchers analyze the responses. Correspondence studies—which represent by far the largest share of field experiments on discrimination—do the same but control for more variables by creating fictitious applicants (often for jobs or apartments) who correspond via mail. We summarize the findings of this body of work (which clearly demonstrate the pervasiveness of discrimination) and discuss its key limitations.

In this section of the chapter, we also discuss a few alternative methods to measure discrimination, many of them having developed in the psychology literature for use in the lab: Implicit Association Tests, Goldberg paradigm experiments, and List Randomization—as well as measures of willingness to pay to interact with minority group members. We argue that these alternative methods deserve more consideration by economists interested in measures of discrimination for their field research.

Section 3 reviews the work that addresses the costs of being discriminated against or stereotyped. In particular, we review the experimental work that has studied how the threat of being viewed through the lens of a negative stereotype can have a direct negative effect on performance. We also review the experimental literature on expectancy effects, the goal of which has been to understand how stereotypes and biases against minority groups may end up being self-fulfilling.

We round up the second part of the chapter by reviewing what is a surprisingly thin field-based literature on the costs (and benefits) of the limited diversity in organizations and groups that directly result from discrimination. This allows us to discuss field work that has considered the consequences of discrimination not just from the perspective of the group that is discriminated against but also from the perspective of society as a whole.

The third and final section of this chapter, Section 4, is related to the review of various interventions and policies that have been proposed to undo or weaken discrimination. This section covers topics such as the impact of role models, how contact and exposure to the minority groups may change prejudice, as well as a large psychology literature on both sociocognitive and technological debiasing strategies. We argue that there is a lot of promising future research that is "ripe for the picking" in this area, given the large amount of theoretical and lab-based work that has not yet been taken to the field.

2. MEASURING DISCRIMINATION IN THE FIELD

Earlier research on discrimination focused on individual-level outcome regressions, with discrimination estimated from the "minority" differential that remains unexplained after including as many proxies as possible for productivity.[2]

The limitations of this approach are well known. The interpretation of the estimated "minority" coefficient is problematic due to omitted variables bias. Specifically, results of a regression analysis might suggest differential treatment by race or gender even if the decision maker (say, an employer) never used group membership in her decision of how much to pay an employee. However, it could be the case that race or gender is correlated with other proxies for productivity that are unobservable to the researcher but observed by the employer. It is therefore impossible to conclude that the employer used group membership in her decision-making process using this method.

The traditional answer has been to saturate the regression with as many productivity-relevant, individual-level characteristics as are available. But, of course, ensuring that the researcher observes all that the decision maker observes is a hopeless task.

Moreover, adding more and more controls to a regression could ultimately obscure the interpretation of the evidence. Consider the labor market context: minority workers might be best responding to the discrimination they know to exist and could have simply sorted into industries where there is no or limited discrimination. Hence, finding no racial gap in earnings after controlling for industry or employer fixed effects in a regression may indicate that there is no discrimination at the margin, which is very different from no discrimination on average.

Also, as pointed out in the study by Guryan and Charles (2013), the variables the researcher controls for might themselves be affected by discrimination. That is,

---

[2] For a review of this earlier literature on the narrower topic of labor market discrimination, see Chapter 48 in the study by Altonji and Blank (1999).

disadvantaged groups may not have access to high-quality schools because of discrimination, yet they might, given their low human capital accumulation, be paid the "fair market wage." While one might still be tempted to conclude from this that there is no discrimination in the labor market but instead discrimination in the education market, that might not be right if the minority group's expectations about labor market discrimination drive their educational decision. In other words, minority group members may decide to underinvest in education if they expect that they will not be able to obtain labor market returns for this education.

Audit and correspondence methodologies were developed to address these core limitations of the regression approach to measure discrimination. We review in the following section both types of studies, discuss the extent to which they address these limitations of the regression approach, and also consider new issues they create.

2.1 Audit studies

In the best-known collection of audit studies exploring the extent of discrimination, Fix and Struyk (1993) describe the method as follows:

Two individuals (auditors or testers) are matched for all relevant personal characteristics other than the one that is presumed to lead to discrimination, for example, race, ethnicity, gender. They then apply for a job, a housing unit, or a mortgage, or begin to negotiate for a good or service. The results they achieve and the treatment they receive in the transaction are closely observed, documented, and analyzed to determine if the outcomes reveal patterns of differential treatment on the basis of the trait studied and/or protected by antidiscrimination laws...

Discrimination is said to have been detected when "auditors in the protected class are systematically treated worse than their teammates" (Yinger, 1998).[3]

A well-known early example of the audit method is offered by Ayres and Siegelman (1995). In this study, pairs of testers (one of whom was always a white male) were trained to bargain uniformly and then were sent to negotiate for the purchase of a new automobile at randomly selected Chicago-area dealerships. Thirty-eight testers bargained for 306 cars at 153 dealerships. Testers were chosen to have average attractiveness, and both testers in a pair bargained for the same model of car, at the same dealership, usually within a few days of each other. Dealerships were selected randomly, testers were randomly assigned to dealerships, and the choice of which tester in the pair would be the first to enter the dealership was also randomly made. The testers bargained at different dealerships for a total of nine car models, following a uniform bargaining script that instructed them to focus quickly on one particular car and start negotiating over it. Testers were

---

[3] Results from the earliest audit studies can be found in the study by Newman (1978), McIntyre et al. (1980), Galster (1990), Yinger (1986), Cross et al. (1990), James and DelCastillo (1991), Turner et al. (1991), and Fix and Struyk (1993).

further instructed to tell dealers at the beginning of the bargaining that they could provide their own financing for the car. In spite of the identical approach to bargaining, Ayres and Siegelman (1995) find that white males are quoted lower prices than white women and blacks (men or women). While ancillary evidence suggests that the dealerships' disparate treatment of women and blacks may be caused by dealers' statistical inferences about consumers' reservation prices, the data do not strongly support any single theory of discrimination.

Another well-known audit study of the labor market is the study by Neumark et al. (1996), which investigates the role of sex discrimination in vertical segregation among waiters and waitresses. Specifically, two male and two female college students were sent to apply in person for jobs as waiters and waitresses at 65 restaurants in Philadelphia. The restaurants were divided into high-, medium-, and low-price categories, with the goal of estimating sex differences in the receipt of job offers in each price category. The study was designed so that a male and female pair applied for a job at each restaurant and so that the male and female candidates were on average identical. The findings are consistent with discrimination against women in high-price restaurants and discrimination in women's favor in low-price restaurants. Of the 13 job offers from high-price restaurants, 11 were made to men. In contrast, of the 10 job offers from low-price restaurants, 8 were made to women. In addition, information gathered from restaurants included in the study suggests that earnings are substantially higher in high-price restaurants, meaning that the apparent hiring discrimination has implications for gender-based differences in earnings among waitpersons. Results are interpreted as consistent both with employer discrimination and customer discrimination.

Another interesting application of the audit method is the study by Pager (2003) who matched pairs of individuals applying for entry-level positions and probed the impact of a criminal record, conditional on race. The author employed two black testers who formed a team and another pair of white testers. Within each team, one auditor was "assigned" a criminal record (this assignment was random and rotating—i.e., each tester played the role of an ex-convict at some point).[4] In total, 350 employers were audited. The effect of the criminal record was both statistically significant and meaningful in magnitude: 17 percent of attempts with whites who had a supposed criminal record received a call back, compared to 34 percent of tries with whites who said they had no criminal record. That is, an equally qualified white candidate was about half as likely to receive a call back if he was believed to be an ex-convict. For black applicants, the effect was notably larger: 5 percent of attempts with blacks who were supposedly ex-convicts received a call back,

---

[4] Pager argues that "[b]y varying which member of the pair presented himself as having a criminal record, unobserved differences within the pairs of applicants were effectively controlled for."

compared to 14 percent of applications with blacks that had no record, meaning an equally qualified black candidate was about one-third as likely to receive a call back if he had a criminal record. Furthermore, these estimates show that a black applicant without a criminal record was about as likely to receive a call back as a white applicant with a criminal record.

Most audit studies do not explicitly test which theory of discrimination has most explanatory power, even if they often informally discuss what forms of discrimination might or might not be consistent with the observed patterns in the data. A notable exception is the study by List (2004) who recruited buyers and sellers at a sports cards market and documented that minority buyers receive lower offers when they bargain for a collectible card. One finding by List (2004) is that in this context lack of information—and the expectation that minorities are inexperienced—drives discriminatory behavior. Experienced dealers discriminate more. Among experienced buyers, final offers to minorities are similar to offers received by white men; but minorities require more time to achieve this outcome. Moreover, List tries to rule out taste-based explanations for the data by combining the field data with results from a dictator game conducted in the lab with these card dealers. He finds that nonwhite males receive roughly as many positive allocations in this game as white males and interprets this pattern as evidence for the absence of taste for discrimination. Of course, while a laboratory experiment is a useful complement to the field study, the behavior of dealers in the dictator game, on its own, does not prove that taste-based discrimination is absent during the actual market transactions.

2.1.1 Limitations of audit studies

Many of the weaknesses of audit studies have been discussed in Heckman and Siegelman (1993) and Heckman (1998). First, these studies require that both members of the auditor pair be identical in all dimensions that might affect productivity in employers' eyes, except for the trait that is being manipulated. To accomplish this, researchers typically match auditors on several characteristics (height, weight, age, dialect, dressing style, and hairdo) and train them for several days to coordinate interviewing styles. Yet, critics note that this is unlikely to erase the numerous differences that exist between the auditors in a pair.

Another weakness of the audit studies is that they are not double blind: auditors know the purpose of the study. As Turner et al. (1991) note: "The first day of training also included an introduction to employment discrimination, equal employment opportunity, and a review of project design and methodology." This may generate conscious or subconscious motives among auditors to generate data consistent or inconsistent with their beliefs about race or gender issues. As psychologists have documented, these demand effects can be quite strong. It is very difficult to insure that auditors will not want to do "a good job." Even a vague belief by auditors that employers treat minorities differently can result in measured differences in treatment. The possibility of such a demand effect is further magnified by the fact that auditors are not in fact seeking jobs (or trying to buy a car for themselves) and are therefore more free to let their beliefs affect the bargaining or interview process.

2.2 Correspondence studies

Correspondence studies have been developed to address some of the more obvious weaknesses of the audit method. Rather than relying on real auditors or testers that physically meet with a potential employer or potential landlord, correspondence studies rely on fictitious applicants. Specifically, in response to a job or rental advertisement, the researcher sends (many) pairs of résumés or letters of interest, one of which is assigned the perceived minority trait. Discrimination is estimated by comparing the outcomes for the fictitious applicants with and without the perceived minority trait. The most common (but not the only) way to manipulate the perceived minority trait has been through the names of the applicants (e.g., female names, African-American names, Arabic Names, etc.). Outcomes studied in a correspondence study have been mainly, but not exclusively, limited to measuring call backs by employers or landlords in response to the mailed or emailed fictitious application.[5]

The correspondence method presents several advantages over the audit method. First, because it relies on résumés or applications by fictitious people and not real people, one can be sure to generate strict comparability across groups for all information that is seen by the employers or landlords. This guarantees that any observed differences are caused solely by the minority trait manipulation. Second, the use of paper applications insulates from demand effects. Finally, because of the relatively low marginal cost, one can send out a large number of applications. Besides providing more precise estimates, the larger sample size also allows researchers to examine the nature of the differential treatment from many more angles and hence promises to link it more closely to specific theories of discrimination.[6]

Although Guryan and Charles (2013) call correspondence tests a "significant methodological advance" and a review of discrimination in the marketplace published about 15 years ago discussed only observational and audit studies (Yinger, 1998), the method is actually not that new. Fictitious applications and résumés have been sent to employers in order to uncover racial or religious discrimination nearly half a century ago.[7] However,

---

[5] See Sections 2.3.2 and 2.3.3 for cases of different approaches.

[6] We discuss in Section 2.5 other weaknesses that are shared by the correspondence studies, as well as added weaknesses of the correspondence method compared to the audit method.

[7] See Jowell and Prescott-Clarke (1970), Jolson (1974), Hubbuck and Carter (1980), Brown and Gay (1985), and Riach and Rich (1991) for early studies. One caveat is that some of these studies fail to fully match skills between minority and nonminority résumés.

the number of correspondence studies in economics has greatly increased following the study by Bertrand and Mullainathan (2004), who study race discrimination in the labor market by sending fictitious résumés in response to help-wanted ads in Boston and Chicago newspapers. To manipulate perceived race, they randomly assigned very white-sounding names (such as Emily Walsh or Greg Baker) to half the résumés and very African-American-sounding names (such as Lakisha Washington or Jamal Jones) to the other half. In total, they responded to over 1300 employment ads in the sales, administrative support, clerical, and customer services job categories and sent out nearly 5000 résumés. They find that white names receive 50 percent more call backs for interviews.

2.2.1 Correspondence studies in the labor market
The main results of labor market correspondence tests are reviewed in Table 1.

As is clear from Table 1, labor market correspondence studies have by now been carried in many countries around the world and have focused on a variety of perceived traits that can be randomized on a résumé. In the following, we review some of these studies in more detail, focusing in particular on those that have attempted to go beyond simply documenting whether or not differential treatment occurs based on the manipulated traits and move toward understanding which theory may best fit the patterns in the data. However, one of our bottom lines will be that, unfortunately, the studies have tended to be fairly close replications of the study by Bertrand and Mullainathan (2004) for different populations or contexts. With a few exceptions, the literature has failed to push the correspondence methodology to design approaches to more formally test for various theories of why differential treatment is taking place.

2.2.1.1 Race and ethnicity
Studies of labor market discrimination based on race and ethnic background have been by far the most popular application of the correspondence method to date. While publication bias is always a concern, the results of correspondence studies where the trait of interest is race or ethnicity offer overwhelming evidence of discrimination in the labor market against racial and ethnic minorities. Evidence has been accumulated from nearly all continents: Latin America (e.g., Galarza and Yamada (2014) compare whites to indigenous applicants in Peru), Asia (e.g., Maurer-Fazio (2012) compares Han, Mongolian, and Tibetan applicants in China), Australia (e.g., where Booth et al. (2011) compare whites to Chinese applicants), Europe (e.g., Baert et al. (2013) compare immigrants to nonimmigrants in Belgium), Ireland (e.g., where McGinnity et al. (2009) compare candidates with Irish names to candidates with distinctively non-Irish names), etc.

Attempts to adapt the correspondence method to learn more about which theory of discrimination best fits the patterns in the data have been mainly focused on trying to provide corroborative evidence for (or against) statistical discrimination. The most common approach has been to investigate whether the gap in call backs is responsive to the amount

Continued

Table 1 Labor market correspondence studies

Paper	Country	CVs / apps	Vacancies	Effect (call-back ratio)	Theory
Galarza and Yamada (2014) Trait: Ethnicity; attractiveness	Peru	4820	1205	White-to-indigenous ratio: 1.8 Low attractiveness hurts white females	No
Eriksson and Rooth (2014) Trait: Unemployment duration	Sweden	8466	–	Employed to long-term unemployed: 1.25	No
Blommaert et al. (2014) Trait: Arabic name	Netherlands	636	–	Dutch-to-foreign: 1.62 (unconditional ratio). No difference, if views held fixed	No
Nunley et al. (2014) Trait: Race	United States	9396	–	White-to-black: 1.18 (unconditional)	Inconsistent with statistical discrimination, consistent with taste-based discrimination
Ghayad (2013) Trait: Unemployment duration	United States	3360	600	Employed-to-unemployed: 1.47	No
Bartoš et al. (2013)	Czech Republic and Germany	274 (Czech R.) 745 (Ger.)	–	Czech-to-Vietnamese: 1.34 Lower requests for CVs if candidate is Turkish	Consistent with attention discrimination
Trait: Ethnicity (Roma, Asian, Turkish)					
Wright et al. (2013) Trait: Religion/ethnicity	United States	6400	1600	White-to-Muslim: 1.58	Consistent with theoretical models of secularization and cultural distate theory
Kroft et al. (2013) Trait: Unemployment duration	United States (largest 100 MSAs)	12,054	3040	1 log point change in unemployment duration: 4.7 percentage points lower call-back probability	No

Table 1 Labor market correspondence studies—cont'd

Paper	Country	CVs / apps	Vacancies	Effect (call-back ratio)	Theory
Baert et al. (2013) Trait: Nationality (Turkish-sounding name)	Belgium	752	376	Flemish-to-Turkish: 1.03 to 2.05, depending on the occupation	No
Bailey et al. (2013) Trait: Sexual orientation	United States	4608	1536	No effect	No
Ahmed et al. (2013) Trait: Sexual orientation	Sweden	3990	–	Heterosexual-to-homosexual (male): 1.14 Heterosexual-to-homosexual (female): 1.22	No
Acquisti and Fong (2013) Traits:Sexual orientation and religion	United States	4183	–	Christian-to-Muslim: 1.16	No
Patacchini et al. (2012) Traits: Sexual orientation and attractiveness	Italy	2320	–	Heterosexual-to-Homosexual: 1.38	No
Kaas and Manger (2012) Trait: Immigrant (race/ethnicity)	Germany	1056	528	German-to-Turkish: 1.29 (if no reference letter is included)	Consistent with statistical discrimination
Maurer-Fazio (2012) Trait: Ethnicity	China	21,592	10,796	Han-to-Mongolian: 1.36 Han-to-Tibetan: 2.21	No
Jacquemet and Yannelis (2012) Trait: Race/nationality	United States	330	990	English-to-foreign names: 1.41	Consistent with patterns of ethnic homophily
Ahmed et al. (2012) Trait: Age	Sweden	466	–	English-to-Black names: 1.46 31-year old to 46-year old: 3.23	No
Oreopoulos (2011) Trait: Nationality (and race)	Canada	12,910	3225	English name-to-Immigrant: ranged from 1.39 to 2.71 (against Indian Pakistani and Chinese applicants)	No
Carlsson (2011) Trait: Gender	Sweden	3228	1614	Female-to-male: 1.07	No
Booth et al. (2011) Trait: Ethnicity	Australia	Above 4000	–	White-to-Italian: 1.12 White-to-Chinese: 1.68	No

Study / Trait	Country			Findings	Consistent
Booth and Leigh (2010) Trait: Gender	Australia	3365	–	Female-to-male: 1.28 (female-dominated professions)	No
Riach and Rich (2010) Trait: Age	United Kingdom	1000+	–	2.64 favoring younger candidates	No
Rooth (2009) Trait: Attractiveness/obesity	Sweden	1970	985	Nonobese/attractive-to-obese/unattractive: ranged from 1.21 to 1.25 (but higher for some occupations)	No
McGinnity et al. (2009) Trait: Nationality/race	Ireland	480	240	1.8, 2.07, 2.44 in favor of Irish and against Asians, Germans, and Africans, respectively	No
Banerjee et al. (2009) Traits: Caste and religion	India	3160	371	Upper caste-to-other backward castes: 1.08 (software jobs, insignificant), 1.6 (call-center jobs)	No
Lahey (2008) Trait: Age	United States	App. 4000	–	Young-to-older: 1.42	No
Petit (2007) Traits: Age, gender, number of children	France	942	157	Ranged from 1.13 to 2.43 against 25-year old, childless women	No
Bursell (2007) Trait: Ethnicity	Sweden	3552	1776	Swedish-to-foreign names: 1.82	Inconsistent with statistical discrimination
Bertrand and Mullainathan (2004) Trait: Race	United States	4870	1300+	White-to-African-American: 1.5 (1.22 for females in sales jobs)	No
Jolson (1974) Trait: Race and religion	United States	300	–	White-to-black: 4.2 for selling positions	No

MSAs; Metropolitan Statistical Areas.

of information provided to employers about the job applicants, as was first done in the study by Bertrand and Mullainathan (2004), in which they studied how credentials affect the racial gap in call back. In particular, Bertrand and Mullainathan (2004) experimentally varied the quality of the résumé used in response to a given ad. Higher quality applicants had on average a little more labor market experience and fewer holes in their employment history; they were also more likely to have an email address, have completed some certification degree, possess foreign language skills, or have been awarded some honors. The authors sent four résumés in response to each ad: two higher quality and two lower quality ones. They randomly assigned an African-American-sounding name to one of the higher and one of the lower quality résumés. They find that whites with higher quality résumés receive nearly 30 percent more call backs than whites with lower quality résumés. On the other hand, having a higher quality résumé has a smaller effect for African-Americans. In other words, the gap between whites and African-Americans widens with résumé quality. While one may have expected improved credentials to alleviate employers' fear that African-American applicants are deficient in some unobservable skills under a statistical discrimination explanation for the overall discrimination, this was not the case in their data. Bertrand and Mullainathan argue that one simple alternative model that may best explain the patterns in their data is some form of lexicographic search by employers:

> Employers receive so many résumés that they may use quick heuristics in reading these résumés. One such heuristic could be to simply read no further when they see an African-American name. Thus, they may never see the skills of African-American candidates and this could explain why these skills are not rewarded.

These findings are replicated in the study by Nunley et al. (2014): blacks received 14 percent fewer call backs compared to whites, and discrimination was not mitigated when productive characteristics were added to a résumé. However, some studies report results that are more in line with the predictions of statistical discrimination models. Oreopoulos (2011) submitted 12,910 résumés in response to 3225 job postings in Canada. First, he compares (fictitious) applicants who had a foreign name but who attended a Canadian (or foreign) university and had work experience in Canada. The call-back rate is 1.39 for Canadian (English-sounding names) versus foreigners if they went to a Canadian university and 1.43 if they went to a foreign university. However, the call-back rate falls dramatically if the foreigners' job experience was purely international (2.71 call-back ratio). Moreover, if candidates who had foreign job experience and education had a Chinese last name with an English first name (Allen and Michelle Wang), their prospects on the job market improved. This raises the possibility that a fraction of the "discrimination" is statistical, for example, with employers making inference about the candidate's English skills. Perhaps even more striking, Kaas and Manger (2012) sent out 528 pairs of applications in Germany to study the effect of a Turkish-sounding name. The German-to-Turkish call-back rate was 1.29 when no reference letter was included. Discrimination was eliminated when a reference letter, containing indirect information about productivity (such as conscientiousness and agreeableness) was added, which the authors interpret as evidence of consistency with statistical discrimination. It is interesting that such "soft information" presented in the reference letter appears to remove the difference in call-back rates even though "harder information" presented in a résumé (such as employment history or honors) does not in other studies. It would be interesting to probe this contrast further.

2.2.1.2 Gender

There are fewer studies on gender, and discrimination against women at the call-back stage is much less apparent in general. Some studies attempt to show whether the degree (and nature) of discrimination depends on the nature of the profession. Carlsson (2011) sent paired applications for positions of IT professionals, drivers, construction workers, sales assistants, high school teachers, restaurant workers, accountants, cleaners, preschool teachers, and nurses. Overall, women are called back slightly more often than men; in male-dominated professions, males have a slight (insignificant) advantage. Booth and Leigh (2010) focused on female-dominated professions (waitstaff, data entry, customer service, and sales jobs) and found a call back of 1.28 in favor of women.

A topic of interest for future work would be to apply the correspondence method to measure the extent to which a bias exists against women with children or against young women who may have children in the future. To our knowledge, only one study, Petit (2007), studies this aspect. In order to shed light on the role of family constraints in gender discrimination, Petit sent résumés for male and female applicants, with or without children, of age 25 or 37. Discrimination against women is detected for young workers in higher skilled positions (in the French finance industry) but not among prime-age workers.

2.2.1.3 Caste and religion

Banerjee et al. (2009) study the role of caste and religion in India's software and call-center sectors. They sent 3160 fictitious résumés with randomly allocated caste-linked surnames in response to 371 job openings in and around Delhi (India) that were advertised in major city papers and online job sites. They find no evidence of discrimination against non—upper-caste (i.e., Scheduled Caste, Scheduled Tribe, and other backward castes) applicants for software jobs. But, in the case of call-center jobs, they do find larger and significant differences between call-back rates for upper castes and other backward castes (and to a lesser extent Scheduled Castes) in favor of upper castes. They find no discrimination against Muslims.

The potential impact of religion on job prospects in the United States is explored by Wright et al. (2013). Affiliation with a religion was signaled through student activities that were listed on résumés.[8] The control group had no religious identification in his/her résumé. Compared to the control group, Muslim applications were 24 percent less likely to receive at least one contact by either email or phone, and they received 33 percent fewer total contacts than did those from the control group.

2.2.1.4 Unemployment spells

More recently, researchers have applied the correspondence model to better understand patterns of labor market discrimination against the unemployed. In Sweden, Eriksson and Rooth (2014) randomly assigned various characteristics (contemporary unemployment, past unemployment immediately after graduation, past unemployment between jobs, work experience, and number of employers). Long-term unemployment did not harm job candidates' chances, as long as the applicant had subsequent work experience. However, if the applicant was unemployed in the preceding 9 months, his or her call-back probability fell by 20 percent.[9] In the United States, Ghayad (2013) finds that (current) unemployment spell longer than 6 months are particularly harmful: the rate of interview requests for résumés with similar firm experience drops 1.13 percentage points for each additional month of nonemployment up to 6 months, and once the candidate experienced 6 months of unemployment, interview requests fell by an extra 8 percentage points.

Kroft et al. (2013) relate these results to the inference problem faced by the prospective employers. The authors replicate the result that longer employment duration reduces call-back rate but also show that this depends on the labor market conditions. Duration dependence is stronger in tight labor markets, suggesting that employers use the information on the length of unemployment as a signal of productivity but recognize that the signal is less informative when the labor markets conditions are weak.[10]

2.2.1.5 Other characteristics: sexual orientation and age

Résumé studies are now also being used to try to detect discrimination in a number of less obvious domains.

A literature has tried to estimate discrimination against Lesbian, gay, bisexual, and transgender (LGBT) candidates; however, most studies have focused only on lesbians

---

[8] It is tricky to signal only religion on a résumé. The manipulation through student activities may reveal more than just religion, an issue we will come back to in Section 2.4.

[9] One caveat, as the authors acknowledge, is that not all employers necessarily view the gaps on the CVs as implying unemployment.

[10] This may also explain the finding in the study by Eriksson and Rooth (2014) (mentioned previously) since that particular study was carried out between March and November 2007, that is, during the global financial crisis.

and gay men.[11] One of the challenges with estimating discrimination against LGBT candidates is how to provide information that identifies a candidate as a member of that minority, when telling such details are not normally solicited in job applications. In the study by Ahmed et al. (2013), which was carried out in Sweden, sexual orientation was indicated by the mention of a "spouse" of either gender in the cover letter and voluntary work in either an LGBT rights organization (gay identity) or the Swedish red cross (heterosexual identity). Targeted occupations included male-dominated ones (construction worker, motor vehicle driver, sales person, and mechanic worker), female-dominated ones (shop sales assistant, preschool teacher, cleaner, restaurant worker, and nurse), and more neutral ones (high school teacher). The authors find some mild evidence of discrimination (ratio of 1.14), which ultimately could be due to the nature of the signaling (e.g., working in LGBT rights, as opposed to the red cross, may be seen as a political gesture, not just revealing an identity). In Italy, Patacchini et al. (2012) performed a correspondence study that revealed "homosexual preferences" through internships in pro-gay advocacy groups and finds higher discrimination against gay men (1.38) but not lesbian candidates. In the United States, Bailey et al. (2013) find no evidence of discrimination against gay men or lesbians candidates.

The issue of discrimination by age has also attracted some attention, and several papers (Ahmed et al., 2012; Lahey, 2008; Riach and Rich, 2010) find that younger candidates are generally preferred to older ones. A fundamental issue with this work is that it is hard to argue that age is not necessarily a proxy for productivity. Lahey (2008) tries to control for physical fitness with hobbies (e.g., racquetball is supposed to indicate fitness), but this is ultimately only moderately convincing.

Finally, physical appearance has also been studied: Rooth (2009) studies obesity in the Swedish labor market and Patacchini et al. (2012) investigate the beauty premium in Italy. Using manipulated facial photos to show an otherwise identical candidate as obese, Rooth (2009) shows there is a significantly lower call-back response for obese people: obese men had a six percentage points lower call-back rate, while the call-back rate for obese women was eight percentage points lower. Patacchini et al. (2012) find a small, but significant, beauty premium for "pretty" females (2 percent); however, they do not find a beauty premium for men. Interestingly, the beauty premium disappears for high-skilled attractive women: low-skilled attractive women are more likely to be called back than high-skilled attractive women. On the other hand, Hamermesh and Biddle (1994) do find the existence of a beauty premium in the United States. We discuss the rationale for a beauty premium further in Section 2.9.

---

[11] To the best of our knowledge, no study has been done that specifically looks at discrimination against transgender people using the correspondence method.

2.3 Correspondence studies in other settings

2.3.1 Rental markets

Correspondence studies in the housing market have very much followed the same approach as those in the labor market. The main findings from the literature are summarized in Table 2.

The rental market studies replicate, in methodology and basic results, those in the labor market. The researchers typically identify rental ads and send inquiries, manipulating the trait of interest. Discrimination against Arabic names is found in Sweden (Carlsson and Eriksson, 2014; Ahmed and Hammarstedt, 2008; Ahmed et al., 2010). Discrimination against blacks and other minority ethnicities in the United States is found in the study by Ewens et al. (2014), Hanson and Hawley (2011), and Carpusor and Loges (2006). Discrimination against immigrants (particularly Muslims) is found in Italy (Baldini and Federici, 2011) and Spain (Bosch et al., 2010). Discrimination against LGBT people is found in Ahmed and Hammarstedt (2009).

Another popular variation, parallel to the labor market literature, has been to provide more information (e.g., job, etc.) about some of the applicants. Positive information (e.g., "I do not smoke and I work full time as an architect") tends to reduce the call-back ratios between white and the minority group, while negative information ("I am a smoker and I have a less than perfect credit score") or small spelling mistakes in the email tend to increase it.

2.3.2 Retail

The expansion of online platforms allows researchers to use the correspondence method to also study discrimination in retail markets. There are currently much fewer such studies, but the door is wide open for more to be performed.

Zussman (2013) studies the mechanisms behind ethnic discrimination in the online market for used cars in Israel. This paper uses an innovative, two-stage approach. First, about 8000 paired emails are sent to sellers of second-hand cars. An enquiry coming from somebody with a Jewish-sounding name was 22 percent more likely to receive a response than an enquiry emailed by an interested buyer with an Arab-sounding name. Second, a follow-up phone survey was used to elicit sellers' attitudes about minorities to tease out potential mechanisms for this effect. The researchers found that Jewish car sellers who strongly disagree with the statement that "the Arabs in Israel are more likely to cheat than the Jews" do not discriminate against the Arab buyer, while others sellers do. That is, expectations about the quality of the transactions are correlated to the differential (average) treatment of Arabs.

Pope and Sydnor (2011) reports evidence from peer-to-peer lending sites. They find that loan listings with an attached picture of a black individual are 25−35 percent less likely to receive funding than those of white individuals with similar credit profiles.

Table 2 Rental market papers

Study	Country	Inquiries	Effect	Theory
Carlsson and Eriksson (2014) Trait: Minority status (Arabic name)	Sweden	5827	Swedish-to-Arabic (females): 1.37 Swedish-to-Arabic (males): 1.62	No
Ewens et al. (2014) Trait: Race	United States	14,237	White-to-black: 1.19	Consistent with statistical discrimination, inconsistent with taste-based discrimination
Bartoš et al. (2013) Trait: Minority status (Roma or Asian name)	Czech Republic and Germany	1800	Czech-to-minority: 1.27 (site available), 1.9 (pooled Asian and Roma names)	Consistent with attention discrimination
Hanson and Hawley (2011) Trait: Race	United States	9456	White-to-African–American: 1.12 (varied by neighborhood and unit type)	Consistent with statistical discrimination
Baldini and Federici (2011) Trait: Immigrant status; Language ability	Italy	3676	Italian-to-East European: 1.24 Italian-to-Arab: 1.48	No
Ahmed et al. (2010) Trait: Minority status (Arabic name)	Sweden	1032	Swedish-to-Arab/Muslim: 1.44 (no information), 1.24 (detailed information about the applicant)	No
Bosch et al. (2010) Trait: Immigrant status	Spain	1809	Spanish-to-Moroccan: 1.44 (no information), 1.19 (with positive information)	No
Ahmed and Hammarstedt (2009) Trait: Sexual orientation	Sweden	408	Straight-to-gay: 1.27	No
Ahmed and Hammarstedt (2008) Trait: Immigrant (race/ ethnicity/religion)	Sweden	1500	Swedish-to-Arab male: 2.17	No
Carpusor and Loges (2006) Trait: Race/ethnicity (Arab, African–American)	United States (Los Angeles County)	1115	White-to-Arab: 1.35 White-to-black: 1.59, conditional on hearing back, 1.98 unconditional	No

2.3.3 Academia

Milkman et al. (2012) ran a field experiment set in academia with a sample of 6548 professors. Faculty members received emails from fictional prospective doctoral students seeking to schedule a meeting either that day or in 1 week; students' names signaled their race (Caucasian, African-American, Hispanic, Indian, or Chinese) and gender. When the requests were to meet in 1 week, Caucasian males were granted access to faculty members 26 percent more often than were women and minorities; also, compared with women and minorities, Caucasian males received more and faster responses. However, these patterns were essentially eliminated when prospective students requested a meeting that same day. The authors argue that their finding of a temporal discrimination effect is consistent with the idea in psychology that subtle contextual shifts can alter patterns of race- and gender-based discrimination (a topic we return to in the last section of this chapter, Section 4.4).

2.4 Beyond the résumés

With the rise of the Internet, employers can easily find more information online about a job applicant besides his or her résumé. A few recent studies enrich the correspondence methodology by allowing employers to search for more (and different) information than that which would typically be available in a résumé.

Given the increasing popularity of online social networks, the contribution of Acquisti and Fong (2013) is particularly interesting. They employ the correspondence method by submitting applications to job postings and extend their experiments by creating either personal websites of social networking profiles for the fictitious applicants, which allow employers to gather additional information if they wish to. The additional information that can be gleaned online about the job applicants relates to their religion and sexual orientation. The question the paper is asking is whether extra information available online but not on the résumé leads to discrimination: Would applicants whose identity is not revealed in the application but who appear to be Muslim (vs. Christian) or gay (vs. straight) on a popular social network, suffer unequal treatment?

To do so, they created distinct online profiles: one profile on a professional network site, and another profile on a social network site where the emphasis is on sharing photographs or leisure-related comments, not job opportunities. The profile on the professional network site was identical across treatments (even the photograph was the same). The name used by researchers (selected after careful testing) was one not commonly associated with a particular race or religion. That is, the name of the "Muslim candidate" was non-Arabic, but the candidate's religion could be inferred after some search on the social network site. Only the profile on the social network site contained clues (e.g., Christian vs. Muslim or straight vs. gay).

The experiment finds that only a small fraction of employers use social media to conduct additional inquiry about job candidates.[12] Given the limited search efforts by employers, the effects of group membership are generally small. The total effect of trait manipulation is not statistically significant: 12.6 percent of applicants who appeared to be Christians received call backs, compared to 10.9 percent of candidates who appeared to be Muslims. About 10.6 percent of candidates who appeared to be straight males received call backs, and the share of call backs for seemingly gay males was nearly identical.

The strength of this type of study is that researchers are able to study more naturally the impact of traits that traditionally are not revealed on a résumé. While some correspondence tests have tried to signal religious affiliation or sexual orientation through "extracurricular activities" described on CVs, this type of disclosure might reveal more than religion or sexual identity: the employers might be reacting to someone's activism regarding their religion or sexuality, not their religion or sexuality per se.

While Acquisti and Fong (2013) focus on the impact of gay status for males and religion, their methods could be used to study the effect of other interesting and until now mostly unexplored characteristics. For example, would the size of a candidate's network have an effect? Would employers infer that a "popular" candidate has valuable social skills? Would attractive-seeming candidates receive more call backs, or would attempts to "choreograph" one's online presence be viewed as an undesirable trait? Would candidates who reveal their family status be treated differently than candidates who are more private? Clearly, online field experiments offer a rich landscape for studying "what employers want."

2.5 Limitations of correspondence studies

While correspondence studies address some key weaknesses of the audit methodology, they share other weaknesses with audit studies and have some unique limitations of their own.

Both types of studies can only inform us about the average differences in hiring behavior. But, we generally think that applicants care about the marginal response. Real job seekers are likely to adjust their behavior during the search process in a strategic manner: in other words, they will not apply for positions in a random fashion. So, while informative about discrimination on average in a given setting, correspondence and audit studies are not informative about discrimination at the margin, when real job seekers have fully optimized their job search strategy to the realities of the workforce. This is related to a criticism raised by Heckman and Siegelman in their contribution to "Clear and

---

[12] Measuring the exact number of visits to a social or professional networking profile is not possible for several reasons. However, using Google Adwords "Keyword Tool" statistics and Professional Network "Premiere" account statistics, the authors estimate that at most one-third of the employers tried to access the profile of the candidates.

Convincing Evidence: Measurement of Discrimination in America" when they challenge the use of newspaper advertisements in audit studies, referring to previous findings that most jobs are found through direct contact with a firm or via informal channels like family and friends:

> [C]ollege students masqueraded as blue collar workers seeking entry-level jobs. Apart from the ethical issues involved, this raises the potentially important problem that the Urban Institute actors may not experience what actually occurs in the these labor markets among real participants (Fix and Struyk, 1993).

Another drawback of field studies (both audit and correspondence) is that fictitious applicants typically only apply to entry-level jobs. There are a few exceptions, and some of the studies we describe previously use applications to skilled and experienced positions. But the bottom line is that many jobs are never advertised, and the extent of discrimination in the workplace overall may be quite different from the discrimination that is measured at the entry point in the labor market.

Yet another limitation of field studies (both audit and correspondence) is that the outcome variables that can be studied are typically very coarse. In fact, in this regard, the correspondence studies are inferior to the audit studies. Most of the time, interview invitations or rental offers ("call-back rates") are the only outcomes captured by field experiments (one exception being Doleac and Stein, 2013, who were able to track transactions—sales of iPods through local online markets—all the way to completion). Obviously, because there is no real applicant, the correspondence study methodology cannot be taken to the interview stage, job-offer stage, or wage-setting stage—or to the stage at which people sign a lease on an apartment. Theoretically, all of this can be measured when auditors are used. However, even audit studies do not allow one to track other important outcomes, such as work hours, working conditions, or promotions. The binary outcome in the typical correspondence studies (call back or not) raises important issues about how to conduct some of the analysis. What should be inferred about discrimination for the employers that do not call back any of the fictitious applicants? Is that evidence of "symmetric treatment"? Riach and Rich (2002) argue that if both the majority and minority candidate are rejected, that does not constitute evidence of equal treatment. Only with more continuous outcome variables—ones that typically are not available to the researcher, such as the ranking of the job candidates by the employer—would it be possible to resolve this tension.

Both correspondence and audit studies have also raised ethical concerns. Employers' time is bound to be a scarce resource, and researchers who carry out these studies are using it without the involved parties' consent. A positive take on this ethical issue is the study by List (2009) who argues that "[w]hen the research makes participants better off, benefits society, and confers anonymity and just treatment to all subjects, the lack of informed consent seems defensible." However, many people outside the scientific community would probably disagree (In fact, List (2009) refers to experiments where subjects are compensated; in the case of correspondence tests, we did not come across experiments where employers were actually compensated for their time.).[13]

Another underappreciated ethical issue is that when the "applicant" declines an offer, things other than the anticipated consumption of the employer's attention can occur. The employer may "learn" (become convinced) that applicants with the attributes similar to those of the fictitious candidate are unlikely to accept offers. If this really happens, it is possible that some real job applicants will be treated differently (possibly less favorably) due to prior communication with the researcher pretending to be a job candidate. But it is also possible that after observing a rejection or two from fictitious candidates, an employer may end up having the impression that the market is tighter than he or she thought; screening could then become less intense, which might be beneficial for real jobless candidates (but potentially detrimental for the employers).[14]

A subtler criticism of the correspondence and audit methods by Heckman and Siegelman (1993) has been recently revisited by Neumark (2012). Heckman and Siegelman (1993) show that a troubling result emerges in audit or correspondence studies because the outcome of interest is not linear in productivity (as it might be for a wage offer) but instead is nonlinear. That is, we think that in the hiring process firms evaluate a job applicant's productivity relative to a standard and offer the applicant a job (or a callback) if the standard is met. This nonlinear relationship can raise issues for any inferences of discrimination based on call backs if employers believe that blacks and whites differ in the variance of their unobserved productivity.

Consider, for example, the case where employers believe that the variance of unobserved productivity is higher for whites than for blacks. The correspondence and audit methods make black and white applicants equal on observable productivity characteristic X_1. However, no information is conveyed on a second, unobservable productivity-related characteristic, X_2. Because an employer will offer a job interview only if it perceives or expects the sum $\beta_1 X_1 + X_2$ to be sufficiently high, when X_1 is set at a low level the employer has to believe that X_2 is high (or likely to be high) in order to offer an interview. Even though the employer does not observe X_2, if the employer knows that the variance of X_2 is higher for whites, the employer correctly concludes

[13] The method of correspondence studies has also been taken to the dating market (e.g., Ong and Wang, 2015). We do not review these contributions here because it is a bit difficult to talk about discrimination when referring to the choice of whom to date, but the ethical dilemma of putting fake applications on a dating website also seems particularly acute. As a conceptual aside, it is also not at all clear that one needs to create a fictitious profile on dating websites, as it is already possible for the researchers to observe exactly the same information that the user has when making a decision. There is thus no "unobserved" variable biasing the analysis and no information to be gained from fictitious résumés. The exercise can be performed with observational data (Fisman et al., 2008; Hitsch et al., 2010; Banerjee et al., 2009). This makes the ethical concern particularly salient.

[14] This particular issue can be at least partially addressed by debriefing employers ex-post about them having been part of a research study.

that whites are more likely than blacks to have a sufficiently high sum of $\beta_1 X_1 + X_2$, by virtue of the simple fact that fewer blacks have very high values of X_2. Employers will therefore be less likely to offer jobs to blacks than to whites, even though the observed average of X_1 is the same for blacks and whites, as is the unobserved average of X_2. The opposite holds if X_1 is set at a high value: in this case, the employer only needs to avoid very low values of X_2, which will be more common for the higher variance whites. In other words, Heckman and Siegelman (1993) show that, even when there are equal group averages of both observed and unobserved variables, an audit or correspondence study can generate biased estimates, with spurious evidence of discrimination in either direction or spurious evidence of its absence.

Building constructively on this criticism, Neumark (2012) shows that if a correspondence study includes variation in observable measures of applicants' quality that affect hiring outcomes, an unbiased estimate of discrimination can be recovered even when there are group differences in the variances of the unobservables. Neumark explains how his method can be easily implemented in any future correspondence study. All that is needed is for the résumés or applicants to include some variation in characteristics that affect the probability of being hired.[15]

Finally, it is remarkable that after literally dozens of correspondence studies, there has been only limited refinement of the methodology to help discriminate between different theories of the differential treatment that is being consistently observed. Employers must try their best to infer future productivity of a candidate based on limited information. That is, applicants who belong to different groups may experience different treatment even if discrimination, as understood by Becker (differential treatment is motivated by prejudice), is absent and only statistical discrimination is at play. Attributes beyond those intended by the researcher may be inferred by the recipient. For example, Fryer and Levitt (2004) suggest that black names may "provide a useful signal to employers about labor market productivity after controlling for information on the résumé." This is clearly true for age, as we noted, but this may also be true for race if the choice of a black name is a political statement by the parent, accompanied by a different attitude toward schooling and obedience. More broadly, as we already mentioned several times, even if in general employers do not see a particular identity as a sign of lower productivity (or want to discriminate based on it), they may infer something from the fact that the person is wearing it on their sleeves. After all, there was no difference in call-back rate according to

---

[15] The method rests on three types of assumptions. First, it is based on an assumed binary threshold model of hiring that asks whether the perceived productivity of a worker exceeds a standard. Second, it imposes a parametric assumption about the distribution of unobservables. Finally, it relies on an additional identifying assumption that some applicant characteristics affect the perceived productivity of workers, and hence hiring, and that the effects of these characteristics on perceived productivity does not vary with group membership.

either religion or sexuality when the information was available to the employer online but not directly reported in the résumé (Acquisti and Fong, 2013).

The only approach that has been used repeatedly by researchers to try to separate statistical from taste-based discrimination has been to compare differential gaps in outcomes between pairs of minority and nonminority applicants with weaker or stronger productivity attributes on their résumés or applications. As more productivity-relevant information is included on the résumé, average differences in unobservable characteristics between the minority and nonminority applicants are reduced, and statistical discrimination should also be reduced; however, it is clear that this remains a very indirect way to try to isolate taste-based discrimination among employers or landlords.

In this regard, a recent paper that breaks the mold of the typical correspondence study and deserves particular attention is the study by Bartoš et al. (2013). This paper is remarkable in its ability to push the correspondence study methodology forward, think beyond the pure call-back data, and refine our theories of discrimination.

The paper links two important ideas: attention is a scarce resource, and lack of information about individual candidates drives discrimination in selection decisions— or, in other words, statistical discrimination is an important factor in selection decisions. While the existing models of statistical discrimination implicitly assume that individuals are fully attentive to available information, the paper develops and tests a model in which knowledge of minority status impacts the level of attention to information about an individual and how the resulting asymmetry in acquired information across groups—denoted "attention discrimination"—can lead to discrimination. In particular, the authors argue that in markets where only a small share of applicants is considered above the bar for selection, such as the labor market, negative stereotypes are predicted to lower attention. On the other hand, the effect is opposite in markets where most applicants are selected, such as the rental housing market.

Bartoš et al. (2013) test for such "attention discrimination" in two field experiments: one in the labor market and one in the rental market, where they can monitor the decision maker's information acquisition about applicants through visits to hyperlinks containing résumés and personal websites (respectively). They created personal websites for fictitious applicants and submitted rental applications in the Czech Republic and job applications in both Germany and the Czech Republic. The advantage of using hyperlinks to résumés and personal sites is that the researchers were able to track the exact number of visitors to the personal profile and, therefore, the share of landlords and employers who allocated additional attention to an applicant. Hence, the study was able to assess whether a minority-sounding name (1) leads to differential call backs and (2) causes less or more search.

Like the prior literature, Bartoš et al. (2013) find evidence of discrimination against minority applicants in both the housing and labor markets. Most interesting, though, are their findings regarding attention allocation. In the labor markets, in both Germany and the Czech Republic, employers put more effort in opening and reading résumés of majority compared to minority candidates. In contrast, in the rental housing market, landlords acquire more information about minority compared to majority candidates through their personal sites.

The findings can best be explained by a model where attention is endogenously determined by the type of the market. When the choosing entity needs to select "top candidates," it will allocate attention to candidates belonging to the group that, according to its priors, is stronger. In markets where most candidates are accepted, some kind of a threshold rule might be used, and the choosing entity will want to eliminate the weakest candidates. In that case (e.g., a housing market), more attention would optimally be allocated to members of the group that is a priori viewed less favorably. The model implies persistence of discrimination in selection decisions, even if information about individuals is available and there are no differences in preferences. The model also implies lower returns to employment qualifications for negatively stereotyped groups (as their credentials are less likely to be reviewed). From a policy perspective, the model and results of this paper also highlight the crucial role of the timing of when a group attribute is revealed.

Bartoš et al. (2013) represents a great example of how the résumé study infrastructure can be pushed forward to deliver deeper learning, cleaner links to specific theories of why differential treatment is taking place, and suggestions about policies that might be most effective to address it. More efforts along these lines would help revitalize this literature.

We now turn to other approaches to measuring discrimination, often more "lab-based" and more closely tied to a particular model of the root of discrimination.

2.6 Implicit association tests

The implicit Association Test (IAT) is a computer-based test that was first introduced by Greenwald et al. (1998). Developed by social psychologists Greenwald, Nosek, and Banaji, as well as other collaborators, the IAT provides a method to indirectly measure the strength of association between two concepts. This test relies on the idea that the easier a mental task is, the quicker it can be performed. When completing an IAT, a subject is asked to classify, as rapidly as possible, concepts or objects into one of four categories with only two responses (left or right). The logic of the IAT is that it will be easier to perform the task when objects that should get the same answer (left or right) somehow "go together".[16]

The typical IAT consists of seven "phases," including practice phases to acquaint the subject with the stimuli materials and rules. Consider, for example, an IAT designed to assess association strengths between categories of black and white and attributes of good and bad. The practice phases are used with the materials and sorting rules. In the first,

---

[16] See Lane et al. (2007) for an excellent introduction to IATs.

subjects would only be presented with faces as stimuli and be asked to assign white faces to one side and black faces to the other; in the second, subjects would only be presented with words as stimuli and be asked to assign pleasant words to one side and unpleasant words to the other. In the test phases, subjects are asked to simultaneously sort through stimuli representing the four concepts (black, white, good, and bad) but with again only two responses (left side or right side). In two of the test phases (the "stereotypical" test phases), items representing white and good (e.g., white faces and words such as wonderful) need to be placed on one side of the screen and items representing the concepts black and bad (e.g., black faces and words such as horrible) on the other. In the other two test phases (the "nonstereotypical" phases), items representing the concepts of black and good need be placed on one side of the screen and items representing the concepts of white and bad on the other. The extent to which an individual dislikes black faces (in this case) is then measured by the difference in milliseconds in response time between the stereotypical phases and the nonstereotypical phases.[17]

Two broad kinds of IAT are pertinent to discrimination: if attitudes or overall preferences are the issue, the category (e.g., black/white) is associated with words that represent good/bad (as in the example we just gave). Alternatively, one may be interested in the association between a category (e.g., male/female) and a particular trait or attribute (e.g. career/family).[18] The first kind is called an attitude IAT and the second a stereotype or belief IAT. Other types include self-esteem IATs (e.g., categories are self and other and words are either positive or negative).

Since the publication of the original IAT, there have been hundreds of IAT studies, many of which try to capture attitudes that could give rise to discrimination (against black people, Muslims, women etc.) or phenomena more akin to statistical discrimination (women and math, women and career, women and politics, etc.). The IAT has been extremely influential both within and outside academic psychology. Greenwald, McGhee, and Schwartz's original 1998 article introducing the IAT has 6689 citations in Google Scholar, as of August 2015. The findings of IAT research on discrimination have been cited to propose changing the law, educating judges, and students, etc. IATs are used increasingly as a convenient tool to measure whether attitudes respond to any particular intervention, since they can be conducted remotely, with large samples of online participants to experiments. As such, they are often used as end points in psychology experiments, as experimentation moves to online platforms.[19]

---

[17] In practice, of course, a number of choices must be made about how to use the data, and this is reviewed in the study by Greenwald et al. (2003).

[18] For example, Nosek et al. (2002) find stereotypical associations connecting male terms with traits related to science and a career, whereas female terms are found to be associated with liberal arts and family.

[19] For examples of IATs used as end points, see Lai et al. (2014).

There are a number of meta-analyses, review articles, and critical papers on the use of IATs. It is not in the scope of this paper to review all of this literature; however, the key question that is raised is what the IAT actually picks up and, relatedly, whether it is effectively associated with other predictors of discriminatory behavior and discriminatory behavior itself. Some individual studies show promising links. For example, implicit bias predicts a more negative judgment of ambiguous actions by a black target (Rudman and Lee, 2002), as well as more negative nonverbal "microbehavior" (less speaking time, less smiling, etc.) during an interaction with a black subject (McConnell and Leibold, 2001). This is important, as these microbehaviors are often posited to be the channel through which implicit bias would translate into different behavior, even among people who do not report explicit discrimination.

Some studies have also shown some mechanisms for those effects, for example, showing that participants who exhibited greater implicit distaste of black people were more likely to detect aggression in a black (but not white) face (Hugenberg and Bodenhausen, 2004). Only a few studies have investigated whether these differences in implicit attitudes are associated with different behaviors in the field. In Atlanta and Boston, doctors with stronger anti-black implicit attitudes were less likely to prescribe thrombolysis for myocardial infarction to African-American patients, compared to white patients (Green et al., 2007). Rooth (2010) tried to relate the behavior of recruiters in a correspondence study in Sweden (focusing on Arab-Muslim vs. Christian) to recruiter-level measures of implicit discrimination they collected later. Unfortunately, they were only able to interview 26 percent of the recruiters they were targeting, but among those, they did find a correlation between implicit distaste of Arabs as measured in an IAT test and the tendency to not call back a resume with an Arab-Muslim name on it.

An initial meta-analysis, conducted on 122 research reports, found that the IAT does seem to be capturing something about attitudes, perhaps more accurately than self-reports (Greenwald et al., 2009). They show that there is a strong correlation between implicit and more standard explicit measures. Moreover, the IAT appears to be a better predictor of actual behavior than explicit reports, particularly for sensitive subjects such as racial preferences (for which they have 32 samples with IAT measure, explicit measure, and questions about behavior).

However, a more recent meta-analysis by Oswald et al. (2013) questions these initial findings. Using a larger sample (which includes newer studies as well as some studies that were omitted from the earlier meta-analysis), and a slightly different aggregation method, they find much lower correlation of the IAT with various measures of discrimination than had been initially found in the 2009 meta-analysis. Explicit measures perform equally poorly, to be sure, but not much worse.

Beyond this debate (which is probably the core one to be had), IATs have been subject to a number of criticisms and questions, mainly regarding their interpretation. First, to the extent that they differ from explicit attitudes, do they reflect something "deeper" about the individuals and are they more "true" than the self-description in any sense or simply another type of attitude? Interestingly, the meta-analysis by Oswald et al. (2013) shows that there is in fact a strong correlation between different brain activities when seeing black and white faces and the IAT. This suggests that the IAT does reflect something fundamental about psychological processes. But our behavior is mediated by the social environments, exactly as our answer to a question on prejudice is mediated by this environment.

So do IATs really identify prejudice or just some raw psychological "material" that we then transform? What does it mean for someone to feel that they are not prejudiced against blacks but have their IAT showing automatic white preferences (Arkes and Tetlock, 2004)? On this last question, Banaji et al. (2004) argue that conscious unbiased attitudes cannot be relied upon in all circumstances, and that IATs may capture unconscious attitudes that may be more relevant in explaining behaviors in other circumstances. Hence, they reject the idea that "if prejudice is not explicitly spoken, it cannot reflect a prejudicial feeling" (Banaji et al., 2004). In this respect, though, the low correlation between the IAT and microbehavior is a bit troubling, as this theory would suggest that the unconscious bias translates into actual acts of discrimination via unconscious behavior.

Also, do IATs measure the prevalent culture or individual attitudes? For example: if a person identifies women with family more than with career, is she making a value judgment or stating, in a sense, a fact of life?

Whatever the resolution of these debates, the measured implicit attitudes vary considerably across people, and the robust correlations—between implicit and explicit attitudes, between the different IATs in similar domains—do seem to indicate IATs capture some signal about the individual. This does not mean that the IAT can be considered a reliable measure of the attitude of any particular individual (at best, it measures attitudes with considerable noise). However, it does mean that the IAT may be a good measurement tool for the propensity for groups to discriminate toward each other.

In this context, whatever the predictive value of the IAT for behavior, the extent to which it is affected by a particular manipulation is of interest. As economists, we may be more interested in the extent to which attitudes can be influenced (by experiences, the environment, or specific interventions), than in their pure measurement at a point in time. Using IATs as an outcome variable also helps side stepping the question of whether they represent any deep truth about anybody: while the signal may be noisy, to the extent that there is signal, this may be a useful measurement tool. As noted, after more than a decade of using the IAT mainly as a descriptive tool, studies in psychology started using them as outcomes. For example, Lai et al. (2014) set up a research contest on debiasing, where teams are given a budget of 5 minutes to interact with participants, and the outcome is the scores on a black-white attitude IAT.

In recent years, economists have also started using IATs as dependent variables. For example, Beaman et al. (2009) design and implement two IATs in West Bengal, India, to measure preferences toward female leaders and stereotypical association of women with domestic rather than political activities. They then examine the impact of exposure to female leaders on these two measures (we will discuss the results below in Section 2.7).

Lane et al. (2007) provide detailed and helpful instructions on how to build an IAT. The software that is needed to construct and analyze the test (millisecond software) is available for purchase. IATs can be designed with only verbal or image stimuli for subjects who are not literate (this is what Beaman et al., 2009 use), and although, they are more difficult in populations that have had no experience with computers and for older participants, they can be a very useful tool. As studies increasingly use electronic data collection methods (on tablets or notebooks), the extra cost of adding an IAT diminishes.

Of course, the debate in psychology does not suggest that the IAT should be considered a "magic bullet," suitable to replace any other measure of discrimination. In particular, it is probably not a substitute for good measures of actual behavior in policy interventions. Nevertheless, it can be an extremely useful intermediate variable, to understand the mechanisms beyond a result (in Beaman et al., 2009 the final end point of interest is actual voting) or, potentially, if collected beforehand, as a covariate of interest. For example, in the study by Glover et al. (2015), the IAT is used as a proxy measure of latent employer discrimination (see further details in Section 3.2.2).

2.7 Goldberg paradigm experiments

Goldberg paradigm experiments are laboratory versions of audit or correspondence studies. They are named after a 1968 experiment by Goldberg where students graded written essays, which were identical except for the male or female name of their author (Goldberg, 1968). This initial experiment demonstrated a bias: female got lower grades unless the essay was on a feminine topic. Since then, a large literature in psychology has used the Goldberg paradigm to identify discrimination against different groups and, in particular, in the resistance to female leaders.[20]

In the typical lab experiment, a group of subjects is asked to review a vignette, describing the behavior of a female or male manager, for example, or witness a confederate (male or female) simulating a leadership situation. The participants are then asked to evaluate the leader's competence or to say whether they would have liked to have them as leader for a task they may collectively perform. Reviewing a large number of such studies, Eagly et al. (1992) do not find that, on average, female leaders are evaluated significantly more negatively than male leaders. However, there are in some circumstances where they do find that female leaders are evaluated more negatively: for

---

[20] See Eagly et al. (1992) for a review and meta-analysis of the literature on such resistance to female leaders.

example, when the leadership was carried out in a masculine style (in particular, when the leader was projected to be authoritative). This supports Eagly's hypothesis of "role congruence": what people dislike is when women behave in a nonfeminine way. Since strong leaders must be assertive, but women must be demure, it makes it difficult for women to be appreciated as strong leaders.

The fact that the circumstances are artificial, and answers have minimal stake associated with them, make those experiments less relevant, on their own, than field-based correspondence tests. But one advantage of the Goldberg-style experiments is that they can be easily and, finely, manipulated, which makes them good outcome measures in field research (or field experiments). They can also be easily added to a standard survey instrument. For example, Beaman et al. (2009) seek to find out how discrimination against female leaders is affected by prior exposure. They administer two Goldberg-style experiments. In one, they ask the participants to listen to a speech by a political leader, which is read either by a female or a male actor (note that it is important that there are several male and female actors). In the second one, they discuss vignette where women or men leader make decisions that are either pro-male (investment in irrigation) or pro-female (investment in drinking water). Each individual receives a randomly selected version of the speech and vignette. The randomization is stratified by village and, hence, by prior exposure to a female leader (due to a policy of gender reservation). While this does not tell us the extent to which any single person discriminates, one can learn whether, on average, exposure to a female leader affects the extent to which individuals give lower grades to women in response to the same speech or vignette. Beaman et al. (2009) find that both men and women, but men more than women, tend to discriminate against female leaders (additional results from this study are discussed further in Section 4.1.2).

2.8 List randomization

Like correspondence tests or Goldberg experiments, list randomization (also known as item count technique, unmatched count, or list response) does not provide a measure of individual bias but can provide an estimate of the extent of discrimination in a population. They are a way of eliciting accurate answers to questions of discrimination in the presence of social desirability bias. The idea is to present the subjects with a list of N statements which are generally noncontroversial but could be true or false (e.g., I had coffee at breakfast; I like popcorn).[21] Then, a randomly selected group of people are asked a potentially controversial statement (e.g., "I would be upset if an African-American family moved next door") on top of the N noncontroversial statements. The subject only states

---

[21] As we explain below there is a tension in the choice of those questions: for maximum precision they should be behavior that almost everyone says yes or no to, but then they do not give any cover to the subject.

the number of statements with which he or she agrees. Comparing the fraction of yes among those who got N and those who got N + 1 statements gives a good measure of discrimination. And clearly no one (including the interviewer) will know how a given subject answered the controversial statement. Unlike the IAT, this method will not reveal biases that are unconscious or biases that the subject wants to deny even to himself or herself, but it will prevent the results from being affected by social desirability bias.

Early applications of list randomization to measure discrimination are Kuklinski et al. (1997a,b). Both studies found considerable racial prejudice in the American South using list randomization techniques (though not in the North). Furthermore, they found higher level of measured discrimination using this method than using direct elicitation methods; for example, respondents are more likely to disagree with a statement such as, "I am comfortable with a black family moving next door" when asked via list randomization than with a traditional survey. Likewise, Coffman et al. (2013) show that stated discrimination against gay populations is much lower in response to a direct question in the control group than when it is elicited through the list randomization method. For example, respondents were 67 percent more likely to express disapproval of an openly gay manager at work when the question is part of a list than when the question is asked directly.

A few papers have used the method to elicit attitudes toward presidential candidates. Kane et al. (2004) find no discrimination against a Jewish presidential candidate (Joe Lieberman). Martinez and Craig (2010) find that few whites in Florida seem distressed by the possibility of having a black president. However, list randomization revealed much more opposition toward the idea of a female president than opinion polls (Streb et al., 2008). As noted previously, several studies suggest that the randomized list technique yields different answers than direct elicitation. In a meta-analysis across 48 comparisons of direct report and list randomization, Holbrook and Krosnick (2010) found that 63 percent of the estimates for socially undesirable behaviors were significantly larger when elicited through list randomization. On the other hand, responses on nonsensitive behavior tend to be more similar (Tsuchiya et al., 2007).

The list randomization method is however not without issues. As we alluded to earlier, there is a fundamental tension between precision (which would require having statements to which everybody responds yes or no) and providing "cover" to the subject (which would require the opposite). The implication is that the results from list randomization methods are often quite imprecise. Gosen (2014) has also shown results tend to systematically depend on how many noncontroversial statements are included in the list, although the opposite was found in Tsuchiya et al. (2007).

In summary, list randomization could be a promising method to measure discrimination as it is less subject to social desirability bias, but since few economists have used it,[22]

---

[22]   See Karlan and Zinman (2012) for an example of an application in economics.

more work needs to be done to ascertain its usefulness in the field. In comparison to other indirect methods, list randomization is often more simple to administer (both for surveyors and respondents) but risks having low power (Droitcour et al., 1991). It would be interesting to see more research comparing measures of discrimination obtained through list randomization compared to an IAT or Goldberg-style experiment. It would also be interesting to compare how noisy these different measures are. The fact that the list randomization method can only provide an aggregate (and not individual) measure of discrimination complicates its use as an outcome variable (say, for a randomized experiment) but no more than any of the other methods we have already discussed that also only give group-level outcomes, such as the Goldberg-style experiments.

2.9 Willingness to pay

A key prediction of Becker's model of taste-based discrimination is that people should be willing to pay to interact with people of their own group. Somewhat surprisingly this prediction has not given rise to a large literature trying to evaluate the willingness to pay to discriminate. As we noted, the correspondence and audit tests tend to be based on a binary measure (interview or not, hire or not).

Until recently, the body of work that came closest to measuring such willingness to pay was a literature on the "beauty premium" motivated by Hamermesh and Biddle's (1994) finding that workers with better-than-average looks earn 10–15 percent higher wages. Analogous to the black-wage race gap, the beauty premium could be due to the fact that more beautiful workers are more productive, say because consumers prefer to interact with beautiful people (Biddle and Hamermesh, 1998; Pfann et al., 2000) or because beautiful people are more confident. Or employers may be wrong in their belief.

Mobius and Rosenblat (2006) set up a laboratory experiment where undergraduates and graduates from Tucuman, Argentina, were randomly assigned into groups of "employers" and "workers." In the experiment, "employers" had to hire "workers" to perform a maze-solving task. After a practice test (which was recorded and became the digital "resume" of the worker) and a question where the workers estimated the number of mazes they could solve in 15 minutes, each worker was matched to five employers, who saw either (1) just the resume, (2) the resume and a photo, (3) the resume and a phone interview, or (4) the resume plus an interview, plus the photograph.[23] The employers in turn saw five workers, and for each of them they decided how many mazes they thought the worker could solve. This estimate contributed to the employer's own payment. It also entered into the calculation of the actual wage of most of their workers.

---

[23] The wages of "workers" were affected by the difference between their estimation of the number of mazes and what they actually competed, therefore they were incentivized to tell the truth.

Mobius and Rosenblat show that productivity at the task is not affected by beauty (as evaluated by 50 high school students on the basis of the photograph), although worker confidence is. A rise of one standard deviation in beauty increases confidence by 13—16 percent. However, employers are willing to pay more employees who are considered to be more beautiful: in all the treatments where they can see beauty, employers are willing to pay workers more. The premium ranges between 12 and 17 percent depending on the treatment. Decomposing the beauty premium by comparing treatments, the authors estimate that 15 percent is due to the confidence channel and 40 percent each through the visual and oral stereotype channels (the fact that beauty still affects wages when the employer does not see the employee but talks to her on the phone indicate that beauty is correlated with speaking skill, perhaps another feature of the beauty channel). Interestingly, employer's estimated productivity is not affected by whether or not they know that it will actually contribute to the worker's wage. This suggests that there is little pure taste-based discrimination in this lab experiment. Employers give a premium to beautiful people because they believe (wrongly) that they will be more productive.

There are a number of limitations of this experiment, not least of all, from the point of view of this chapter, that it is a lab experiment. It is also limited to a one-shot interaction at the hiring stage. Nevertheless, it sets an interesting template for what a field experiment leveraging this methodology might look like and, in particular, does an excellent job laying out the various pieces that are needed to establish discrimination and understand the mechanism behind it.

One paper which has recently followed in Mobius and Rosenblat's footstep is the study by Rao (2013), which seeks to measure the extent to which well-off kids in India discriminate against poorer kids (in order, as we will discuss in more detail in Section 4.2, to estimate the extent to which any such discrimination is affected by forced exposure to poorer kids through an affirmative action program in education). To do so, Rao sets up an ingenious field experiment, based around team selection for a relay race. First, students from a rich private school and a poor public school, who were all present at a sporting event to support their classmates, were randomized in different sessions with different prizes for winning the race (from Rs 50 to Rs 500, which are very high stakes). After mixing for 15 minutes, they watched a series of one-on-one sprints (most of them pitting a poor student against a rich one), and then each was asked to indicate on a worksheet which of the two he wanted as teammate for the relay race. After these choices were revealed, one of the choices was picked, the teams were formed, and the relay race was run. To make sure that there was a "cost" to picking out a poorer students (if students did not like them), students had to spend 2 hours socializing with their teammate, which was announced prior to team selection. This experiment has a number of clever features. It presents children with a real choice, and by varying the stakes, it makes it clear how much (on average) students are willing to sacrifice to avoid interacting with a poor student. The sprint phase entirely and unambiguously reveals ability, so the setup is targeted to pick up pure taste-based discrimination (e.g., dislike of hanging out with a poor teammate).

The results show that there is substantial taste-based discrimination in this context: in 19 percent of the cases where the poor students is the fastest, rich students prefer to pick the rich student as a teammate anyway.[24] Discrimination does decline as the stakes increase: discrimination falls from 35 percent with the lowest stake, to 27 percent with the intermediate stake, and 5 percent in the highest stake. Fitting a structural model to the data, Rao estimates that, for students without prior exposure to poor classmates, the distaste of interacting with a poor student is worth Rs 37. That is, a student is willing to give up to Rs 37 in expected prize money to hang out with a rich student rather than a poor one.

3. CONSEQUENCES OF DISCRIMINATION

3.1 Self-expectancy effects

3.1.1 Stereotype threat and underperformance

Models of statistical discrimination explain the differential treatment of disadvantaged groups in say, hiring decisions, due to employers' inability to perfectly predict a given worker's future productivity and hence their rational decision to assign some weight to the average productivity of the worker's racial group. For example, African-Americans as a whole are categorized as less productive than whites, and employers take this supposed average difference in productivity into account when deciding whether or not to hire any African-American job candidates, given their inability to precisely predict each specific candidate's future productivity.

While discrimination emerges under the logic above as a consequence of average differences in productivity across groups, research in social psychology has provided convincing evidence for the reverse causal channel. In particular, the simple process of categorizing or "stereotyping" some groups as less productive appears to cause these groups to be less productive. This research suggests that individuals from some groups may suffer negative performance outcomes (such as lower test scores or less engagement with academics) because of the burden of the "stereotype" or "stereotype threat" (Steele and Aronson, 1995).[25] The key conjecture is that the threat of being viewed through the lens of a negative stereotype can create an anxiety that disrupts cognitive performance.

In a seminal study, Steele and Aronson (1995) demonstrated in a lab setting that inducing stereotype threat—by asking test takers to indicate their race before the

---

[24] In contrast, if a rich student is the fastest, he is picked 97 percent of the time and among two students of the same background, the fastest is picked 98 percent of the time.

[25] Defined by Steele and Aronson (1995) as a "risk of confirming, as self-characteristic, a negative stereotype about one's group."

test—significantly undermines African-Americans' performance on intellectual tasks. They also showed that reducing stereotype threat—by convincing test takers that the test was not being used to measure their abilities—can significantly improve African-Americans' performance, dramatically reducing the racial gap.

Numerous lab studies have since replicated the effects of stereotype threat both with respect to social identities other than race (e.g., gender, income class, etc.) and with respect to mediating outcomes (such as blood pressure, heart-rate variability, performance expectations, effort, etc.).[26]

The rest of the social psychology research on the stereotype threat has also focused on documenting methods that can undo or undermine the threat of the stereotype. One line of research has addressed the underlying message of the stereotype—that stereotyped individuals are inherently limited because of their group membership. Thus, if participants can be convinced that intelligence is not a fixed trait, but a malleable quality that can be increased with hard work and effort, they may be less prone to stereotyping. Levy et al. (1998) present evidence consistent with this idea. Descriptively, they find that people holding an entity theory of intelligence (i.e., intelligence is a fixed trait) made more stereotypical trait judgments of ethnic and occupational groups than those who believed that intelligence is malleable. Moreover, in a small lab experiment, they found that manipulating implicit theories affected the level of stereotyping, at least temporarily. In the experiment, 155 introductory to psychology students were randomly assigned to a fake "scientific" article that either presented evidence for an entity (fixed) or an incremental (malleable) view of personality. After reading the article, they were presented with questions in which they had to rate the extent to which a series of 15 traits accurately describe certain occupational groups (teachers, doctors, lawyers, and politicians) and ethnic groups (African-Americans, Asians, and Latinos). To try to reduce the likelihood of participants recognizing the link between the article and the questions, the researchers told participants that the questions were for a separate study and that they would be asked questions on the content of the article later. The experiment found a small but significant effect: those who read the article that argued for fixed personality were less likely to

---

[26] While most of these lab studies have been conducted by social psychologists, a few have been performed by economists. For example, Dee (2009) ran a lab experiment with student athletes and nonathlete students at Swarthmore College, randomly assigning some of them to a treatment that primed their awareness of a stereotyped identity (i.e., student athlete). He finds that the treatment reduced the test-score performance of athletes relative to nonathletes by 14 percent. Also, Hoff and Pandey (2006) present evidence from a caste priming experiment in Uttar Pradesh, India. Among 321 high-caste and 321 low-caste junior high school male student volunteers, there were no caste differences in performance in an incentivized maze-solving task when caste was not publicly revealed, but making caste salient created a large and robust caste gap in performance. However, the mechanisms for the underperformance in this case seems quite different from the hypothesized mechanism in the social psychology literature. In particular, the authors find that when a nonhuman factor influencing rewards received for the maze-solving task (a random draw) was introduced, the caste gap disappeared. The results suggest that when caste identity is salient, low-caste subjects anticipate that their effort will be poorly rewarded.

believe traits can change and more likely to rate stereotypical traits as highly descriptive of their respective groups.

Similarly, in a lab experiment, Aronson et al. (2002) assign white and black students to one of three conditions to assess the impact of an intervention designed to reduce stereotype threat. In two conditions, students were asked to write a letter of encouragement to a younger student who was experiencing academic struggles. In one of these conditions, students were prompted to endorse a view of intelligence as malleable, "like a muscle" that can grow with work and effort. In the second condition, students endorsed the view that there exist different types of intelligence. The third condition served as a control condition in which students were not asked to compose a letter. Several days after the intervention, all students were asked to indicate their identification with and enjoyment of academics. Results showed that black students in particular were more likely to report enjoying and valuing education if they had written a letter endorsing malleable intelligence. In addition, grades collected 9 weeks following the intervention were significantly higher for blacks in the malleable intelligence condition. Whites showed a similar, though statistically marginal, effect.[27]

While most research on stereotype threat, and how to undo it, has taken place in the lab, a few interesting field studies have also been conducted by social psychologists. Schools, where test-taking and performance measurements are part of normal operations, have provided a natural setting for much of this field research.

Good et al. (2003) performed a field experiment to test methods for helping female, minority, and low-income adolescents overcome the effects of stereotype threat and, consequently, improve their standardized test scores. Specifically, seventh-grade students in the experimental conditions were mentored by college students who encouraged them either to view intelligence as malleable or to attribute academic difficulties in the seventh grade to the novelty of the educational setting. Results showed that females in both experimental conditions earned significantly higher math standardized test scores than females in the control condition. Similarly, the students—who were largely black or Hispanic and low-income adolescents—in the experimental conditions earned significantly higher reading standardized test scores than students in the control condition. Blackwell et al. (2007) based a field experiment on the laboratory finding on "malleable intelligence." They randomly selected half of a group of 95 mainly African-American and Hispanic seventh graders to participate in an 8-week training on the theory of malleable intelligence based on interventions that had been successful in the lab (25 minutes per week, in the students' classroom). In the control condition, student also received small

---

[27] It is important to note that for this experiment, while the randomized interventions took place in the lab, outcomes are measured (1) on naturally occurring tasks outside the lab and (2) quite a long time after the interventions took place; both of these features are important strengths of this experiment compared to the standard "stereotype threat" lab experiments.

group coaching but not on this theory. Students in the experimental conditions obtained higher grades.

Good et al. (2008) also conducted a field experiment where they explored stereotype threat and its negation in high-level college math courses that typically serve as gateways to careers in math and science. Male and female students in the last course of an advanced university calculus sequence were given a practice test containing items similar to those found on the Graduate Record Examination (GRE) standardized test. All students were told that the test was "aimed at measuring your mathematical abilities" (stereotype threat) but half of the students additionally were assured that "this mathematics test has not shown any gender differences in performance or mathematics ability" (stereotype threat negation). Test performance was higher for women than men in the stereotype threat negation condition but was equivalent in the stereotype threat condition.

In a related field study, Cohen et al. (2006) reduced the black–white Grade point average (GPA) gap among low-income middle school students by affirming the students' self-concepts (and presumably inoculating them from stereotype threat) at the beginning of the school term. The intervention is very light touch: students are asked to write a series of short essays focusing on a self-affirming value. The authors first found short-term impacts, and then, most remarkably, fairly large long-term impacts: over 2 years after the intervention, the average GPA of an African-American student who participated in the essay writing was 0.24 higher than that of the control group (Cohen et al., 2009). Most of the effects is concentrated among those who were initially low achieving. These are remarkable numbers, especially since the effects of most education interventions tend to fade. The authors speculate that the long-term benefits may be due to the fact that initial psychological state sets out a self-fulfilling trajectory.

Cohen's work has since then been replicated and extended in other similar contexts, and Dweck and Cohen's initial insights have helped jumpstart a subfield of psychology called "mindset studies." Yeager et al. (2014) experiment with "wise feedback," an intervention where high school students are given critical feedback on their written work, alongside with a note emphasizing the high standard of the teachers and the belief that the student can succeed. The intervention reduces mistrust among African-American students and improves the quality of the final product.[28]

3.1.2 Identity and preferences
The "stereotype threat" literature can be viewed as part of a broader literature on how self-identity considerations may affect behavior and preferences of disadvantaged groups and

---

[28] A background paper written for a White House conference gives a good overview of the literature on mindset studies (Yeager et al., 2013).

ultimately may perpetuate gaps in economic outcomes. The same way that women may do poorly on a math test when reminded of their gender (due to the anxiety-inducing burden of the stereotype of "girls not being good at math"), they may also show low risk preferences when reminded of their gender (if nurtured with the behavioral norm that "girls should not take risk" by gender-biased parents and/or teachers).

Against the backdrop of a large literature in social psychology that has tested the self-categorization theory and the cognitive mechanisms through which it operates,[29] a few recent papers in economics have leveraged the lab environment to learn more about how various social identities relate to preference parameters, such as risk, time, and social preferences.

For example, Benjamin et al. (2010) explore the effect of racial and gender category norms on time and risk preferences. In a laboratory setting, they study how making salient a specific aspect of one's social identity affects subjects' likelihood to make riskier choices or more patient choices. From a methodological perspective, the study consists of temporarily making more salient ("priming") a certain social category (as is done in the "stereotype threat" literature) and seeing how the subjects' choices are affected. For example, the gender identity salience manipulation is done through a questionnaire included in the beginning of the experiment in which subjects are asked to identify their gender and their opinion regarding living on a coed versus single-sex dormitory floor. The study uncovers some interesting patterns with respect to racial identity. For example, priming a subject's Asian-American identity makes the subject more patient. Hence, an Asian-American identity might partly contribute to the higher average level of human capital accumulation in this racial group.

However, making gender salient appears to have no significant effects on either men's or women's patience or their level of risk aversion. Of course, it is possible that the priming performed in this experiment was too weak to temporarily affect preferences. In other words, it is difficult to affirmatively conclude from these nonresults that gender identity norms are not culturally reinforcing whatever biological differences may exist between the sex in the willingness to take risks.

Another lab study aimed at assessing how social preferences are affected by gender identity is the study by Boschini et al. (2009). The question under study here is whether gender identity priming affects subjects' level of altruism. The experiment consists of comparing behavior in a dictator game for subjects whose gender identity has been primed versus not primed. The results indicate that the priming does affect behavior but only when the subjects are assigned to mixed-gender groups. Moreover, the effect is driven by males: men are sensitive to priming and become less generous in a mixed-gender setting when primed with their male identity. Women do not appear to respond to the treatment.

---

[29] See for example Reicher and Levine (1994), Forehand et al. (2002), and LeBoeuf et al. (2010).

As far as we are aware of, no field experiment exists on how social identity affects preferences and behaviors outside of the mindset literature discussed previously, which focuses on education and on adolescents. It seems worthwhile for future research to consider such work. Interventions might be designed to emphasize a "default" social identity that may be counterproductive for that social group's performance against an "alternative" social identity. For example, while deciding to work hard toward completing college coursework for a young black father might be uncool because it is "acting too white," the decision might resonate much more when his identity as a "father" is being primed. Moreover, specific interventions might be designed to simply undo or undermine the power of the social identity norms when they work toward reinforcing differences in behaviors and outcomes between groups. If women decide against applying for a job in a high-risk but also high-return occupation because of internalized conservative social norms about "what is appropriate work for a woman," it might be possible to undermine the pull of this conservative norm with counteractive "messaging," in the same spirit as what has been done to undermine the burden of the stereotype in the "stereotype threat" literature. Such interventions might be particularly powerful if the timing of the counteractive "messaging" is close to when women are making these important career choices (e.g., when applying for school or on a job search website or when considering which contact in their LinkedIn network to reach out to).

3.2 Expectancy effects and self-fulfilling prophecies
3.2.1 Pygmalion and Golem effects

Suppose minority and majority workers have similar inherent abilities. How could differential beliefs about their abilities persist? One explanation is that employers' beliefs that minorities are on average less productive are self-reinforcing (Arrow, 1973; Coate and Loury, 1993). This could happen for two reasons. First, minority and majority workers may rationally make different skill investment or effort choices in the face of the beliefs of their employers. A minority worker may see less value in investing in her skills if she knows that the employers will be slow in updating their beliefs and hence less likely to promote her. Second, the employers themselves may invest less in the minority workers (e.g., investing in training) if they do not believe that the workers will be "up to the task." In both cases, employers' beliefs about minority workers will be self-fulfilling.

The social psychology literature offers multiple demonstrations of such self-fulfilling prophecies.[30] Interestingly, most of these demonstrations took place in the field.

---

[30] The first self-fulfilling prophecy to be investigated extensively in psychology was the experimenter effect. The experimenter effect refers to the possibility of the experimenter influencing subjects to respond to the treatment in a way that conforms to the experimenter's expectations. Rosenthal (1963) summarized a dozen experimenter-effect studies and wondered whether similar interpersonal expectation effects occur among physicians, psychotherapists, employers, and teachers.

The earlier work on self-fulfilling prophecies in the social psychology focused on how heightened expectations can be self-fulfilling. In a seminal study, Rosenthal and Jacobson (1968) conducted a field experiment in a US public elementary school (Oak School). Teachers were deceived into believing that a set of one-fifth of their class were expected to develop ("blossom and spurt") much faster than the rest, as measured by IQ points (supposedly measured by the Harvard test of inflicted acquisition). In fact, this set was randomly selected. The main outcome measure was an IQ test (Test of General Ability), administered at the start of the school year (pretest) and at 4 months (end of first semester), 8 months (end of second semester and of first year of school), and 20 months (end of second school year with a different teacher). Rosenthal and Jacobson showed that the students for whom teachers had raised expectations had faster IQ gains than control students in the same classes (the treatment children gained 12 IQ points over the course of the year, and the control children gained 8), with the biggest effect on first and second grade children by the end of the first year. Rosenthal and Jacobson dubbed this boost in achievement driven by teachers' beliefs the "Pygmalion effect."

The Pygmalion effect in the classroom was subsequently studied intensively[31] and criticized extensively. Snow (1995) reanalyzed the data from the original experiment, highlighting that approximately 35 percent of the IQ observations fall out of the normal range and that there are several observations which have rapid growth in pretest and post-test scores (e.g., increasing from 17 to 110). He finds that the expectancy effect on IQ disappears when these outlier scores are omitted. A relatively recent review of the literature (including a balanced review of the meta-analysis and the various critics) concludes that while the Pygmalion effect in the classroom is real, it is probably fairly modest (Jussim and Harber, 2005).

Since this early work, social psychologists have demonstrated the self-fulfilling nature of leaders' expectations in several other field settings and have tried to better understand the underlying mechanisms. Rosenthal (1994) and Eden (1992) provide a review of much of the work in this literature. For example, Eden and Shani (1982) replicated the original design and results of Rosenthal and Jacobson (1968) in the Israeli Defense Forces. But they also concluded, based on additional survey work to complement the randomized controlled trial, that leadership behavior was a key mediator in generating the Pygmalion effect.

Also using the Israeli Defense Forces as a field, Eden and Ravid (1982) interestingly combined expectancy and self-expectancy manipulations in a single study. Trainees included 60 men in the first half-year of military duty enrolled in a 7-week clerical course divided into five training groups, each instructed by a commander. To produce the

---

[31] See Dusek et al. (1985) and Rosenthal and Rubin (1978), which was one of the first meta-analysis in psychology and was based on 345 studies and Rosenthal, 1994, which updates it for reviews.

Pygmalion effect, a random quarter of each instructor's trainees were described to the instructor as having high success potential. Another random quarter was told directly by a psychologist in a brief personal interview that they had high success potential, in order to induce high self-expectancy. The remaining trainees served as controls. Learning performance was significantly higher in both high expectancy groups than in controls, confirming the Pygmalion hypothesis and the additional hypothesis that inducing high self-expectations similarly enhances trainee performance. Interestingly, while several instructors were unexpectedly relieved midway through the course, the hypothesized performance differentials continued even though the authors abstained from refreshing the expectancy induction among the substitute instructors, reflecting the possible durability of expectancy effects. Finally, Eden and Ravid (1982) also showed that equity considerations among the trainees likely played a mediating role: trainees in both of the high expectancy conditions reported feelings of overreward, which may have motivated them to improve their performance.

While the Pygmalion literature shows that the self-fulfilling nature of raising leaders' expectations, another branch of this literature also demonstrated the self-fulfilling nature of lowering those expectations. Psychologists have dubbed this the "Golem effect".

There have been far fewer studies on the Golem effect than the Pygmalion effect, given the trickier ethical issues associated with lowering leaders' expectations (Reynolds, 2007). This challenge has led to research designs that are not quite as "clean" as those used to demonstrate the Pygmalion effect. For example, Oz and Eden (1994) randomly led treatment-assigned squad leaders (n = 17) in a military unit to believe that low scores on physical fitness tests were not indicative of subordinates' ineptitude, while control squad leaders (n = 17) were not told how to interpret test scores. Tests indicated that low-scoring individuals in the experimental squads improved more than those in the control squads. While the researchers employed a respectable research design and were cautious to abide by ethical standards, the sample was extremely small and the researchers did not directly attempt to lower supervisors' expectations.

Given the challenge of doing research on the Golem effect, an alternative approach in the literature has been to rely on natural variation in leaders' expectations, rather than exogenously varying those expectations. For example, Babad et al. (1982) studied expectation effects among physical education student teachers. They found that pupils about whom they imparted high expectations to the instructors performed best (i.e., the standard design for a demonstration of the "Pygmalion effect"). However, they also found that pupils toward whom instructors naturally harbored low expectations performed worse than those regarding whom they had high or intermediate natural expectations, consistent with a "Golem effect."

A recent paper (Kondylis et al., 2015) demonstrates the power of self-fulfilling prophecy. In villages, either women or men were randomly selected to learn a new technology and teach it to others. Women retained more information from the training and those who were trained by them did in fact learn more. But women ended up performing much worse in terms of the number of farmers they convinced because other farmers perceived women as less able and, hence, paid less attention to their messages.

3.2.2 Endogenous responses to bias

While the Pygmalion and Golem effects demonstrate the self-fulfilling nature of leaders' expectations about performance on that performance, they are not directly tied to discrimination. Are leaders' biases against some groups also endogenously affecting the performance of these groups? Two recent field studies in the economics literature provide what we believe is the first field-based answers to this question. Conceptually, these studies follow a very similar research approach to that in the study by Babad et al. (1982) to demonstrate the relevance of self-fulfilling prophecies as an explanation for persistent differences in performance between different groups of workers or students. Specifically, rather than "artificially" priming leaders to vary their level of bias, the analysis relies on randomly assigning those trainees to leaders who are known to have different levels of bias. To be clear, the limit of this design compared to the preferred "Pygmalion design" is that any unobserved factors that are systematically correlated to different levels of biases among leaders cannot be formally ruled out as an explanation for the findings. However, the two papers below take several ingenious steps to deal with this concern.

Glover et al. (2015) studied cashiers in a French grocery store chain, a sizable share of whom were of North African and Sub-Saharan African origin. They assess whether cashiers performed worse on the days when they were assigned to a manager who was more biased against their group. They measured managers' bias toward workers of different origins using an IAT test. The cashiers in these stores worked with different managers on different days and had virtually no control over their schedule, allowing the authors to use the quasi-randomness of the schedules to assess the causal effect of being paired with a more biased manager. To address the difficulty raised previously of manager bias being correlated with some other manager characteristics that might also affect employee performance (for example, more biased managers might also be less skilled), they use a difference-in-difference methodology, comparing the change in minority workers' performance under biased and nonbiased managers with the change in nonminority workers' performance under these two types of managers. They find that on days when they are scheduled to work with biased managers, minority cashiers are more likely to be absent. When they do come to work, they spend less time at work; in particular, they are much less likely to stay after their shift ends and they scan articles more slowly and take longer between customers.

Glover et al. (2015) also report interesting complementary survey evidence to better understand mechanisms. They do not find that minority workers report that they dislike working with biased managers more, or that biased managers dislike them, or that biased managers make them feel less confident in their abilities. However, they do find evidence that biased managers put less effort into managing minority workers. Minority workers report that biased managers were less likely to come over to their cashier stations and that biased managers demanded less effort from them. Consistent with this, they find that the effect of manager bias grows during the contract, perhaps as workers may learn that they are not being monitored by biased managers.

Lavy and Sand (2015) estimate the effect of primary school teachers' gender biases on boys' and girls' academic achievements during middle and high school, as well as on the choice of advanced-level courses in math and sciences during high school. In particular, they tracked three cohorts of students from primary school to high school in Tel-Aviv, Israel. They measured teachers' gender-biased behavior by comparing their average marking of boys' and girls' in a "nonblind" classroom exam to the respective means in a "blind" national exam marked anonymously. For identification, the authors rely on the conditional random assignments of teachers and students to classes within a given grade and a primary school. They compare outcomes for students who attended the same primary school but were randomly assigned to different teachers, who have different degrees of stereotypical attitudes. They find that being assigned to a more gender-biased teacher at early stage of schooling has long-run implications for occupational choices and hence likely subsequent earnings in adulthood. Specifically, teachers' overassessment of boys in a specific subject has a positive and significant effect on boys' achievements in the national test on that subject administered during middle and high school, while it has a significant negative effect on girls'. In addition, assignment to primary school math teachers favoring boys over girls encourages boys and discourages girls from engagement in advanced math courses offered in high school.

3.3 Discrimination in politics and inequality across groups

A direct consequence of discrimination in politics and other leadership positions is that there are fewer members of the discriminated group with the power to act in the interests of others in their group. In a standard median voter world, the underrepresentation of women or other subordinate groups in politics would matter less, as elected politicians would endeavor to represent the interest of the median voter. But if politicians cannot commit to a particular political platform, and their group membership eventually determines the type of policies they will implement, then the lack of representation at the top means that the underrepresented groups in society will get worse outcomes (Besley and Coate, 1997; Pande, 2003). This would also occur if the absence of a leader means that the underrepresented groups find that they cannot express their preferences in the political arena.

The best evidence on the consequences of discrimination in politics comes from studies that have evaluated what happens to the underrepresented groups when they finally gain political representation. A few observational studies have exploited exogenous shocks to representation due to close elections; a few other papers have also studied nonrandomized variation in mandates.[32] There have also been a set of studies that exploit the random selection of places that have to elect a leader from a historically underrepresented group (caste, tribe, or gender) in India's local governments. Comparing villages that were randomly selected to receive either a male or female head, Chattopadhyay and Duflo (2004) find that female leaders spend more on goods that women prefer, compared to those that men prefer. Beaman et al. (2010) replicate the results over a longer period. Using a data set that covers a larger number of states, they find that the results persist over time, and that investments in drinking water (a preferred good for women) continue to be higher even after the seat is not reserved anymore and women have (generally) left power.[33] Iyer et al. (2012) show that greater female representation (in local governments) is related to more crimes against women; using a household-level crime victimization survey in Rajasthan; they however show that the increase is not due to an actual increase in the amount of crimes but rather greater willingness to report such crimes. Finally, Chattopadhyay and Duflo (2004) further find that village leaders from scheduled castes invest more in scheduled castes hamlets.[34]

3.4 Benefits of diversity?

Discrimination leads to less-diverse firms, legislative assemblies, etc., but does diversity in itself matter for society? What are the implications of the low diversity that discrimination may generate for the performance of organizations and society in general?

3.4.1 Does homogeneity hurt or help productivity?

A long literature in political economy and development has tended to emphasize the cost of diversity, in particular ethnic diversity. If members of different groups do not like each other, diversity creates holdups, breeds conflicts, makes it difficult to agree on public good provision, etc.

Lang (1986) proposes that the roots of discrimination are communication difficulties across different groups (what he calls "language communities"). A similar argument is made by Lazear (1999). In that view of the world, segregation arises naturally, because homogenous groups are more productive (since communication within them is faster and easier). More homogeneous groups will create a trusting environment where people can work better together. While the minority will suffer as a result, the short-run

---

[32] See Pande (2003), Clots-Figueras (2009, 2011), and Rehavi (2007) for examples.

[33] Bardhan et al. (2010) compare places before and after reservation and do not find a difference in what leaders do, but since there seems to be a lingering effect of quota on pro-female policies, this finding might not be so surprising.

[34] Dunning and Nilekani (2013) find little impact of the reservation on distribution of goods by ethnic group and a strong impact of parties, but they use a regression discontinuity design strategy rather than focusing on a states where the assignment is random.

356 Handbook of Field Experiments

equilibrium is efficient, and policies directly aimed at increasing diversity would be socially counterproductive. The role of policy should be instead to diminish language barriers between groups (e.g., through the education system).

Others have emphasized the benefits of diversity and potential drawbacks of "homophily" (or the tendency to want to associate only with people like oneself). One powerful argument is that similar people will tend to have similar information and perspectives, and if people only interact with people like themselves, lots of valuable information will be not transmitted across groups. Arguments along these lines have been made, more or less formally, in the human resources and management literature. More formally, Golub and Jackson (2012) show that, when agents in a network prefer to associate with those having similar traits (homophily), it may take a very long time for participants in a network to converge to a consensus.

Ultimately, there is thus a tradeoff between the cost of communication and collaboration and the benefits of diverse viewpoints, which means that diversity (and hence homophily) may in theory hurt or improve productivity (Hamilton et al., 2003; Alesina and Ferrara, 2005).

While there is a large nonexperimental literature on the impact on diversity on public good provision[35] and a sizeable lab experimental literature,[36] the field experimental literature is more nascent. There are nevertheless a few interesting recent papers that we review in the following section.

Hoogendoorn and Van Praag (2012) and Hoogendoorn et al. (2013) experimentally varied the composition of teams of undergraduate student required to start a business venture as part of a class. In teams of 12, students start up, sell stock, and run a real company with a profit objective and shareholders for a year. They ran the experiment on 45 teams and 550 students.

The composition of teams was varied by gender (men only, women only, or mixed) and ethnicity (the fraction of non-Dutch ethnicity varied from 20 percent to 90 percent). Students then had a year to choose their venture, elect officers, conduct meetings, produce, sell, make money, and liquidate. This was a field experiment; the program played out over a year, and the incentives to do well were very high. Students' ability to graduate, their grades, and potentially some money, were all on the line.

There is a clear benefit to gender diversity in the experiment. The performance as a function of the share of women in the team is inverse U-shaped, with the peak reached when the share of women is approximately 0.55. The authors attribute this effect to greater monitoring in gender-diverse groups. This in itself is an interesting finding as

---

[35] See Alesina and Ferrara (2005) for a review of the literature on diversity.
[36] For example, see Woolley et al. (2010) and Engel et al. (2014).

this is not a mechanism that is emphasized in the theoretical literature: perhaps when communication is too easy, workers become more complacent.

For ethnic diversity, the result is more subtle: Hoogendoorn, Oosterbeek, and Van Praag find that the marginal effect of increasing diversity on performance is zero or perhaps even negative when the teams are least 50 percent Dutch. However, once the teams are less than 50 percent Dutch, further increases in the share of other groups are associated with better performance. The authors also identify evidence for the different channels proposed in the theoretical literature (including higher communication costs in more diverse groups but also more diverse knowledge in more diverse teams), but these results are not extremely precise.

Hjort (2013) analyzes a natural experiment where a flower firm in Kenya randomly assigned workers to teams. Kenya offers a context with heightened ethnic tensions and where the level of distrust among different groups may be particularly high. In the experiment, an upstream worker distributed flowers to a team of two downstream workers. The upstream worker earned w per flower packed and the downstream worker, $2w$ per flower packed. Hjort finds that, conditional on productivity, upstream workers distribute fewer flowers to teams when one or both are not from his ethnic group, at the cost of lower wages for him, and lower production overall. Furthermore, within mixed teams, upstream workers give more flowers to the worker from their same ethnic group. Interestingly, the output gap between homogenous and ethnically mixed teams doubled during the period in 2008 when ethnic conflict intensified. In response to this, the firm introduced team pay for the downstream workers (not randomized) and subsequently experienced an increase in the productivity of the ethnically mixed teams.

Also in Kenya, Marx et al. (2015) randomly assigned enumerators to pairs, and each pair to a supervisor. The job of the enumerator was to make contact with a household and administer an intervention. They find that homogenous pairs have higher productivity and they attribute that to higher trust in those teams. However, when a pair is further matched with a supervisor of the same ethnic group, the productivity is lower (not higher). The contrast between the (negative) impact of diversity in horizontal teams and the (positive) impact in vertical relationships in the Marx et al. (2015) experiment hints at a different potential negative impact of discrimination: in-group preference may create room for cheating and corruption. In their setting, the coethnic supervisor was willing to let the enumerators cheat.

3.4.2 Discrimination and corruption

Prendergast and Topel (1996) provide a theoretical analysis of the influence of favoritism on optimal compensation and extent of authority for the manager. The point extends further than the firm: discrimination may lead to misallocation of resources by politicians (to members of their ethnic group) or conversely to willingness to put up with corrupt or incompetent politicians from one's own group (rather than less corrupt ones from another group) (Key, 1949; Padro i Miguel, 2007). More generally, voters' preferences for a group may diminish the role of issues in campaign and by implication the quality of government (Dickson and Scheve, 2006).

Besley et al. (2013) provide nonexperimental evidence of this effect: they show that in Sweden, after the social democratic party imposed gender balance by requiring that all candidates be selected in a "zipper" pattern (one man/one woman), the quality of the male candidates greatly increased (they call this the "crisis of the mediocre man").

Experimental evidence of the link between homophily and the quality of politicians or corruption level is rare. One interesting experiment took place in Uttar Pradesh, India's most populous state, where the rise in caste-based politics has been accompanied by a staggering criminalization of politics (Banerjee et al., 2010). On the eve of the 2007 election, 206 of the sitting members of the legislative assemblies had a criminal case pending against them (Banerjee and Pande, 2009). Prior to the 2007 election, the authors conducted a field experiment in which villages were randomly selected to receive nonpartisan voter mobilization campaigns (street plays, puppet shows, or discussions). One type of campaign encouraged citizens to vote on issues, not on caste, while the other encouraged them to not vote for a corrupt candidate. They found that the caste campaign led to a reduction of the (reported) votes on caste and to a reduction in the vote share going to candidates with a criminal record. It, thus, seems that successfully reducing discrimination (in this case, to be more precise, reducing lower caste group members' tendency to systematically discriminate against higher caste candidates) does lead to an improvement in the quality of elected leaders.

The natural experiment in India discussed in Section 3.3 that introduced quotas for women in politics shed interesting light on this question as well. In the short run at least, reservation for women politicians reduced bribe taking (Beaman et al., 2010). Of course, in the short run, quotas do not increase competition (since on the contrary the pool is reduced to women only, whereas it was initially open to women and men), and the observed reduction of corruption could be due to inherent characteristics of women or to their lack of experience. However, quotas do tend to increase political competition in the medium run because once a woman leaves office and her seat is open, she (or her relative) has the option to run again, but the field is now more open to competition than if she were a traditional incumbent. Moreover, when Banerjee et al. (2013) collected data on what happens in previously reserved places, they found that female incumbents whose seats became free were less likely to run than male incumbents whose seat became free, but that this effect disappeared when they considered not only the incumbent but the incumbent and his or her family. In other words, the probability to elect someone from the incumbent's dynasty remains the same in places that just have experienced a quota or not. Also, they found that the probability of reelection of someone from the incumbent's family is more sensitive to past performance in the previously reserved places. Thus, the best politicians' dynasties are more likely to be reelected after reservation, and the worst ones less likely to. To the extent this effect persists, it does suggest that policies that constrain voters to vote outside of their "comfort" zone may improve the quality of the decision-making process overall even after these constraints are lifted.

3.4.3 Law of small numbers

Even if discrimination does not lead to outright corruption, it may restrict the pool of available candidates. Research shows that the leader quality matters both for firms (Bertrand and Schoar, 2003) and for countries (Jones and Olken, 2005). If discrimination implies that leaders have to be selected from a relatively small pool, it reduces the chance that the most talented person will be picked, and it thus may have negative productivity consequences.

The empirical evidence (even nonrandomized) on any such consequence of discrimination is thin at best: Ahern and Dittmar (2012) and Matsa and Miller (2013) examine the impact of the Norway 2006 law which mandated a gender quota in corporate board seats. They both find negative consequences on profitability and stock prices. However, these are short-run impacts. It could be that women are temporally less effective because they are less experienced or that they maximize something else other than short-run shareholder value, which may turn out to be profitable in the long run.

Unfortunately, we do not see an experiment on this nor can we think of an obvious design for one. But this would be a very intriguing avenue for further research.

4. WHAT AFFECTS DISCRIMINATION?

4.1 Leaders and role models

One effect of discrimination against a group is that few leaders emerge from it into the mainstream. This has potentially three consequences. First, mechanically, fewer people from this group are in a position to make a decision regarding others. To the extent that leaders discriminate against members from other groups, discrimination will persist. Second, the majority group may be reinforced in their belief that the minority group is incapable of success, since they have rarely, if ever, observed success of the minority in practice. And third, members of the minority group may then feel that either they are incapable of succeeding, or that the world is rigged against them, and there is no point in even trying.[37] Given all this, discrimination could be lessened by forcing exposure to

---

[37] See, for example, Lockwood and Kunda (1997).

leaders from groups that are traditionally discriminated against, which is often achieved through quotas. This section reviews the evidence for this and also points out the gaps.

4.1.1 Does diversity in leadership positions directly affect discrimination?

Mechanically, discrimination may breed discrimination because the decision-making power is concentrated with the majority group. For example, if managers are mostly males, they may tend to favor other males in their recruiting or promotion decisions. This may happen because they themselves discriminate (consciously or unconsciously) or because they know more males and are more likely to promote or hire people they know or who are more similar to them.[38] This tendency is part of the rationale for requiring a certain fraction of women on corporate boards, in academia or in appointment, evaluation, and promotion committees.

It is, however, not obvious that minority group leaders, or committees that contain such minority leaders, would necessarily favor others from the minority: faced with their own discrimination, they may feel the need to go to lengths to avoid being perceived as biased. In several observational studies, women were not inclined to judge other women more favorably than men.[39] In group decisions, there may also be a response of other members of the committee, who may try to "undo" any agenda they perceive (rightly or wrongly) the minority group members to have.

The empirical evidence of the impact of minority representation on selection committees largely comes from a series of very interesting papers by Bagues et al. Bagues and Esteve-Volart (2010) examine the impact of the gender composition of the evaluation committee for the entry exam in the Spanish judiciary on the success of women in that exam. A causal study is made possible by the fact that people are randomly assigned to a committee. They find that women are less likely to succeed at the exam when the committee they are assigned to has more women, while the opposite is true for male candidates. Additional evidence in the study suggest that these results might be driven at least in part by the fact that female evaluators tend to overestimate the quality of male candidates.

Zinovyeva and Bagues (2011) and Bagues et al. (2014) present interesting evidence from randomized academic evaluation committees in Spain and Italy, respectively. In both countries, candidates for promotion appear in front of a centralized committee to

---

[38] Bagues and Perez-Villadoniga (2012) provide evidence from entry exams into the judiciary in Spain that support the latter effect; Bagues and Zinovyeva (2015) show that the former effect also applies in the case of academic promotions.

[39] See Booth and Leigh (2010) for an audit study in Australia, where they find no interaction between the gender on the résumé and the gender of the recruiter. See also Broder (1993) for similar evidence in the context of NSF proposal reviews, and Abrevaya and Hamermesh (2012) for referee reports.

be qualified. Files are assigned to randomly composed committees. In the Spanish case, the authors find no impact of an additional female committee member on the promotion likelihood of female candidates. In the Italian case, they find a negative effect: in a five-member committee, with each additional female member added to the committee, the success rate of female applicants relative to that of male applicants decreases by around two percentage points. Analyzing the voting records, they find both that (1) the same female candidate is scored on more harshly by females than by males, and (2) male committee members grade female candidates more harshly when there are women on the committee, perhaps because they are trying to compensate for a perceived bias in favor of women on such committees [even though in reality the opposite appears to be true given (1)].

This evidence on academic and recruitment committees is striking and suggest that some type of affirmative action may in fact hurt promising female candidates. It would be interesting to see if it also carries through in other settings, such as management or political decisions. The study by Bursell (2007) is an audit study that makes some progress in this direction (although the specific comparison it focuses on is itself not experimental). He sent 3552 applications to 1776 jobs in Sweden, including applications to more skilled positions, such as senior/high school teachers, IT professionals, economists, and engineers and compares, among other things, the call-back rates for applicants with Swedish-sounding and non–Swedish-sounding names according to the name of the CEO. He finds, consistent with the evidence previously mentioned that, when the "CEO of a company has a foreign-sounding name, the applicants with a Swedish-sounding name have a 2.4 times higher probability to receive a call-back. If the CEO has a Swedish-sounding name, the probability is 1.7 times higher" (Bursell, 2007).

4.1.2 Minority leaders and the attitude of the majority

Even if there is no direct effect of having women or minority members in on leadership decisions, it could still affect discrimination against the minority because those minority individuals in leadership positions will change the beliefs, or precision of the beliefs, of the majority about the competence of the minority group.

In a working paper version of Beaman et al. (2009), the authors propose a model where taste and statistical discrimination reinforce each other. Suppose that there are strong tastes (or social norms) against having a female leader. Then, it is very likely that citizens have never observed a female leader in action. This makes female leaders riskier as a group: even if citizens believe that female leaders are equally competent on average, they have much more precise priors about male leaders, and to the extent they are risk averse, this will lead them to avoid women leaders. This is of course reinforced if citizens start with the prior that women are less competent: they will never have the occasion to find out that in fact they are wrong. In this world, forcing exposure to minority leaders (political leaders, board members, colleagues in academic departments, students at top colleges, etc.) will have a persistent negative impact on discrimination, even if it does not affect the underlying taste for the community, simply by affecting beliefs about the competence of the minority group.[40]

The impact might be reinforced if the image of what constitutes a good leader also evolves in response to what people see. The "role incongruity" theory by Eagly and Karau (2002) stipulates that one reason why people prefer male leaders is that the traits associated with leadership (strength, assertiveness) are not traits that are associated with women under prescriptive gender norms (such as being nice, accommodating, etc.). Yet, as people get to see many (not just one or two token) women leaders who are strong, but also nice, or who have an effective, but also more accommodating, leadership style, then people may change their attitude toward female leaders. As inconsistencies between the female gender stereotype and qualities associated with leadership diminish, so will prejudice toward female leaders.

Of course, a potential force in the opposite direction is the possibility of backlash against minority leaders, in particular, if there is a perception that they got into their leadership role because of special treatment (Coate and Loury, 1993).

Beaman et al. (2010) study a natural experiment in the context of local electoral politics in India and are able to provide more evidence for the mechanism underlying the persistent effect of temporary affirmative action policies. In a context where local village councils are randomly selected, by rotation, to be forced to elect female leaders, the authors show that after a cycle of reservation (and even more when the same place happened to be reserved for a woman for two cycles in a row), more women run, and are elected, on unreserved seats. While there could be many reasons for this (including the fact that women may have become more willing to run, or that networks of women may have been created), they provide evidence that it is probably at least in part due to a change in attitude in the villages that were previously subjected to reservation. They collect evidence on attitudes in various ways: with a Goldberg-type experiment and with two IATs, one for like or dislike for female leader (a more "hardwired" attitude that their model takes no stance on) and one for a stereotype associating women with domestic activities and men with leadership activities (in the spirit of the assessing whether "role incongruity" effects diminished). They find that the experience with the past quota does not affect preferences (as measured by the taste IAT), although it tends to harden stated preferences against women in leadership. However, citizens

---

[40] In an observational study, Miller (2014) finds evidence consistent with such effects in the context of affirmative action programs in the United States. US government contractors are forced to hire minority workers. Miller finds that, after an establishment is no longer subject to such affirmative action because it stops being a government contractor, the black employment share nevertheless continues to grow.

(particularly men) update on measures of perception of women's competence. For example, their rating of a speech pronounced in female voice converges to that of a speech given by a male voice if they have been exposed to a quota either in this cycle or in the previous cycle. Moreover, the stereotypical IAT also shows a decrease of the stereotype that associates women with domestic activity rather than with leadership. This provides reasonably strong field evidence that exposure to role models from another group affect attitudes. The evidence seems quite robust: Bhavnani (2009) also finds that women continue to be more likely to be elected after a seat was reserved for a while (in urban Maharashtra). Banerjee et al. (2013) also find, in Rajasthan, that women are more likely to run (and win) on a previously reserved seat.

Although there is a vast laboratory literature that test the role incongruity theory and its implications and laboratory studies that show, for example, that college students asked to screen candidates for a typical male job (e.g., finance manager trainee) are less likely to discriminate against a female résumé after reading an editorial documenting women's success in this type of job (Heilman and Martell, 1986), we are not aware of field experiments that investigate these types of effect in other contexts (e.g., exposure to a female or black manager, minority teachers, etc.). It would be valuable to establish whether such impact on the majority's attitude can also be documented in some of these other contexts.

4.1.3 Role models, aspirations, and the attitude of the minority

Leaders issued from disadvantaged groups, in addition to their direct decision-making power and to the effect they may have on the opinion of the majority could also serve as role models and trailblazers. They might affect the attitudes of the minority group about their own ability to succeed or their aspirations to do so. Seeing successful women or blacks may lessen stereotype threat (as discussed in Section 4.1.2) or the belief among those groups that society is rigged against them so there is no point in trying anyway. In both cases, exposure to role models may increase effort and lead to better outcomes for the minority, even without direct changes in the majority attitude (though this could of course trigger subsequent change in the majority's beliefs and attitudes as well). However, as noted by Lockwood and Kunda (1997), these positive effects might be moderated by how fixed minority group members view their ability and how personally relevant and attainable they consider the achievement of the role models.

As in the case of the impact of exposure on the attitudes of the majority, there is both a descriptive and a laboratory literature on this question. The observational literature looks for correlation between either outcome (e.g., teen pregnancy) or measure of stereotyping (e.g., IAT) to naturally occurring exposure (e.g., black teachers). For example, Dasgupta and Asgari (2004) show that women who have been exposed to female teachers and role models are more likely to associate women and leadership. A laboratory experiment literature explores the extent to which exposure to stereotypically feminine role model in a science, technology, engineering, and math (STEM) career (Betz and Sekaquaptewa, 2012) or exposure to a nonstereotypical computer science role model (Cheryan et al., 2011) increases the likelihood that girls will present themselves as interested in STEM. Interestingly, and maybe in line with the cautionary note in the study by Lockwood and Kunda (1997), these studies show that a role model that simply belongs to the minority group might not be sufficient, and that the "type" of role model appears to matter significantly.

Cheryan et al. (2011) find that exposure to a nonstereotypical computer science role model (e.g., someone who dresses fashionably, enjoys sports and hanging out with friends, and watches "normal" TV shows, such as "The Office") through a "getting to know each other" task in the lab increases female subjects' beliefs of succeeding in the field, and that this is true regardless of the gender of that role model. Similarly to the discussion in Section 3.1.2 on "social identity," the authors argue that this is because women feel the stereotypical characteristics of a computer science major (e.g., social isolation, obsession with computers, social awkwardness) do not align with what they see as their female gender role (e.g., helping others, having social skills, attending to physical appearance), and a nonstereotypical role model, whether man or woman, can thus influence young girls' preferences and beliefs. On the other hand, Betz and Sekaquaptewa (2012) find that counterstereotypic-yet-feminine STEM role models (as signaled by characteristics such as wears makeup and pink clothes, enjoys reading fashion magazines, etc.) discourage middle school girls' success expectations in STEM relative to gender-neutral STEM role models (as signaled by characteristics such as wears dark-colored clothes and glasses, enjoys reading books, etc.). The authors find that this is particularly the case for girls who did not identify with STEM subjects and conclude that this subgroup of girls viewed the combination of both STEM success and femininity as unattainable.

Reviewing either literature fully is outside the scope of this chapter, but the mixed results of the lab experiments provide interesting directions for field research.

Here again, however, the field experiment work so far appears to be quite limited. Beaman et al. (2012) study the same randomized natural experiment for women in leadership positions in India and look at the impact on girls' educational attainment and career aspirations. They give evidence of impact on parents' hopes for daughters. Compared to never-reserved villages, parents in reserved villages were more likely to state that they would like their girl to graduate or study beyond the secondary school level and more likely to state that they would like their daughter to have a career. Parental aspirations for boys did not change. Furthermore, in villages with reservation, girls were more likely to stay in middle school, which cannot be directly attributed to any direct action of the leader because middle schools are not under their jurisdiction. This is therefore strongly suggestive of a causality running from role model to change in aspirations and actual change in behavior.

Overall, this literature seems to us surprisingly thin, compared to the larger literature on "horizontal exposure" (e.g., roommates or classmates) which we discuss in Section 4.2. Part of the explanation for this is practical: there is probably more naturally occurring variation in peer groups than in supervisors, leaders, or teachers. Another issue is that in many settings, female teachers or leaders may take actions that can translate directly into behavioral changes for female students (or trainees) even absent any effect on aspirations, so that isolating the impact on minority aspirations is tricky. While this was not the case in the quota experiment in India, it could have been. Nevertheless, we suspect that the lack of more field studies in this area is also a reflection of too little attention devoted to this important and exciting topic, and that much more probably can be done to explore how exposure to role models affects minority groups' aspirations.

4.2 Intergroup contact

Allport (1954) developed the contact hypothesis, also known as intergroup contact theory. Allport argued that, under appropriate conditions, interpersonal contact is an effective method to reduce prejudice: if majority group members have the opportunity to communicate with minority group members, they are able to understand and appreciate them, and prejudice will diminish. In particular, according to Allport, prejudice will be reduced through intergroup contact if four features of the contact situation are present: equal status between the groups in the situation, common goals, intergroup cooperation, and the support of authorities, law, or custom.

Much of the psychology literature on the contact hypothesis has focused on lab experiments that have helped refine Allport's original theory. An unresolved issue in psychology is whether specific conditions for the contact situation are needed to ensure that contact will have the theorized effect. For example, is it important for the contact to take place in a cooperative environment with peers of equal status (e.g., two roommates in a university dorm working together on a math homework) for contact to be effective at reducing discrimination? In a meta-analysis combining observational and experimental studies of the intergroup contact theory, Pettigrew and Tropp (2000) find that intergroup contact reduces prejudice in 94 percent of the 515 studies reviewed. Their meta-analysis also suggests that the contact effect generalizes to a broad range of minority groups (not just racial and ethnic minorities but also the elderly, the mentally ill, LGBT, etc.) as well as a broad range of contact settings (schools, homes, etc.). Pettigrew and Tropp (2000) also assess whether the optimal conditions for contact stated by Allport are necessary for positive contact outcomes. They find that the inverse relationship between contact and prejudice persists, though not as strongly, even when the contact situation is not structured to match Allport's conditions. Hence, while Allport's conditions may not be necessary for prejudice reduction, some combinations of them might be relevant. Psychologists are still debating and investigating the specific negative factors that may prevent intergroup contact from diminishing prejudice.

While much of the experimental research on the contact hypothesis has taken place in the lab, there have also been quite a few field experiments. Green et al. (2016) identify 56 field experiments.

The best-known field work within economics has focused on contact between college roommates. Sacerdote (2000) was the first to exploit the random assignment of roommates at college for a study of peer effects on test scores. More relevant to us, Boisjoly et al. (2006) leveraged random roommate assignment at Harvard to study the impact of shared experiences at college on opinions about the appropriateness of keeping affirmative action policies. They find that white students who are randomly assigned African-American roommates are significantly more likely to endorse affirmative action. Hence, mixing with African-Americans tends to make individuals more empathetic to them. They also find that white students who were assigned roommates from any minority group are more likely to continue to interact socially with members of other ethnic groups after their first year.

What remains unclear from Boisjoly et al. (2006) is whether contact to a minority roommate reduced stereotype or bias. Empathy might increase even if bias is unaffected. Burns et al. (2015) leveraged the same design to get at this question, and hence, their paper is closest to a field test of the contact hypothesis. Specifically, they exploit random assignments of roommates in double rooms at the University of Cape Town to investigate whether having a roommate of a different race affects interethnic attitudes but also cooperative behavior and academic performance. They find that living with a roommate from a different race significantly reduces prejudice toward members of that group, as measured by an IAT. The reduction in stereotype is accompanied by a more general tendency to cooperate, as measured in a Prisoner's dilemma game, but smaller effects on trust, as measured in a trust game. The paper also reports interesting results on grades. Black students that are assigned a nonblack roommate experience higher GPAs; white students that are assigned a nonwhite roommate experience lower GPAs.

Related findings are reported in the study by Shook and Fazio (2008). Participants were white freshmen who had been randomly assigned to either a white or an African-American roommate in a university college dormitory system. Students participated in two sessions during the first 2 and the last 2 weeks of their first quarter on campus. During these sessions, they answered questions about their satisfaction and involvement with their roommates and completed an inventory of intergroup anxiety, as well as an IAT test. Automatically activated racial attitudes (as measured with the IAT) and intergroup anxiety improved over time among students in interracial rooms but not among students in same-race rooms. However, participants in interracial rooms reported less satisfaction and less involvement with their roommates than did participants in same-race rooms.

Several field experiments in psychology have also examined contact effects between classmates. In particular, psychologists have looked at cooperative learning techniques—which are designed so that students must teach to one another and learn from one another and place a strong emphasis on the academic learning success of each member of the group—and tested whether these help reduce prejudice (Johnson and Johnson, 1989; Slavin, 1995). The rational is that because cooperative learning encourages positive social interactions among students of diverse racial and ethnic backgrounds, it creates some of the conditions hypothesized in Allport as beneficial to reducing discrimination: as students work cooperatively, they have the opportunity to judge each other on merits rather than stereotypes. Slavin and Cooper (1999) provide a review of the field evidence on cooperative learning, which has been generally supportive of cooperative learning being a useful tool to improve intergroup relations.

For example, Slavin (1977, 1979) study one particular approach to cooperative learning, called Student Teams Achievement Divisions. Under this approach, the teacher presents a lesson, and students then study worksheets in four-member teams. Following this, students take individual quizzes, and team scores are computed based on the degree to which each student has improved over his or her own past record. The team scores are published in newsletters. He finds that the students who had experienced such cooperative learning over periods of 10—12 weeks gained more cross-racial friendships than did control students. In a follow-up 1 year later, Slavin (1979) found that the students that experienced cooperative learning named an average of 2.4 friends outside their own race, compared to an average of less than one in the control group. Also, Slavin and Oickle (1981) found significant gains in whites' friendships toward African-Americans as a consequence of using the same cooperative learning method, but, interestingly, no difference in African-American friendships toward whites.

A recent paper in economics also brings the contact hypothesis to the classroom but under conditions that are not tailored to be as optimal as possible for prejudice reduction to occur, at least as hypothesized by Allport. Starting in 2007, some elite private schools in Delhi were required to offer places to poor students. Rao (2013) exploits this policy change and uses a combination of experimental and administrative data to study whether exposure of rich students (from 14 private schools in New Delhi) to poorer students affects (1) tastes for socially interacting with or discriminating against the poor, (2) generosity and prosocial behavior, and (3) learning and classroom behavior. Core to his identification strategy is a comparison of outcomes for treated and nontreated student cohorts within a school. Rao also exploits a second identification strategy that is closer to a randomized design. Some schools in his sample used the alphabetic order of first name to assign students to study groups and study partners. Hence, in those schools, the number of poor children with names similar to a given rich student provides plausibly exogenous variation in personal interactions with a poor student. This second identification strategy is obviously more appealing as a test of the contact hypothesis because it focuses more centrally on changes in personal interactions between students and rules out other confounds (such as changes in teacher behavior, changes in the curriculum, etc.).

Rao (2013) finds that economically diverse classrooms cause wealthy students to discriminate less against other poor children outside school. As discussed in Section 2.9, Rao's approach to measure discrimination is quite unique. First, he relies on a field experiment in which rich participants select teammates for a relay race and are forced to reveal how they tradeoff more-athletic poor students versus less-athletic rich students. Using this measure of discrimination, Rao finds that exposure to poor students at school reduces discrimination by 12 percentage points. Rao also conducts a second field experiment. He invites students to attend a play date at a school for poor students and elicit incentivized measures of their willingness to accept. He finds that having poor classmates makes students more willing to attend the play dates with poor children. In particular, it reduced the average size of the incentive that is required to attend the play date by 19 percent. Having a poor study partner (e.g., contact alone) explains 70 percent of the increase in this "willingness to play."

When Rao (2013) turns to how exposure to poor students affects prosocial behavior and learning in the classroom, he finds that having poor classmates makes students more prosocial, as measured by their history of volunteering for charitable causes at school, as well as their behavior in dictator games conducted in the lab. The findings reveal that exposure to poor students does not just make rich students more charitable toward the poor; instead, it affects generosity and notions of fairness more generally. Finally, Rao shows that exposure to poor classmates has limited effects on the wealthy students' test scores: while he detects marginally significant but meaningful decreases in rich students' English test scores, he finds no effects on Hindi or Math scores or on a combined index over all subjects.

The studies reviewed previously suggest that intergroup contact is an effective tool to reduce prejudice, even though more work remains to be done to ascertain the specific conditions under which contact will be most effective. Yet, some recent work in psychology (Dixon et al., 2012) suggests new angles through which the contact hypothesis should be evaluated and, more specifically, the possibility that its impact on the ultimate goal of achieving a more inclusive society might be less obvious than what would immediately appear. One of the observations made under this new line of work is that prior research on the contact hypothesis has paid little attention on how the minority group reacts to contact, with the focus being on how contact changes prejudice level among majority group members. In this context, Dixon et al. (2012) mention a few observational studies suggesting that, while majority group members may demand more social change toward inclusiveness subsequent to intergroup contact, minority group members may actually become less demanding of social change, as they perceive that discrimination and social injustice have lessened. A few recent studies (Saguy et al., 2009; Dovidio et al., 2009; Glasford and Calcagno, 2012) provide lab results consistent with this observational data, with minority group members under the contact condition appearing lulled into believing that the majority group is more just minded than it really is. If these effects are real, one can easily imagine how contact may backfire at the societal level, with the theoretically more powerful advocates for the minority group (e.g., African-Americans at Ivy League Universities experiencing positive intergroup contact) decreasing their level of political activism. At the very least, this provocative new research in psychology suggests that future field work on the intergroup contact hypothesis should be more systematic in collecting evidence on how minority group members react to contact and broadening the definition of a successful intervention outcome.

4.3 Sociocognitive debiasing strategies

In the absence of direct contact, is it possible to teach individuals to become less biased against the minority group?

We start with the discussion of a field experiment in Rajasthan, India, which offers a cautionary tale about how easy it might be to simply tell people to overcome their stereotypes. Banerjee et al. (2013) set up a large-scale randomized experiment designed to test whether citizens can learn from others' experiences about the quality of female leaders. This is an environment where, we have already shown, there is a large bias against the ability of women to be decision makers. Using high-quality street theater troupes, they set up a street play followed by a discussion of the performance of local leaders a few weeks ahead of the 2010 panchayat (local government) election. Following up on the work we discussed previously in Section 4.1.2, which showed that direct experience with a female leader does change attitude toward female leaders (and willingness to vote for one), this study sought to test whether the process could be accelerated by providing citizens objective information that, in fact, women and men are about equally good at carrying out a key task in the local government. The experiment took place in 382 panchayats: in randomly selected ones, a street play emphasized the importance of the local leader in making key decisions and encouraged citizens to vote for a competent leader. It then showed information on the average performance of all leaders in providing employment under the flagship employment guarantee scheme. In another group of villages, the play and the information were almost the same, but the script of the play emphasized the fact that citizens are often biased against women leaders but that women also can be good leaders. The statistics provided on leader performance were also disaggregated by gender (as it turns out, women do about as well as men in the sample districts).

There are two main results: first, the play and information campaign, when it does not emphasize gender, does appear to move priors. More candidates enter and the incumbent is less likely to enter and to win. For example, the incumbent vote share declines by 6 percentage points (or a remarkable 60 percent) in villages where the general campaign was run. Moreover, the vote share for the incumbent become more sensitive to past performance in places where the gender-neutral campaign was run. Second, however, these effects disappear in places where the campaign introduces the "gender" theme: in those villages, there is very little effect of the intervention on any outcomes (including on the probability that a female runs or wins or on the vote share for women). It is as if, when citizens understood that the campaign was about convincing them to consider women, they lost interest. These findings underscore the challenge of fighting discrimination in an environment where discrimination is rife.[41]

It is possible that this experiment failed because it did not pay enough attention to the structure of the bias and ways to overcome it. Over the last 20 years, social psychologists have designed and tested in the laboratory setting a series of strategies to reduce bias and stereotypical thinking. These include (following the categorization in Paluck and Green, 2009): consciousness raising; targeting emotions through perspective taking; targeting value consistency and self-worth; expert opinion and accountability interventions; as well as recategorization, decategorization, and cross-categorization techniques.

Consciousness-raising strategies are inspired by the large body of work (in particular the IAT literature) suggesting that prejudice can operate without the person's awareness or endorsement of it. The most promising consciousness-raising strategies emerging from the psychology literature to date include counter-stereotype training and approach-avoidance training.

For example, in the study by Kawakami et al. (2000), lab subjects received extensive training in negating specific stereotypical thinking toward elderly people and skinheads (young individuals with closed cropped or shaven heads who typically wear heavy boots, are often part of the working class, and stereotypically perceived as aggressive). In the elderly stereotype negation condition, subjects were instructed to respond "NO" on the trials in which they saw a picture of an elderly person paired with an elderly stereotypic trait and "YES" when they saw a picture of an elderly person with a nonstereotypic trait. In the skinhead stereotype negation condition, subjects were to respond "NO" on trials in which they saw a picture of a skinhead paired with a skinhead stereotypic trait and "YES" on trials in which they saw a picture of

---

[41] Note that the effect of reservation in this sample on the probability that a woman runs or wins after the reservation is canceled is still positive, as in West Bengal or Mumbai: so the results are not due to the fact that people in Rajasthan are so hell bent against women that they cannot learn about them. It just appears they cannot learn about them from this intervention.

a skinhead paired with a nonstereotypic trait. Kawakami et al. (2000) show that such training in negating stereotypes was able to reduce the stereotypical activation. These results were obtained even when participants were no longer instructed to "not stereotype" and, importantly, for stereotypic traits that were not directly involved in the negation training phase. This reduced activation level was still clearly visible 24 hours following the training session.[42]

Dasgupta and Greenwald (2001) report on two experiments where they examined whether exposure to pictures of admired and disliked exemplars can reduce automatic preference for white over black Americans and younger over older people. In experiment 1, participants were exposed to either admired black (e.g., Denzel Washington) and disliked white individuals (e.g., Jeffrey Dahmer), disliked black (e.g., Mike Tyson) and admired white (e.g., Tom Hanks) individuals, or nonracial exemplars. Immediately after exemplar exposure and 24 hours later, they completed an IAT that assessed automatic racial attitudes and two explicit attitude measures. Exposure to admired black and disliked white exemplars significantly weakened automatic pro-white attitudes for 24 hours beyond the treatment but did not affect explicit racial attitudes. Experiment 2 provided a replication using automatic age-related attitudes. Also, Wittenbrink et al. (1997) examined the effects of watching videos of African-Americans situated either at a convivial outdoor barbecue or at a gang-related incident. Situating African-Americans in a positive setting produced lower implicit bias scores.

In a series of papers reviewed by Madva (2015), Kawakami and his colleagues have also demonstrated how counter-stereotype training and approach-avoidance training can reduce bias. For example, Kawakami et al. (2007a) perform a lab experiment where subjects undergo gender counter-stereotype training by being asked to pair male faces with words such as "sensitive" and female faces with words such as "strong." The subjects next evaluated four job applications (two with male names, two with female names) for a position as "chairperson of a District Doctor's Association." Sixty-one percent of the subjects that had received counter-stereotype training chose a woman for the position, compared to only 35% among the subjects that had not received the training.

In another experiment, Kawakami et al. (2007b) demonstrated the debiasing potential of "approach-avoidance" conditioning. In this experiment, white and Asian participants repeatedly pulled a joystick toward themselves when they saw black faces and pushed it away when they saw white faces. The participants demonstrated reduced implicit bias on the IAT subsequent to completing this training. Kawakami et al. (2008) also showed that "approach-avoidance" conditioning training might be a promising approach to deal with the stereotype threat: female undergraduates trained in repeatedly

---

[42] Follow-up studies have partially replicated but also qualified the original findings. See Gawronski et al. (2008).

"approaching" math-related images ("e.g., calculators, equations") subsequently showed stronger preferences for math on implicit measures and answered more questions on a math test. Forbes and Schmader (2010) replicated Kawakami et al. (2008) in a study that allowed for a longer delay (24—30 hours) between the debiasing training and the math test and also showed that counter-stereotype training seemed more effective than approach-avoidance training in this context.[43]

Because emotional states can influence the expression of prejudice, psychologists have hypothesized that interventions that encourage the perceiver to experience the emotions of the minority group might be effective debiasing strategies. What does it feel like to have your intelligence automatically questioned or to be trailed by detectives each time you walk into a store? Perspective taking involves stepping into the shoes of a stereotyped person and can be useful in assessing the emotional impact on individuals who are constantly being stereotyped in negative ways.

There are now multiple studies attesting to the merits of perspective taking as a strategy for reducing intergroup bias. Some have linked perspective taking to decreased activation and application of negative group stereotypes (Galinsky and Moskowitz, 2000; Todd et al., 2011); others have shown that adopting the perspective of a particular out-group target leads to more positive evaluations of other individual members of the target's group (Shih et al., 2009) and of the target's group as a whole (Stephan and Finlay, 1999). For example, Todd et al. (2011) conducted a series of lab experiments examining the impact of perspective taking on several outcomes: automatic evaluations, approach-avoidance reactions, and behaviors displayed during face-to-face interactions. In one of the experiments, participants watched a video depicting a series of discriminatory acts directed toward a black man versus a white man. As they watched the video, participants either adopted the black man's perspective or they attempted to remain objective and detached (control group). The researchers included two different perspective-taking conditions in this experiment. Some participants tried to imagine the black man's thoughts, feelings, and experiences (other condition) as they watched the video; others tried to imagine their own thoughts, feelings, and experiences as if they were in the black man's situation (self-condition). After watching the video, participants completed a variant of the IAT that assesses automatic evaluations of black relative to white

---

[43] Interestingly, these effects were only observed when the task of choosing the best candidate came second, after the trait evaluation. When this choice task was first, only 37 percent of those who had undergone the training chose a female candidate. A similar pattern emerged when the order of the tasks was switched, in that participants were consistently biased on the first task and debiased on the second, regardless of which task actually came first. One possible explanation for this effect is that participants seem to recognize that the researchers are trying to debias them and then try to correct for this perceived influence by deliberately responding in more stereotypical ways, at least at first. Once they have an opportunity to explicitly counteract the debiasing, they stop trying to resist the training and then the effects emerge. Subsequently, they respond in counterstereotypical ways.

Americans. Subjects in both of the perspective-taking conditions (other and self-conditions) exhibited significantly weaker pro-white bias than the control subjects.

Strategies targeting value consistency and self-worth rely on the theory that individuals' desire to maintain consistency between valued cognitions and behaviors or protect their self-worth may be leveraged to lead them to repress their prejudice (Paluck and Green, 2009). Debiasing strategies in this area have leveraged cognitive dissonance and self-affirmation theories. For example, in a lab experiment, Leippe and Eisenstadt (1994) apply cognitive dissonance theory to get subjects to see prejudice as inconsistent with their own values: college students softened their antiblack positions on social policies and reported more egalitarian attitudes and beliefs after agreeing to write a public statement in favor of pro-black policies. Also, Fein and Spencer (1997) report that lab subjects who have "self-affirmed" by circling values that were most important to them were more likely to give positive ratings to a Jewish job candidate.[44]

A body of research in social psychology suggests that prejudice and discrimination might also be influenced by expert opinion and greater accountability to others for one's beliefs and behaviors. Levy, Stroessner, and Dweck (1998) show that telling lab subjects that experts believe that personality is malleable reduces stereotyping against minority groups. Dobbs and Crano (2001) report that subjects allocated more points to a fictitious out group when they were required to justify their allocations to others; similarly, Bodenhausen et al. (1994) show that students involved in a school disciplinary case were less likely to stereotype the student if they believed they would be accountable to their peers for their evaluation of the case.

Individuating is another sociocognitive debiasing strategy that involves gathering very specific information about a person's background, tastes, hobbies, and family, so that one's judgments will be based on the particulars of that person, rather than on group characteristics. This approach is grounded in the social identity and categorization literature and essentially is a decategorization effort, where subjects are instructed to focus on the individual rather than the group (Brewer, 1988; Fiske and Neuberg, 1990). Lebrecht et al. (2009) provide an interesting take on the individuation exercise. In their study, two groups of Caucasian subjects were exposed equally to the same African-American faces in a training protocol run over five sessions. In the individuation condition, subjects learned to discriminate between African-American faces; specifically, they received "expertise training" with other-race faces—defined by the authors as a procedure that improves observers' ability to individuate objects within the training domain and hence reduce the degree to which other-race faces are stereotyped. In contrast, in the categorization condition, subjects learned to categorize faces as African-American or not. Subjects in the individuation condition, but not in the categorization condition,

---

[44] Note that participants who were Jewish were excluded from this part of the study.

showed improved discrimination of African-American faces with training. Also, subjects in the individuation condition, but not the categorization condition, showed a reduction in their implicit racial bias. For the individuation condition only, the degree to which an individual subject's implicit racial bias decreased was significantly correlated with the degree of improvement that the subject showed in their ability to differentiate African-American faces.

Other debiasing strategies inspired by the social identity and categorization literature include recategorization and crossed-categorization techniques, where participants are encouraged to think of people from different groups as part of one subordinate group using cues such as same shirt colors or shared prizes, or participants are made aware of their common membership in a third group. Such recategorization and cross-categorization efforts have shown some success in reducing favoritism for the in-group and improving cooperation between groups (Dovidio and Gaertner, 2000; Gaertner et al., 1999).

An exciting recent study in the sociocognitive debiasing area is by Lai et al. (2014), who sought to determine the effectiveness of various methods for reducing implicit bias. Structured as a research contest, teams of scholars were given 5 minutes in which to enact interventions that they believed would reduce implicit preferences for whites compared to blacks, as measured by an IAT, with the goal of attaining IAT scores that reflect a lack of implicit preference for either of the two groups. Teams submitted 18 interventions that were tested approximately two times across three studies, totaling 11,868 non-black participants. Half of the interventions were effective at reducing the implicit bias that favors whites over blacks. Most effective were the following interventions: (1) participating in a sports game in which all of the teammates were black while the opposing team was all white and engaged in unfair play and being subsequently instructed to recall how their black teammates helped them while their white opponents did not; (2) reading a graphic story in which one is asked to place oneself in the role of the victim who is assaulted by a white man and rescued by a black man; and (3) practicing an IAT with counterstereotypic black (e.g., Michael Jordan, Martin Luther King, Jr.) and counterstereotypic white (e.g., Timothy McVeigh, Jeffrey Dahmer) exemplars.

A concern one may have about the relevance of this lab evidence for the field is that it can only document fairly short-term effects (up to 24 hours) and hence might be of limited relevance to the real world. However, even such a short time frame might be relevant to some important decisions that have been shown to be subject to bias, such as human resource managers' decision on whether to pass on a given résumé or teachers' grading decisions. Therefore, we believe that even short-term effects could be of real-world relevance.

What this lab evidence does not allow us to assess, however, is how these short-term impacts would differ if the same person (e.g., an HR manager) was repeatedly exposed to such debiasing strategies (e.g., every time he or she sits down to start reviewing résumés or grading exams).

Some other debiasing work in psychology has taken seriously this concern about one-shot, short-term interventions and has asked whether related strategies can be built to produce enduring reductions in bias. Work by Devine and a series of coauthors is of particular interest. Devine (1989) proposes a habit-breaking approach to prejudice reduction and likens implicit biases to deeply entrenched habits developed through socialization experiences. "Breaking the habit" of implicit bias therefore requires learning about the contexts that activate the bias and how to replace the biased responses with responses that reflect one's nonprejudiced goals. Devine and Monteith (1993) and Plant and Devine (2009) argue that the motivation to break the prejudice habit stems from two sources. First, people must be aware of their biases and they must also be concerned about the consequences of their biases before they will be motivated to exert effort to eliminate them. Second, people need to know when biased responses are likely to occur and how to replace those biased responses with ones more consistent with their goals.

Devine et al. (2012) develop and test a longer term intervention to help people reduce implicit biases and "break the prejudice habit." The participants were 91 non-black introductory psychology students, who completed a 12-week longitudinal study for course credit. The key elements of the intervention were as follows. First, to ensure awareness of their bias, all participants completed a measure of implicit bias and received feedback about their level of bias. People assigned to the treatment group were also presented with a bias education and training program, the goals of which were to evoke a general concern about implicit biases and train people to eliminate them. The program lasted 45 minutes. The education component likened the expression of implicit biases to a habit and provided information linking implicit bias to discriminatory behaviors across a wide range of settings (e.g., interpersonal, employment, health). The training component described how to apply a variety of bias reduction strategies in daily life. The training section presented participants with a wide array of strategies (covering many of the strategies discussed in the following section, such as taking the perspective of stigmatized others, imagining counterstereotypic examples, training in negating stereotypical associations, and individuation) as well as opportunities to engage in positive interactions with members of the minority group (e.g., intergroup contact). This enabled participants to flexibly choose the strategies most applicable to different situations in their lives.

Following the intervention, treated participants had lower IAT scores than control group participants at 4 and 8 weeks after the intervention; moreover, the effects at 4 and 8 weeks were not systematically different from each other, indicating that the reduction in implicit race bias persisted over time. These data provide the first evidence that a controlled, randomized intervention can produce enduring reductions in implicit bias. The intervention created no changes in the participants' reported racial attitudes, but it did affect participants' concern about discrimination and their awareness of their personal bias. Also, concerns about discrimination emerged as a moderator for the interventions' effects. The intervention appears to have raised concerns about discrimination at week 2, and the biggest reduction in implicit bias in the treatment group was among those subjects who experienced growing concerns.

Despite the large amount of both theoretical and lab-based work in psychology on these various sociocognitive debiasing techniques, it is remarkable how few evaluations of these techniques have been performed in the field.

Paluck and Green (2009) perform a thorough literature search of the randomized field evidence on the debiasing techniques listed previously. While the number of field experiments they identify is nontrivial (71), much of the work they survey is not directly guided by the psychology literature or directory transposable into the specific lab-based strategies reviewed previously. Moreover, very few of the existing field studies are designed to track changes in behavior outcome measures. The modal existing field study also involves a very short-term follow-up (often within the day) and takes place in a class-room setting with a student population, hence quite "lab-like" even if not explicitly in the lab.

By far, most common have been interventions relying on various forms of entertainment (books, movies, cartoons, etc.) to create a persuasive narrative aimed at altering stereotypical thinking. In many cases though, the entertainment content is not based on the specific psychological theories that have guided the lab work, and it is hence difficult to make a direct link between the lab and the field evidence. For example, Paluck and Green (2009) identify several randomized field experiments performed in schools to measure the impact of reading on prejudice. This work suggests reduction in self-reported bias associated with reading content that portrays contact between children who are similar to the studied population and children of different race (e.g., intergroup friendship), as well as reading content that emphasizes a minority characters' individual characteristics rather than group membership (e.g., individuating). But is also possible that reading interventions might be effective because of the emotional reaction they induce through perspective taking (e.g., putting oneself in the shoes of the minority character in a book) or because they are a channel to communicate social norms (e.g., descriptions of what others are doing and hence what the reader should do).

Paluck and Green (2009) also identify a few instruction-based (rather than narrative based) field interventions. In this case again, though, the content of the interventions is rarely directly guided by the lab evidence, and a lack of theoretical foundations may explain in part a lack of impressive findings. One exception is the study by Lustig (2003), which evaluates a training program in Israel that aims to encourage perspective taking and empathy to reduce prejudice against Palestinians among Jewish 12th graders. Lustig (2003) reports encouraging findings among Jewish students who were asked to write an essay about the Israeli-Palestinian conflict from the Palestinian viewpoint.

The randomized field studies designed to directly test consciousness raising, value consistency, and self-worth, as well as recategorization, decategorization and cross-categorization techniques can essentially be counted on one hand.[45] All have been performed on student populations and have produced mixed results.

At the same time, we are confident that hundreds of antiprejudice interventions directly inspired by the lab-based literature described previously must be taking place yearly not only in schools but also in business and government settings but are not being rigorously evaluated. It would be of first-order importance for researchers to strike up partnerships with organizations interested in better understanding the value of the diversity training programs they are investing resources in, both in terms of their immediate impact on bias and their ultimate impact on organizational performance. Human resource departments, police departments, and courtrooms are only a few of the possible real-world settings where a much-needed field validation of this large lab-based literature could be performed.

For example, the US Department of Justice is funding the development of a curriculum for police staff that reflects on the Fair and Impartial Policing perspective. This training program applies the modern science of bias to policing: it trains officers on the effect of implicit bias and gives them the information and skills they need to reduce and manage their biases. The curriculum addresses not just racial/ethnic bias but biases based on other factors such as gender, sexual orientation, religion, socioeconomic status, etc. Officers are taught skills, inspired by the lab-tested methods described previously to reduce and manage their own biases. Social psychologists from around the nation who conduct the research on human biases are members of the team that help design the curriculum. While this program has been implemented with various target audiences (recruits/patrol officers, first-line supervisors, mid-level managers, command staff, and law enforcement trainers), to our knowledge, it has not been the subject of a rigorous evaluation.

As another example, there has been much discussion in the recent years about how the sociodebiasing techniques described previously could be used to debias judges and jurors. Kang et al. (2012) discuss possible ways to import these techniques to the courtroom. They argue that:

In chambers and the courtroom buildings, photographs, posters, screen savers, pamphlets, and decorations ought to be used that bring to mind counter-typical exemplars or associations for participants in the trial process—for jurors, then,—he hope would be that by reminding them of counter-typical associations, we might momentarily activate different mental patterns while in the courthouse and reduce the impact of implicit biases on their decision-making.

---

[45] See Houlette et al. (2004) for recategorization, Rokeach (1971, 1973) for value consistency, Katz and Zalk (1978) and Katz (2000) for cognitive retraining, and Lustig (2003) for perspective taking.

Also, Elek and Agor (2014) show how debiasing strategies could be feasibly brought to the courtroom with simple alterations to the standard instructions delivered by the judge to the jury, such as including a recognition of the universality of bias and explicit encouragement of perspective taking.

4.4 Technological debiasing

Stanovich and West (2000) put forward an important distinction between System 1 and System 2 cognitive functioning. System 1 corresponds to intuitive reasoning, which tends to be fast, implicit, and emotional. In contrast, System 2 reasoning tends to be slower, more explicit, and more logical. In situations where we know that implicit biases are likely to prop up, such as when evaluating diverse candidates for a job posting, relying exclusively on System 1 might be dangerous.

Prior research has shown conditions under which System 1 reasoning is more likely to occur. Ambiguous or unfamiliar situations tend to be associated with System 1: without concrete criteria for decision-making, individuals will rely on the information that is most easily accessible, including stereotypes, to make decisions (Dovidio and Gaertner, 2000; Johnson et al., 1995). Emotional states such as anger or disgust have also been shown to induce more bias against minority group members, even if those emotions were not triggered by the minority group members themselves or directly related to the decision-making situation (DeSteno et al., 2004; Dasgupta et al., 2009). Interesting, even happiness has been shown to produce more stereotypic judgments, though the exact mechanism for this is unclear (Bodenhausen et al., 1994). Importantly, states of fatigue, time pressure, heavy workload, stress, emergencies, or distraction also trigger more System 1 reasoning and more stereotypic judgments (Eells and Showalter, 1994; Hartley and Adams, 1974; Keinan, 1987; Van Knippenberg et al., 1999; Bodenhausen and Lichtenstein, 1987; Gilbert and Hixon, 1991; Sherman et al., 1998).

For instance, Correll et al. (2002) have used videogames in the lab to assess the effect of race on shoot/do not shoot decisions of targets who are either holding guns or holding nonthreatening objects. While all subjects are instructed to shoot the armed targets but not shoot the unarmed targets, subjects make errors and these errors are systematically correlated with the race of the target: they disproportionately shoot unarmed Blacks and do not shoot armed Whites. Subsequent work has shown this "shooter bias" to be more prevalent in situations where subjects are tired (Ma et al., 2013), rushed (Payne, 2006), or cannot see well (Payne et al., 2005).

The field study by Danziger et al. (2011) of parole decisions made by judges provides another interesting illustration. They study a sample of 1112 parole board hearings in Israeli prisons over a 10-month period. The rulings are made by eight experienced Jewish—Israeli judges, with each judge considering between 14 and 35 cases each day and spending around 6 min on each decision. The judges take two food breaks, hence dividing their day into three sessions. Danziger et al. (2011) find that the percentage of favorable rulings drops from 65% to nearly zero within each decision session, returning to 65% after a food break. The researchers attribute their results to the repeated task draining the judges' mental resources: when drained, the judges start opting for the easy default option, which is to deny parole. Taking a food break helps to replenish the judges' energy. However, the researchers did not find any evidence that the timing of the decision within each session affected discrimination, either based on gender and ethnicity or the severity of the crime.

Casey et al. (2012) study how one could build on this knowledge of what triggers System 1 versus System 2 thinking to help technologically debias the courtroom. For example, the authors discuss how jurors might be allowed more time on cases in which implicit bias might be a concern by, for example, spending more time reviewing the facts of the case before committing to a decision. Also, courts may review situations where judges and other decision-makers are likely to be overburdened and consider options (e.g., reorganizing court calendars) to provide more time for decision-making. Also, jurors may be asked to commit to decision-making criteria before reviewing a case. Furthermore, courtrooms could consider using judges with special expertise to handle more ambiguous cases. Many of the possible strategies that Casey et al. (2012) discuss for the courtroom setting could naturally be applied to other real-world settings where biases in decision-making have been documented.

When historical data on inputs and outcomes associated with a particular decision process are available (e.g., whether or not to grant parole to a prisoner), another strategy for moving toward System 2 reasoning might be to construct statistical models that will automatically map inputs (e.g., past criminal history) into a forecast about the relevant outcome (e.g., likelihood of recidivism). Such statistical models can produce predictions that outperform those of experts (Dawes, 1971).[46] As importantly, the use of simple statistical models or more complex machine learning models may equip decision-makers with a tool that will help debias their choices. More research should be devoted to testing the feasibility of this approach across a variety of domains.

With better knowledge of why discrimination occurs in a particular setting, it will become easier to design appropriate technological debiasing strategies. As we discussed earlier in Section 2.5, Bartoš et al. (2013) convincingly demonstrate racial gaps in attention allocation by HR managers. Once they see a minority name on a résumé, they pay less attention to that résumé. These findings confirm the merit of requiring separate rankings of applicants from nonminority and minority groups (or across gender lines) followed by a comparison of leading candidates across the groups. One can think of this rule as providing quotas in the preselection process. We do not know of any systematic evaluation of such a strategy.

---

[46] The value of linear models in hiring, admissions, and selection decisions are highlighted by research that Moore et al. (2010) conducted on the interpretation of grades by graduate admission officers.

Also, since the earlier a decision maker learns a group attribute, such as name, the larger the asymmetry in attention to subsequent information such as education or qualification, the findings by Bartoš et al. (2013) strengthens the case for suppressing the signals of a group attribute during the part of the selection process. This particular technological approach has been receiving quite a lot of attention from policymakers in the recent years and has been evaluated in the field. In particular, the large number of correspondence studies have raised interest in the possibility of using "blind" hiring procedures. In some recruiting circumstances, the full hiring process can take place anonymously. Goldin and Rouse (2000) famously showed that American orchestras conducting blind auditions hired more women. In most other cases, though, only the first stage of the recruitment is made anonymous: this is the case in anonymous application procedures, such as the masking of identifying characteristics in résumés at the first selection stage.

In several European countries, pilot studies of the impact of such anonymization of résumés have been conducted, including relatively large-scale field experiments in France, the Netherlands, Sweden, and Germany. These experiments are summarized in the study by Krause et al. (2012b). Only a subset were truly randomized, and we focus our discussion on this subset.[47]

In 2010, 2011, the French government initiated an experiment, which was implemented by the French public employment service. It involved about 1000 firms in eight local labor markets, and it lasted in total for about 10 months (Behaghel et al., 2014).

Among volunteer firms, résumés were either transmitted anonymously or nonanonymously. The experiment's main findings can be summarized as follows. First, women benefit from higher call-back rates with anonymous job applications—at least if they compete with male applicants for a job. Second, and most interestingly, migrants and residents of deprived neighborhoods suffer from anonymous job applications. Their call-back rates are lower with anonymous job applications than with standard applications. This adverse effect on minority candidates is the exact opposite effect to what policymakers had hoped, and a surprising result given existing evidence from correspondence testing in France (Duguet et al., 2010), which shows discrimination against minority

---

[47] Åslund and Skans (2012) analyze an experiment conducted in parts of the local administration of the Swedish city of Gothenburg between 2004 and 2006. Based on a difference-in-differences approach, the authors find that anonymous job applications increase the chances of an interview invitation for both women and applicants of non-Western origin when compared to standard applications. These increased chances for minority candidates in the first stage also translated into a higher job offer arrival rate for women but not for migrants. In the Netherlands, two experiments took place in the public administration of one major Dutch city in 2006 and 2007 (Bøg and Kranendonk, 2011). The experiments focused on ethnic minorities. The lower call-back rate for minority candidates with standard applications disappears with anonymous job applications. With regard to job offers, however, the authors do not detect any differences between minority and majority candidates—irrespective of whether or not their résumés are treated anonymously.

candidates for some jobs, no discrimination for others, but never discrimination against majority candidates. Behaghel et al. (2014) explain these surprising results by the self-selection of firms that agreed to participate in the field experiment. Among firms that were contacted to participate in the experiment, 62 percent accepted the invitation. While participating firms were very similar to refusing firms in most observable dimensions, there was one significant exception: participating firms tended to interview and hire relatively more minority candidates (when using standard résumés). The anonymization therefore prevented selected firms from treating minority candidates more favorably during the experiment. Hence, the results of the experiment cannot be viewed as representative of what anonymization might have achieved if it had been mandated to all firms. Methodologically, this paper offers a valuable illustration of one danger when trying to generalize the findings of a field experiment. External validity is far from guaranteed if there is sizable room for selection or self-selection of subjects into the experiment (Heckman, 1992; Allcott, 2015).

Another large-scale randomized field experiment took place in Germany in early 2010 (Krause et al., 2012a). The publication of a correspondence testing study for Germany (Kaas and Manger, 2012) triggered a lively public debate about discrimination in the hiring decisions of German firms.[48] Against this background, the Federal Anti-Discrimination Agency initiated a field experiment with anonymous job applications in Germany to investigate their potential in combating hiring discrimination. This experiment was also subject to selection in participation, with eight organizations voluntarily joining the experiment. The characteristics that were made anonymous include the applicant's name and contact details, gender, nationality, date and place of birth, disability, marital status, and the applicant's picture.[49] Unlike the French study, the authors find that the anonymization leads to less discrimination against minority groups. Moreover, anonymizing applications is not too difficult administratively, with standardized application forms that are completed by the applicants appearing as the most effective and efficient way to make applications anonymous.

---

[48] The study finds that applicants with a Turkish-sounding name are on average 14 percentage points less likely to receive an invitation for a job interview than applicants with a German-sounding name who are otherwise similar. In small- and medium-sized firms, this difference is even larger and amounts to 24 percentage points.

[49] The study was further designed to assess the practicality of different methods to remove identifiers from applications; practicality was assessed from interviews with the HR specialists at the firms. Four methods were considered: (1) standardized application forms in which sensitive information is not included; (2) refinements of existing online application forms such that sensitive information is disabled; (3) copying applicant's nonsensitive information into another document; and (4) blacking out sensitive information in the original application documents.

5. CONCLUSION

We have organized this chapter along three overarching themes: the measurement of discrimination, the consequences of discrimination, and factors and policies that may help undermine it. It is apparent from our review of the existing field experiments under each of these themes that there remain more unanswered or unexplored questions than there are settled ones.

By far, the bulk of the field experiments that have been conducted in this area relate to the measurement of discrimination using the correspondence method. This body of work has demonstrated how remarkably pervasive the differential treatment of minority groups is throughout the world (at least in the labor market and rental market). These studies, most often focusing on a single minority group in a single country, have been important in generating debates in the local media and local public opinion and, from that perspective, each has added value. In many fields of inquiry, researchers shy away from replication, but this is refreshingly not the case here—most likely because demonstrating differential treatment in the given country seemed a sufficiently important goal. On the other hand, researchers' ability to push the correspondence method further to go beyond pure measurement of differential treatment has been more limited. Disappointingly, there has been minimal methodological innovation in the way correspondence studies are being carried out. The main innovation might have been in leveraging the method to study differential treatment across other characteristics than race, gender, or ethnicity, such as in the set of recent studies using the method to study discrimination against the long-term unemployed. While one might conclude from this that the correspondence method might have reached its full potential, recent papers such as by Bartoš et al. (2013) which demonstrate how it can used to study the dynamics of discrimination (endogenous attention allocation in this case) suggest there remain unexplored avenues for more creative uses.

Perhaps, because so much of economists' attention has been devoted to using field experiments to measure the extent of discrimination, there has been much less activity in designing creative ways to better document either its consequences or ways to undermine it. The dearth of field-based evidence on these last two themes is particularly striking given the rich theoretical and lab-based literature (mainly in psychology) that such work could build upon. On the topic of consequence of discrimination, we are heartened to see a few recent papers such as the study by Glover et al. (2015) that develop a creative field design to demonstrate how discrimination can be self-perpetuating. We believe that the last theme in our chapter, interventions to undermine discrimination, is particularly ripe for more field experimentation. It is striking that most of the research in economics on this question has centered around the contact hypothesis and exposure effects, while so many other strategies to debias people have been proposed by psychologists and evaluated in the lab. We strongly encourage researchers to take on this work in the near future. Creating more partnerships with organizations that are willing to provide the testing ground for different debiasing strategies will be particularly useful for this work to move forward. More generally, while field experiments in the last decade have been instrumental in documenting the prevalence of discrimination, field experiments in the future decade should aim to play as large of a role in isolating effective methods to combat it.

REFERENCES

Abrevaya, J., Hamermesh, D.S., 2012. Charity and favoritism in the field: are female economists nicer (to each other)? Rev. Econ. Statistics 94 (1), 202–207.

Acquisti, A., Fong, C.M., 2013. An Experiment in Hiring Discrimination via Online Social Networks. http://dx.doi.org/10.2139/ssrn.2031979. Available at SSRN: http://ssrn.com/abstract=2031979.

Ahern, K.R., Dittmar, A.K., 2012. The changing of the boards: the impact on firm valuation of mandated female board representation. Q. J. Econ. 127 (1), 137–197.

Ahmed, A.M., Hammarstedt, M., 2008. Discrimination in the rental housing market: a field experiment on the internet. J. Urban Econ. 64 (2), 362–372.

Ahmed, A.M., Hammarstedt, M., 2009. Detecting discrimination against homosexuals: evidence from a field experiment on the internet. Economica 76 (303), 588–597.

Ahmed, A.M., Andersson, L., Hammarstedt, M., 2010. Can discrimination in the housing market be reduced by increasing the information about the applicants? Land Econ. 86 (1), 79–90.

Ahmed, A.M., Andersson, L., Hammarstedt, M., 2012. Does age matter for employability? A field experiment on ageism in the Swedish labour market. Appl. Econ. Lett. 19 (4), 403–406.

Ahmed, A.M., Andersson, L., Hammarstedt, M., 2013. Are gay men and lesbians discriminated against in the hiring process? South. Econ. J. 79 (3), 565–585.

Aigner, D.J., Cain, G.G., 1977. Statistical theories of discrimination in labor markets. Industrial Labor Relat. Rev. 175–187.

Alesina, A., Ferrara, E.L., 2005. Ethnic diversity and economic performance. J. Econ. Literature 43, 762–800.

Allcott, H., 2015. Site selection bias in program evaluation. Q. J. Econ. 130 (3).

Allport, G.W., 1954. The Nature of Prejudice. Addison-Wesley, Cambridge, MA.

Altonji, J.G., Blank, R.M., 1999. Chapter 48: race and gender in the labor market. Handb. Labor Econ. 3 (C), 3143–3259.

Arkes, H.R., Tetlock, P.E., 2004. Attributions of implicit prejudice, or "would Jesse Jackson 'fail' the implicit association test?". Psychol. Inq. 15 (4), 257–278.

Aronson, J., Fried, C.B., Good, C., 2002. Reducing the effects of stereotype threat on African American college students by shaping theories of intelligence. J. Exp. Soc. Psychol. 38 (2), 113–125.

Arrow, K.J., 1973. The theory of discrimination. Discrimination Labor Mark. 3 (10), 3–33.

Åslund, O., Nordströum Skans, O., 2012. Do anonymous job application procedures level the playing field? Industrial Labor Relat. Rev. 65 (1), 82–107.

Ayres, I., Siegelman, P., 1995. Race and gender discrimination in bargaining for a new car. Am. Econ. Rev. 85 (3), 304–321.

Babad, E.Y., Inbar, J., Rosenthal, R., 1982. Pygmalion, Galatea, and the Golem: investigations of biased and unbiased teachers. J. Educ. Psychol. 74 (4), 459.

Baert, S., Cockx, B., Gheyle, N., Vandamme, C., 2013. Do employers discriminate less if vacancies are difficult to fill? Evidence from a field experiment. In: IZA Discussion Paper, pp. 1–30.

Bagues, M., Perez-Villadoniga, M.J., 2012. Do recruiters prefer applicants with similar skills? Evidence from a randomized natural experiment. J. Econ. Behav. Organ. 82 (1), 12–20.

Bagues, M., Zinovyeva, N., 2015. The role of connections in academic promotions. Am. Econ. J. Appl. Econ. 7 (2), 264–292.

Bagues, M., Sylos-Labini, M., Zinovyeva, N., 2014. Do gender quotas pass the test? Evidence from academic evaluations in Italy. In: Scuola Superiore Sant'Anna, LEM Working Paper Series, vol. 14.

Bagues, M.F., Esteve-Volart, B., 2010. Can gender parity break the glass ceiling? Evidence from a repeated randomized experiment. Rev. Econ. Stud. 77 (4), 1301–1328.

Bailey, J., Wallace, M., Wright, B., 2013. Are gay men and lesbians discriminated against when applying for jobs? A four-city, internet-based field experiment. J. Homosex. 60 (6), 873–894.

Baldini, M., Federici, M., 2011. Ethnic discrimination in the Italian rental housing market. J. Hous. Econ. 20 (1), 1–14.

Banaji, M., Nosek, B.A., Greenwald, A.G., 2004. No place for Nostalgia in science: a response to Arkes and Tetlock. Psychol. Inq. 15 (4), 279–310.

Banaji, M.R., Greenwald, A.G., 1995. Implicit gender stereotyping in judgments of fame. J. Personality Soc. Psychol. 68 (2), 181.

Banerjee, A., Pande, R., 2009. Parochial politics: ethnic preferences and politician corruption. In: CEPR Discussion Paper No. DP6381.

Banerjee, A., Bertrand, M., Datta, S., Mullainathan, S., 2009. Labor market discrimination in Delhi: evidence from a field experiment. J. Comp. Econ. 37 (1), 14–27.

Banerjee, A., Green, D., Green, J., Pande, R., 2010. Can Voters Be Primed to Choose Better Legislators? Experimental Evidence from Rural India. Unpublished manuscript, available at:http://www.povertyactionlab.org/node/2764.

Banerjee, A., Duflo, E., Imbert, C., Pande, R., 2013. Entry, exit, and candidate selection: evidence from India. In: Mimeo, 3ie Grantee Final Report.

Bardhan, P.K., Mookherjee, D., Torrado, M.P., 2010. Impact of political reservations in West Bengal local governments on anti-poverty targeting. J. Glob. Dev. 1 (1).

Bartoš, V., Bauer, M., Chytilová, J., Matějka, F., 2013. Attention discrimination: theory and field experiments. In: CERGE Working Paper, 1211-3298.

Beaman, L., Chattopadhyay, R., Duflo, E., Pande, R., Topalova, P., 2009. Powerful women: does exposure reduce bias? Q. J. Econ. 124 (4), 1497–1540.

Beaman, L., Duflo, E., Pande, R., Topalova, P., 2010. Political reservation and substantive representation: evidence from Indian village councils. In: Berry, S., Bosworth, B., Panagariya, A. (Eds.), India Policy Forum 2010–11, Volume 7. SAGE Publications Inc.

Beaman, L., Duflo, E., Pande, R., Topalova, P., 2012. Female leadership raises aspirations and educational attainment for girls: a policy experiment in India. Science 335 (6068), 582–586.

Becker, G.S., 1957. The Economics of Discrimination. University of Chicago Press.

Behaghel, L., Crépon, B., Barbanchon, T.L., 2014. Unintended effects of anonymous resumes. In: CEPR Discussion Paper No. DP10215.

Benjamin, D.J., Choi, J.J., Joshua Strickland, A., 2010. Social identity and preferences. Am. Econ. Rev. 100, 1913–1928.

Bertrand, M., Mullainathan, S., 2004. Are Emily and Greg more employable than Lakisha and Jamal? A field experiment on labor market discrimination. Am. Econ. Rev. 94 (4), 991–1013.

Bertrand, M., Schoar, A., 2003. Managing with style: the effect of managers on firm policies. Q. J. Econ. 118 (4), 1169–1208.

Bertrand, M., Chugh, D., Mullainathan, S., 2005. Implicit discrimination. Am. Econ. Rev. 94–98.

Besley, T., Coate, S., 1997. An economic model of representative democracy. Q. J. Econ. 85–114.

Besley, T.J., Folke, O., Persson, T., Rickne, J., 2013. Gender quotas and the crisis of the mediocre man: theory and evidence from Sweden. In: IFN Working Paper.

Betz, D.E., Sekaquaptewa, D., 2012. My fair Physicist? Feminine math and science role models demotivate young girls. Soc. Psychol. Personality Sci. 3 (6), 738–746.

Bhavnani, R.R., 2009. Do electoral quotas work after they are withdrawn? Evidence from a natural experiment in India. Am. Political Sci. Rev. 103 (01), 23.

Biddle, J.E., Hamermesh, D.S., 1998. Beauty, productivity and discrimination: lawyers' looks and lucre. J. Labor Econ. 15, 172–201.

Blackwell, L.S., Trzesniewski, K.H., Dweck, C.S., 2007. Implicit theories of intelligence predict achievement across an adolescent transition: a longitudinal study and an intervention. Child. Dev. 78 (1), 246–263.

Blommaert, L., Coenders, M., van Tubergen, F., 2014. Discrimination of Arabic-named applicants in The Netherlands: an internet-based field experiment examining different phases in online recruitment procedures. Soc. Forces 92 (3), 957—982.

Bodenhausen, G.V., Lichtenstein, M., 1987. Social stereotypes and information-processing strategies: the impact of task complexity. J. Personality Soc. Psychol. 52 (5), 871.

Bodenhausen, G.V., Kramer, G.P., Süsser, K., 1994. Happiness and stereotypic thinking in social judgment. J. Personality Soc. Psychol. 66 (4), 621.

Bøg, M., Kranendonk, E., 2011. Labor market discrimination of minorities? Yes, but not in job offers. In: MPRA Paper No. 33332.

Boisjoly, J., Duncan, G.J., Kremer, M., Levy, D.M., Eccles, J., 2006. Empathy or antipathy? The impact of diversity. Am. Econ. Rev. 96 (5), 1890—1905.

Booth, A., Leigh, A., 2010. Do employers discriminate by gender? A field experiment in female-dominated occupations. Econ. Lett. 107 (2), 236—238.

Booth, A.L., Leigh, A., Varganova, E., 2011. Does ethnic discrimination vary across minority groups? Evidence from a field experiment. Oxf. Bull. Econ. Statistics 74 (4), 547—573.

Bosch, M., Angeles Carnero, M., Farré, L., 2010. Information and discrimination in the rental housing market: evidence from a field experiment. Regional Sci. Urban Econ. 40 (1), 11—19.

Boschini, A., Muren, A., Persson, M., 2009. Constructing Gender in the Economics Lab. Technical report. Stockholm University, Department of Economics.

Brewer, M.B., 1981. Ethnocentrism and its role in interpersonal trust. Sci. Inq. Soc. Sci. 214.

Brewer, M.B., 1988. A dual process model of impression formation. In: Wyer, R., Srull, T. (Eds.), Advances in Social Cognition, vol. 1. Lawrence Erlbaum Associates, Inc., Hillsdale, NJ, pp. 1—36.

Broder, I.E., 1993. Review of NSF economics proposals: gender and institutional patterns. Am. Econ. Rev. 964—970.

Brown, C., Gay, P., 1985. Racial Discrimination: 17 Years After the Act. Policy Studies Institute.

Burns, J., Corno, L., La Ferrara, E., 2015. Interaction, Prejudice and Performance. Evidence from South Africa. Working Paper.

Bursell, M., 2007. What's in a name? A field experiment test for the existence of ethnic discrimination in the hiring process. SULCIS WP 7.

Carlsson, M., 2011. Does hiring discrimination cause gender segregation in the Swedish labor market? Fem. Econ. 17 (3), 71—102.

Carlsson, M., Eriksson, S., 2014. Discrimination in the rental market for apartments. J. Hous. Econ. 23, 41—54.

Carpusor, A.G., Loges, W.E., 2006. Rental discrimination and ethnicity in names. J. Appl. Soc. Psychol. 36 (4), 934—952.

Casey, P.M., Warren, R.K., Cheesman, F.L., Elek, J.K., 2012. Helping Courts Address Implicit Bias. Technical report. National Center for State Courts, Williamsburg, VA.

Charles, K.K., Guryan, J., 2008. Prejudice and wages: an empirical assessment of Becker's "the economics of discrimination". J. Political Econ. 116 (5), 773—809.

Chattopadhyay, R., Duflo, E., 2004. Women as policy makers: evidence from a randomized experiment in India. Econometrica 72, 1409—1443.

Cheryan, S., Oliver Siy, J., Vichayapai, M., Drury, B.J., Kim, S., 2011. Do female and male role models who embody STEM stereotypes hinder women's anticipated success in STEM? Soc. Psychol. Personality Sci. 2 (6), 656—664.

Clots-Figueras, I., 2009. Are Female Leaders Good for Education? Evidence from India. Universidad Carlos III de Madrid, Mimeo.

Clots-Figueras, I., 2011. Women in politics: evidence from the Indian states. J. Public Econ. 95 (7—8), 664—690.

Coate, S., Loury, G., 1993. Antidiscrimination enforcement and the problem of patronization. Am. Econ. Rev. 92—98.

Coffman, K.B., Coffman, L.C., Keith, M., 2013. Marzilli Ericson. The size of the LGBT population and the magnitude of anti-gay sentiment are substantially underestimated. In: NBER Working Paper No. 19508.

Cohen, G.L., Garcia, J., Apfel, N., Master, A., 2006. Reducing the racial achievement gap: a social-psychological intervention. Science 313 (5791), 1307—1310.

Cohen, G.L., Garcia, J., Purdie-Vaughns, V., Apfel, N., Brzustoski, P., 2009. Recursive processes in self-affirmation: intervening to close the minority achievement gap. Science 324 (5925), 400—403.

Correll, J., Park, B., Judd, C.M., Wittenbrink, B., 2002. The police Officer's dilemma: using ethnicity to disambiguate potentially threatening individuals. J. Personality Soc. Psychol. 83 (6), 1314—1329.

Cross, H., Kenney, G., Mell, J., Zimmerman, W., 1990. Employer hiring practices: differential treatment of Hispanic and Anglo job seekers. In: Urban Institute Report 90-4.

Danziger, S., Levav, J., Avnaim-Pesso, L., 2011. Extraneous factors in judicial decisions. Proc. Natl. Acad. Sci. U.S.A. 108 (17), 6889—6892.

Dasgupta, N., Asgari, S., 2004. Seeing is believing: exposure to counterstereotypic women leaders and its effect on the malleability of automatic gender stereotyping. J. Exp. Soc. Psychol. 40 (5), 642—658.

Dasgupta, N., Greenwald, A.G., 2001. On the malleability of automatic attitudes: combating automatic prejudice with images of admired and disliked individuals. J. Personality Soc. Psychol. 81 (5), 800.

Dasgupta, N., DeSteno, D., Williams, L.A., Hunsinger, M., 2009. Fanning the flames of prejudice: the influence of specific incidental emotions on implicit prejudice. Emotion 9 (4), 585.

Dawes, R.M., 1971. A case study of graduate admissions: application of three principles of human decision making. Am. Psychol. 26, 180—188.

Dee, T.S., 2009. Stereotype Threat and the Student-Athlete. NBER Working Paper No. 14705.

DeSteno, D., Dasgupta, N., Bartlett, M.Y., Cajdric, A., 2004. Prejudice from thin air: the effect of emotion on automatic intergroup attitudes. Psychol. Sci. 15 (5), 319—324.

Devine, P.G., 1989. Stereotypes and prejudice: their automatic and controlled components. J. Personality Soc. Psychol. 56, 5—18.

Devine, P.G., Monteith, M.J., 1993. The role of discrepancy-associated affect in prejudice reduction. In: Mackie, D.M., Hamilton, D.L. (Eds.), Affect, Cognition, and Stereotyping: Interactive Processes in Group Perception. Academic Press, San Diego, CA, pp. 317—344.

Devine, P.G., Forscher, P.S., Austin, A.J., Cox, W.T.L., 2012. Long-term reduction in implicit race bias: a prejudice habit-breaking intervention. J. Exp. Soc. Psychol. 48 (6), 1267—1278.

Dickson, E.S., Scheve, K., 2006. Social identity, political speech, and electoral competition. J. Theor. Polit. 18 (1), 5—39.

Dixon, J., Levine, M., Reicher, S., Durrheim, K., 2012. Beyond prejudice: are negative evaluations the problem and is getting us to like one another more the solution? Behav. Brain Sci. 35 (6), 411—425.

Dobbs, M., Crano, W.D., 2001. Outgroup accountability in the minimal group Paradigm: implications for aversive discrimination and social identity theory. J. Personality Soc. Psychol. 27, 355—364.

Doleac, J.L., Stein, L.C.D., 2013. The visible hand: race and online market outcomes. Econ. J. 123 (572), F469—F492.

Dovidio, J.F., 2001. On the nature of contemporary prejudice: the third wave. J. Soc. Issues 57 (4), 829—849.

Dovidio, J.F., Gaertner, S.L., 2000. Aversive racism and selection decisions: 1989 and 1999. Psychol. Sci. 11 (4), 315—319.

Dovidio, J.F., Gaertner, S.L., Isen, A.M., Rust, M., Guerra, P., 1998a. Positive affect, cognition, and the reduction of intergroup bias. In: Sedikides, C., Schopler, J., Insko, C.A. (Eds.), Intergroup Cognition and Intergroup Behavior. Lawrence Erlbaum Associates, Mahwah, NJ, pp. 337—366.

Dovidio, J.F., Gaertner, S.L., Validzic, A., 1998b. Intergroup bias: status, differentiation, and a common in-group identity. J. Personality Soc. Psychol. 75 (1), 109.

Dovidio, J.F., Gaertner, S.L., Saguy, T., 2009. Commonality and the complexity of "We": social attitudes and social change. Personality Soc. Psychol. Rev. 13 (1), 3—20.

Droitcour, J., Caspar, R.A., Hubbard, M.L., Ezzati, T.M., 1991. The item count technique as a method of indirect questioning: a review of its development and a case study application. In: Beimer, P.B., Groves, R.M., Lyberg, L.E., Mathiowetz, N.A., Sudman, S. (Eds.), Measurement Errors in Surveys. John Wiley & Sons, Inc, Hoboken, NJ, pp. 185—211.

Duguet, E., Leandri, N., horty, Y.L., Petit, P., 2010. Are young French jobseekers of ethnic immigrant origin discriminated against? A controlled experiment in the Paris area. Ann. Econ. Statistics 187—215.

Dunning, T., Nilekani, J., 2013. Ethnic quotas and political mobilization: caste, parties, and distribution in indian village councils. Am. Political Sci. Rev. 107 (01), 35—56.

Dusek, J.B., Hall, V.C., Meyer, W.J., 1985. Teacher Expectations. Lawrence Erlbaum Associates, Hillsdale, NJ.

Eagly, A.H., Karau, S.J., 2002. Role congruity theory of prejudice toward female leaders. Psychol. Rev. 109 (3), 573.

Eagly, A.H., Makhijani, M.G., Klonsky, B.G., 1992. Gender and the evaluation of leaders: a meta-analysis. Psychol. Bull. 111 (1), 3.

Eden, D., 1992. Leadership and expectations: pygmalion effects and other self-fulfilling prophecies in organizations. Leadersh. Q. 3 (4), 271—305.

Eden, D., Ravid, G., 1982. Pygmalion vs. Self-Expectancy: effects of instructor- and self-expectancy on trainee performance. Organ. Behav. Hum. Perform. 30, 351—364.

Eden, D., Shani, A.B., 1982. Pygmalion goes to boot camp: expectancy, leadership, and trainee performance. J. Appl. Psychol. 67 (2), 194.

Eells, T.D., Robert Showalter, C., 1994. Work-related stress in American trial judges. J. Am. Acad. Psychiatry Law Online 22 (1), 71—83.

Elek, J.K., Agor, P.H., April 28, 2014. Can Explicit Instructions Reduce Expression of Implicit Bias? New Questions Following a Test of a Specialized Jury Instruction. Available at SSRN: http://ssrn.com/abstract=2430438.

Engel, D., Williams Woolley, A., Jing, L.X., Chabris, C.F., Malone, T.W., 2014. Reading the mind in the eyes or reading between the lines? theory of mind predicts collective intelligence equally well online and face-to-face. PLoS One 9 (12), e115212.

Eriksson, S., Rooth, D.-O., 2014. Do employers use unemployment as a sorting criterion when hiring? evidence from a field experiment. Am. Econ. Rev. 104 (3), 1014—1039.

Ewens, M., Tomlin, B., Wang, L.C., 2014. Statistical discrimination or prejudice? A large sample field experiment. Rev. Econ. Statistics 96 (1), 119—134.

Fein, S., Spencer, S.J., 1997. Prejudice as self-image maintenance: affirming the self through derogating others. J. Personality Soc. Psychol. 73 (1), 31.

Fiske, S.T., Neuberg, S.L., 1990. A continuum of impression formation from category-based to individuating processes: influences of information and motivation on attention and interpretation. Adv. Exp. Soc. Psychol. 23, 1—74.

Fisman, R., Iyengar, S.S., Kamenica, E., Simonson, I., 2008. Racial preferences in dating. Rev. Econ. Stud. 75 (177—32).

Fix, M., Struyk, R.J., 1993. Clear and Convincing Evidence: Measurement of Discrimination in America. Urban Institute Press.

Forbes, C.E., Schmader, T., 2010. Retraining attitudes and stereotypes to affect motivation and cognitive capacity under stereotype threat. J. Personality Soc. Psychol. 99 (5), 740.

Forehand, M.R., Deshpandé, R., Reed II, A., 2002. Identity salience and the influence of differential activation of the social self-schema on advertising response. J. Appl. Psychol. 87 (6), 1086—1099.

Fryer, R.G., Levitt, S.D., 2004. The causes and consequences of distinctively black names. Q. J. Econ. 119 (3), 767—805.

Gaertner, S.L., Dovidio, J.F., Rust, M.C., Nier, J.A., Banker, B.S., Ward, C.M., Mottola, G.R., Houlette, M., 1999. Reducing intergroup bias: elements of intergroup cooperation. J. Personality Soc. Psychol. 76 (3), 388.

Galarza, F.B., Yamada, G., 2014. Labor market discrimination in Lima, Peru: evidence from a field experiment. World Dev. 58, 83—94.

Galinsky, A.D., Moskowitz, G.B., 2000. Perspective-taking: decreasing stereotype expression, stereotype accessibility, and in-group favoritism. J. Personality Soc. Psychol. 78 (4), 208.

Galster, G., 1990. Racial discrimination in housing markets during the 1980s: a review of the audit evidence. J. Plan. Educ. Res. 9 (3), 165—175.

Gawronski, B., Deutsch, R., Mbirkou, S., Seibt, B., Strack, F., 2008. When "just say No" is not enough: affirmation versus negation training and the reduction of automatic stereotype activation. J. Exp. Soc. Psychol. 44 (2), 370—377.

Ghayad, R., 2013. The jobless trap. In: Job Market Paper, pp. 1–39.

Gilbert, D.T., Gregory Hixon, J., 1991. The trouble of thinking: activation and application of stereotypic beliefs. J. Personality Soc. Psychol. 60 (4), 509.

Glasford, D.E., Calcagno, J., 2012. The conflict of harmony: intergroup contact, commonality and political solidarity between minority groups. J. Exp. Soc. Psychol. 48 (1), 323–328.

Glover, D., Pallais, A., Pariente, W., 2015. Discrimination as a Self-Fulfilling Prophecy: Evidence from French Grocery Store. Working Paper.

Goldberg, P., 1968. Are women prejudiced against women? Society 5 (5), 28–30.

Goldin, C., Rouse, C., 2000. Orchestrating impartiality: the impact of "blind" auditions on female musicians. Am. Econ. Rev. 90, 715–741.

Golub, B., Jackson, M.O., 2012. How Homophily Affects the Speed of Learning and Best Response Dynamics. FEEM Working Paper.

Good, C., Aronson, J., Inzlicht, M., 2003. Improving adolescents' standardized test performance: an intervention to reduce the effects of stereotype threat. J. Appl. Dev. Psychol. 24 (6), 642–662.

Good, C., Aronson, J., Harder, J.A., 2008. Problems in the pipeline: stereotype threat and women's achievement in high-level math courses. J. Appl. Dev. Psychol. 29 (1), 17–28.

Gosen, S., 2014. Social Desirability in Survey Research: Can the List Experiment Provide the Truth? (Ph.D. Dissertation) Philipps-Universität, Marburg.

Green, A.R., Carney, D.R., Pallin, D.J., Ngo, L.H., Raymond, K.L., Iezzoni, L.I., Banaji, M.R., 2007. Implicit bias among physicians and its prediction of thrombolysis decisions for black and white patients. J. Intern. Med. 22 (9), 1231–1238.

Green, S., Green, D.P., Dias, K., Paluck, B.L., 2016. The contact hypothesis re-examined. (in progress, forthcoming).

Greenwald, A.G., Banaji, M.R., 1995. Implicit social cognition: attitudes, self-esteem, and stereotypes. Psychol. Rev. 102 (1), 4.

Greenwald, A.G., McGhee, D.E., Schwartz, J.L.K., 1998. Measuring individual differences in implicit cognition: the implicit association test. J. Personality Soc. Psychol. 74 (6), 1464.

Greenwald, A.G., Banaji, M., Nosek, B.A., 2003. Understanding and using the implicit association test: I. An improved scoring algorithm. J. Personality Soc. Psychol. 85 (2), 197–216.

Greenwald, A.G., Andrew Poehlman, T., Luis Uhlmann, E., Banaji, M., 2009. Understanding and using the implicit association test: III. Meta-analysis of predictive validity. J. Personality Soc. Psychol. 97 (1), 17–41.

Guryan, J., Kofi Charles, K., 2013. Taste-based or statistical discrimination: the economics of discrimination returns to its roots. Econ. J. 123 (572), F417–F432.

Hamermesh, D.S., Biddle, J.E., 1994. Beauty and the labour market. Am. Econ. Rev. 84, 1174–1194.

Hamilton, B.H., Nickerson, J.A., Owan, H., 2003. Team incentives and worker heterogeneity: an empirical analysis of the impact of teams on productivity and participation. J. Political Econ. 111 (3), 465–497.

Hanson, A., Hawley, Z., 2011. Do landlords discriminate in the rental housing market? Evidence from an internet field experiment in us cities. J. Urban Econ. 70 (2–3), 99–114.

Hartley, L.R., Adams, R.G., 1974. Effect of noise on the stroop test. J. Exp. Psychol. 102 (1), 62.

Heckman, J., 1992. Randomization and social policy evaluation. In: Manski, C., Garfinkel, I. (Eds.), Evaluating Welfare and Training Programs. Harvard University Press, Cambridge, MA, pp. 201–230.

Heckman, J.J., 1998. Detecting discrimination. J. Econ. Perspect. 101–116.

Heckman, J.J., Siegelman, P., 1993. The urban Institute audit studies: their methods and findings. In: Fix, M., Struyk, R. (Eds.), Clear and Convincing Evidence: Measurement of Discrimination in America. Urban Institute Press.

Heilman, M.E., Martell, R.F., 1986. Exposure to successful women: antidote to sex discrimination in applicant screening decisions? Organ. Behav. Hum. Decis. Process. 37 (3), 376–390.

Hitsch, G.J., Hortaçsu, A., Ariely, D., 2010. Matching and sorting in online dating. Am. Econ. Rev. 130–163.

Hjort, J., 2013. Ethnic divisions and productions in firms. In: CESifo Working Paper Series.

Hoff, K., Pandey, P., 2006. Discrimination, social identity, and durable inequalities. Am. Econ. Rev. 206–211.

Holbrook, A.L., Krosnick, J.A., 2010. Social desirability in voter turnout reports: test using the item count technique. Public Opin. Q. 74, 37–67.

Hoogendoorn, S., Van Praag, M., 2012. Ethnic diversity and team performance: a field experiment. In: Tinbergen Institute Discussion Paper 2012-068/3.

Hoogendoorn, S., Oosterbeek, H., Van Praag, M., 2013. The impact of gender diversity on the performance of business teams: evidence from a field experiment. Manag. Sci. 59 (7), 1514–1528.

Houlette, M.A., Gaertner, S.L., Johnson, K.M., Banker, B.S., Riek, B.M., Dovidio, J.F., 2004. Developing a more inclusive social identity: an elementary school intervention. J. Soc. Issues 60 (1).

Hubbuck, J., Carter, S., 1980. Half a Chance?: a report on job discrimination against young blacks in Nottingham. Comm. Racial Equal.

Hugenberg, K., Bodenhausen, G.V., 2004. Ambiguity in social categorization the role of prejudice and facial affect in race categorization. Psychol. Sci. 15 (5), 342–345.

Iyer, L., Mani, A., Mishra, P., Topalova, P., 2012. The power of political voice: women's political representation and crime in India. Am. Econ. J. Appl. Econ. 4 (4), 165–193.

Jacquemet, N., Yannelis, C., 2012. Indiscriminate discrimination: a correspondence test for ethnic homophily in the Chicago labor market. Labour Econ. 19 (6), 824–832.

James, F., DelCastillo, S.W., 1991. Measuring Job Discrimination by Private Employers Against Young Black and Hispanic Seeking Entry Level Work in Denver Metropolitan Area. Unpublished report. University of Colorado, Denver.

Johnson, D.W., Johnson, R.T., 1989. Cooperation and Competition: Theory and Research. Interaction Book Company, Edina, MN.

Johnson, J.D., Whitestone, E., Anderson Jackson, L., Gatto, L., 1995. Justice is still not colorblind: differential racial effects of exposure to inadmissible evidence. Personality Soc. Psychol. Bull. 21 (9), 893–898.

Jolson, M.A., 1974. Employment barriers in marketing. J. Mark.

Jones, B.F., Olken, B.A., 2005. Do leaders matter? National leadership and growth since world war II. Q. J. Econ. 120 (3), 835–864.

Jowell, R., Prescott-Clarke, P., 1970. Racial discrimination and white-collar workers in Britain. Race Class 11 (4), 397–417.

Jussim, L., Harber, K.D., 2005. Teacher expectations and self-fulfilling prophecies: knowns and unknowns, resolved and unresolved controversies. Personality Soc. Psychol. Rev. 9 (2), 131–155.

Kaas, L., Manger, C., 2012. Ethnic discrimination in Germany's labour market: a field experiment. Ger. Econ. Rev. 13 (1), 1–20.

Kane, J.G., Craig, S.C., Wald, K.D., 2004. Religion and presidential politics in Florida: a list experiment. Soc. Sci. Q. 85 (2).

Kang, J., et al., 2012. Implicit bias in the courtroom. UCLA Law Rev. 59 (5).

Karlan, D.S., Zinman, J., May 2012. List randomization for sensitive behavior: an application for measuring use of loan proceeds. J. Dev. Econ. 98 (1), 71–75.

Katz, P.A., 2000. Intergroup Relations Among Youth: Summary of a Research Workshop. Research Summary. Carnegie Corp, New York.

Katz, P.A., Zalk, S.R., 1978. Modification of children's racial attitudes. Dev. Psychol. 14 (5), 447.

Kawakami, K., Dovidio, J.F., Moll, J., Hermsen, S., Russin, A., 2000. Just say No (to stereotyping): effects of training in the negation of stereotypic associations on stereotype activation. J. Personality Soc. Psychol. 78 (5), 871.

Kawakami, K., Dovidio, J.F., Van Kamp, S., 2007a. The impact of counterstereotypic training and related correction processes on the application of stereotypes. Group Process. Intergr. Relat. 10 (2), 139–156.

Kawakami, K., Phills, C.E., Steele, J.R., Dovidio, J.F., 2007b. (Close) distance makes the heart grow fonder: improving implicit racial attitudes and interracial interactions through approach behaviors. J. Personality Soc. Psychol. 92 (6), 957.

Kawakami, K., Steele, J.R., Cifa, C., Phills, C.E., Dovidio, J.F., 2008. Approaching math increases math=me and math=pleasant. J. Exp. Soc. Psychol. 44 (3), 818–825.

Keinan, G., 1987. Decision making under stress: scanning of alternatives under controllable and uncontrollable threats. J. Personality Soc. Psychol. 52 (3), 639.

Key, V., 1949. Southern Politics in State and Nation. University of Tennessee Press.

Kondylis, F., Mobarak, M., Ben Yishay, A., Jones, M., 2015. Are Gender Differences in Performance Innate or Social Mediated? Working Paper.

Krause, A., Rinne, U., Zimmermann, K.F., 2012a. Anonymous job applications in Europe. IZA J. Eur. Labor Stud. 1 (1), 1–20.

Krause, A., Rinne, U., Zimmermann, K.F., 2012b. Anonymous job applications of fresh Ph.D. Economists. Econ. Lett. 117 (2).

Kroft, K., Lange, F., Notowidigdo, M.J., 2013. Duration dependence and labor market conditions: evidence from a field experiment. Q. J. Econ. 128 (3), 1123–1167.

Kuklinski, J.H., Cobb, M.D., Gilens, M., 1997a. Racial attitudes and the "new South". J. Polit. 59 (2), 323–349.

Kuklinski, J.H., Sniderman, P.M., Knight, K., Piazza, T., Tetlock, P.E., Lawrence, G.R., Mellers, B., 1997b. Racial prejudice and attitudes toward affirmative action. Am. J. Political Sci. 41 (2), 402–419.

Lahey, J.N., 2008. Age, women, and hiring: an experimental study. J. Hum. Resour. 43 (1), 30–56.

Lai, C.K., Marini, M., Lehr, S.A., Cerruti, C., Jiyun-Elizabeth, L.S., Joy-Gaba, J.A., Ho, A.K., Teachman, B.A., Wojcik, S.P., Koleva, S.P., et al., 2014. Reducing implicit racial preferences: I. A comparative investigation of 17 interventions. J. Exp. Psychol. General.

Lane, K.A., Banaji, M.R., Nosek, B.A., Greenwald, A.G., 2007. Implicit measures of attitudes. In: Wittenbrink, B., Schwarz, N. (Eds.), Understanding and Using the Implicit Association Test: IV. Guilford, New York, pp. 59–102.

Lang, K., 1986. A language theory of discrimination. Q. J. Econ. 101, 363–382.

Lavy, V., Sand, E., 2015. On the Origins of Gender Human Capital Gaps: Short and Long Term Consequences of Teachers' Stereotypical Biases. NBER Working Paper No. 20909.

Lazear, E., 1999. Language and culture. J. Political Econ. 107 (6), S95–S126.

LeBoeuf, R.A., Shafir, E., Bayuk, J.B., 2010. The conflicting choices of alternating selves. Organ. Behav. Hum. Decis. Process. 111 (1), 48–61.

Lebrecht, S., Pierce, L.J., Tarr, M.J., Tanaka, J.W., 2009. Perceptual other-race training reduces implicit racial bias. PLoS One 4 (1), e4215.

Leippe, M.R., Eisenstadt, D., 1994. Generalization of dissonance reduction: decreasing prejudice through induced compliance. J. Personality Soc. Psychol. 67 (3), 395.

Levy, S.R., Stroessner, S.J., Dweck, C.S., 1998. Stereotype formation and endorsement: the role of implicit theories. J. Personality Soc. Psychol. 74 (6), 1421–1436.

List, J.A., 2004. The nature and extent of discrimination in the marketplace: evidence from the field. Q. J. Econ. 119 (1), 49–89.

List, J.A., 2009. Informed consent in social science. Science 322 (5902), 672.

Lockwood, P., Kunda, Z., 1997. Superstars and me: predicting the impact of role models on the self. J. Personality Soc. Psychol. 73 (1), 91.

Lustig, I., 2003. The Influence of Studying Foreign Conflicts on Students' Perceptions of the Israeli-Palestinian Conflict (Unpublished Masters thesis). University of Haifa.

Ma, D.S., Correll, J., Wittenbrink, B., Bar-Anan, Y., Sriram, N., Nosek, B.A., 2013. When fatigue turns deadly: the association between fatigue and racial bias in the decision to shoot. Basic Appl. Soc. Psychol. 35, 515–524.

Madva, A., 2015. Biased Against Debiasing: On the Role of (Institutionally Sponsored) Self-Transformation in the Struggle Against Prejudice. Working Paper, California State Polytechnic University.

Martinez, M.D., Craig, S.C., 2010. Race and 2008 president politics in Florida: a list experiment. Forum 8 (2).

Marx, B., Pons, V., Suri, T., 2015. Homogeneous Teams and Productivity. Unpublish manuscript, available at: http://www.novasbe.unl.pt/images/novasbe/files/INOVA_Seminars/Vincent_Pons.pdf.

Matsa, D.A., Miller, A.R., 2013. A female style in corporate Leadership? Evidence from quotas. Am. Econ. J. Appl. Econ. 5 (3), 136–169.

Maurer-Fazio, M., 2012. Ethnic discrimination in China's internet job board labor market. IZA J. Migr. 1 (12), 1–24.

McConnell, A.R., Leibold, J.M., 2001. Relations among the implicit association test, discriminatory behavior, and explicit measures of racial attitudes. J. Exp. Soc. Psychol. 37 (435–442).

McGinnity, F., Nelson, J., Lunn, P., Quinn, E., 2009. Discrimination in recruitment. Equal. Res. Ser.

McIntyre, S., Moberg, D.J., Posner, B.Z., 1980. Preferential treatment in preselection decisions according to race and sex. Acad. Manag. J. 23 (4), 738—749.

Milkman, K.L., Akinola, M., Chugh, D., 2012. Temporal distance and discrimination: an audit study in academia. Psychol. Sci. 23 (7), 710—717.

Miller, C., 2014. The Persistent Effect of Temporary Affirmative Action. Job Market Paper.

Mobius, M.M., Rosenblat, T.S., 2006. Why beauty matters. Am. Econ. Rev. 222—235.

Moore, D.A., Swift, S.A., Sharek, Z.S., Gino, F., 2010. Correspondence bias in performance evaluation: why grade inflation works. Personality Soc. Psychol. Bull. 36 (6), 843—852.

Neumark, D., 2012. Detecting discrimination in audit and correspondence studies. J. Hum. Resour. 47 (4), 1128—1157.

Neumark, D., Bank, R.J., Van Nort, K.D., 1996. Sex discrimination in restaurant hiring: an audit study. Q. J. Econ. 111 (3), 915—941.

Newman, J.M., 1978. Discrimination in recruitment: an empirical analysis. Industrial Labor Relat. Rev. 32 (1), 15—23.

Nosek, B.A., Banaji, M., Greenwald, A.G., 2002. Harvesting implicit group attitudes and beliefs from a demonstration website. Group Dyn. Theory, Res. Pract. 6 (1), 101—115.

Nunley, J.M., Pugh, A., Romero, N., Alan Seals, R., 2014. An Examination of Racial Discrimination in the Labor Market for Recent College Graduates: Estimates from the Field. Working Paper.

Ong, D., Wang, J., 2015. Income attraction: an online dating field experiment. J. Econ. Behav. Organ. 111 (C), 13—22.

Oreopoulos, P., 2011. Why do skilled immigrants struggle in the labor market? A field experiment with thirteen thousand resumes. Am. Econ. J. Econ. Policy 3 (4), 148—171.

Oswald, F., Mitchell, G., Blanton, H., Jaccard, J., Tetlock, P.E., 2013. Predicting ethnic and racial discrimination: a meta-analysis of IAT criterion studies. J. Personality Soc. Psychol. 105 (2), 171—192.

Oz, S., Eden, D., 1994. Restraining the Golem: boosting performance by changing the interpretation of low scores. J. Appl. Psychol. 85, 314—322.

Padro i Miguel, G., 2007. The control of politicians in divided societies: the politics of fear. Rev. Econ. Stud. 74 (4), 1259—1274.

Pager, D., 2003. The mark of a criminal record. Am. J. Sociol. 108 (5), 937—975.

Paluck, E.L., Green, D.P., 2009. Prejudice reduction: what works? A review and assessment of research and practice. Annu. Rev. Psychol. 60 (339—367).

Pande, R., 2003. Can mandated political representation increase policy influence for disadvantaged minorities? Theory and evidence from India. Am. Econ. Rev. 93 (4), 1132—1151.

Patacchini, E., Ragusa, G., Zenou, Y., 2012. Unexplored Dimensions of Discrimination in Europe: Religion, Homosexuality and Physical Appearance. Unpublished manuscript: http://www.frdb.org/upload/file/FRDB_Rapporto_PATACCHINI.pdf.

Payne, B.K., 2006. Weapon bias: split-second decisions and unintended stereotyping. Curr. Dir. Psychol. Sci. 15, 287—291.

Payne, B.K., Shimizu, Y., Jacoby, L.L., 2005. Mental control and visual illusions: toward explaining race-biased weapon misidentifications. J. Exp. Soc. Psychol. 41 (1), 36—47.

Petit, P., 2007. The effects of age and family constraints on gender hiring discrimination: a field experiment in the French financial sector. Labour Econ. 14 (3), 371—391.

Pettigrew, T.F., Tropp, L.R., 2000. Does intergroup contact reduce prejudice? Recent meta-analytic findings. Reducing Prejudice Discrimination 93 (114).

Pfann, G.A., Biddle, J.E., Hamermesh, D.S., Bosman, C.M., 2000. Business success and businesses' beauty capital. Econ. Lett. 67 (2), 201—207.

Phelps, E.S., 1972. The statistical theory of racism and sexism. Am. Econ. Rev. 659—661.

Plant, E.A., Devine, P.G., 2009. The active control of prejudice: unpacking the intentions guiding control effects. J. Personality Soc. Psychol. 96, 640—652.

Pope, D.G., Sydnor, J.R., 2011. What's in a picture? Evidence of discrimination from Prosper.com. J. Hum. Resour. 46 (1), 53—92.

Prendergast, C., Topel, R., 1996. Favoritism in organizations. J. Political Econ. 104, 446—461.

Rao, G., 2013. Familiarity Does Not Breed Contempt: Diversity, Discrimination and Generosity in Delhi Schools. Job Market Paper.

Rehavi, M.M., 2007. Sex and Politics: Do Female Legislators Affect State Spending? Unpublished manuscript University of Michigan.

Reicher, S., Levine, M., 1994. Deindividuation, power relations between groups and the expression of social identity: the effects of visibility to the out-group. Br. J. Soc. Psychol. 33 (2), 145–163.

Reynolds, D., 2007. Restraining golem and harnessing pygmalion in the classroom: a laboratory study of managerial expectations and task design. Acad. Manag. Learn. Educ. 6 (4), 475–483.

Riach, P.A., Rich, J., 1991. Testing for racial discrimination in the labour market. Camb. J. Econ. 239–256.

Riach, P.A., Rich, J., 2002. Field experiments of discrimination in the market place. Econ. J. 112 (483), F480–F518.

Riach, P.A., Rich, J., 2010. An experimental investigation of age discrimination in the english labor market. Ann. Econ. Statistics/Annales d'Économie de Statistique 169–185.

Rokeach, M., 1971. Long-range experimental modification of values, attitudes, and behavior. Am. Psychol. 26 (5), 453.

Rokeach, M., 1973. The Nature of Human Values, vol. 438. Free Press, New York.

Rooth, D.-O., 2009. Obesity, attractiveness, and differential treatment in hiring: a field experiment. J. Hum. Resour. 44 (3), 710–735.

Rooth, D.-O., 2010. Automatic associations and discrimination in hiring: real world evidence. Labour Econ. 17 (3), 523–534.

Rosenthal, R., 1963. On the social psychology of the psychological experiment: the Experimenter's hypothesis as unintended determinant of experimental results. Am. Sci. 268–283.

Rosenthal, R., 1994. Interpersonal expectancy effects: a 30-year perspective. Curr. Dir. Psychol. Sci. 176–179.

Rosenthal, R., Jacobson, L., 1968. Pygmalion in the classroom. Urban Rev. 3 (1), 16–20.

Rosenthal, R., Rubin, D.B., 1978. Interpersonal expectancy effects: the first 345 studies. Behav. Brain Sci. 1 (3), 377–386.

Rudman, L.A., Glick, P., 2001. Prescriptive gender stereotypes and backlash toward agentic women. J. Soc. Issues 57 (4), 743–762.

Rudman, L.A., Lee, M.R., 2002. Implicit and explicit consequences of exposure to violent and misogynous rap music. Group Process. Intergr. Relat. 5 (2), 133–150.

Sacerdote, B., 2000. Peer Effects with Random Assignment: Results for Dartmouth Roommates. NBER Working Paper No. 7469.

Saguy, T., Tausch, N., Dovidio, J.F., Pratto, F., 2009. The irony of harmony intergroup contact can produce false expectations for equality. Psychol. Sci. 20 (1), 114–121.

Sherman, J.W., Lee, A.Y., Bessenoff, G.R., Frost, L.A., 1998. Stereotype efficiency reconsidered: encoding flexibility under cognitive load. J. Personality Soc. Psychol. 75 (3), 589.

Shih, M., Wang, E., Trahan Bucher, A., Stotzer, R., 2009. Perspective taking: reducing prejudice towards general outgroups and specific individuals. Group Process. Intergr. Relat. 12 (5), 565–577.

Shook, N.J., Fazio, R.H., 2008. Roommate relationships: a comparison of interracial and same-race living situations. Group Process. Intergr. Relat. 11 (4), 425–437.

Slavin, R.E., 1977. How student learning teams can integrate the desegregated classroom. Integr. Educ. 15 (6), 56–58.

Slavin, R.E., 1979. Effects of biracial leaning teams on cross-racial friendships. J. Educ. Psychol. 71 (381–387).

Slavin, R.E., 1995. Cooperative Learning: Theory, Research, and Practice, second ed. Allyn & Bacon.

Slavin, R.E., Cooper, R., 1999. Improving intergroup relations: lessons learned from cooperative learning programs. J. Soc. Issues 55 (4), 647–663.

Slavin, R.E., Oickle, E., 1981. Effects of cooperative learning teams on student achievement and race relations: treatment by race interactions. Sociol. Educ. 54 (3), 174–180.

Snow, R.E., 1995. Pygmalion and intelligence? Curr. Dir. Psychol. Sci. 169–171.

Stanovich, K.E., West, R.F., 2000. Advancing the rationality debate. Behav. Brain Sci. 23 (5), 701–717.

Steele, C.M., Aronson, J., 1995. Stereotype threat and the intellectual test performance of African Americans. J. Personality Soc. Psychol. 69 (5), 797—811.

Stephan, W.G., Finlay, K., 1999. The role of empathy in improving intergroup relations. J. Soc. Issues 55 (4), 729—743.

Streb, M.J., Burrell, B., Frederick, B., Genovese, M.A., 2008. Social desirability effects and support for a female American president. Public Opin. Q. 72 (1), 76—89.

Tajfel, H., 1970. Experiments in intergroup discrimination. Sci. Am. 223 (5), 96—102.

Tajfel, H., Turner, J.C., 1979. An integrative theory of intergroup conflict. Soc. Psychol. Intergr. Relat. 33 (47), 74.

Todd, A.R., Bodenhausen, G.V., Richeson, J.A., Galinsky, A.D., 2011. Perspective taking combats automatic expressions of racial bias. J. Personality Soc. Psychol. 100 (6), 1027.

Tsuchiya, T., Hirai, Y., Ono, S., 2007. A study of properties of the item count technique. Public Opin. Q. 71 (253—272).

Turner, M.A., Fix, M., Struyk, R.J., 1991. Opportunities Denied, Opportunities Diminished: Racial Discrimination in Hiring. The Urban Institute.

Uhlmann, E.L., Cohen, G.L., 2005. Constructed criteria redefining merit to justify discrimination. Psychol. Sci. 16 (6), 474—480.

Van Knippenberg, A.D., Dijksterhuis, A.P., Vermeulen, D., 1999. Judgement and memory of a criminal act: the effects of stereotypes and cognitive load. Eur. J. Soc. Psychol. 29 (2—3), 191—201.

Wittenbrink, B., Judd, C.M., Park, B., 1997. Evidence for racial prejudice at the implicit level and its relationship with questionnaire measurements. J. Personality Soc. Psychol. 72, 262—274.

Woolley, A.W., Chabris, C.F., Pentland, A., Hashmi, N., Malone, T.W., 2010. Evidence for a collective intelligence factor in the performance of human groups. Science 330 (6004), 686—688.

Wright, B.R.E., Wallace, M., Bailey, J., Hyde, A., 2013. Religious affiliation and hiring discrimination in New England: a field experiment. Res. Soc. Stratif. Mobil. 34, 111—126.

Yeager, D.S., Paunesku, D., Walton, G.M., Dweck, C.S., 2013. How can we instill productive mindsets at scale? A review of the evidence and an initial R&D agenda. In: White Paper for White House Meeting on "Excellence in Education: The Importance of Academic Mindsets".

Yeager, D.S., Vaughns, V.P., Garcia, J., Apfel, N., Brzustoski, P., Master, A., Hessert, W.T., Williams, M.E., Cohen, G.L., 2014. Breaking the cycle of mistrust: wise interventions to provide critical feedback across the racial divide. J. Exp. Psychol. General 143, 804—824.

Yinger, J., 1986. Measuring racial discrimination with fair housing audits: caught in the act. Am. Econ. Rev. 881—893.

Yinger, J., 1998. Evidence on discrimination in consumer markets. J. Econ. Perspect. 23—40.

Zinovyeva, N., Bagues, M., 2011. Does Gender Matter for Academic Promotion? Evidence from a Randomized Natural Experiment. IZA Discussion Paper 5537.

Zussman, A., 2013. Ethnic discrimination: lessons from the Israeli online market for used cars. Econ. J. 123 (572), F433—F468.

CHAPTER 9

Field Experiments on Voter Mobilization: An Overview of a Burgeoning Literature

A.S. Gerber[*,1], D.P. Green[§,1]
*Yale University, New Haven, CT, United States
§Columbia University, New York, NY, United States
[1]Corresponding authors: E-mail: alan.gerber@yale.edu; dpg2110@columbia.edu

Contents

Abstract

This essay reviews the ways in which field experiments have been used to study political participation. We begin by charting the intellectual history of field experimentation in political science. We explain why the advent of field experimentation in recent years represents an important advance over previous work, which relied principally on nonexperimental survey research. Our review of the

Handbook of Economic Field Experiments, Volume 1
ISSN 2214-658X, http://dx.doi.org/10.1016/bs.hefe.2016.09.002

experimental literature on political participation focuses on two broad research domains related to voter mobilization: the effects of different modes of communication (e.g., face-to-face conversations, phone calls, and mail) and the effects of different messages (e.g., those that stress social norms, express gratitude, or urge the expression of implementation intentions). In the final section, we discuss some open questions and new ways that field experiments may illuminate the study of voter turnout and political behavior more generally.

Keywords
Field experiments; Political participation; Voter mobilization; Voting behavior

JEL Codes
C93; D72

In recent years the focus of empirical work in political science has begun to shift from description to an increasing emphasis on the credible estimation of causal effects. A key feature of this change has been the growing prominence of experimental methods, and especially field experiments.

In this chapter we review the use of field experiments to study political participation. Although several important experiments address political phenomena other than voter participation (Bergan, 2009; Broockman and Butler, 2015; Butler and Nickerson, 2011; Broockman, 2013, 2014; Grose, 2014; Kalla and Broockman 2016), the literature measuring the effect of various interventions on voter turnout is the largest and most fully developed, and it provides a good illustration of how the use of field experiments in political science has proceeded. From an initial focus on the relative effects of different modes of communication, scholars began to explore how theoretical insights from social psychology and behavioral economics might be used to craft messages and how voter mobilization experiments could be employed to test the real world effects of theoretical claims. The existence of a large number of experimental turnout studies was essential, because it provided the background against which unusual and important results could be easily discerned.

We begin by describing the intellectual context of the modern emergence of field experiments to study voter turnout. We discuss the state of the literature on campaign effects and voter mobilization around the time of the reintroduction of field experimentation to study political behavior. We discuss some of the methodological reasons why this change represents an important advance over previous work. Our literature reviews focus on two broad areas of research: the effects of different modes of communication (face-to-face conversations, phone calls, and mail) and the effects of different messages. In the final section we discuss some open questions and new directions for applications of field experiments to the application of field experiments to voter turnout and the study of political behavior more generally.

1. INTELLECTUAL CONTEXT FOR EMERGENCE OF FIELD EXPERIMENTS IN POLITICAL SCIENCE

1.1 The development of field experimentation in political science

The first political-science field experiments were conducted by Harold Gosnell in the 1920s. Gosnell, one of the foremost empirical political scientists of the first half of the 20th century, showed an early appreciation for the challenge of identifying the effects of voter mobilization efforts. He notes that the fall of 1924 featured a great deal of get-out-the-vote (GOTV) activity, including a National League of Women Voters' door-to-door canvassing effort and a campaign by two million Boy Scouts to remind citizens of their duty to vote. However, he recognized that any correlation between turnout and mobilization activity cannot be taken to demonstrate that a causal relationship exists. Foreshadowing the concerns about causal identification that now suffuse work on voter turnout, Gosnell writes:

> What was the net effect of all this publicity regarding the election? Did a higher proportion of the eligible voters take part in the electoral process? The only candid answer to these questions is that we do not know... It is true that in some states a larger portion of the adult citizens voted in 1924 than in 1920, but what part of this increase, if any, can be traced to a single factor like the get-out-the-vote movement?
>
> **Gosnell (1927, p. 2)**

Gosnell took up this challenge and conducted the earliest field studies of voter mobilization. He investigated the effects of GOTV mailings on turnout in the presidential election of 1924 and the 1925 Chicago mayoral election (Gosnell, 1927). Although it remains unclear whether Gosnell employed random assignment of the GOTV treatment in his study, other aspects of his research protocol such as measurement of outcomes using the administrative voter records have become familiar features in the modern experimental literature.[1] Three decades after Gosnell, Eldersveld (1956) conducted a series of randomized field experiments to measure the effects of different modes of campaign contact on voter turnout. Eldersveld assigned treatments at the household level and, using post-election administrative records, measured the effect of mail, phone, and canvassing on voter turnout in Ann Arbor, Michigan. While these early experiments have many features of contemporary work, the studies were seldom cited and had little effect on the trajectory of subsequent research. In the decades after Eldersveld, field experimentation was treated as an unusual curio and, when the method was considered at all, it was dismissed as impractical or of limited application. Although lab and survey experiments gained popularity during the 1980s and 1990s, experiments in naturalistic settings

---

[1] Gosnell canvassed some Chicago neighborhoods and assembled a collection of matched pairs of streets. He selected one of the pair to get the treatment, but it is not clear what method Gosnell used to decide which of the pair was to be treated.

remained rare; no field experiment on any subject was published in a major political science journal during the 1990s.

The modern tradition of political-science field experimentation began with a series of experimental studies of campaign activity (Gerber and Green, 2000; Gerber et al., 2001). The turn to field experiments can be understood in part as a response to persistent methodological concerns regarding the then-dominant approaches employed in important political behavior literature. To provide an appreciation for the context in which field experimentation developed in political science, we briefly review the state of the literature on campaign effects at the time of the authors' 1998 field experiment on voter turnout in New Haven. Although this literature includes some of the very best empirical studies of their time, the work suffered from important methodological weaknesses and often produced sharply conflicting results. The appeal of field experiments stems in part from its ability to address many of the deficiencies in the prior literature.

At the time of the New Haven field experiments, the literature that attempted to measure the effect of campaign spending on election outcomes included perhaps a dozen major studies using a variety of empirical strategies. With few exceptions, one common feature of this literature was that the studies did not examine the effect of particular campaign activities but rather explored the correlation between reported campaign spending [as compiled by the Federal Election Commission (FEC)] and candidate vote shares.[2] The pioneering work employing the newly available FEC data was conducted by Jacobson, who estimated spending effects by regressing election outcomes on incumbent and challenger spending levels (Jacobson, 1978, 1985, 1990, 1998). A key assumption of this approach is that spending levels do not adjust to unmeasured aspects of the political context. Intuition, however, suggests that incumbents tend to increase their spending when facing a tough race. This concern was heightened by the major finding of this line of work that incumbent spending frequently had a negative relationship with incumbent vote share. There were two major responses to the threat of bias. First, some studies proposed instrumental variables for candidates spending levels (Green and Krasno, 1988; Gerber, 1998). Second, it was proposed that omitted variables regarding election conditions could be eliminated through a panel approach. Levitt (1994) examined the subset of races that involved the same candidates facing each other in the same district on more than one occasion. Using the subset of races involving repeat-pairs, Levitt measured the relationship between the change in vote share and the change in spending levels, producing estimates that were unrelated to differences in candidate or district attributes that might be lurking in the error term of a cross-sectional regression.

---

[2] There were some exceptions, for example, Ansolabehere and Gerber (1994).

Using the results from several of the leading studies, we can calculate the implied cost per vote.[3] Table 1 shows that the results produced by alternative estimation strategies are dramatically different. The estimated cost of moving the vote margin by a single vote ranges from as little as 20 dollars to as much as 500 (Gerber, 2004). This range seems to span all plausible estimates. Further, it is not clear which study ought to be believed, as each relies on assumptions that, while plausible, are far from airtight. The dramatically inconsistent results, and the sensitivity of the estimates to modeling assumptions, suggest the usefulness of attempting a fresh approach to measuring campaign effects.

The turn to experiments represents one such attempt. The campaign-spending literature attempts to draw conclusions about the effectiveness of spending using overall campaign spending as the independent variable. However, overall spending is the sum of spending on a variety of different activities. Thus, it might be possible to gain insight into the effect of spending overall by measuring the effectiveness of spending on particular components of campaigns, such as voter mobilization efforts. This suggests the usefulness of obtaining a ballpark estimate of the cost of inducing a supporter to cast a ballot. As the literature on campaign-spending effects developed, a parallel literature examining the effects of campaign mobilization was developing as well. This literature progressed on an independent track and, despite its relevance, no connection was drawn to the aggregate spending literature. What did the observational and experimental works on voter mobilization say about the votes that could be produced through voter mobilization efforts?

Prior to the 1998 New Haven experiments, a small field experimental literature addressed the effects of campaign activity on voter turnout. Table 2 lists and summarizes the results of these studies. Gosnell's study in the 1920s was by far the largest. Gosnell measured the effect of a nonpartisan mail campaign in Chicago's 1924 and 1925 elections. Eldersveld followed three decades later with studies of the effect of different modes of contact on turnout levels. He examined the effect of voter mobilization in a pair of local

Table 1 Approximate cost of adding one vote to candidate vote margin

	Incumbent	Challenger
Jacobson (1985)	$278/vote	$18/vote
Green and Krasno (1988)	$22/vote	$19/vote
Levitt (1994)	$540/vote	$162/vote
Erikson and Palfrey (2000)	$68/vote	$35/vote

2015 dollars. Calculations are based on 190,000 votes cast in a typical House district. For House elections, this implies that a 1% boost in the incumbent's share of the vote increases the incumbent's vote margin by 3800 votes.
Adapted from Gerber, A.S., 2004. Does campaign spending work?: Field experiments provide evidence and suggest new theory. Am. Behav. Sci. 47, 541–574.

[3] The cost-per-vote in this context refers to the cost of reducing the vote margin by one vote. In the context of the turnout literature described below, cost-per-vote refers to the cost of mobilizing one additional voter.

Table 2 Voter mobilization experiments prior to 1998 New Haven experiment

Study	Date	Election	Place	No. of subjects (including control group)	Treatment	Effects on turnout (%)[a]
Gosnell (1927)	1924	Presidential	Chicago	3969 registered voters	Mail	+1
Gosnell (1927)	1925	Mayoral	Chicago	3676 registered voters	Mail	+9
Eldersveld (1956)	1953	Municipal	Ann Arbor	41 registered voters	Canvass	+42
				43 registered voters	Mail	+26
Eldersveld (1956)	1954	Municipal	Ann Arbor	276 registered voters	Canvass	+20
				268 registered voters	Mail	+4
				220 registered voters	Phone	+18
Miller et al. (1981)	1980	Primary	Carbondale, IL	79 registered voters	Canvass	+21
				80 registered voters	Mail	+19
				81 registered voters	Phone	+15
Adams and Smith (1980)	1979	Special city council	Washington, DC	2650 registered voters	Phone	+9
Greenwald et al. (1987)	1984	Presidential	Columbus, Ohio	60 registered voters	Phone	+23

[a]These are the effects reported in the tables of these research reports. They have not been adjusted for contact rates. In Eldersveld's 1953 experiment, subjects were those who opposed or had no opinion about charter reform. In 1954, subjects were those who had voted in national but not local elections. The Greenwald et al. results are those for which Greenwald and colleagues count as voting those who in a follow up call say they voted outside the jurisdiction of the study. Alternative treatments of these cases has no material effect on the results. Note that this table includes only studies that use random experimental design [or (possibly) near-random, in the case of Gosnell (1927)].
Adapted from Gerber, A.S., Green, D.P., Nickerson, D.W., 2001. Testing for publication bias in political science. Polit. Anal. 9, 385–392.

elections in Ann Arbor. Greenwald et al. (1987) investigated the psychological hypothesis that predicting one's behavior had a causal effect on future action. They constructed a brief series of questions that had the effect of inducing treated subjects, a random subset of 32 treated subjects drawn from a collection 60 Ohio State undergraduates, to state that they intended to vote in the next day's 1984 presidential election. They measured the effect of this treatment on their subsequent turnout and found the intervention produced more than a 20 percentage point boost in turnout. In 1980, Adams and Smith measured the effect of a 30 s phone call on turnout and vote choice in a District of Columbia special election. In the same year, Miller et al. (1981) measured the turnout effects of door-to-door canvassing, phone calls, and direct mail on randomly targeted voters in a Carbondale, Illinois primary election.

Summarizing the early experiment literature, prior to 1998, there were a few studies conducted over many decades and across a range of political contexts. Nevertheless, when the small literature is viewed as a whole, a few conclusions emerge. First, it appears that campaign interventions are highly effective. Short phone calls produce turnout increases of 10 or even 20 percentage points. According to these studies, visits from canvassers or even a single letter also tend to produce effects of this same magnitude. These are very large estimated effects; to put this treatment effect into context, the falloff in turnout between a presidential election and a midterm election is about 10 percentage points. Second, these large treatment effects are observed in both general elections, such as the 1984 presidential election, and less high profile contests. Third, treatment effects show no tendency to decrease over time.

Another important and related line of research employed laboratory experiments to assess the effect of campaign activity. A leading example of this work is the influential study by Ansolabehere and Iyengar (1996), who brought subjects into a laboratory setting designed to mimic a typical living room and measured the effect of political advertisements inserted into mock newscasts. They found that advertisements that attacked the opposing candidate reduced the likelihood that subjects, when interviewed later, said they would vote, an effect that was especially strong among independent voters. Like field experiments, these studies use random assignment to estimate the causal effect of campaign communications. However, it is hard to translate the results from the laboratory experiments into quantitative estimates of the impact of actual campaign activity on actual voter turnout. Despite the researchers' best effort to simulate the typical viewer experience and measure outcomes reliably, the context in which subjects receive the treatment and express outcomes (intention to vote) differs from natural settings in so many ways, both obvious and subtle, that it is unclear how the lab result indicates either the magnitude or even the direction of the campaign effects being studied.[4]

---

[4] As Gerber (2011) notes, it is not necessarily the case that estimates obtained in the lab indicate the direction of effects in field settings. There are often plausible arguments for why a lab effect might go in the opposite direction from the real world effect. One major difference between the lab and field is that in the real world individuals have additional choices and exposures. Applying this to laboratory studies of negative campaigning, outside the lab individuals may be inspired by a negative advertisement to seek additional information about the claim or to pay more attention to campaign related stimuli, leading to greater interest and higher participation levels.

In contrast to the occasional experimental study, the vast majority of work on campaigns and turnout was (and is) observational. During the 1990s, the most influential scholarship on the causes of turnout were studies that measured the relationship between voter turnout and voter demographics, attitudes, and reported campaign contacts using survey data. Research by Rosenstone and Hansen (1993) is an exemplar of this line of work. Their book was extremely influential and remains a standard reference (its Google scholar citation count exceeded 3700 as of the start of 2016). The book is cited by all turnout scholars, and the research design they employ is still common in current research. The American National Election Study is a federally funded biennial survey research project that began in 1952 and continues to this day. Questions about voter turnout and campaign contact have been asked since the earliest surveys, and Rosenstone and Hansen use the American National Election Studies (ANES) to measure the effect of reported campaign contacts on various measures of participation. Using estimates from a pooled cross-sectional analysis of ANES data, they calculate the incremental contribution of many different factors, including campaign contacts, on reported participation in presidential and midterm years (see Tables 5.1 and 5.2 in Rosenstone and Hansen, 1993). They find that the estimated effect of campaign contact on reported voter turnout is approximately a 10 percentage point increase in turnout probability.

The 10 percentage point turnout boost from campaign contact found by Rosenstone and Hansen is similar in magnitude to the effects estimated by many of the early field experiments. However, despite this agreement, there are grounds for skepticism. As we point out in the next section, respondents' exposure to campaign contact is neither randomly assigned nor accurately measured. The move to field experiments in the late 1990s was motivated in part by concern about the potential bias in the dominant survey-based research tradition.

2. HOW DO EXPERIMENTS ADDRESS THE PROBLEMS IN THE PRIOR VOTER TURNOUT RESEARCH?

In this section we present a basic framework for defining causal effects and apply the framework to explain how field experiments eliminate some of the key sources of bias in observational studies. To fix ideas, we will use the classic Rosenstone and Hansen (1993) survey analysis as a running example. In Rosenstone and Hansen, some respondents report that they are "treated" (contacted by a campaign) and some report that they are "untreated" (not contacted by the campaign). The key challenge in estimating the treatment effect of campaign contact on those who are truly contacted is that the analyst must use available data to construct an estimate of a counterfactual quantity, the turnout rate of the contacted in the event they had not been treated. We express this challenge using potential outcomes notation (Rubin, 1978). For each individual i, let Y_{i0} be the outcome if i does not receive the treatment (in this example, contact by the mobilization effort), and Y_{i1} be the outcome if i receives the treatment. The treatment effect for individual i is defined as

$$\tau_i = Y_{i1} - Y_{i0}. \tag{1}$$

We define the treatment effect for individual i as the difference between the outcome for i in the two possible, but mutually exclusive, states of the world: one in which i is treated, and another in which i is not. Moving from a single individual, the average treatment effect for the treated (ATT) is defined as

$$\text{ATT} = E(\tau_i | T_i = 1) = E(Y_{i1} | T_i = 1) - E(Y_{i0} | T_i = 1), \tag{2}$$

where the E() operator stands for a group average and $T_i = 1$ when a person is treated. The quantity $Y_{i1} | T_i = 1$ is the posttreatment outcome for those who are actually treated, and $Y_{i0} | T_i = 1$ is the outcome that would have been observed for the treated had they, in fact, not been treated.

In Rosenstone and Hansen, as in the rest of the nonexperimental literature, the comparison group for the treated are subjects who are untreated. When covariate adjustment is used, the comparison group is the set of subjects who are untreated but resemble the treated with respect to their background attributes. This approach is susceptible to selection bias when the potential outcomes among the untreated are systematically different from those of the treated. Stated formally, in expectation the observational comparison of the treated and the untreated estimates yields

$$E(Y_{i1}|T_i = 1) - E(Y_{i0}|T_i = 0) = [E(Y_{i1}|T_i = 1) - E(Y_{i0}|T_i = 1)]$$
$$+ [E(Y_{i0}|T_i = 1) - E(Y_{i0}|T_i = 0)]$$

$$= \text{ATT} + \text{Selection Bias}. \tag{3}$$

Under what conditions does the selection bias term disappear? The critical assumption for identification of the average treatment on treated in observational work is that—controlling for covariates (whether through regression or through matching), $E(Y_{i0}|T_i = 1) = E(Y_{i0}|T_i = 0)$, that is, apart from their exposure to the treatment—the treated and untreated group outcomes are on average the same in the untreated state. In the absence of some unusual as-if random circumstance by which some units came to be treated and other remained untreated, this assumption is not credible. Consider the case at hand, estimating the effect of campaigning on voter turnout. Campaigns typically have extensive information available about a jurisdiction's voters based on both administrative records of voter turnout and demographics along with insider information about individuals and neighborhoods. This information, which may not be fully available to the data analyst, is typically used in campaign targeting strategies. Campaigns commonly target those who have shown a tendency to participate, and this characteristic is, from the standpoint of the analyst, an omitted variable. The ANES, for example, does not record respondents' vote history, although voter files available to campaigns do contain this information. Second, previous turnout records are highly predictive of the outcome variable, turnout. Therefore, $E(Y_{i0}|T_i = 1)$ may be substantially higher than $E(Y_{i0}|T_i = 0)$. Although in this case it is possible to guess the direction of the bias, analysts rarely have a firm basis to speculate about the magnitude of the bias, and so it is not possible to correct the estimates.[5]

Beyond selection bias, field experiments mitigate a variety of other common methodological concerns regarding observational studies of political behavior. In observational studies the researcher controls neither the treatment assignment nor the design of the treatment. At the most basic level, a key feature of field experimentation is that the researcher controls the assignment to treatment and therefore knows which subjects are assigned to treatment and control conditions. Observational studies often attempt to measure whether an individual is treated or not, but survey measures may be unreliable. Commonly, whether a subject is treated or not relies on the subject's self-report (of campaign contact, of advertising exposure, of media usage, etc.). Consider again the example of attempts to measure the effects of campaign mobilization on voter turnout. In this literature, contact is self-reported, and misreporting leads to a treatment group that is a mixture of the treated and untreated. If this misreporting is random misclassification, the estimated average treatment effects will be attenuated, but if those who misreport campaign contact tend to be the more politically engaged, this nonrandom measurement error may exaggerate the effects of campaign contacts. This bias will be heightened when, as is often the case, the subject's turnout is itself based on self-report. There is empirical evidence of both substantial misreporting and a positive correlation between misreporting campaign exposure and misreporting having voted (Vavreck, 2007; Gerber and Doherty, 2009). It should be noted that although from time to time previous observational work has employed validated vote (the ANES used public voting records to add this variable into the survey datasets for the years 1964, 1972, 1974, 1976, 1978, 1980, 1984, 1986, 1988, and 1990[6]), one of the important innovations brought about by the advent of field experimentation in this area is that it has become common for studies of political behavior to use administrative data rather than self-reports.

A further problem that is avoided by field experiments is ambiguity about what intervention is being assessed. Turning again to the case of the voter mobilization research, the ANES item used for campaign contact in the Rosenstone and Hansen study asks

---

[5] Further, when "correcting" for bias, this uncertainty about the size of bias is not contained in the reported standard errors and, unlike sampling variability, it remains undiminished as the sample size increases (Gerber et al., 2004). The conventional measures of coefficient uncertainty in observational research thereby underestimate the true level of uncertainty, especially in cases where the sample size is large.

[6] See http://www.electionstudies.org/overview/dataqual.htm.

respondents: "Did anyone from one of the political parties call you up or come around and talk to you about the campaign?" Taken literally, this question asks the respondents about partisan phone or face-to-face contact leading to a conversation about the campaign, which omits all campaign contact through mail, all contact about political issues outside the campaign, and possibly all manner of nonpartisan contact urging turnout. It is unclear whether survey respondents attend to these nuances when answering the question, which only deepens the ambiguity surrounding the treatment effect that survey-based regressions are estimating.

In experimental analysis, it is now standard to account for noncompliance. In the context of voter mobilization, noncompliance most commonly occurs when individuals who were assigned to the treatment group remain untreated. The rate at which failure to treat occurs varies across modes of contact, the intensity of the effort to contact, the difficulty of contact, and attributes of the subjects and context. Noncompliance arises for a variety of reasons, such as the subject relocating, not answering the door or phone when the campaign attempts contact, or the campaign running out of resources before attempting to contact all subjects assigned to be treated. The failure to treat is immediately apparent in field experiments, and the observed difference in average outcomes for the treatment and control groups is adjusted for the proportion of the treatment group contacted to estimate the average treatment effect among compliers (Angrist et al., 1996), which is the same as the average effect of the treatment on the treated when experiments encounter one-sided noncompliance.

Properly accounting for noncompliance in voter mobilization experiments is an innovation of recent work, as experimental studies prior to 1998 either dropped the untreated subjects in the treatment group from the analysis or reclassified them as control group observations (Adams and Smith, 1980; Eldersveld, 1956) or made no mention of the issue (Miller et al., 1981). Such approaches produce biased estimates of the effect of the treatment on the treated if those who cannot be contacted in the treatment group have a different average untreated potential outcome than the entire pool of subjects. Because failure to treat may stem from factors related to propensity to turnout, such as recently relocating, being out of town around election day, being busy or anti-social, or any of a number of other possibilities, noncompliance is unlikely to be ignorable. In studies of GOTV phone calls, those who are hard to contact often prove to be much less likely to vote than the average subject (Gerber and Green, 2005; Arceneaux et al. 2006). In observational studies, those whom the campaign cannot reach will tend to report that they were untreated and will therefore be grouped with those the campaign did not attempt to reach. Thus, in addition to selection bias due to the campaign targeting, there is also bias due to the campaign's failure to treat some of its targets.

In sum, field experiments have at least three important advantages over survey-based observational studies of voter turnout. Random assignment of the treatment eliminates the threat of selection bias. Direct manipulation of the treatment also allows researchers to have more control over what the treatment is and to more accurately ascertain whether subjects received it. The use of administrative data to measure outcomes helps ensure symmetry between those assigned to the treatment and control groups. A commonly noted limitation of field experiments is that they seldom encompass a random sample of a national electorate (but see Fieldhouse et al., 2013), which raises the question of whether experimental results generalize across subjects, treatments, and contexts. One way to address this concern is through extensive replication of experiments, a practice that has become common in voter mobilization research. Indeed, one of the distinctive features of the experimental literature on voter mobilization is the large and ever growing number of studies that replicate and extend existing research. The next section describes the evolution of the experimental literature, which now encompasses studies conducted in Europe, Asia, and Latin America.

3. AN OVERVIEW OF THE EXPERIMENTAL LITERATURE ON VOTER MOBILIZATION[7]

The modern voter mobilization literature can be divided into two main classes of studies. The early work focused on the relative effectiveness of different modes of contact. This focus was in part inspired by a concern that the shift from the more personal campaigning of a previous era to modern campaigns conducted through mailings and television were contributing to a decline in turnout. Although some studies introduced experimental variation in message content, this was not the major focus of the research. A second line of research aimed to measure the effect of alternative messages employed in the communications. Often inspired by psychological theories or political folk wisdom, these studies examined how the impact of the communication changed according to the words and images used in the campaign material. For some influential theories in social psychology, this literature, although published largely in political science journals, provides some of the most telling empirical evidence.

3.1 Modes of contact

The New Haven 1998 study examined the relative effectiveness of three common campaign tactics: door-to-door canvassing, calls from commercial phone banks, and direct mail. The study found that face-to-face canvassing produced an 8 percentage point increase in turnout among those contacted, each piece of mail raised turnout by half a percentage point in households receiving the mail (the number of mailings varied from 0 to 3), and a phone call produced no increase in turnout. A substantial follow

---

[7] This section is adapted from Green and Gerber (2015).

up literature measured the effect of each of these three modes of communication across a range of contexts and extended this line of research to include GOTV appeals communicated via television, radio, and social media.

3.1.1 Canvassing studies

After the New Haven Study, basic questions of generalizability abounded. Would canvassing work elsewhere? Would it work in competitive as well as uncompetitive municipal races? We first summarize studies that, like the New Haven Study, canvassed using nonpartisan GOTV appeals. In 2001 a multisite evaluation was carried out in six cities: Bridgeport, Columbus, Detroit, Minneapolis, Raleigh, and St. Paul. Baseline turnout rates in the control groups varied considerably across sites, from 8.2% to 43.3%. Despite the varying electoral and demographic contexts, results were no more variable than one would expect by chance. In all six sites, turnout was higher in the assigned treatment group than the control group, although the increase was negligible in one site. Analyzing the data for the six sites with a single regression model raised turnout among those contacted by 7.1 percentage points with a standard error of 2.2 percentage points (Green et al., 2003).

Another mobilization experiment conducted in 2001 extended previous work in three important directions (Michelson, 2003). First, the canvassing effort achieved a remarkable 75%-contact rate. Second, it showed how mobilization works in a rural setting. The study took place in a low-turnout municipal election in a largely Latino California farming community. Third, it varied the campaign message between appeals that stressed either civic duty, ethnic solidarity (for Latino voters), or community solidarity (for non-Latino voters). Regardless of the message used, the team of Latino canvassers proved highly effective at mobilizing Latino voters. For all Latinos, turnout increased from 13.8% (N = 298) to 18.5% (N = 466). For non-Latinos, turnout increased from 25.7% (N = 758) to 28.2% (N = 1243). Canvassers contacted 73% of Latinos and 78% of non-Latinos. The scripts were not significantly different in terms of the effectiveness with which they mobilized voters.

Again examining the effects of alternative messages in addition to the effects of Latino and non-Latino canvassers, Herbert Villa and Melissa Michelson (2003) focused on a sample of voters under the age of 26, encouraging them to vote in the 2002 state and federal elections. Turnout among Latino subjects rose from 7.2% (N = 1384) to 9.3% (N = 1507), and among non-Latino subjects it rose from 8.9% (N = 1438) to 10.0% (N = 1455). The contact rates were 51% and 39%, respectively. Again, Michelson and Villa found no evidence that the content of the canvassing script made an appreciable difference. Michelson returned to Fresno in 2003, using students from her classes to conduct an experiment on the differential effects of partisan and nonpartisan appeals. Like the Bennion study of the 2002 midterm election, which also used students canvassing as part of a course assignment, this study found weak treatment effects (Bennion, 2005).

Overall, the control group (N = 2672) turned out at a rate of 15.2%, compared to 14.9% in the treatment group (N = 3371), which was contacted at a rate of 34%.

Unlike other studies of door-to-door canvassing, Nickerson (2008) used a placebo control design. Half of those contacted were urged to recycle; the other half, to vote in the 2002 primary elections held in Denver and Minneapolis. Turnout increased from 47.7% (N = 279) to 56.3% (N = 283) among those urged to vote. Since by design the contact rate was 100%, the study had reasonable statistical power despite the small sample size. Perhaps the most interesting aspect of this experiment was Nickerson's demonstration that turnout among housemates of persons in the treatment group was significantly higher than turnout among housemates of those in the control group, suggesting that the mobilizing effects of a face-to-face conversation with canvassers may have been transmitted to other members of the household.

In 2004, Carrie LeVan (2016) organized a nonpartisan canvassing campaign aimed at mobilizing voters in low-turnout, low-income, and largely Latino precincts in Bakersfield, California. The study comprised 727 voters, 423 of whom lived in households that were assigned to the treatment group. The contact rate among those assigned to the treatment group was 50%. The study found strong canvassing effects. Among voters living in one-person households, for example, turnout was 41.0% in the control group and 54.5% in the treatment group. Gregg Murray and Richard Matland (2012) also conducted a canvassing study in a largely Latino area, Brownsville, Texas. Turnout among the 3844 individuals assigned to the control group was 33.3%, compared to 34.9% among the 7580 assigned to the canvassing group, of whom 22% were actually contacted.

Lisa García Bedolla and Melissa Michelson (2012) collaborated with several nonpartisan groups participating in the California Votes Initiative, which sought to mobilize low-propensity voters in a series of elections from 2006 through 2008. The effort is noteworthy because of the number of organizations that conducted door-to-door outreach, the range of ethnic groups that were targeted, and the range of electoral contexts during which canvassing took place. In all, 117 distinct experiments were conducted. Although the authors note that many of the participating organizations contacted voters primarily to spread the word about the organization's activities or administer issue surveys rather than to engage in voter mobilization (p. 127), the treatment voted at a higher rate than the control group in 77 of these experiments, which would occur by chance with $p < .001$.

By comparison to partisan canvassing, which tends to occur on a vast scale in closely contested states in presidential elections, nonpartisan canvassing is relatively rare. However, since partisan campaigns always have the option of using nonpartisan appeals to mobilize their partisan supporters, experimental evaluations of nonpartisan canvassing are potentially informative even to campaigns that seek to advocate on behalf of a candidate or ballot measure. Nevertheless, the question arises as to whether the results would differ if canvassers attempted to urge voters to support a particular candidate or cause. Although no experiments have attempted a head-to-head comparison between nonpartisan and advocacy appeals, a series of advocacy experiments suggest that such canvassing may produce widely varying effects.

Two experiments conducted in 2003 gave early indications that advocacy campaigns could be quite effective in mobilizing voters. In Kansas City, the ACORN organization canvassed extensively in predominantly African American precincts. Its aim was to identify and mobilize those supportive of a ballot measure designed to preserve local bus service. Unlike most other canvassing experiments, this one was randomized at the level of the precinct, with 14 assigned to the treatment group and 14 to the control group. Among voters assigned to control precincts (N = 4779), turnout was 29.1%, compared to 33.5% in the treatment group, 62.7% of whom were contacted (Arceneaux, 2005). At roughly the same time, ACORN canvassed in Phoenix on behalf of a ballot measure to determine the future of the county hospital (Villa and Michelson, 2003). ACORN conducted two rounds of canvassing, the first to identify voters sympathetic to the ballot measure and a second to urge supportive voters to vote. The canvassing effort targeted voters with Latino surnames who had voted in at least one of the previous four elections. ACORN made multiple attempts to contact voters (including making a small number of phone calls), the result being that 71% of those living in one-voter households were contacted at least once. This figure rose to 80% among two-voter households. This mobilization campaign had a powerful effect on turnout. Among one-person households, turnout rose from 7.4% in the control group (N = 473) to 15.9% in the treatment group (N = 2666). Among two-person households, turnout rose from 6.9% in the control group (N = 72) to 21.0% in the treatment group (N = 2550).

On the other hand, advocacy campaigns have been known to produce disappointing results. Strategic Concepts in Organizing and Policy Education (SCOPE) in Los Angeles canvassed in opposition to the "three-strikes" statewide ballot measure but generated no apparent turnout effect (Arceneaux and Nickerson, 2009). Gray and Potter (2007) found weak mobilization effects in a small canvassing experiment on behalf of a candidate for local magistrate. In their study of canvassing on behalf of a local candidate, Barton et al. (2012) find an unexpectedly negative effect on turnout. Larger candidate advocacy experiments show positive effects, although the treatment-on-treated estimates are smaller than those obtained in the ACORN studies. A sizable experiment on behalf of a Democratic gubernatorial candidate in 2005 generated a treatment-on-treated estimate of 3.5 (SE = 2.4), and a series of experiments in 2014 on behalf of state legislative candidates in Republican primary runoff elections generated a treatment-on-treated estimate of 3.1 (SE = 1.8).

3.1.2 Commercial phone banks

In 1998 the authors conducted two nonpartisan campaigns using a single commercial phone bank (Gerber and Green, 2000, 2001). The smaller of the two campaigns was conducted in New Haven; a larger study was conducted in neighboring West Haven. In both cities, the elections were rather quiet affairs, with relatively little campaign activity. In both experiments, the group receiving phone calls voted at rates that were no greater than the rates of the control group receiving no calls. None of the three scripts—one stressing civic duty, another, neighborhood solidarity, and a third, the possibility of deciding a close election—had any appreciable impact.

In order to assess whether these results were specific to the context or the calling house, we replicated the 1998 experiments on a grand scale in 2002 (Arceneaux et al., 2006). Congressional districts in Iowa and Michigan were divided into two categories, depending on whether they featured competitive or uncompetitive races. Within each category, 15,000 randomly selected individuals at distinct addresses were called by one of two commercial phone banks, each delivering the same nonpartisan message. Thus, 60,000 people in all were called in the treatment group, and more than 1 million names were placed in the control group. In the 2002 study, the treatment effects were just barely on the positive side of zero, implying that these phone banks mobilized one additional voter for every 280 people they spoke with. Another massive study in Illinois, which called voters before the 2004 November election using a similar nonpartisan script, found somewhat larger effects (Arceneaux et al., 2010). This time one vote was generated per 55 completed calls. However, this study is counterbalanced by a pair of large nonpartisan experiments in North Carolina and Missouri, which found conventional calls to have meager effects, just one vote generated per 500 contacts (Ha and Karlan, 2009).

Calls that advocate on behalf of a candidate or ballot measure have been found to produce similarly weak average treatment effects among compliers. Close to 30,000 calls (about half resulting in successful contact) were made by a commercial phone center on behalf of a ballot measure in a San Francisco municipal election. Consistent with other findings concerning the delivery of brief scripts by commercial phone banks, one vote was produced for every 200 successful contacts (McNulty, 2005). Similar results were found in a relatively small study of a 2002-gubernatorial primary (Cardy, 2005). A much larger experiment conducted by the 2006 general elections also found weak effects, regardless of whether these calls were made using nonpartisan messages or messages advocating support for a minimum wage measure (Mann, 2008). A head-to-head experimental comparison between partisan and nonpartisan scripts indicated that neither had an appreciable effect on turnout (Panagopoulos, 2008).

Several scholars have investigated the hypothesis that the effectiveness of these calls hinges on the manner in which the scripts are delivered. Commercial vendors are paid according to the number of targets they reach, not the number of votes they generate. The callers, who can forge through 50 or so completed calls per hour, behave much as one would expect given the incentives of piecework and the eagerness of supervisors to move on to the next calling campaign.

In 2002 David Nickerson evaluated a youth-oriented voter mobilization campaign in which a commercial phone bank was paid top dollar to deliver its GOTV appeal in a chatty and unhurried manner. The script required the reader to pause for questions and to invite respondents to visit a website in order to learn more about their polling location. A good deal of coaching ensured that this appeal was read at the proper speed. Between one and four calls were made to randomly selected subgroups of young people over the four-week period leading up to election day. The phone bank kept records of each person they contacted, so that when respondents were contacted a second time, the script took notice of the fact that the previous conversation was being resumed. The calls produced a substantial and statistically significant increase in voter turnout in the target group, but only among those called during the final week of the campaign. In other words, calls made during the first three weeks of a month-long GOTV campaign had no apparent effect on voter turnout. Calls made during the last week produced one vote for every 20 contacts (Nickerson, 2007). This finding set in motion a series of experiments designed to sort out whether the strong effects reflect timing, the use of repeated calls, or the conversational style in which the scripts were delivered.

As to the timing and sequencing of calls from commercial phone banks, a large study conducted across battleground and non-battleground states in the weeks leading up to the 2008 presidential election found that neither first round nor second round calls by themselves boosted turnout but that turnout rose significantly when voters who in round 1 said they planned to vote were later called back and asked whether they could still be counted on to vote. This finding echoes the unusually strong effects found in four follow-up call experiments conducted by volunteer phone banks (Michelson et al., 2009). However, this effect did not replicate in a large commercial phone bank experiment in 2014, which found follow-up calls to have much weak effects (Gerber et al., 2016).

These results tentatively suggest that the active ingredients in a successful call are the scripts and the manner in which they are delivered. This scripts hypothesis was tested in prior to the presidential election of 2004 with calls directed at residents of a battleground and non-battleground state (Ha and Karlan, 2009). A large phone bank deployed three kinds of nonpartisan scripts: a standard script akin to the ones used above; a longer, chattier script in which people were asked whether they knew their polling location, which was provided on request; and a still longer script in which people were encouraged both to vote and to mobilize their friends and neighbors to vote. The results are suggestive, if a bit puzzling. As expected, the standard script had weak effects, raising turnout by just 1.2 percentage points among those contacted. Also as expected, the medium script had a fairly large effect, producing a complier average casual effect (CACE) estimate of 3.4 percentage points. This statistically significant increase implies that one vote was generated for every 30 completed calls. The puzzling result is the fact that the chatty recruit-your-friends script had an unexpectedly weak effect, as one vote per 69 completed calls.

The call-quality hypothesis was tested in 2010 in a head-to-head competition among different phone banks (Mann and Klofstad, 2015). On the high side of the quality spectrum were phone banks that specialized in fundraising or political calls; on the low side were phone banks whose business consisted of a wide array of nonpolitical as well as political clients. Mann and Klofstad reason that firms on the low end of the quality spectrum are incentivized to push through a high volume of calls in a mechanical fashion, whereas the focus and reputation of the high-quality firms required them to recruit and retain callers with a knack for political persuasion. Each of the four phone banks called more than 100,000 voters across several states. All the phone banks used the same "chatty" script, which blended several of the ideas discussed in Section 4: gratitude, implementation intentions, and positive descriptive norms. Consistent with the quality hypothesis, the two low-quality phone banks generated weak results, raising turnout among those they spoke with by just 0.2 percentage points. By contrast, the two high-quality phone banks raised turnout among those they reached by 0.9 and 1.4 percentage points. Although the high-quality phone banks proved far less effective than the average volunteer phone bank or the vaunted high-quality phone bank in the Nickerson study, they were significantly more effective than the low-quality phone banks. (Ironically, the lower quality phone banks also reported a higher rate of contacts, which meant that they ended up being more expensive on a cost-per-vote basis.) Given the immense size of this experiment and the tight controls that the authors imposed on the scripts used by the different phone banks, this study offers the most convincing evidence to date about the importance of that intangible ingredient, quality.

3.1.3 Mailings

We begin our summary of the direct mail literature by focusing on "standard" nonpartisan appeals, deferring the discussion of mailings that exert social pressure and other psychological tactics until Section 4. During the four weeks leading up to the 1998 election, we conducted an experiment in which registered voters in New Haven received one, two, or three pieces of nonpartisan direct mail. Each batch of mail reflected one of three themes: the need to do one's civic duty, the responsibility to stand up for one's neighborhood so that politicians will take an interest in its problems, or the importance of voting in a close election. Turnout in the control group, which received no mail, phone calls, or door-to-door canvassing, was 42.2% (N = 11,596). Turnout was 42.6% (N = 2550) among those receiving one mailer, 43.3% (N = 2699) among those receiving two, and 44.6% (N = 2527) among those receiving three. For the sample as a whole (N = 31,098), regression estimates that controlled for the effects of phone and door-to-door canvassing put the effects of each additional mailer at 0.5 percentage point

(SE = 0.3), which was narrowly significant at the 0.05 level using a one-tailed test. No significant differences were found among the three messages.

In New Haven's 1999 mayoral election, nonpartisan mailings patterned after the civic duty and close election mailings used in the 1998 earlier study were sent to a random sample of the 1998 voter list. The innovation of this study was to send up to eight mailings in order to assess diminishing returns. The close election message had no effect (the election was not remotely close), but the civic duty message performed on par with the 1998 results. The results suggest that returns from mailings begin to diminish after six mailings per household.

Given these encouraging initial results, a series of subsequent experiments tested the effectiveness of nonpartisan mailings as a means of encouraging turnout among ethnic minorities. In a field experiment conducted before the 2002 election, Janelle Wong (2005) classified Los Angeles County voters by last name into one of several Asian American groups: Chinese, Filipino, Indian, Japanese, and Korean. Chinese Americans were sent one piece of bilingual nonpartisan direct mail encouraging them to vote. Other ethnic groups were sent one piece of direct mail in English. Among Chinese Americans, turnout in the control group was 29.0% (2924); the treatment group turned out at a rate of 31.7% (1137). Among other Asian groups, the control group voted at a rate of 38.5% (N = 5802), compared with the treatment group rate of 39.4% (N = 2095). Also in the 2002 election, a much larger multisite experiment sought to mobilize Latino voters in Los Angeles County, Orange County (California), Houston, New Mexico, and Colorado (Ramirez, 2005). The content of the bilingual mailers was developed in collaboration with consultants using focus groups. The number of mailers varied across sites from two to four. Despite the high quality of the printing and graphics, they were found to have weak turnout effects.

Several other scholars have attempted to gauge whether ethnic communities can be mobilized using direct mail in 2004. Trivedi (2005) tested alternative nonpartisan messages and graphic themes designed to mobilize Indian American voters living in New York City. Her postcards conveyed ethnic, pan-ethnic, or civic duty appeals, but no message stood out as particularly effective. Richard Matland and Gregg Murray (2012) conducted a nonpartisan mail campaign in largely Latino Brownsville, Texas. Households were randomly assigned a postcard with one of two messages. One emphasized greater power for Latinos if they became more politically active and voted. The other emphasized civic duty and the closeness of the election as the reasons for the recipients should go to the polls and vote in the upcoming presidential election. Both found weak effects.

Bedolla and Michelson (2012) conducted 38 direct mail experiments in California from 2006 through 2008 in an effort to mobilize minority voters using a combination of generic and ethnic appeals. They found weak effects overall, with 19 of the 38 experiments producing positive estimates. Neither voter guides nor hand-written postcards seemed to boost turnout.

Two further strands of the nonpartisan mail literature deserve mention. The first is the simple reminder that an election is imminent. This tactic has repeatedly been shown to have negligible effects and has come to be used as a placebo condition in several experiments (Panagopoulos, 2014, 2013, 2011). Another tactic is to pique voters' interest in an election by calling attention to certain ballot measures. One such experiment sent a single mailing to registered voters both across Florida and specifically in Leon County (Barabas et al., 2010). Each mailing alerted voters to the importance of one ballot measure. The authors compared the mobilization effects of these mailings to those of a generic GOTV mailing and found small differences in effects across different issues or appeals.

The literature gauging the turnout effects of advocacy mailings is essentially a string of null findings. The first large-scale experiments were conducted in 1999 in state legislative and municipal elections on behalf of Democratic candidates (Gerber et al., 2003). The state legislative experiments divided the target population into "prime" Democrats (those with a high propensity to vote), "nonprime" Democrats and Independents, and a random sample of the list of registered voters. The mailings boosted turnout among prime Democrats, but not among other Democrats. Turnout in the random sample rose with the number of mailings, but the effects were small given the number of mailings sent to each household. Combining all of the New Jersey samples suggests that mail did not significantly increase voter turnout. Some slight evidence for demobilization may be found in the negatively toned mayoral campaign, which sent nine mailings to each household.

Another early study evaluated the mobilizing effects of advocacy mail from an abortion-rights interest group, which backed a pro-choice candidate in a gubernatorial primary campaign (Cardy, 2005). The group targeted strongly pro-choice voters whose stances had been previously identified by the phone interviews. The treatment group (N = 1974) received five mailings that were printed in full color on glossy paper and mailed between 19 and 6 days before the election. Turnout in the control group (N = 2008) was slightly higher than in the treatment group. Other small studies produced results that, on average, suggest little effect on turnout (Cho et al., 2006; Gray and Potter, 2007; Niven, 2006). This conclusion was bolstered by a massive study that sent up to nine pieces of mail on behalf of a Democratic gubernatorial candidate in 2005, as well as a large test on behalf of Republican state legislative candidates in 2014 that sent up to 12 mailers (Cubbison, 2015). The lack of effect is not altogether surprising given that the mailers focused on issues and candidates rather than turnout. Nevertheless, the findings drive home the point that advocacy communications per se do little to stimulate voter turnout.[8]

---

[8] Somewhere between nonpartisan mail and advocacy mail are mailers from advocacy groups that target ideologically allied voters but appeal to them using nonpartisan language. See, for example, Mann (2008). These studies tend to produce effects that are somewhere between the noneffects of partisan mail and the weak effects of nonpartisan mail.

3.1.4 Other modes of communication

Compared to the extensive experimental literature on canvassing, phone banks, and direct mail, the literature on other modes of communication looks relatively thin. Some of the most robust findings concern the weak effects of some widely used tactics. For example, David Nickerson (2007) reports the results of 13 experiments in which almost a quarter of a million people—college students, registered voters who did not opt out of email communication, or visitors to websites who agreed to be reminded to vote—were urged via email to vote in an upcoming election. These nonpartisan appeals produced negligible effects, even when 20% or more of the recipients opened the GOTV email on an HTML-compatible browser. Malhotra et al. (2012) found that small but statistically significant effects were found when emails were sent out by the registrar of voters, but identical emails sent by a nonpartisan group has no effect. Alissa Stollwerk collaborated with the Democratic National Committee to assess the effects of three emails encouraging voter turnout in support of the Democratic mayoral candidate in the 2005 New York City general election. The emails were sent in the late afternoon on election eve, on the morning of Election Day, and during the midafternoon of Election Day. The subject lines referred to voting, and the text of the email itself implored Democrats to "vote to ensure that our representatives protect the values and beliefs that we all treasure." Of the 41,900 people in the treatment group, 13% opened at least one of the emails. The partisan reminders, however, had no effect on voter turnout. Among the 41,900 people in the treatment group, the turnout rate was 58.7%. Among the 10,513 in the control group, turnout was 59.7%. When Stollwerk replicated this study in the days leading up to the 2013 mayoral election, she found positive but insignificant effects (Stollwerk, 2015). Overall, it appears that GOTV email does little to raise turnout.

Another growing literature evaluates the effects of messages conveyed via social media, such as Facebook. The most well-known study was conducted by a team of academics and Facebook researchers. Prior to the 2010 midterm election, Bond et al. (2012) randomly assigned millions of Facebook users to one of three conditions. The first was a control group that received no encouragement to vote. The second group received an information treatment that consisted of several elements: users were shown a banner at the top of their news feed announcing that "Today is Election Day," encouraged to indicate whether they voted by clicking an "I Voted" graphic, provided a link to locate their polling place, and presented with a counter tabulating the cumulative vote count among Facebook users. The third group received a social treatment: they received the same encouragement as the information group and were also shown the faces of up to six friends who had voted along with a count of friends who had voted. Data gleaned from Facebook users' personal profiles allowed the research team to assess actual turnout for about one in 10 subjects, which nevertheless left approximately 60,000 subjects in the control and information conditions and millions in the social condition. Two key findings emerged. The first is that the information treatment had precisely zero effect on turnout. This finding reaffirms the finding from direct mail experiments suggesting that reminders to vote have little effect on turnout. The second is that the social treatment increased turnout by 0.39 percentage points, which is small but statistically significant. Turnout in the social group is significantly higher than in the control condition or the information condition. Evidently, the active ingredient in social condition is the presentation of friends' turnout, a theme that foreshadows the results discussed in Section 4.1.1.

The idea of putting an "I-voted" widget on Facebook user's news feeds is a creative one, but this intervention is not something that those outside Facebook are at liberty to do, even for a fee. The fallback position is to buy ads on Facebook. In a pair of large-scale experiments, Collins et al. (2014) tested whether "Rock The Vote" ads placed in the news feed in fact raised turnout. In 2012, they assigned approximately 365,000 people to an untreated control group and another 365,000 to a treatment group that received encouragements to vote via sidebar ads and in their news feeds (the latter were actually delivered to 41% of the assigned treatment group). These encouragements showed, for example, the number of days left before the election and a display of friends who "liked" this countdown. Because "Rock The Vote" enjoyed a positive image among the subjects who received its message, having helped many of them register to vote, it was a credible source of information and encouragement. However, voter turnout records later revealed that the treatment and control groups voted at identical rates, 56.5%. The following year, a follow-up experiment using the same design was conducted in 14 states where November elections were being held. Roughly 46,500 voters were assigned to an untreated control and a like number to the treatment group exposed to "Rock The Vote" advertising. This time, a slightly higher proportion of the assigned treatment group, 54%, received ads embedded in their news feeds. Turnout, however, was 14.6% in the control group and 14.0% in the treatment group. In both elections, Facebook ads proved ineffective on increasing turnout.

The experimental literature on email and social media, while disappointing to those who hoped that votes could be mobilized on a grand scale at low marginal cost, is theoretically informative. Evidently, a stream of reminders to vote are ineffective, even when they come from credible sources (e.g., a civic group on whose website one registered to vote or opted in for voting reminders). There is some evidence that more personalized peer-to-peer interaction via social media may foster an interest in politics and increase turnout (Teresi and Michelson, 2015). Further testing is needed to assess whether new media stimulate turnout to the extent that they mimic direct personal interaction.

3.1.5 Conclusion

We conclude this section by taking note of one of the striking features of the experimental literature on voter turnout—the sheer volume of similar studies employing each of the modes of contact. To illustrate this, consider the example of GOTV mailings. Table 3, which is adapted from our recent book reviewing the experimental literature (Green and Gerber, 2015), collects the results of 85 distinct studies conducted between 1998 and 2014.[9] The table reports the average treatment effect for each study, and includes information about the political context (e.g., general election, primary election, etc.), date, location, and content of the mailing (e.g., mail that supported a candidate or a cause, mail that employed strategies to exert social pressure).

These studies can be used to explore how treatment effects vary with differences in subject pools, election contexts, messages scripts, and other details of the experiment. Table 4 shows the results of several meta-analyses performed using Table 3 data and presents the results for the overall effect of mailings and for some subsets of studies formed by partitioning the studies by the message scripts that appeared on the mailing. Pooling all mail studies together shows that sending a piece of mail to a voter increases the subject's turnout rate by about $^3/_4$ of a percentage point. Further, there is some evidence that the content of the mailings influences the size of the treatment effect. Messages that exert social pressure are substantially more effective than the typical nonpartisan GOTV message, for example, and pooling across the social pressure studies shown in Table 3 produces a treatment effect estimate of a 2.3 percentage point increase in voting rates. Two things should be kept in mind when interpreting the results from these meta-analyses. First, there is substantial heterogeneity in both the estimated treatment effects and the experimental conditions within the groupings used to form the sets of studies included in each of the rows of Table 4. Second, because there are relatively few studies that conduct a "horserace" between messages in which scripts vary but the other experimental conditions are held constant, it is possible that some of the observed differences in message effectiveness are due to variation in conditions other than the message, a possibility highlighted by the variability of the treatment effects across studies that use similar messaging approaches.

4. THE EFFECT OF MESSAGING

We next review studies that assess the effectiveness of alternative messages. The New Haven study varied message as well as mode of contact. The study tested the effect of including three different messages based on the calculus of voting and folk theories about campaign messaging: pictures and text that urged voting on the grounds that it is a civic duty, that one's vote might be pivotal in deciding a close race, and that one's neighborhood benefits from higher turnout and the attention that attracts among elected officials. There were some differences in the estimated effects, but these fell short of statistical

---

[9] These 85 table entries are produced from an analysis of 220 distinct treatment and control comparisons. See Green and Gerber 2015, Table B-1 for details of how study results were condensed for this table.

Table 3 Results of direct mailing experiments in the United States from 1998 to 2014

Context	Study	Estimated turnout effect per mailer	SE	Advocacy used	Social pressure (S) or gratitude (G)
1998G	Gerber & Green—New Haven	0.51	0.3		
1999G	Gerber & Green—New Haven	0.30	0.18		
1999G	Gerber et al.—Connecticut and New Jersey	−0.01	0.09	X	
2000G	Green—NAACP	−0.02	0.46	X	
2002G	Ramirez—NALEO	0.05	0.07		
2002G	Wong—Los Angeles county	1.3	1		
2002M	Gillespie—Newark	−1.1	2.5	X	
2002P	Cardy—Pennsylvania	−0.23	0.50	X	
2002P	Gerber—Pennsylvania	−0.05	0.31	X	
2002S	Gillespie—Newark	−1.6	2	X	
2003M	Niven—West Palm Beach	1.42	2.07		
2004G	Anonymous—Minnesota	−0.86	0.74		
2004G	Matland & Murray—Brownsville	2.94	1.09		
2004G	Trivedi—Queens county	1.13	1.67		
2005G	Anonymous—Virginia	0.2	0.05	X	
2006G	Barabas et al.—Florida	0.25	0.62		
2006G	Bedolla & Michelson—APALC	1.15	0.53		
2006G	Bedolla & Michelson—OCAPICA	−0.45	0.79		
2006G	Bedolla & Michelson—PICO	−3.17	0.97		
2006G	Gray & Potter—Franklin county	−2.92	2.73	X	
2006G	Mann—Missouri	−0.06	0.04	X	
2006G	Anonymous—Maryland	−0.41	0.32	X	
2006P	Bedolla & Michelson—APALC	0.01	0.34		
2006P	Bedolla & Michelson—PICO	1.09	0.82		
2006P	Gerber et al.—Michigan	1.8	0.3		S★
2006P	Gerber et al.—Michigan	5.23	0.17		S
2007G	Gerber et al.—Michigan	1.78	0.87		S★
2007G	Gerber et al.—Michigan	5.15	0.46		S
2007G	Mann—Kentucky	2.73	0.20		S
2007G	Panagopoulos—Gilroy	−0.3	1.4		
2007G	Panagopoulos—Iowa and Michigan	2.20	0.84		S
2008G	Keane & Nickerson—Colorado	−0.67	0.29		

Table 3 Results of direct mailing experiments in the United States from 1998 to 2014—cont'd

Context	Study	Estimated turnout effect per mailer	SE	Advocacy used	Social pressure (S) or gratitude (G)
2008G	Nickerson—APIA Vote	−1.2	0.6		
2008G	Nickerson—FRESC	−0.2	0.7		
2008G	Nickerson—Latina Initiative	0.23	0.26		
2008G	Nickerson—NCL	1.47	0.63		
2008G	Nickerson—Voto Latino	−0.59	0.33		
2008G	Rogers & Middleton—Oregon	−0.03	0.48	X	
2008P	Enos—Los Angeles county	2.05	1.13		
2008 PP	Barabas et al.—Florida	−2.73	0.62		
2008 PP	Nickerson & White—North Carolina	0.8	0.7		
2008 PP	Nickerson & White—North Carolina	0.96	0.26		S
2009G	Larimer & Condon—Cedar falls	0.74	2.38		S
2009G	Mann—Houston	1.2	0.6		G
2009G	Panagopoulos—New Jersey	2.5	0.5		G
2009G	Panagopoulos—New Jersey	2	0.5		S
2009S	Abrajano & Panagopoulos—Queens	1.10	0.40		S
2009S	Mann—Houston	1.1	0.5		G
2009S	Panagopoulos—Staten Island	2	0.98		G
2009S	Sinclair et al.—Chicago	4.4	0.6		S
2010G	Anonymous—Nevada	0.15	0.45		S
2010G	Barton et al.—unknown state	−2.23	1.65	X	
2010G	Bryant—San Francisco	1.75	1.99		
2010G	Gerber et al.—Connecticut	2.00	0.53	X	
2010G	Gerber et al.—Connecticut	0.39	0.64		
2010G	Mann & Mayhew—Idaho, Md., N.C., and Ohio	2.00	0.42		
2010G	Murray & Matland—Texas and Wisconsin	1.75	0.66		
2010G	Murray & Matland—Texas and Wisconsin	1.46	0.66		S
2010M	Panagopoulos—Lancaster	−1.08	0.96		
2010P	Binder et al.—San Bernardino county	−0.11	0.50	X	
2010P	Panagopoulos—Georgia	2.5	0.5		G
2011G	Mann & Kalla—Maine	2.40	0.58		
2011G	Panagopoulos—Lexington	0.97	0.75		
2011G	Panagopoulos et al.—Hawthorne	−0.40	0.71		
2011G	Panagopoulos et al.—Hawthorne	2.17	0.58		S

Continued

Table 3 Results of direct mailing experiments in the United States from 1998 to 2014—cont'd

Context	Study	Estimated turnout effect per mailer	SE	Advocacy used	Social pressure (S) or gratitude (G)
2011M	Panagopoulos—Key West	1.1	0.5		S
2011M	Panagopoulos—Key West	−0.05	0.35		
2011S	Mann—Nevada	0.85	0.28		G
2011S	Panagopoulos—Charlestown	−0.30	0.53		
2012G	Citrin et al.—Virginia and Tennessee	0.74	0.41		
2012G	Doherty & Adler—battleground state	0.05	0.20	X	
2012G	Levine & Mann—Georgia and Ohio	0.24	0.30		G
2012M	Panagopoulos—Virginia	0.03	0.62		
2012P	Condon et al.—Iowa	2.85	0.64		S
2012P	Condon et al.—Iowa	0.4	0.9	X	
2012P	Condon et al.—Iowa	2.7	0.9		
2012R	Gerber et al.—Wisconsin	1.1	0.7		
2012R	Rogers et al.—Wisconsin	1.05	0.27		S
2013G	Biggers—Virginia	0.11	0.18		
2013G	Matland and Murray—Minn., Ohio, Tex., and Va.	0.41	0.32		
2013M	Matland & Murray—El Paso	0.12	0.39		
2014G	Broockman & Green—California	0.35	0.13	X	
2014G	Cubbison—North Carolina	−0.12	0.07	X	
2014P	Green et al.—Texas	0.12	0.53	X	
2014P	Hill & Kousser—California	0.49	0.08		

Context refers to the election year and type, where G, general; M, municipal; P, primary; PP, presidential primary; R, runoff; S, special election; SE, standard error. Advocacy refers to appeals that urge support for candidates or causes. Social pressure refers to appeals that emphasize compliance with the social norm of civic participation. Social pressure entries marked with an asterisk forcefully assert the norm of voting but do not tell recipients that whether they vote is a matter of public record. Gratitude mailers thank recipients for voting in a prior election or for their past involvement in elections.

When a given study involved multiple pieces of mail or varying quantities of mail, regression was used to estimate the per-mailer turnout effect. The number of significant digits in the table may vary depending on how the studies' authors reported their results. When a given author or authors report multiple mail tests by the same organization in the same election, we calculated the overall estimated effect and standard error by taking the precision-weighted average, which is equivalent to a fixed effects meta-analysis.

APALC, Asian Pacific American Legal Center; APIA, Asian and Pacific Islander American Vote; FRESC, Front Range Economic Strategy Center; NAACP, National Association for the Advancement of Colored People; NALEO, National Association of Latino Elected Officials; NCL, National Council of La Raza; OCAPICA, Orange County Asian and Pacific Islander Community Alliance; PICO, People Improving Communities through Organizing. This table uses information from Green, D.P., Gerber, A.S., 2015. Get Out The Vote: How to Increase Voter Turnout, third ed. Brookings Institution Press (Table B-1).

Table 4 Meta-analysis of direct mail experiments in the United States, 1998–2014

Type of direct mail	Estimate	95% Confident interval	No. of studies
Advocacy (excludes social pressure)	0.010	(−0.101, 0.120)	19
Nonadvocacy (excludes social pressure)	0.523	(0.299, 0.748)	51
Social pressure	2.280	(1.259, 3.301)	15
All	0.759	(0.530, 0.988)	85

Results obtained using the metan command in Stata 12, with the random effects option. Estimates are in percentage points. Advocacy includes mailings that urge support for ballot issues or candidates. Social pressure refers to mailings that emphasize compliance with the social norm of civic participation and present recipients with information about their record of voting in past elections. The nonadvocacy category includes mailings the express gratitude for past turnout or stress the norm of voting but do not present or refer to past or future turnout records. Excluding these studies reduces the estimate to 0.366, with a confidence interval ranging from 0.136 to 0.596.

significance, and it appeared that messaging effects were, if present, relatively modest. A large number of subsequent field experiments investigated message effects and some approaches, especially those that employ a treatment that is designed to induce social pressure to participate, have shown large and reproducible increases in turnout.

Here we focus on studies in which the messaging is closely related to or explicitly inspired by leading social psychological theories and for which there is a sufficiently large literature to get a sense for the robustness of the findings.[10] It is useful to compare the mechanisms that might be at work in these psychological approaches to the more standard elements emphasized in the classic accounts of rational participation.

When voting is analyzed from the standpoint of rational decision theory, an individual votes if $pB > C$, where p is the probability the vote changes the outcome (one vote makes or breaks a tie), B is the private benefit to the individual from the preferred candidate winning, and C is the cost of voting. This is the decision theoretic account, since in this account the "pivot probability" is a belief and there is no effort to justify it as the endogenous outcome of game among voters. Because the empirical probability of being pivotal in a large election is miniscule, elections that attract tens of millions of voters represent an anomaly. As long as there is even a modest amount of noise regarding turnout, for any symmetric rule mapping voter costs and benefits into voting, as a theoretical matter the chances that the election in a large electorate will be an exact tie (or within one vote) is essentially zero, which leads to a zero expected return for participation. To account for substantial turnout rates, the basic theory was expanded to include an explicit term for the benefits from voting: $pB + D > C$, where D stands for a sense of civic duty (Riker and Ordeshook, 1968). Some of the messaging strategies can be

[10] Rogers et al. (2013) provide an argument for why voter mobilization field experiments are an excellent environment to test social psychology theories and provide a description of some early findings.

relatively easily incorporated into the standard decision theoretic framework for rational participation or modest extensions of it. Messages employed might affect citizens' beliefs about the components of the formula or the weight should be placed on them.

An alternative source of theoretical inspiration is social psychology, which emphasizes the ways in which behavior may be induced by raising the salience of certain ideas and norms. For example, it has been argued that behaviors such as obtaining an immunization become more likely when people think about how where and when they would be immunized (Milkman et al., 2011). As described below, similar approaches have been used to mobilize voters. One might express this hypothesis using the language of $pB + D > C$ by arguing that rehearsing the steps by which one will cast a ballot reduces the cognitive costs encompassed by C. Similarly, it may be argued that one of the benefits of voting (D) is that it raises one's esteem in the eyes of others, who look down on those who do not perform this civic obligation. We next consider experimental tests of these propositions.

4.1 Self-prophecy and implementation intentions

Both the theory of "self-prophecy" (Greenwald et al., 1987) and the theory of "implementation intentions" (Gollwitzer, 1999) hypothesize that the trajectory of an individual's behavior can be altered by inducing the individual to state that he or she will take a certain action. We will discuss each of these theories and their application to voter turnout.

The notion of self-prophecy is inspired by the idea that some kinds of prediction errors may be self-correcting (Sherman, 1980). There are many things that a person feels he or she ought to do but, for some reason, the individual's actions do not match his or her putative goals. Contributing something to charity, getting more exercise in the coming year, and voting in the next election would be examples of such aspirations. When asked to predict whether they expect to undertake the desirable action, people frequently say they will. According to Sherman (1980) and subsequent authors, inducing individuals to predict their behavior produces "self-erasing error" or an example of "self-prophecy," as the prediction itself induces a sense of obligation to follow through, which then leads to a higher level of adherence to the predicted course of action. Applying this argument to voter mobilization suggests that merely by asking individuals if they expected to vote, a question that is overwhelmingly answered in the affirmative, one can raise turnout.[11]

The "self-prophecy effect" was first applied to voting behavior by Greenwald and colleagues. Prior to the 1984 presidential election, several dozen college students were phoned and asked some questions about the upcoming election. They found that the

---

[11] It is possible that such a question could also serve as a reminder to vote, but, as noted in our earlier discussion of reminder phone calls and email, there is ample evidence that reminding people that an election is coming has negligible effects on turnout. Simple reminders are often used as the placebo condition in messaging studies involving direct mail.

incremental effect adding an item that asked subjects to predict their participation was a stunning 23 percentage point increase in the voting rate (Greenwald et al., 1987).[12] Subsequent studies were much less supportive. When the same setup was repeated by the original authors in a 1986 senate election and a 1987 state primary, they found no effect. Studies of self-prophecy by other scholars have found treatment effects similar to those produced by a typical commercial turnout phone call (on the order of a 1% turnout increase). In a replication study approximately 10 times the size of the original Greenwald study, Smith et al. (2003) organized a phone bank to call registered voters in advance of the 2000 presidential primary. They compared the turnout of subjects asked if they knew where and when to vote with those asked these questions and whether they expected to vote on Tuesday; the incremental effect of the self-prophecy treatment was −0.1 percentage points. Dustin Cho (2008) replicated this experiment at a larger scale during the 2008 presidential primary and found a 2.2 percentage point turnout increase from the self-prophecy treatment. A large study by Nickerson and Rogers (2010), also conducted during the 2008 presidential primary, found a 2 percentage point effect. Although the effect of self-prophecy each of these three follow up studies was not significant, pooling these findings together suggests that self-prophecy might produce a small boost in turnout, although nothing close to the finding reported in the sentinel study.

In addition to the studies that directly test self-prophecy, several studies provide indirect evidence about self-prophecy's effectiveness. In some studies the question about vote prediction is just one component of the treatment. Christopher Mann (2005) studied the effect of being administered a multiquestion preelection survey that included questions about turnout intention. He found that those registered voters assigned to be asked about their vote intentions and other political attitudes by major news media pollsters voted at the same rate as the randomly selected control group who were not called for the survey. A recent study by Green et al. (2015) found that canvassing door to door with a script that merely asked residents how they intend to vote produced no increase in turnout. Commercial phone banks often conclude their GOTV appeals with the query "can I count on you to vote?" As noted above, the overall turnout effect of these calls is small, typically finding less than a 1 percentage point increase in turnout.

A theory closely related to self-prophecy is the "implementation-intentions" hypothesis, which posits that there is a weak but consequential cognitive barrier between an individual's goals and taking the actions needed to accomplish those goals. According to this theory, getting a person to state the goal and then elaborate the steps necessary to achieve the goal makes accomplishing the goal more likely. The exercise of elaboration makes the steps required more salient and illuminates the path for successful goal-oriented

---

[12] There are some studies of self-prophecy in other domains. For example, Morwitz et al. (1993) detect an effect of asking people about their plans to buy a car on subsequent car purchases.

action. A messaging strategy based on this theory has been applied to voter turnout by supplementing the self-prophecy item (do you expect to vote?) with follow-up questions about what subjects need to do to achieve their (now stated) intention to vote.

An early effort to test implementation intentions in a field setting was Nickerson and Rogers (2010). Their study asked subjects if they intended to vote and then, for a subset of those subjects, proceeded to a series of questions about actions related to casting a ballot. Those who stated they planned to vote were asked: Around what time do you expect you will head to the polls on Tuesday? Where do you expect to be coming from when you head to the polls on Tuesday? What do you think you will be doing before you head out to the polls?[13] Nickerson and Rogers report that the implementation intentions script (which combines a standard GOTV message, an inquiry about intention to vote, and the implementation intentions questions) boosted turnout by 4.1 percentage points, and that the incremental effect of the three questions implementation battery was 2.1 percentage points.[14]

Several other studies have investigated the effect of elaborating a voting plan. These include Dustin Cho (2008) and Gerber et al. (2015), who found an implementation intentions phone call script to have negligible effects, and Rogers and Ternovski (2015), who tested a version of implementation intentions using a mailing and found a statistically significant 0.5 percentage-point effect from a single mailer.[15] Overall, it appears that scripts that evoke self-prophecy and implementation intentions may nudge turnout upward, but the effects tend to be much smaller than suggested by the sentinel studies.

4.1.1 Social pressure, pride, and shame

If we restrict ourselves to a theoretical model that focuses exclusively on the pivot probability, the benefits from being decisive, and the costs of participation, it is impossible to produce a robust explanation for the observed high levels of turnout in mass elections.

One response to this gap between prediction and model is to extend the set of considerations used by the voter to evaluate whether to vote. An example of this approach is Coate and Conlin (2004), in which two groups of strategic voters incorporate a group identity and then adhere (for unmodeled psychological or social reasons) to a behavioral rule that maximizes group welfare. The particular voting rule (the cut point for the cost of

---

[13] Slightly over 85% of subjects said that they planned to vote in the upcoming election.

[14] Further exploration of treatment effect by Nickerson and Rogers revealed that, unexpectedly, the effect of implementation was concentrated among those who resided in households with one eligible voter, for whom the overall effect of the implementation script was 9.1 percentage points and the incremental effect of the implementation questions in particular was 8 percentage points. The authors speculated that this finding was consistent with the idea that implementation planning was unnecessary for those living in multiple voter households because, due to the relative centrality of politics in these households and other aspects of the multiresident social context, these individuals were more likely to already have a voting plan.

[15] The Rogers and Ternovski mailing also included a "gratitude treatment," a message strategy described below.

voting that separates voters from nonvoters) that is considered normatively desirable for each group emerges as an equilibrium outcome. How these implied norms of proper voter behavior for members of each group—rules that make sense for the group but are not rational for the individual—are enforced is either a psychological or social matter.

A complementary but alternative strategy has been to examine the norms that support voting directly and study how these norms are enforced. Survey evidence indicates that voting behavior appears to be embedded in a set of social norms that support voting. Simple reflection suggests that there is some social dimension to voting, but how important is this consideration? It may be that people merely pay lip service to ideas of voting and civic duty, but perhaps the norms regarding voting are more deeply rooted. If individuals are susceptible to feelings of pride and shame regarding their voting behavior, interventions that heighten these feelings may affect turnout. Conversely, if heightening social pressure leads to a large change in turnout, this lends plausibility to social pressure as a mechanism that is working to produce the observed levels of mass participation.

Experiments have explored the effectiveness of "social pressure," that is, strategies crafted to tap into the basic human drive to win praise or avoid scolding. Social pressure is exerted by praising those who uphold a social norm or by chastising those who violate them. The level of social pressure exerted can be varied through variation in the intensity of the message or through disclosure of the individual's level of compliance with the norm. In the voter mobilization literature, social pressure messages typically involve three components: exhorting the receiver to comply with the social norm, stating that the receiver's behavior will be monitored, and warning that the receiver's compliance may be disclosed to others.

In a large experiment conducted in a primary election in Michigan in 2006, Gerber et al. (2008) evaluated a set of four mailers that conveyed varying doses of social pressure. The first mailer employed a hectoring tone to encourage citizens to do their civic duty and vote. The second mailer added to this message an element of surveillance by telling people that they were part of an academic study and that their turnout in the upcoming election would be monitored. The third mailing, labeled the "self" mailer, included information from the voter files listing the voting behavior of household members in recent elections and contained a promise to send an updated mailing after the election reporting whether the listed individuals voted or not. Finally, the "Neighbors" mailing increased the social pressure by including the turnout history of the household as well as that of the neighbors on the recipient's block. Thus, the four mailings represented a (steep) gradation in social pressure.

The results show a very strong effect of social pressure on voter turnout. Bear in mind that a typical nonpartisan GOTV mailing raises turnout by half a percentage point. The first mailing, a forceful civic duty appeal, raised turnout by 1.8 percentage points, while the "self" mailing raised turnout by 4.9 percentage points. The "neighbors" mailing produced a remarkable 8.1 percentage point boost in turnout. These quantities are all distinguishable from zero and each other, since the treatment groups each comprised 20,000 households and the control group comprised 100,000 households.

Follow up studies have confirmed the basic contours of these results.[16] The main effort has been to replicate and extend the "self" mailing. The social pressure mailings, especially those that confronted voters with their voting record and those of their neighbors (the highly effective "Neighbors" mailing), provoked outrage among some recipients (Murray and Matland, 2014), prompting a search for messaging strategies that produced the turnout effect without as much agitation. These efforts led to a few different approaches. First, there was an attempt to build on the "self" treatment, a strong message that produced an outsized increase in vote but only a modest level of resistance. Table 5 shows the results of several studies testing messages employing the "self" approach. Pooling the results of these studies, which were conducted across a variety of political contexts, shows that the "self" mailing is a powerful treatment, with especially strong effects in low-to-medium salience elections. The results across these studies are similar to the 16% boost (+4.9 from a base of 29.7 in the control group) observed in the 2006 Michigan primary election study. In addition to the higher base rate of voting in a general election, the cases in which the mailing had weaker effects may also be related to the mechanism of the social pressure treatment; the Texas and Wisconsin studies by Matland and Murray used a version of the mailer that did not scold voters for failing to vote.[17]

A second strategy is to employ social norms to praise rather than scold. Panagopoulos (2013) used this approach and encouraged subjects to join an "honor roll" of perfect voters. A collection of voters identified as African American, Hispanic, or unmarried women were randomly assigned to receive a mailing that presented the perfect voting history of 10 neighbors. The text included this language:

There is no action more important to our democracy than going to the polls to vote. That's why Our Community Votes, a non-profit organization that encourages voting, is recognizing citizens in your neighborhood who have perfect voting records in general elections over the past four years. These neighbors deserve our recognition and congratulations for doing their civic duty and making

[16] Although the neighbors' mailing has been used from time to time in campaigns, to date, there is only one academic follow-up to the Michigan neighbors' mailing. In the very high turnout of Wisconsin governor election, a neighbors' mailing produced a one-percentage point increase overall and a 3 percentage point increase among those whose base turnout rate was 30%, a subgroup with participation levels more similar to the Michigan subjects than the overall Wisconsin subject pool (Rogers et al. 2015).

[17] No turnout gains were produced by a partisan version of the self mailing, in which subjects were presented with their turnout record and told that it was important for Democrats and Independents to vote because of the negative effects of having Republicans in power (Schwenzfeier, 2014). This may be related to the mechanism thought to be at work. A partisan message is typical in politics and does not cause the subject to reflect on civic duty and the social implications of participation. Nonpartisan mailers that threaten to shame/praise nonvoters/voters by putting their names in a local newspaper seem to produce large effects, although these experiments are somewhat underpowered (Panagopoulos, 2010).

Table 5 The effects of the self mailer on voter turnout across multiple studies

Study	Election type	Setting	Control	Self	Percentage increase in turnout
1[b]	2006 August primary	Michigan	29.7 (191,243)	34.5 (38,218)	16%[a]
2[c]	2007 Municipal	Michigan	27.7 (772,479)	32.4 (27,609)	17%[a]
3[d]	2007 Gubernatorial general (previous nonvoters)	Kentucky	6.8 (19,561)	8.9 (13,689)	31%[a]
3[d]	2007 Gubernatorial general (previous voters)	Kentucky	13.2 (25,037)	16.3 (17,731)	23%[a]
4[e]	2009 Municipal special	New York city	3.2 (3445)	4.2 (3486)	36%[a]
5[f]	2010 General	Texas	40.5 (63,531)	43.1 (1200)	6%
5[f]	2010 General	Wisconsin	49.0 (43,797)	50.8 (801)	4%
6[g]	2011 Municipal	California	10.6 (13,482)	12.0 (1000)	13%

[a]Statistically significant at $p < .01$, one-tailed test. This Table is adapted from Table 11-1, Get out the Vote, Green and Gerber (2015).
[b]Gerber, A.S., Green, D.P., Larimer, C.W., 2008. Social pressure and voter turnout: evidence from a large-scale field experiment. Am. Polit. Sci. Rev. 102 (1), 33–48.
[c]Gerber, A.S., Green, D.P., Larimer, C.W., 2010. An experiment testing the relative effectiveness of encouraging voter participation by inducing feelings of pride or shame. Polit. Behav. 32, 409–422.
[d]Mann, C.B., 2010. Is there backlash to social pressure? A large-scale field experiment on voter mobilization. Polit. Behav. 32, 387–407.
[e]Abrajano, M., Panagopoulos, C., July 2011. Does language matter? The impact of Spanish versus English-language GOTV efforts on latino turnout. Am. Polit. Res. 39, 643–663.
[f]Murray, G.R., Matland, R.E., 2014. Mobilization effects using mail: social pressure, descriptive norms, and timing. Polit. Res. Q. 67, 304–319. The table reports only the results of the Self mailer with no additional information about the voting rate of the community.
[g]Panagopoulos, C., Larimer, C.W., Condon, M., 2014. Social pressure, descriptive norms, and voter mobilization. Polit. Behav. 36, 451–469.

their voices heard. And with New Jersey's election for governor taking place on November 3rd, we hope that you will go to the polls and join your neighborhood's Civic Honor Roll of perfect voters. Voting records show that you voted in the presidential election of 2008 but not in the 2005 election for governor. Voting records are public information, so people know when you voted, but never how you voted. By voting on November 3rd, you will join the following voters as perfect voters.

Panagopoulos (2013, p. 275)

This approach, an extensive modification of the self-message, raised turnout significantly, albeit less than the original self-mailer; turnout rose by 2.3 percentage points among African American and Hispanic subjects and by 1.3 percentage points among women.

A third variation includes language that hints at the possibility that the subjects might be contacted after the election and asked to explain their participation or failure to participate. An example of this approach is Rogers and Ternovski's (2015) large-scale study of turnout on the 2010 midterm election, which included a box in the corner stating that "You may be called after the election to discuss your experience at the polls." They find that the incremental effect of adding this to the mailing was a statistically significant quarter-percentage point increase in turnout.[18]

4.1.2 Gratitude

Gratitude is thought by some to have evolutionary roots and to have developed in a manner to facilitate social exchange and reciprocity (Trivers, 1971). Drawing on the extensive and growing literature on the power of gratitude and the reciprocity caused by expressions of gratitude (McCullough et al. (2008), Bernstein and Simmons (1974), Clark et al. (1988), Rind and Bordia (1995)), Panagopolous (2011) proposed a voter mobilization message in which the subject is thanked for prior participation. Part of the motivation for the gratitude mailing was to explore a method of making the self mailing, which has the subject's vote history as a centerpiece, more palatable. Thanking the voter provides an explanation for why the subject's vote history has been looked up and presented.

Panagopolous tested the gratitude mailing in three very different elections: a 2009 special election in Staten Island, New York, the November 2009 Governor's Election in New Jersey, and a 2010 Georgia Primary. He found sizeable effects for the gratitude mailings, with a turnout boost of 2.4 percentage points in Staten Island, a 2.5 percentage point increase in New Jersey, and a 2.4% increase in Georgia. The effects of the gratitude mailing were approximately two-thirds as large as the self mailer. An unexpected feature of this trio of studies emerged in the Georgia study, where Panagopolous included two additional treatment arms: (1) a mailing in which the vote history was discussed but there was no mention of official records of voter turnout and (2) a mailing that included just a generic expression of gratitude for the subjects attention to politics, but did not mention anything about the individual or their voting record. The key portion of the basic gratitude message was:

THANK YOU FOR VOTING!

We realize voting takes time and effort.

Official voter records indicate that you voted in the last midterm election in November 2006, and we just wanted to say "thank you."

---

[18] Another field experiment that reports the results of an intervention that includes a similar message ("researchers will contact you within three weeks of the Election to conduct a survey on your voter participation") is DellaVigna et al. (2014).

Our democracy depends on people like you exercising their right to vote. We appreciate the fact that you made it a priority to cast a ballot.

We also remind you that the primary elections in Georgia will take place on

Tuesday, July 20, 2010. *You are eligible to vote.*

The version that makes no mention of official records is identical except the sentence about official records is excluded. The text for the generic gratitude treatment is:

THANK YOU!

Our democracy depends on people like you paying attention to politics and getting involved in the political process. We appreciate the fact that you make this a priority.

We also remind you that the primary elections in Georgia will take place on

Tuesday, July 20, 2010. *You are eligible to vote.*

These three arms fielded in Georgia were approximately equally effective, producing turnout increases of over 2 percentage points. Remarkably, the point estimate for the generic expression of gratitude was a 3.1 percentage point turnout increase, implying that the gratitude mailer is not simply a veiled self mailer but rather taps into a distinct set of psychological mechanisms. More research is needed to verify this potentially important discovery and to assess whether GOTV messages delivered in person or by phone are enhanced by expressions of gratitude.

4.1.3 Descriptive norms

In contrast to prescriptive norms, which assert that people ought to vote, descriptive norms center on what others do, with the implication you should do likewise. For example, the statement "Everyone else is voting, and you should, too" suggests that you should conform to others' example, either because others know best or because there are personal advantages to going along with the crowd. Conversely, a statement of the form "Turnout is low, so we hope that you will vote" sends a mixed message; voting is encouraged, but the descriptive norm seems to militate in favor of not voting.

In comparison to the literature on prescriptive norms, the literature on descriptive norms rests on fewer studies, and the experiments tend to be smaller in size. An early study by Gerber and Rogers (2009) showed that voting intentions are affected by information about whether turnout is likely to be high or low. Subsequent studies have gauged the effects of such information on subjects' actual turnout. Panagopoulos et al. (2014) presented voters in a 2011 municipal election with either a standard mailer or a self mailer. Each type of mailer was distributed with different variants. In the high turnout condition, the mailer included the wording "THE MAJORITY OF YOUR NEIGHBORS DO THEIR CIVIC DUTY. DO YOURS TOO." Following this statement, individuals were told "TURNOUT IN YOUR COMMUNITY: 70%" in reference to turnout in the 2008 general election. In the low turnout condition, the wording was reversed: "THE MAJORITY OF YOUR NEIGHBORS DO NOT DO THEIR CIVIC DUTY. BUT YOU SHOULD DO YOURS." Following this statement, individuals were told "TURNOUT IN YOUR COMMUNITY: 35%" in reference to turnout in the 2006 election. In the self condition, wording with either the high or low norm boosted turnout slightly but not significantly; estimated effects were essentially zero in the standard condition. Another study by Murray and Matland (2014) presented parallel experiments conducted in Lubbock, Texas and Kenosha, Wisconsin. Standard or self-mailers sent to subjects in the low descriptive norm condition included the following passage:

> In the Lubbock city elections earlier this year, voter turnout was around 10%, among the lowest levels recorded in the past twenty years. While there are many opportunities to participate, millions of people in Texas never take advantage of these opportunities. Many experts are discouraged by how few voters they expect for the upcoming election. We encourage you to buck this trend among your fellow Lubbock citizens and vote on Tuesday, November 2nd.

By contrast, the high descriptive norm language expressed optimism:

> In the General Election in Lubbock in 2008, voter turnout was over 70% of registered voters and among the highest levels recorded in the past twenty years. Throughout the country there has been a surge in voter participation. Many experts are encouraged by this trend and are expecting another large turnout in the upcoming election. We encourage you to join your fellow Lubbock citizens and vote on Tuesday, November 2nd.

Again, the results were ambiguous. In Lubbock, the mailers were equally effective regardless of whether they conveyed high or low norms or none at all. In Kenosha, the high-norm language boosted turnout significantly, whereas the low-norm language had no effect. Although larger replication studies are needed in order to estimate these effects with more precision, it appears that descriptive norms exert weaker effects than prescriptive norms.

4.1.4 Discussion

Our summary of the literature has highlighted a number of empirical regularities. One is that encouragements to vote tend to be more effective when delivered in person than via direct mail or email. Another is that advocacy messages that give voters reasons to support or oppose a given candidate or cause tend not to increase turnout. Yet another is that messages that forcefully assert the social norm of civic participation are often highly effective at stimulating turnout, especially in low salience elections.

4.2 Voter mobilization outside the US

Although these conclusions emerge from a robust experimental literature, the studies described above were all conducted in the context of American elections, which leaves open the question of whether the results hold outside the United States. The last decade has seen a steady increase in the number of GOTV experiments conducted in other countries. One of the earliest large-scale experiments assessed the effects of nonpartisan phone calls and canvassing in the United Kingdom (John and Brannan, 2008), and several follow-up studies have extended this experimental work to nationally representative samples (Fieldhouse et al., 2013) and to partisan campaigns (Foos and John, 2016). Within the domain of nonpartisan campaigns, these studies confirm the effectiveness of personal GOTV tactics and, if anything, suggest that volunteer phone banks work especially well in the UK, where landlines are less overburdened by telemarketing calls. On the other hand, impersonal tactics such as direct mail have been found to be effective, too, both in the UK (Fieldhouse et al., 2013) and Ireland (Regan, 2013), again perhaps due to the lower volume of commercial junk mail in those countries. Interestingly, partisan canvassing and phone calls have produced mixed results, with studies in the UK, France, and Spain finding no increase in turnout (Foos and John, 2016; Pons, 2014; Ramiro et al., 2012) or heterogeneous effects that are positive only among supporters (Foos and de Rooij, 2013).

Although studies conducted outside the United States have the potential to shed light on the interaction between interventions and electoral context, the lack of individual-level administrative data on voter turnout often presents an impediment to field experimental research. One response has been to conduct an experiment in a single precinct, stationing poll workers to observe who votes in that location, as Guan and Green (2006) did when studying door-to-door canvassing among students in a Chinese university. Occasionally, research collaboration with government agencies gives scholars access to extraordinarily rich data on both turnout outcomes and the social attributes of the study participants. For example, in their study of voter mobilization in Denmark, Bhatti et al. (2016) had access to detailed family data linking parents and offspring, enabling the research team to assess whether the text messages they sent to young voters affected turnout among family members and housemates. Another approach is to randomize at the polling station or city level, a research strategy that has been used in Brazil (De Figueiredo et al., 2011), Italy (Kendall et al., 2013), and Mexico (Chong et al., 2015). Although this type of experimental design tends to be less powerful than one based on individual assignment, it allows the researcher to estimate treatment effects on both turnout and vote share. Some of the most interesting studies are those that show how persuasive campaign messages affect vote share even when they do not affect turnout (Pons and Liegey, 2013), a finding reminiscent of analogous experiments in high-salience US elections (Rogers and Middleton, 2015).

4.3 Downstream effects

One of the most interesting findings to emerge from GOTV research in the US and UK is that voter mobilization campaigns have enduring effects. The New Haven residents who were randomly assigned to receive direct mail or face-to-face canvassing in 1998 were more likely to vote in both the election held in November 1998 and the mayoral election held in November 1999. This type of persistent effect has since been replicated repeatedly (Coppock and Green 2016). For example, voters assigned to receive mailings in the Michigan social pressure experiment not only voted at higher rates in the 2006 August primary; they were also significantly more likely to vote in August primaries in 2008, 2010, and 2012. The self mailing generated approximately 1850 votes in August 2006, plus an additional 900 votes over the next three August primaries. This pattern of over time-persistence holds for other large social pressure studies (Davenport et al., 2010; Rogers et al., 2015), for nonpartisan efforts to mobilize ethnic minority voters in California (Bedolla and Michelson, 2012), and for GOTV efforts in Britain (Cutts et al., 2009).

The enduring impact of voter mobilization is subject to multiple interpretations. One interpretation is that voting is a habit-forming activity. Someone who votes in this election is more likely to vote in the next election. Someone who skips an election is less likely to vote in the future. America's low turnout rates may reflect the fact that we have the most frequent elections on earth. One might liken sleepy municipal elections to gateway drugs; by enticing so many people to abstain from voting, they weaken voting habits. Another interpretation is that voting in the initial election attracts the attention of political campaigns, which direct extra attention to recent voters, thereby promoting their continuing participation. The one study to track campaign activity—using contact records from the campaigns themselves—found that those assigned to the treatment group prior to a spring election were more likely to receive mail but no more likely to receive phone calls or personal visits prior to the fall general election (Rogers et al., 2015). Still another interpretation is that mobilization effects endure because subjects continue to remember the communication that mobilized them initially, a hypothesis that has some plausibility when the initial mobilization takes the form of strongly worded social pressure mailers.

4.4 Future directions

Much of the existing experimental work on stimulating voter turnout is inspired by theoretical accounts of why people vote or psychological theories of how individuals might be persuaded to take an action. These frameworks make directional predictions about the effects of interventions, but there is rarely any effort to estimate parameters of the subjects' utility function. An important avenue for future research is to use field experiments to estimate parameters in explicit structural models. An example of this work is Della Vigna et al. (2014), which incorporates a "social-image" motivation for voting into the subject's utility function and designs a set of experiments that identifies the monetary value of voting in order to avoid having to say you failed to vote (lying is costly). Based on their experimental results and some assumptions (including an evidence-based assumed cost to subjects of lying), Della Vigna et al. estimate that the monetary cost of admitting failure to vote is between $5 and $15 for the 2010 congressional election, a plausible estimate given the observed level of turnout and the modest time and effort cost of voting.

A noteworthy feature of Della Vigna et al. is that, as a side benefit to their search for interventions designed to estimate model parameters, the authors conduct novel experiments that are interesting in their own rights. Misreporting of voting is a common source of measurement error in surveys. Della Vigna et al. examine the effect of providing the subject an incentive to tell the interviewer she did not vote; a random subset of survey respondents are told after 2 min of a 10-min survey that if they answer that they did not vote in the recent congressional election, the survey will end rather than continue for eight more minutes. Della Vigna et al. find that providing the incentive to say you did not vote has a small, statistically insignificant effect on reported voting by respondents who had voted, but nonvoters are substantially more likely to admit (that is, report truthfully) having not voted. Thus, very little misreporting of turnout is induced by the incentive, while the net degree of misreporting is substantially reduced in the incentive condition.

Another path for further research is to explicitly consider the implications of the accumulating corpus of academic work on voter mobilization for the "applied work" done by campaigns and elections. Most directly, there is the question of how campaign activity might be optimized given the experimental evidence on the relative effectiveness of alternative communications' strategies or the differences in treatment response across individuals. Imai and Strauss (2011), continuing a line of work pioneered by Kramer (1966), consider the question of crafting the optimal GOTV campaign. They use data from existing experiments to estimate treatment effect heterogeneity and then compare the relative effectiveness of strategies that begin by targeting the individuals who are expected to have the largest turnout response versus a strategy that assumes zero-treatment effect heterogeneity. They find that there are often large expected gains from incorporating treatment-effect heterogeneity into the prioritization of mobilization targets.

A second question (perhaps better labeled a puzzle) regarding the relationship between the experimental work and real world campaign activity is to understand how accumulating experimental evidence affects industry practice. What accounts for the continued reliance by candidates and parties on methods with little evidence to support their use, despite the fact that elections have important stakes and are often sharply competitive? Some scholars have argued that the continued ubiquity of techniques experimentally demonstrated to produce small returns for large expenditures (early TV advertising, for example) stems from the financial windfalls the spending produces for campaign consultants (Sheingate, 2016). This explanation, while somewhat persuasive, seems at best incomplete, because all marketers, political or otherwise, would be interested in selling worthless things at a high price, but this is probably not often a sustainable business model.

REFERENCES

Adams, W.C., Smith, D.J., 1980. Effects of telephone canvassing on turnout and preferences: a field experiment. Public Opin. Q. 44, 389–395.

Angrist, J.D., Imbens, G., Rubin, D.B., 1996. Identification of causal effects using instrumental variables. J. Am. Stat. Assoc. 91, 444–472.

Ansolabehere, S.D., Gerber, A.S., 1994. The mismeasure of campaign spending: evidence from the 1990 US House elections. J. Polit. 56, 1106–1118.

Ansolabehere, S.D., Iyengar, S., 1996. Going Negative: How Political Advertising Divides and Shrinks the American Electorate. The Free Press, New York.

Arceneaux, K., 2005. Using cluster randomized field experiments to study voting behavior. Ann. Am. Acad. Polit. Soc. Sci. 601 (1), 169–179.

Arceneaux, K., Gerber, A.S., Green, D.P., 2006. Comparing experimental and matching methods using a large-scale voter mobilization experiment. Polit. Anal. 14, 1–36.

Arceneaux, K., Nickerson, D., 2009. Who is mobilized to vote? A re-analysis of eleven randomized field experiments. Am. J. Polit. Sci. 53, 1–16.

Arceneaux, K., Gerber, A.S., Green, D.P., 2010. A cautionary note on the use of matching to estimate causal effects: an empirical example comparing matching estimates to an experimental benchmark. Sociol. Methods Res. 39, 256–282.

Barabas, J., Barrilleaux, C., Scheller, D., 2010. Ballot Initiative Knowledge and Voter Turnout: Evidence From Field Experiments and National Surveys. Florida State University (unpublished manuscript).

Barton, J., Castillo, M., Petrie, R., 2012. Going Negative: The Persuasive Effect of Tone and Information on Campaign Fundraising and Voter Turnout. No. 1037 (unpublised manuscript).

Bedolla, L.G., Michelson, M.R., 2012. Mobilizing Inclusion: Transforming the Electorate Through Get-Out-the-Vote Campaigns. Yale University Press.

Bennion, E.A., 2005. Caught in the ground wars: mobilizing voters during a competitive congressional campaign. Ann. Am. Acad. Polit. Soc. Sci. 601 (1), 123–141.

Bergan, D.E., 2009. Does grassroots lobbying work?: A field experiment measuring the effects of an e-mail lobbying campaign on legislative behavior. Am. Polit. Res. 37, 327–352.

Bernstein, D.M., Simmons, R.G., 1974. The adolescent kidney donor: the right to give. Am. J. Psychiatry 131.

Bhatti, et al., 2016. http://cvap.polsci.ku.dk/publikationer/arbejdspapirer/2015/SMS_spillover.pdf.

Bond, R.M., Fariss, C.J., Jones, J.J., Kramer, A.D.I., Marlow, C., Settle, J.E., Fowler, J.H., 2012. A 61-million-person experiment in social influence and political mobilization. Nature 489 (7415), 295–298.

Broockman, D.E., 2013. Black politicians are more intrinsically motivated to advance blacks' interests: a field experiment manipulating political incentives. Am. J. Polit. Sci. 57 (3), 521–536.

Broockman, D.E., 2014. Mobilizing candidates: political actors strategically shape the candidate pool with personal appeals. J. Exp. Polit. Sci. 1 (2), 104–119.

Broockman, D.E., Butler, D.M., 2015. The causal effects of elite position-taking on voter attitudes: field experiments with elite communication. Am. J. Polit. Sci. http://onlinelibrary.wiley.com/doi/10.1111/ajps.12243/epdf.

Butler, D.M., Nickerson, D.W., 2011. Can learning constituency opinion affect how legislators vote? Results from a field experiment. Q. J. Polit. Sci. 6 (1), 55–83. http://dx.doi.org/10.1561/100.00011019.

Cardy, E.A., 2005. An experimental field study of the GOTV and persuasion effects of partisan direct mail and phone calls. Ann. Am. Acad. Polit. Soc. Sci. 601 (1), 28–40.

Cho, D., 2008. Acting on the Intent to Vote: A Voter Turnout Experiment. Available at: SSRN 1402025. Yale University (unpublished manuscript).

Cho, W.K.T., Gimpel, J.G., Dyck, J.J., 2006. Residential concentration, political socialization, and voter turnout. J. Polit. 68 (1), 156–167.

Chong, A., Ana, L., Karlan, D., Wantchekon, L., 2015. Does corruption information inspire the fight or quash the hope? A field experiment in Mexico on voter turnout, choice, and party identification. J. Polit. 77 (1), 55–71.

Clark, H.B., Northrop, J.T., Barkshire, C.T., 1988. The effects of contingent thank-you notes on case Managers'visiting residential clients. Educ. Treat. Child. 45–51.

Coate, S., Conlin, M., 2004. A group rule-utilitarian approach to voter turnout: theory and evidence. Am. Econ. Rev. 94 (5), 1476–1504.

Collins, K., Keane, L., Kalla, J., 2014. Youth voter mobilization through online advertising: evidence from two GOTV field experiments. In: Paper Presented at the Annual Meeting of the American Political Science Association, Washington, DC (unpublished manuscript).

Coppock, A., Green, D.P., 2016. Is voting habit forming? New evidence from experiments and regression discontinuities. Am. J. Polit. Sci. 60 (4), 1044–1062.

Cubbison, W., 2015. The marginal effects of direct mail on vote choice. In: Paper Presented at the Annual Meeting of the Midwest Political Science Association, Chicago, IL (unpublished manuscript).

Cutts, D., Fieldhouse, E., John, P., 2009. Is voting habit forming? The longitudinal impact of a GOTV campaign in the UK. J. Elections Public Opin. Parties 19 (3), 251–263.

Davenport, T.C., Gerber, A.S., Green, D.P., 2010. Field experiments and the study of political behavior. In: Leighley, J.E. (Ed.), The Oxford Handbook of American Elections and Political Behavior. Oxford University Press, New York.

De Figueiredo, M.F.P., Daniel Hidalgo, F., Kasahara, Y., 2011. When Do Voters Punish Corrupt Politicians? Experimental Evidence From Brazil. University of California Berkeley (unpublished manuscript).

Della Vigna, S., List, J.A., Malmendier, U., Rao, G., 2014. Voting to Tell Others. NBER Working Paper No. 19832 (unpublished manuscript).

Eldersveld, S.J., 1956. Experimental propaganda techniques and voting behavior. Am. Polit. Sci. Rev. 50, 154–165.

Erikson, R.S., Palfrey, T.R., 2000. Equilibria in campaign spending games: theory and data. Am. Polit. Sci. Rev. 94, 595–609.

Fieldhouse, E., Cutts, D., Widdop, P., John, P., 2013. Do impersonal mobilisation methods work? Evidence from a nationwide get-out-the-vote experiment in England. Elect. Stud. 32 (1), 113–123.

Foos, F., de Rooij, E., 2013. Does Candidate Party Affiliation Affect Turnout? University of Zurich (unpublished manuscript).

Foos, F., John, P., 2016. Parties are no civic charities: voter contact and the changing partisan composition of the electorate. Polit. Sci. Res. Methods. http://dx.doi.org/10.7910/DVN/EWISS3 (forthcoming).

Gerber, A.S., 1998. Estimating the effect of campaign spending on senate election outcomes using instrumental variables. Am. Polit. Sci. Rev. 92, 401–411.

Gerber, A.S., 2004. Does campaign spending work?: Field experiments provide evidence and suggest new theory. Am. Behav. Sci. 47, 541–574.

Gerber, A.S., 2011. New directions in the study of voter mobilization: combining psychology and field experimentation. In: Gerken, H.K., Charles, G.U.E., Kang, M.S. (Eds.), Race, Reform. Cambridge University Press.

Gerber, A.S., Doherty, D., 2009. Can Campaign Effects Be Accurately Measured Using Surveys?: Evidence From a Field Experiment. Yale University (unpublished manuscript).

Gerber, A.S., Green, D.P., 2000. The effects of canvassing, direct mail, and telephone contact on voter turnout: a field experiment. Am. Polit. Sci. Rev. 94, 653–663.

Gerber, A.S., Green, D.P., 2001. Do phone calls increase voter turnout? A field experiment. Public Opin. Q. 65, 75–85.

Gerber, A.S., Green, D.P., September 2005. Do phone calls increase voter turnout? An update (with Green). Ann. Acad. Polit. Soc. Sci. 601.

Gerber, A.S., Green, D.P., Green, M., 2003. Partisan mail and voter turnout: results from randomized field experiments. Elect. Stud. 22 (4), 563–579.

Gerber, A.S., Green, D.P., Kaplan, E.H., 2004. The illusion of learning from observational research. In: Shapiro, I., Smith, R., Massoud, T. (Eds.), Problems and Methods in the Study of Politics. Cambridge University Press, New York.

Gerber, A.S., Green, D.P., Larimer, C.W., 2008. Social pressure and voter turnout: evidence from a large-scale field experiment. Am. Polit. Sci. Rev. 102, 33–48.

Gerber, A.S., Green, D.P., Nickerson, D.W., 2001. Testing for publication bias in political science. Polit. Anal. 9, 385–392.

Gerber, A.S., Hill, S.J., Huber, G.A., 2015. Small cues and large effect: the results from a collection of simultaneous field experiments. In: Paper Presented at the Annual Meeting of the Midwest Political Science Association, Chicago, IL (unpublished manuscript).

Gerber, A.S., Huber, G.A., Fang, A.H., Reardon, C.E., 2016. When Does Increasing Mobilization Effort Increase Turnout? New Theory and Evidence from a Field Experiment on Reminder Calls. Institution for Social and Policy Studies, Yale University (unpublished manuscript).

Gerber, A.S., Rogers, T., 2009. Descriptive social norms and motivation to vote: everybody's voting and so should you. J. Polit. 71 (01), 178–191.

Gollwitzer, P.M., 1999. Implementation intentions: strong effects of simple plans. Am. Psychol. 54 (7), 493.

Gosnell, H.F., 1927. Getting-Out-the-Vote: An Experiment in the Stimulation of Voting. University of Chicago Press, Chicago.

Gray, J., Potter, P., 2007. Does signaling matter in elections? Evidence from a field experiment. In: Paper Presented at the Annual Meeting of the American Political Science Association (unpublished manuscript).

Green, D.P., Gerber, A.S., 2015. Get Out the Vote: How to Increase Voter Turnout. Brookings Institution Press, Washington, DC.

Green, D.P., Gerber, A.S., Nickerson, D.W., 2003. Getting out the vote in local elections: results from six door-to-door canvassing experiments. J. Polit. 65 (4), 1083–1096.

Green, D.P., Krasno, J.S., 1988. Salvation for the spendthrift incumbent: reestimating the effects of campaign spending in house elections. Am. J. Polit. Sci. 32, 884–907.

Green, D.P., Zelizer, A., Kirby, D., 2015. Testing the Effesct of Mail, Phone, and Canvassing Treatments in Partisan Primary Runoff Elections. Columbia University (unpublished manuscript).

Greenwald, A.G., Carnot, C.G., Beach, R., Young, B., 1987. Increasing voting behavior by asking people if they expect to vote. J. Appl. Psychol. 72 (2), 315.

Grose, C.R., 2014. Field experimental work on political institutions. Annu. Rev. Polit. Sci. 17.

Guan, M., Green, D.P., 2006. Non-coercive mobilization in state-controlled elections: an experimental study in Beijing. Comp. Polit. Stud. 39, 1175–1193.

Ha, S.E., Karlan, D.S., 2009. Get-out-the-vote phone calls does quality matter? Am. Polit. Res. 37 (2), 353–369.

Imai, K., Strauss, A., 2011. Estimation of heterogeneous treatment effects from randomized experiments, with application to the optimal planning of the get-out-the-vote campaign. Polit. Anal. 19, 1–19.

Jacobson, G.C., 1978. The effects of campaign spending in congressional elections. Am. Polit. Sci. Rev. 72, 469–491.

Jacobson, G.C., 1985. Money and votes reconsidered: congressional elections, 1972–1982. Public Choice 47, 7–62.

Jacobson, G.C., 1990. The effects of campaign spending in house elections: new evidence for old arguments. Am. J. Polit. Sci. 34, 334–362.

Jacobson, G.C., 1998. The Politics of Congressional Elections. Longman, New York.

John, P., Brannan, T., 2008. How different are telephoning and canvassing? Results from a 'get out the vote' field experiment in the British 2005 general election. Br. J. Polit. Sci. 38, 565–574.

Kalla, Broockman, 2016. http://onlinelibrary.wiley.com/store/10.1111/ajps.12180/asset/ajps12180.pdf; jsessionid=822F8F1CAE0F9A97C646C147CD02C675.f03t01?v=1&t=itfpo37d&s=51a51e9cae44 80b5d78bf9141dec01497ef187de.

Kendall, C., Nannicini, T., Trebbi, F., 2013. How Do Voters Respond to Information? Evidence From a Randomized Campaign. No. w18986. National Bureau of Economic Research (unpublished manuscript).

Kramer, G.H., 1966. A decision theoretic analysis of a problem in political campaigning. In: Bernd, J.L. (Ed.), Mathematical Applications in Political Science, vol. 2. Southern Methodist University Press, Dallas, Texas, pp. 137—160.

LeVan, C., 2016. The Neighbor Effect: Spillover Effects of an Experimental Intervention to Increase Turnout Amongst Voters in Low-Income Neighborhoods. University of California, Los Angeles (unpublished manuscript).

Levitt, S.D., 1994. Using repeat challengers to estimate the effect of campaign spending on election outcomes in the US House. J. Polit. Econ. 102, 777—798.

Malhotra, N., Michelson, M.R., Valenzuela, A.A., 2012. Emails from official sources can increase turnout. Q. J. Polit. Sci. 7 (3), 321—332.

Mann, C.B., 2005. Unintentional voter mobilization: does participation in preelection surveys increase voter turnout? Ann. Am. Acad. Polit. Soc. Sci. 601 (1), 155—168.

Mann, C., 2008. Field Experimentation in Political Communication for Mobilization (Ph.D. dissertation). Yale University, Department of Political Science.

Mann, C.B., Klofstad, C.A., 2015. The role of call quality in voter mobilization: implications for electoral outcomes and experimental design. Polit. Behav. 37 (1), 135—154.

McCullough, M.E., Kimeldorf, M.B., Cohen, A.D., 2008. An adaptation for altruism the social causes, social effects, and social evolution of gratitude. Curr. Dir. Psychol. Sci. 17 (4), 281—285.

McNulty, J.E., 2005. Phone-based GOTV—What's on the line? Field experiments with varied partisan components, 2002—2003. Ann. Am. Acad. Polit. Soc. Sci. 601 (1), 41—65.

Michelson, M.R., 2003. Getting out the latino vote: how door-to-door canvassing influences voter turnout in rural central California. Polit. Behav. 25, 247—263.

Michelson, M.R., Bedolla, L.G., McConnell, M.A., 2009. Heeding the call: the effect of targeted two-round phonebanks on voter turnout. J. Polit. 71, 1549—1563.

Miller, R.E., Bositis, D.A., Baer, D.L., 1981. Stimulating voter turnout in a primary: field experiment with a precinct committeeman. Int. Polit. Sci. Rev. 2, 445—460.

Milkman, K.L., Beshears, J., Choi, J.J., Laibson, D., Madrian, B.C., 2011. Using implementation intentions prompts to enhance influenza vaccination rates. Proc. Natl. Acad. Sci. 108 (26), 10415—10420.

Morwitz, V.G., Johnson, E., Schmittlein, D., 1993. Does measuring intent change behavior? J. Consum. Res. 46—61.

Murray, G.R., Matland, R.E., 2014. Mobilization effects using mail social pressure, descriptive norms, and timing. Polit. Res. Q. 67 (2), 304—319.

Nickerson, D.W., 2007. Quality is job one: volunteer and professional phone calls. Am. J. Polit. Sci. 51 (2), 269—282.

Nickerson, D.W., 2008. Is voting contagious? Evidence from two field experiments. Am. Polit. Sci. Rev. 102, 49—57.

Nickerson, D.W., Rogers, T., 2010. Do you have a voting plan? Implementation intentions, voter turnout, and organic plan making. Psychol. Sci. 21 (2), 194—199.

Niven, D., 2006. A field experiment on the effects of negative campaign mail on voter turnout in a municipal election. Polit. Res. Q. 59 (2), 203—210.

Panagopoulos, C., 2008. Partisan and nonpartisan message content and voter mobilization: field experimental evidence. Polit. Res. Q. 62.

Panagopoulos, C., 2010. Affect, social pressure and prosocial motivation: field experimental evidence of the mobilizing effects of pride, shame and publicizing voting behavior. Polit. Behav. 32 (3), 369—386.

Panagopoulos, C., 2011. Social pressure, surveillance and community size: evidence from field experiments on voter turnout. Elect. Stud. 30 (2), 353—357.

Panagopoulos, C., 2013. Positive social pressure and prosocial motivation: evidence from a large-scale field experiment on voter mobilization. Polit. Psychol. 34 (2), 265—275.

Panagopoulos, C., 2014. Raising hope: hope inducement and voter turnout. Basic Appl. Soc. Psychol. 36 (6), 494—501.

Panagopoulos, C., Larimer, C.W., Condon, M., 2014. Social pressure, descriptive norms, and voter mobilization. Polit. Behav. 36 (2), 451—469.

Pons, V., 2014. Does Door-to-Door Canvassing Affect Vote Shares? Evidence From a Countrywide Field Experiment in France. Harvard University (unpublished manuscript).

Pons, V., Liegey, G., 2013. Increasing the electoral participation of immigrants. Experimental evidence from France. Massachusetts Institute of Technology (unpublished manuscript).

Ramirez, R., 2005. Giving voice to Latino voters: a field experiment on the effectiveness of a national nonpartisan mobilization effort. Ann. Am. Acad. Polit. Soc. Sci. 601 (1), 66—84.

Ramiro, L., Morales, L., Jiménez Buedo, M., 2012. Assessing the electoral payoffs of partisan mobilization. A field experimental study of the 2011 Spanish local elections. In: Paper Presented at the Annual Meeting of the International Political Science Association.

Regan, J., 2013. The Effects of Direct Mail on Voter Turnout: A Randomized Field Experiment. University of Birmingham Department of Economics (unpublished manuscript).

Riker, W.H., Ordeshook, P.C., 1968. A theory of the calculus of voting. Am. Polit. Sci. Rev. 62 (01), 25—42.

Rind, B., Bordia, P., 1995. Effect of server's "thank you" and personalization on restaurant tipping. J. Appl. Soc. Psychol. 25 (9), 745—751.

Rogers, T., Fox, C.R., Gerber, A.S., 2013. Rethinking Why People Vote. In: The Behavioral Foundations of Public Policy, vol. 91.

Rogers, T., Green, D.P., Ternovski, J., Ferrerosa-Young, C., 2015. Social Pressure and Voting: A Field Experiment Conducted in a High-Salience Election. Harvard University (unpublished manuscript).

Rogers, T., Middleton, J., 2015. Are ballot initiative outcomes influenced by the campaigns of independent groups? A precinct-randomized field experiment showing that they are. Polit. Behav. 37 (3), 567—593.

Rogers, T., Ternovski, J., 2015. 'We May Ask if Your Voted': Accountability and a Behavior's Importance to the Self (unpublished manuscript).

Rosenstone, S.J., Hansen, J.M., 1993. Mobilization, Participation, and Democracy in America. MacMillan, New York.

Rubin, D.B., 1978. Bayesian inference for causal effects: the role of randomization. Ann. Stat. 6, 34—58.

Schwenzfeier, M., 2014. When Social Pressure Fails: Evidence From Two Direct Mail Experiments. College of William & Mary Undergraduate Honors Theses. Paper 69 (unpublished manuscript).

Sheingate, A., 2016. The Rise of Political Consulting and the Transformation of American Democracy. Oxford University Press.

Sherman, S.J., 1980. On the self-erasing nature of errors of prediction. J. Personal. Soc. Psychol. 39 (2), 211.

Smith, J.K., Gerber, A.S., Orlich, A., 2003. Self-prophecy effects and voter turnout: an experimental replication. Polit. Psychol. 24 (3), 593—604.

Stollwerk, A., 2015. Does Partisan E-mail Affect Voter Turnout? An Examination of Two Field Experiments in New York City. Columbia University, Department of Political Science (unpublished manuscript).

Teresi, H., Michelson, M.R., 2015. Wired to mobilize: the effect of social networking messages on voter turnout. Soc. Sci. J. 52 (2), 195—204.

Trivers, R.L., 1971. The evolution of reciprocal altruism. Q. Rev. Biol. 35—57.

Trivedi, N., 2005. The effect of identity-based GOTV direct mail appeals on the turnout of Indian Americans. Ann. Am. Acad. Polit. Soc. Sci. 601 (1), 115—122.

Vavreck, L., 2007. The exaggerated effects of advertising on turnout: the dangers of self-reports. Q. J. Polit. Sci. 2, 287—305.

Villa Jr., H., Michelson, M., 2003. Mobilizing the Latino Youth Vote. The Field Experiments Website, No. 00311.

Wong, J.S., 2005. Mobilizing Asian American voters: a field experiment. Ann. Am. Acad. Polit. Soc. Sci. 601 (1), 102—114.

CHAPTER 10

Lab in the Field: Measuring Preferences in the Wild

U. Gneezy*,§,1, A. Imas¶

*University of California, San Diego, La Jolla, CA, United States
§University of Amsterdam, Amsterdam, Netherlands
¶Carnegie Mellon University, Pittsburgh, PA, United States
1Corresponding author: E-mail: ugneezy@ucsd.edu

Contents

Abstract

In this chapter, we discuss the "lab-in-the-field" methodology, which combines elements of both lab and field experiments in using standardized, validated paradigms from the lab in targeting relevant populations in naturalistic settings. We begin by examining how the methodology has been used to test economic models with populations of theoretical interest. Next, we outline how lab-in-the-field studies can be used to complement traditional randomized control trials in collecting covariates to test theoretical predictions and explore behavioral mechanisms. We proceed to discuss how the methodology can be utilized to compare behavior across cultures and contexts, and test for the external validity of results obtained in the lab. The chapter concludes with an overview of lessons on how to use the methodology effectively.

Keywords

Experimental economics; Field experiments; Laboratory experiments; Risk preferences; Social preferences; Time preferences

JEL Codes

B40; C91; C92; C93; D01; D03

Lab experiments and field experiments differ on several core dimensions. Lab experiments are typically conducted in environments that attempt to abstract from the naturalistic setting where individuals typically make their decisions. Factors orthogonal to the theoretical problem being studied such as context and background are removed so

Handbook of Economic Field Experiments, Volume 1
ISSN 2214-658X, http://dx.doi.org/10.1016/bs.hefe.2016.08.003

that the experimenter can maintain tight control and eliminate potential confounds from the study. These experiments are typically conducted on university campuses with convenient populations of students who are aware that their actions are being studied. While the high level of experimenter control has benefits such as reducing noise and ease of replicability, abstracting from the naturalistic setting and using student populations brings into question whether students in the lab making abstract decisions are a good representation of the types of decisions made by individuals actually relevant to the economic theory.

We have learned quite a lot from carefully designed experiments that impose a strict structure on decision-making. Yet, it is important to explore how individuals' preferences in theoretically relevant settings shape behavior. When studying performance under different incentive schemes, output on a real-effort task could be a more appropriate measure than an induced value design.[1] Similarly, manipulating incentives for charitable giving with actual donors to study social preferences may yield more insightful results for charities than the same manipulation in an anonymous giving game in the lab.[2]

Field experiments are conducted in naturalistic environments and typically use a nonstudent population that is not aware that their decisions are being studied. By targeting a population of theoretical interest in its natural environment, the experimenter can be more confident that the results are applicable to the relevant context. However, field experiments sacrifice experimenter control that may inject noise into the data and introduce potential confounds that bias the results. It is also harder to replicate results from field experiments as they are often inherently situation specific. Replicating a dictator game in the university lab with student participants is easier than replicating the same game with a tribe in a remote area. This situation-specific element also makes it difficult to generalize the results and make direct comparisons to other environments and populations.

In this chapter, we discuss a methodology termed "lab-in-the-field" and argue that by combining elements of both lab and field experiments, it provides researchers with a tool that has the benefits of both, while minimizing the respective costs. We define a lab-in-the-field study as one conducted in a naturalistic environment targeting the theoretically relevant population but using a standardized, validated lab paradigm. Targeting the relevant population and setting increases the applicability of the results. Employing a standardized paradigm permits the experimenter to maintain tight control, while allowing for direct comparisons across contexts and populations. Importantly, the use of lab-in-the-field is an important additional tool in understanding preferences in the wild that could be employed alongside traditional field work.

---

[1] See Fehr et al. (1998) and Gneezy and List (2006) for the qualitative difference in effort and reciprocity depending on methodology used.

[2] See Andreoni and Miller (2002) and Karlan and List (2007) for qualitative differences in price sensitivities in giving depending on the methodology used.

In some cases, the method that we consider is similar to that of Harrison and List (2004). According to their taxonomy, lab-in-the-field is a type of field experiment. What we call lab-in-the-field using nonstandard populations is similar in spirit to what they termed an artefactual field experiment, which they define as "…the same as a conventional lab experiment but with a nonstandard subject pool." As an example of such artefactual field experiment, Harrison and List (2004) discuss the paper by Harrison et al. (2002) who use a standard lab experiment but instead of running it at a university run it in hotels in order to be able to attract a representative sample of the Danish population. Following Charness et al. (2013), we argue that the physical location of the lab is not what defines a method, and laboratory experiments that are run outside of the university are not best described as field experiments.

While there is no clear cut difference here between lab experiments and lab in the field, we argue that the population itself does not make a study a field experiment. For example, Cappelen et al. (2015) conducted a social preference experiment with a representative population in their lab. In our classification, that would be a lab experiment. According to Harrison and List (2004), this would be an artefactual field experiment.

1. THEORETICALLY-RELEVANT POPULATIONS

One of the limitations of standard experiments in the lab is the use of a narrow set of participants, typically university students, with similar cognitive abilities, low variance in age, education, income, etc. A natural concern is whether results obtained in this specific population would be representative of behavior in a more relevant population. Henrich et al. (2010) argue that participants in laboratory experiments are typically drawn from Western, Educated, Industrialized, Rich, and Democratic (WEIRD) societies, and results obtained from such studies may not generalize to other populations and settings. For example, in fairness and social preference experiments, WEIRD subjects tend to be more generous and make fewer income maximizing offers than participants drawn from other societies.

The issue of generalizability is particularly important for using experimental data for informing economic theory. For example, economic models of financial decision making such as of asset pricing and household consumption and saving were often developed to capture the behavior of market participants like finance professionals (e.g., traders) and individuals investing to save for retirement. Experiments to test these models in the lab typically used a convenient sample of undergraduates and implicitly assumed that behavior in the lab would generalize to the relevant population of experienced traders and financial market participants.

Locke and Mann (2005) discuss the applicability of studying behavior of nonprofessional traders in the context of information cascades and herd behavior in financial decisions, stating that individuals without experience in financial markets are too far removed from the price discovery process and may therefore behave differently than the population of market professionals. In the paper, the authors study the disposition effect—the tendency to hold on to losing stocks longer than winning stocks—in a population of professional traders and retail traders. Although they find that both groups display a pronounced disposition effect, the former group does not suffer financial losses as a result whereas the latter group does. This discrepancy in how a well-studied behavioral phenomenon effects different populations is taken as evidence for the importance of studying the theoretically relevant population rather than a convenient sample. Theorists examining herding and information cascades similarly argue that to examine herding behavior requires a population of individuals "who trade actively and act similarly" (Bikhchandani and Sharma, 2000).

Alevy et al. (2007) aimed to address this issue by comparing behavior of market professionals and undergraduate students in a paradigm typically used to study information cascades and herding (Anderson and Holt, 1997). In this setting, individuals make decisions based on a noisy private signal and a public signal based on the behavior of others who faced the same decision before them. Cascades are said to form when individuals ignore their private signal to follow the public signal and can be either statistically justified or not depending on the quality of the public and private signals. Students were recruited for a lab study on a university campus, while traders participated in the experiment at the Chicago Board of Trade (CBOT). The behavior in the experiment differed significantly between the two populations. Market professionals were more likely to use their private signal and were more sensitive to the quality of the public signal, making better use of it than the undergraduates. In turn, the professionals were involved in (weakly) fewer cascades overall and significantly fewer suboptimal cascades (reverse cascades).

But professionals do not always "fix" biases. In a similar vein to the information cascade study, Haigh and List (2005) compared the propensity of market professionals (traders on the CBOT) and students to exhibit myopic loss aversion. Myopic loss aversion, which combines two behavioral concepts of loss aversion and mental accounting, predicts that people will take on more risk over a sequence of gambles than when the same gambles are presented in isolation (Benartzi and Thaler, 1995). It has been proposed as an explanation for the equity premium puzzle, suggesting that the high risk premium on stocks is due to traders evaluating asset performance over too narrow of a frame. Using a standard laboratory paradigm from the myopic loss aversion literature (Gneezy and Potters, 1997), Haigh and List (2005) found that rather than displaying less myopic loss aversion than the students, traders were even more likely to take on greater risk when gambles were framed together rather than separately.

Both papers offer insight on the extent to which behavior of relevant populations differ from convenient populations typically used in lab experiments. The results of using the lab-in-the-field methodology in these cases suggest that the students were not qualitatively different than the relevant population and offer a step in the direction of showing the degree to which behavioral phenomena were applicable outside of the student population.

Policy is often designed to target a specific population. For example, initiatives such as Medicare Part D are aimed at improving the healthcare outcomes of retirees while programs to increase student retention and the development of human capital are targeted towards young children and adolescents. For these policies to be effective, it is important to examine how the preferences of these populations differ from those assumed in standard economic theory.

In the tradition of developmental psychology, Harbaugh et al. (2001) examine the question of whether age and greater market experience mitigates behavioral phenomena such as the endowment effect—the gap in valuations of a good between buyers and sellers. If age and market experience brings behavior closer to the predictions of the neoclassical model, then adults are expected to show a lower gap than children. The participants in the experiment were kindergarten children and undergraduates enrolled in an introductory economics class. Using the standard paradigm of Knetsch (1989), participants were randomly endowed with one of two objects and then asked whether they would like to keep the object or trade it for the other. The school-aged students made choices between different goods than the college students: the former kept or traded toys and school supplies while the latter made choices over chocolates and coffee mugs. The main finding was no difference in the propensity to choose the endowed item between the age groups, suggesting that exposure to markets between kindergarten and college does not diminish this behavioral phenomenon.

In a paper titled "GARP for Kids," Harbaugh et al. (2001) further studied the relationship between age and rationality by presenting groups of children aged 7 and 11 and undergraduate students with a series of choices between bundles of goods while varying relative prices and budget. Andreoni and Miller (2002) have previously used this experimental paradigm in a standard lab setup to test whether preferences are transitive and consistent with the Generalized Axiom of Revealed Preference (GARP). The authors find that children as young as seven already display a high degree of choices consistent with GARP. By age 11 years, the choices of children appear just as consistent as those of adult undergraduates, suggesting that models of economic behavior can be applied to children as well as adults.

The study of social preferences is a rapidly growing literature in economics. Several models (see Charness and Kuhn, 2011 for a recent survey) aim to capture the systematic violations of the purely selfish, money-maximizing actor, which used to be a typical assumption in neoclassical economics. People have been observed to share money with strangers (Forsythe et al., 1994), sacrifice money by rejecting unfair offers in ultimatum bargaining games (Guth et al., 1982), and cooperate with others even in one-shot interactions (Andreoni, 1989).

However, an important question for both theory and policy is when such preferences develop. Fehr et al. (2008) sought to answer this question by examining the allocation decisions of young children. Groups of children aged 3—4, 5—6, and 7—8 at local preschools and elementary schools participated in the study. Each child was paired with another and asked to make decisions on how to allocate candy between themselves and their partner in three games. In the prosocial game, the child chose whether to receive one candy and give nothing to their partner, (1, 0), or for both to receive one candy each, (1, 1). This game was designed to examine whether the child would be willing to benefit another at no cost to themselves. In the envy game, the child chose between an equal split of candy, (1, 1), or disadvantageous inequality, (1, 2). Since allocating an extra candy to their partner came at no cost to the child, the envy game aimed to measure participants' inequity aversion. Finally, in the sharing game, children chose between an equal split, (1, 1), or a selfish allocation of, (2, 0). The authors found that preferences for equal splits increased significantly with age. While young children 3—4 years of age preferred selfish allocations, a large fraction of children aged 7—8 years chose the equal split of (1, 1) in each of the three games. These results suggest that rather than being innate, preferences for outcomes consistent with norms such as fairness develop with exposure to culture. In related work, Almås et al. (2010) show that a significant development in morality happens in adolescence, as a response to culture, and Almas et al. (forthcoming) show that family background is crucial for understanding levels of competitiveness.

Dohmen et al. (2012) jointly elicit preferences of both children and their parents. Their goal was to examine the extent to which willingness to take risks and trust others are traits that children inherit from parents, the influence of positive assortative matching on this intergenerational transmission and whether the local attitudes in the environment affects preferences. Children and parent pairs were interviewed at their homes. In order to maintain control and avoid potential confounds, each child and parent were interviewed separately to ensure that each answers questions individually and independent of the others. By studying children and their parents in their homes instead of using a convenient population of undergraduates, the authors were able to gain access to all members in a family. Results suggest significant intergenerational transmission of risk and trust attitudes, which is strengthened by positive assortative matching between the parents. The prevailing attitudes in the environment also play a significant but independent role in shaping children's risk and trust preferences.

On the other end of the age spectrum, as life expectancy in the developed world increases, there is greater pressure to push forward the retirement age and for individuals to keep working later into their years. However, employers are often reluctant to hire older workers (Bendick et al., 1999) due to the notion that seniors are less productive than their younger counterparts. While this belief is common (Kovalchick et al., 2005), evidence for it has been lacking in the economics literature. Using a lab-in-the-field design, Charness and Villeval (2009) aimed to directly compare the preferences and behavior of older individuals such as retirees to those of a younger population. Particularly, whether the two populations differed in their willingness to cooperate and compete with others.

The first set of experiments took place at two large French firm work sites. To measure cooperation, juniors (under 30) and seniors (over 50) were invited to participate in a team production game that was akin to a public goods game typically studied in lab experiments. In the game, participants were endowed with a private sum that they could choose to either contribute to the public good (cooperate), where it is multiplied and split evenly amongst the group, or to keep it. Given the potential of free riding on the contribution of others, the equilibrium of the game under the assumption of selfishness is to keep the entire endowment while the efficient outcome is for everyone to contribute the maximum amount. To measure competitiveness, juniors and seniors engaged in a real-effort task (solving anagrams) and could choose to either be paid at a piece-rate for every anagram solved or to compete with others in a tournament, where the one who solved the most anagrams would win a large prize and the others would win a much smaller prize. The choice of compensation scheme (piece rate versus tournament) served as the measure of competitiveness. Attitudes towards financial risk-taking were also collected.

Charness and Villeval (2009) found that both juniors and seniors responded strongly to competition and that seniors were more willing to cooperate than juniors. The groups did not differ in their willingness to engage in financial risk taking. Moreover, groups containing both juniors and seniors were better off than more homogeneous groups because seniors responded to the presence of juniors by being even more cooperative. The authors replicated these findings in a traditional lab experiment with a student population and retirees. These findings suggest that age diversity in the work place may potentially be beneficial for both employees and employers.

These experiments comparing decision-making in children and adults of different age groups can teach us about the origin of violations of standard models as well as the development of behavior policy makers may either want to encourage or prevent. By using a standardized experimental paradigm, the authors were able to maintain tight control over the study and make direct comparisons between the populations of interest.

More generally, the evidence reviewed here shows that it is important to elicit behavior and preferences with nonstandard populations that are closer to the theoretically relevant target population. The method of lab-in-the-field is a useful tool to achieve this aim since it is often difficult or impossible to get these nonstandard populations into the standard laboratory environments (Table 1).

2. USING LAB-IN-THE FIELD FOR COLLECTING COVARIATES AS COMPLEMENTS TO RCTs AND FOR TARGETING POLICY

One criticism of randomized control trials (RCTs) is that they are often limited in discerning the mechanism driving the observed results. Because researchers are often

Table 1 Theoretically relevant populations

Article	Population and setting	Study
Harbaugh et al. (2001)	125 Children in kindergarten, third grade, and fifth grade, and 38 undergraduates in classrooms	Testing whether endowment effect changes with age/market experience.
Harbaugh et al. (2001)	Seven-year and 11-year-old children and college undergraduates in classrooms	Testing whether age affects rationality and consistency of preferences in line with GARP.
Alevy et al. (2007)	Market professionals at the Chicago Board of Trade and college students in lab	Testing for differences in cascade behavior and herding between students and market professionals.
Dohmen et al. (2012)	Families—children and their parents—interviewed at their homes	Testing whether willingness to take risks and trust are inherited from parents.
Frijters et al. (2015)	Chinese migrants interviewed in hotel rooms and over the phone	Examining selection bias for lab in field studies conducted on representative population of migrants versus self-selected population of migrants.
Marette et al. (2011)	201 Households—with women between 25 and 35 years old, with at least one child under 15, who eat fish at least 2× a week. Interviews conducted in home and preferences elicited at market	Welfare effects of regulatory tools such as labels and/or taxes.
Grossman and Baldassarri (2013)	2597 Ugandan farmers in rural communities	Tested whether group attachment and relative position in social networks affects prosocial behavior towards in-group.
Gilligan et al. (2014)	Residents in conflict-plagued regions	Used incentivized behavioral activities to measure Nepal communities' social capital. Took advantage of Nepal's natural landscape to study communities which are exposed to uncertainty of violence.

Table 1 Theoretically relevant populations—cont'd

Article	Population and setting	Study
Spears (2010)	Informal day market laborers in Rajasthan, India	Studies whether poverty causes impulsive behavior through a "store" game and behavioral test. Test was designed to mimic analogous decisions in the real world.
Chandrasekhar et al. (2014)	Villagers in Karnataka, India	Studies how real-world social networks may substitute for formal contract enforcement by conducting experiments in villages. Imitate real-world relation network as subjects have real-world relationships with each other. These relationships were observable from available detailed social network data for each household in the village.
Attanasio et al. (2012)	Residents in Columbia	Studies how risk-sharing group formation is affected by pre-existing social network and individual's risk attitude. Real-world relations were studied as friendship and kinship already existed among participants, many of whom came from the same community.
Binzel and Fehr (2013)	Residents in Cairo, Egypt	Studies how prosocial behavior is influenced by people's social distance and anonymity by conducting dictator game in Cairo communities. Utilizes pre-existing social relations to mimic real-world social networks.
Alexander and Christia (2011)	Students from Mostar, Bosnia-Herzegovina	Studies the effect of ethnic diversity on cooperation. Subjects were drawn from populations that have historically been in conflict (Croats and Bosnians).
Charness and Villeval (2009)	Juniors (under 30) and seniors (over 50) at two large French firms	Examine differences in competitiveness and cooperation amongst younger and older individuals.

limited in the number of treatments they can run due to costs or access to the required sample size, RCTs frequently cannot identify a particular theoretical model while ruling out alternative explanations on their own (Viceisza, forthcoming). In this section, we build the case for using lab-in-the-field methodology to collect explanatory covariates that can be used in conjunction with RCTs to inform researchers about the mechanism leading to the observed behavior. In general, lab-in-the-field can be used in two complimentary ways when conducting an RCT. First, lab-in-the-field could be used as a part of the RCT baseline, which allows the researcher to study whether treatment effects depend on behavior measured in experiments. Second, the researcher can conduct a lab-in-the-field as a part of the outcome of the RCT, studying whether the intervention affected related behavior, such as overconfidence or competitiveness.

Ashraf et al. (2006) ran an RCT exploring the effectiveness of commitment devices on savings behavior. The authors offered some bank clients in the Philippines commitment savings account with limited access to deposits. The account was designed to be appealing to clients who are sophisticated about their self-control problems, and in turn, would like to restrict access to their savings in order to limit impulsive purchases. Of the 710 clients who were offered this account, 202 (28.4%) opted in. Moreover, the intervention successfully increased savings: for those clients offered the commitment savings account, the average savings balances increased by 81% in the following year relative to clients who were in the control group and not offered the account.

While the nonzero take-up rate of the commitment savings device is interesting in its own right, it is not sufficient evidence for the hypothesis that people chose the account in order to overcome their self-control problems. In order to provide support for this mechanism, Ashraf et al. (2006) conducted a time discounting experiment before the RCT. They report that clients who exhibited lower discount rate for future relative to current trade-offs in the experiment were, consistent with the hypothesis, more likely to choose the commitment savings account.

Jakiela et al. (2015) sought to examine the causal impact of an education intervention on cultural values, norms, and social preferences. Although many have claimed that human capital gains lead to more equitable attitudes and support for democratic institutions, causal evidence for this relationship was largely absent. A Dutch NGO ICS Africa introduced a scholarship program to a random sample of sixth grade girls in Western Kenya. The program led to significant improvements in performance on academic tests relative to the control group (Kremer, 2009). Jakiela et al. (2015) ran a lab-in-the-field experiment with girls who were in the treatment group of the Girls Scholarship Program (GSP) and girls who were in the control group, and hence did not receive access to the scholarship program. Both groups participate in a modified dictator game where the dictator decides how to allocate money between themselves and another individual. Critical to the design, the sum to be divided was earned by the latter individual through a real effort task, creating an informal "property rights" over the money.

The authors found that participants in the treatment group exhibited superior academic performance relative to the control group. Moreover, the GSP group allocated significantly more to the other, with a greater shift towards 50-50 splits, than girls who were not in the program. These results suggest that the randomized education intervention had medium to long-run effects not only on academic performance but on social preferences and cultural values as well.

In a study on microentrepreneurship, Berge et al. (2015a) examine the effects of business training and business grants on economic outcomes such as business performance, practice, and investment. The authors collaborated with an established microfinance institution in running the RCT which recruited small scale entrepreneurs in Dar es Salaam, Tanzania. Participants were randomized to either be enrolled in a business training course focusing on basic principles such as customer service, pricing, and accounting, or to receive a business grant equivalent to the cost of the training course; performance of both groups were compared to a control. In conjunction with the RCT, lab-in-the-field experiments were run to elicit participants' risk and competitiveness preferences, as well as their confidence and willingness to share information.

The authors found that business training had a significant and positive effect on outcomes such as sales, profit, and reported happiness—but only for the male entrepreneurs; business grants had no significant impact for either. Exploring this gender effect further using collected lab-in-the-field measures revealed that female participants were less willing to share income information with their spouse, suggesting a significant levy on their earnings that may make business expansion less worthwhile. Additionally, they were less competitive than their male counterparts, which the authors argue is an important factor in the entrepreneurial mind-set.

In order to optimally target policy and RCT interventions towards those who are most likely to experience positive impact, it is important to understand what traits and preference measures are associated with economic behavior. Burks et al. (2008) examined how elicited measures relate to and influence labor outcomes, specifically job attachment. A sample of 1000 trainee truckers at a company operated training facility took part in the study on how cognitive skills (CS) affect economic preferences and behavior. The authors elicited three measures of CS (IQ, planning ability, quantitative literacy) from each individual and examined the relationship between CS and standard measures of economic preferences (choice consistency, time and risk preferences). The lab-in-the-field method allowed them to examine how CS relates to actual economic behavior by linking the elicited measures to human resource records and the relationship between the measures and job attachment. CS was found to have a positive and significant correlation with patience and the willingness to take calculated risks.

Importantly, higher CS, particularly in the ability to plan, was significantly related to job attachment: participants who displayed better abilities to plan stayed at the job longer, which was profitable for the company. By using the lab-in-the-field methodology to link experimentally elicited measures to real-world behavior, these findings are able to inform policy by highlighting a series of traits relevant for labor market outcomes.

Another important use of the lab-in-the-field methodology is to examine how the environment and prior experiences of population shape their preferences in order to improve the targeting of policy measures and RCT interventions. Bchir and Willinger (2013) exploit natural variation in the potential for lahars (mudflows from volcanoes) in Arequipa, Peru to examine how living with greater ex ante background risk affects preferences for financial risk. The authors utilize a commonly employed method of eliciting risk preferences in the lab, a multiple price list over lotteries (Holt and Laury, 2002; see Charness et al., 2013 for review), to compare the preferences of individuals living in high-risk areas to those living with lower levels of background risk. In this method, individuals make a series of decisions between safer lotteries with smaller variances and riskier lotteries with greater variances; an individual's risk attitude is measured by the number of times he or she chooses the safer option. The authors find that, contrary to standard economic intuition, individuals living with greater background were more risk seeking than those in less exposed areas. However, this difference only held for low-income participants—there was no significant relationship between lahar exposure and risk preferences amongst those with higher incomes.

Eckel et al. (2009) document an analogous relationship between natural hazards and risk attitudes for individuals who experienced a natural disaster versus those who did not. Particularly, they elicited risk attitudes from a sample of individuals being evacuated from the aftermath of Hurricane Katrina and compared their responses to a similar group of people who did not experience the disaster. Risk preferences were measured using the Eckel and Grossman (2002) method which offered individuals a choice between six lotteries that differed in their expected return and variance; a given lottery choice could be used to classify the individual as risk-averse, risk neutral, or risk-seeking. Eckel et al. (2009) found that those who had experienced Hurricane Katrina were significantly more risk-seeking than the comparison group.

Similarly, Voors et al. (2012) examined how prior exposure to violence on the community level-shaped risk preferences. The authors identified communities in Burundi who had been exposed to violent conflict and matched them to comparable communities who were not exposed to the conflict. Individuals in both groups were asked to make choices between safe and risky lotteries in a multiple price list format. They found that, similar to exposure to natural disasters, exposure to violence also leads individuals to make riskier choices.

To summarize, collecting covariates using the lab-in-the-field methodology as part of an RCT helps in two ways. First, it can help identify the theoretical mechanism driving

Table 2 Lab-in-the-field as compliment to randomized control trials

Article	Population and setting	Study
Ashraf et al. (2006)	Banking customers in the Philippines	Significant portion of customers offered commitment savings vehicle limiting their access to cash opted in, especially those with higher elicited discount rates.
Berge et al. (2015a)	Microentrepreneurs in Tanzania	Evaluated effect of business training and business grants on performance. Business training had significant short and long-term effects for male entrepreneurs, business grants did not. Separately elicited measures suggest null effect for female entrepreneurs due to greater spousal levies and lower competitiveness.
Jakiela et al. (2015)	School-aged Kenyan women	Sixth-grade girls randomly assigned to girls scholarship program (GSP), explored whether intervention changed social preferences and norms. More educated girls found to be less likely to appropriate others' income and adhere to fair financial allocations.
Lahno et al. (2015)	Pairs of individuals in 30 villages in rural Uganda	Studies the external validity of elicited risk measures in predicting interpersonal conflict. Finds risk-aversion per se does not explain level of conflict but rather differences in risk attitudes strongly predict interpersonal conflict.
Voors et al. (2012)	Villagers from Burundi	Studies how exposure to violence affects risk preferences.

Continued

Table 2 Lab-in-the-field as compliment to randomized control trials—cont'd

Article	Population and setting	Study
Bchir and Willinger (2013)	Communities in Arequipa, Peru	Studies how differing exposure to background risk in the form of mudslides affects risk preferences.
Eckel et al. (2009)	Individuals who were evacuated after Hurricane Katrina	Studies how exposure to natural disasters affects risk attitudes.
Burks et al. (2008)	1000 Trainee truckers at company operated trainee facility.	Studies effect of cognitive skills on three tests of preferences, strategic behavior, and perseverance in the job.
Ward and Singh (2015)	Farmers in rural India	Examines how elicited risk preferences, loss, and ambiguity aversion relate to the propensity to adopt new risk-reducing farming technologies.
Liu (2013)	Farmers in rural China	Studies how elicited risk preferences, loss aversion, and probability weighting relate to adoption of new agricultural biotechnology.
Karlan (2005)	Individuals in rural Peru	Examines how elicited trustworthiness in a trust game predicts propensity to default on microfinance loans.

the success or failure of the program. Second, this data can assist policy makers in targeting future interventions to participants who are most likely to adopt/benefit from it (Table 2).

3. COMPARING BETWEEN CONTEXTS AND CULTURES

Another benefit of the lab-in-the-field methodology relative to other methods is the ability to make direct comparisons between different populations and contexts. This advantage is exemplified in studies examining the role of culture on decision-making. Henrich et al. (2006) study whether willingness to engage in costly punishment is universal amongst cultures, arguing that a possible mechanism for such cooperation could be the use of costly punishment of defectors. To test this conjecture, they compare the use of costly punishment between industrialized (using a standard student population) and nonindustrialized populations.

A total of 1762 adults in 15 different societies participated in the experiment. Populations ranged from Western educated students at Emory University to nomadic adults in the Amazon. Each individual participated in three games aimed to capture willingness to engage in costly punishment and altruism. In the Ultimatum Game, one participant was endowed with a day's wage and chose how to split it with his or her partner. The partner could engage in costly punishment by rejecting allocations deemed too low—this would result in both players getting nothing. In the Third-Party Punishment game, participants observed the dictator game allocation decisions of another pair and could sacrifice part of his or her endowment to punish a greedy Dictator. Last, all participants played the dictator game where they decided how to split a sum of money between themselves and another participant (who did not have a choice).

Henrich et al. (2006) found substantial costly punishment in every culture. In the Ultimatum game, willingness to reject an offer decreased as the size of the offer increased from 0% to 50% of the endowed cash. Rejection rates differed substantially by population: in some societies only 15% were willing to reject a low offer while in others 60% were willing to reject. A similar pattern was found in the Third-Party Punishment game: all societies were willing to punish low offers to some extent, but this punishment rate ranged from 28% in Tsimane to 90% in Gusii. In each society, punishment rates in both games were highly correlated with each other as well as the measure of altruism in the dictator game.

Examining the data set of Herrmann et al. (2008) which used the standardized protocol of a public goods game across 16 subject pools and six distinct cultures, Gachter et al. (2010) analyze rates of contribution and cooperation between cultures in a public goods game with and without punishment. They find little variation in behavior amongst the subject pools within a culture. Consistent with prior findings (e.g., Gachter and Fehr, 2000), contributions were positive and dropped significantly at the end of the game. However, contribution rates as well as responses to the ability to punish differed significantly between cultures. Contributions in English-speaking cultures and Protestant Europe were higher than in Southern Europe and the Arab-speaking cultures. Additionally, English-speaking, Protestant Europe, and Confucian cultures contributed significantly more when players had the ability to punish free riders while those in Southern Europe, Arab-speaking, and ex-communist cultures did not respond to the potential to punish others.

By using the same experimental methodology across a variety of cultures, researchers were able to make direct comparisons between how social preferences developed in each of the societies studied. Despite similar social standing within their respective societies, individuals made vastly different choices in their willingness to cooperate with others, share resources, and punish defectors. This suggests that environmental factors and the culture in which individuals develop have a critical influence on how they interact with others. Particularly, the presence of stable institutions and effective means of sanctioning violators of social norms appear to play a key role in people's willingness to engage in costly behavior that is beneficial for others. These findings have significant implications for the development of policy and interventions aimed at fostering such behavior.

In some cases, lab-in-the-field is useful to test a hypothesis regarding parameters that cannot be randomized in the lab. For example, Gneezy et al. (2009) examined whether culture influences the gender gap in willingness to compete or if the gap was due to innate differences in preferences. Gneezy et al. (2003) and Niederle and Vesterlund (2007) showed that women react less to competitive incentives and are significantly less likely to enter competitions than men even when their ability and performance would have allowed them to win.

This gender difference in preference with respect to competitiveness has been replicated many times in laboratory experiments (see Croson and Gneezy, 2009 for review). However, it is impossible to know from these experiments if the difference in preferences originated from innate biological differences between men and women ("nature") or due to the culture men and women are raised at ("nurture"). In order to disentangle the two explanations, Gneezy et al. (2009) examined gender differences in competitive preferences between a patriarchal society in Tanzania (the Maasai) and a matrilineal society in India (the Khasi). The Khasi tribe is special because it is organized around the women who own the property and make many of the substantive decisions. Participants in the experiment were asked to choose between a piece rate per success (landing a tennis ball in a basket 3 meters away) or compete with others on the number of successful tosses such that the winner would get three times more per success than in the piece rate payment and the losers would get nothing (in case of a tie both participants were paid the same as in the piece rate).

Results revealed that similar to gender differences in the west, Maasai men were significantly more likely to choose competition over piece rate than the women. However, this gap disappeared for the Khasi—women were just as likely to compete as men. The results were robust to a variety of controls including separately elicited risk attitudes. These findings suggest that culture could affect gender differences in preferences up to a point of eliminating them.

Hoffman et al. (2011) similarly examine the effect of culture on the gender gap in spacial ability. Voyer et al. (1995) demonstrate that women perform significantly worse than men on tasks requiring spacial reasoning. Spacial ability is related to performance on engineering and problem-solving tasks (Poole and Stanley, 1972), and the gender gap in these abilities has been used to explain the relative dearth of women in science jobs (Spelke and Pinker, 2005). Hoffman et al. (2011) tested whether the gender gap was

Table 3 Comparing between contexts

Article	Population and setting	Study
Henrich et al. (2006)	Random sample across 15 diverse populations around the world	Willingness to engage in costly punishment
Gachter et al. (2010)	120 Participants across 6 different cultures	Willingness to contribute and cooperate in public goods games with and without punishment
Herrman et al. (2008)	120 Participants across 6 different cultures	Willingness to engage in antisocial punishment in public goods games
Gneezy et al. (2009)	Members of the patrilineal Maasai tribe and the matrilineal Khasi tribe	Whether gender gap in competitive preferences is due to nature versus nurture
Hoffman et al. (2011)	Members of the patrilineal Karbi tribe and the matrilineal Khasi tribe	Whether gender gap in spatial ability is due to nature versus nurture
Hui et al. (2004)	33 Nations for study 1, Canada and People's Republic of China for studies 2 and 3	How cultural perceptions of power moderates the effect of empowerment on job satisfaction
Jakiela et al. (2015)	Residents of rural villages in western Kenya	Social preferences governing distribution of earned versus unearned income, finds unlike with western student samples, village populations do not distinguish between earned and unearned income

due to nature versus nurture by having two genetically similar participant pools (the Khasi and the Karbi) complete a puzzle task involving special abilities. Importantly, as described above, the Khasi are a matrilineal tribe while the Karbi are patriarchal. The authors found a strong and significant gender gap amongst the Karbi where men were more successful in solving the puzzle than women. However, there was no significant gender gap in the Khasi. The results were robust to a variety of controls such as education and income.

By comparing performance on the same task across different cultures, these findings suggest that like the gender gap in competitiveness, the gap in spatial reasoning is largely influenced by nurture rather than nature. If the gap in performance and preference is due to cultural and environmental factors rather than innate differences between genders, this leaves room for policy and external interventions aimed at closing that gap (Table 3).

4. EXTERNAL VALIDITY

A common concern with traditional lab experiments is whether findings would generalize to the relevant environments and contexts. Take, for example, the gift exchange model of labor contracts first proposed by Akerlof (1982). In the model, firms pay wages above the market-clearing rate in expectation that workers will reciprocate the higher wages by putting in greater effort. Fehr et al. (1993) provided an early test of the model by randomizing participants into the role of employer and employee in the lab. The employer's earnings were based on an exogenously assigned profit function of the employee's chosen level of effort minus the wage paid to them. The employee's earnings were calculated as the wage offered by the employer minus the effort cost, which was also determined by an exogenous function. The task proceeded with the employer choosing a number corresponding to the wage and the employee responding by either accepting the wage and choosing a number corresponding to effort or rejecting the wage contract. The authors found that higher wage offers were reciprocated with higher choices of effort—suggesting evidence for gift exchange. A very large literature based on lab experiments replicated and extended these early findings (Charness and Kuhn, 2011)

Gneezy and List (2006) studied gift exchange by examining whether employees reciprocated higher-wage offers by putting in greater effort. However, unlike Fehr et al. (1993), the authors used a lab-in-the-field setting where employees were recruited to complete an assignment and chose how much real effort to exert for a certain wage. Employees were recruited to perform actual work on a task for a specified amount of time at a wage of $12 an hour. When the employees arrived to complete the task, one group was told that instead of being paid $12 an hour, they would instead be paid $20. A second group worked for the expected wage. The authors found that although employees in the first group started out working harder than the second, the effort of the two groups quickly converged. The employers in the experiment would have been better off paying the market-clearing wage rather than attempting to encourage reciprocity by offering a higher wage.

In order to explore the external validity of experimentally elicited risk attitudes, Hanoch et al. (2006) studied the domain specificity of willingness to take risk or how people's perception and chosen course of action in dealing with risk vary depending on the domain: a person may appear risk seeking in one domain (finance) but risk averse in another (sports). The type of risk spans across different domains—divers and bungee jumpers in the recreational domain, gym members from the health-conscious domain, smokers from health-risk domain, casino visitors from the gambling domain, and stock traders from investment domain.

Hanoch et al. (2006) elicited risk perception and likelihood of engaging in risky activity across these domains. The results suggest that the domain-specific elicitation method is externally valid since it correlates with actual risk-taking in that domain by the target population. Moreover, risk attitudes themselves appear domain specific: risk taking in one domain does not appear to be correlated with risk taking in another. For example, gamblers who are risk seeking in casinos are not necessarily risk seeking in the health and recreation domains. The authors conclude that a general measure of risk fails to capture people's behavior across domains, and as such both theory and experiments should utilize more domain-specific measures.

Dohmen et al. (2012) explore a similar question of what measure of risk is optimal for predicting and describing behavior. They study how risk-taking propensity is affected by various biological and socioeconomic factors such as gender, age, height, and family background, and examine the stability of elicited risk attitudes across domains of real-life behavior.

The data used was from a national survey, the German Socio-Economic Panel (SOEP), which collects data from a large, representative sample. The survey asked general risk questions about people's willingness to take risk and recorded information on savings, investment behavior, health expenditures, etc. Responses were not incentivized. The authors conducted a complementary experiment where participants' answers on the SOEP survey could be compared with choices on standardized experimental paradigms used in the literature to elicit preferences in an incentive compatible manner.

The results suggest that incentivized lottery experiments typically used to elicit risk attitudes lack predictive power over the unincentivized general survey questions in predicting relevant real-world behavior such as investment choices. Similar to Hanoch et al. (2006), Dohmen et al. (2012) find that domain-specific questions are best at predicting risky behavior in the respective domain. Additionally, the general risk question that consists of a scale representing how willing participants are to take on risk in general explains a substantial amount of variance across domains of risky behavior, outperforming the incentivized lottery task. By using the lab-in-the-field methodology, the authors were able to directly test the external validity of commonly used measures of risk preference, finding that the general and domain specific questions to be more representative of individuals' willingness to take risk in theoretically relevant contexts.

In a similar vein, Barr and Zeitlin (2010) investigate how well measures of social preferences elicited using the dictator game reflect actual prosocial behavior in real-life "specific, naturally occurring, policy-relevant decision-making." Participants were primary school teachers in Uganda who took part in dictator game with their students' parents serving as recipients. The chosen allocation game was compared to teachers' allocation of time to teaching, which served as a real-life proxy for prosocial behavior. The results

Table 4 External validity

Article	Population and setting	Study
Insurance versus savings for the poor: why one should offer either both or none	Rural villagers in the Philippines	Study residents in developing countries' decisions regarding insurance, saving and risk-sharing. Sample is more compatible with the idea of risk sharing at the village level and strengthens external validity of results.
Galizzi and Martinez (2015)	University students and alumni (London School of Economics and Political Science)	Compare results from lab experiments, field experiments and self-reports of the past behavior to assess the external validity of social preference games.
Ligon and Schechter (2012)	Villagers in Paraguay	Studies the motive for sharing in rural villages. Participants from rural Paraguay communities so that their sharing decisions are closer to real-world results. Examined money transfer data from both the experiment and real-world record to examine external validity of experiment.
Benz and Meier (2008)	Students at the University of Zurich	Conducted donation experiments in order to compare students' behavior in games with their behavior in an unconnected decision situation about donating to social funds. Studies the relationship between participants' behavior in experiment and decisions outside the laboratory.
Hanoch et al. (2006)	Decision-makers who are regularly subjected to risks	Studies the domain specificity of risk-taking behavior. Subjects drawn from different real-life risk-taking domains for external validity.

Table 4 External validity—cont'd

Article	Population and setting	Study
Dohmen et al. (2012)	Representative sample of German population	Compared results from national survey and lab-in-the-field experiment to examine how well people's responses to general risk questions (and therefore their risk attitudes) reflect people's actual decision when facing real risks in life.
Barr and Zeitlin (2010)	Primary school teachers in Uganda	Studies the external validity of dictator game by comparing school teachers' responses in the games with their actual prosocial behavior in real life (extra time allocated to teaching).
Berge et al. (2015b)	Small-scale entrepreneurs in Salaam, Tanzania	Studies the external validity of competitiveness measures by comparing entrepreneurs' competitive choices in lab-in-the-field measures to their employment choices in the field, finding a significant correlation.

showed a weak correlation between the two measures, suggesting that behavior in the dictator game may be capturing a preference orthogonal to decisions involving allocations of time to teaching (Table 4).

5. CONCLUSION

In this paper, we consider an important element in the toolbox of researchers who are interested in behavior in the "real world"—lab-in-the-field. Such experiments can be used to inform researchers and policy makers about individual preferences, mechanism design, and best practices. Good studies take into account that, as argued by Harrison et al. (2015), "Any data generated by an experiment needs to be interpreted jointly with considerations from theory, common sense, complementary data, econometric methods and expected applications."

Using carefully designed lab-in-the-field experiments can increase our understanding of the mechanisms behind behavior, inform the design of field experiments and increase the effectiveness of policies at a relatively low cost to the researcher. This method can bridge the gap between traditional lab experiments and field experiments, as well as take the powerful tool of lab experiments to new, theoretically relevant subject pools and environments.

Running lab-in-the-field experiments brings with it new challenges not present in traditional laboratory environments. In this section, we outline several lessons that we have learned from conducting lab-in-the-field studies.

1. *Simpler is better*

Nonstandard populations, especially in developing countries, can exhibit large variation in their level of literacy and mathematical ability. With that in mind, it is important to develop methodology that is easy for participants to understand and mirrors real-world decision making. As an example, consider the elicitation of risk preferences from a population in rural Senegal using a series of validated methods, with some more complex than the others. Charness and Villeval (2009) found that presenting participants with a complicated list of choices between lotteries yielded inconsistent, noisy data more than 50% of the time; in contrast, a simpler measure analogous to a choice of how much resources one is willing to expose to risk yielded more precise estimates that correlated with real-world behavior.

2. *Use standardized, validated methods*

When designing a study to take to the field, it is important to use standardized, validated methods to ensure that results are comparable and replicable across contexts. As outlined in Section 3, one of the main advantages of the lab-in-the-field methodology is the ability to compare results across contexts and cultures. Using new methods to elicit preferences in a standard student population is less of a concern because one can readily have access to a similar context and population again in order to validate the novel methodology and compare it to prior work either directly in the same experiment or across studies. In the field, however, using novel methods that have not been validated may handicap the researcher in arguing that the elicited measure corresponds to the construct of interest.

3. *Be aware of cultural factors when developing methodology*

It is critical to be aware of cultural differences when developing the methodology for a study. A design that can be carried out easily in one context, e.g., the United States, may be impossible to implement in another, e.g., Tanzania. In turn, it may be useful to include an individual deeply familiar with the culture and environment for a given study as a part of the research process. For example, the four countries experiment of Roth et al. (1991) compared the market and bargaining behavior amongst participants in the United States, Yugoslavia, Israel, and Japan. The authors found that while market behavior was consistent between countries, bargaining behavior diverged. The research team came up with a number of design modifications in order to be able to argue that culture rather than flaws in the experimental design drove the results. For example, in order to ensure that language in the instructions was consistent between countries, the

English instructions were first translated to the respective language, e.g., Hebrew. The Hebrew instructions were then translated back to English to ensure that meaning was not lost in the translation.

For a lab-in-the-field study, one of us (Gneezy) wanted to draw blood from villagers near Shillong in India, in order to correlate biological markers with measures of competitiveness. When arriving to the research site, it turns out that the participants refused to have their blood drawn because of a belief that "people from the mountains will come over, take their blood, and feed it to snakes."

Religious factors can play a role as well. For example, for a study in Bosnia on the effects of post-war partitioning on investment behavior, Imas et al. planned to use a validated risk measure to proxy for individuals' willingness to invest that involved a financial gamble. However, financial gambling was against custom in the predominantly Muslim population so another method needed to be devised. At the end, the authors settled on a hypothetical scenario involving willingness to invest in either a risky business venture with both a high upside and downside or a safer venture involving less variance.

4. *Plan out logistics ahead of time*

When going into the field, it is vital to plan out the logistics well ahead of time and factor delays into your timeline. Obtaining the right permissions and getting the relevant people on board early is critical for successfully running a lab-in-the-field experiment.

For example, in many contexts, it will be difficult to follow-up with a population if your study involves a delayed payment. In such situations, it may be more effective to design a study where a random subset of the subjects is selected to be paid rather than taking on the impossible task of tracking everyone down. Similarly, busy people such as financial professionals may not care about the low stakes involved in typical incentivized lab experiments. Since incentivizing an experiment for the very rich would make the stakes consequential is outside the budget of most experimentalists, it may be more effective to run a hypothetical study with large stakes.

REFERENCES

Akerlof, 1982. Labor contracts as partial gift exchange. Q. J. Econ. 97 (4), 543–569.

Alevy, Haigh, List, 2007. Information cascades: evidence from a field experiment with financial market professionals. J. Finance 62 (1), 151–180.

Alexander, Christia, 2011. Context modularity of human altruism. Science 334 (6061), 1392–1395.

Almås, I., Cappelen, A.W., Salvanes, K.G., Sørensen, E.Ø., Tungodden, B., 2010. Fairness and the development of inequality acceptance. Science 328, 1176–1178. Management Science.

Almås, I., Cappelen, A.W., Salvanes, K.G., Sørensen, E.Ø., Tungodden, B., 2016. Willingness to compete: family matters. Manag. Sci. (forthcoming).

Anderson, Holt, 1997. Information cascades in the laboratory. Am. Econ. Rev. 87 (5), 847–862.

Andreoni, 1989. Giving with impure altruism: applications to charity and Ricardian equivalence. J. Polit. Econ. 97 (6), 1447–1458.

Andreoni, Miller, March, 2002. Giving according to GARP: an experimental test of the consistency of preferences for altruism. Econometrica 70 (2), 737−753.

Ashraf, N., Karlan, D., Yin, W., May 2006. Tying Odysseus to the Mast: evidence from a commitment savings product in the Philippines. Q. J. Econ. 121 (2), 635−672.

Attanasio, Barr, Cardenas, Genicot, Meghir, 2012. Risk pooling, risk preferences, and social networks. Am. Econ. J. Appl. Econ. 4 (2), 134−167.

Barr, Zeitlin, 2010. Dictator Games in the Lab and in Nature: External Validity Tested and Investigated in Ugandan Primary Schools. Mimeo.

Bchir, Willinger, 2013. Does the Exposure to Natural Hazards Affect Risk and Time Preferences? Some Insights From a Field Experiment in Peru. Mimeo.

Benartzi, Thaler, 1995. Myopic loss aversion and the equity premium puzzle. J. Econ. 110 (1), 73−92.

Bendick, Brown, Wall, 1999. No foot in the door: an experimental study of employment discrimination against older workers. J. Aging Soc. Policy 10 (4), 5−23.

Benz, Meier, 2008. Do people behave in experiments as in the Field? − Evidence from donations. Exp. Econ. 11 (3), 268−281.

Berge, L.I.O., Pires, A., Bjorvatn, K., Tungodden, B., 2015a. Competitiveness in the lab, successful in the field. J. Econ. Behav. Organ. 118, 303−317.

Berge, L.I.O., Bjorvatn, K., Tungodden, B., 2015b. The role of human and financial capital in microenterprise development: experimental evidence from Tanzania. Manag. Sci. 61 (4), 707−722.

Bikhchandani, Sharma, 2000. Herd behavior in financial markets. IMF Staff Pap. 47 (3), 279−310.

Binzel, Fehr, 2013. Giving and sorting among friends: evidence from a lab-in-the-field experiment. Econ. Lett. 121 (2), 214−217.

Burks, Carpenter, Gotte, Rustichini, 2008. Cognitive skills explain economic preferences, strategic behavior, and job attachment. PNAS 106 (19), 7745−7750.

Cappelen, A.W., Nygaard, K., Sørensen, E.Ø., Tungodden, B., 2015. Social preferences in the lab: a comparison of students and a representative population. Scand. J. Econ. 117 (4), 1306−1326.

Chandrasekhar, Kinnan, Larreguy, 2014. Social Networks as Contract Enforcement: Evidence From a Lab Experiment in the Field. NBER Working Papers, 20259.

Charness, G., Kuhn, P., February, 2011. Lab labor: what can labor economists learn in the lab? Handb. Labor Econ. 4a, 229−330.

Charness, Villeval, 2009. Cooperation and competition in intergenerational experiments in the field and laboratory. Am. Econ. Rev. 99 (3), 956−978.

Charness, Gneezy, Imas, 2013. Experimental methods: eliciting risk preferences. J. Econ. Behav. Organ. 87, 43−51.

Croson, Gneezy, 2009. Gender differences in preferences. J. Econ. Lit. 47 (2), 448−474.

Dohmen, Falk, Huffman, Sunde, U., 2012. The intergenerational transmission of risk and trust attitudes. Rev. Econ. Stud. 79 (2), 645−677.

Eckel, Grossman, 2002. Sex differences and statistical stereotyping in attitudes toward financial risk. Evol. Hum. Behav. 23 (4), 281−295.

Eckel, El-Gamal, Wilson, 2009. Risk loving after the storm: a Bayesian-Network study of Hurricane Katrina evacuees. J. Econ. Behav. Organ. 69 (2), 110−124.

Fehr, Bernhard, Rockenbach, 2008. Egalitarianism in young children. Nature 454, 1079−1083.

Fehr, Kirchsteiger, Riedl, 1993. Does fairness prevent market clearing? An experimental investigation. Q. J. Econ. 108 (2), 437−459.

Fehr, Kirchler, Weichbold, Gachter, 1998. When social norms overpower competition: gift exchange in experimental labor markets. J. Labor Econ. 16 (2), 324−351.

Frijters, Kong, Liu, 2015. Who Is Coming to the Artefactual Field Experiment? Participation Bias Among Chinese Rural Migrants. NBER Working Papers, 20953.

Forsythe, Horowitz, Savin, Sefton, 1994. Fairness in simple bargaining experiments. Games Econ. Behav. 6 (3), 347−369.

Gachter, Fehr, 2000. Cooperation and punishment in public goods experiments. Am. Econ. Rev. 90 (4), 980−994.

Gachter, Herrmann, Thoni, 2010. Culture and cooperation. Philos. Trans. R. Soc. B Biol. Sci. 365 (1553), 2651–2661.

Galizzi, Martinez, 2015. On the External Validity of Social-Preference Games: A Systematic Lab-Field Study. Working Papers 802. Barcelona Graduate School of Economics.

Gilligan, Pasquali, Samii, 2014. Civil war and social cohesion: lab-in-the-field evidence from Nepal. Am. J. Polit. Sci. 58 (3), 604–619.

Gneezy, List, 2006. Putting behavioral economics to work: testing for gift exchange in labor markets using field experiments. Econometrica 74 (5), 1365–1384.

Gneezy, Potters, 1997. An experiment on risk taking and evaluation periods. Q. J. Econ. 112 (2), 631–645.

Gneezy, Leonard, List, 2009. Gender differences in competition: evidence from a matrilineal and a patriarchal society. Econometrica 77 (5), 1637–1664.

Gneezy, Niederle, Rustichini, 2003. Performance in competiitive environments: gender differences. Q. J. Econ. 118 (3), 1049–1074.

Grossman, Baldassarri, 2013. The effect of group attachment and social position on prosocial behavior – evidence from lab-in-the-field experiments. PLoS One 8 (3), e58750.

Guth, Schmittberger, Schwarze, 1982. An experimental analysis of ultimatum bargaining. J. Econ. Behav. Organ. 3 (4), 367–388.

Henrich, Heine, Norenzayan, 2010. The weirdest people in the world? Behav. Brain Sci. 33, 61–135.

Hui, Au, Fock, 2004. Empowerment effects across cultures. J. Int. Bus. Stud. 35 (46–60), 46–60.

Haigh, List, 2005. Do professional traders exhibit myopic loss aversion? An experimental analysis. J. Finance 60 (1), 523–534.

Hanoch, Johnson, Wilke, 2006. Domain specificity in experimental measures and participant recruitment. Psychol. Sci. 17 (4), 300–304.

Harbaugh, Krause, Berry, 2001a. GARP for kids: on the development of rational choice behavior. Am. Econ. Rev. 91 (5), 1539–1545.

Harbaugh, Krause, Vesterlund, 2001b. Are adults better behaved than children? Age, experience, and the endowment effect. Econ. Lett. 70 (2), 175–181.

Harrison, G., Lau, M., Williams, 2002. Estimating individual discount rates for Denmark: a field experiment. Am. Econ. Rev. 925, 1606–1617.

Henrich, et al., 2006. Costly punishment across human societies. Science 312 (5781), 1767–1770.

Harrison, G.W., List, J.A., 2004. Field experiments. J. Econ. Lit. 42 (4), 1009–1055.

Harrison, G.W., Lau, M.I., Rutström, E.E., 2015. Theory, experimental design and econometrics are complementary. In: Frechette, G., Schotter, A. (Eds.), Methods of Modern Experimental Economics. Oxford University Press, Oxford, UK.

Herrmann, Thoni, Gachter, 2008. Antisocial punishment across societies. Science 319 (5868), 1362–1367.

Hoffman, Gneezy, List, 2011. Nurture affects gender differences in spatial abilities. PNAS 108 (306), 14786–14788.

Holt, Laury, 2002. Risk aversion and incentive effects. Am. Econ. Rev. 92 (5), 1644–1655.

Jakiela, P., Miguel, E., te Velde, V.L., 2015. Youve earned it: estimating the impact of human capital on social preferences. Exp. Econ. 18 (3), 385–407.

Karlan, December 2005. Using experimental economics to measure social capital and predict real financial decisions. Am. Econ. Rev. 95 (5), 1688–1699.

Karlan, List, 2007. Does price matter in charitable giving? Evidence from a large-scale natural field experiment. Am. Econ. Rev. 97 (5), 1774–1793.

Knetsch, 1989. The endowment effect and evidence of nonreversible indifference curves. Am. Econ. Rev. 79, 1277–1284.

Kovalchick, et al., 2005. Aging and decision-making: a comparison between neurologically healthy elderly and young individuals. J. Econ. Behav. Organ. 58 (1), 79–94.

Kremer, M., Miguel, E., Thornton, R., 2009. Incentives to learn. Rev. Econ. Stat. 91 (3), 437–456.

Lahno, A., Serra-Garcia, M., D'Exelle, B., Verschoor, A., 2015. Conflicting risk attitudes. J. Econ. Behav. Organ. 118, 136–149.

Ligon, Schechter, 2012. Motives for sharing in social networks. J. Dev. Econ. 99 (1), 13–26.

Liu, 2013. Time to change what to sow: risk preferences and technology adoption decisions of cotton farmers in China. Rev. Econ. Stat. 95 (4), 1386—1403.

Locke, Mann, 2005. Professional trader discipline and trade disposition. J. Financ. Econ. 76 (2), 401—444.

Marette, Roosen, Blanchemanche, 2011. The combination of lab and field experiments for benefit-cost analysis. J. Benefit-Cost Anal. 2 (3), 1—34.

Niederle, Vesterlund, 2007. Do women stay away from competition? Do men compete too much? Q. J. Econ. 122 (3), 1067—1101.

Poole, Stanley, 1972. A factorial and predictive study of spatial abilities. Aust. J. Psychol. 24 (3), 317—320.

Roth, A.E., Prasnikar, V., Okuno-Fujiwara, M., Zamir, S., December 1991. Bargaining and market behavior in Jerusalem, Ljubljana, Pittsburgh, and Tokyo: an experimental study. Am. Econ. Rev. 81, 1068—1095.

Spears, 2010. Economic Decision-Making in Poverty Depletes Behavioral Control. CEPS Working Paper, 213.

Spelke, Pinker, 2005. The Science of Gender in Science: A Debate. Edge Foundation.

Viceisza, A., 2016. Creating a lab in the field: economics experiments for policymaking. J. Econ. Surv. (forthcoming).

Voors, Nillesen, Verwimp, Bulte, Lensink, van Soest, 2012. Violent conflict and behavior: a field experiment in Burundi. Am. Econ. Rev. 102 (2), 941—964.

Voyer, Voyer, Bryden, 1995. Magnitude of sex differences in spatial abilities: a meta-analysis and consideration of critical variables. Psychol. Bull. 117, 250—270.

Ward, P.S., Singh, V., 2015. Using field experiments to elicit risk and ambiguity preferences: behavioural factors and the adoption of new agricultural technologies in rural India. J. Dev. Stud. 51 (6), 707—724.

CHAPTER 11

Field Experiments in Marketing

D. Simester
MIT Sloan School of Management, Cambridge, MA, United States
E-mail: simester@mit.edu

Contents

Handbook of Economic Field Experiments, Volume 1
ISSN 2214–658X, http://dx.doi.org/10.1016/bs.hefe.2016.07.001

Abstract

In the last 20 years the marketing literature has seen a sharp increase in the number of papers reporting findings from field experiments. This can be partly explained by the ease of conducting field experiments in Internet settings. However, we have also seen an increase in field experiments in physical stores and other non-Internet settings. While many of these papers focus on pricing and advertising topics, there are also a broad range of other topics represented, including several papers that use field experiments to provide model-free validation of optimization models. We review the requirements to publish a field experiment paper in the marketing literature. We also identify topics that remain relatively understudied. In particular, there is a notable absence of papers studying channel relationships or business-to-business markets. Perhaps more surprisingly, there is also a lack of papers investigating the feasibility of using field experiments to optimize marketing decisions.

Keywords

Advertising; Field experiments; Marketing; Model validation; Pricing; Randomization; Sales force; Word of mouth

JEL Codes

D12; D4; M3

Marketing is a diverse field that draws from a rich array of disciplines and a broad assortment of empirical and theoretical methods. One of those disciplines is economics and one of the methods used to investigate economic questions is field experiments. The history of field experiments in the marketing literature is surprisingly long. Early examples include Curhan (1974) and Eskin and Baron (1977), who vary prices, newspaper advertising, and display variables in grocery stores. This chapter reviews the recent history of field experiments in marketing by identifying papers published in the last 20 years (between 1995 and 2014). We report how the number of papers published has increased during this period and evaluate different explanations for this increase. We then group the papers into five topics and review the papers by topic. This chapter concludes by reflecting on the design of field experiments used in marketing and proposing topics for future research.

1. PAPERS THAT REPORT FIELD EXPERIMENTS

We focus on the five leading marketing journals that publish papers with an economics focus. They include the *Journal of Marketing* (JM), the *Journal of Marketing Research* (JMR), *Marketing Science* (MktSci), *Quantitative Marketing and Economics* (QME), and the marketing department of *Management Science* (MngSci).[1] To identify relevant papers, we first had a research assistant read every issue of the journals published between 1995 and 2014. We then supplemented this initial list with a Web of Science topic search.

---

[1] The two major marketing journals not included in this list are *Journal of Consumer Research* (JCR) and the *Journal of Consumer Psychology* (JCP). Papers published in these two journals have a strongly psychological perspective.

This process yielded over 300 papers. We then read and screened these papers to generate a final sample of 61 papers.[2] In this screening, we restricted attention to studies in which the response measure represented a behavioral response in the "field." We excluded studies in which the response was a survey or perceptual measure, such as customer evaluations or purchase intentions. We also excluded studies where the responses were obtained in a laboratory setting, including studies where the response environment was created by the researchers.

The screening also restricted attention to studies that reported experiments, rather than just analysis of historical data. An experiment includes at least two experimental conditions, with exogenous variation introduced by the researchers. In most cases, this exogenous variation results from variation across randomly selected customer samples. In other cases, it involves rotation of treatments over time or matched pairs of products in an auction setting.

The 61 papers actually report findings from a total of 86 field experiments, with 18 (30%) of the papers reporting multiple field experiments. This includes 12 papers that report 2 experiments, 5 papers that report 3 experiments, and 1 paper that reports findings from 4 experiments.

1.1 Date of publication

Our first investigation was to compare the dates the papers were published. The publication dates are summarized in Fig. 1. Papers reporting field experiments were rare between 1995 and 1999, with just three examples identified. The frequency has since increased sharply; between 2010 and 2014 a total of 37 field experiment papers were identified.

There are likely to be multiple reasons for this trend. One explanation is that the field has become a lot more concerned about endogeneity when interpreting results estimated using historical data. Before 2000, the marketing literature contained numerous econometric papers studying historical supermarket scanner data.[3] Many of these early papers paid little attention to the endogeneity of the independent variables. This has since changed. The quantitative marketing field now pays a considerable attention to the limitations inherent in interpreting endogenous variables. The focus on endogeneity can partly be attributed to a 1999 paper that highlighted these limitations (Villas-Boas and Winer, 1999). The change also coincides with the development of structural models in the new empirical IO literature. Publication in a leading quantitative marketing journal now requires that the authors justify the source of their identification. Many papers

---

[2] Although we believe that the list of 61 papers is extensive, it is unlikely to be complete. We recognize that we will have overlooked some papers that report field experiments and apologize to these authors.

[3] This literature traces its origins to Guadagni and Little (1983), which demonstrated how to apply multinomial logit to scanner data.

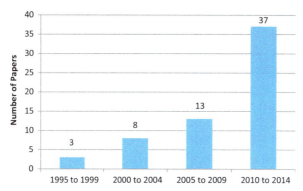

Figure 1 *Publications by year.* This figure reports the number of papers published by 5-year period. The sample size is 61 (papers).

using econometrics methods now use structural models to address this concern. Field experiments provide researchers with an alternative mechanism to overcome this hurdle. The increased prominence of concern about endogeneity may have contributed to the sharp increase in the number of published field experiments.

A second explanation for the growth in the number of published field experiments is that it has become easier to conduct field experiments. The development of the Internet coincides with the growth in the number of reported experiments. It is now possible to conduct field experiments using eBay and Google AdWords, without requiring active participation from a cooperating company. Even for studies that do require cooperation, this cooperation is often much easier to obtain in an Internet setting because the cost of conducting the experiments is relatively low, and because many firms already conduct their own experiments. Firms that conduct experiments as part of their own operations have implicitly revealed that they understand the value of field experiments and are likely to have invested in infrastructure to support their implementation.[4]

We can evaluate this explanation by investigating whether the format used to implement experimental variation has changed over time. In particular, we grouped the studies into three categories according to the type of experimental manipulation:

Physical	in-person interactions in a home, at a workplace, or in a bricks and mortar retail store (including shelf-signage or product assortments)
Direct mail	telephone, catalog, or other direct mail
Internet	search or display advertising, eBay, email, Twitter, Website content, or another computer or Internet interaction.

---

[4] We might expect that if it is easier to conduct field experiments in Internet settings then papers that use this setting are more likely to report findings from multiple experiments. It turns out that the reverse is true; papers reporting findings from Internet-based field experiments are actually less likely to report multiple studies.

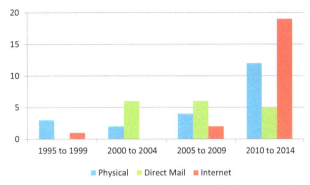

Figure 2 *Publications by type of experimental manipulation.* This figure reports the number of papers published using each type of experimental manipulation in each 5-year period. The sample size is 60.

In Fig. 2, we report how use of these manipulations has changed over time. The total sample size is 60 observations.[5]

In the 5 years between 2010 and 2014, there were 19 papers published that used the Internet to implement experimental variation, representing more than half of the field experiment paper published during this period. Nineteen papers in this 5-year period contrasts with just three papers in the previous 15 years. We conclude that it is likely the Internet contributed to the growth in field experiment papers across the data period.

However, it is notable that we also see growth in the number of papers implementing experiments through physical manipulations in home, at the workplace, or in physical retail stores. There were 12 papers reporting physical manipulations between 2010 and 2014, compared to a total of just nine papers in the previous 15 years. It seems that the ease of conducting experiments on the Internet is not a complete explanation for the growth in the number of published papers.

A third explanation is that the top marketing journals are publishing more papers (not just more field experiment papers). In 2006, *MktSci* increased from four issues a year to six issues a year, and in 2008, *JM* and *JMR* made the same transition. In addition, *QME* began publication in 2003. The result is an increase in the total number of published papers. To investigate the extent to which this explains the increase in the frequency of field experiment papers, we counted the total number of papers published across the 20-year period (1995–2014) and report a histogram of the proportion published in each 5-year

---

[5] In four papers the description of the treatment was insufficient to allow classification. Moreover, three papers either reported multiple studies using different types of variation or used different types of variation across different treatments within the same study. These three papers were coded as appearing in multiple categories.

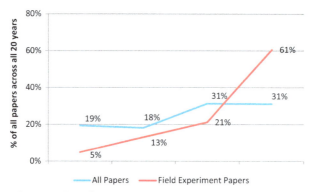

Figure 3 *Histogram of the number of papers published in each 5-year period. All papers compared to field experiment papers.* This figure reports a histogram of how many papers were published in each 5-year period. We separately report the findings for all papers, and for just those papers that report findings from a field experiment. The sample size is 3250 for all papers and 61 for the field experiment papers. The percentages within each curve add to 100%.

period. We do this separately for all papers, and for just those papers that report field experiments.[6] The findings are reported in Fig. 3.

While there has been growth in the total number of papers published, this growth is a lot smaller than the growth in the number of field experiment papers. When counting all of the papers published between 1995 and 2014, we find that 31% were published in the last 5 years (2010–2014). In contrast, 64% of all field experiment papers were published in that period.

We conclude that the sharp growth in the number of marketing papers reporting field experiments can be attributed to several factors. The field itself has grown and so there has been growth in the number of papers published, including field experiment and nonfield experiment papers. Second, the ease of conducting field experiments over the Internet may also have contributed to the phenomenon. Finally, the marketing field now pays more attention to the endogeneity of independent variables. Field experiments are an effective mechanism for resolving confounds due to endogeneity.

1.2 Choice of topics

In the Fig. 4, we categorize the 61 papers into general topic areas. This categorization reveals that the papers are dominated by two topics: pricing and advertising.

---

[6] The total number of papers in *MktSci, JM,* and *JMR* is calculated using entries in the Web of Science. We excluded papers published in *MngSci* as the Web of Science does not identify which department editor accepted the paper. Unfortunately the Web of Science does not index the first few issues of *QME,* and so for this journal we manually counted the number of papers published in each issue.

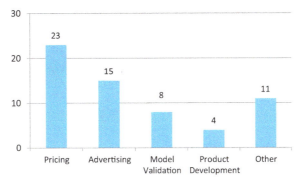

Figure 4 *Choice of topics.* This figure reports the number of published papers by topic. The sample size is 61 papers.

Further investigation also reveals clear differences in the distribution of topics over time. Prior to 2010, half of the papers (12 of 24) addressed pricing topics, with only two papers investigating advertising issues. However, this dominance has reversed, with more papers in the last 5 years studying advertising issues (13) than pricing issues (11).

Understandably, the recent focus on advertising has been dominated by research questions related to Internet advertising. Many of these papers study characteristics of Internet advertising that simply did not exist at the start of the data sample. For example, dynamic retargeting of advertising (targeting advertisements using individual browsing behaviors on other websites) was not possible earlier in the data period. Similarly, personalizing advertising using information posted on Facebook pages is a relatively recent advertising technique.

In the sections that follow we briefly survey the papers on each of these topics. We also summarize all of the papers, grouped by topic, in a table as an Appendix to this chapter.

2. PRICING TOPICS

The 23 papers investigating pricing issues can be grouped into four subtopics:
1. Who to target with discounts?
2. What types of discounts are most effective?
3. Price as a signal
4. Multipart tariffs and other pricing schemes

The effectiveness of discounts has been a favorite research topic in the marketing field. This in part reflects both the pervasiveness of discounts, and recognition that they can have tremendous positive and negative impacts on unit sales and firm profits. For example, Ailawadi et al. (2007) study the unit sales and profit impact of every discount offered by the national pharmacy chain CVS in 2003. They report that more than 50% of the promotions are unprofitable because the loss of margin is not fully offset by the incremental sales. Using a very large-scale 13-week field test, in which they simply withheld promotions in 15 product categories in 400 stores, they demonstrated that CVS could improve its profits by over $50 million.

2.1 Who to target with discounts?

Three field experiments contribute to our understanding of who should receive discounts. Dholakia (2006) shows that sending a $5-off discount coupon to customers who previously paid full price can actually lead to less demand. This study was conducted using randomly selected customers of a large automobile servicing firm.[7] Anderson and Simester (2001a) report that offering extended payment terms to customers of a prestigious jewelry catalog can lower demand. The authors interpret this effect as an adverse quality signal, with the installment billing signaling that the products are suitable for customers who are more sensitive to price than quality. In a later study with a different catalog retailer, the same research team reports that deep discounts have more positive long-term externalities when targeted at new customers compared to existing customers (Anderson and Simester, 2004). For the existing customers the long-term effects were negative; the deep discounts resulted in these customers accelerating their purchases and becoming more price sensitive. In contrast, deeper discounts increased future purchases by new customers, apparently due to more favorable expectations about future prices. Collectively, these studies suggest that discounts are most effective when targeted at customers who are newer, who have paid lower prices in the past, and who are relatively more concerned about price than quality.

2.2 Which discounts are most effective?

Field experiments have been used to address not just who should receive discounts but also what form the discounts should take. The literature now provides a rich answer to this question. In the oldest paper in our sample, Dhar and Hoch (1996) report the findings from two field experiments conducted at 86 supermarket stores in the Dominick's Finer Foods supermarket chain.[8] They showed that coupons lead to a 35% larger increase in unit sales than an equivalent discount in the shelf-price. Moreover, because redemption of coupons is incomplete, this leads to a 108% larger increase in profits. In

---

[7] Related findings from two field experiments are reported by Anderson and Simester (2010), which is published in an economics journal. Customers of a publishing catalog and an apparel catalog were less likely to place a subsequent order if they received a catalog containing lower prices than they had recently paid for the same item.

[8] This is the same retailer that provided the data for the now widely used Dominick's scan data panel.

two large-scale field experiments conducted at the (apparently) same 86 supermarkets, Wansink et al. (1998) illustrate two ways that retailers can increase the number of units that customers purchase. Imposing a quantity limit of 12 units per customers led to customers purchasing twice as many units (per buyer) compared to a quantity limit of 4 units. Framing discounts using multiple unit promotions (e.g., 2 for $1.50) instead of single unit promotions (75-cents each) also increased the number of units that customers purchased. Both of these effects are interpreted as examples of customers anchoring on retailer-provided cues to decide how many units to purchase. In another example of framing, Chen et al. (2012) show that describing a discount as "50% more free" is more effective than "33% off the regular price," even though both are economically equivalent. Their study is motivated by related evidence that customers tend to focus on the % magnitude of the discount and neglect the base over which the percentage is calculated.

Ramanathan and Dhar (2010) present findings suggesting that the impact of different types of promotions may vary according to the customer's psychological orientation. Customers entering a Chicago grocery store were primed to think of either enjoying themselves or acting sensibly. Those primed to enjoy themselves purchased more items when they received coupons with longer expiration dates, and when the coupons were framed as "Get $x Off" rather than "Save $x." In contrast, customers primed to act sensibly purchased more items when they received coupons with shorter expiration dates and when the coupons read "Save $x."

There have been several studies investigating the impact of framing discounts as "free samples" or "free gifts." Bawa and Shoemaker (2004) use two field experiments to disentangle three effects of offering free samples: demand acceleration (temporal substitution), cannibalization, and demand expansion. They show that unlike coupons, free samples can generate positive long-term effects that can endure for as much as 12 months after the event. In a longitudinal study in the financial services sector, Haisley and Loewenstein (2011) investigated how offering customers unexpected gifts affected their subsequent deposit balances. They found that an increasing sequence of gifts ($35 then $100) had a more positive impact on subsequent balances than a decreasing sequence ($100 then $35). They described this as an "aversion to deterioration." Shu and Gneezy (2010) study how expiration dates on gift certificates affect redemption rates. Participants who received gift certificates with a longer expiration data had more favorable perceptions of the firm but were actually less likely to redeem the certificates. They attribute this profitable coincidence to procrastination and support this claim using a follow-up survey. Laran and Tsiros (2013) investigate how uncertainty about which free gift will be offered influences the effectiveness of these promotions. If customers were primed to think about their decisions, they responded more favorably if they knew what free gift they would receive. In contrast, if they were primed to make more emotional decisions then the uncertain gift was more effective.

We also highlight three particularly innovative studies. Hui et al. (2013) investigate the impact of sending discounts through mobile phone technology. They show that sending coupons for products that are located further away from the customers' planned in-store shopping paths are effective at increasing unplanned purchases. Tsiros and Hardesty (2010) study how to most effectively *remove* discounts. They show that phasing out a discount gradually is more effective at raising unit sales than removing the discount all at once. They attribute this in part to higher customer expectations about future price levels. Gaurav et al. (2011) study the adoption of rainfall insurance in rural Indian villages. The insurance is a relatively sophisticated financial product, and they find that training customers about the products is generally more effective than offering other forms of marketing promotions. The exception is a "MoneyBack" guarantee if the farmers never have cause to claim on the insurance, which works almost as effectively as the training programs.

2.3 Price as a signal

A third group of pricing studies focuses on the signaling role of prices. Using data from an apparel catalog, Anderson and Simester (2001b) highlight the importance of rationing how often sale signs are used. They motivate this study as a test of an earlier paper that argues that sale signs serve a credible signaling role, enabling poorly informed customers to evaluate which prices are low relatively to other prices in the market (Anderson and Simester, 1998). A key feature of that model is that the sale signs are self-regulating; any one sign becomes less credible the more often it is used. In a related study, Anderson and Simester (2003) measure the impact of 9-digit price endings (e.g., $1.99 or $49). Using a series of three field experiments conducted at two different women's apparel catalogs, they show that $9 price endings increase demand, and that this demand increase is stronger on newer items than for established items. However, the effect appears to be weakened when the $9 price ending is accompanied by a "sale" sign. They interpret these findings as evidence that the price endings serve a similar signaling role to "sale" signs, revealing to customers which items are discounted compared to other prices in the market.

Gneezy et al. (2014) investigate the information that prices signal about quality. When customers see high prices they anticipate higher quality and so react more adversely if quality is low. As a result, customers evaluate a low-quality product with a high price more negatively than a low-quality product with a low price. They establish this result using a field experiment at a small California vineyard.

Two other papers in this signaling stream have already been discussed as contributions to the discounting literature. Recall that Anderson and Simester's (2001a) evidence that extended payment terms lowered sales at a prestigious jewelry catalog was interpreted as evidence that targeting price-sensitive customers can undermine the credibility of a retailer's quality claim. Similarly, the evidence that deeper discounts to first-time customers can make these customers more loyal also had a signaling interpretation (Anderson and Simester, 2004), although in this case the signal was about future prices rather than quality.

2.4 Multipart tariffs and other pricing schemes

The fourth stream of pricing-related field experiments addresses multiperiod and multi-part tariffs together with other innovative pricing schemes. Lambrecht and Tucker (2012) report one of the few field experiments conducted in a business-to-business setting. They collaborate with a web hosting provider in the United Kingdom to investigate the impact of varying both the monthly price and the framing of "hassle costs" in the first period of a multiperiod contract. Rather than evaluating the entire contract term, they show that customers in this market evaluate the outcome in each distinct period. As a result, they show that if customers incur hassle costs in the first period, then it is more effective to lower the first period price and defer some of this revenue until later periods.

Anderson and Simester (2008) show that price differentiation can lower demand if it is perceived to be unfair. Their field experiment was conducted in a women's apparel catalog that sells plus sizes. Because the cost of producing very large garments is higher than the cost of producing smaller garments, the retailer sought to charge higher prices on its largest sizes. The results revealed an asymmetry; there was no change in demand at the smaller sizes, but demand fell sharply for the larger sizes (even after controlling for the absolute price itself). They interpret these findings as evidence that price differentiation can lower demand if it is perceived to be unfair. However, customers actually have to experience the unfairness; it is not sufficient to see other customers treated unfairly.

Two papers focus on multipart tariff schemes. Danaher (2002) uses the exogenous variation introduced through a field experiment in the telecommunications market to develop an optimal pricing model for a two-part tariff. The scheme includes both a monthly access fee, together with a per-minute usage rate for cellular phone service. The results highlight the importance of accounting for both usage and customer retention. Solely focusing on usage and ignoring attrition will substantially underestimate the sensitivity of revenue to price. Yao et al. (2012) also study cellular phone pricing, although in their case they use a field experiment to recover estimates of customer discount rates (rather than revenue price sensitivity). Customers' plan choices reveal much faster consumer discounting of future periods than we normally assume.

Perhaps the most unusual pricing scheme represented in the literature is a "pay-what-you-want" (PWYW) scheme. Kim, Natter, and Spann report three field experiments conducted in German restaurants and a movie theatre. The firms rotated PWYW schemes and their standard pricing schemes on different days. In general, customers chose to pay lower prices than the prices which firms regularly charged. However, this was not always the case. Customers in one of the experiments chose to pay an average of $1.94 for a hot beverage, compared to the regular price of $1.75. In another experiment, customers on average chose to pay less for a buffet lunch ($6.44) than the regular price ($7.99), but the PWYW scheme attracted enough extra demand to generate significantly higher daily revenue.

3. ADVERTISING TOPICS

The 15 papers that focus on advertising-related issues can be grouped into three broad subtopics:
1. Does advertising impact purchasing?
2. Which advertising messages are most effective?
3. Optimizing paid search advertising

3.1 Is there an impact on purchasing?

Four papers investigate whether advertising can impact purchasing, including two papers that reach a relatively negative conclusion. Lewis and Reiley (2014) study whether display advertisements at Yahoo! caused offline purchases at a department store. Despite a controlled randomized environment and a sample size of 1.6 million customers, they are only just able to establish a statistically significant effect. Lambrecht and Tucker (2013) study the effects of "dynamic retargeting" of advertisements. Dynamic retargeting describes the widely used practice of using browsing history from other websites to select which advertising content to display. They find that this practice does not increase advertising effectiveness. The exception is when the browsing history indicates that a customer is relatively close to making a purchase. It is only then that dynamic retargeting is effective.

Another paper with a key finding that is effectively a null result focuses on the impact of digital video recorders (DVRs) on advertising effectiveness. The introduction of DVRs led to concern that television advertising would become less effective because customers could filter out advertising. In this very large-scale study, the authors found no evidence that this was the case. Instead the authors concluded that filtering out advertisements occurs relatively infrequently. In contrast to the two previous papers, this could be considered a relatively positive paper about the impact of advertising. It suggests that the widespread consumer adoption of DVR technology will not diminish the impact of TV advertising.

The fourth paper in this sequence investigates the impact of competitive advertising. Competing catalog retailers share the names and addresses of their best customers on a reciprocal basis to lower the costs of prospecting for new customers. Using a randomized field experiment, Anderson and Simester (2013) measure how allowing competitors to target your customers with competing catalogs impacts a firm's own sales to those customers. Although we might expect a negative effect due to substitution, they actually find that for many customers the competitors' advertising increased purchases from the original firm. This positive effect was particularly strong in product categories in which customers learn product sizes that are firm-specific (such as footwear). This leads the authors to attribute their findings to the importance of product standards, customer learning, and switching costs.

3.2 Which messages are most effective?

An additional nine papers focus on improving messaging to increase advertising response rates. They include several papers that address targeting or personalization of advertising messages. For example, Tucker (2014) reports a field experiment conducted on Facebook that studies how customers react to advertisements that are personalized based on a customer's posted personal information (see also Lambrecht and Tucker, 2013; which is discussed earlier). Fortuitously, the experiment coincided with a widely publicized change in Facebook's privacy policies, which gave users more control over their personalization settings. The findings reveal that giving customers the option of controlling their personalization settings greatly improved the performance of targeted advertisements. Schumann et al. (2014) study how to mitigate adverse customer reactions to targeted Internet advertising. They show that reciprocity appeals ("Our service is free of charge to you — targeted advertising helps us fund it") are more effective than relevance claims ("You will see more interesting and less irrelevant advertisements in the future").

Three studies investigate how messaging should be customized to different customer segments using dimensions other than prior browsing behavior. Berger and Schwarz (2011) study messages that prompt customers to recommend products to other customers (word-of-mouth, WOM). They show that messages that link a brand to a product cue are more effective when customers do not already have strong associations between the brand and the cue. Using a Google AdWords field experiment conducted in Israel, Kronrod et al. (2012) demonstrate that the use of assertive messages ("You must save the Mediterranean") are more effective when customers already believe in the cause, but are less effective for more general causes, for which customers' preferences are weaker.

Beyond Kronrod et al. (2012), two other studies investigate how to design messaging that encourages customers to engage in more environmentally friendly behavior. In an ambitious study, White and Simpson (2013) collaborate with a large metropolitan city to encourage residents to leave their grass clippings on the ground, rather than disposing them through the municipal waste system (which sends the clippings to landfills). Using hangers placed on the front doors of resident's home, they tested six different messaging conditions, together with a control condition. They then measured the reduction in waste. Varying the type of appeal after priming a focus on either individual or social benefits had a significant effect on residents' behavior. Spangenberg et al. (2003) report two studies. In the first study, they investigate how messages in outdoor advertising media (billboards) can increase recycling. In the second study, they vary the content of messages inserted in a health club's monthly newsletters and billing statement, with the goal of increasing member visits to the club. They show that framing an appeal as a self-prediction increases its effectiveness. Specifically, in the fitness club study, the message "Fitness guilt?" was more effective at increasing member visits than the alternative treatment "Work out at [fitness club name]."

Two other examples of messaging tests were reported by Tucker and Zhang (2010, 2011). Both of these studies investigate how reporting participation in a two-sided network increases participation in the network. The first example is Tucker and Zhang (2010), which is another rare example of a study in a business-to-business market. The setting was a Website that resembles craigslist.org, and the outcome measure was the number of sellers who chose to list on the site. The field experiment randomized whether to display the number of buyers and/or sellers and (if so) the number of buyers and/or sellers to claim. They find that a large number of sellers can deter additional listings, unless only the number of sellers is revealed (not the number of buyers). Displaying many buyers will attract more sellers as long as the number of sellers is also revealed. They conclude that markets with more competitors can appear more attractive to entrants, as there must be sufficient demand to attract so many competitors (a positive network externality). The second study, Tucker and Zhang (2011), uses data from a Website that lists wedding service vendors. They randomize whether the Website reveals the previous number of clicks on a vendor. We might expect that revealing this information would increase the popularity of the vendors with the most clicks. Instead, they show that the same level of historical clicks results in a larger lift for brands with a niche market position, compared to a brand with a mainstream position. Customers appear to infer that these brands must provide high quality to overcome their narrow reach.

The final paper investigating the impact of advertising messages includes a pair of studies conducted using matched pairs of music CD auctions on eBay. Dholakia and Simonson (2005) study the impact of messaging that explicitly recommends that potential bidders "compare the price of this CD with the prices of similar CDs listed next to this one." They find that these messages lead to more cautious bidding behavior. The winning bidders tended to submit later bids, submit fewer bids, and avoid participating in simultaneous auctions. They interpret the findings as evidence that making competing options more salient makes customers more risk averse because opportunity costs become more prominent.

3.3 Optimizing paid search advertising

Two papers by different teams investigate how to optimize paid search advertising. Yang and Ghose (2010) begin by using an historical panel data set to investigate how the response to paid search advertising is affected by the presence of organic (unpaid) search results. They then test the robustness of the model predictions using an 8-week field experiment on Google. They confirmed that when paid search is present, so that customers can see both paid and organic search results, the combined click-through rate (CTR) was 5.1% higher compared to when there was no paid search present. The conversion rate (probability of a purchase) also increases by 11.7%.

Agarwal et al. (2011) investigate the importance of position in paid search advertising. Specifically, they ask whether being the first search result, second result, or a lower result, impacts both CTRs and conversion (purchases). As we might expect, the closer to the first position, the higher the CTR. However, the opposite is true for conversion rates. Appearing lower in the rank of search results can actually increase conversion rates because conversion is conditional on clicking. As a result, only the most motivated customers click on lower results, and these are the customers that are more likely to convert. Given advertisers generally pay for clicks irrespective of conversions, it may be optimal for many advertisers to prefer lower positions in the search order.

4. PRODUCT-RELATED TOPICS

We identified seven papers that present field experiments addressing product-related topics. This includes four studies focused on market research and product development issues, and three papers focused on product sizes.

4.1 Market research and product development

Two studies investigate the role that *mere measurement* can have on customer purchasing behavior. Chandon et al. (2005) asked 251 customers of an online grocer about their purchase intentions. A second randomly selected set of 140 consumers served as the control (and were not asked any questions). The study revealed that the customers who were surveyed were significantly more likely to make a subsequent purchase and were significantly more profitable for the retailer. Two years later, a different research team conducted a related study in the automotive services industry (Borle et al., 2007). A telephone survey was administered to 3773 randomly selected customers. Subsequent service visits by these customers were then compared with a randomly selected control sample of 1227 customers. This comparison revealed that participating in the survey increased purchases and made customers more responsive to firm promotions.

The other two studies on this topic use field experiments to validate new market research methods. Urban et al. (1997) validate a method for conducting research very early in the product development process. Forecasts of new product sales are more valuable the earlier they are available. The authors investigate the possibility of using multimedia representations of potential new products to provide earlier and less costly forecasts. They conduct two field experiments, which confirm that multimedia computer interactions can both realistically portray customers' information sources and yield forecasts that are not significantly different from traditional methods. Neslin et al. (2009) propose a model that is designed to maximize response rates to online market research panels. The model is dynamic, optimizing over a discrete number of studies in a finite period, where this finite period can be extended using a rolling horizon. They compare their model against the current managerial heuristic and report significantly higher response rates.

4.2 Product sizes and bundling

Consumers' assessments of relative package volumes are often biased when packages have different shapes. Krider et al. (2001) investigate this bias by comparing how customers react to product packages that have the same volume but different shapes. In a university cafeteria that sells cream cheese to complement bagels, the authors compare demand for a $^3/_4$ oz round tub of cream cheese and a $^3/_4$ oz square tub of the same cream cheese. Customers were significantly more likely to purchase two tubs of cream cheese for their bagel on days that only the round tubs of cream cheese were available. This finding is consistent with other evidence in their paper that customers perceive round containers to be smaller than rectangular containers of the same volume.

Leszczyc and Haubl (2010) report findings from three field tests that investigate the profitability of product bundling. Using a series of eBay auctions of collectable postage stamps, they compare the profitability of bundling-related and -unrelated items. Their findings reveal that bundling substitutes or unrelated items in an auction are less profitable than selling them separately, but bundling is more profitable when the items are complementary. A third study related to product bundling has already been discussed as an example of a pricing-related paper. Recall that in an experiment conducted at 86 supermarket stores, Wansink et al. (1998) compared the effectiveness of multiple unit promotions (e.g., 2 for $1.50) versus single unit promotions (75 cents each). The multiple unit promotions increased the number of units that customers purchased by an average of 32%.

5. MODEL VALIDATION

The marketing field has a long tradition of developing models that optimize marketing decisions. Traditionally, these models are validated by measuring goodness-of-fit, either in-sample or with holdout samples. A limitation of this validation is that it generally relies on assumptions inherent in the models, and so errors in the assumptions are also introduced to the validation process.

Because of these limitations, researchers have begun using field experiments as a means of validating marketing models. Field experiments provide an almost ideal validation setting; different polices can be implemented in treatment and control settings and their outcomes compared. This provides a "model-free" basis for validation, together with a comprehensive test of all of the assumptions in the model.

For example, Simester et al. (2006) propose a model for dynamically optimizing catalog (and other direct marketing) mailing decisions. Catalog firms regularly send catalogs to customers and must decide who should receive each catalog. Traditionally, these decisions have been made myopically; the companies send catalogs to customers who are most likely to respond to that catalog. The model proposed in this paper optimizes a sequence of mailing decisions over an infinite horizon. The model begins by proposing a method for dividing customers into discrete Markov states using a set of variables describing each customer's purchasing and mailing histories. Transition probabilities and rewards are then estimated for each strategy (mail or not mail) in each state space. Finally, a standard policy-iteration algorithm is used to calculate the optimal policy in each state. The authors then test their proposed method by varying catalog mailing decisions for 60,000 customers of an apparel catalog over a period of 6 months including 12 catalog mailing dates. The findings revealed that the model performed well for low-valued and moderately valued customers. However, during the initial months of the experiment, the results were less favorable for the most valuable customers in the sample. Further investigation revealed an explanation for the poor initial outcome for these customers: in the training data, there were too few occasions in which the firm had not mailed to these customers to provide a reliable estimate of the outcome.

These comparisons not only validate the proposed models but have also proved valuable as a source of insights about the underlying phenomenon.[9]

In addition to Simester et al. (2006), we identified seven other papers published in the last 20 years that employ field experiments to validate optimization models. These include two pricing models, three advertising models, and two new market research methods. All but one of these papers was published in 2006 or later, suggesting growing interest in this approach. Although some of the papers involve relatively small numbers of participants (see, for example, Urban et al., 1997; and Belloni et al., 2012), others include large numbers of participants and extended treatment periods. For example, Mantrala et al. (2006) compare the outcome when implementing an optimal pricing model in 200 experimental stores over a period of 8 weeks.

6. OTHER TOPICS

Our search revealed an additional 10 studies that do not fit easily within the previous four topics. Notably, these papers are all relatively recent, with the first published in

---

[9] The findings in the Simester et al. (2006) field experiment led to a subsequent paper (Shie et al., 2007) in which the authors documented the potential for positive bias when applying dynamic programming models to field data.

2008, and eight of them published in the last 5 years. We have grouped these papers into five topics:

1. Sales force optimization
2. WOM and referrals
3. Participation in online communities
4. Encouraging positive behaviors
5. Other topics.

6.1 Sales force optimization

Kumar et al. (2008) report findings from two large-scale field experiments. One experiment was conducted with a multinational business-to-business technology firm, while the second study was conducted with a firm in the telecommunications industry that sells to both businesses and retail consumers. The studies compared a "customer focus" in which the timing of sales calls was coordinated with forecasts of customers' purchasing decisions. In this condition, sales calls were also coordinated across product categories, so that if a customer was expected to purchase multiple categories assigned to different sales teams, the customer received a joint visit from both teams. This coordinated policy was compared with a standard policy, which lacked coordination. The two treatments were randomly assigned within matched pairs of customers. The findings revealed that coordination led to significantly higher profits and return-on-investment. Lim et al. (2009) also investigate sales force optimization issues using randomized field experiments, although they focus on sales force incentives. Specifically, they compare the impact of different prize structures in sales contests. Their findings indicate that a sales contest should include multiple prize winners and rank ordering prizes in contests with multiple winners does not increase sales or revenues.

6.2 Word-of-mouth and referrals

In a widely cited paper, Godes and Mayzlin (2009) investigate whether firm actions designed to encourage WOM lead to higher sales. They find that WOM is more effective at increasing sales if it comes from relatively less loyal customers. They also report that WOM generates more sales if it comes from acquaintances, rather than close friends. Kumar et al. (2010) use four field experiments conducted with a financial services firm to identify which customers a firm should target when designing customer referral programs. They use the findings to validate an approach for computing the "customer referral value" for each customer.

6.3 Participation in an online community

In a study conducted in Germany involving eBay users, Algesheimer et al. (2010) measure the impact of a program designed to increase participation in the firm's online community. Customers in the randomly assigned treatment group received multiple email messages inviting participation, while those in the control group did not receive these messages. Over the next year customers in the treatment group spent less and listed fewer items than customers in the control group.

Two years later an overlapping research team conducted a follow-up study again using German eBay users (Zhu et al., 2012). Email messages to a randomly selected treatment group were again used to invite participation in the firm's online community. The findings reveal that participants engage in more risk-seeking bidding behavior. This effect is only true when community members have strong ties to other members of the community. The findings are replicated in a second field experiment conducted with prosper.com.

Toubia and Stephen (2013) study why people contribute to the microblogging site Twitter (see also our earlier discussion of Berger and Schwarz, 2011, who ask why customers contribute WOM). They experimentally manipulated the number of Twitter followers and compared their posting activities to a randomly assigned controlled group. Their findings suggest that many users contribute because they care about how people perceive them, rather than because they derive intrinsic utility from the activity.

6.4 Encouraging positive behaviors

We earlier described two papers that study how advertising messages can lead to prosocial behavior (White and Simpson, 2013 study waste reduction, and Spangenberg et al., 2003 study recycling behavior). Two other papers have focused on encouraging positive behaviors. Raju et al. (2010) examine how to encourage children to choose healthier food options. The most effective intervention was to establish a "friendly healthful eating competition with students at the same grade level from other participating schools." Asking the children to sign a pledge to eat more fruits and vegetables and providing direct incentives for healthy choices (e.g., pencils, stickers, key chains) also led to improved eating habits, even up to 10 weeks after the interventions ended.

Soman and Cheema (2011) compare methods for improving savings rates among low-income laborers in rural India. Financial planners visited the 146 families in the study for 15 weeks, and gave them a savings goal, which was placed in a sealed envelope. Experimental variations included the size of this goal, whether their pictures of their children were printed on the envelope, and whether the savings goal was pooled into a single envelope or split between two envelopes. Although the size of the goal did not affect the savings rate, savings were significantly higher in the photograph condition, and when the savings were partitioned into multiple envelopes.

6.5 Other topics

The remaining two papers study diverse topics. Dagger and Danaher (2014) report findings from field experiments designed to measure how remodeling a store impacts store demand. The first of these studies was conducted at an "equipment retailer and service provider" that retained its original retail space, while remodeling new space in the building to serve as a replacement retail space. The researchers randomly rotated the retail operations between the new and old spaces for a period of 6 weeks. They found that the remodeled space increased sales significantly more for new customers than for existing customers. They replicate their findings in a second study conducted in a large department store.

Haruvy and Leszczyc (2010) conducted a series of experiments using pairs of simultaneous auctions to measure the impact of a range of auction features, including: auction durations, shipping costs, the level of open reserve prices, and the use of secret reserve prices. The results reveal considerable price dispersion within the auction pairs. They also confirm that the auction features had significant effects on final prices, which the authors attribute to the role of search costs.

7. DESIGNING EXPERIMENTS AND FUTURE TOPICS

We conclude by reflecting on what is required to publish field experiments in the marketing literature. We also discuss the range of topics that have been studied and identify topics that remain relatively understudied.

7.1 Designing experiments for the marketing literature

Field experiments published in marketing obviously share many of the same characteristics as field experiments published in economics journals. However, there are some distinguishing features. Publishing any empirical study in the marketing literature requires more than merely documenting an effect. Researchers are expected to also shed light on the mechanism that causes the effect. For example, it is not sufficient to just show that multiple unit promotions (e.g., 2 for $1.50) are more effective than single unit promotions (75 cents each). Wansink et al. (1998) were also expected to explain this result as an example of a more general phenomenon. They interpreted their finding as an example of "anchoring and adjustment."

This requirement can be a formidable obstacle for field experiments, as it is often not possible to interview customers, or to otherwise collect intermediate process measures that can reveal underlying causes. Instead, there are four approaches that researchers have generally used to investigate the cause of their effects, and they often use these approaches in combination.

First, many papers report interactions rather than just main effects. For example, Tucker and Zhang (2011) do not just report the main effect of revealing popularity information on a Website. Instead, they compare these effects for niche versus mainstream brands. Similarly, Berger and Schwarz (2011) compare the effect of advertising message on WOM for customers who have strong and weak associations between the brand and the message. For researchers seeking to publish field experiments in marketing, it is important to give careful thought to what interactions they can measure and how those interactions will help clarify the cause of their effects. Insightful interactions are often viewed as the "clever" element of a study. Ideally the interactions are consistent with a proposed argument and are difficult to reconcile with alternative explanations. Indeed, this is the benefit of reporting interactions; they are more likely to be immune from alternative explanations.

To estimate interactions, researchers sometimes use multiple field experiments (recall that 30% of the papers report results from multiple field experiments). Although the additional studies are occasionally positioned as replications (e.g., Danaher, 2002), they are also often used to investigate interactions (e.g., Anderson and Simester, 2003). Other studies report a single experiment but include a large number of experimental treatments. For example, in Gaurav et al. (2011) study of demand for rainfall insurance among rural Indian farmers, they include 14 different experimental conditions. In general, studies either report multiple experiments or multiple treatments (and not both).[10]

Where a paper reports a single field experiment with just two conditions, it is common to complement the field experiment with one or more laboratory experiments. Examples include Kronrod et al. (2012), who add two laboratory experiments, and Krider, Raghubir, and Krishna, who report five laboratory experiments. In papers that include multiple laboratory experiments, the field experiment often serves a less prominent role. In particular, the laboratory experiments may establish the main effect, replicate the effect, and investigate interactions, whereas the field experiment is relegated to confirming generalizability in a field setting.

A third approach used to investigate explanations is to combine the field experiment with a customer survey. For example, recall that Anderson and Simester (2001a) measured how customers react to an installment billing offer in a premium jewelry catalog. Customers did not purchase as much in the installment billing condition, which they interpreted as an adverse quality signal, revealing that the products are targeted at customers who are more sensitive to quality than price. To support this interpretation, they mailed catalogs similar to those used for the experimental treatments to other randomly selected customer samples, together with a short survey. Customers who received the installment billing version were more likely to express concern about product quality. One respondent wrote on the survey instrument: "It makes [catalog name] look tacky to have installment plans — kind of like Franklin Mint dolls" (at page 326). Shu and Gneezy (2010) provide a similar example of using a survey to validate an explanation for their experimental findings.

---

[10] The pairwise correlation between the number of experiments and the (maximum) number of conditions is −0.14.

The fourth approach is to use field experiment data to estimate a structural model. For example, in a recent working paper, Dubé et al. (2016) report findings from two field experiments in which they sent SMS (text) messages to Chinese mobile phone users offering promotions on movie tickets. They randomly varied (1) the size of the discount, (2) whether the text indicated the service provider would donate to a local charity for every ticket purchased, and (3) the size of the donation (if any). Surprisingly, they show that customers are less responsive to larger donations when the discounts are large. They estimate a structural model to provide evidence that this effect results from "self-signaling"; larger price discounts prompt consumers to infer that their purchases are no longer altruistic. The authors observe that without the structural model there is no obvious way to test this mechanism and disentangle it from alternative explanations. This approach of using a structural model to explain the findings in a field experiment is still relatively novel in the marketing literature. The structural modeling and field experiment literature have grown at similar times, perhaps partly because they offer alternative solutions to resolving endogeneity concerns (see earlier discussion). This paper recognizes that the two approaches are not just alternatives; they can also complement each other. Given the rapid growth in interest in both methods, once the benefits of combining the methods are more widely recognized we should anticipate many more papers using this combination of methods.

7.2 Randomization

Randomization offers well-documented statistical advantages when comparing treatment and control conditions. However, randomization is not required to publish field experiments in the marketing literature. In 29% of the papers, experimental treatments were *not* assigned by randomization (in three papers it was unclear whether the studies used randomization). In some cases, randomization could have led to contagion between the experimental treatments. For example, in Soman and Cheema's (2011) study of how to increase savings levels among rural Indian laborers, participants were assigned to conditions "according to geographic and social clusters to minimize the possibility of households from different treatment conditions meeting and discussing their participation" (at page S17). In other cases, it is not obvious how randomization could be achieved. For example, in the studies involving matched pairs of auctions on eBay (Dholakia and Simonson, 2005; Leszczyc and Haubl, 2010'; Haruvy and Leszczyc, 2010), the matched pairs serve as treatment and control samples. Randomizing the experimental treatments between products within a pair would not be meaningful, either because the products are identical or because the experimental variation involves differences in the product bundles themselves.

In the absence of randomization, a common approach is to rotate treatments across time. For example, in Dagger and Danaher's (2014) study of a store remodeling, "the original retail environment served as the control, used in weeks 1, 4 and 5. The new environment, which represented the treatment condition, was in place for weeks 2, 3 and 6" (page 66).[11] Other examples include Yang and Ghose (2010), where the treatment was implemented by rotating sponsorship of key words in 2 week intervals, and Krider et al. (2001), who rotate across days the shape of cream cheese packages in a store.

7.3 Future topics

This survey of the recent marketing literature reveals a remarkable diversity in field experiment topics. This mirrors the diversity of topics in the field generally. Firms have a wide range of levers that they can use to influence demand, and the marketing literature consequently has a wide range of topics to choose from. Notably, the Internet has increased the range of levers available to firms, and this has further broadened the topics that are studied.

While the diversity of available topics makes the field attractive to researchers, it is also a weakness. Almost without exception, the papers we have discussed raise new research questions, rather than building on previous research. Other fields benefit from greater focus in their research topics, such as the study of price rigidity in the monetary economics literature. This is not the case in marketing, which lacks broad agreement about the research questions that should be prioritized. As a result, there has not been a tradition of extending previous findings and comprehensively answering well-defined problems. Although there are some exceptions to this observation, many of the exceptions reflect a dedication to a research question by a single research team (or by teams with overlapping researchers).

Despite the diversity of topics, there are topics that are clearly underrepresented. None of the papers investigate issues related to managing upstream or downstream channel partnerships. For example, none of the papers investigate the benefits of exclusivity in supply or distribution relationships, or the role of standardization to facilitate coordination. The absence of studies on these topics may in part reflect the difficulty of implementing experimental variation. Variation in channel relationships almost always requires conflict, which disrupts relationships that firms have often spent considerable time building.

There is also relatively little research studying business-to-business markets. Only five of the papers report field experiments in which firms target other businesses (this includes one study targeting rural farmers in India). This paucity of studies may reflect difficulties in generating sufficient sample in these markets. Experimentation may also be hindered by greater transparency, which could lead to business customers in the different

---

[11] Dagger and Danaher (2014) did randomly assign the treatments to the 6 weeks, although it is common for rotation to occur without randomization.

experimental conditions becoming aware of the experimental variation (although this limitation would also seem relevant in several of the Internet studies). A third possibility is that the time required to implement change and observe outcomes could be longer in business-to-business settings than in consumer markets.

What is perhaps most surprising is the lack of papers investigating the feasibility of using field experiments to optimize marketing decisions. As we have already recognized, the marketing field has a long history of developing models to optimize marketing decisions. Indeed, eight of the papers that we reviewed report on field experiments designed to *validate* example of optimization models. However, field experiments are themselves an optimization method. By experimentally changing marketing variables and comparing the outcomes, firms could in principle use field experiments to improve profits by searching across the space of possible decisions.

None of the empirical papers we surveyed investigate the feasibility of this approach. Perhaps the closest example is Danaher (2002), which uses the data from a field experiment implemented by a telecommunications company to develop a statistical model that optimizes a two-part tariff (pricing) scheme. However, in this example the field experiment is used as a source of data, while the optimization is pursued using more traditional methods.

Although we could find no empirical papers that study whether firms could use field experiments as a practical optimization method, there is a recent theoretical paper. Li et al. (2015) investigate how many experiments are needed to set prices in a product category, as the size of the category grows. Setting prices across a product category requires estimating a large matrix of cross-product demand elasticities (because items in the same category may be substitutes or complements). They show that if the category has a favorable structure, the number of experiments needed may grow just logarithmically with the number of products. They conclude that firms may be able to obtain meaningful estimates using a practically feasible number of experiments, even in categories with a large number of products. To our knowledge, this is the only paper that formally investigates when it is feasible to optimize marketing variables using field experiments alone. However, this paper presents theoretical results using information theory; it does not report the results of any field experiments.

8. CONCLUSIONS

Field experiments are no longer a rarity in the marketing literature. The sharp growth in the number of papers, particularly in the last 5 years, means that they are now a mainstream method for undertaking empirical research. The growth in the number of papers is matched by tremendous growth in the number of authors who are participating in these studies. Between 1995 and 1999, just 11 authors authored or coauthored a paper using a field experiment (in our sample). Between 2010 and 2014, there were 75 authors represented.[12]

There appear to be at least three reasons for this growth in the number of field experiment papers. First, the marketing field has become increasingly concerned about the interpretation of endogenous independent variables. This concern does not arise if experimental treatments are exogenously manipulated. Second, the field has grown generally, and so there are more papers of all types being published. Third, the Internet has made it easier to implement field experiments, often without the need for cooperation from firms.

Our survey reveals that before 2010, field experiment papers in marketing were dominated by pricing topics. Since 2010, at least some of this focus has shifted from pricing to advertising, with many of the recent papers investigating topics related to Internet advertising. However, even within the pricing and advertising topics, there is a remarkable level of diversity in the research questions. Very few of the papers build on a previous field experiment paper. We recognize this as both a strength and weakness of the field.

An important criterion for publishing a field experiment in a top marketing journal is the ability to extend the findings beyond documenting a main effect and to also provide insights about the cause of that effect. Although explaining effects is obviously valued in economics journals, this objective receives even greater emphasis in the marketing field. Field experiments are not always well-suited to evaluating competing explanations. For this reason, many of the papers report interactions, rather than just main effects. Other researchers complement their field experiments with laboratory experiments or customer surveys to provide support for their interpretations.

Although an explanation for an effect is generally necessary, randomization is not. Almost 30% of the field experiments published in marketing do not employ randomization to assign experimental treatments. When treatments are not randomized, they are generally rotated over time. We also identified three papers that report field experiments using matched sets of products auctioned on eBay.

Although we have highlighted the diversity in topics, our review also identified several topics that are yet to receive attention. These include the problems of motivating and coordinating upstream and downstream channel relationships. There are also very few studies of business-to-business markets. Finally, we recognized that field experiments are themselves an optimization method; firms could use field experiments to improve profits by searching across the space of possible decisions. Although there is some initial theoretical work in this area, the feasibility of using field experiments in this role remains an important but understudied topic.

---

[12] Across all 20 years there are 123 unique authors or coauthors of papers in the sample.

APPENDIX: SUMMARY OF THE PAPERS

Pricing issues

Who to target with discounts?

Avoid sending discounts to customers who previously paid full price	Dholakia (2006)
Avoid offering discounts to customers who are more sensitive to quality than price	Anderson and Simester (2001a)
Deep discounts have a more favorable long-term impact for new customers than for existing customers	Anderson and Simester (2004)

What types of discounts are most effective?

More than 50% of the promotions are unprofitable because the loss of margin is not fully offset by the incremental sales	Ailawadi et al. (2007)
Coupons are more effective for increasing sales and profits than discounts off the regular price	Dhar and Hoch (1996)
Multiple unit promotions (e.g., 2 for $1.50) are more effective than single unit promotions (75 cents each). Larger quantity limits increase the number of units that customers buy	Wansink et al. (1998)
Framing a discount as "50% more free" is more effective than "33% off the regular price"	Chen et al. (2012)
The optimal design of a coupon depends upon the customer's psychological orientation	Ramanathan and Dhar (2010)
Free samples can lead to positive long-term demand effects	Bawa and Shoemaker (2004)
A sequence of increasing customer bonuses is more effective at driving usage and retention than a sequence of decreasing bonuses	Haisley and Loewenstein (2011)
Longer deadlines on gift cards lead to lower redemption rates	Shu and Gneezy (2010)
Uncertainty about a free gift can influence the effectiveness of promotions, depending upon whether customers are primed to make emotional or thoughtful decisions	Laran and Tsiros (2013)
Returning promoted prices to regular levels gradually will generate more demand	Tsiros and Hardesty (2010)
Promotions that extend store trips can lead to an increase in unplanned expenditure	Hui et al. (2013)
Training customers to appreciate the benefits of the product can be more effective than promotions	Gaurav et al. (2011)

Price as a signal

Nine-digit price endings can signal a price is discounted, particularly for new products	Anderson and Simester (2003)
"Sale" signs are a less credible signal when they are used too often	Anderson and Simester (2001b)
Higher prices set higher expectations, and so customers evaluate a low-quality product more negatively when it has a higher price	Gneezy et al. (2014)
Promotions can lower demand by signaling that a product is suitable for customers who are more sensitive to quality than price	Anderson and Simester (2001a)
Using discounts to attract first-time customers can make these customers more loyal by signaling that the firm offers good value	Anderson and Simester (2004)

Multipart tariffs and other schemes

Customers evaluate outcomes within a period, rather than across the entire contract	Lambrecht and Tucker (2012)
A multipart pricing system can lower demand if customers interpret it as unfair	Anderson and Simester (2008)
When designing a revenue maximizing two-part tariff in the telecommunications market, it is important to account for both usage and customer retention, as solely focusing on usage will substantially underestimate the sensitivity of revenue to price	Danaher (2002)
Consumers are surprisingly short term focused when choosing between linear price schemes and three-part tariffs	Yao et al. (2012)
How do customers respond to a pay-what-you-want pricing scheme?	Kim et al. (2009)

Advertising issues

Is there an impact on purchasing?

It takes a lot of data to measure the impact of Internet advertising on consumer spending	Lewis and Riley (2014)
Retargeting is generally ineffective, unless consumers are close to purchasing	Lambrecht and Tucker (2013)
DVR's do not appear to affect household spending	Bronnenberg et al. (2010)
Competitors' advertising can increase your demand	Anderson and Simester (2013)

Continued

Which messages are most effective?	
Framing an appeal as a self-prediction increases its effectiveness	Spangenberg et al. (2003)
Matching the type of appeal with a focus on either individual versus social benefits can improve advertising effectiveness	White and Simpson (2013)
Highlighting the benefits of targeting is less effective than emphasizing reciprocity for free access	Schumann et al. (2014)
Control over personalization can make personalized advertisements more effective	Tucker (2014)
Markets with more competitors can appear more attractive to entrants, as there must be sufficient demand to attract so many competitors	Tucker and Zhang (2010)
Advertising popularity information can benefit niche brands because customers recognize that these brands must offer high quality to overcome their narrow reach	Tucker and Zhang (2011)
Appeals to explicitly compare an offer with competing offers produces more cautious bidding behavior in auctions	Dholakia and Simonson (2005)
The effect of advertising on word-of-mouth is stronger for those who do not already associate the brand with the message	Berger and Schwartz (2011)
Assertive messaging is more effective if customers believe in the cause but less effective if they are not yet convinced	Kronrod et al. (2012)
Optimizing paid search advertising	
Clicks and revenues for organic search are higher in the presence of paid search	Yang and Ghose (2010)
Clicks decrease with search position but conversion may increase with search position	Agarwal et al. (2011)

Market research and product development issues

Market research	
Mere measurement of purchase intentions may increase the correlation between stated purchase intentions and actual purchase probabilities	Chandon et al. (2005)
Participation in customer satisfaction surveys increases subsequent purchase likelihoods	Borle et al. (2007)

Multimedia computer interactions can realistically portray customer's information sources and provide forecasts that are not significantly different from traditional methods	Urban et al. (1997)
An optimal contact model for increasing response rates to online marketing research panels	Neslin et al. (2009)

Product sizes and bundling

If a customer needs a fixed quantity, they will purchase more units when the product is in a round package compared to a square package of equal volume	Krider et al. (2001)
Bundling substitutes or unrelated items in an auction is less profitable than selling them separately, but bundling is more profitable for complementary products	Leszczyc and Haubl (2010)
Multiple unit promotions (e.g., 2 for $1.50) are more effective than single unit promotions (75 cents each)	Wansink et al. (1998)

Validating optimization models

Pricing models

Category pricing of automobile parts	Mantrala et al. (2006)
Scholarships and university admission decisions	Belloni et al. (2012)

Advertising models

Optimizing search engine advertising bids	Skiera and Nabout (2013)
An advertising contact model for catalog mailing	Simester et al. (2006)
Estimating the incremental impact of marketing activities in different channels	Li and Kannan (2014)
Banner-advertising optimization	Urban et al. (2014)

Market research and product development models

Increasing response rates to online marketing research panels	Neslin et al. (2009)
Forecasting customer demand for really new products	Urban et al. (1997)

Other topics

Sales force optimization

Coordinating sales calls to match forecasts of customers' purchasing decisions can increase profits	Kumar et al. (2008)
Sales force and sales contest should include multiple prize winners, and rank ordering prices in contests with multiple winners do not increase sales or revenues	Lim et al. (2009)

Continued

Word-of-mouth and referrals	
Word-of-mouth is more effective at increasing sales if it comes from relatively less loyal customers and from acquaintances instead of friends	Godes and Mayzlin (2009)
Which customers should a firm target when designing customer referral programs?	Kumar et al. (2010)

Participation in an online community	
Participation in an online community leads to less spending and fewer listings	Algesheimer et al. (2010)
Participation in an online community makes customers more willing to engage in risky bidding behavior, particularly when ties to other community members are strong.	Zhu et al. (2012)
Users contribute to Twitter because they care about how people perceive them, rather than because they derive intrinsic utility from the activity	Toubia and Stephen (2013)

Encouraging positive behaviors	
Competitions, pledges, and incentives can all improve children's food choices	Raju et al. (2010)
Earmarking earnings can increase savings rates	Soman and Cheema (2011)

Other	
Remodeling a retail space increases sales more for new customers than established customers	Dagger and Danaher (2014)
Auction outcomes can be influenced by shipping costs, secret reserve prices, and other auction features	Haruvy and Leszczyc (2010)

REFERENCES

Agarwal, A., Hosanagar, K., Smith, M.D., December 2011. Location, location, location: an analysis of profitability of position in online advertising markets. J. Mark. Res. XLVIII, 1057—1073.

Ailawadi, K.L., Harlam, B.A., César, J., Trounce, D., 2007. Quantifying and improving promotion effectiveness at CVS. Mark. Sci. 26 (4), 566—575.

Alexandre, B., Lovett, M.J., Boulding, W., Staelin, R., 2012. Optimal admission and scholarship decisions; choosing customized marketing offers to attract a desirable mix of customers. Mark. Sci. 31 (4), 621—636.

Algesheimer, R., Borle, S., Dholakia, U.M., Singh, S.S., 2010. The impact of customer community participation on customer behaviors: an empirical investigation. Mark. Sci. 29 (4), 756—769.

Anderson, E.T., Simester, D.I., 1998. The role of sale signs. Mark. Sci. 17 (2), 139—155.

Anderson, E.T., Simester, D.I., 2001a. Research note: price discrimination as a signal: why an offer to spread payments may hurt demand. Mark. Sci. 20 (3), 315—327.

Anderson, E.T., Simester, D.I., 2001b. Are sale signs less effective when more products have them? Mark. Sci. 20 (2), 121—142.

Anderson, E.T., Simester, D.I., 2003. Effects of $9 price endings on retail sales: evidence from field experiments. Quantitative Mark. Econ. 1 (1), 93—110.

Anderson, E.T., Simester, D.I., 2004. Long run effects of promotion depth on new versus established customers: three field studies. Mark. Sci. 23 (1), 4—20.

Anderson, E.T., Simester, D.I., 2008. Research note: does demand fall when customers perceive that prices are unfair? the case of premium pricing for large sizes. Mark. Sci. 27 (3), 492—500.

Anderson, E.T., Simester, D.I., 2010. Price stickiness and customer antagonism. Q. J. Econ. 125 (2), 729—765.

Anderson, E.T., Simester, D.I., 2013. Advertising in a competitive market: the role of product standards, customer learning and switching costs. J. Mark. Res. 50 (4), 489—504.

Bawa, K., Shoemaker, R., 2004. The effects of free sample promotions on incremental brand sales. Mark. Sci. 23 (3), 345—363.

Berger, J., Schwarz, E.M., October 2011. What drives immediate and ongoing word of mouth. J. Mark. Res. XLVIII, 869—880.

Borle, S., Dholakia, U.M., Siddharth, S.S., Westbrook, R.A., 2007. The impact of survey participation on subsequent customer behavior: an empirical investigation. Mark. Sci. 26 (5), 711—726.

Bronnenberg, B.J., Dubé, J.-P., Mela, C.F., 2010. Do digital video recorders influence sales? J. Mark. Res. XLVII, 998—1010.

Chandon, P., Morwitz, V.G., Reinartz, W.J., April 2005. Do intentions really predict behavior? self-generated validity effects in survey research. J. Mark. 69, 1—14.

Chen, H., Marmorstein, H., Tsiros, M., Rao, A.R., July 2012. When more is less: the impact of base value neglect on consumer preferences for bonus packs over price discounts. J. Mark. 76, 64—77.

Curhan, R.C., 1974. The effects of merchandising and temporary promotional activities on the sales of fresh fruits and vegetables in supermarkets. J. Mark. Res. XI, 286—294.

Dagger, T.S., Danaher, P.J., May 2014. Comparing the effect of store remodeling on new and existing customers. J. Mark. 78, 62—80.

Danaher, P.J., 2002. Optimal pricing of new subscription services: analysis of a market experiment. Mark. Sci. 21 (2), 119—138.

Dhar, S., Hoch, S.J., January 1996. Price discrimination using in-store merchandising. J. Mark. 17—30.

Dholakia, U.M., Simonson, I., 2005. The effect of explicit reference points on consumer choice and online bidding behavior. Mark. Sci. 24 (2), 206—217.

Dholakia, U.M., February 2006. How customer self-determination influences relational marketing outcomes: evidence from longitudinal field studies. J. Mark. Res. XLIII, 109—120.

Dubé, J.-P., Luo, X., Fang, Z., 2016. Self-signaling and prosocial behavior: A cause marketing experiment. working paper, University of Chicago.

Eskin, G.J., Baron, P.H., 1977. Effects of price and advertising in test-market experiments. J. Mark. Res. XIV, 499—508.

Gaurav, S., Cole, S., Tobacman, J., 2011. Marketing complex financial products in emerging markets: evidence from rainfall insurance in India. J. Mark. Res. XLVIII, S150—S162. Special Issue 2011.

Gneezy, A., Gneezy, U., Lauga, D.O., April 2014. A reference-dependent model of the price-quality heuristic. J. Mark. Res. LI, 153—164.

Godes, D., Mayzlin, D., 2009. Firm-created-word-of-mouth communication: evidence from a field test. Mark. Sci. 28 (4), 721—739.

Guadagni, P.M., Little, J.D.C., 1983. A logit model of brand choice calibrated on scanner data. Mark. Sci. 2 (3), 203—238.

Haisley, E., Loewenstein, G., February 2011. It's not what you get but when you get it: the effect of gift sequence on deposit balances and customer sentiment in a commercial bank. J. Mark. Res. XLVIII, 103—115.

Haruvy, E., Peter, T., Popkowski, L., 2010. Search and choice in online consumer auctions. Mark. Sci. 29 (6), 1152—1164.

Hui, S.K., Inman, J.J., Huang, Y., Suher, J., March 2013. The effect of in-store travel distance on unplanned spending: applications to mobile promotion strategies. J. Mark. 77, 1—16.

Kim, J.-Y., Natter, M., Spann, M., January 2009. Pay what you want: a new participative pricing mechanism. J. Mark. 73, 44—58.

Krider, R.E., Priya, R., Aradhna, K., 2001. Pizzas: π or square? psychological biases in area comparisons. Mark. Sci. 20 (4), 405–425.

Kronrod, A., Grinstein, A., Wathieu, L., 2012. Go green! Should environmental messages Be so assertive? J. Mark. 76, 95–102.

Kumar, V., Venkatesan, R., Reinartz, W., September 2008. Performance implications of adopting a customer-focused sales campaign. J. Mark. 72, 50–68.

Kumar, V., Andrew Peterson, J., Leone, R.P., September 2010. Driving profitability by encouraging customer referrals: who, when, and how. J. Mark. 74, 1–17.

Lambrecht, A., Tucker, C., 2012. Paying with money or effort: pricing when customers anticipate hassle. J. Mark. Res. XLIX, 66–82.

Lambrecht, A., Tucker, C., October 2013. When does retargeting work? information specificity in online advertising. J. Mark. Res. L, 561–576.

Laran, J., Tsiros, M., 2013. An investigation of the effectiveness of uncertainty in marketing promotions involving free gifts. J. Mark. 77, 112–123.

Leszczyc, P.T.L.P., Haübl, G., 2010. To bundle or not to bundle: determinants of the profitability of multi-item auctions. J. Mark. 74, 110–124.

Lewis, R.A., Reiley, D.H., 2014. Online ads and offline sales: measuring the effects of retail advertising via a controlled experiment. Quantitative Mark. Econ. 12, 235–266.

Li, H., Kannan, P.K., February 2014. Attributing conversions in a multichannel online marketing environment: an empirical model and a field experiment. J. Mark. Res. LI, 40–56.

Li, J.Q., Rusmevichientong, P., Simester, D.I., Tsitsiklis, J.N., Zoumpoulis, S.I., 2015. The value of field experiments. Manag. Sci. 61 (7), 1722–1740.

Lim, N., Ahearne, M.J., Ham, S.H., 2009. Designing sales contests: does the prize structure matter? J. Mark. Res. XLVI, 356–371.

Mantrala, M.K., Seetharaman, P.B., Kaul, R., Gopalakrishna, S., Stam, A., November 2006. Optimal pricing strategies for an automotive aftermarket retailer. J. Mark. Res. XLIII, 588–604.

Mannor, S., Simester, D.I., Sun, P., Tsitsiklis, J.N., 2007. Bias and Variance in Value Function Estimates. Manag. Sci. 53 (2), 308–322.

Neslin, S.A., Novak, T.P., Baker, K.R., Hoffman, D.L., 2009. An optimal contact model for maximizing online panel response rates. Manag. Sci. 55 (5), 727–737.

Raju, S., Rajagopal, P., Gilbride, T.J., May 2010. Marketing healthful eating to children: the effectiveness of incentives, pledges and competitions. J. Mark. 74, 93–106.

Ramanathan, S., Dhar, S.K., June 2010. The effect of sales promotions on the size and composition of the shopping basket: regulatory compatibility from framing and temporal restrictions. J. Mark. Res. XLVII, 542–552.

Schumann, J.H., von Wangenheim, F., Groene, N., January 2014. Targeted online advertising: using reciprocity appeals to increase acceptance among users of free web services. J. Mark. 78, 59–75.

Shu, S.B., Gneezy, A., October 2010. Procrastination of enjoyable experiences. J. Mark. Res. XLVII, 933–944.

Simester, D.I., Sun, P., Tsitsiklis, J.N., 2006. Dynamic catalog mailing policies. Manag. Sci. 52 (5), 683–696.

Skiera, B., Nabout, N.A., 2013. PROSAD: a bidding decision support system for profit optimizing search engine advertising. Mark. Sci. 32 (2), 213–220.

Soman, D., Cheema, A., 2011. Earmarking and partitioning: increasing saving by low-income households. J. Mark. Res. XLVIII, S14–S22. Special Issue 2011.

Song, Y., Mela, C.F., Chiang, J., Chen, Y., December 2012. Determining consumers' discount rates with field studies. J. Mark. Res. XLIX, 822–841.

Spangenberg, E.R., Sprott, D.E., Grohmann, B., Smith, R.J., July 2003. Mass-communicated prediction requests: practical application and a cognitive dissonance explanation for self-prophecy. J. Mark. 67, 47–62.

Toubia, O., Stephen, A.T., 2013. Intrinsic vs. image-related utility in social media: why do people contribute content to twitter? Mark. Sci. 32 (3), 368–392.

Tsiros, M., Hardesty, D.M., January 2010. Ending a price promotion: retracting it in one step or phasing it out gradually. J. Mark. 74, 49–64.

Tucker, C.E., Zhang, J., 2010. Growing two-sided networks by advertising the user base: a field experiment. Mark. Sci. 29 (5), 805–814.

Tucker, C.E., Zhang, J., 2011. How does popularity information affect choices? a field experiment. Manag. Sci. 57 (5), 828–842.

Tucker, C.E., October 2014. Social networks, personalized advertising, and privacy controls. J. Mark. Res. LI, 546–562.

Urban, G.L., Hauser, J.R., Qualls, W.J., Weinberg, B.D., Bohlmann, J.D., Chicos, R.A., February 1997. Information acceleration: validations and lessons from the field. J. Mark. Res. XXXIV, 143–153.

Urban, G.L., Liberali, G., MacDonald, E., Bordley, R., Hauser, J.R., 2014. Morphing banner advertising. Mark. Sci. 33 (1), 27–46.

Villas-Boas, M.J., Winer, R.S., 1999. Endogeneity in brand choice models. Manag. Sci. 45 (10), 1324–1338.

Wansink, B., Kent, R.J., Hoch, S.J., February 1998. An anchoring and adjustment model of purchase quantity decisions. J. Mark. Res. XXXV, 71–81.

White, K., Simpson, B., March 2013. When do (and don't) normative appeals influence sustainable consumer behaviors? J. Mark. 77, 78–95.

Yang, S., Ghose, A., 2010. Analyzing the relationship between organic and sponsored search advertising: positive, negative or zero independence? Mark. Sci. 29 (4), 602–623.

Zhu, R., Dholakia, U.M., Xinlei (Jack), C., Algesheimer, R., June 2012. Does online community participation foster risky financial behavior? J. Mark. Res. XLIX, 394–407.

INDEX

'*Note:* Page numbers followed by "f" indicate figures and "t" indicate tables.'

CPSIA information can be obtained
at www.ICGtesting.com
Printed in the USA
BVHW012301110922
646649BV00043BA/556